Introduction to
COMMUNITY RECREATION

PREPARED FOR THE

National Recreation Association

BY

GEORGE D. BUTLER

FIRST EDITION
EIGHTH IMPRESSION

McGRAW-HILL BOOK COMPANY, INC.

NEW YORK AND LONDON

1940

THE MAPLE PRESS COMPANY, YORK

PREFACE

Many books have been written on the theory and significance of recreation, on recreation activities and leadership methods, on recreation areas and facilities, and on the content and conduct of various parts of the community recreation program. There has long been a need, however, for a comprehensive volume interpreting community recreation, its significance, functions, objectives, program content, methods of operation, and relationships. This book has been written to meet this particular need.

The term "community recreation" is applied in this volume to recreation services that are provided for the benefit of all the people. Special consideration is given to those forms of recreation which require a considerable degree of organization and leadership and in which participation plays an important role. Because governmental agencies are providing a large and increasing proportion of such services, this book is devoted primarily to the work of these agencies. It deals with recreation as a function of local government, like health, education, and other essential public services. Yet to a large degree the material presented in the following pages applies equally well to those recreation services of private and semipublic agencies, which are made available to all the people without restriction as to membership, creed, or race. Commercial recreation, which is motivated more by the desire for profit than by interest in the welfare of the people served, is not included as a part of community recreation.

Throughout the volume major consideration is given to problems of community recreation as related to the town and city rather than the rural community. Although the provision of recreation in rural districts gives rise to problems which require solutions different from those which are applied in cities, much of the material presented here should be useful to rural recreation leaders.

The volume opens with a general discussion of recreation—its nature, significance, and extent—and a brief history of municipal recreation in this country. Then follows a consideration of the essential elements in the community recreation program—leadership, areas and facilities, activities, and organization methods. The recreation system is then treated from two points of view, one dealing with the operation of different physical units in the system, the other with distinct program features

v

and services. A description of recreation programs in several representative cities gives a well-rounded picture of the service of local government in the recreation field. The concluding section of the book deals with several important administrative aspects and functions essential to the effective operation of the recreation department.

The special interests and needs of three groups have been kept in mind in preparing this volume—students and teachers of recreation courses, professional recreation workers, and lay individuals interested in the significance of this increasingly important field. The material is especially designed for use in the large number of colleges, universities, and special teacher-training institutions that have established recreation courses. It should give the student who is contemplating a professional career in recreation a background for further specialized study. To persons who are preparing for the field of education, either as classroom teachers or as specialists in a subject like crafts, music, or physical education, or who are looking forward to a career in social work or government service, it should furnish an understanding of community recreation, a field closely related to the one in which they will be working.

Because the book has drawn heavily upon the experience of outstanding leaders in the recreation field, contains numerous accounts of local recreation developments, describes activities and methods that have proved successful in conducting various parts of the recreation program, and presents trends, standards, and administrative procedures, recreation authorities and individuals engaged in recreation leadership should find in it much of value. It should be pointed out, however, that it is not a manual of procedure. It is not intended to equip the reader to conduct a playground, lay out a tennis court, organize an athletic league, plan a training institute for leaders, prepare a recreation budget, or perform other duties that a trained recreation worker is expected to undertake. As its title indicates, it is an introduction to the entire subject, and detailed information as to specific methods and procedures must be sought in other publications.

Much of the material in this volume has been adopted from records of local experience. It is obvious that many recreation agencies do not measure up to the standards recommended or follow the policies and practices described in this book. Nevertheless, it presents the best thinking of leaders in the profession and points out the procedures that are proving most successful. In selecting illustrative material, an attempt has been made to draw upon reports of recreation departments in cities of various sizes, in different parts of the country, and administered under several types of managing authorities. The name of the city or agency has been given, in referring to local developments, only where they were considered unusual or significant or were described in detail.

The recreation movement is comparatively new and is undergoing rapid changes and expansion, and its significance and extent are far from being fully realized. Because this is true, in presenting this volume one can merely give a picture of past achievements, point out present trends and objectives, and realize that the future will necessitate many revisions in order that the book may keep abreast of new patterns and unexpected developments.

GEORGE D. BUTLER.

NEW YORK CITY,
April, 1940.

ACKNOWLEDGMENTS

The cooperation of a large number of recreation workers throughout the country has helped to make this volume possible. Grateful acknowledgment is made to the many individuals who contributed to the book by sharing their experiences with the National Recreation Association and to the recreation departments which supplied information concerning their work.

Special thanks are extended to the following: Raymond W. Robertson of Oakland, California, and members of his staff, who read the entire manuscript and submitted many excellent suggestions; Dorothy C. Enderis of Milwaukee, Wisconsin, whose criticisms of a large part of the manuscript were particularly helpful; V. K. Brown of Chicago, Illinois, and the several workers on his staff who read one or more chapters each and offered comments of much value; Lewis R. Barrett of Washington, D.C., and James S. Stevens of Greenwich, Connecticut, whose suggestions on parts of the manuscript were greatly appreciated.

Several members of the National Recreation Association staff have had a direct share in preparing this volume. Special acknowledgment is made to Mary J. Breen, whose constructive criticisms and suggestions influenced a considerable portion of the work and who had a large part in the preparation of Chap. VI; to Weaver W. Pangburn, who assisted in the preparation of several chapters, especially Chap. XXXIII, and whose reading of the manuscript yielded many valuable suggestions; and to Arthur Williams, who assembled much of the material in Chaps. XXVIII, XXIX, and XXXI. Thanks are due also to Howard S. Braucher, to whose advice may be attributed the clarity and accuracy of many passages, and to the many other workers who criticized specific parts of the manuscript and assisted in various ways in preparing it for publication.

GEORGE D. BUTLER.

CONTENTS

PART I

RECREATION—ITS NATURE, EXTENT, AND SIGNIFICANCE

The many diverse opinions as to the nature and scope of recreation make it desirable at the start to indicate briefly its essential characteristics. This part also considers the reasons why recreation is important in modern life and its relationship to other essential functions. After a review of the numerous types of agencies which in America provide recreation in varied forms, the place of local government among these agencies is treated in some detail. A résumé of the significant steps leading up to the present status of the municipal recreation movement completes this introductory part.

CHAPTER I

WHAT IS RECREATION?

The word "recreation" is heard today on every hand. Yet widely different meanings are attributed to it, and it is applied to a great variety of activities. It would doubtless be helpful at the very beginning of this study of recreation and its development to suggest a simple, brief definition of the word. It is believed, however, that the significance of recreation can be better understood after a consideration of its more important implications and of the theories that have been formulated to explain it as a form of human activity.

Recreation is usually considered as the antithesis of work. It is true that relatively few people today find recreation in their work, but there are individuals whose vocation is so absorbing and satisfying as to make it a form of recreation. The late Thomas A. Edison, for example, gave himself so completely to creative work in his laboratory that he felt no need for recreation outside his working hours. Occasionally one finds others, such as artists or businessmen engaged in a new enterprise, who find in their work the kind of satisfaction that is commonly associated with recreation. As a rule, however, recreation is a leisure-time activity and for most people the opportunities for it are largely confined to their leisure hours.

Recreation has been variously defined as refreshment, diversion, or as "the less serious and more passive types of playful activity," but these definitions are too general or too limited in scope to be adequate. The term is sometimes applied to activities of young people and adults to differentiate them from the play of young children. This contrast in the meaning of the two words "play" and "recreation" is not universally employed in defining them, but in common usage "recreation" is usually accepted as being more comprehensive. As Dr. John H. Finley has pointed out, "the word 'recreation' is broad enough to include 'play' in its every expression and also many activities that are usually not thought of as play—music, the drama, the crafts, every free activity and especially creative activity for the enrichment of life."[1]

Activities considered as recreation take a great variety of forms. To many people recreation means fishing, sailing, camping, singing, skating,

[1] *Recreation*, November, 1933, p. 367.

photography, dancing, or taking part in a play.   Nevertheless, an activity which is recreation for one individual may be drudgery for another; for example, building a boat may be an ideal form of recreation to one, whereas to another it would be work.   Even in the case of the same individuals an activity that affords recreation at one time or under certain conditions does not always yield the satisfaction which would make it recreation.   Sometimes a person feels like playing golf or joining a square dance group; at other times he does not.   Furthermore, recreation takes a multitude of forms which have an appeal varying according to the age, interests, and desires of the individual.   It comprises activities that are engaged in by a person apart from his fellows as well as others that involve group activity.   In some forms it consists of active participation; in others of quiet relaxation, listening, or watching.

The child playing in the sandbox, the girl keeping house with her dolls, playing hopscotch, or collecting butterflies, the boy making a model airplane or taking a swim, the young couple canoeing in the moonlight, youth hiking, dancing, or producing a play, the family on a picnic, at the theatre, or having an evening of music at home, the "old folks" reading, playing croquet, or collecting first editions—these few examples suggest the wide variety of activities which are known as recreation. Like education, it is for people of every country and of every age.

ESSENTIAL CHARACTERISTICS

Although there are countless activities that may be considered recreation, it is generally agreed that all recreation activity has certain basic characteristics.   One is that the person engages in it because he desires and chooses to do so, without compulsion of any type other than an urge from within.   Fishing is the most alluring occupation for many a boy on an April morning; at the same time there is nothing his young sister would rather do than play with her dolls.   It is this urge to take part in the activity that makes fishing for one, and doll play for the other, forms of recreation activity.   And it is the lack of this urge which prevents the girl from considering fishing as a form of recreation and which for her older brother eliminates doll play from his list of recreation activities.

Another characteristic is that the activity brings immediate and direct satisfaction to the individual.   Playing in a string ensemble or orchestra brings to the violinist a thrill, a challenge, a· sense of group membership, and a satisfaction which he gains in no other way.   The fourteen-year-old boy needs no other inducement to play baseball than the excitement, the zest, and the fun which he gets from taking part in this competitive activity.   Thus recreation is activity that is satisfying and engaged in for its own sake.   In recreation the individual finds opportunity for self-expression and from it he derives fun, relaxation, or pleasure.

A Matter of Attitudes.—The fact that an individual gains direct satisfactions from certain activities makes these activities forms of recreation for him, and the varying nature and intensity of the satisfactions resulting from different forms of activity give them varying recreation values for the individual. The types of satisfactions which certain activities yield and which therefore make participation in them a form of recreation are considered in Chap. XIV. Because many people gain satisfying experiences from the same kinds of activity, these have come to be considered as forms of recreation, yet essentially recreation is the attitude characterizing participation in these activities. It is the spirit which finds expression in them and which through them contributes to satisfying, joyous, abundant living.

Dr. James S. Plant, the noted psychiatrist, has pointed out that recreation is "interested in the things which people are doing, rather than in the finished product . . . It is in the doing of the thing rather than in the final result that we have the real elements of recreation."[1] It is this characteristic of recreation that differentiates it from many other aspects of American life which are evaluated in terms of results. It must be recognized, however, that with some forms of activity there may be a direct relationship between the recreational possibilities of the activity and "the finished product." The satisfaction which an individual obtains from participating in them is not likely to persist unless it includes a sense of achievement. For a time a boy may find satisfaction in the making of model airplanes, regardless of their quality or efficiency. Yet if his attempts to fly the planes result in repeated failure, his interest in making them is likely to diminish or disappear entirely. The appeal of certain activities which are forms of recreation for large numbers of people lies in their challenge to the development of increasing skill on the part of the individual and in the satisfaction that results from attaining higher levels of achievement.

Dr. Plant has further emphasized the fact that "recreation is an integrating experience for the individual because it catches, strengthens, and projects his own rhythm." In illustrating this he points to the difference between the tool and the machine. The former is an extension of the individual, it is subject to his control, and it moves on the basis of his own rhythm. The machine, on the other hand, imposes its rhythm on the individual who must adjust himself to its demands. Recreation, according to this interpretation, is any form of activity in which an

[1] "Recreation and the Social Integration of the Individual," *Proceedings of the Twenty-second National Recreation Congress*, New York, National Recreation Association, 1937.

individual feels a sense of freedom and of self-forgetfulness and to which he gives himself freely and wholeheartedly because it elicits from him a harmonious and satisfying response. Participation in such an activity is characterized by lack of compulsion, restriction, or pressure from outside the individual. This conception of recreation helps to explain why for certain individuals such activities as laboratory research or the study of archaeology have the characteristics of recreation, although for most people they do not.

THEORETICAL EXPLANATIONS

The many theoretical explanations of play and recreation which have been developed from time to time have been discussed thoroughly in other publications.[1] A brief consideration of some of these theories, however, may be helpful in better understanding the modern conception of recreation. It will be observed that whereas these various theories have not proved adequate, it has been because they were partial and incomplete rather than incorrect. It is of interest to note, too, that most of these theories were based upon and related to the play of children rather than the recreation of people of all ages.

One of the oldest theories, that of surplus energy, held that play was the expression of animal spirits, that the individual was so charged with muscular energy that he could not keep still. According to this theory, play is aimless; this obviously is untrue of much observed play activity. It is also obvious that many activities are entered into in spite of largely depleted physical or mental energy. The motivation behind them cannot be explained by surplus energy. In partial contrast with the surplus-energy theory is the one which viewed play as recuperative activity, required for restoration of physical and mental energies and providing rest and relaxation after work. This theory may be applied to certain forms of adult recreation but much of the play of children and young people occurs at the peak of their physical and mental energies.

Somewhat related to the surplus-energy theory is the catharsis theory which views play as a safety valve for pent-up emotions, such as anger. Although it has some validity it in no sense explains the nature of play. It is negative, while much of observed play is positive. Furthermore, most individuals under the stress of intense emotion seem to be inhibited from play rather than inclined to it.

According to Karl Groos, play arises in the child as a result of the appearance of certain instincts that impel him to a great variety of activities, for example, to run, jump, fish, or swim. He interprets play as Nature's preparation of children for adult life. Yet childhood is life,

---

[1] See especially *The Theory of Play*, by Elmer D. Mitchell and Bernard S. Mason, A. S. Barnes & Company, 1934.

something to be fulfilled for its own sake, not simply as a preparation for adulthood. The play experiences of childhood do contribute to the individual's effectiveness in later years but they cannot adequately be interpreted as merely training for the functions of adult life.

G. Stanley Hall's explanation of play as the result of biological inheritance rests on his unsustained conception of "play as the motor habits and spirit of the past of the race." His theory further contends that the growing child passes through a series of stages which recapitulate the "culture epochs" in the development of the race. It holds that in play the child at certain ages relives the animal, savage, nomad, agricultural, and tribal life stages and rehearses the activities of his ancestors. This explanation assumes the inheritance of acquired characteristics and makes insufficient allowance for the reconditioning of play interests and habits by environment.

Play has also been interpreted as activity called forth by the needs of the growing body. Yet numerous individuals play at tennis, golf, swimming, music, and drama after full organic growth has been attained. This theory obviously can relate only to children and youth. The relaxation theory, on the other hand, is applicable primarily to adults.

The Self-expression Theory.—A theory of play as self-expression has been widely accepted. This theory recognizes the nature of man, his anatomical and physiological structure, his psychological inclination, his feeling of capacity, and his desire for self-expression. It accepts the point of view of Hart that the motive of life is to function and that "joy —real happiness, the thing people are after in all experience—is to act, to do things, to function."[1] It further takes into account the fact that the forms of activity through which man achieves this joy are conditioned by his mechanical possibilities of behavior, his physical condition, and his attitudes and habits. Thus play activities are those for which his body structure is well adapted, such as running, climbing, or singing. Man's inclination to activity and the satisfaction he gains from it at a particular time are also influenced by the abundance of his physical energy or the nature of his desire for mental or emotional gratification. At one time he may desire strenuous activity, at another relaxation. Under certain conditions he may seek adventure through new experiences, under others he may crave the satisfaction attained through old associations.

According to this theory play is a form of activity, an attempt at self-expression, resulting from man's urge to be active and to use his equipment to the utmost. It is through play that man finds the satisfaction of his desires to achieve, create, win approval, and express his

[1] Hornell Hart, *The Science of Social Relations*, p. 15, Henry Holt & Company, Inc., 1927.

personality. The great variety of forms which play takes is accounted for by the complexity of man's nature and of his social environment. While the self-expression theory is somewhat general, it is in line with modern thinking. It is true that man seeks to express himself in work, in religious experience, and in study, as well as in play. However, in work, religious experience, and study he often seeks rewards outside these activities themselves. In play he seeks no outside reward. Thus play is activity, self-expression, carried on for its own sake.

The term "play" has been generally employed in the foregoing discussion of theories, yet the word "recreation" might have been substituted. The fact that in the past play rather than recreation received major consideration indicates that recreation has only recently emerged as a recognized aspect of human life. In this book, the word "recreation" is used primarily because it is considered more inclusive and satisfactory than the word "play." The two terms may be used synonymously, however, for if the conception of play as self-expression is accepted as most adequate, then the spirit which characterizes the recreation of adults is much the same as that found in the play of children.

THE RECREATION MOVEMENT

Recreation is not a tangible, static thing but a vital force influencing the lives of people. It is essential to happiness and satisfaction in living. Through recreation the individual grows and develops his powers and personality. As Harry A. Overstreet has expressed it, "The man who plants his garden or plays his violin or swings lustily over the hills, or talks ideas with his friends, is already, even though in small degree, investing life with the qualities that transform it into the delightful and adventurous experience it ought to be."[1]

Recreation is so essential that it is a matter of public concern that recreation opportunities should be available for all the people. Because conditions in modern life, as outlined in the following chapter, have denied to many outlets for self-expression through recreation, leaders have recognized the resulting danger both to individuals and to society. Out of the realization of this need there arose the recreation movement. In the words of its leader, Joseph Lee, its purpose is "to liberate the power of expression of people and communities . . . to help the men and women and children of America to find their voice—to set forth in drama, art, and music and in the hundred other forms of play what it is they have all along been trying to say which could not get itself expressed within the confines of their daily work."[2]

---

[1] *A Guide to Civilized Leisure*, p. 29, W. W. Norton & Company, Inc., 1934.

[2] Augustus D. Zanzig, *Music in American Life*, Oxford University Press, 1932.

The significance of the recreation movement, its relationships to other movements, and yet its independence of them are clearly pointed out in the following quotation:

The joy in living movement is a movement for the centuries and not just for today and tomorrow. It belongs to and is a part of religion, education, industry, social work, health movements, prevention of crime movements, character building, citizenship movements—yet it belongs exclusively to no one of these for it is in itself one side of life.[1]

The difficulty in defining or contrasting recreation with other fields such as education is due in part to the fact that recreation is sometimes considered in terms of activity and sometimes as an attitude or spirit. Recreation and adult education programs, for example, include many activities in common and these "overlapping" activities cannot be allocated exclusively to one field or the other. They have a place in both. Their differences are primarily in the attitudes of the people engaging in them, in the objectives sought, and in the methods by which the activities are conducted. Some of these differences are clear cut and widely accepted; others are difficult to distinguish and are variously interpreted. These differences, as well as the areas of coincidence and the closely interwoven relationships between recreation and other essential aspects of life, need to be recognized. Nevertheless, the important thing to remember is that recreation is an attitude or spirit which finds expression in varied forms of activity and which brings "a way of rich and joyful living" to children, youth, and adults.

[1] Howard S. Braucher, *Recreation*, August, 1936, p. 233.

CHAPTER II

THE IMPORTANCE OF RECREATION

Since earliest times recreation, like work, love, and worship, has been a form of human activity. Festivals, dances, games, and music have always been a part of life, although at times they have been looked upon with disapproval by certain groups. During the past few decades, however, recreation in its various forms has expanded to an unprecedented degree. Large areas have been set aside for recreation use; facilities for a wide range of recreation activities have been developed; new forms of recreation have been devised; a new profession of recreation leadership has arisen. The significance and values of recreation are being heralded widely in the press, from the pulpit, and by leaders in all walks of life. The desire for recreation opportunities is so widespread and insistent that the American people, even during a depression, have been spending several billion dollars annually for them.

Why has man always sought recreation and why is he demanding it so insistently today? What are the reasons for the remarkable developments in the field of recreation, especially since the beginning of the century? What are the factors which have given rise to the widespread recognition of the need and importance of recreation in modern life? Why are the leaders in many other major fields of human activity turning to recreation for help in the solution of their own problems? In this chapter an attempt is made to suggest an answer to these questions and to point out why recreation is serving an increasingly important function in the life of individuals and society.

RECREATION—A FUNDAMENTAL HUMAN NEED

The preceding chapter made it clear that recreation is a fundamental and universal human need. Among all peoples and in all stages of history, man has found outlets for self-expression and personal development in forms of recreation which have a striking similarity. As Joseph Lee has said, in referring to the different songs, games, art, drama, and literature of the various nations, "The muses that have whispered to us are the same." Recreation is a common heritage of all peoples, though its expression does take varied forms.

In all lands, play is the chief occupation of the young child during his waking hours. Through play the child attains growth and experience

10

—it is the major business of life for him. It is nature's way of affording outlets to the great biological urge for activity. At play the child does a variety of interesting things with complete absorption.

As he grows older, other forms of activity make increasing demands on his time, energy, and attention. Nevertheless, as John Dewey has pointed out, "the two dominant impulses of youth are toward activity and toward some kind of collective association." Both of these impulses find expression in forms of recreation. In adult life the duties and responsibilities of earning a living, caring for a family, and maintaining a place in human society tend to relegate recreation to a place of minor significance on the margin of life. Too often it is crowded out of people's lives or is present only in harmful or negative forms. Yet the urge for recreation is so fundamental and universal that it will not be entirely suppressed.

Recreation Contributes to Human Happiness.—In the last analysis, everyone wishes to be happy. Happiness was recognized by our forefathers as a fundamental and worthy objective for every individual. It can seldom be attained, however, by any one kind of activity. When sought consciously as an end in itself it is most elusive. For happiness is essentially a by-product which can best be achieved in a balanced life—and recreation holds an important place in the balanced life along with work and rest, love and worship. Life would indeed be incomplete and drab without it. The significance of play to man's well-being was emphasized by Dr. Austin Fox Riggs when he wrote:

> The function of play is to balance life in relation to work, to afford a refreshing contrast to responsibility and routine, to keep alive the spirit of adventure and that sense of proportion which prevents taking oneself and one's job too seriously, and thus to avert the premature death of youth, and not infrequently the premature death of the man himself.[1]

For large numbers of people most of life is drab, discouraging, harnessed to material things, and devoid of joy or satisfactions. Rabbi Silver has repeatedly stressed the fact that because this is so there is need for people to create their own inner world where they can truly live during their leisure hours. Among the needs for real living, he cites "beauty, knowledge, and ideals; books, pictures, and music; song, dance, and games; travel, adventure, and romance; friends, companionship, and the exchange of minds."[2] Recreation holds its place of importance in modern life because it has afforded and continues to afford opportunities for the attainment of these basic human needs.

[1] *Play*, Doubleday, Doran & Company, Inc., 1935.
[2] Abba Hillel Silver, "Recreation and Living in the Modern World," *Recreation*, January, 1931, p. 531.

Man is the kind of animal that must have adventure, excitement, and romance. The pursuit of happiness, the love of adventure, and the desire for achievement are great motivating forces which, for large numbers of people, are realized most fully in recreation. The sense of achieving and feeling alive is attained by certain individuals at certain periods of life—while sailing in a heavy breeze, playing polo or football, riding horseback, creating an object of beauty, playing a difficult piece of music on a violin, or watching the sunrise from a mountaintop. The significance of these experiences "in sport, in art, and in the processes of beauty" is enhanced by the fact that they "give almost as much of satisfaction in memory as at the time." Because it makes such experiences possible for large numbers of people the recreation movement, in the opinion of Dr. Hugh M. Woodward, "is still the nearest approach to a practical program for carrying into effect and keeping alive a philosophy of happiness."[1]

RECENT CHANGES AFFECTING RECREATION

Recreation has ever afforded an outlet for self-expression, for release, and for the attainment of satisfaction in life. However, the marked and rapid changes that have taken place in our social, industrial, economic, and political life during the last few decades have magnified the importance of recreation and have greatly affected the recreation life of the people. Some of these changes and their significance for recreation will be presented briefly.

The Growth of Cities.—The playground movement in America was a direct result of the development of large cities with crowded, congested neighborhoods in which children had no place to play in safety. As long as the country was largely rural in character many of the simpler forms of recreation were at hand and available to all, even though many rural people had little opportunity for social contacts and fellowship, for cultural activities, or even for reading. Nevertheless, large open areas enabled children to play near their homes, while the fields, forests, and waters offered adults opportunities for hunting, fishing, and other sports. Folks knew their neighbors, and the occasions for working and playing together were not infrequent. In their work many people gained satisfactions which today must be sought in leisure. The need for special provisions for recreation was consequently less urgent than under urban conditions.

With the growth of cities, streets became crowded and unsafe for play, vacant lots were built upon, and the habitual recreation spaces were used for other purposes. Streams and lakes were polluted, forests were cut down, and large areas were closed to public use. With the complexity of

[1] "Recreation—A Philosophy of Joyful Living," *Recreation*, January, 1938, p. 590.

city life neighborliness all but disappeared and living became more artificial and stratified. People became largely dependent upon special agencies to provide opportunities for outdoor recreation. Man, essentially an outdoor animal, needs recreation spaces, facilities, and leadership to compensate for the natural resources which crowded city life now denies him. He also needs, more than before, companionship with his neighbors and with others whose interests are similar to his own. Under conditions of urban living opportunities for such companionship are found largely through organized recreation.

Changing Home Conditions.—Changes have occurred in the home as well as the community. Laborsaving devices such as washing machines, electric lights, gas stoves, vacuum cleaners—to mention only a few—have revolutionized housekeeping methods. The hours formerly spent in drudgery can now be used for other activities, including recreation. Children who formerly had many chores about the home now find few tasks to perform. The oil burner has eliminated the necessity for shoveling coal and carrying out ashes—chores which in turn replaced the task of chopping and carrying in wood. The rapid increase in the number of multiple-family dwellings not only eliminated the back yard—the main playground of the small children—but also reduced the opportunity for indoor forms of family recreation. The garage has replaced the garden, and the automobile the family horse and buggy. The reduction in the size of families has made it necessary for children to seek outside the home those experiences and values of cooperative and social activity which once they could get at home. The playground, club, recreation center, and moving-picture theater owe their popularity in part to changes in home conditions, especially in the cities. The commercial amusement interests have been alert to the opportunities and needs resulting from the lack of facilities for recreation in the modern home. One modern invention, however, which has contributed greatly to home recreation is the radio, the very popularity of which reflects the meagerness of other home activities.

Speed of Modern Living.—The greatly accelerated speed of modern life has resulted in a nervous tension and pressure to which human beings have not been accustomed and for which they are unprepared. "The nervous organism has been built up over tens of thousands of years to meet conditions in which no human being could move faster than a horse." The strain to which people are subjected, especially in our cities, owing to the crowding, the noise, and the rushing about, "uses up our strength without giving us time for recovery." Under such conditions the need for recreation of the right sort has become exceedingly important. Only as people have a chance to relax, to get their minds off the daily routine, and to give themselves over fully to some form of satisfying recreation activity can they hope to counteract the effects of the abnormal conditions under which they are living.

Increase in Leisure.—When man worked 12 to 14 hours a day, 6 days a week, the problem of the recreational use of leisure, so vital today, was nonexistent. For most people, time for recreation was very short and opportunities were very few. But according to President Hoover's Research Committee on Social Trends[1] the normal work week in American industry was probably decreased by 20 hours during the 50 years preceding 1932. This reduction of working hours to less than 40 hours per week and the wide adoption of the 5-day week have entirely changed conditions as related to leisure and have given rise to an unprecedented situation. The acquisition by millions of men and women of large quantities of leisure which many of them had not been prepared to use intelligently, created a new problem.

Wisely used, this leisure offers promise of becoming a great boon to the individual and to society. On the other hand, it may become a liability, if not a menace, provided it is dissipated or used for unsocial ends. In this new leisure Joseph Lee saw the most extraordinary opportunity ever granted to a nation, and at the same time the heaviest responsibility.

We may employ it in revisiting, in the woods and by the streams, and at the playing fields, the ancient sources of our strength and may seek in the pursuit of beauty and of understanding, our great inheritance; or we may spend the gift in the frenzied seeking of sensation and in barren pleasures. We may choose the path of life or pass it by.[2]

Grave concern has been expressed by some leaders over the prospects of a wasted or misused leisure, yet there is evidence that people appreciate forms of recreation on a high cultural level and avail themselves of these forms if opportunities are made easily accessible and at a cost within their means. The new leisure presents a direct challenge to each community to provide for the recreation needs of the present and to plan intelligently to meet the increasing demands of the future. In accepting or ignoring this challenge each community will help decide whether the leisure of its citizens is to become an asset or a liability.

Unemployment.—Unemployment is not a new phenomenon but the problem of providing gainful occupation for young people and adults has become a matter of grave national concern. Technological developments have been an important factor in creating this unemployment and, according to a report of the National Resources Committee, there are no signs to indicate that new inventions are diminishing in number.[3]

[1] *Recent Social Trends*, p. 828, McGraw-Hill Book Company, Inc., 1933.

[2] Joseph Lee, "Leisure," *Recreation*, May, 1931, p. 57.

[3] *Technological Trends and National Policy*, National Resources Committee, 1937.

The report also implies that unemployment is not likely to be eradicated, but on the contrary is likely to increase. Young men and women are not being absorbed in paid positions at as early an age as heretofore, and the retirement age is being lowered in many industries.

Recreation plays an important part in this picture in that these added years before employment afford youth opportunities for gaining recreative skills and interests which will continue through life. These years can be used not only for constructive, worth-while recreation activities but for giving youth training and experience in volunteer recreation leadership. Furthermore, men and women who use their leisure to develop hobbies and recreation interests will find them a great source of satisfaction and a constructive way to spend their time when their working years are over. People need music, athletics, art, games, and social recreation even more when unemployed than they do under normal conditions.

Specialization and Mechanization in Industry.—The changes in working conditions which have come about due to technological inventions, the development of highly automatic machinery, and specialization of work in both industry and business are well known. In large measure the demands upon the worker's physical and mental energy are less than before, but as a rule the nervous tension is greater. Formerly the worker was fatigued in body at the end of the day's work, but today he is frequently merely bored with the hours of dull monotony. Today most workers are denied the satisfaction which once came from creating an object. What is more, the degree to which they are controlled by the machine or the system tends to develop a sense of inferiority and often results in a degree of nervous tension which is not beneficial either to the individual or to society.

Man is not a machine and "his nature is not adapted to long hours of repetitive tasks." For centuries man has been essentially an outdoor animal whose daily activities have called into play the use of his entire body. Today the development and maintenance of a well-balanced physique must be attained for a large percentage of our people outside their working hours. Harold Butler, while director of the International Labour Office, made a plea for a shorter working week because of the increasing need for greater leisure and more sport. He argued that the nervous strain caused by machines on the human organism made this necessary.[1] Psychologists have repeatedly claimed that for people whose energies are used mechanically and uncreatively, recreation becomes a matter of "absolute necessity." An additional reason why recreation is so important is the tendency for man to carry over into other phases of life the regimentation and standardization which characterize so much of

[1] See *The New York Times*, June 15, 1937.

business and industrial life.   Recreation, with its freedom of spirit and action, affords an effective antidote for this unwholesome tendency.   It is significant that the New York Department of Labor, in determining its basic wage scale, makes specific provision for recreation which it recognizes as essential in the life of industrial workers.

A Stable Population.—The National Resources Committee in 1935 predicted that the United States could look forward to a stable population in 1960 with twice as many citizens over sixty years of age as in 1935.   If this prophecy is realized and if a large percentage of this age group is unemployed, the country will face the comparatively new and challenging problem of developing an adequate leisure-time program for our older people.   The importance of this problem is recognized in the committee's comprehensive report on population trends issued in 1938, which states, "There should be consideration of further possibilities for adult education and other measures for enhancing the usefulness and increasing the joy of persons in the later middle and last years of life."[1]

Other Factors.—The introduction of music, arts, drama, and sports into the school curriculum has a far-reaching significance for the recreation movement.   Each year the schools are turning out a host of young people who have acquired skill in recreation activities and who desire, and are going to demand, opportunity for continued participation in them.   The development of the low-cost automobile, followed by the construction of a system of hard-surfaced roads, has revolutionized the recreation habits of millions of Americans.   It has been one of the most important factors in the acquisition and improvement of public parks and private resorts within a few hours' ride of our large population centers and it has swelled the ranks of the visitors to the national and state parks and forests.   The influence of the airplane upon recreation has only begun to be realized.   The change in the United States from an agricultural to an industrial nation, the decline in religious intolerance, the increase in the employment of women and girls, and the rapid development of commercial recreation are other factors that have affected the significance of recreation in the life of America.

RECREATION'S CONTRIBUTION TO OTHER COMMUNITY FORCES

Although recreation is a distinct phase of human activity, characterized by a particular spirit or attitude, which brings direct satisfaction to human beings, it does not function in a watertight compartment but is closely related to and integrated with other phases of life.   The value of recreation to the individual and the community is due in part to the contribution which it makes to other major human interests and forces.   The fact that recreation affords direct benefit to the individual and at the

[1] *The Problems of a Changing Population*, National Resources Committee, 1938.

same time serves other constructive purposes explains why it is receiving such widespread recognition as an essential factor in modern life.

Many claims have been made for recreation as a means of reducing delinquency and crime, of building health, of developing character, and of bringing about other desirable results. A word of warning needs to be given, however, concerning such statements. In the first place, every local situation involves so many varied forces and factors that it is exceedingly difficult to estimate the influence of any single one such as recreation or to evaluate the part which it has played in bringing about changes in the situation. For instance, a decrease in the crime rate after the establishment of a recreation center in a neighborhood cannot be attributed to the center, except after careful consideration of housing, schools, churches, employment conditions, and many other neighborhood factors.

The individual who has a rich recreation life is more likely to be a healthy, well-balanced, law-abiding citizen than the person who is deprived of recreation opportunities. It needs to be strongly emphasized, however, that recreation is not primarily a means for attaining some objective such as health, good conduct, or morale, much as it may contribute to these ends. The contributions of recreation to other community forces, important as they are, should be considered as by-products. The chief value of recreation lies in its power to enrich the lives of individuals.

Recreation and Health.—The fact that participation in wholesome forms of recreation contributes to the physical well-being of the individual is widely recognized. Medical authorities testify that big-muscle activity stimulates growth and is absolutely essential for the growing child, and that athletic games and sports contribute largely to the proper development of the vital organs. Certain forms of recreation cause increased circulation, greater respiratory activity, better elimination of waste, and improved digestion. Recreation which is vigorous, which is carried on in the open air, and which makes use of the fundamental muscles is the best known means of developing and maintaining healthy organs. Certain forms of recreation contribute to emotional stability by affording rest and relaxation; others give tone to the body by a healthful stimulation of nerve centers.

The health value of play for children has been pointed out by Herbert S. Jennings of Johns Hopkins University as follows:

The young child perhaps learns more and develops better through its play than through any other form of activity. Opportunity for varied play under healthful outward conditions is beyond doubt the chief need of children; comparative study of the physical and mental development of children to whom opportunity for such play is given shows striking superiority, as compared with children to whom such opportunities are denied.

The importance of recreation to health does not mean that recreation is only a part of health or should be considered a phase of health education. Such a relationship was pointed out as a "misconception" by a committee of the White House Conference on Child Health and Protection.[1] The fallacy of considering recreation primarily as a tool for the attainment of health is further emphasized by Dr. Richard Cabot: "When we give play, recreation, and the other popular arts their proper place beside the fine arts, we shall avoid, then, the popular error which degrades play to a medical instrument."[2]

The value of recreation as a means of healthful physical development is not limited to children and youth but applies also to the adult. Many physicians prescribe forms of recreation for their patients, but the effectiveness of the treatment is likely to depend largely upon the extent to which the spirit of recreation prevails in the individual's participation in the activity. The daily round of golf taken under the doctor's orders has much less value when performed as a duty than as a game. The importance of building up recreation interests which will carry into adult life has been stressed by Dr. Charles Loomis Dana of Cornell Medical College who said, "When the young folks are taught the worth and ways of recreation, they are taking out an insurance policy against nervous disorders and in middle age, when they come to collect, they will find themselves reimbursed a hundred fold."[3]

Recreation and Mental Health.—Today in the hospitals of the United States, according to reliable reports, there are more patients suffering from mental diseases than from all other diseases combined. The rapid increase in the number of mental patients is alarming. The National Committee for Mental Hygiene stated that in 1936 the prospect for residents in New York City was that 1 out of every 18 would at some time be confined to an insane asylum or sanitarium because of mental ill-health. The rate for the United States as a whole is 1 out of every 22. It is therefore significant that Col. H. E. Bullis of this Committee, in discussing community factors favorable to the creation of a mentally healthful environment, states, "Among these none is more important than those which have to do with the development of recreation and other resources of the community that serve the leisure-time needs of our people and contribute to the preservation of their physical health."[4]

---

[1] *Recreation*, September, 1932, p. 273.
[2] *The Soul of Play*, National Recreation Association, 1910.
[3] *Play and Health*, National Recreation Association.
[4] "Mental Health and Recreation," *Recreation*, November, 1933, p. 370.

The preventive values of recreation from the point of view of mental health have been indicated as follows by Dr. Arthur H. Ruggles, Chairman of the Executive Committee, National Committee for Mental Hygiene:

Recreation is an important element in our efforts for the prevention and cure of mental disease. For the normal individual it tends to sustain a healthful, happy outlook on life. Games, sports, music, dramatics, folk dances, and other social activities provide healthful releases for pent-up physical and mental energy. Success in recreations also gives the individual a sense of achievement and power, and thus helps to avoid the growth of a feeling of inferiority which may oppress him throughout life and even lead to serious mental maladjustments. Furthermore, the feverish nervous strain of modern urban existence is relieved by regular recourse to play, especially outdoor recreation in close contact with the soothing influence of nature.[1]

Besides contributing to the maintenance of mental health, recreation is used increasingly in the mental rehabilitation of the individual. People suffering from mental disorders have been found to react quickly to the stimulus of play. Music in particular, recorded in the Old Testament as a soother of troubled spirits, has been used with remarkable success as a therapeutic agent in institutions for mental patients. Crafts and hobbies are likewise proving valuable and athletics have proved an effective stabilizing factor.

Recreation and Character Development.—Recreation activity, like many other forms of individual or social action, may be either moral or immoral. It presents the same opportunities for lying or truthfulness, cheating or honesty, cruelty or kindness, and all the other vices and virtues of life. Vigorous forms of recreation under normal conditions nevertheless tend to be a moral force and under wise direction may be a very strong one. Recreation not only develops individual qualities, but it strongly influences the growth of social attitudes which affect the individual as a member of the group. In recreation there is repeated opportunity for expression of the ideals of sportsmanship. "Respect for rules, fair play and courage, an ability to subordinate the selfish interests of the individual to the welfare of the group, a capacity for team play, and experience in leadership may be among the values which recreation may give."

The civic qualities—involved in the attitude of the individual toward organized society—are also fostered. Many forms of recreation, especially team games, drama, and music, require social cooperation, loyalty, and a group consciousness. Through them children and adults may learn to recognize the right of others and discover the meaning of freedom through cooperative action. "Recreation," according to a well-known leader, "is a force of tremendous consequence for the personal character

[1] *Recreation.* November, 1932, p. 372.

and the national culture." Yet character development is not an objective specifically sought by persons engaging in recreation activities, but rather a natural by-product of such participation.

Recreation and Crime Prevention.—Since recreation helps to build character, it is obviously a potent agent in the prevention of crime and delinquency. Little wonder then that agencies directly concerned with this problem are turning to recreation as an effective ally! Because recreation activities have a strong appeal for youth, delinquency and crime are less likely to flourish in communities where such opportunities are abundant and attractive than in cities or neighborhoods where adequate facilities are lacking. While children or young people are engaged in recreation activities on the playground, they cannot at the same time be robbing a bank, breaking into a home, or perpetrating some other crime. Because the playground leader helps them develop wholesome interests and furnishes opportunities for pursuing them, the chances of their becoming criminals are materially reduced. The boy who "makes" the playground baseball team or who excels in the model aircraft club, and the girl who earns a part in the cast for the drama guild play or who is a leader in the nature group, are finding outlets for the normal desire for recognition, success, and achievement and do not need to seek such satisfactions in unsocial ways.

Idle time is not an asset to any community. Most delinquent and criminal acts are committed during leisure time and a large percentage of them are performed in order to get the means for the enjoyment of leisure. Prison wardens testify to the desire of young men and women to do daring things. Many crimes are committed because of a desire to buy pleasures which are much less satisfying than other forms of recreation which might be provided by the community at little cost. Studies have shown that a majority of children are brought into court because of the lack of adequate community provision or direction of leisure-time activities. Dr. Sheldon T. Glueck and Dr. Eleanor T. Glueck, in their analysis of the lives of 500 delinquent women,[1] found that only 9.7 per cent of them had had any constructive recreation at any time in their lives. Probation officers, police officials, and prison authorities in large numbers have testified from their experience that much delinquency and crime result from inadequate recreation opportunities. On the other hand, their testimony and juvenile court records offer conclusive evidence of the beneficial effects of wholesome recreation on children and young people.

A single instance shows how a group of boys who had started on criminal careers responded to a sympathetic interest in their play life:

[1] *Five Hundred Delinquent Women*, Alfred A. Knopf, Inc., 1934.

In a Midwestern city of 100,000, eight boys who had done $300,000 worth of damage and had committed 470 crimes were brought before the court. They were organized into a Rangers' Athletic Club under a competent leader. In the course of the next three years only two of them came back to the court. These two were reported by the club members themselves and one of them proved to be a mental case.

The lack of adequate recreation facilities is considered by the National Resources Committee[1] an outstanding contributing cause of the delinquency which in its opinion is one of the primary problems our cities will have to face and solve in the future. None can doubt the seriousness of the conditions when delinquency and crime, according to J. Edgar Hoover, are costing the country 15 billion dollars a year. Recreation has much to offer toward the solution and is being used more and more by the agencies concerned with the problem.

A word of caution is needed, however, as to the results which may be expected from recreation. It is not a cure-all and it is only one of the forces that influence the lives of people. It makes its contribution, but the importance of these other factors cannot be overlooked. As Dr. Henry M. Busch has said, "Don't expect recreation to stem or reverse the antisocial forces of an unplanned society, but look to it to illuminate personal and social life and to make the world a somewhat better place in which to live."[2]

Recreation and Community Solidarity.—Many forces in modern life tend to separate people into distinct and often hostile groups, based on differences in their economic status, social position, race, creed, nationality, education, or cultural background. The natural outcome of this situation is a growing suspicion, distrust, and dislike of our fellow men and a lack of neighborliness and unity of interest. Recreation affords a common ground where differences may be forgotten in the joy of participation or achievement. Recreation is essentially democratic; interest and skill in sports, drama, or art are shared by all groups and classes. The young man who excels in swimming or basketball is recognized by all followers of these sports, and the woman who can act or paint scenery is welcomed by the drama group, regardless of her social position. The banker and the man on relief are found singing in the community chorus or taking part in the activities of the municipal sketch club. An excellent example of the extent to which recreation activities draw people together from various walks of life is the municipal orchestra in a Mid-

---

[1] *Our Cities—Their Role in the National Economy,* National Resources Committee, 1937.

[2] "Contributions of Recreation to the Development of Wholesome Personality," *Recreation,* October, 1933, p. 311.

western city, in which 35 vocations or professions are represented. Its membership includes a broker, electrician, physician, boilermaker, housewife, salesman, shoemaker, beauty parlor operator, manufacturer, barber, and color artist—truly a cross section of the community. In many a hiking club the college professor, the factory worker, the salesgirl, and the office clerk tramp over the hills together.

Playground workers frequently tell of feuds which either have entirely disappeared or have been converted into enthusiastic competitions through the effects of organized games and sports. Demonstrations of the crafts, games, and music of other countries, presented by national groups, have done much to win respect for the foreign born. There is perhaps no more effective means by which people come to a friendly understanding of each other than by taking part in a recreation activity to which they are devoted. Any force which helps build such an understanding makes for a community solidarity that is greatly needed in the country today.

Recreation and Morale.—During the World War the value of recreation as a means of building and sustaining morale was convincingly demonstrated. In periods of insecurity, depression, and unemployment, man is more than ever in need of activity which brings satisfaction and a sense of accomplishment. Dr. George K. Pratt has developed this truth in his book, *Morale: The Mental Hygiene of Unemployment*, in which he states:

> One of the two convictions essential to a feeling of emotional security is that one can do something really well . . . It matters little what. Anything in the whole range of human endeavor will suffice—repairing an auto, managing the children, writing poetry, building a house, or mastery of a hobby of some kind: golf, stamp collecting, amateur gardening.[1]

It cannot be doubted that one of the most potent forces making for individual and community morale during the prolonged period of depression was the increased opportunity for recreation afforded by local and Federal agencies.

Man also needs outlets for draining off pent-up nervous energy. In furnishing opportunities for recreation the community is providing a safety valve. The wisdom of doing so is attested by Dr. Pratt who states:

> Communities will do well to make ample provision for organized group recreation (particularly activities in which whole groups participate, as contrasted with isolated participation by single individuals); concerts, spectacles of

[1] *Morale: The Mental Hygiene of Unemployment,* The National Committee for Mental Hygiene, 1933.

one sort or another—historical episodes, parades, boxing matches, and generous showings of movies.[1]

This is true not merely during periods of unemployment. During normal times and under favorable conditions man needs inspiration to keep from becoming mentally and emotionally stale.

Recreation and Safety.—Safety officials consider that adequate provision for recreation, especially in the form of playgrounds under leadership, supervised swimming, and winter sports centers, contribute definitely to the reduction of accidents. A single instance may be cited to illustrate the relationship between playgrounds and children's safety. In a Midwestern city of 65,000 it was considered necessary, because of limited funds, to close the playgrounds two weeks before school opened in the fall. During this period the Bureau of Accident Prevention of the Police Department kept a separate record of the accidents occurring to children of playground age. Between September 1 and 12, 14 such accidents took place. All occurred while children were running or playing in the street. After hearing the report the local Safety Council went on record as favoring the continuance and further promotion of playgrounds, convinced that the increase in accidents was due entirely to their early closing.

The playgrounds themselves are remarkably safe when operated under competent leadership. A report of playground and playfield accidents during a period of one year in a group of Western cities showed that the ratio of accidents to attendance was only 1.19 to each 100,000 visits. Comparable figures have been reported by other cities.

According to the Metropolitan Life Insurance Company, drownings rank fourth in the number of accidental deaths in the United States. The loss of life in this way, however, is negligible in the hundreds of public pools, lakes, and beaches operated under competent management. The serious hazards presented by unsupervised swimming emphasize the importance of providing more opportunities for engaging in water sports under safe conditions.

Recreation and Economy.—One of the strongest arguments for municipal appropriations for recreation is that the investment pays dividends in dollars and cents as well as in intangible returns. When it is remembered that it costs a city several hundred dollars per year to care for one delinquent whereas a playground, which may prevent children from becoming delinquents, can be operated at an annual cost of only a few dollars per child served, the economy of providing playgrounds is clear. The saving of a single life justifies many times over the cost of operating a playground. If, as medical authorities state, physical and mental health are dependent upon forms of wholesome recreation activity, the city is wise which spends money for recreation rather than for mending broken minds and bodies resulting from inadequate opportunities for the recreational use of leisure hours. Reducing the recreation budget is likely to prove shortsighted economy.

Industrial leaders realize the cost which results from "working time lost by people who, for want of stimulating outdoor play, have lost steadiness of nerves and muscular tone." This has been a factor in the location of many new industries. The president of the General Motors Company was asked why he selected a certain city for a new plant rather than several others which offered equal manufacturing facilities. He replied that the city was chosen because the company was bringing a great many of its workers to the city and that it was a good place for them and for their children since the city was taking care of their leisure time. The mayor of an Eastern industrial city in which the recreation budget was increased by 25 per cent in 1937 stated that the good will of industrial leaders who are large taxpayers had been built up for the recreation program. Real estate men and chambers of commerce recognize that one of the best means of attracting "live" people to a community is through advertising its parks, playgrounds, bathing beaches, recreation centers, schools, and libraries. Attractive play areas used throughout the year by children, youth, and adults are "evidences of a city's greatness quite as impressive as smoking factory chimneys." Studies in a number of cities have indicated that such areas and facilities, if well maintained and wisely administered, have caused marked increase in property values and have yielded correspondingly increased municipal income.

Even though it has not been possible in this chapter to treat fully the significance of recreation or to consider all its many and varied relationships, the preceding pages have indicated why recreation has gained a place of importance in modern life and have pointed out several ways in which it is contributing to individual and community welfare.

CHAPTER III

AGENCIES PROVIDING RECREATION

In view of the universal need and desire for recreation and of its diversified forms, it is not surprising that there is a multitude of agencies which provide recreation opportunities of widely different types. Some of these serve only their members; others serve the entire community. Many are concerned with a single form of recreation, while others offer a wide range of activities. Some agencies exist for the financial profit which accrues from providing the public with recreation; the sole purpose of others is the enrichment of life. Recreation is the exclusive or primary concern of many agencies, whereas it is merely an incidental activity in the case of others.

A simple and logical grouping can be made under the following headings: (1) governmental agencies, which include the various ones created and maintained by Federal, state, and local governments; (2) semipublic agencies, those supported primarily by private funds but which are nonexclusive in their membership or afford recreation opportunities to individuals who are not members; (3) private agencies, which comprise the innumerable clubs and associations organized for the benefit of their members and in which membership is on a selective basis; (4) commercial agencies, including many business organizations which are catering to the public demand for leisure-time activities and which have developed commercial recreation into a billion-dollar industry. A knowledge of the contribution which these various groups are making in the field of recreation is essential to an understanding of the scope and significance of recreation in the life of America.

INDIVIDUAL AND HOME RECREATION

It is well at the start to remember the extent to which recreation activity is initiated and carried on by individuals and family groups. Many forms of recreation are essentially individual activities and are engaged in apart from others and independent of any recreation agency —for example, walking, nature study, reading, hobbies, creative writing, painting, sculpturing, sketching, gardening, caring for pets, woodworking, and making collections. Automobile riding, cycling, hunting, boating, and fishing also belong in this group. Many of these activities are more enjoyable when engaged in cooperatively, but some individuals have neither the desire nor the opportunity to share them with others. It is not always recognized as such, but the home is doubtless the chief center of recreation for most people. Activities in and around the home occupy more hours than those away from home. The back yard is still the daily playground of most children under six or eight years of age and the home is where much of their indoor play activity takes place whether it is quiet games, reading, playing with dolls or mechanical trains, playing an instrument, or having a party. Young people tend to seek their recreation elsewhere but much adult recreation takes place at home. Listening to the radio, reading, visiting and entertaining, playing cards and other quiet games, caring for the garden, pitching horseshoes in the backyard, singing or playing in family groups, making things in the basement workshop, and sewing for pleasure are only a few of the many forms which home recreation takes. Some of these are not available to apartment dwellers but even in our large cities the home activities of many people occupy a larger percentage of their leisure hours than forms of recreation provided by outside agencies. Nevertheless, the limitations of the home are such that many kinds of recreation are possible only as they are provided by the outside agencies considered briefly in the following pages.

GOVERNMENTAL AGENCIES

Before the World War the Federal and state governments paid relatively little attention to the recreation needs of the people. Public provision for such activities consisted primarily of parks, playgrounds, and recreation programs afforded by municipal authorities. However, recreation is now considered a major concern of government—Federal, state, and local—and through a variety of agencies government is contributing to the recreational use of the people's leisure.

The Federal Government.—The significant part which Federal agencies are playing in the field of recreation was emphasized at a session of the Twentieth Recreation Congress, held in Washington, D. C., in 1934, when the recreation service of the national government was presented by representatives of several departments and bureaus. The concern of Federal agencies with problems relating to recreation has grown until in 1937 according to the Technical Committee on Recreation "approximately thirty-five units scattered throughout twelve departments of the Federal government were engaged in promoting sixty to seventy separate programs affecting the citizens' use of leisure time."[1] The committee groups these programs in the following manner:

[1] *Report of the Technical Committee on Recreation,* Interdepartmental Committee to Coordinate Health and Welfare Activities, 1937.

1. Conserving natural resources to be used for recreational purposes
2. Constructing recreational facilities
3. Maintaining and administering recreational areas
4. Making surveys of recreational facilities and needs
5. Planning and advising on standards of recreation
6. Furnishing information concerning recreation through correspondence, publications, and conferences
7. Conducting educational programs designed to promote recreation
8. Providing recreational supervision and leadership
9. Training for recreational leadership
10. Furnishing employment on projects designed to make additional recreation facilities available to the public

Although these programs in many instances are incidental to the primary function of the agencies conducting them, taken together they represent a significant contribution to the field of recreation. Space does not permit a listing of all these agencies but a few of them will be mentioned briefly.

National Park Service.—For many years the national parks have been recognized as among the foremost recreation assets of this country and have attracted millions of visitors annually. The National Park Service was created to administer these areas of national scenic or historical significance so they might be preserved for all time and render the maximum benefit and enjoyment to the people. To this end the service has made parks easily accessible by roads and trails, has provided transportation and hotel accommodations for park visitors, and has maintained in many of them a nature guiding service which adds greatly to the public's interest in and appreciation of the parks and their natural features. The total acreage of the parks and other areas administered by the National Park Service exceeds 17 million acres. Because most of the national parks are located far from the centers of greatest population, their maximum use is during vacation periods.

The interest of the Park Service in recreation facilities and their organized use has been greatly enlarged because of its responsibility for the Civilian Conservation Corps work program in the national parks and also in state parks and reservations. The extent and significance of this program are mentioned later in the chapter. Another feature of its work is the acquisition and development of recreation demonstration areas. Sixty-two areas consisting of submarginal lands with some degree of scenic attractiveness, within a reasonable distance of large centers of population, and with a total area of 400,000 acres, had been acquired by the end of 1937. They are intended to provide group camps, cabins for family use, and facilities for water sports, picnicking, hiking, and other day uses. More than 50 of these group camps were completed for use during the 1938 season by agencies selected by local camp advisory committees. The service also began in 1936 a nationwide survey of parks and recreation areas, which is being carried on with the cooperation of state authorities.

U. S. Forest Service.—By far the most extensive recreation areas in the country are the national forests which comprise nearly 173 million acres and which are administered by the U. S. Forest Service. Large sections of the national forests are relatively inaccessible and in them wilderness conditions will be perpetuated for those who would seek the primitive and find communion with nature untouched by the hand of man. In many forests, however, definite, accessible areas have been developed for such forms of recreation as camping, picnicking, fishing, hiking, winter and water sports. Most of these facilities are available without charge and with a minimum of restrictions. A number of hotels and resorts have also been established to accommodate vacationists. The tremendous popularity of the national forests as vacation and recreation centers is indicated by the fact that of the 71 million people who visited or passed through them in 1936, about 24 million actually used national forest recreation opportunities.[1] Their use is mounting rapidly as more facilities for recreation are developed and as the people come to know and appreciate them.

Works Progress Administration.—Between 1933 and 1939 no Federal agency afforded recreation opportunities to a greater number of people in a wider range of activities and in more communities than the Works Progress Administration and the emergency relief agencies such as the Civil Works Administration and the Federal Emergency Relief Administration which it superseded. Through its Leisure-time Division, thousands of unemployed received training and were used as recreation leaders in playgrounds, indoor recreation centers, institutions, and for a variety of community-wide activities. These workers served under local recreation agencies or under special committees organized to sponsor the recreation program. Through its Federal art, drama, and music projects the administration not only provided employment but enabled large numbers of people—many of them for the first time—to enjoy fine music and to watch dramatic programs at little or no charge. Hundreds of communities today have playgrounds, athletic fields, swimming facilities, picnic areas, winter sports facilities, and other valuable recreation features which have been constructed with WPA funds. Furthermore, many communities for the first time enjoyed the benefits of an organized recreation program because leadership was made available by the Federal relief agencies. In other cities the service of recreation departments has been expanded through the use of recreation personnel

[1] Harold E. Curtiss, "Opportunities for Recreation in the National Forests," *Recreation*, January, 1938, p. 592.

paid from emergency funds. The recreation service of the WPA is reported more fully in Chap. V.

Other Federal Agencies.—The Bureau of Biological Survey, in its efforts to conserve and protect wild life and to restore native conditions, is benefiting hunters with gun and camera and also lovers of nature. It is helping "to restore America to itself." Some of the bird sanctuaries which it administers also afford facilities for picnicking and day camping. The Children's Bureau has employed a specialist in recreation, conducted recreation studies, published literature on games and recreation programs, and assisted state and local groups in recreation projects. The Office of Education is a promoter of recreation in a great variety of forms, encouraging school authorities to place more emphasis upon music, physical education, art, play, and library service. It has urged the extension of the camping movement, selected the teaching personnel for the education-recreation program in CCC camps, and assisted in the development of the nationwide emergency adult education program in which recreation activities have had a prominent part. The Housing Division of the PWA and its successor, the U. S. Housing Authority, have established play areas and facilities in their developments and have emphasized the importance of recreation in housing projects.

One of the most notable contributions to the enrichment of life in the rural districts has been rendered by the Extension Service of the Department of Agriculture. In the words of its director,

The social and recreational phases of the Extension programs include such activities as community singing and music appreciation, plays, games and pageants, camps, contests and exhibits, debates and public speaking, reading, tours, achievement days, vesper services, picnics, folk dancing, and other ways of bringing rural people together, both young and old, for social enjoyment.

The Service, with the help of the National Recreation Association, during a 10-year period conducted 1,026 training institutes for rural recreation leaders, the total enrollment reaching 63,424. An important feature of its 4-H Club program is its summer camps which number nearly 3,000 and which provide leadership training in games, music, and other play activities. Recreation also has an important place in the camps which the service conducts for rural women.

Through the CCC recreation opportunities are being provided in two ways. In the first place, the CCC has constructed most of the recreation facilities developed in the Federal and state parks and forests during the depression period. It has been estimated that as a result of this program, facilities for recreation have been constructed in these areas a decade or more in advance of ordinary expectations and that some of them would not otherwise have been seen or enjoyed by the present generation. In addition, the young men enrolled in the camps have been provided with wholesome recreation as well as educational activities through a corps of trained advisers. "From the beginning an important aspect of CCC life has been recreation." Boxing, athletic games and sports, dramatics, debating, music, minstrel shows, and a variety of hobbies and craft projects have supplemented the out-of-doors work program.

A picture of the service of the Federal government in the field of recreation would not be complete without a reference to the recreation areas and programs established by the Tennessee Valley Authority, the service of the Bureau of Public Roads in making the parks and forests accessible, of the Federal Radio Commission, the Bureau of Fisheries, the National Youth Administration, and many others. It is evident therefore that Federal agencies are making a varied and valuable contribution to the recreational life of the people and that recreation has come to be recognized as an important Federal function.

The State Governments.—New York has been a leader among the states in the acquisition and development of land suitable for recreation use. In 1885 it began acquiring, as permanent forest and recreation preserves, the Adirondack and Catskill areas which comprise more than 2,100,000 acres. Other states subsequently acquired land specifically designated as parks and with the assistance of the National Conference of State Parks the movement to acquire park areas grew slowly but steadily. The establishment of the CCC provided a great stimulus to the acquisition and development of state parks and between 1933 and 1936 more than 600,000 acres were added. At the end of 1937, parks and related recreation areas totaling more than 1,700,000 acres were owned by 47 states. With the help of the National Park Service the movement is gaining headway, although the ultimate total of 10 million acres of state and county parks suggested by the National Resources Board[1] is far from realization.

Rapid progress has also been made in the development of state parks for the recreational use of the people through the construction of swimming pools and bathing beaches, boat houses and docks, hiking, bridle, and nature trails, winter sports facilities, nature museums, and areas for a variety of games and sports. Some of the parks located near large centers of population have been designed for intensive use; larger outlying areas have been primarily preserved in their natural state. Approximately 500,000 campers are accommodated annually on the free camp sites in New York. Authorities are just beginning to appreciate the value of recreation leadership in enriching state park programs.

[1] *National Resources Board Report*, December 1, 1934, p. 113.

Other state properties such as forests, reservations, or game preserves, which are usually administered by a Conservation Department, have varied recreation uses. The total area of state-owned forest lands in 48 states on June 30, 1937, was 17,815,772 acres. Fish and game commissions are enlarging the opportunities for hunting and fishing by stocking streams and hunting grounds and by opening new areas to public use. In New Jersey a Farmer-Sportsman Cooperative Plan has been inaugurated whereby 70,000 acres that had been "posted" for years have been stocked with game and opened to the public. In this industrial state, over 90 per cent of the streams and lakes are open for public fishing and over 50 per cent of the hunting areas of the state are open for public hunting.

State education departments also are giving consideration to the question of recreation, partly as a result of developments during the depression. A comprehensive program of adult education and community recreation has been carried on with emergency funds in several states under the sponsorship of the educational authorities. Steps have been taken to provide funds for carrying over this program on a permanent basis, and in New York an appropriation has been made to the State Education Department "for the purpose of increasing state supervisory service in the department to develop more satisfactory preventive and corrective physical education and recreation programs for children and adults." Through their control over the acquisition and development of new school sites, buildings, and facilities, several state education departments have been instrumental in securing more adequate provision of indoor and outdoor recreation facilities in local school-building programs.

The employment of recreation specialists by the extension departments of state agricultural colleges has contributed significantly to the enrichment of the recreational life of people in the rural districts. In 1938 at least 16 states were being served by such workers, some employed on a full-time and others on a part-time basis. The chief functions of these state workers who serve rural communities are to train persons for local recreation leadership, to assist local groups in planning recreation programs and conducting recreation activities, and to prepare and distribute literature.

County Agencies.—Taking the country as a whole and excluding the work done with emergency funds, county governments do not make an important contribution to recreation. A number of counties, however, are rendering a service in this field, primarily through their park systems. The most outstanding systems are in metropolitan districts but in several counties the parks serve as recreation centers for rural areas. There are more than 80 counties which own one or more parks and the total acreage of these properties exceeds 175,000.[1] Although relatively small in comparison with most national and state parks, county parks in general are more highly developed and receive more intensive use. This is especially true of areas close to or within the boundaries of large cities, which serve essentially as municipal parks. Picnic centers are most numerous, and other common facilities are bathing beaches, baseball diamonds, swimming pools, winter sports facilities, hiking, bridle, and nature trails, tennis courts, golf courses, and children's playgrounds.

The promotion and administration of activities and programs on a county-wide basis have been undertaken by only a few counties. Union County, New Jersey, furnishes an outstanding example of a successful program of this type, administered under the auspices of a park commis·sion. In Westchester County, New York, widely known for its park system, a Recreation Commission for many years has conducted a variety of county-wide activities and has assisted communities in the development of their recreation service. In many rural counties recreation programs have been sponsored by local organizations with the help of Federal agents, but the county authorities have had little if any responsibility for them. During the depression recreation programs have been established on a county basis in many of the states, in some instances with the cooperation and financial aid of the county governments, but for the most part they have been made possible by emergency relief funds.

Municipal Agencies.—Recreation programs under municipal auspices include a greater variety of interests and are more closely related to the day-by-day life of the people than those provided by other governmental agencies. Most municipal recreation facilities are near the homes of the people they serve and therefore are used more frequently than state and Federal properties. Park, recreation, and school departments furnish most of the municipal recreation programs, although libraries and museums provide special services and other departments sometimes have a place in the recreation picture. In the larger cities there are few recreation interests which cannot find outlets for expansion in the facilities provided by the municipal agencies. Large sections of the population make use of these services, many of which are available without direct cost to the individuals enjoying them. This book is devoted primarily to a consideration of the recreation services furnished by municipal agencies and of the relationships of these agencies to individuals and community groups.

Recreation programs of park, school, and recreation departments are similar in many respects. Playground and indoor center programs are essentially the same whether conducted under park, recreation, or school

[1] *Municipal and County Parks in the United States*, 1935, National Park Service, 1937.

department auspices but, because each of these departments tends to emphasize certain types of activities, their services are described separately. It should be kept in mind, however, that most of the activities listed under each of these agencies are more or less frequently included in the programs of the other two. A more detailed consideration of the service and programs of these departments will be found in later chapters.

The Park Department.—Many park departments own or control extensive properties, some of which were selected and developed primarily for active recreation use. At the end of 1935 the total area in municipal parks in 1,200 communities was approximately 380,000 acres,[1] about one-third of which had been acquired during the preceding decade. To meet the growing demand for more recreation opportunities, park authorities, especially during the past two decades, have developed their properties for the recreational use of the people by constructing and laying out countless facilities for games, sports, and other activities. The quality and extent of park recreation service have been enhanced by an enlarged recognition of the importance of competent recreation leadership. The program has been gradually extended beyond the limits of the park properties and is frequently conducted on a community-wide basis.

A few examples of the activities which park departments make possible are: picnicking by individuals or groups at areas provided with such conveniences as running water, firewood, fireplaces, tables, and benches; boating or canoeing on streams or lakes, with equipment available at a nominal fee; swimming, diving, and water sports at natural or artificial pools and beaches; skating, skiing, and tobogganing at ponds, hills, rinks, or specially constructed facilities; hiking along park trails or through the woods; horseback riding on bridle trails; playing golf, tennis, archery, baseball, horseshoes, bowling on the green, or roque on park courts; testing one's skill at trap shooting or archery; dancing at outdoor, lighted pavilions; listening to band concerts; observing animal, fish, or plant life at zoo, aquarium, or botanical garden or along the nature trail; taking part in or listening to plays, pageants, or operettas in an outdoor theater; and enjoying the beauty of park landscape. The richness, variety, and value of these activities, most of them carried on out of doors, are obvious. A complete picture of the recreation service of park departments must, in addition, take into account the programs at children's playgrounds and the many indoor activities provided at park buildings.

The Recreation Department.—In many cities special departments have been created, usually under a board or commission, for the purpose of developing recreation service for the people. Often the department

[1] *Ibid.*

uses park and school property; sometimes it also controls special recreation areas. Like the schools, its program is often built around the operation of children's playgrounds and indoor centers but many additional features are also provided. Typical of these activities are: conducting city-wide athletic programs with teams in baseball, soccer, softball, volley ball, field ball, football, or ice hockey; arranging institutes at which volunteer recreation leaders learn the techniques of game leading, play production, or song leading; organizing choral societies or symphony orchestras where amateur musicians may sing or play for the joy of participation; conducting city-wide learn-to-swim campaigns, gift-making classes, one-act play tournaments, community holiday celebrations, playdays for industrial women and girls, municipal tournaments in tennis, horseshoes, archery, fly casting, swimming, and other sports; providing picnic and party equipment for outings and socials conducted by various groups in the city; assisting in the organization of programs for industrial and mercantile workers; sponsoring backyard playground contests; providing entertainment programs at city institutions; sponsoring hiking, nature, and garden clubs; and organizing groups around various hobby interests.

The School Department.—Community recreation programs under school auspices sometimes include many of the features described in the preceding paragraphs, but considering the country as a whole, they center around children's playgrounds, athletic fields, and indoor recreation centers. Among the activities made possible on the playgrounds are: singing, running, circle, low organized, and highly organized team games; folk dancing; handicraft of many kinds; athletic tests and stunts; storytelling; quiet games; wading pool, apparatus and sandbox play; art activities such as poster making and soap modeling; dramatics such as puppetry, story acting, and the production of children's plays; music activities including ukulele clubs, harmonica bands, and whistling quartets; publishing a playground newspaper; and a wide range of feature events such as a pet show, circus, track and field meets, hobby show, doll show, model aircraft contest, or playground festival. Athletic fields are used for highly organized team games and for track and field events. At the school recreation centers which are conducted for community groups during nonschool hours, young men and women engage in league and team games such as basketball, volley ball, and indoor baseball; social evenings are arranged where all participate in community singing, games, and social activities; dances are held for club or community groups; classes are formed in arts and crafts such as millinery, woodworking, china painting, modeling, or basketry; forum discussions are conducted; and groups are organized in a variety of music, drama, or educational activities.

School departments are also contributing directly to the development of recreation interests through their regular school programs. The play-interest motive is being introduced widely into the school curriculum, and educators, recognizing the importance of play in the life of the child, are providing recess and afterschool play. programs. The modern curriculum includes such subjects as music, manual and speech arts, physical education, and natural science, which offer opportunities for the development of interests and skills in activities that may be continued as forms of recreation after the students leave school. Requirements of this varied school program include a large outdoor play area, a gymnasium or playroom, auditorium, clubrooms, laboratories, library, and workshops. Since these facilities are also needed for the community recreation program, they serve a double purpose when school authorities make them available for the use of young people and adults outside the regular school hours. Reference has already been made to the adult education programs featuring many recreation activities, which have been initiated by a large number of school authorities.

The Public Library.—The primary service and function of the library is to provide opportunities for reading—the most common of all recreation activities. Not only does the library supply books and magazines for people to read but it offers guidance in the selection of suitable reading material and literature dealing with all forms of hobbies and leisure-time pursuits. It is a "community storehouse of avocational information." The library bulletin board carries announcements of activities, events, and cultural and recreational opportunities in the city. It prepares reading lists and exhibits of timely hobbies and recreation activities. In many cities storytelling hours are regularly conducted for children at the library; in others storytellers are sent to the playgrounds. Occasionally special craft groups or dramatic activities are a part of the library program.

Library buildings are being equipped with auditoriums and lecture halls which are available—usually without charge—to study groups, discussion clubs, and radio listening groups, and for forums, musicales, exhibits of all kinds, lectures, and educational movies.[1] Other special library services are the operation of outdoor libraries in city parks, branch or traveling libraries at city playgrounds, and the libraries-on-wheels which have proved so valuable and popular in many rural counties. Some libraries maintain collections of plays and of vocal and instrumental music which are lent to individuals and community groups.

The Museum.—The museum is a building in which are displayed works of art or collections of natural, scientific, literary, or historic

[1] See "The Public Library in the Program of Leisure Time," by the American Library Association, *Recreation*, February, 1935.

interest.   It attracts large numbers of visitors who come to study or merely to view the displays and exhibits.   At the art museum master-pieces in painting, sculpture, and other art forms can be enjoyed by all the people.   At the natural history museum people gain a knowledge of life in other lands, observe earlier cultures, and study forms of plant and animal life under varying conditions.   Historical museums record the early story of the city, state, or region.   The highly popular zoo-logical and botanical gardens in a sense belong under this general category.

The educational efforts of museum authorities are directed primarily toward attracting visitors, center chiefly about school children, and are mostly limited to daylight hours.   There are museums, however, that offer other valuable recreation and cultural services to the community.   These include afternoon and evening concerts by outstanding local artists; lecture courses for children and for adults on travel, science, art, music, and special subjects related to museum projects; workshops for classes and for informal participation in sketching, painting, modeling, crafts, and hobbies; junior nature clubs, collections, hikes, and trips; children's gardens; music appreciation and listening groups; field trips; children's story hours; industrial, craft, and special exhibits; and cam-era clubs.   The use of museum auditoriums, workrooms, and other facilities is occasionally granted to local civic, cultural, nature, and other organizations.

In these ways the museum of today is not only creating a wider appreciation of its own work and program but is also developing interests, abilities, and hobbies which are enriching the lives of an ever widening group of people.

Other Municipal Agencies.—As previously stated, there are other city departments that play a part in the city's recreation life.   Police departments, for example, have established centers for boys and young men in neighborhoods where recreation facilities are lacking.   Water department properties have been developed and made available for golf, picnicking, fishing, hiking, and related activities.   Special depart-ments are sometimes created to administer a golf course, swimming pool, or other facility.   Recreation is sometimes a responsibility of the welfare, public works, or public service department, although in such cases the program is usually limited in scope.

SEMIPUBLIC AGENCIES

Recreation has an important place in the programs of most semi-public agencies which include the Y.M.C.A., the Y.W.C.A., boys' clubs, settlements, Boy and Girl Scouts, Y.M.H.A., Y.W.H.A., Camp Fire Girls, and many others.   These agencies serve varying age groups— children, young people, and adults.   They operate largely on a membership basis but membership is seldom exclusive and in some cases participation in parts of their program is not restricted to members. The cost of financing the facilities and program is usually met in part through contributions from individuals or community chests and in part from membership fees. Only a few of these agencies which constitute a significant force in leisure-time service can be mentioned here.

The Settlement.—This agency is primarily "a group of people resident in a neighborhood where community needs are obvious—discovering and developing, in local or wider spheres, opportunities and resources which may lead toward higher standards of living, broader cultural interests, social justice, and education for a better day."[1] Its welfare features, its resident staff, and the various fields which comprise its program differentiate the settlement from the community house or municipal recreation center. Although it serves children and young people primarily, its program also includes activities for adults. In many instances the settlement is the chief or only source of wholesome recreation activity in the neighborhood.

Since its early days the settlement has emphasized the development of cultural skills. It was a pioneer in the little-theater movement and many settlement buildings have auditoriums with stages well equipped for dramatic and music productions. Plays are studied, written, and completely produced by drama workshop groups. Music is a regular feature of many settlement functions and, in addition, music classes in various instruments, vocal instruction, and group music activities are often a part of the program. Gymnasiums are used for a variety of games, gymnastics, and athletic events. Arts and crafts groups, often utilizing the special aptitudes and techniques of foreign-born members, produce many objects of remarkable beauty. Forums or discussion groups are arranged for the consideration of topics of special interest or significance. Summer camps are conducted which afford opportunities to engage in woodcraft, nature study, and other outdoor activities which are seldom otherwise available to the people served by the settlement.

Youth Service Organizations.—Typical of the agencies in this group are the Y.M.C.A., the Y.W.C.A., and the Jewish Community Centers. The development of interests and skills essential to the enrichment of leisure is one of their objectives. Their well-equipped buildings afford facilities for a wide range of recreation activities and social relationships, participation in which is extended to both young men and young women. The magnitude of their facilities and services is indicated by the fact that in 1938 the Y.M.C.A. alone reported a total of 717 buildings, not including camp buildings, valued at 250 million dollars and used by a constituency of nearly 2 million individuals. Among the features of the

[1] Lea D. Taylor, *Social Work Year Book*, p. 446, Russell Sage Foundation, 1937.

Y.M.C.A. program are its Hi-Y organization for high-school boys, its activities for industrial workers, and its leadership in the fields of athletics and camping. The Y.W.C.A. membership numbered 407,000 in 1937 and it is estimated that 2,475,000 individuals had some kind of continuing relationship with the organization in 1935. Its well-equipped buildings afford a place for a great variety of social, cultural, and recreational projects.

The following statement concerning the Jewish Community Center gives a fair summary of the content of the recreation program of this and other youth service organizations:

> The Center provides for its membership a well-rounded program of health activities, including gymnasium and swimming classes, socials, games, dances and entertainments and a variety of cultural and educational activities, including dramatics, music, art, discussion groups, unit courses, lectures, concerts, forums, and lyceums.[1]

Hostels.—Among the youth agencies concerned with a particular form of recreation is the American Youth Hostels which furnishes overnight facilities for young people in different parts of the country and conducts trips through the United States and into foreign countries. In 1938 a total of 11,379 individuals held membership in the organization and during a one-year period 26,495 "overnights" were accommodated in its 184 hostels. It has been the means of stimulating the growing interest in hiking and bicycling, especially in New England and the North Central states.

Boys' and Girls' Work Organizations.—Recreation plays an important part in the programs of organizations serving boys and girls, typical of which are the Boy Scouts, Girl Scouts, and Camp Fire Girls. These agencies emphasize out-of-door activity and afford opportunity for participation in a wide range of projects. Nature study, woodcraft, games, athletics, service, camps, water sports, and craft activities, which feature their programs, appeal strongly to boys and girls and provide a basis for the development of interests that carry over into later life. The recent expansion of their camping service to include day, week-end, and winter, as well as summer, camps has a distinct recreation value.

Another group of organizations is represented by the boys' clubs and girls' clubs. They differ from the agencies in the Scouting group in that they have no standardized program prepared by a national organization; most of them have a special club building in which their activities are centered, and in many instances they are located in and serve underprivileged neighborhoods. The programs vary according to local inter-

[1] Harry L. Glucksman, *Social Work Year Book*, p. 555, Russell Sage Foundation, 1935.

ests and facilities but they are often built around informal groups and include a wide variety of recreation activities appealing to boys and girls. Their buildings serve as clubhouses where boys or girls may spend a quiet evening reading or playing games with a few friends, where entertainments and social programs are arranged and carried out, and where individuals or clubs may engage in a variety of craft, athletic, or cultural activities. Some clubs include in their programs parties, dances, and other social activities for mixed groups but for the most part participation is restricted to the sex which the club is organized to serve.

PRIVATE AGENCIES

Recreation has a part in the program of innumerable private agencies and organizations. Programs are generally restricted to members and, unlike the semipublic agencies, these agencies are not dependent upon outside public or private support. A few of the more important agencies in this group are stores, industries, churches, country clubs, service clubs, fraternal organizations, labor unions, women's clubs, outing and athletic clubs, and groups organized to carry on special recreation activities. Only a few of these agencies can be considered in this chapter.

Industry.—Industrial plants, especially those which employ large numbers of workers or which largely dominate small communities where they are located, often furnish elaborate recreation facilities for their employees. Similarly, department stores, insurance companies, banks, and other commercial organizations sometimes provide recreation facilities and programs. Athletic fields are used for company leagues and teams; recreation rooms equipped with piano, victrola, magazines, and tables for quiet games are popular during the noon hour; playgrounds are equipped for the workers and their families; vacation and week-end camps afford many attractive forms of activity, and libraries provide books for leisure hours. In many mill towns and villages well-equipped community houses have been erected and are operated by the factory management. Dances, outings, music, and dramatic entertainments are arranged for the workers and their families. Frequently, too, teams or other groups representing firms which employ them participate in activities conducted by the local recreation department or some other local recreation agency. In spite of the growing tendency for municipal agencies to provide such facilities and programs for workers, industry is still contributing to the recreation life of employees in many communities.

The Church.—The church has always been concerned with the way its members used their leisure hours, but through the centuries and from one denomination to another, there has been a great variation in its attitude toward recreation and its willingness to provide recreation for its members. Today most churches encourage their members to participate in wholesome recreation activities and many of them conduct programs that promote good fellowship among their members and afford a wise use of their leisure time. The church supper and the Sunday school picnic have long been high spots in the social program of the church but today it offers more varied attractions. The dramatic group may present a play, the Young People's Society a program of folk songs and folk dances, or the church choir an operetta. Frequently such occasions include group singing or games in which everyone participates. In addition, many a church social calendar includes dinners, holiday entertainments, athletic leagues, outings, and play nights. Games, music, crafts, and other play activities form an important part of the Vacation Bible School program.

To provide facilities for such varied programs many churches, not only in large cities but in small communities, have buildings fully equipped for an indoor recreation program. In other churches the special facilities are limited to bowling alleys, clubrooms, and a library or kitchen. Apparatus for children's play, tennis courts, and facilities for other games have been built on many church properties. Recreation activities hold a place of growing importance in the programs of church-sponsored organizations for young people, of which the Epworth League, the Catholic Youth Organization, and the Mutual Improvement Association are typical.

Sports Organizations.—The tremendous popularity of games and sports such as golf, tennis, boating, track and field athletics, boxing, fishing, hunting, polo, hiking, water and winter sports has resulted in the formation of thousands of clubs or organizations devoted to one or more of these activities. Membership in these groups is exceedingly high and the acreage of their properties exceeds that of public recreation areas in many communities. Some of these groups such as yacht clubs, golf clubs, polo clubs, and the more exclusive athletic clubs are open only to people of considerable wealth or to individuals who have attained prominence in the particular sport. Many others, however, serve persons with moderate incomes. Emphasizing only one or a few types of activity, they appeal to persons who have a deep interest in these particular sports and whose desires are not fully satisfied by existing public facilities. In addition to these local groups, practically every type of competitive game or sport has a state and a national organization which sets up standard rules for the activity and in many cases promotes or conducts state and national tournaments or competitions.

Other Clubs.—Comparable to the sports organizations are the many clubs which are organized about other activities or interests. Merely to mention a few of them suggests the wide scope of their activity and the variety of their membership. Among them are social clubs, dancing clubs, folk dance groups, chess and checker clubs, camera, stamp, and hobby clubs, players' guilds and little-theater groups, glee clubs, orchestral societies, garden clubs, bridge and whist clubs, youth hostels, discussion groups, civic improvement associations, marionette clubs, bird clubs, sketch clubs, various craft groups, and a host of others. Many of these organizations have a relatively small local membership but because they are formed around a common interest they often influence the lives of the individual members more than some of the larger agencies with a more varied program. Like the sports organizations, many are served by state and national agencies which promote the particular activity by issuing publications or by sponsoring meetings, exhibits, or competitions on a state or national basis.

No picture of recreation as it affects the women of our country would be complete without reference to the programs of the women's clubs with their groups devoted to dramatic activity, music, gardening, art, literature, civics, and current problems. As a rule, the programs of men's community clubs are more restricted in scope, with emphasis upon civic, social, and entertainment features. Lodges with their initiations, ritual, social functions, and good fellowship reach large, though decreasing numbers.

Recreation plays an important part in the activities of the many societies comprising foreign-born groups. It outranks discussions of agricultural problems as a means of attracting rural folk to meetings of the farm bureau and the grange. It has a place in the program of the labor union and in the meetings of service organizations, civic and luncheon clubs—organizations which also frequently sponsor community recreation projects. Intercollegiate and intramural athletic, music, and literary programs, dramatic groups, debates, lectures, social functions, "proms," outing clubs, discussion and special interest groups have a conspicuous place in college and university life. In fact the private agency that does not carry on some form of recreation is exceptional.

COMMERCIAL AGENCIES

The universal urge for recreation, relaxation, and release from the daily routine has been capitalized by commercial agencies which have built up a recreation business totaling several billion dollars per year. This gigantic development testifies to the public demand for recreation and also to the inadequacy of the recreation facilities and opportunities which have been afforded by the agencies mentioned in the preceding pages. Unlike these agencies which aim to give individuals a chance for self-expression, the philosophy of commercialism, as applied in the field of recreation, is "buy something." The commercial agencies are primarily motivated by profits rather than service and many of their offerings help to make the American people "the world's greatest consumers of passive recreation." On the other hand, some of the most popular forms of commercial recreation involve strenuous physical activity.

In comparison with the amounts spent for certain commercial sports events, expenditures for other forms of recreation seem insignificant. For example, the "gate" at a predepression world's championship prize fight exceeded $2,500,000—which of course does not include the enormous amount spent for travel, hotels, and other items by persons attending it. This amount is more than four times as large as the total expenditure of the Los Angeles Playground and Recreation Department for the year 1937 when the total attendances recorded at its playgrounds, indoor centers, camps, beaches, and other facilities exceeded 25 million. Commercial agencies account for a large percentage of the nation's annual recreation expenditures which, it has been estimated, totaled as high as 21 billion dollars shortly before the depression.[1]

Amusements.—Under this heading may be grouped moving pictures, the radio, the theater, night clubs, and dance halls. The radio and moving picture, comparatively recent developments, have become two of the most popular and widely accepted mediums for leisure-time activity. Of 37,677 places of amusement recorded in the Census of Business: 1935, nearly one-third were motion-picture theaters and they accounted for 72.7 per cent of the total receipts of all amusement places, which were $669,051,000.[2] The hold which this industry has upon the American public is evident from the total weekly attendance at motion-picture theaters, estimated in 1929 to be between 100 million and 115 million and in 1939 approximately 85 million.

The radio also has become a powerful factor in the everyday leisure time of the American people. Its various offerings of dance music and symphony concerts, descriptions of sporting events, dramas, news comments, lectures, skits, and stories afford unprecedented possibilities for recreation and education. According to a 1938 estimate, there were some 33 million radios in the homes, cars, and meeting places of the nation and between 84 million and 90 million people listened to the radio each day. With the possible exception of reading, it is the most widespread form of leisure-time activity—if indeed it can be classed as "activity." For this reason the nature and quality of the programs broadcast over the air are matters of great public concern.

The degree to which the motion picture has monopolized the amusement field in most cities is emphasized by the fact that the Business Census reported only 158 theaters used for the production of legitimate drama and opera. Few in number and located principally in a few large

[1] Stuart Chase, "Play" in *Whither Mankind* by C. A. Beard, Longmans, Green & Company, 1928.

[2] Census of Business: 1935, U. S. Department of Commerce, 1937.

cities, they still make a valuable contribution to the cultural life of America. In addition to such other forms of amusement as the rodeo, circus, vaudeville, and many amusement park features, are the traveling carnival, burlesque, and peep shows which have very questionable recreation value. The popular desire to dance is capitalized by dance halls, dine-and-dance restaurants, cabarets, night clubs, and excursion boats. At a convention of dancing teachers held in New York in 1937 it was reported that the public is spending more than 100 million dollars yearly for dancing lessons and that more than 6 million adults and children are enrolled in dancing schools.

Athletics and Sports.—Professional sports exhibitions have become a common feature of American life. Public interest in athletics has made profitable the development of professional baseball on a national scale, the growth of professional football, and the current popularity of wrestling, ice hockey, and winter sports exhibitions. Championship fights attract spectators from all parts of the country. Horse racing and, more recently, dog racing have a large and enthusiastic following, as do automobile, motorcycle, and bicycle racing. In recent years tennis has joined golf in the field of professional sports. College basketball and track teams, although composed of amateurs, are attracting capacity crowds at commercial arenas and college football has many characteristics of a professional sport.

But it is not as spectators alone that the American people are being served by commercial recreation agencies. The failure of public agencies to keep pace with the demand for recreation facilities has resulted in their development by private interests. Swimming pools, bathing beaches, tennis courts, picnic areas, golf courses, roller and ice skating rinks, boating facilities, bowling alleys, and billiard parlors under commercial auspices outnumber the public facilities in many cities. In the Census of Business: 1935, 12,412 billiard and pool parlors and bowling alleys were reported, 698 swimming pools, 645 riding academies, and 939 boat and canoe rental services. This development, coupled with the marked increase in municipal recreation facilities, may explain in part the apparent downward trend, even before the depression, in spectator interest in sports as compared with the upward trend in participant interest.[1]

Travel.—Travel, including the use of the automobile for pleasure, accounts for by far the largest recreation expenditure of the American people. President Hoover's Committee on Social Trends estimated that between 1928 and 1930 the annual expenditure by Americans for vacation travel at home and abroad and for the pleasure use of automobiles, motorboats, motorcycles, and bicycles was nearly 6½ billion dollars.[2] Hotels,

---

[1] *The Index,* July, 1936.
[2] Jesse F. Steiner, *Americans at Play,* McGraw-Hill Book Company, Inc., 1933.

camps, gas stations, and resorts primarily serving people on vacation help make recreation one of the country's largest business undertakings. A study conducted by the New England Council showed that 3 million visitors and summer residents spend 500 million dollars annually in New England. In 1935 some 37 million people took the highroad to "see America."[1]

The unparalleled development of recreation facilities in the national and state parks and forests during the depression would have yielded only limited returns if an extensive road-building program had not furnished the means by which large numbers of people could reach them. It has also stimulated the travel and transportation companies to devise new ways of inducing people to make use of these new facilities. Snow trains, first introduced by a New England railroad in 1930 when they carried only 197 passengers, attracted 24,240 passengers 6 years later. This feature has been copied by several railroads and its success has prompted other similar ventures. Bicycle and hiking trains have been run by a number of railroads; a hobby train took 600 people from Detroit for a day's outing; a group of New York camera and sketching enthusiasts were taken to Saybrook, Connecticut, on a train which provided a darkroom and instructors; husking-bee trains have given many New Yorkers their first introduction to a grange supper, husking bee, and country dance. An Eastern airline has scheduled vacation flights in the form of 9-day, all-expense tours from New York to a winter sports resort in Idaho. Rail and steamboat excursions and the special cruises conducted by many steamship companies are well known. All these features provide an income not only for the transportation agencies but also for the communities which are visited by the travelers and for the companies producing sports apparel and equipment. Private camps for children and adults, dude ranches, and other vacation centers also contribute to the total of recreation travel.

THE NEED FOR COOPERATIVE PLANNING

The multiplicity of agencies undertaking some form of recreation activity or serving some recreation interest is largely the result of independent attempts to meet specific recreation desires and needs rather than of concerted action to render recreation service according to a carefully devised, cooperative plan of action. The rapidity and extent of the changes which have given recreation a place of prominence in American life—some of which were mentioned in the preceding chapter—account in part for the relative lack of coordination among recreation agencies

---

[1] Recreation, *Building America*, April, 1936.

in the past. With the emergence of recreation as a major factor in modern life, however, the need for cooperative planning has become apparent and notable progress has been made in this direction.

Reference was made earlier in the chapter to a committee which was appointed to study the problem of coordinating the work of the Federal agencies in the field of recreation. Federal legislation has authorized cooperation between the National Park Service and state and local park and recreation authorities in the acquisition, development, and operation of areas and facilities. For the first time in many states planning boards have been studying the states' recreation resources under public and private auspices and have been suggesting programs of action. The National Education-Recreation Council, composed of representatives of twenty national agencies interested in some phase of the leisure-time problem, serves as a medium for discussing common problems, considering effective methods of joint action, and conducting local studies of agencies serving the people through recreation. Recreation councils, committees of councils of social agencies, and other representative groups have been created in many cities to study this problem and to work out ways in which the people can best be provided with recreation. Organizations of this type will be considered in a later chapter.

Closer cooperation or central control has been achieved also by many of the private recreation groups. A number have established national organizations or federations for the setting of standards, the promotion of activities on a uniform national basis, or for some other purpose. For example, the Amateur Athletic Union, which includes among its objectives the improvement and promotion of amateur sports, the development of uniform rules, and the supervision of athletic championships, comprises among its membership state and district sports bodies as well as 36 allied national organizations promoting various amateur sports programs. The desirability of uniform practices and centralized control has also been recognized by the major commercial recreation interests, notably professional baseball and the motion-picture industry.

The many agencies mentioned in this chapter are all contributing to a greater or lesser degree to the enrichment of the leisure time of people. Some of them are serving large numbers without regard to their social, religious, economic, or racial background; others are reaching only limited, homogeneous groups. It is clear that recreation—like education and health—is so vital to the life and welfare of the people that government must assume some responsibility for assuring recreation opportunities for all the people. Private and commercial agencies cannot be expected to meet this universal need. Therefore, the municipality has a place of primary importance in furnishing recreation for all the people and in giving them opportunity to share their common recreation interests in a democratic leisure-time experience. Furthermore, there is much to be gained by cooperative planning and action on the part of all agencies furnishing recreation, public and private, to the end that the greatest opportunities for wholesome and satisfying recreation may be extended to all.

CHAPTER IV

RECREATION—A MUNICIPAL FUNCTION

A century ago local government was relatively simple and concerned itself with few functions. The complex organization which controls our cities today is the result of the gradual absorption by the municipality of a variety of functions and services. Many of these services were initiated and carried on for a time by private agencies, but as their need and value became recognized they were gradually taken over by the municipal authorities who created special agencies to provide and administer them. Education, which before 1850 was largely under private auspices, has been accepted without question as an essential function, justifying not only public financial support and administrative control but compulsory school attendance. About 1880, cities began to recognize that health was a major problem, the solution of which required municipal action. Social welfare, long considered a philanthropic service to be rendered by private agencies, has been taken over by the local government increasingly since 1900.

THE EXPANSION OF MUNICIPAL SERVICES

To understand fully the manner in which municipalities added to the range and variety of their functions, it is necessary to remember that the local government is not a completely independent unit. It is rather an entity created by the state, and its functions are dependent on legal authority from the state. Fortunately, along with the need for new municipal services, there also developed a liberal attitude toward municipal functions, especially those concerned with human well-being and happiness. The opinion of Charles A. Beard, that "nothing human is alien, for in the wide range of its activities, the city summons every power of human mind and character,"[1] is representative of the broad viewpoint which evolved during the course of the years.

Many local governments, taking advantage of this liberal attitude toward municipal functions, added new services without resorting to special legislation, by invoking the police powers with which they were vested by the state. The police power was utilized because it includes "the right to frame and enforce reasonable measures for the protection of

[1] Charles A. Beard, *American Government and Politics*, p. 731, The Macmillan Company, 1931.

health, life, property and morals." Furthermore, as A. G. Truxal writes, "modern jurisprudence is giving a more liberal interpretation to this power so that it may include measures adopted to promote the common welfare, convenience, and prosperity."[1] During a long period recreation was felt to be a matter of no public concern, and the early attempts to provide play opportunities were carried on through private initiative and funds. Like the other municipal services which grew out of "the increasing complexity of civilization and the growing tendency to invoke governmental aid for the satisfaction of wants not previously met, or if felt, met by voluntary action,"[2] recreation passed through the stages from private to municipal support and established itself as one of the functions of local government.

Recreation Is Recognized as a Function of Government.—Some of the larger cities first established playgrounds as they did certain other services, under the broad interpretation of the police power granted them by the state. In other cities existing park or school legislation was deemed sufficient authority for operating playgrounds, or special laws were enacted to give them such authority. As the recreation movement grew in scope, however, and as the demand for such facilities and services increased, there developed a need for specific legislation giving municipalities power to appropriate funds for a comprehensive recreation program. Laws of this type have been passed in many states. Chapter XXVIII, which considers more fully the legal aspects of recreation, reviews existing legislation of this kind and the extent to which the courts have upheld it, establishing recreation as an essential function of government.

The acceptance of recreation as a reasonable concern of government has had strong support from leaders in many fields of public life. When Newton D. Baker was Mayor of Cleveland, he stated, "The control and financing of recreation activities of almost every kind, I believe, is a definite and proper city function."[3] While President, Calvin Coolidge said, "Play for the child, sport for youth, and recreation for adults are essentials of modern life. It is becoming generally recognized that the creation and maintenance of outdoor recreation facilities is a community duty in order that the whole public might participate in their enjoyment. This presents a particular challenge to municipal and county administrations."[4] In the report of the Committee on Municipal Parks and Playgrounds to the President's Conference on Outdoor Recreation held in May,

[1] A. G. Truxal, *Outdoor Recreation Legislation and Its Effectiveness*, p. 21, Columbia University Press, 1929.

[2] James Brice, *American Commonwealth*, p. 625, The Macmillan Company, 1923.

[3] *The Playground*, September, 1912, p. 186.

[4] From an introduction to *Parks: A Manual of Municipal and County Parks*, prepared by the National Recreation Association.

1924, the committee held that these factors are necessary for normal life: play for the child, sport for youth, and recreation for adults, and "that to promote these ends an immutable moral duty rests upon all persons, as well as upon each community and our Nation."

Dean William F. Russell of Teachers College concluded an address on Leisure and National Security with these words: "Education for leisure and the enrichment of adult life . . . is no incidental task. It is rather a fundamental problem affecting the welfare of the State and its perpetuity; and as such should receive major consideration."[1] While he was Governor of New Hampshire, John G. Winant said:

> If life, liberty, and the pursuit of happiness are the ends for which governments are created, surely the opportunity to use leisure that we may prolong life and to play that we may better understand the rights of others, and to do both so that our children and ourselves may enjoy greater happiness, lies well within the province of the State.[2]

REASONS FOR MUNICIPAL RECREATION

In fact, in law, and in public opinion, recreation is recognized today as a suitable and essential function of government. Yet the question may still be raised as to whether local government is necessarily the best or most effective agency for providing recreation facilities and service. Some of the reasons why recreation is distinctly a part of the city's job will be considered here.

1. **Municipal recreation affords a large percentage of the people their only opportunity for forms of wholesome recreation.**—People of wealth can belong to country clubs, travel, attend the theater and opera, own their own yachts, and secure for themselves many recreation opportunities. Those with moderate means can also, to a considerable degree, provide many attractive and satisfying recreation activities for themselves through individual or group effort. For a great many people, however, recreation opportunities are very limited except as facilities, areas, activities, and leadership are provided by the government or semipublic agencies. Especially in the cities, simple, traditional ways of spending leisure have been abandoned, if not made impossible, so that organization and the provision of facilities by the government become necessary. The benefits society gains from participation in recreation will be largely lost if public funds do not make possible recreation programs and services.

2. **It is only through government that adequate lands can be acquired.** It is not possible for most individuals or private organizations to acquire

[1] *Recreation*, July, 1932, p. 174.
[2] *Recreation*, January, 1927, p. 535.

and develop for recreation the areas necessary for an adequate program. Only through governmental action can the city be supplied with ample and properly located playgrounds, parks, and other outdoor areas. Through city planning, subdivision control, eminent domain, transfer of properties between governmental units, the acceptance of gifts of land, and its ability to issue bonds, the local government has the means for acquiring them. These powers enable cities to secure waterfront properties suitable for recreation, large outlying reservations, stream valleys, and areas of scenic interest. Such problems as eliminating the pollution of streams, lakes, or beaches in order that they may be used for recreation by the people can be dealt with only by governmental action.

The municipality's essential responsibility in this respect was stressed by Walter Rauschenbusch who said:

Public property is the only thing that can beat commercialized amusements. I am for taking the sewage out of our rivers and putting boys and girls into them to swim . . . I am for stocking the waters inside of the city limits with perch, rock bass, and bullheads . . . The spirit of adventure is essential to childhood and nothing but public property creates freedom enough in big cities to invite adventure.[1]

3. Municipal recreation is democratic and inclusive.—Unlike most of that provided by other agencies, municipal recreation is for all the people. In large measure it is equally available for rich and poor, for people of all ages, racial backgrounds, social status, political opinions, and religious preference, for boys and girls, men and women. It gives to all the opportunity to engage in activities of their choice. Municipal recreation conforms with the American spirit and way of living.

Since all the people benefit either directly or indirectly, it is fitting that the burden should be distributed upon the entire community. There is no more reason why the entire cost of providing recreation for the people should be borne by public-spirited individuals or by a fee-paying public than that the schools should be financed privately or on a basis of self-support. One recreation department reported that during 1936 a total of 1,750 special groups made use of the city recreation centers for such activities as handicraft, dancing, music, dramatics, social recreation, sports, hobbies, and character-building clubs. It is difficult to believe that such widespread participation could have resulted except under a governmental agency.

4. Municipal recreation is comparatively inexpensive.—Through a pooling of resources and the provision of service on a city-wide basis the municipality can furnish recreation at a much lower cost than would otherwise be possible. In Los Angeles, for example, in 1936–1937, it

[1] *The Playground*, March, 1916, p. 468.

cost the taxpayers only 3.5 cents every time an individual used a municipal playground, slightly more than ½ cent for every bather at the city's ocean beaches, and 7.8 cents for every swim at its municipal pools. As Roy Smith Wallace pointed out, "A tax of $2 or $3 per householder for the provision of public recreation will buy day-by-day recreation indoor and outdoor, of a great variety of kinds, for the whole family for the whole year, at a cost of one theater ticket or eight or ten attendances at the movies."[1]

Even with the growth of municipal recreation since the World War, the expenditures for the country are comparatively small. According to the Recreation Year Book[2] which records local expenditures for organized recreation activities and programs and for the construction, operation, and maintenance of facilities and areas used for active recreation, the total amount spent for these purposes in 1,258 communities in 1938 was less than $29,400,000, not including expenditures from relief or emergency funds. This total indicates that only a fraction of a dollar was spent per capita in these communities for municipal recreation during the year. *Financial Statistics of Cities*, issued by the Bureau of the Census, records all governmental cost payments by large cities for the operation and maintenance of parks, recreation, museums, music, and other related services. According to the latest figures available, for the year 1934, the average per capita expenditure for all these purposes in the 94 largest cities of the country was only $1.29.

5. The municipal government gives permanency to recreation.—Private agencies are dependent for their continuance upon the interest and support of individuals or special groups. The government, on the other hand, is a perpetual agency and can alone assure the continuance of the recreation program. As Mayor H. H. Burton of Cleveland stated, "The children of one family outgrow the recreation problem, but the public's children are there forever." Permanent, but subject to the changing needs of the people, the local government stands out as the best equipped agency for meeting the recreation needs, not only of the present but of the future. Furthermore, recreation areas acquired and developed by the government are dedicated to public use in perpetuity whereas private property may be withdrawn from public use at any time.

6. The job is too large for any private agency.—With the increase in leisure, the prospect of considerable permanent unemployment, and the growing need and demand for recreation, the task of providing recreation for all the people is too large for any agency except the government. Only by utilizing the government's powers of acquiring land and raising

---

[1] "How Much Public Recreation is Essential?" *Recreation*, November, 1932, p. 375.

[2] *Recreation*, June, 1939, p. 132.

funds, and by taking advantage of the low cost which city-wide, nonprofit service makes possible, can a large portion of the public secure the recreation it will demand and which, in the public interest, it should have. Failure to provide it will close the avenues of recreation to countless individuals except in forms which contribute little or nothing in positive values to them or to society. Some of the activities which have the greatest citizenship and cultural value are small-group activities, but they frequently require considerable expenditures for expert guidance or special facilities. Opportunities for such activities cannot be made extensive enough to compete with less desirable forms of commercial recreation except as the municipality makes them convenient, attractive, and inexpensive.

7. The municipality cannot afford not to provide recreation.—The frequent emphasis which has been placed upon the economy of maintaining recreation budgets even during the depression has borne testimony to the importance of recreation to the municipality. The relationship between the maintenance of an adequate recreation program and the city's crime bill has been pointed out repeatedly. Robert Moses, New York City Commissioner of Parks, has stated the case clearly and emphatically in an article from which the following is quoted:

No matter how difficult the problem of providing these increased [recreation] facilities may be, and afterwards maintaining and controlling them, it must be met. It does not matter how conservative a citizen may be or how much he may deprecate the expansion of government facilities into new fields, recreation in cities and municipalities is not a new field and must be recognized as a vital necessity. There is neither justice, nor economy, nor common sense in dodging this issue. This is a real field, some of it measurable in dollars and a great deal more which can be gauged only in terms of human misfortune. The problem can be solved by proper planning and financing. We know from experience that the answer will be reflected directly in a more healthful nation, a reduction in street accidents and a curtailment in crime . . .

The demand for all these new facilities in the park system has unquestionably existed. The evidence that these new facilities have improved health, decreased juvenile delinquency and accidents is beyond dispute. I am not referring merely to the claims of exuberant reformers . . . I have already stated my conviction that the non-revenue as well as the new self-supporting activities of the Park Department are an actual economy, and that they bring about a directly traceable reduction in the cost of policing, crime prevention, operation of accident wards and health administration. The beneficial effects of park and parkway improvements on adjacent property also needs no proof.[1] .

One of the principles of democracy is that, except as all the people have a fair opportunity for the good life, the nation as a whole cannot

[1] "Who Will Pay the Piper?" *The Survey Graphic*, June, 1937.

prosper. The public education system is based on the principle that it is essential for all the people to be able to read, write, and think. It is unsafe for part of the population to be without health services. Just so it has been demonstrated and is being recognized that the city cannot afford to have a part of its people deprived of opportunities for wholesome recreation and that it is good economy to spend public funds to provide them.

CAN RECREATION BE ENTRUSTED TO GOVERNMENT?

No argument for a tax-supported recreation program is complete which ignores this question. Some people do not trust local government because they fear corrupt practices and believe that political considerations rather than the public good may dominate important functions. In a democracy such as ours faith in government and in its ability to render efficient service to all the people is fundamental. Except as people believe in government and are willing to work to make government something to be believed in, there is no hope for democracy.

"Government after all is all of us working together for the common good" and to abandon government is to give up faith in ourselves. To admit that city departments under present conditions cannot successfully carry out the undertakings of the people and truly express their will is fundamental pessimism. It is true that there have been cities in which recreation, like other functions, has been thwarted by the selfishness, lack of vision, or dishonesty of public officials. On the other hand, many of the finest achievements in recreation, as in other fields, have been developed within the government. If it is true that recreation for all the people can best be achieved through government, as suggested in the preceding pages, it is clear that all who are concerned with this problem should work together for the achievement of higher standards in city administration. The results will be measured not merely in terms of greater municipal efficiency but in terms of greater concern by city officials for the welfare of the people.

Strengthening and raising the standards of the public agencies is not only good theory in a government such as ours but it is also a wise procedure in view of recent developments and trends. In an address before the Governmental Research Association in 1937, Clifford W. Ham, late Executive Director of the American Municipal Association stated:

Throughout the tough days since 1929, one thing stands out with strong emphasis; government does not—cannot retreat. One direction only is possible and public services do not diminish in number or intensity . . . Even at the low point of public revenue and finance, enlarged government services were insisted upon and the tempo of these services was stepped up.

Prominent educators and other public leaders are prophesying that present provisions for recreation and education are insignificant in comparison with what they will be in the future. If this be true, as indications seem to imply, the building up of a strong, honest, efficient, municipal recreation service is a wise and forward-looking plan of action.

LOCAL GOVERNMENT CANNOT DO THE ENTIRE JOB

The municipality does not aim to meet, and can never hope to serve, all the recreation needs of all the people. These particular interests and needs of any community are too diverse and too extensive to be the sole province of any one agency. Freedom of choice is inherent in recreation, and individuals are best served when there are a number of agencies offering a variety of recreation opportunities from which they may choose. There are certain recreation services which can be furnished only—or most advantageously—by the states or the Federal government; individuals will continue to form private membership groups for the purpose of engaging in recreation activities, and the commercial field will, in all probability, reach even greater proportions in the years ahead. If this is the case, what part of the entire field of recreation constitutes the particular responsibility of the municipality, and what is the relation of municipal recreation to the other similar agencies?

There is no definite or commonly accepted answer to this question. It is generally agreed that the municipality should provide, maintain, and operate for the use of the people a system of major areas and facilities, such as parks, golf courses, water and winter sports facilities, playgrounds, athletic fields, indoor recreation centers, playfields, and reservations. It is also widely recognized that the public should provide leadership not only in the use of these facilities but also in the promotion of a city-wide program of athletics, music, drama, social recreation, crafts, and other activities. Art and nature are being included in municipal recreation programs more than before; somewhat more slowly camping is being recognized as an important activity for the whole community. There are few forms of recreation that can be carried on in a locality which are not included in the program of one or more municipalities. Some of the suggested criteria for a municipal recreation activity are that it should be constructive, be recognized as an acceptable public service, be made available to all citizens, be reasonable in cost in proportion to the values received, and that participation should not be restricted by political, religious, or other considerations.

The Place of Other Governmental Agencies.—Most municipalities cannot provide for their citizens areas of outstanding scenic beauty or extensive properties which afford opportunities for camping, nature study, and hiking, like the national and state parks and forests. The provision of such areas which serve the people in a region, state, or the country as a whole, is a Federal or state, and not a municipal, responsibility. The problem of conserving wild life and of developing large-scale opportunities for hunting and fishing cannot be met primarily through municipal action but is a matter for the Federal or state authorities. In all probability, if the millions of children, youth, and adults in the rural communities are to enjoy the benefits of recreation programs, it will continue to be a result of assistance received primarily through state and Federal agencies rather than through action of the local government.

The Semipublic Agency.—The function of the semipublic agencies in the leisure-time field has been the subject of much consideration during the past decade. The rapid extension of municipal recreation programs has absorbed many activities which were formerly available largely if not entirely through these agencies. Yet it is commonly agreed that even though the local government takes over many of the recreation functions of the semipublic agencies, these agencies will continue to meet definite leisure-time needs. Opinions differ as to the specific nature of the recreation services which these agencies are best equipped to render, just as the personnel, objectives, facilities, and financial resources of these agencies differ from city to city. However, unlike the municipal agency which must consider the recreation needs of all the people, the semipublic agency usually restricts its primary service to a limited group. It is therefore especially fitted to serve the special interests of individuals who desire to engage in forms of recreation with others of a similar religious, social, economic, or racial background. In some cases it is more free than the municipal agency to experiment, to explore the possibilities of new activities, the value of which has not demonstrated and for which public funds are not available, and to provide opportunities for the discussion of controversial issues and questions.

Semipublic agencies realize that they have a responsibility for helping to strengthen public recreation programs. This is clearly reflected in a report of the Committee on Correlation of Public and Private Leisure Time Activities at the Southern Institute for Social Work Executives in 1931. Agencies supported by philanthropic funds and concerned with the problem of leisure-time activities were held to have the following functions:

1. To help in initiating and establishing public or tax-supported leisure-time agencies.
2. To continue their interest in order to help ensure the permanency and growth of such agencies.
3. To help develop favorable public opinion and sentiment in favor of an adequate public leisure-time program.

4. To demonstrate the value of a needed piece of work and the necessity of definite standards for the administration and conduct of all phases of public leisure-time programs. In this connection we believe that participation on the part of public departments in such demonstrations will bring about better results than where there is no participation in such demonstrations.

5. To be constantly on the alert to reshape their policies and programs, in order that such programs in whole or in part may be transferred to public or tax-supported agencies.

The Private Agencies.—It is neither possible nor desirable for the government to take the place of the private agencies of many types which afford recreation for their members and constituents. People who can afford membership in exclusive clubs or who desire to join with their friends in restricted recreation groups, will continue to enjoy such privileges. One of the outstanding functions of municipal recreation is to stimulate, encourage, and assist the provision of more and better recreation opportunities in homes, churches, industries, clubs, and other private groups. In this way the municipality can render a most important and valuable service and can reach a large number of people who may not make direct use of public recreation facilities or participate in municipal recreation programs. Instances of cooperation with both semipublic and private agencies and of service rendered them by public authorities are recorded in later chapters.

The Commercial Agencies.—In most cities the only direct relationship between the municipality and the commercial recreation agencies has been one of regulation. Through a system of licenses, fees, or regulations, the city has placed restrictions upon forms of commercial recreation in the interest of public safety, morals, health, or welfare. There has been little if any attempt to relate or coordinate municipal and commercial recreation services. The types of service rendered by the commercial interests are not as a rule the ones which the municipal agency promotes as having the greatest value to the people. There is a sound basis for the belief that by establishing high standards and attractive programs within the means of the people the city can render its best service and at the same time help raise the standards of commercial recreation agencies.

The municipal recreation program must be equally available to all; the commercial agency, on the other hand, can set up restrictions which give its offerings an added appeal to individuals who are able to afford them. There are activities of doubtful value which the municipality could not justifiably include in its program but which offer a financial return that makes them attractive business enterprises. Recreation is, therefore, likely to continue as a profitable undertaking. The municipality seldom directly competes with the commercial recreation agency, but there have been instances where the public provision of swimming pools, the conducting of community dances, and other projects have been opposed by commercial interests. The recreation needs in most cities are so great that if existing commercial activities are reasonably acceptable, the municipal department may well turn its attention to other forms of activity. On the other hand, if the opportunities are unwholesome, inadequate, or too expensive, the city should not be deterred from fulfilling its responsibility to the people by the opposition of the commercial agencies.

CHAPTER V

THE HISTORY OF MUNICIPAL RECREATION IN THE UNITED STATES

Recreation has played a role of varying importance in the life of all peoples. The earliest known races had their games, dances, music, and ceremonials just as the savage Bushmen today engage in similar activities. The Chinese, Egyptian, Aztec, Babylonian, and other early civilizations have left evidences of varied forms of recreation. The high esteem in which games, athletics, and the cultural arts were held by the Greeks at the height of their achievements is well known. During the Dark Ages certain forms of recreation fell into disrepute, but the ideal of chivalry as well as the minstrels, through song and story, helped maintain the play tradition. With the Renaissance and Reformation there returned a popular interest in the arts and sports which has grown steadily up to the present time, in spite of attempts of small groups to suppress it. This advance was aided by the philosophers and educators who since the sixteenth century have advocated recreation as an activity of social and educational value.

New England was settled chiefly by people whose primary concerns were to make a living and build a new home in the wilderness. Consequently, during the colonial period forms of recreation in New England were comparatively few though quilting and cornhusking parties, apple bees, and similar gatherings provided diversion at the same time they were serving practical ends. Life in other colonies, however, was brightened by a great variety of sports and amusements. Horse racing, dancing, cards, backgammon, bowling, cock fighting, contests of skill and strength, hunting, fishing, and excursions are among the forms of recreation engaged in during colonial times and the early part of the nineteenth century. Some of these were limited largely to the "well-to-do," although there were many occasions when all could take part.

During the early half of the nineteenth century, according to Jesse F. Steiner, popular amusements followed in the main the patterns set during the colonial period and were looked upon with disfavor by many influential leaders.[1] Recreation continued to be chiefly a matter of individual concern, although numerous sports clubs were organized, especially among the wealthy. The country was still essentially a pioneer nation in

[1] *Americans at Play*, McGraw-Hill Book Company, Inc., 1933.

which rural influences played a dominating part and in which wealth and leisure were relatively scarce. The period therefore gave no indication of the subsequent development of recreation as a major activity and as an organized service of local government.

SIGNIFICANT EVENTS IN THE RECREATION MOVEMENT

The history of municipal recreation in the United States, like that of other movements of social significance, cannot be told fully in terms of a series of specific events which mark distinct stages or periods of evolution. The recreation movement was the result of a combination of ideas, experiments, and developments. Some of them were closely related to each other in time, place, and influence; others seem to have had little connection with preceding, simultaneous, or subsequent happenings. Events now regarded as significant had only a remote relationship with other events immediately preceding them, yet they all contributed to the growth of the recreation movement. For this reason the following table, which points out some of the significant happenings, serves as a guidepost in tracing the history of this uniquely American movement:

1820–1840 Opening of outdoor gymnasiums at several schools and universities
1853 Purchase of land for Central Park in New York City
1866 Vacation School started in Old First Church of Boston
1872 Brookline, Mass., purchased land for two playgrounds
1885 The first sand garden conducted in Boston
1889 The Charlesbank Outdoor Gymnasium for men and boys opened in Boston
1892 A "model" playground established at Hull House, Chicago
1898 School buildings in New York City opened as evening recreation centers
1903 $5,000,000 voted for creation of "small parks" by South Park Commission in Chicago
1904 Board of Playground Commissioners appointed in Los Angeles
1905 Opening of ten South Park centers in Chicago
1906 April 12th, Organization of the Playground Association of America in Washington, D. C.
1907 Opening of "social and civic" centers in Rochester schools
1907 First Play Congress held in Chicago
1909 First Normal Course in Play published
1911 Name of Playground Association of America changed to Playground and Recreation Association of America
1917 P.R.A.A. organized work for servicemen for the War Department, later known as War Camp Community Service
1919 Community Service established
1924 Conference on Outdoor Recreation called by President Coolidge
1926 National Recreation School organized
1930 White House Conference on Child Health and Protection called by President Hoover
1930 Name of Playground and Recreation Association of America changed to National Recreation Association
1931–1932 Dr. L. P. Jacks's lecture tour of United States

1932 First International Recreation Congress in Los Angeles
1933 Federal government established first nationwide emergency works program, including expansion of recreation facilities and services
1938 The Society of Recreation Workers of America organized

EARLY DEVELOPMENTS

The event generally accepted as distinctly marking the beginning of the recreation movement in this country was the opening of the Sand Garden in Boston in 1885. However, the events listed in the preceding table which took place before this date are regarded as important because they influenced the recreation life of the people and focused attention upon the value of a public recreation program. The opening of outdoor gymnasiums at several schools and universities between 1820 and 1840, largely the result of German influence, served to bring formal gymnastics and physical education to the attention of the people in this country. The experience of English schools and universities was utilized soon after the middle of the century in the introduction of games and athletics as an important part of school and college life. Many athletic and sporting clubs were organized during this period. All these had their effect on the development of recreation as a distinct movement.

Of great significance, too, was the purchase of a large tract of land by New York City in 1853, later developed and known as Central Park. This is reported to be the first municipal park in the United States to be established as a result of a "conscious effort of a democratic body to meet a proven need."[1] Many cities followed New York's example in acquiring large parks, but for years these properties were considered to be for rest and contemplation and not for recreation activity although horseback riding, boating, skating, walking, and picnicking were provided for in Central Park and a special center for the play of young children was established. Another important event which preceded the beginning of the recreation movement was the opening of the first vacation school on record in the Old First Church in Boston in 1866. Twenty years later Newark made such schools a part of the city school system. Singing, "manual work," and nature study—typical play activities—had an important place in the program of these schools.

Arising as the recreation movement did out of a great social need, it is not surprising that social workers played a great part in launching the projects which were the forerunners of the recreation movement as we know it today. As was shown in Chap. II, the social problems attendant upon the industrialization of the country focused attention upon the need for wholesome recreation opportunities for all the people. Bad housing conditions resulting from the growth of tenement slum areas, the

[1] Frederick Law Olmsted, Jr., and Theodora Kimball, *Central Park—As a Work of Art and as a Great Municipal Enterprise*, G. P. Putnam's Sons, 1928.

great influx of immigrants, the rising tide of juvenile delinquency, the increase in factories accompanied by the evils of child labor and unsanitary and unsafe working conditions, the spread of commercialized amusements which were often associated with vice—all helped to create a condition which made the provision of wholesome recreation a necessity.

Play Centers in Boston.—The year 1885 is memorable in playground history because of the outdoor play center for children established in Boston in that year and the influence of this center on later playground developments in other cities. In 1885 a large sand pile was placed in the yard of the Children's Mission on Parmenter Street in Boston through the efforts of the Massachusetts Emergency and Hygiene Association. This was the direct result of a visit by Dr. Marie Zakrzewska to Berlin where she observed the sand gardens which had been established for the children of that city. Each day an average of 15 children attended this first Boston playground which was open 3 days a week for 6 weeks during July and August. They dug in the sand, sang songs, and marched about under the guidance of a woman who lived in the neighborhood.

This experiment was continued in succeeding years and its success is indicated by the fact that in 1887 ten centers were opened. In this year paid matrons were employed for the first time. It was not until 1893 that a supervisor and trained kindergarteners were used to conduct the play activities. During the first years the sand piles were in mission yards but schoolyards soon replaced the private areas and in 1894 all the sand gardens—or playgrounds as they came to be called—were on school property. Funds for operating the playgrounds were provided by the Massachusetts Emergency and Hygiene Association until 1899 when the city council appropriated $3,000 toward meeting their cost. In this same year 3 of the 21 centers were designated as playgrounds for boys between twelve and fifteen years of age and were equipped with a limited amount of gymnastic apparatus. The Boston School Committee in 1901 took over the operation of several playgrounds although the Association continued to conduct activities at many areas. Much of the credit for the success of this first playground effort belongs to Miss Ellen M. Tower, for many years chairman of the Playground Committee of the Massachusetts Emergency and Hygiene Association.

Since the experience in Boston had a direct influence upon the opening of playgrounds in other cities and gave definite direction to the development of the entire movement, it is worth while reviewing the stages which marked the evolution of the Boston experiment:

1. Started as a private project, it was later taken over and operated as a public responsibility.

2. Financed in the beginning through private philanthropy, support from public funds was later secured.

3. The playgrounds were originally on private property but were gradually transferred to public areas.

4. At first under volunteer leaders, soon matrons were employed, and subsequently kindergarteners and other trained workers were used as play leaders.

5. The first centers were merely sand piles for little children but apparatus and areas for older boys were later provided.

The experiment in Boston proved to be a forecast of the course the recreation movement as a whole was to follow. Each of these developments—from private to public financial support, management, and areas, from untrained to trained leaders, from young children to boys and girls of all ages—has been characteristic of the growth of the movement throughout the country.

The Movement Spreads to Other Cities.—With the impetus the sand gardens of Boston gave to similar efforts elsewhere, at least ten other cities had established playgrounds before the end of the century. In practically every instance the initiative and funds were provided by philanthropic individuals or social agencies. A playground was opened in New York in 1889. In 1892 a "model" playground was opened in connection with Hull House in Chicago. The development of this playground was influenced by the efforts, under the guidance of Miss Octavia Hill, to supply playing space for the children of East London. In addition to sandboxes it provided apparatus and areas for playing handball and indoor baseball. Because it was larger and had more varied facilities it served older children than the earlier sand gardens. In 1893 two summer kindergarten playgrounds, one of them in a schoolyard, were established in Philadelphia, and the following year sand gardens were started in Providence. Other cities which made a beginning in playgrounds before 1900 were Pittsburgh, Brooklyn, Baltimore, Milwaukee, Cleveland, Minneapolis, and Denver. As in Boston, these playgrounds although started and financed by private initiative were taken over by city or school authorities after their value had been demonstrated. In New York City in 1899, ten years after the first playground was opened in that city, the School Board conducted 31 school play centers.

Cities Acquire Recreation Areas.—The close of the nineteenth century saw an awakening on the part of city officials to the importance of acquiring and developing special areas for play and recreation use. An early instance of action to acquire land for playground purposes was in 1871 when the voters of the town of Brookline, Massachusetts, authorized the purchase of land "for public commons or playgrounds." Two properties were acquired but nothing was done to develop them. In 1876 Washington Park in Chicago was opened as a recreation park but it was not used for this purpose until ten years later when two tennis courts were built in it. By 1892 over 100 cities were known to have made provision for municipal parks but few of these areas were used for active recreation.

In 1889 the Boston Park Department converted a 10-acre tract along the Charles River in a congested section of the city into an open-air gymnasium for boys and men. Two years later a section was provided for women and girls. This area, known as the Charlesbank Outdoor Gymnasium, established a playground pattern which had a widespread influence. It was fenced and landscaped, and was equipped with swings, ladders, seesaws, a sand garden, and a ⅕ mile running track. Wading, bathing, and rowing facilities were also provided, and supervisors were appointed to conduct the program.

Other cities also took steps to acquire public playgrounds, largely because of the insistence of social workers and influential citizens. In New York City a tract of 2⅝ acres, covered with five- and six-story tenements, was purchased in 1897 at a cost of $1,800,000. But only after a most determined effort led by Jacob A. Riis was this area, now known as Seward Park, developed as a well-equipped demonstration playground and opened in 1899. In addition to apparatus, wading pool, and game spaces, a gymnasium with baths was constructed, and seats were provided for spectators. It was intended that the playground should be a "neighborhood affair." So successful was this experiment that the Park Department was induced to provide similar equipment and facilities in other parks in congested sections of the city.

By 1900 there were four play parks constructed and in operation in Louisville, Kentucky, and in 1901 a Special Park Commission opened four municipal playgrounds in Chicago. The value of providing large athletic fields was also recognized at this period, an outstanding example of this type of area being Franklin Field, Boston, which was purchased in 1894. The first recreation pier was opened in New York City in 1897.

Chicago's Neighborhood Recreation Parks.—Chicago, through its South Park playgrounds and centers, influenced the development of playgrounds and recreation in the United States more than any other city, with the possible exception of Boston. In 1903, a $5,000,000 bond issue was voted for the acquisition and development of small recreation parks in the crowded neighborhoods of South Chicago. The creation of these parks, ten of which were opened in 1905, was called by Theodore Roosevelt "the most notable civic achievement of any American city." They established a new standard in park and playground building. Heretofore facilities were mostly out of doors; they were used only a few months of each year; they were designed primarily for athletics and other physical activities, and they were not related closely to the needs of the people in the neighborhoods which they served. The South Parks, on the other hand, were designed to serve persons of all ages and with varied interests throughout the entire year; they afforded both indoor and outdoor facilities available for a wide range of recreation uses; and they were intended to supplement the meager facilities for happy, wholesome living which many of the neighborhoods afforded.

These parks varied from 7 to 300 acres in size, and although large portions were used for active recreation, a high degree of landscape beauty was attained through effective planting. Field houses provided facilities for indoor recreation, including an assembly hall with stage and dressing rooms, gymnasiums for men and women, shower and locker rooms, refectory, clubrooms, and a branch of the public library. The cost of some of these buildings exceeded a quarter of a million dollars. The outdoor plants were equally elaborate, including fully equipped children's playgrounds, separate "outdoor gymnasiums" for men and women with equipment and game courts, fields for a variety of games and sports, bandstands, and outdoor swimming pools. The employment of trained directors under a general director of field houses and playgrounds made possible a wise use of these plants through the organization of a program of varied recreation activities.

The widespread favorable publicity which these parks received, especially at the time of the first playground convention in Chicago in 1907, held under the auspices of the Playground Association of America, was a powerful influence in extending the recreational use of parks in other cities. It also contributed to the growing conception of the indoor recreation center for young people and adults. The South Park example was soon followed by the West Chicago and Lincoln Park Commissioners, and when these three park boards, with 17 other small districts, were consolidated into the present Chicago Park District in 1934, the city possessed 137 parks with 85 field houses equipped for recreation use.

A Playground Board.—The appointment of a Board of Playground Commissioners in Los Angeles in September, 1904, was a significant event in that a city had recognized play and recreation as of sufficient importance to justify the creation of a special department to take charge of these functions. This step, like many of the others previously mentioned, resulted from the initiative of several local organizations. The first playground was opened in 1905, and a superintendent of recreation was employed by the board. Several playgrounds were acquired and, although most of them were under ten acres, they were equipped with diversified outdoor facilities and with clubhouses including an assembly hall, clubroom, kitchen, and quarters for the director. Like the Chicago centers, they served all ages and were open under leadership the year round. These were among the first, if not the first, tax-supported playgrounds not on park or school property. During the decade following 1905, recreation buildings were erected in the parks of many cities, as well as indoor gymnasiums and public baths which afforded facilities for only a limited program.

School Buildings Are Opened for Recreation.—Paralleling the development of the municipal recreation centers was the tendency to use school buildings for community recreation. In many cities the school plant contained an auditorium, gymnasium, swimming pool, library, and special rooms which were suitable for recreation purposes but which were generally idle during the evening, week ends, and in vacation periods. The economy of opening these facilities to the public rather than spending money to duplicate them in special recreation buildings was apparent and many states prior to 1900 had passed laws permitting school buildings to be used as civic or social centers. As early as 1898, schools were opened under leadership for evening recreation in New York City as a continuation of the summer playground program. By 1907, 26 schools were being used as evening recreation centers in that city. The movement received nationwide attention and a great impetus when in 1907 a school extension committee was organized in Rochester, an appropriation of $5,000 was made for a school center demonstration, and a supervisor was employed to direct the program under the auspices of the school board. The name "social and civic centers" which was adopted suggests the attempt to encourage better citizenship through a democratic method of operation. Although only moderately successful, the experiment stimulated in other cities the wider use of the school plant and the gradual introduction into school buildings of features which serve both school and community recreation use. In 1911, Wisconsin passed legislation authorizing school authorities to levy a 0.2 mill tax for recreation purposes. Milwaukee took advantage of this law in establishing its widely known playground and community center program.

THE PLAYGROUND ASSOCIATION OF AMERICA IS ORGANIZED

As playgrounds were established even before the turn of the century, leaders in the cities where unusual playground plans had been worked-out were deluged with requests for advice and information. It was natural, therefore, that they should come together to discuss ways in which help could be given to other communities. A small group, including such prophetic spirits as Jane Addams, Henry S. Curtis, and Luther H. Gulick, met in Washington, D. C., in April, 1906, and for three days considered the nation's play needs and particularly those of the children in the large cities. During the course of these meetings, one of them held at the White House, the group decided to organize a national body to help towns and cities develop adequate playground systems and to create public sentiment for their extension and support. The purpose of the Playground Association of America, as stated in its constitution, was "to collect and distribute knowledge of and promote interest in playgrounds throughout the country, to seek to further the establishment of playgrounds and athletic fields in all communities and directed play in connection with the schools." President Theodore Roosevelt gave his hearty endorsement to the new Association which launched the recreation movement on a nationwide basis and he was elected honorary president. Other officers of the Association were Jacob Riis, honorary vice-president, Dr. Luther H. Gulick, president, and Dr. Henry S. Curtis, secretary.

No single event has had greater significance for the recreation movement than this Washington meeting. Joy Elmer Morgan of the National Education Association has said, "America owes a priceless debt to the men and women who in 1906 organized the recreational forces of America."[1] Invaluable help in starting the work of the association was received from the Russell Sage Foundation.

Up to this time the movement for playgrounds had received no concerted guidance or support. With the formation of the Playground Association of America, it received new impetus and competent national leadership. A monthly magazine, *The Playground*, was started; field workers were employed who went from city to city meeting with committees and public officials, exchanging experiences, and assisting in the establishment of playgrounds and recreation programs; a central clearinghouse for information was established; publications were issued and annual play congresses were organized. Among the early activities of the association was the preparation of a Normal Course in Play which was widely used by schools and colleges in the training of play leaders.

In 1910, Joseph Lee, "the philosopher of the movement for creative recreation," was elected president of the association, a position in which he served with practical wisdom, social insight, loyalty, and generosity until his death in 1937. In April, 1909, Howard S. Braucher was appointed secretary, in which position he is still serving. The name of the organization was changed in 1911 to Playground and Recreation Association of America. This change indicated the enlarging scope of the movement which was then concerned not only with children's playgrounds but with providing recreation facilities and programs for young people and adults. Years later the name was again changed to the National Recreation Association which is its present name.

A testimony as to the Association's influence upon the recreation movement is contained in the following quotation from a bulletin issued by the Recreation Commission in a large Western city:

[1] "Twenty-five Years of Prophetic Achievement," *The Journal of the National Education Association*, May, 1931.

The National Recreation Association is to playground departments what the Federal Reserve is to member banks—a sustaining influence, a source of information, and an able representative on matters of national import. For nearly thirty years the National Recreation Association, serving as the clearinghouse for the recreation movement in America, has been the means for focusing the attention of the nation upon the need for and the importance of public recreation. It has worked to determine needs, to plan adequate programs, train leaders, and raise standards of service and leadership. It has put its resources behind private and governmental agencies interested in recreation, and has served as a unifying force for all who are working through recreation to make life in America a rich, joyous experience.

SUBSEQUENT DEVELOPMENTS

One indication of the association's accomplishments is the marked increase in the number of cities which established playgrounds in the years immediately after it was founded. During the 6 years prior to 1906, 26 cities had established playgrounds, or an average of 4 cities a year. In the next 6 years a total of 158 cities started playgrounds, or an average of 26 cities a year. The association's emphasis upon the responsibility of the municipality to provide playgrounds and recreation centers helped to bring a general acceptance of the idea of public support.

In the years preceding the World War, the scope of the recreation movement was gradually enlarged. As its value was demonstrated, recreation came to be accepted as serving a universal need and not merely a need of congested or underprivileged communities. From the idea of providing a program of activities at playgrounds and centers alone emerged the conception of recreation service for the entire community. More emphasis was laid upon music, drama, arts, and civic activities. Projects of a city-wide nature, such as holiday celebrations, pageants, and festivals, were carried out. Neighborhood groups were organized to help plan and conduct the program. Comprehensive city recreation surveys conducted by workers of the association and of the Russell Sage Foundation disclosed facts concerning existing opportunities for recreation, unmet recreation needs, delinquency, accidents, street play, and other related subjects. They helped greatly to focus public attention upon the need for city-wide recreation systems. These surveys also provided a fund of valuable information which was useful in organizing programs in the cities in which they were conducted.

Influence of the World War.—The trend toward city-wide recreation systems with varied opportunities for everyone in the community received a further impetus after War Camp Community Service was organized by the Playground and Recreation Association of America at the request of the War Department. The task of this service was to mobilize the recreation resources of communities near the military camps and to provide wholesome recreation activities for the men in uniform. Community singing, games and sports, social recreation, and entertainments afforded a welcome relief from the daily camp routine. These activities also demonstrated the value of a recreation program under competent leadership, not only for servicemen but for civilians as well. In order to conserve the values which had been created in the war camp communities and to extend this type of program to other cities, a national organization known as Community Service was established in 1919. With its assistance, recreation programs, financed through community effort, were established in a large number of cities.

Although the recreation service conducted by War Camp Community Service came to an end with the closing of the army camps, and the programs established with the help of Community Service were gradually taken over by municipal recreation agencies, these two nationwide efforts during and after the war exerted a great influence upon the recreation movement. Servicemen who had become accustomed to out-of-door life and sports and who had enjoyed the recreation programs provided in the war camps desired the same opportunities in their home communities. The people who saw during the war what such activities as community singing, pageants, athletic meets, and neighborhood parties could mean in community life were insistent that means be devised for continuing them. Influential citizen groups and committees which had played such a large part in these programs had been brought face to face with the significance of recreation and had come to realize the value of volunteer recreation service and the satisfaction obtained from it. Social, civic, and religious agencies had acquired common interest in and a sense of responsibility for community recreation. Many communities for the first time had observed the vital contribution made by a worker who gave his full time to planning the effective utilization of the community's recreation resources. The rapid expansion of the municipal movement in the 1920's, with its enriched programs and enlarged public support, was in no small measure an outcome of these earlier influences and developments.

Community Houses Are Erected.—The widespread construction of community houses, especially during the years following the war, was partly due to this emphasis upon neighborhood and community recreation, but also to the stimulus of a nationwide campaign for the erection of buildings as war memorials. In most cases, these buildings were financed through private funds, managed by boards of directors, and contained meeting rooms for local organizations, an assembly hall for community gatherings, and recreation facilities for the use of individuals and groups. In a few instances a trained recreation director was employed, but as a rule the leadership was furnished chiefly by members of the groups using the building. Many of the community houses were erected in small towns and rural communities and serve as centers for their social and cultural life. Some consisted merely of an assembly hall with platform or stage and perhaps a kitchen; others, like the one in Whiting, Indiana, contain elaborate recreation facilities. Erected in 1919 as a war memorial at a cost of nearly $550,000, the Whiting Community House has two gymnasiums and an auditorium, all completely equipped, a swimming pool, American Legion headquarters, bowling alleys, showers and lockers, billiard room, reading rooms, refreshment lobby, dining hall, large clubroom, and Memorial Hall. In several cities the war memorial took the form of a municipal auditorium which generally provided some recreation facilities.

The Importance of Leisure Is Recognized.—As early as 1912 the Playground and Recreation Association of America had issued pamphlets discussing the relation of recreation and leisure. In 1918 the National Education Association focused attention upon leisure as a major community problem by declaring that the training for the worthy use of leisure was one of the seven objectives of education. It was not until the late 1920's, however, that the important place which recreation can play in the rapidly increasing leisure time of the people was widely heralded in books, magazine articles, and the daily press. The tour of Dr. L. P. Jacks, noted English educator, who in 1931-1932 visited cities from coast to coast under the auspices of the National Recreation Association, interpreting the significance of recreation and leisure, did much to call attention to this problem. Nationwide publicity resulted from the 3-day hearings arranged by the New York Leisure Time Committee of the National Recovery Administration in 1933 during the course of which such outstanding figures as Newton D. Baker, Alfred E. Smith, and Nicholas Murray Butler gave testimony to the need of public planning for the recreational use of leisure.

The Expanding Recreation Movement.—"No phase of American life is more interesting than the rising tide of recreation during the 1920's," according to Jesse F. Steiner, who adds that during this period "play for the first time took its place alongside of work and was recognized as one of the major interests of life."[1] This decade was characterized by a growing appreciation of the importance of leisure and a marked expansion in public recreation services. The rapid increase in community recreation areas and facilities accompanied the acceptance of recreation as an essential factor in city planning. Recreation programs were greatly enlarged in scope and in the number of individuals participating. Recreation budgets increased. Leadership training was emphasized and there

[1] "Research Memorandum on Recreation in the Depression," p. 38, Social Science Research Council, 1937.

was a marked increase in the volume of recreation literature. State legislation authorized municipalities to establish and to maintain recreation systems and there was a tendency on the part of cities to create a special recreation department to handle the expanding recreation programs. An evidence of the growing recognition of the place of recreation in our national life was the Conference on Outdoor Recreation called by President Coolidge in 1924, which helped to focus national attention on the importance of municipal recreation as well as on various other phases of outdoor leisure-time activity.

Areas and Facilities.—During the decade beginning in 1920, the number and variety of recreation facilities increased by leaps and bounds. Not only playgrounds but golf courses, swimming pools, bathing beaches, picnic areas, winter sports facilities, and game fields were constructed in unprecedented numbers. The growth in municipal park acreage, especially during the latter half of the decade, unquestionably exceeded that in any other period of equal length. Part of this growth was due to the fact that many cities began to acquire and develop parks outside the city limits. In addition to the expansion in municipal recreation areas, several county park systems providing a variety of recreation facilities were established. The growth in recreation areas focused attention upon the importance of relating them to other features of the city plan. The practice of dedicating space for recreation in real estate developments, actively stimulated by William E. Harmon, the Harmon Foundation, and the National Recreation Association, resulted in the dedication of splendid recreation areas in many cities.

Programs.—The decade is also significant as a period of expanding programs. Music, drama, arts and crafts, and nature activities received increasing emphasis. More recreation opportunities were provided for older girls and women, and more adequate consideration was given to the recreation needs of Negroes. New types of services which found their place in the recreation department program were picnic and party service to organized groups, the organization of activities for workers in stores and industries, and the extension of recreation service to public institutions and to shut-ins. Guidance to parents in providing home-play facilities and in the promotion of play in the home was included in the service of many recreation departments.

Leadership.—With the expansion of recreation facilities and programs, the need for trained, competent leadership became increasingly apparent. The number of employed recreation leaders, according to the *Recreation Year Book,* increased from 10,218 in 1920 to 22,920 in 1929. Greater emphasis was laid upon the provision of training courses for both paid and volunteer leaders. The growing recognition of recreation leadership as a profession and the difficulty in securing properly trained recreation personnel led to the establishment of the National Recreation School in New York City in 1926. This graduate course provided training for persons preparing for executive leadership in the recreation field. Of special significance was the extension of training opportunities to rural community leaders through institutes conducted by workers of the National Recreation Association under the auspices of the Extension Service of the U. S. Department of Agriculture.

Expenditures.—Inevitably the growth in facilities, programs, and leaders led to greater expenditures for municipal recreation service. According to the *Recreation Year Book*, expenditures for organized community recreation service rose from $7,199,430 in 1920 to $33,539,-806 in 1929. Reports of the Bureau of the Census show that municipal expenditures for all types of municipal recreation service including parks, museums, and public celebrations, also increased to a remarkable degree during this period. Between 1919 and 1929 the total amount spent by cities of 30,000 and over for the operation and maintenance of all forms of recreation service increased from $24,204,797 to $61,863,327. Recreation was one of the few functions of local government that accounted for a larger percentage of total municipal expenditures in 1929 than it did ten years before.

Research.—To meet the needs of the recreation profession and to serve more adequately the growing movement, research projects in many special fields were undertaken during this period. Nationwide studies of organized camps, municipal and county parks, music in American life, and leisure and the public schools, were made by the National Recreation Association and were followed by the publication of comprehensive reports. Publications on various forms of recreation activity, such as crafts, drama, and social recreation, swelled the rapidly increasing library of recreation literature. Committees of recreation executives, after a thoughtful pooling of experiences and opinions, issued authoritative reports on widely different subjects. President Hoover's Committee on Social Trends issued comprehensive reports based on nationwide surveys in the field of recreation and the cultural arts. Local recreation survey reports afforded a basis for local planning and action and also contributed valuable data on many aspects of recreation.

RECREATION IN THE DEPRESSION

The depression and the unemployment which accompanied it inevitably had their effect upon the municipal recreation movement. An added burden was thrown upon public facilities and leadership. People without work or with limited funds turned from more expensive forms of recreation to the playgrounds, recreation centers, beaches, and picnic areas. The unprecedented attendance at indoor and outdoor recreation centers placed a heavy load upon the operating and leadership personnel and created new demands for additional facilities and services and for the adaptation of existing facilities to more diversified and continuous uses. The rapid expansion in municipal sports programs provided opportunities for individuals to participate in the activities and also afforded enjoyment to increasing numbers of spectators. Instead of expanding their budgets, however, many cities were obliged to make deep cuts in their appropriations for recreation because of the financial crisis. As a result, in several cities the leadership staff was reduced to a point where it was impossible to operate playgrounds and centers. Realizing the seriousness of the situation, citizens offered to serve as volunteer leaders during the period of stress so that recreation services could be maintained without interruption. After a period of training, volunteers took the places of the workers who had been dropped. In 1932 and 1933 especially, the operation of playgrounds and indoor centers in many cities was made possible to a large degree by the service of volunteer leaders working under a limited staff of paid workers.

In the early days of the depression some of the larger cities established special centers for the unemployed, and programs for the families of persons out of work were also provided in a number of smaller communities. On the whole, however, it was considered better to encourage the unemployed to take part in the recreation activities provided for the entire community than to conduct special programs for this group. Many playgrounds and centers were kept open for longer periods than before in order to serve the unemployed, and the tremendous increase in attendance at municipal recreation areas was due in no small measure to their use by this group.

The depression necessitated a retrenchment of individual expenditures for recreation and reduced the attendance at most places of commercial amusement, such as the legitimate theaters and motion-picture houses. People turned to forms of recreation which were inexpensive or available at no cost. There was an increase in home activities, such as listening to the radio, reading, gardening, and hobbies.[1] On the other hand, activities carried on outside the home involving considerable expense or elaborate equipment, were engaged in by fewer people. The value of sporting goods produced in this country, as reported by the *Census of Manufactures*, decreased from $58,289,000 in 1929 to $25,267,-000 in 1933, a decline of 57 per cent. The fact that for a great many people the use of leisure was determined not by their desires but by economic limitations threw an added burden of responsibility upon governmental agencies in the recreation field. Local recreation author-

---

[1] See *The Leisure Hours of 5,000 People*, a report of a survey conducted by the National Recreation Association.

ities did their utmost to provide the greatest possible service with the curtailed funds at their disposal, but the recreation needs of the people would have been unmet had it not been for the financial resources made available by emergency agencies.

The Use of Emergency Funds for Recreation.—Early in the depression cities used persons on relief to work on projects for the improvement of recreation areas, and in a few states comprehensive recreation leadership programs were worked out by the relief authorities. The object of these programs was to provide employment for "white collar" workers as recreation leaders and also through the programs to furnish recreation opportunities to the localities, especially for the unemployed and their families. These earlier efforts pointed the way to the subsequent Federal projects carried on by the Civil Works Administration, the Federal Emergency Relief Administration, and the Works Progress Administration which supplanted them, and by the National Youth Administration. Most of the Federal recreation projects may be classified in two groups, (1) those involving the construction and development of recreation areas and facilities, and (2) those providing leadership for recreation activities.

Recreation Facilities Projects.—Through the use of local, state, and Federal relief funds, communities throughout the United States have been able to improve existing parks, playgrounds, and school sites and to develop them for recreation uses. In addition, hundreds of athletic fields, swimming pools, tennis courts, golf courses, and winter sports facilities have been constructed throughout the country. Many communities, large and small, expanded their recreation facilities to a degree which without the relief funds would not have been attained for another decade. The estimated total cost of 12,348 projects classified as "parks and other recreational facilities" initiated under the Works Program, placed in operation through September 30, 1937, was $536,778,961 or 6 per cent of the total cost of the entire program.[1] In addition the program provided for the construction of 3,267 "social and recreational buildings" involving a total expenditure of $79,869,011. More than 16,000 or about 13 per cent of the young people engaged in NYA work projects in the fall of 1937 were helping with the construction of parks and other recreational facilities.

Recreation Leadership Projects.—An important feature of the emergency relief program has been the recreation service carried on, primarily through Federal funds, under the sponsorship of state agencies and local governmental units or lay committees. In many cities relief workers serving as leaders have enabled recreation agencies to maintain programs which otherwise would have been curtailed; in others, workers have made

---

[1] *Report on Progress of the Works Program*, Works Progress Administration, December, 1937.

it possible for agencies to operate their enlarged facilities. Because many of these workers had been specially trained in music, crafts, drama, dancing, or other activities, they have often been used to introduce or to extend the activities in these particular fields. Leaders paid from emergency funds have given many small towns and rural communities their first opportunity to know and appreciate the benefits of a recreation program under leadership. In the spring of 1937 there were 49,000 persons employed by the Recreation Division of the WPA. Educational projects under the WPA were also employing leaders of adult groups in programs including recreation activities. The NYA shared in the leadership program and in October, 1937, almost 12 per cent of its youth were serving as recreation leaders in parks and play centers.

It is clear, therefore, that even though municipal recreation budgets were reduced during the depression, emergency leadership made expansion of the recreation program possible in most cities and enabled many communities to secure the benefits of a recreation program for the first time.

SOME TRENDS IN MUNICIPAL RECREATION SINCE 1930

Careful research is needed to appraise accurately the effects of the depression upon the recreation movement; only a few observations are noted here. Very few cities dismissed their recreation executives or eliminated their programs; in fact, recreation budgets have been restored to predepression levels in several cities and partly restored in many others. The need for greater citizen interest and a more generous public support in order that the enlarged program might be continued and the new facilities maintained and operated adequately, led to the widespread formation of advisory councils or lay committees. In a number of cities attempts were made to bring about a change in the form of municipal recreation organization or a consolidation of recreation and some other department, allegedly in the interest of greater efficiency and economy. Few such changes have been put into effect, however, and, as indicated in Chap. XXIX, in general, municipal organization for recreation in American cities does not differ greatly from that in 1930.

Adults are taking a more active part in municipal recreation programs than ever before, and many of the new facilities are primarily for adult use. Large numbers of school buildings have been opened for community recreation use for the first time. The success of Federal music and drama projects has demonstrated the possibilities of similar activities in the municipal recreation program and has given hundreds of thousands of people opportunity to hear fine music and to see well-produced plays. The value of recreation in sustaining morale and in affording joyous, constructive, healthful use of leisure time has been more widely demonstrated and is more generally appreciated than ever before. Municipal recreation leaders, having observed the public response to such activities as winter sports, roller skating, bicycling, and camping promoted on a commercial basis, are expanding their facilities to afford more opportunities for the public to enjoy these activities. Significant trends in municipal recreation programs have been the widespread introduction of music, nature, crafts, and drama activities, and the greater emphasis upon co-recreation for youth. Many cities conducted such activities before 1930, but there has been a marked enrichment of programs throughout the country since that date.

Universities and colleges have become deeply interested in recreation and have considered the desirability of establishing courses to prepare individuals for recreation leadership. The significance attached to adequate training for this service is indicated by the conferences arranged by university, Federal, and local leaders in 1937 and 1939 for a discussion of training principles and methods. The organization of the Society of Recreation Workers of America at the Recreation Congress in 1938 is a further indication that recreation leadership is approaching the status of a profession.

Since 1930, in spite of the depression, the public recreation movement has gone forward and is looking ahead to a period of greatly increased service. Much progress has been achieved, but still far from realization is the purpose of the National Recreation Association: "That every child in America shall have a chance to play. That everybody in America, young or old, shall have an opportunity to find the best and most satisfying use of leisure time."

PART II

LEADERSHIP

Leadership, more than areas and facilities, activities and programs--important as they are—determines the success of municipal recreation service. In a field where human relationships and values are so important creative, intelligent, trained leaders are absolutely essential. Part II is concerned with the nature, objectives, and methods of recreation leadership, and with the general and special qualifications for various positions in the recreation department. Other aspects of the subject receiving consideration are preliminary and in-service training and methods of selecting and maintaining a leadership staff. Because volunteer leadership plays an important part in municipal recreation programs, a chapter is devoted to the problems involved in the use of volunteers and to the significance of citizen groups in the recreation field.

CHAPTER VI

RECREATION LEADERSHIP

In the early days of the recreation movement the question "Why teach a child to play?" was frequently asked. Even civic leaders and parents who readily recognized the need for providing playgrounds in crowded cities felt that leaders were unnecessary. "Play is natural," they asserted. "Children don't have to be taught to play." This particular argument is now raised less frequently, but it is still heard. Individuals who object in this way do not realize that while the impulse to play is natural, the forms of play are not. A child is born with the ability to talk, but the words he uses are taught him by his mother, his father, and his companions. It is the same with play. A baby does not inherit his finger plays and nursery rhymes, but learns them from his mother or older sister. A boy learns to play baseball from his father, his older brothers, or his companions on the playground. He is not born with the knowledge or skill which enables him to play the game. Even a little girl's doll play is an imitation of her mother's activity. Play has always been taught.

WHY PLAY LEADERSHIP?

Parents, sisters, brothers, and companions are still teaching children to play either by offering an example for them to imitate or by actually instructing them. But valuable as it is, this natural, informal, and often unconscious teaching is not sufficient. In supplementing the teaching of parents and companions, the play leader gives a deeper significance to the child's play life by bringing it to a wider experience and trained understanding. This would have been true even in a more leisurely age, as modern education with its great emphasis on the importance of child life has revealed. Today it is especially true, for the conditions which made playgrounds and recreation centers a necessity have also made the play leader indispensable.

As play spaces have become limited, children's play opportunities have grown more restricted. With the disappearance of the wide fields and streams went the child's chance to roam adventurously with his playmates, to climb trees, to fish, and to swim. The street with its limited and hazardous play resources became his playground. As houses became smaller and the farm was replaced by the back yard—

79

and for many children by the crowded city tenement with no place for play either indoors or out—the opportunity to play games, to build things, to have pets and gardens, was lost to many children. Group play among brothers and sisters decreased as families became smaller. Work in factories and offices took fathers long distances from home for the greater part of the day, and as children were forced to seek much of their play outside the home, mothers too lost touch with a large part of it. Consequently many parents no longer were able to share so frequently and intimately in their children's play.

Because children have always been taught even the most simple play forms and because they no longer have the opportunity of learning these in the home, children must be given the guidance in their play activities which city living has taken from them.

Play without Guidance.—Children will play without guidance. The impulse to play is too strong to be short-circuited by a change of living conditions. But if the environment frustrates its free expression, play activities are just as likely to be destructive as they are constructive. Play itself is neither good nor bad. A boy who throws a stone through a store window so the storekeeper will chase him may be obeying the same urge to adventure as the boys in the open country when they play "Run Sheep Run" on a summer evening. But the storekeeper and the police do not excuse the boy's transgression of law and order just because he is playing. If the boy is caught, he is regarded either as a juvenile delinquent or well on the way to becoming one.

Juvenile court records are full of cases of misdirected play, the right expression of which would have meant much to the boy or girl involved and to society. Take for example the group of boys about whom George E. Johnson writes in his monograph, *Why Teach a Child to Play?*[1]

Some boys were brought before our juvenile court on the charge of malicious mischief. They had built a hut in a vacant lot. They were bad boys, I understand, and their methods were wrong, but their act comes out of the very heart of the instinct of workmanship. What would this world be if it had not been for this instinct of construction? In this act the boys centered several immemorial streams of heredity, like our great rivers into the Ohio; the instincts of shelter, of construction, of companionship. Had these play instincts been supervised and these acts allowed proper expression, the majesty of the law would not have been offended and the divine right of these boys would not have been violated.

Discussing the subject of misdirected play further, Mr. Johnson continues:

It may seem a striking statement, but it is nevertheless perfectly true that no case ever appeared in the Pittsburgh juvenile court or any other juvenile court

[1] Published by the National Recreation Association.

in which the act committed was not prompted wholly or in part by some impulse which under other relations and other associations could not but be both right and desirable.

Streets and back alleys are usually the places where children run afoul of the law in their play. Playgrounds take the children off the streets and give them a place where they can play freely and without interference from objecting neighbors. But playgrounds without leadership are no guarantee against rowdyism and unsocial conduct. They are the city's answer to the question, "Where shall we play?" But playgrounds present more difficulties to the child than the open fields where he can roam with his friends. On the city playground a child must learn to adjust his activities to the limitations of space and equipment, and to share the facilities with large numbers of other children. He must take turns using the swings or playing on the ball diamond, and he must acquire the ability to cooperate with children he has never seen before.

Children cannot be expected to cope with such complex problems without help. They do not have the necessary self-discipline, social experience, or maturity of judgment to appraise each situation properly, or the ability to deal with it satisfactorily. There must be an adult present to see that rowdies do not monopolize the playground, that the shy, retiring child has a chance to play, and that little children have a place in which to play safely while the older boys are engaged in vigorous activities.

THE NATURE OF PLAY LEADERSHIP

Leadership on the playground assures the maintenance of discipline and order, but it does much more than that. Park guards can look after the equipment, and policemen, who represent organized force and authority to the child, can enforce good behavior by threatening to arrest him for improper conduct. But this discipline can have only negative results. It can never have the vital, positive influence on the growing child which a competent leader brings to the playground. On a playground where there is no leader the police or guards act only when some disciplinary problem already exists. If two boys get into a fight the policeman separates them or throws them off the playground. Such action does not solve the problem nor does it keep the boys from continuing their battle around the corner or starting it again when the officer's back is turned. And more important than that, the policeman's exhibition of force causes resentment and does nothing to prevent future uprising.

Since the policeman is not called upon until the problem already has come to a crisis, his handling of it cannot be expected to accomplish lasting good. The leader, on the other hand, is in constant association with the children. He maintains order in an environment of willing cooperation by keeping the child happily engaged in activities which interest him deeply. His is not the discipline of suppression achieved by enforcing rules and regulations set up according to adult standards. He avoids fights and disagreements by keeping the boys and girls happy and busy and by conducting activities in such a way that occasions for dispute are minimized. When fights do occur—and they sometimes do—the leader helps the combatants settle their difficulties and reach a solution through understanding. Unlike the policeman who coerces and suppresses, the play leader seeks to enlist the children's active cooperation in curbing an undesirable activity for an understandable and worthy end. In this way children learn self-control and restraint in their social relationships and the likelihood of future disputes is minimized. Children learn the value of discipline by experiencing the good it brings them—not by fighting against its restraints.

Leadership and Character.—The playground under competent leadership is an excellent place for a child to learn right conduct. The social situations a child meets there bear a close resemblance to the situations he must cope with in later life. The child comes into free association with other children as individuals and in groups. He is rarely compelled to attend or participate in the program of activities. If he does choose to participate, however, and the playground is under the guidance of a good leader, the child learns to give and take with others, to win graciously, and to accept defeat without complaint. The rules that govern the child's conduct are chiefly the rules of the game and the rules of social living. The child may even have a share in preparing these rules and in enforcing them. The leader helps the child to conform to them, not through coercion but through the indirect, effective, and more lasting guidance of suggestion. He remains in the background and exercises direct control only when it is absolutely necessary. Consequently, the children learn by firsthand experience how to get along with others. If a boy chooses to drop out of a game rather than to abide by its rules he is compelled, by his own choice, to stand on the sidelines and watch the game proceed without him. The results of his actions are immediate and direct, and the play experiences afford valuable lessons in social conduct.

Under the guidance of a capable leader the child has the opportunity on the playground to develop desirable character traits, individual as well as social. Since the playground is essentially free from compulsion the child makes his own decisions and experiences the results, good or bad, that come directly from them. He has the opportunity to initiate and to lead activities, and through actual practice he acquires judgment, self-reliance, and the ability to handle responsibilities.

LEADERSHIP OBJECTIVES AND METHODS

Character building is not the essential purpose of play leadership, although there are people who claim that it should be. Play leadership involves a recognition of the fact that a happy childhood through play is essential to a child's normal growth and personal development. Self-discipline and right conduct are natural results of a situation in which a child engages in activities of absorbing interest under wise guidance. The chief purpose of play leadership, therefore, is to fill the child's play hours with gripping, creative, varied activities which foster the free expression of his play interests, and to conduct these activities in such a way that every child on the playground is assured of a happy and richly satisfying playtime. To the extent that the leader succeeds in achieving this objective, he is contributing to the children's happiness and personal development.

According to Glenn Frank the problem of leisure for children is "so to organize a kind of play life for children that out of it the skills will be developed, the capacity for cooperation developed which will make them function more intelligently and more effectively as individuals and as members of social groups as they move on into maturity."[1] The methods and specific objectives of leadership are designed to achieve this result.

The play leader provides not merely the opportunity for children to play the games, to sing the songs, and to make the things they want, but the infectious enthusiam which gives a zest to the activities. Neither he nor the children are hampered by a fixed schedule or curriculum. Direct guidance is given chiefly where it is needed to take care of particular difficulties or to make participation more enjoyable. The leader sees that the necessary equipment, playing space, and materials are provided for the activities in which the children have a definite interest. He organizes the program in such a way as to minimize quarrels arising out of the conflicting desires of different children and to effect solutions through understanding when they do occur. In planning and conducting the program, the leader is guided by the factors which facilitate self-expression by the children and make for personality and character development. He takes into account the children's individual interests and abilities; he preserves initiative by allowing ample opportunity for self-directed activities; and he takes into consideration each child's need for recognition and for experiencing success. He fosters the children's creative planning ability and encourages exploration in new fields of activity. By getting acquainted with all the children he tries to discover interests which are not immediately apparent. He pays special

[1] "Citizen Leadership in Today's Leisure Time," *Recreation*, February, 1938, p. 635.

attention to the needs of the timid and awkward child. He introduces new activities so the children will have a greater range of choices than they would have if left entirely to themselves. By helping them develop skills, he increases the satisfaction and enjoyment which they gain from taking part in the activities.

Leadership Teaches Skills.—The importance of these last two objectives—teaching skills and providing a variety of play opportunities —is sometimes overlooked by people who do not understand the nature and purpose of leadership. The acquisition of skill is a prerequisite to satisfactory participation in many forms of recreation. To a degree, skill is acquired by trial and error, but trained leaders can save individuals costly and discouraging experimentation.

A boy who has no one to instruct him in correct swimming methods may learn the dog paddle, then the side stroke, and may even attempt to swim the crawl. These self-taught strokes seem satisfactory to the boy as long as he swims with a group who have no greater ability in the water than he has. However, if at a later period he swims with boys who have been taught by skillful teachers and who swim the crawl with speed and form, he at once realizes his inferiority in the water. His awkwardness may prove embarrassing and take away the enjoyment which he formerly gained from his swimming. In fact, some boys may even give up swimming entirely. On the other hand, if the boy has had the benefit of leadership in other activities and has learned that he can acquire skills through guidance and training, he may be challenged to seek leadership which will enable him to become a capable swimmer.

The man who is a "dub" at tennis or baseball is usually the man who did not have the opportunity to learn the game as a boy. People enjoy most the activities which they perform well, and they tend to avoid those in which they have little skill. By arousing in children a desire for self-improvement and by helping them to learn better ways of playing old games and the best ways of performing new activities, the leader increases the satisfaction and fun which they derive from participation. In addition he is helping overcome the reluctance of many children as well as adults to take part in activities which they do not perform well and is preparing them for a richer recreation experience in later life.

Leadership Makes Variety Possible.—Variety is essential in a child's play life for the fullest development of his interests and of his personality. Some adults seem to think that because children are always active they are never at a loss to know what to do. Parents who repeatedly hear children say, "There's nothing to do," know this is not the case. Often when children get into mischief it is because they are bored with playing the same old games. "Life is so full of a number of things, I am sure we should all be as happy as kings," said Robert Louis Stevenson when he was writing for children. Playtime is the time to play games of all kinds, to explore the world of fairies and make-believe and adventure in stories, to become acquainted with the world of song, to build things, to produce plays and learn about drama and the stage, to dance, to discover nature and the world of growing things. Leadership makes possible a variety of such experiences.

Children learn best when they are free from compulsion, when the motive comes from within themselves, not from the outside. Playtime is the time when the child is most free, the time when he is most himself. Therefore, the lessons of the playground are quickly learned and long remembered. Suggestion and imitation are powerful influences in determining children's behavior and because on the playground the child sees others playing happily in various ways, he has the desire and incentive to join them. In this way he tries out new play activities and gains play experiences which otherwise might never be his. On the playground the child has the opportunity to experiment with many different activities and to discover the interests which for him have the greatest value and which are likely to afford rich leisure-time resources in later life. The discovery and development of latent skills and potential play interests are among the primary functions of the playground leader.

Carry-over Values.—Leadership for children's play activities is primarily provided by the recreation department on the playground, but it is not concerned with activities on the playground alone. The real test of playground leadership is the extent to which the activities engaged in and the attitudes taught at the playground are carried over into the child's play life at home and in the neighborhood. Its influence is also indicated by the degree to which interests developed on the playground persist in later life and afford rich leisure-time resources. In teaching skills and acquainting children with a variety of activities, the playground leader awakens and encourages interests which may last a lifetime and make the difference between richness and drabness in adult living.

Leadership and Freedom.—The objection has sometimes been made that play leadership encroaches on a child's freedom, destroying the spontaneity of his play and initiative. This argument reveals a failure to understand the nature of freedom and of play leadership. As was pointed out earlier in the chapter, a child is made more free to enjoy his activities as he is helped to acquire skills. He is also made free as a social being when he learns the submissions necessary to successful group living. Freedom involves, indeed is based upon, restraint and sacrifice. As John Dewey has said, "Without rules there would be no game . . . rules are a part of the game."[1] In every game a child gives up some of

[1] *Experiences in Education*, p. 55, The Macmillan Company, 1938.

his freedom to the other players.　If he insists on being "It" all the time, the game breaks up, and he loses not only the chance of being "It" according to the rules but all the fun of playing.　As Hughes Mearns has written in his article, "Discipline and the Free Spirit:" "Freedom without restraint is like a game without rules.　The free spirit is most free which has been taught to accept willingly the necessary restrictions of human living."[1]

Freedom is inherent in the playground situation.　A child is always free to come or not as he chooses.　But on a playground under competent leadership he is more free to play his own games and to follow his own inclinations than on a playground monopolized by older children or dominated by bullies.　He learns control, but most of the restraints are inherent in the activities themselves or are established by the play group. If he wants to play he must recognize the rights of his comrades and abide by the rules.　When he submits, he does so voluntarily.

The leader creates an environment in which the children are free to play, and in which the expression of their play interests assumes forms which make it easier for them to function as individuals and as social beings.　Far from destroying freedom, play leadership increases the only freedom which matters—freedom with control based on understanding, willing acceptance, and cooperation.

Leadership Must Be of High Quality.—To accomplish the purposes and attain the objectives described in the preceding pages, it is obvious that trained leaders of intelligence and high moral caliber are necessary. The playground leader is in a strategic position to inspire children with the enthusiasm to participate in games and play activities, and to influence child character.　What children play and how they respond to group play situations on the playground are often the direct result of the leader's own enthusiasms and of his personal attitudes and conduct. Certainly the children cannot be expected to develop desirable character traits on the playground unless the leaders themselves possess and demonstrate such qualities in their varied, daily relationships.

The tendency for children to "hero-worship" an adult whom they admire either personally or for his accomplishments is well known.　Lindbergh's flight over the Atlantic gave rise to a host of youthful Lindberghs who imitated their hero's manners, his speech, his interests, and his attitudes.　The playground leader by the circumstances of his position is a natural object of hero worship.　His chief concern is to serve the children's interests and to increase their enjoyment of the activities. Children are therefore kindly disposed toward him and are more amenable to his influence than they would be if he compelled them to perform tasks which they found disagreeable.　The whole association between the

[1] *Progressive Education*, December, 1931, p. 633.

leader and the children is a happy one. Since the leader helps the children to have fun, it is natural for them to like him, and liking easily becomes admiration. If the playground leader has a record of success in high-school or college sports, or in some other field which interests the children, or if he has personal qualities which impress them, their admiration for him is that much greater, and they imitate him in countless ways.

Since the leader through his position on the playground can exert such a profound influence on the children, only the best and highest quality of play leadership is acceptable.

DO CHILDREN WANT LEADERSHIP?

The idea that play leadership is necessary is not mere theory. What boys and girls themselves think of leadership has been demonstrated repeatedly. For instance, as an experiment a playground in a city of 300,000 was thrown open without play leadership. Fifteen or twenty children used it. Unannounced, a play leader appeared. The attendance increased to between 75 and 80. A thoroughly qualified leader was then placed in charge and the daily attendance mounted to 448. When the experienced leader was later withdrawn and an untrained person substituted, the attendance at once began to fall off.

The history of playgrounds at which no leadership has been provided has been universally disappointing and the experience has been little better where incompetent persons were employed as leaders. Children have shown that they want more than just a place in which to play. They want a leader who can make the place interesting and exciting with challenging activities.

THE NEED OF RURAL CHILDREN FOR PLAY LEADERSHIP

The need for variety in play and for acquiring skill makes play leadership just as important in rural as in urban communities. Most rural children have ample play space and a rich and potentially stimulating play environment. The rural child has the materials for play in abundance, but he needs leadership to help him make the most of his resources. Parents with wide experience and with cultivated imaginations can make living in the country richly creative for their children. But since many parents lack the experience, understanding, or time, there is need in rural areas as well as in the city for play leadership to be provided by some outside agency—whether school, church, grange, or club. Such leadership enables children to play happily with other children of the same age, acquaints them with play resources at their disposal, and helps them make use of these resources in the best and most satisfying way.

RECREATION LEADERSHIP FOR YOUTHS AND ADULTS

Many communities fail to realize that modern city living has created the need for recreation leadership for youth and adults as well as for children. The argument is frequently raised that young people and adults should have the maturity to look after their own recreation. This short-sighted viewpoint completely overlooks the fact that youth and adults are restricted in their recreation opportunities by the conditions of urban living just as much as the children are. Admittedly many adults have the maturity to choose and the ability to direct their own activities. But they cannot play in a baseball league unless they have access to a diamond; they cannot play tennis if there are no courts; they cannot swim if there are no pools or bathing beaches; nor can they play in a community orchestra unless someone takes the initiative to organize one and to provide a meeting place.

Leadership is necessary to provide recreation opportunities. The young people and adults who need recreation most can seldom secure the facilities for themselves. Leadership is necessary to bring together people of similar tastes, for in a modern city people often do not know other individuals who are interested in the same activities. Leadership also furnishes young people and adults the opportunity and experience of conducting their own activities and provides instruction in these activities when it is needed. Most adults have fewer recreation interests than children, usually because in their early years they were denied opportunities to play and to develop recreation skills. Countless individuals will never experience the joy of participating in recreation activities except as leadership extended to adult groups makes such participation possible.

The Value of Instruction.—Adults who can afford to secure instruction or assistance in organizing their recreation activities do not hesitate to do so. Private athletic clubs employ directors and instructors in various sports. Country clubs have their managers and golf "pro's," riding masters, and tennis instructors. Sketch clubs have their art teachers, and dramatic groups, their coaches and directors. Unfortunately the majority of people are not able to afford such assistance. But where communities have made recreation leadership generally available, adults have demonstrated by their enthusiastic participation in the program that they want not only the type of leadership which provides facilities but the leadership which organizes activities and furnishes instruction when it is needed.

The number of older boys and men playing baseball, softball, and other team games has grown by leaps and bounds in cities where athletic directors have been provided to organize and promote teams, leagues, and contests. The attendance at city golf courses and tennis courts has shown a marked increase in cities where the recreation authorities have opened golf and tennis schools. People who did not know how to play were reluctant to use the facilities at hand but were eager to learn when offered the opportunity. Others attended the schools because they were anxious to improve their skills. Similar results have been experienced in the case of other types of activity. For example in one city hundreds of adults who had formerly taken no part in the recreation program joined a newly organized drama group as soon as a trained director was added to the department staff.

Leadership Methods.—People who question the value and need of providing recreation leadership for youth and adult groups ignore the fact that every such group involves leadership either from within or from the outside. This leadership may be represented by one individual or it may be exerted by the cooperative action of certain members, but no group can function without it. "There is no question of whether there shall be leaders or not; that was settled when man began."

The chief function of professional recreation leadership for young people and adults is to draw out, strengthen, and put into action the leadership capacities inherent in the members of the group. It is common for the recreation leader gradually to withdraw from continuous direct leadership of an adult group after an activity has been started and the group has learned to carry on successfully under its own leadership. It is in this respect that the functions of leaders of adult groups differ most from those of the playground leaders. Because in general adults are more disciplined than children, more experienced in group relationships, and have more defined though fewer recreation interests, they can take greater responsibility for determining and directing their own activities. They can assume a larger measure of self-government and self-organization, and the paid recreation leader does not need to give as continuous or direct guidance as is necessary in dealing with children's groups. Young people may often select and direct their own activities but it "requires skillful leadership to inspire them to seek perfection." In many instances the most valuable service which the paid leader can render is to advise and assist people in forming their own recreation groups and to help their lay leaders acquire the skills and techniques which are essential to effective self-leadership within these groups.

Group leadership of youth and adults is involved in the organization and promotion of athletic leagues, orchestras, drama groups, and social and hiking clubs. Its functioning is perhaps best demonstrated by the community center leader who like the playground leader comes into direct relationship with individuals and groups of diversified interests. He must be able to help the participants discover interests, introduce variety when it is needed, and furnish instruction where it seems advisable. But the community center leader, because he is working primarily with adults, is more often able to remain in the background. He assists individuals in getting together with others who have a similar interest, and he helps groups in organizing their activities and getting their programs under way, after which he withdraws except for occasional contacts and help with specific problems. When he offers suggestions he usually does so as one of the group so that in the active sharing of ideas the participants acquire the experience of functioning as a group and increase their skill in managing their own activities. This experience, especially in recreation activities, is denied to large numbers of young people and adults except as leadership is provided by the recreation department.

OTHER ASPECTS OF RECREATION LEADERSHIP

So far the discussion has dealt only with the leadership of group activities for children, youth, and adults. Several types of leadership are required for the successful operation of a well-rounded community recreation program. Activities such as picnicking, horseback riding, bathing, tennis, and golf are largely self-directed, and are engaged in by individuals rather than groups, but the provision of the necessary facilities requires a certain form of leadership. This type of leadership involves little, if any, direct contact between the leader and the participants in the activities which these facilities make possible. Effective operation of these facilities, however, calls for a close and friendly relationship between the persons using them and the officials in immediate charge of them.

Sometimes individuals want specific instruction in recreation activities but are not interested in joining a highly organized group. They want to learn to dance, to play a musical instrument, to make jewelry or some other type of handicraft. Here the leader's primary function is to give instruction, but he also has an opportunity to develop a feeling of fellowship among the members of the class and to make its meetings a pleasant social experience. Furthermore, by introducing the class to related, diversified activities the leader is often able to arouse the members' interest in other parts of the program and to broaden their field of recreation activity.

Leaders Serve Many Functions.—In serving the varied recreation interests of individuals and groups, leaders are required to function in several different capacities. Most members of the recreation department leadership staff, as the following chapter points out, have titles and duties which relate primarily to some specific function. Their chief responsibility is that of executive, supervisor, organizer, director, instructor, or activity leader. However, the types of leadership which these terms suggest are exerted to a certain degree in most recreation positions. The superintendent of recreation, for instance, has responsibilities which are chiefly executive in nature, but he must also inspire, supervise, and oversee the work of his staff, assist in training his workers, and perhaps personally direct certain parts of the program. The community center director serves as an executive in managing his staff, as a supervisor in directing the work of his paid and volunteer leaders, and as an instructor or group leader in conducting activities in the center program.

A supervisor of a special activity such as dancing or dramatics, whose chief function is to furnish information and guidance to the playground and center leaders, must first of all be a good teacher, for it is by instructing leaders that he better equips them to teach their particular activities. He functions as a supervisor when he assists them in planing and conducting the phase of the program for which he is responsible; but if he organizes and directs a dance pageant or a drama festival or conducts a craft class, he performs duties commonly associated with the position of director or specialist.

The extent to which a recreation worker is called upon to exercise these various leadership functions depends largely upon the nature of his position and on the size and degree of specialization of the department staff. However, since all types of leadership are involved in most recreation positions, the ability of a worker to function as an executive, supervisor, director, activity leader, or an instructor, as the occasion demands, is a large factor in determining his success.

LEADERSHIP AIMS

Regardless of the capacity or position in which a recreation worker serves, all recreation leadership is governed by the same aims. Whether a person is working with children or adults, with individuals or with groups, or is functioning as a supervisor, executive or instructor, the fundamental purposes of his leadership are: to guide and serve the leisure-time interests of all the people—not to dictate them; to enlarge and deepen interests so that they will be more richly satisfying; to provide organization and instruction where it is desired; to furnish the means for self-expression through recreation activities so the hours of leisure will make for joyous living. The achievement of these objectives is possible only if trained, sympathetic leadership is provided, and their attainment assures the success of a municipal recreation program.

Communities, therefore, which value recreation and expect a fair return on their investment in areas and facilities, cannot afford to stint on providing competent leaders. They must insist on the kind of dynamic leadership that vitalizes and energizes the whole recreation life of the community.

CHAPTER VII

LEADERS IN THE RECREATION DEPARTMENT

The recreation department, like every other phase of municipal service, can function effectively only if it has a staff of competent, loyal workers. Such workers are particularly essential to the recreation department because they have a direct personal relationship with the individuals and groups who use its facilities and participate in its program. To plan and conduct the various activities and services comprising its comprehensive program described in later chapters and to operate and maintain its many areas and facilities, personnel of diversified qualifications, training, experience, and ability is required. Executive leadership is needed in planning and directing the work of the department; supervisors are in charge of special features; directors or managers are responsible for operating areas or facilities; and leaders and instructors conduct activities. Maintenance workers keep the recreation plant in good condition; clerical assistants handle the department records; and many other types of employees serve in varying capacities.

Each worker in the recreation department has an important place to fill, but of special significance are those employed to perform the leadership functions which are peculiar to the recreation department and which differentiate such service from work carried on in other branches of local government. They are the workers who comprise the group which has become recognized as a new and distinct profession. This chapter considers the types of leadership positions in municipal recreation, the duties performed, and some of the essential qualifications for workers in each of these positions.

GENERAL QUALIFICATIONS FOR ALL LEADERS

"The leader must be an individual of well-rounded personality and upright character, with power to influence character and personality in both children and adults." In these words Joseph Lee points out the qualifications without which the recreation leader cannot be successful. He also recognizes the influence which the leader continually exerts in his relations with individuals and groups.

Important as it is to select recreation workers for their technical abilities, it is equally essential to take account of their general qualifications. Experience in the field of leisure-time activity has taught that technical skill in directing activities is of limited value to the recreation leader unless he has the proper attitudes, interests, and native abilities. The more responsibility the recreation worker is to have, the greater should be the emphasis on his personal qualifications. But no worker should be accepted even for the least responsible position in a profession where dealing with people is the prime concern unless he has a broad cultural background and potentialities for growth and development.

As the requirements for recreation service have become higher and higher and as recreation leadership has sought a place among the professions, the educational standards required for employment have taken on greater significance. At present college graduation or its equivalent is considered as a basic qualification for employment in practically all leadership positions in the recreation department and graduate study is recommended for persons planning to serve in an executive capacity. Exceptions are made in the position of play leader where high-school graduation is considered sufficient and in the case of special instructors who because of some technical skill or special ability are able to render valuable service to the department even though their educational background is limited.

Because of the demands which the profession of recreation leadership makes upon those who would undertake it, only those who have the personal qualities essential for success should consider it as a life work. Individuals interested in the possibilities offered by this field will find a valuable guide in an editorial entitled Reasons for Not Becoming a Recreation Leader which contains the following statements:

> The number of men really qualified to find supreme happiness and rewarding service in the recreation movement is not large. It is much easier to teach, to preach, to write, to build bridges and skyscrapers. The quality of leadership possessed by the best recreation workers is found in only a limited number of each million persons born. For these few the rewards are very great.
>
> Until we care enough for the art of living and the art of playing to discover, develop, educate, the individual youngsters who have the natural gifts for recreation leadership it will be necessary to call upon many to serve in the recreation profession who are much better qualified for other work, who would find greater satisfaction elsewhere.
>
> The recreation field is the place for men who want to live and to see every one else live and who have satisfaction in forgetting all about themselves in the common life about them, to which they give themselves completely.[1]

Personal Requirements.—The personal qualifications desirable in any individual serving as a recreation leader have been listed frequently. One of the most critical analyses of such requirements appeared in the report of a committee of recreation executives dealing with qualifications

[1] Howard S. Braucher, *Recreation*, October, 1936.

for community recreation work.[1]   The following list is condensed from this report:

1. Social attitude
   a. Sense of the worth and dignity of every human being and desire to serve
   b. Understanding of people; comprehending their hungers, needs, and aspirations
   c. Personal realization of the art of living
   d. Sense of humor
2. Creative attitude
   a. Interest in the growth and development of individuals
   b. Desire to stimulate the creative impulses in others—initiative, freedom of expression, productive activity
3. Scientific attitude
   a. Understanding of the scientific method
   b. Hospitality to different points of view and diverse personalities
   c. Keen interest in research, experimentation, and human engineering
4. Capacity and zest for learning
   a. An understanding mind
   b. The ability to think; *i.e.*, skill in analyzing and in selecting the significant and in making concepts which will serve human purposes
   c. Insatiable curiosity, especially with reference to discovery and solution of social problems
5. Ability to lead democratically
   a. Belief and enthusiasm for self-government, for democracy in recreation
   b. Understanding of cooperative, democratic recreation procedure as distinguished from arbitrary control
   c. Skill in the techniques of group discussion and group determination of policies
   d. Character and personality (not the dominating type)
   e. Organizing ability
   f. Productive energy
6. Technical skill
   a. Skill in the particular field in which recreation worker is going to lead
   b. Skill in dealing with people to be served

TYPES OF LEADERSHIP POSITIONS

Owing to widely different local conditions there is no uniformity in the types or titles of recreation positions throughout the United States. Nevertheless, there is an increasing tendency for cities to adopt a standard nomenclature.   This is due in no small measure to the work and published reports of a committee of recreation executives appointed by the National Recreation Association, which has been working for several years on the problem.   Many of the statements in this chapter are based upon or adapted from one of the reports of this committee.[2]   The follow-

[1] See *Standards of Training, Experience, and Compensation in Community Recreation Work*, National Recreation Association.   The report was originally issued in 1931 but was revised in 1938.

[2] *Ibid.*

ing is a brief description of the titles generally used and of the major responsibilities usually assigned to the representative positions:

Superintendent, the chief officer in charge of a department or division and its personnel.

General supervisors, executive officers in charge of a group of recreation centers of similar kind, their personnel and the general program of activities carried on therein, or of some special function such as construction and maintenance generally applicable to all centers; *e.g.,* Supervisor of Playgrounds, Supervisor of Community Centers, Supervisor of Construction and Maintenance.

Supervisors of special activities, specialists in charge of special phases of program development.   Examples are Supervisor of Athletics, Supervisor of Music, Supervisor of Drama, Supervisor of Girls' and Women's Activities, Supervisor of Dancing, Supervisor of Arts and Crafts, and Supervisor of Nature Activities.

Directors of centers, executive officers in charge of administering the facilities, staff, and program of a recreation center such as a playground, community center, swimming pool, golf course, or camp.   Examples are Playground Director, Community Center Director, and Camp Director.   The title of Manager, rather than Director, is often applied to the person in charge of a golf course, swimming pool, or bathing beach.

Play leaders, employees who, under the close direction of directors or assistant directors, exercise general oversight over the play of children or adults on a playground or in a community center, lead groups in organized play activities, or assist with special projects.   These employees are often employed part time and frequently they are students preparing for professional work in recreation.

Specialists, employees who serve as instructors in a special activity, usually at more than one center, or on a part-time basis.   Examples are tennis, tap dancing, and archery instructor.

It is clear that many recreation departments do not employ all of the types of workers mentioned in the preceding list.   With the growing diversification in recreation programs and the expansion of recreation facilities, however, cities are finding it necessary to employ more and more workers who are particularly equipped to assume responsibility for special features and services.   A superintendent of recreation is needed as executive director in every recreation department.   In cities where there are more playgrounds and centers than can be supervised effectively by the superintendent, one or more general supervisors are needed.   In case the department operates and maintains its own areas and facilities, it needs a supervisor of construction and maintenance.   Most departments today employ one or more supervisors of special activities to promote and direct special phases of the program such as athletics, music, and drama.   In some of the larger systems there are several such workers.

Playground directors are found in every city, and community center directors are employed by departments operating indoor centers.   In cities having a golf course, municipal camp, or bathing areas, a director or manager is required for each.   Assistant playground and center directors and play leaders are needed in all cities to assist the directors and to help in conducting activities. More and more cities are employing specialists to provide instruction in special activities.

Duties and Special Qualifications.—In the light of experience, recommended standards have been adopted for the several positions listed. These standards set forth the special qualifications, experience, age, and education considered necessary for satisfactory service. They are not to be applied rigidly to given positions, but they set forth normal requirements which should be met by persons being considered for employment in recreation. In general the duties, special qualifications, and education considered essential do not vary according to the size of the city in which the service is to be rendered. In the case of the executive and supervisory positions, however, a differentiation in the minimum age and experience requirements is made between cities of varying populations. As a rule, the larger the community the broader the program and the more complex the executive and supervisory problem; therefore, greater experience and maturity are required in handling them.

The following pages contain brief statements outlining the essential duties of workers in the various leadership positions and a few of the basic qualifications for effective service.

Superintendent. *Duties.*—The superintendent of recreation as chief executive of the department is responsible for assisting and advising his board or superior officer in formulating policies and basic procedures governing the work of the department and for putting them into effect. His duties are comparable in many respects to those of a superintendent of schools. Most of his time is devoted to planning, organizing, supervising, and promoting the work and interests of the recreation department. Among the specific duties which he assumes either directly or through assistants are: planning, care, and management of areas and facilities; determining the activities and services to be provided by the department, and planning of the department's program; selecting, supervising, and training the department staff; preparing the annual budget and supervising the keeping of departmental records and reports; conducting research and special studies relating to the work of the department and the city's recreation needs; interpreting the program to the public and informing it as to the department's objectives and activities; cooperating with other local agencies in developing plans to meet the city's leisure-time needs. In the small community the superintendent also performs duties of a supervisory or directive nature which in the large cities are performed by other workers.[1]

Qualifications.—The superintendent must be well grounded in the philosophy of recreation, fully understand the significance of leisure, be familiar with the many activities comprising the recreation program and

[1] For a classified list of the superintendent's duties, see Chap. XXX.

with the principles and methods essential to effective program building. He must have a general knowledge of recreation areas, facilities, and equipment, and must understand the principles underlying their effective development and use. He must be familiar with personnel practices in order that he may select, organize, supervise, and train his staff and secure their fullest cooperation. He needs to know the principles and methods involved in setting up a recreation budget, cost and service records, in interpreting the work of his department, in handling its business affairs, in conducting studies, and in building up cooperative relationships with other community agencies. In short he must have those qualities which characterize the student, promoter, organizer, and executive. From one to five years' experience in a subordinate executive capacity in recreation is considered essential.

General Supervisor. *Duties.*—Except for the supervisor of construction and maintenance most of these workers are responsible for supervising playground and community center programs either for the entire city or for a given district. Among their specific duties are selecting the areas or centers to be operated, training and supervising the playground and center staff, securing cooperation among workers, assisting them in planning, organizing, and conducting their activities, advising on equipment and maintenance problems, assisting with publicity, cooperating with neighborhood agencies, recommending expansion in areas, facilities, and programs, and assuming general responsibility for the playground and indoor center service. An important duty is that of assisting the special supervisors in developing playground and center projects in music, nature, arts and crafts, and other special services.

Qualifications.—These workers must have a thorough understanding of recreation activities and of the ways in which they may be made available to the people. They must be familiar with principles of supervision and be able to work with others and to inspire, train, and guide them. They must have a thorough knowledge of the philosophy of recreation, of the scope and service of other social agencies, and the ability to meet the public and discuss recreation problems intelligently. From two to four years' experience as a supervisor or director is considered essential.

Supervisor of Construction and Maintenance. *Duties.*—This worker alone among the types mentioned in this chapter has no responsibility for the supervision or conduct of activities, but he is responsible for the design, construction, maintenance, and repair of areas, buildings, and facilities essential to the program. He prepares, or collaborates with technicians not on the department's staff in preparing, detailed plans for the general development of new areas and for the facilities to be provided in them such as buildings, pools, apparatus, and game equipment.

He supervises their development and construction including such operations as planting, grading, surfacing, and drainage. His responsibility includes the general care, upkeep, and maintenance of all types of outdoor areas and of all buildings and other structures. In some cities he builds playground apparatus and much of the other equipment used in the department.

Qualifications.—Originality and resourcefulness in designing areas and facilities to serve a maximum recreation use, and ability to prepare plans for their effective development are essential. This supervisor must have ability to lay out work and to supervise a construction and maintenance staff, and must be in sympathy with the objectives of the department. He should have a practical knowledge of several crafts such as surveying, drafting, plumbing, and carpentry, and construction and horticultural experience are sometimes required.

Supervisors of Special Activities. *Duties.*—These workers are responsible for promoting, introducing, organizing, and conducting activities in some special field such as music, crafts, drama, or athletics. They assist workers at the individual playgrounds and centers in initiating and conducting activities in their special fields, prepare instructions, select materials and develop projects, provide staff instruction, and demonstrate methods of conducting these activities. They sometimes plan and conduct city-wide events and organize groups or classes in their specialty. They assist in evaluating the effectiveness of staff workers and cooperate with other supervisors and directors in working out well-balanced programs. Their function is to expand service in their special fields, not only within the department program, but elsewhere throughout the city. The supervisor of women and girls, who often serves as an assistant superintendent, gives special attention to phases of the program affecting women and girls.

Qualifications.—Among the many qualifications required of all special supervisors are practical knowledge and appreciation of the varied activities within the special field for which the worker is responsible, an appreciation of their recreation values and ability to interpret them, personal skills in several types of activity within the special field, ability to organize and direct groups, to supervise and instruct leaders, and to plan and supervise city-wide events featuring the special activity. These workers seek to secure participation of the rank and file as well as the development of the special abilities of the talented few, and they must be ready to relate their special field to other phases of the recreation program. The position of supervisor of women's and girls' activities, unlike the other types, calls primarily for a person with broad rather than specialized experience, since the worker is called upon to advise and assist directors and supervisors in planning and conducting activities for women and girls in all phases of the department's program. As a matter of fact, the value of any special supervisor is likely to be much greater as his knowledge extends to fields other than his own particular subject.

Playground and/or Community Center Director. *Duties.*—The playground director and the community center director are to the playground and center what the principal is to the school. This type of worker is in direct charge of a single playground or center and is responsible with the help of supervisors and his assistants for making sure that the playground or center renders the maximum recreation service to the people in the neighborhood. To this end he studies the neighborhood's needs, organizes and develops an appropriate program of activities, divides the work among his leaders, assists them in every way possible, keeps playground records and reports, and sees that buildings, facilities, and equipment are properly maintained. He cooperates with other neighborhood agencies in recreation projects, often organizes a neighborhood council, and enlists, trains, and supervises volunteers to help with parts of the program.

Qualifications.—These workers must combine the qualities of an executive with those of a teacher or leader. They must understand the value of such activities as athletics, storytelling, dramatics, nature study, music, handicraft, folk dancing, social recreation, and informal discussion, be familiar with their forms, and know how they may be introduced in the playground or center program. The worker is expected to have personal skills in at least three of these activities. He must know how to develop a well-balanced, diversified program, to direct his assistants in carrying out the work assigned to them, to organize leagues, tournaments, demonstrations, entertainments, and other special features. The director must be able to work with groups at the playground and center, to deal intelligently with parents and neighborhood leaders, to write publicity, and to speak in public. Special interest and ability in children's activities are of primary importance to the playground director. The center director requires, in addition, greater maturity and special ability in working with young people and adults.

Play Leader. *Duties.*—The duties of this worker include organizing and conducting activities such as games, nature study, hiking, crafts, storytelling, dancing, or dramatics. He assists the playground or center director or the camp manager in preparing for special events and programs, gives guidance to clubs and other groups, supervises special rooms or facilities, and assists in various other ways. He works under the director and is never in full charge of a playground or center.

Qualifications.—The play leader should have personal skill in several activities and a knowledge of first-aid methods. Experience as a participant in play activities and as a leader in recreation or a related field is desirable. High-school graduation or its equivalent is the educational requirement for this position, although some recreation executives believe that at least two years of college or specialized training beyond high school are essential for successful work as a play leader.

Specialist. *Duties.*—The chief duties of this worker are to organize classes in a special program feature such as archery, dancing, puppetry, or tennis, and to provide instruction for groups in his special activity. He may work at a single center, but more frequently his time is distributed between groups meeting at various places throughout the city. He is sometimes called upon to instruct other members of the department staff and to organize tournaments or special programs featuring his particular activity. Specialists, who usually serve on a seasonal or part-time basis, are not to be confused with supervisors of special activities who have a much larger responsibility.

Qualifications.—The specialist needs to have ability to interest people in a particular type of activity and to organize and teach it successfully. In most instances the position requires a high degree of personal skill in the activity. The worker must be able to conduct the activity in such a manner that participants find joy in it for its own sake. This calls for ability as an instructor and a readiness to adapt teaching methods to the capacity of the group and to relate it to other phases of the recreation program.

Experience as a participant in the activity and also as an instructor is essential. College graduation is desirable but it is not a strict requirement. Some cities, for example, have employed Indian chiefs as archery instructors, who in spite of their limited schooling have proved successful leaders.

Manager of Special Facilities. *Duties.*—These vary somewhat according to the type of facility—whether camp, golf course, or swimming center—but in general they include broad responsibilities for program planning, supervision of personnel, and property maintenance. This worker supervises the care and maintenance of the areas and facilities in his charge to make sure that they are attractive, safe, and sanitary. He plans for the most effective use of the facilities, arranges an attractive program of activities, and supervises the collection of fees, the handling of funds, and the keeping of essential cost and service records.

Qualifications.—The manager of a special facility must have ability as an administrator and must know something of business management, public relations, the supervision of a staff, and maintenance methods. He requires a special knowledge of the activities carried on at his center. The manager of a bathing center must have expert skill in swimming and lifesaving, and the camp director an understanding of children and of educational methods.

Other Workers.—As mentioned earlier in the chapter there are other types of workers in the recreation department most of whom do not serve in a leadership capacity, but who are responsible for other phases of the department's work. Among such workers are lifeguards at the swimming pools and beaches, cashiers at the golf course and bathing centers, greenkeepers, maintenance foremen, mechanics, janitors, camp cooks, clerical and research personnel. The nature of the tasks performed by many of these workers involves their meeting and dealing with the public; in some cases they have frequent relationships with children. For this reason character, personality, and ability to deal with people in a courteous, friendly, but efficient manner are important. In most of these positions it is not necessary or practical to demand the same educational and personal qualifications as in leadership positions. However, training, skill, experience, and personality traits which make for success in them must be considered in employing personnel for these nonleadership tasks.

CONDITIONS VS. STANDARDS

The general and special qualifications outlined in this chapter for leadership personnel in the recreation department represent standards which have been accepted by the recreation profession. They obtain in practice in some cities; in others local recreation department standards fall far short of meeting them. The chief discrepancies are generally in respect to educational requirements and personal qualifications of the workers. Naturally, many of the workers in a new field like recreation have not received the type of training which is now considered essential. Yet in most cities the executive and supervisory positions in municipal recreation are held by graduates of colleges or special schools and such positions are open only to college graduates with special recreation training and experience. A common requirement for work on the playground is two years of college study; in several cities playground directors must be college graduates. There is also a growing appreciation of the importance of desirable personal qualifications as well as educational background.

Therefore, in spite of unsatisfactory conditions in some cities, a steady advance toward higher standards and toward the acceptance of the standards recognized in the profession is being achieved. More adequate training opportunities, more honest and intelligent methods of selecting workers, and greater assurance of promotion for persons who render satisfactory service, are contributing to this end. Some of these factors affecting recreation leadership will be considered in the chapters that follow.

CHAPTER VIII

TRAINING RECREATION LEADERS

Recreation leadership obviously cannot take its place among the professions unless high standards of training are established and adequate means of furnishing such training are made available. Training opportunities and methods designed to prepare persons for employment as recreation workers are largely provided by schools, colleges, and universities. In-service training after employment, on the other hand, intended to make leaders more effective in their work, is furnished primarily by the recreation department itself and by other agencies in the cities where the individuals are working. Both types of leadership training are essential.

PRELIMINARY TRAINING

As pointed out in Chap. VII, standards adopted by the profession make college graduation or its equivalent in education a basic requirement for most recreation positions and recreation agencies are more and more accepting these standards. Until recent years educational institutions showed little concern over the preparation of men and women for recreation service and training opportunities were comparatively few. Courses offered in schools of education and social work afforded valuable basic preparation, and the art, music, athletic, and other divisions provided instruction in subjects useful to the recreation worker. However, no institution offered an integrated curriculum adequate for the needs of the field, and in the courses offered little consideration was given to the problems involved in the operation and administration of the municipal recreation department. Because of this lack of training opportunities, especially for persons looking toward supervisory or executive positions, the National Recreation School, a one-year graduate course, was established in 1926 by the National Recreation Association. After nine years this course was temporarily suspended when, owing to the depression, great difficulty was experienced in placing its graduates in suitable recreation positions.

The recent increase in people's leisure, the rapid expansion in recreation programs under Federal auspices, and the gradual development of recreation leadership as a profession, have caused educational institutions to face seriously the problem of training workers for this field. Leader-

102

ship training has been a frequent topic of discussion at the National Recreation Congress, and the reports of the Committee on Training and Experience in Recreation Work have helped focus attention upon and secure the acceptance of leadership standards.

A great number of colleges and institutions have established one or more courses dealing with some phase of recreation leadership and a few have developed curricula providing for recreation majors and designed to prepare men and women for the profession. The importance which has been attached to this problem is illustrated by the conferences on the college training of recreation leaders held at the University of Minnesota in December, 1937, and at the University of North Carolina in April, 1939, which were attended by invited delegates from universities in all sections of the country and by representatives of Federal, national, and local agencies concerned with recreation.

Among the questions to be faced in considering the preparation of recreation leaders are the positions for which persons are to be trained, the types of institutions which should provide the training, the nature of the courses that should be offered and of the training methods to be employed, the length of the training period, and the probable demand for trained leaders. Obviously the answers to these questions depend on many factors, a few of which are considered here.

TRAINING FOR EXECUTIVE LEADERSHIP

Increasingly, persons most familiar with the field of community recreation are of the opinion that preparation for executive leadership should consist of a general four-year undergraduate college course supplemented by two years of graduate training. Opinions differ as to the specific subjects which should be included in such a course, but it is believed desirable that the emphasis during the undergraduate years should be upon subjects of cultural or general educational value and that the professional preparation should be limited primarily to the graduate years.

There is considerable agreement as to the types of knowledge which should be possessed by all recreation leaders serving in an executive capacity, and which should therefore be included in any program designed to prepare people for such service. With a few exceptions, the same types of knowledge are essential to all persons engaged in recreation leadership in any capacity. These general subjects may be summarized briefly as follows:

1. *Physical Science.*—A knowledge of the world in which we live, man's environment, and physical nature is of primary importance. Therefore two or more courses in physical sciences should be covered. Subjects such as biology, physiology, geology,

botany, or astronomy have not only a general educational value but an immediate relationship to nature recreation and physical activities.

2. *English and Literature.*—Every recreation worker should be familiar with the best in literature. Reading is perhaps the most universal form of recreation and a knowledge of the personal satisfaction resulting from acquaintance with the best in literature is of great importance. Furthermore, ability to speak and write effectively is essential.

3. *Social Science.*—The recreation worker must have an understanding of the society of which he is a part and be acquainted with its history and the record of man's development as a social being. This is important because he must take his place along with others in whose work social relationships play such an important part. History, government, and sociology should have a part in the training program.

4. *Education.*—In many of its aspects recreation is closely related to education and the recreation leader often functions in the role of a teacher. He must therefore be familiar with educational principles, methods, and procedures in order to enable him to work effectively with individuals and groups. He must understand the child and his various stages of growth and be familiar with the problems of human behavior. Therefore courses in such subjects as principles of education, child psychology, and teaching methods are essential.

5. *Cultural Arts.*—The history of the development of the arts and the study of their significance in civilization have a great contribution to make in the preparation for recreation service. Drama, music, arts and crafts play an increasingly important part in recreation programs. It is important that recreation workers have a general knowledge of the basic arts and of their application in the recreation program and also a considerable degree of skill in at least one of them.

6. *Games and Physical Activities.*—Athletic games and sports, table games, social activities, and forms of outdoor recreation such as hiking, camping, and aquatics, play a major role in recreation programs. Therefore workers must have sound training in a variety of these activities and must develop, in addition to general motor ability, considerable skill in several of them.

7. *Recreation Administration and Theory.*—Among the chief duties of recreation workers are the conducting or management of playgrounds, indoor centers, and facilities, the planning and conducting of recreation programs of various types, and the organizing of community groups for recreation. Basic training in carrying out these functions and in the best methods of administering recreation as a municipal function is of primary importance. Workers also need to have a knowledge of the theory and function of play, of the signiffcance of leisure in the modern world, and of recreation objectives. Practice teaching and group leadership under careful supervision, and participation in study and work projects, are important. Club organization, recreation service to special groups such as homes, industries, churches, and institutions, methods of interpreting recreation service, office management, fiscal policies, budget-making and record-keeping methods are subjects with which a recreation worker should also be familiar and which should be included in training courses.

8. *Recreation Areas and Facilities.*—The recreation worker needs to have a general knowledge of the principles and problems involved in the selection, design, and equipment of recreation areas and facilities such as playgrounds, playfields, athletic fields, and other special areas for winter and water sports, camping, picnicking, and golf. He should be familiar with such problems as the surfacing, lighting, maintenance, and operation of these areas and facilities. The importance and place of recreation planning in the general field of city planning should be understood; also the fundamental principles in planning and operating recreation buildings and in adapting and using school buildings for community recreation purposes.

Many other subjects could be studied to advantage by a person preparing for service as a recreation worker but most of the important ones fall under one of the groupings suggested. In general it is considered advisable for the undergraduate period to be devoted largely to physical science, literature, social science, education, and other fields, which will afford a background for the more professionalized and specialized subjects such as recreation administration and recreation areas and facilities which should largely come in the two years of graduate work.

Much value is derived from extracurricular activities such as athletics, music, dramatics, debating, and clubs of various kinds, either as an active participant or in a leadership or administrative capacity. Of equal importance with the subject matter offered in the professional courses is the development of opportunity for undertaking individual research, experimentation, and investigation of recreation problems and for engaging in laboratory work under competent guidance. By devoting his summers to leadership in camp, club, or playground the student secures valuable practical training which enables him more quickly to assume a position of responsibility upon completion of his course. It is recommended that every recreation student spend at least one of his summers in a recreation position and seek opportunities for volunteer service as a Scout, club, or church group leader, as well as leadership responsibility in college life.

The Demand for Trained Executives.—The establishment of professional graduate courses is justified only as there is a demand for trained workers, particularly in positions of a supervisory or executive nature. Of the 23,975 recreation leaders reported employed by localities for community recreation service in 1938, only 3,345 were serving on a full-time, year-round basis. Many of these were not executives or supervisors but were in subordinate positions. Yet in spite of the small number of openings, there is almost universal agreement that training for supervisory and administrative positions should be on the graduate level. As the Committee on Curriculum at the Minnesota Conference mentioned previously reported, "To offer such curricula at the undergraduate level is to do violence to the significance of the work involved."

The limited demand for executive leadership and the high standard of training required for such work present a practical problem for the training institutions. It is obvious that enrollments in professional courses on the graduate level must be limited and students selected with the greatest care. Some leaders believe that students should be drawn as far as possible from men and women who have had experience in the field of recreation and who have shown the capacity for positions of greater responsibility. A graduate course requires a highly specialized faculty experienced in and familiar with the everyday problems and developments in the recreation field.

The Committee on Teacher Training Institutes at the Minnesota Conference expressed the opinion that possibly three or four properly located schools should offer training courses for full-time administrative positions. Dr. L. P. Jacks on the basis of his observations believed that because the success of such a course demands a faculty in close touch with the field and a freedom to plan and conduct the course without reference to formal educational restrictions, the task should not be assigned to any existing university but could best be performed by an institution created primarily for this specific purpose.

TRAINING FOR ACTIVITY LEADERSHIP

Although a basic cultural undergraduate course followed by professional studies on the graduate level is considered the ideal training for all types of recreation positions, the limited employment opportunities and the salary rates prevalent in many cities make such preparation impracticable for many individuals. To a large extent students must be trained in a four-year course.

Opinions differ as to whether universities or colleges setting up a training course should place it under an existing school or department, should create a special department to administer it, or should appoint a coordinating committee to plan and direct the training program. The first method has been followed in many institutions which have placed the course under a physical education, education, music, social science, or other existing department. This tends to make recreation training subordinate to these other fields and the faculty are seldom selected primarily because of their ability in the field of recreation. The second method, although sound in principle, is impracticable under present conditions because of the limited demand for leaders and the necessarily small enrollment in the course. The coordinating committee assures consideration of the problem from many points of view and makes possible cooperative planning on the part of the various divisions and departments which have some interest in, and contribute to, the training program. This method is being followed in several institutions which are setting up an experimental curriculum.

In any plan for an undergraduate curriculum providing a major in recreation the cooperation of all departments which have a contribution to make should be enlisted. Many believe that such cooperation and a proper organization of the curriculum are of greater importance than the form of administration under which the curriculum is set up. In a particular institution, the plan is conditioned by the types of recreation positions leaders are being trained for, the faculty available, the courses which are already being given, and the essential requirements for graduation. If leaders are to be trained primarily for the rural field, for service in industries or institutions, or with group work agencies, the courses must be adapted to the special needs of these groups. The curriculum must naturally meet the general requirements of the institution governing graduation, majors, minors, and other factors. It is of special importance that the individual courses that deal indirectly with recreation be somehow related definitely to this field. Opportunities for practical leadership experience, problem solving, and personal participation in extracurricular activities are necessary as a supplement to, and testing ground for, classroom work.

A Four-year Undergraduate Curriculum.—The following outline contains a suggested grouping of courses from which a selection is to be made by a student preparing to enter recreation work immediately after graduation. In any institution each individual student would naturally choose the particular available courses which most fully met his own interests and needs. In the allotment of credit hours and the various grouping of courses it is assumed that a total of 120 hours is required for graduation and that the distribution of courses also meets the general requirements for graduation. The figures in the outline represent the number of credit hours for each course.

FROM THIS GROUP AT LEAST 14 HOURS
Astronomy... 6
Biology... 8
Botany... 6
Chemistry... 8
Geology... 6
Physics... 8
Physiology... 6
Zoology... 6

FROM THIS GROUP AT LEAST 15 HOURS
English literature... 6
English composition... 9
Foreign language... 6
Public speaking... 2
Voice training... 2
Debating... 2
Reporting... 2
Special writing... 3
Playwriting... 3

FROM THIS GROUP AT LEAST 20 HOURS
Principles of economics... 3
General sociology... 3
Government... 3

Municipal administration... 3
History... 6
Anthropology... 6
Community organization and relationships... 2
Social surveys... 2
Social problems... 2
Educational sociology... 2
Contemporary civilization... 3
Leisure in the modern world... 2

FROM THIS GROUP AT LEAST 16 HOURS
Psychology... 3 to 6
Social psychology... 3
Educational psychology... 3
Child psychology... 3
Principles of education... 3
History of education... 3
Teaching methods... 3
Educational tests and measurements... 3
Mental hygiene... 2
Adult education... 2
Philosophy... 3
Preschool child... 3

Training for Specialized Service.—It is desirable that supervisors of music, drama, arts and crafts, and athletics have graduate training of a specialized nature following a general college course. In any case these workers as well as the specialists need training in college or in a school offering special instruction in the activity which they are to teach, lead, or supervise. It is very important, however, that these workers supplement the training in their particular field of activity by taking courses that will help them understand the philosophy and practice of recreation and the objectives of community recreation service.

The Probable Demand for Trained Leaders.—The present interest of colleges and other institutions in recreation training is apparently based upon the expectation that there will be a marked increase in employment opportunities in the recreation field. Large numbers of individuals are engaged in recreation under Federal emergency programs, but the expansion in municipal recreation personnel has been slow and gradual. In 1938, for example, a total of 23,975 men and women were reported employed as recreation leaders in community recreation service throughout the United States and Canada as compared with 20,762 leaders 10 years earlier. Opinions differ widely as to the probable demand for trained leaders in the years ahead. Nevertheless, it seems desirable that to a large extent recreation leadership courses be so planned that persons completing them will be prepared to secure positions in some other type of service which may be supplemented by part-time recreation work.

NONPROFESSIONAL COURSES

Perhaps the greatest contribution that colleges and universities can make in the field of training for recreation leadership is by offering courses which will appeal to the entire student body. Such courses would be presented not from the standpoint of vocational opportunities but because of their contribution to the enrichment of the leisure-time resources of the students. Two types of courses would contribute to this end, (1) those dealing with the significance of leisure in modern life and (2) others offering opportunity for participation in crafts, social recreation, drama, music, and related activities. Such courses are helpful in interpreting the significance of student leisure-time activities and create an interest in the recreational arts on the part of the individual students. They have value as a means of introducing students to activities which promise genuine enjoyment and satisfaction in their own leisure hours and they equip students to serve as volunteer recreation leaders and as enthusiastic supporters of recreation in their own communities. Suggestions on the content of such courses are offered in Chap. X.

IN-SERVICE TRAINING

Owing to the limited training opportunities afforded by colleges and universities in the past, a large percentage of the men and women now engaged in recreation work have undertaken their tasks without adequate preparation for the duties and responsibilities which have been placed upon them. Many of these workers had a general cultural education or were trained for other fields such as teaching, physical education, music, social work, religious education, or drama. Their studies have been carried on in departments concerned primarily with training for some other field. Much of the knowledge of recreation activities, organization, facilities, and leadership which these workers have acquired was gained after employment through in-service training. No recreation department can afford to neglect this phase of its training program and the need for in-service training will continue regardless of how adequately institutions may prepare recreation workers in the future. The recreation field is so wide in scope and is changing so rapidly that workers must continue to study, to observe, and to keep abreast of new developments in recreation and in related fields.

The comprehensive in-service training program is not only continuous, but it includes all workers in the department. It is in no sense considered as a substitute for professional education, but it continues the teaching process by "stimulating thought, challenging ideas, developing strength, and encouraging growth."[1] Among the methods most commonly used

[1] Agnes Van Driel, "In-Service Training," *Proceedings of the National Conference of Social Work,* 1937, p. 426.

by recreation departments to accomplish in-service training are institutes, conferences, staff meetings, supervised reading, workers' committees, group discussion, observation trips, and demonstrations.

Training Institutes.—Most recreation departments conduct some form of training institute. Such courses differ widely in nature and purpose, but perhaps the most common type is that for seasonal workers, particularly playground leaders. The institute is commonly held just before the opening of the summer playground season and usually extends over a period of about a week, with all-day sessions. In some cities where appointments are made following the institute, all applicants for positions are required to attend. Workers already employed or individuals who have served in previous seasons are sometimes excused from some of the courses. The program at these institutes generally includes inspirational addresses, discussions of program planning, lectures on safety, first aid, and care of supplies, practice demonstrations and group participation in games and play activities, workshop classes in handicraft and other special subjects, and an interpretation of the objectives, relationships, techniques, rules, procedures, schedules, and assignments to be in effect during the playground season.

In cities with a year-round staff the responsibility for planning the institute is sometimes assumed largely by these workers who also have a large part in the actual conduct of the sessions. Leaders from agencies in the city or recreation officials from other cities are sometimes brought in to present special subjects. The playground institute can in no sense provide the essential training for successful playground leadership but it supplements general training and helps prepare individuals to meet the specific problems which they are expected to deal with in any particular city.

General Recreation Courses.—In a number of cities training courses have been conducted by recreation departments, usually in cooperation with other local agencies, for the purpose of providing general supplementary training for their workers. In one city where such a course was offered the topics presented included cooperation among recreation agencies in the city, responsibility of the municipality for recreation, group organization and clubs, effects of competitive athletics, mental health, community night programs, special playground features, folk dancing, problem children, and the care of equipment. This course was held in the evening and included 15 sessions of two or more hours each. Recreation department employees were encouraged to take the course and all persons seeking employment with the department were required to attend it. It was open, however, to all in the city. Like the playground institutes these general courses include both lectures and participation in activities and afford opportunity for group consideration of special problems.

An outstanding example of the general recreation institute is the type which has been conducted over a period of years in a large number of American cities by the National Recreation Association in cooperation with local recreation departments and other agencies. The major purpose of these institutes has been to bring new inspiration and a fresh point of view to paid and volunteer leaders, present a new interpretation of objectives in the field of recreation, establish high standards of excellence in recreation work, and help workers increase their skills in conducting activities. These institutes have extended over a period of four weeks, classes being held five days per week and comprising a total of approximately 90 hours. Much of the work presented in these institutes has consisted of practice in organizing, performing, and leading. Some of the earlier institutes included courses in several subjects; others have been devoted to a limited number of subjects such as nature activities, arts and crafts, and music. Many recreation authorities have felt that this type of institute has resulted in increased skill and understanding on the part of their leaders.

Institutes in Special Activities.—A third type of course which plays a major part in in-service training programs is the institute in some special phase of activity such as song leading, folk dancing, social recreation, puppetry, or crafts. Such courses are conducted by a specialist in this particular activity, frequently by a national authority in the field. In cases where they are under the leadership of a person from outside the city, they are usually intensive in nature. In other instances they extend over a longer period, with weekly sessions. Music and drama institutes frequently terminate in a production by the persons taking the course. This type of institute affords an excellent means by which staff workers can enlarge and increase their own skills and learn the techniques of group leadership in specific activities and effective methods of organizing special projects. It often helps to initiate an enlarged program in a special field and furnishes an opportunity for training and enlisting volunteer leaders in the activity. New leadership methods learned in this type of course may frequently be applied to advantage in other parts of the department program.

Institutes for Lay Leaders.—Paid workers also receive valuable training either as instructors or participants in the institutes which are frequently arranged primarily for the training of volunteers and for the benefit of the general public. Sometimes in these institutes major emphasis is laid upon interpreting the significance of the recreation movement and the importance of the local recreation program. More frequently, however, they afford opportunities for participation in activities. In one city an annual recreation institute sponsored by a committee of recreation department workers is conducted primarily for men and women who serve as leaders of adult groups. Programs vary from year to year, but the six weekly sessions include instruction and demonstration in such activities as table games, parties for large groups, progressive games, community dancing, informal dramatics, and creative activities. In another city the course comprises several weekly sessions and each of the meetings is divided into three periods. The first consists of a general assembly at which outstanding speakers present subjects of general interest. Following this several section group meetings are conducted in which special topics are considered such as recreation in the home, games and sports, or dramatics. The evening is concluded with a third period when the entire group participates in social recreation, indoor picnics, old-time dances, or campfire programs. Although intended for the general public and for lay leaders, these institutes afford excellent training opportunities for members of the department staff and are also frequently attended by local university students who are preparing for work in recreation.

Local recreation departments frequently cooperate with other local agencies in planning institutes and courses from which their workers receive benefits. A number of recreation executives and other staff workers serve as instructors in courses offered by local colleges or universities. Such courses afford a recruiting and training ground for persons who later are employed in the department. Institutes conducted by the Federal emergency agencies, often in cooperation with the local recreation authorities, have furnished training for large numbers of emergency leaders assigned for service with recreation departments. In a few cities such courses have continued throughout the entire year; in others they have been in the nature of brief intensive institutes.

Staff Meetings.—The staff meeting is a widely used and effective means of in-service training. In cities with a year-round program staff meetings are usually held once a month but during the summer playground season workers in many cities are called together each week. As a rule all workers are obliged to attend staff meetings, which serve the following purposes: to inform the staff as to department rules, regulations, policies, and plans; to afford instruction in specific recreation activities and projects; to plan city-wide and other special events; to confer on staff relationships; to hear reports on special problems submitted by staff members; to discuss community events affecting recreation; and to consider methods of self-improvement. Sometimes outstanding leaders on some phase of recreation address the group.

Members of the department staff increasingly share in the responsibility for planning and conducting staff meetings. Individual workers are assigned topics which are presented before the group; others are called upon to provide instruction in special activities and projects. Committees of workers are appointed to study special problems and to lead discussions at staff meetings. Such methods stimulate study and research, furnish training in public speaking, and keep workers in touch with new developments in the recreation field. The staff meeting, if wisely planned and conducted, affords a splendid opportunity for raising standards of work in the department and for developing a spirit of cooperation among the members of the staff.

Conferences.—Opportunities for exchanging ideas between workers in different cities and of learning about new methods of conducting recreation work are stimulating to workers. Progressive recreation departments therefore encourage their workers to attend national and district conferences where the subject of recreation is discussed. The most outstanding of these gatherings is the National Recreation Congress which is held annually and is attended by hundreds of recreation leaders and representatives of related fields. At the Congress workers gain inspiration from addresses by outstanding speakers, participate in discussions of techniques, trends, and problems at the many section meetings, observe exhibits and displays of recreation products and local recreation service, take part in informal sessions devoted to demonstrations and participation in social recreation, music, and other activities, observe local facilities and activities, and most valuable of all, exchange ideas through informal conferences and meetings with individuals who are confronted by the same kind of problems which they are facing.

Many opportunities arise during the year for workers to benefit by attending other meetings. Conferences of municipal recreation executives, under the sponsorship of the National Recreation Association, are held each year in various sections of the country. Unlike the Congress, attendance at these meetings is restricted largely to professional workers and discussion is limited primarily to technical problems. Local, district, or national meetings of groups interested in some phase of recreation such as camping, athletics, or girls' work afford recreation leaders opportunities for extending their knowledge. Recreation workers are encouraged to take part in local conferences arranged by city-wide groups for discussions of problems touching the recreation field.

Other Training Methods.—Directed reading is used in many cities as a means of in-service training. Workers' attention is called to publications of unusual value and interest, workers are required to devote a certain amount of time each week to professional reading, or special books on recreation are made available through the department, city, or municipal reference library. Many departments subscribe to magazines which are useful to their workers and in a number of cities several copies of *Recreation* are distributed each month among the members of the staff. Reports of publications relating to the recreation field are sometimes submitted at staff meetings.

Supervision provided by the department staff is one of the most effective in-service training methods. Through their visits to centers, through meetings with junior workers, through demonstrations and guidance in the development of projects, supervisors help workers acquire skills and understanding. Some executives make it a point to call the workers' attention to local events and happenings which are in some way related to the work of the department and from which the leaders might gain useful suggestions. Typical of such happenings are exhibits, demonstrations, music, dance, or athletic programs. Short local courses in special subjects related to recreation are called to the attention of the workers, who are sometimes permitted time off to attend them. The value of apprenticeships in the field of local government is becoming widely recognized, but only a beginning has been made in the use of apprentices in recreation departments. However, the National Recreation Association is financing several apprentices each year in local recreation departments in the belief that the training, experience, and guidance which they receive during their apprenticeship will better equip them for positions of responsibility in the field. Likewise the possibilities which an exchange of workers offers for the growth of workers and the benefit of programs have only begun to be appreciated in the recreation field.

In a few cities, especially those with a year-round staff, workers have formed clubs or associations, the objectives of which are to increase the effectiveness of the members, to promote good fellowship, and to further the interests of public recreation. In achieving these objectives problems confronting the department are studied and discussed, and research projects are undertaken. Picnics, outings, week ends in camp, or social recreation evenings are also arranged, when the leaders have an opportunity to serve their own recreation interests. These volunteer organizations of recreation workers are a useful means of developing morale among the members of the department staff and also encourage the workers to suggest ways and means of improving standards of recreation leadership and service.

CHAPTER IX

SELECTING AND MAINTAINING THE LEADERSHIP STAFF

Municipal recreation must compete with other fields of employment for people of the qualifications outlined in Chap. VII. In order to secure and retain the right kind of personnel, the recreation department must make its conditions of employment attractive to qualified workers. Recreation authorities have no task more important than the selection of their leadership staff.

ESSENTIAL FACTORS IN SELECTING WORKERS

Conditions and factors which affect the ability of recreation authorities to select and retain competent leaders include the following:

1. The interpretation of opportunities offered by the recreation field
2. The establishment of broad qualifications for employment in various positions
3. Freedom to select and employ individuals who are most competent
4. The adoption of satisfactory procedure for the selection of workers
5. Ability to pay salaries commensurate with the preparation and responsibilities involved
6. Opportunities for full-time, year-round employment
7. Assurance of reasonable security for workers
8. Ability to make recreation a career service by offering opportunities for advancement
9. Adequate provisions for retirement

The ability of recreation authorities to influence or control these factors varies widely from city to city. In some cases they have the power to fix conditions relative to the selection and retention of their workers; in others these conditions are largely determined by other officials. Because of the limited employment opportunities in the field, recreation authorities have not paid adequate attention to some of these factors. Noteworthy progress is being made, however, toward the attainment of satisfactory conditions as they affect recreation workers.

The report of the Committee on Training, Experience, and Compensation in Community Recreation Work[1] has helped focus attention not only on the need for adequate standards but also on more satisfactory employment practices. The Society of Recreation Workers of America, organized in 1938, lists among its aims and objectives the main-

[1] Published by the National Recreation Association, 1938.

tenance of high standards of professional qualifications, the promotion of adequate programs of professional training, and the protection of the interests of recreation workers as a group. The report of the Commission of Inquiry on Public Service Personnel,[1] outlining procedures for the establishment of career service in government, has received wide publicity and support and will unquestionably aid in meeting the personnel problems in municipal recreation service.

Interpreting the Movement.—The possibilities for professional service which the recreation field offers must be interpreted widely and effectively in order that persons with the proper qualifications for this service may consider recreation leadership as their life work. Methods of interpreting the movement and of advising the public as to the work of the recreation department are considered in Chap. XXXIII. It is especially important that the recreation profession be represented in vocational and guidance conferences arranged for students in schools and colleges. Only as the recreation movement is adequately interpreted will it attract persons interested in a career which demands unselfish personal service, and will it weed out persons interested merely in a job. Interpretation is also essential in order that the public may realize the necessity for well-qualified personnel and may support the recreation department in its insistence upon qualified workers.

Qualifications.—The general and special qualifications for recreation service presented in the committee report[2] are being used more and more by recreation departments as a guide in setting up standards for the selection of its workers. Local conditions sometimes require or justify variations in the qualifications recommended by the Committee but the standards have proved useful in raising the general level of local requirements for employment.

Freedom in Employing Workers.—Because recreation authorities are responsible for the quality and quantity of the service rendered by their workers, they must have freedom to choose the best qualified personnel available. Political pressure and personal favoritism must obviously be eliminated in the selection of workers. Local applicants are entitled to full and fair consideration, but restricting employment to persons residing in the city, county, or state may handicap a locality in securing the best personnel. As a rule, competent workers can be secured locally for the positions of minor responsibility. It is particularly important, however, that the position of chief executive and others of a technical or supervisory nature be open to all regardless of residence, because in many instances suitable candidates are not available within the city. Increas-

[1] *Better Government Personnel,* McGraw-Hill Book Company, Inc., 1935.
[2] *Report of the Committee on Training, Experience, and Compensation in Community Recreation Work,* National Recreation Association, 1938.

ingly, applications from experienced persons outside the city are welcomed, if not actually sought, by recreation authorities.

Salaries.—Competent workers can be secured and retained only when salaries are adequate. The salary scale presented in the Committee report[1] was determined after a careful study of the different positions, the responsibilities involved, and the salaries in related fields of public service requiring comparable training and experience and involving equal responsibilities. Local salary rates in such fields must be kept in mind in fixing the compensation of recreation workers in a particular locality. Unfortunately, in most localities, recreation leaders are paid considerably less than the minimum standards recommended in the report.[2]

Full-time, Year-round Service.—One of the difficulties in attracting competent personnel is that to a great extent the direction of playgrounds and indoor centers and various types of supervisory and executive service still afford only part-time employment. Recreation is only a secondary means of livelihood for part-time workers, so they naturally look to some other field for professional advancement. The percentage of community recreation leaders employed on a full-time basis is increasing but the best interests of the community program demand a further trend in this direction.

SOURCES OF WORKERS

Many persons who are serving successfully in leadership positions with local recreation departments were trained for and gained their experience in other fields. With the growth of the movement, however, a larger percentage of these positions, especially of an executive or supervisory nature, are being filled from within the profession. Furthermore, because more recreation courses are now available, many of the persons who are being employed by recreation departments for subordinate and part-time positions have had some professional training.

The Executive.—Several sources are available to the city seeking a recreation executive or general supervisor. In a large city with a highly organized departmental staff, the position may be filled by the promotion of a worker who has demonstrated his ability and capacity for larger responsibilities. Otherwise, the authorities are likely to canvass the best available personnel in comparable positions in other cities and, if possible, to induce these workers to apply for the position. In a smaller city they utilize the same sources, but in addition they may seek a person in a large city system who has been particularly successful in a less responsible position, such as playground director. When there is a change in exec-

---

[1] *Ibid.*

[2] See *Survey of Salaries Paid to Recreation Workers*, 1938, National Recreation Association, 1939.

utive leadership or when a new department is created, pressure is often brought to bear upon the recreation authorities to appoint a local citizen. Sometimes there is available a worker in a related field such as a supervisor of physical education, a school principal, a Y.M.C.A. or settlement worker, or an athletic director, who has the proper personal qualifications, training, and experience. More often, however, the position can be filled satisfactorily only by appointing an individual experienced in municipal recreation work.

Other Full-time Employees.—Other positions offering full-time employment are those of general supervisor, special activities supervisor, and playground or center director. These positions are sometimes filled from outside the city although competent local applicants for them are more likely to be found than for the executive positions. In selecting a supervisor, the authorities look to the following sources: (1) persons who have served in a similar position on a part-time or seasonal basis, (2) playground or center directors who have demonstrated unusual ability and the capacity for higher responsibility, or (3) instructors or specialists in a particular type of activity, either within the department or in related fields, who have shown a special aptitude for such service in the recreation department. For example, a person who has taught manual training or natural science in the schools, who has worked vacations as a specialist at camps or playgrounds, and who has made a special study of municipal recreation, may be selected for the supervisor of crafts or nature activities. The position of playground and center director, on the other hand, is more likely to be filled by promoting individuals who have successfully served as assistant director, group leader, or special instructor, or by employing recent graduates of colleges offering recreation courses, who have had some experience in recreation leadership.

Part-time Workers.—Because their periods of employment and remuneration are comparatively limited, part-time or seasonal workers are usually recruited from the city employing them. Schoolteachers, kindergarteners, and teachers or supervisors of physical education, music, crafts, and science are employed in large numbers for work during the summer months as supervisors, special teachers, playground directors, and assistants. In many cities summer workers are drawn largely from the ranks of recent college graduates or students who are specializing in recreation or a related field or who formerly served as junior leaders while attending the playgrounds themselves. School, college, and university faculties and student bodies furnish much of the leadership personnel employed at camps, swimming centers, and other special features.

Indoor center directors and assistants, specialists, and club leaders are drawn from a great variety of sources. Day-school teachers of physical education, manual training, and other subjects are often employed one or more evenings a week to conduct center groups or classes. In some cities the use of employed schoolteachers is avoided because of the objection to dual employment and because teachers cannot be expected to give their best service after a day in the classroom. An attempt is therefore made to find other people who are willing to serve on a part-time basis. For example, a professional musician is employed to train the orchestras, a dressmaker to conduct the sewing classes, a craftsman to assist the group making jewelry, and an artist to instruct the sketch club. It is frequently possible to find women who before their marriage were recreation workers or teachers and who are glad to accept such part-time employment. The possibilities for expanding the program are limited in some communities because properly trained workers are not available in the locality.

METHODS OF SELECTING WORKERS

Regardless of the specific method used, it is agreed that recreation workers, especially those employed full-time the year round, should be selected on the basis of merit. Competitive examination is perhaps the most practical and common method of selection, whether under civil service, the recreation authorities, or some other municipal agency. In the case of part-time or seasonal positions, workers are often chosen from individuals who have done satisfactory work in short institute courses and without competitive examination; sometimes a personal interview and references followed up carefully are the chief basis for selection. In rare instances the selection is restricted to persons who have been certified by a designated agency. In any case all applicants must measure up to certain personality and educational requirements considered essential for the particular position.

Civil Service.—On the whole, recreation authorities feel that civil service is probably the most practical method yet devised for the selection of their workers. According to the *Recreation Year Book* for 1937, however, civil service was used in only 103 cities in the selection of recreation personnel. Most of these are large municipalities or are in states where civil service procedure has been widely adopted.

The underlying principle of civil service is the selection of the best qualified personnel available, and to the extent that it achieves this objective it protects the taxpayer as well as the worker. Procedure for putting the plan into effect rests with the local civil service commission. Among its functions are the following: to set up a proper and adequate classification system with the positions clearly defined as to the duties involved and the essential qualifications; to work out adequate minimum entrance requirements; to prepare examination questions after consultation with recreation authorities; to conduct examinations designed to test the applicants' technical knowledge and personal qualifications; to secure information as to the applicants' past record, character, and physical condition; to submit to the recreation authorities a list of satisfactory candidates from which appointments are to be made; to fix a probationary period before the appointments become permanent; and to establish and administer efficiency ratings.

These conditions are being met with varying degrees of satisfaction in different cities. If the civil service authorities are selected with care, and if they give advance publicity to examinations, seek competent advice in setting up qualifications and in preparing and grading examinations, and provide the recreation department with lists of the best qualified candidates, the results are satisfactory. Several recreation departments have extended effective assistance to the civil service authorities who have sought their cooperation. Occasionally recreation authorities from outside the city have been employed to assist in preparing and conducting examinations and in grading the applicants. An alert, informed public opinion is effective in causing civil service authorities to consider carefully the special requirements of recreation service and to adopt acceptable selection methods.

It is worth mentioning that, although they usually set rather high standards for their workers, boards of education do not use civil service generally. Therefore, however effective this method may become as a means of selecting recreation workers with Federal, state, or municipal agencies, there will be many workers, particularly in part-time and seasonal positions, who are not employed through civil service.

Certification.—Certification or licensing of individuals as a prerequisite to employment in recreation is in effect in two states, New Jersey and California, and it affects only recreation workers in school systems. Under this method only persons who have been certified by a central body in the state are eligible for local employment in recreation leadership positions. Few recreation executives favor this method and most of them feel that it can be satisfactory only if it is administered by a body controlled by the recreation profession. Such a body would have administrative freedom to establish classifications for recreation positions and standard requirements for them, and to fix fees and conduct necessary examinations. Special certificates would be issued for each major classification. Persons licensed by this body would provide a reservoir of personnel from which positions might be filled after further examination by the employing agency.

Other Methods.—In cities where there is no civil service commission or certification system, other methods must be developed of ensuring the selection of competent, adequately trained personnel. Many attempts have been successful; others have failed because of powerful and hostile opposition. In cities with a merit system along the lines of civil service, positions are classified, examinations held, and selection based on the best judgment of the recreation authority. Rating scales which eliminate the necessity of examinations have been used in one or more cities where the large number of applicants for summer playground positions makes personal interviews and written examinations impracticable; but this practice is not recommended for general use. Authorities commonly conduct a training course before employing seasonal workers who are selected on the basis of their record during the course.

Some systems select their workers without providing any special training and without any examination. This arrangement has worked out successfully when the managing authority is free from political control and where applicants must meet standard qualifications. In general, however, it is wise to select workers on the basis of an examination which assures competent and unbiased consideration of the merits of all applicants.

EXAMINATIONS

Examinations for the selection of recreation workers generally include three types of tests to determine the fitness of candidates. A *written* test is designed to reveal the applicant's knowledge of the field covered by the examination, his understanding of its relationships to other fields, and his ability to organize and express his thoughts in written form. A *practical* test requires the applicant to organize or lead a group of people in selected activities or to perform some other task related to the particular position. A *personal interview* reveals the applicant's personal qualities, character, general fitness, mentality, and ability to express himself orally. It also affords an opportunity for evaluating the references and records of previous experience which each applicant is required to submit and to appraise his possibilities for growth in the service.

All candidates for positions are expected to meet minimum standards of age, education, and experience before they are permitted to take the examination. Evidence of good character and a certificate of sound physical health are also considered prerequisites. Before appointment physical examinations should be given all who pass the preceding tests.

The relative weight to be given to each of the three tests varies according to the nature of the position. Four out of a ten-point total is allowed for the written test in the case of most positions. The practical test counts for more than the personal in examinations for such positions as lifeguard, play leader, specialist, or supervisor of special activities. The personal interview, however, is considered relatively more important in examinations for the position of superintendent or general supervisor.

Content of Written Examinations.—The questions asked in written examinations are intended to reveal the applicant's knowledge of the problems and responsibilities involved in the position which he is seeking and of the methods of solving them. Examinations for the different positions naturally vary widely. Candidates for executive positions are asked questions relative to the broad scope of municipal recreation and are designed to indicate his knowledge of administrative methods. The activity leader on the other hand is expected to show familiarity with specific leadership methods, activities, and materials.

In an examination applicants for the position of superintendent of recreation may be asked to prepare an organization chart for a recreation department for a city of a given size, to outline a plan of procedure for establishing a year-round recreation program, to prepare a budget, to describe a system of departmental service and business records, to outline a program for interpreting the work of the recreation department, or to discuss an adequate system of recreation areas and facilities for a city. Applicants for this type of position are frequently required to write a thesis on some general phase of the subject such as the relation of organized municipal recreation to other community agencies or the importance of recreation in modern city life.

Candidates for supervisory positions are tested on their fitness for the specific job; for example a supervisor of athletics is required to demonstrate his knowledge of athletics, games, and sports, and also to indicate how these activities may be organized on the individual playground, at the indoor center, or on a city-wide basis. Playground and center workers are asked questions which for the most part relate to problems involved in operating these facilities. Typical subjects are the reasons for playgrounds or indoor centers, play interests at different ages, descriptions of games and other activities, program planning methods, the selection and care of supplies and play materials, safety on the playground, methods of enlisting neighborhood cooperation, the use of volunteer leaders, and methods of solving problems of conduct. Lifeguards, golf course managers, and other special workers are questioned primarily on the particular phases of the work for which they are to be held responsible.

APPOINTMENTS

Under civil service, lists of qualified personnel eligible for appointment on the basis of their rating in the three-fold examination previously described, are prepared by the civil service authorities, and the recreation authorities are required to make their appointments from the names on this list. In any case, if merit is the sole basis for selection, the individuals who have made the most creditable showing in the examination or who have passed some other test receive the appointment. Whether civil service is in effect or not, experience has shown that a probationary period of at least six months is highly desirable for all appointees; many authorities believe a two-year period is necessary in the case of some types of workers. The probationary period enables the department to observe the worker's attitudes, the quality of his work, and his suitability for the position. During the period he should be helped in becoming effective in it. It is desirable for the superintendent of recreation to report regularly to the civil service commission and to his superiors, and to recommend that the worker be dropped if he has demonstrated that he is not fitted for the position. This is highly important because civil service regulations make it difficult to discharge workers after final appointment, except for serious offenses. If at the end of the probationary period the worker has demonstrated his fitness for the position, his appointment becomes permanent.

MAINTAINING STANDARDS OF EFFICIENCY

Practices and policies which enable the recreation department to retain, protect, and promote the successful worker and also to release the ineffective one are just as important as those which assure the securing of competent personnel. A successful personnel program calls for the active cooperation of the civil service commission or other general personnel agency of the city, the recreation authority, and the workers themselves. It involves the adoption of procedures which are fair to the worker, give him reasonable protection on the job, and provide opportunities for advancement. On his part the worker must perform his duties faithfully, maintain a sustained interest in his work, respond to reasonable rules of personal conduct, and continue his professional training. Workers are entitled to reasonable security of tenure and to protection from demotion or dismissal except for legitimate reasons, just as the department employing them has a right to demand effective service on the part of its workers.

Rating Workers.—A system of rating recreation workers is desirable as a basis for salary increases or decreases, promotions, transfers, renewals, and adjustments in the assignments of individual workers. Many recreation authorities have established effective rating systems or are cooperating with civil service commissions in the rating of their workers. In departments where the staff is small, the executive can personally follow the work of each employee closely and with the aid of his supervisors can easily appraise their efficiency. In systems employing large numbers of workers, however, definite rating schemes are required.

It is commonly agreed that ratings should be made frequently and periodically throughout the year, that several competent individuals should have a part in the rating process, that as far as possible ratings be objective and have a uniform basis, that workers be rated on specific qualities or factors, and that rating systems facilitate the checking of individual scores. It is desirable that each worker's record be analyzed at least once a year and that outstanding work be given special commendation and failures be accounted for. Some authorities make it a practice of having each worker's rating reviewed annually with him by the person to whom he is directly responsible.

Advancement.—Promotion of workers within the department is desirable whenever possible because it helps to attract capable individuals to the service and to maintain the morale of workers. Recreation can be developed into a career service only when promotion is on merit and is based upon efficiency, service records, and examinations, rather than on seniority. Definite periodic salary increases offer an incentive to workers, but should be granted only if deserved. Frequently examinations for positions in higher classifications are restricted to persons already employed and giving satisfactory service in subordinate positions. Supplementary training secured by employed workers is sometimes taken into account in making promotions, but it is desirable that such training count only as it is reflected in increased effectiveness on the job. Academic credits alone are not considered a justification for salary increases or the assignment of greater responsibility.

Retirement.—Full-time, year-round recreation workers employed by agencies of the local government are entitled to participate in retirement systems on the same basis as other governmental employees.

CHAPTER X

VOLUNTEER SERVICE IN THE RECREATION DEPARTMENT

Volunteer service has played an important role in the development of community recreation. As pointed out in Chap. V, the sand gardens of Boston were first conducted by volunteer leaders. Many present-day public recreation departments grew out of the work of the voluntary playground or recreation associations which sprang up in the 1890's or later. When the municipality took over the program some of the members of these associations were appointed to serve on recreation commissions, advisory boards, or committees. Each year thousands of individuals contribute time and service to municipal recreation departments. In 1938, more than 300 cities reported the enlistment of 25,000 volunteer workers, one-third of whom served as leaders of activities.

In spite of the large number of volunteer recreation leaders, increase in such service has not kept pace with the growth of the movement and volunteers are used less extensively in municipal recreation than among a number of private leisure-time agencies. Since in the future the public demand for recreation is likely to exceed what municipal governments will be able to supply, there should be opportunity for a vast amount of volunteer recreation service. Every community contains men and women of talent, leisure, and personality who might be drawn into the work. Greater resourcefulness in attracting them and more effective organization for using them are necessary in order that the values and possibilities of volunteer service may be fully realized. As a matter of fact, since the recruiting, training, and guidance of volunteers calls for initiative, tact, and ability, the extent to which a recreation department enlists volunteer service is one indication of the caliber of its leadership. Some of the major problems and methods in the use of volunteers are considered in this chapter.

TYPES OF VOLUNTEER SERVICE

The many different ways in which volunteers serve recreation departments may be grouped according to the following types:

1. *Administrative, Promotional, or Advisory.*—Lay service of this type generally involves membership on boards, councils, or committees. In this group are included the members of the official board or commission responsible for the department's operation, of special departmental committees, or of an advisory group such as a

125

recreation council. Under this type are also the persons who assist with referendum campaigns or who accept assignments to help interpret the work of the department to the local authorities or the public.

2. *Activity or Group Leadership.*—This type involves organizing, guiding, or instructing people, such as advising a hobby club, conducting nature hikes, or teaching a craft class. Other examples of such leaders are playground storytellers, tennis instructors, social recreation leaders, or persons who assume responsibility for organizing and conducting a bowling tournament, softball league, or doll show.

3. *Nonleadership Help with Program Projects.*—Officiating at athletic games or contests, serving as a judge at special events, or helping in the preparation of a playground pageant are examples of such service. In addition, many individuals perform without charge at department entertainments, serve as ushers or help with the scenery or lighting equipment at dramatic productions, or furnish transportation for playground groups on special occasions.

4. *Miscellaneous Services.*—These consist of such services as marking game courts, helping with playground registration, constructing game equipment, or giving clerical assistance in the department office.

It is clear that different kinds of volunteer service require persons of widely different training, experience, and ability. Some tasks involve brief, specific periods of service whereas others make demands upon the individual's time and attention throughout the year. A great variety of possible volunteer services suggest themselves to the alert executive. For example, in one city which used nearly 600 volunteers during the year, 5 were members of the Recreation Commission, 49 served as storytellers at play streets and in institutions, 100 performed for the traveling theater, 8 served as play leaders, 180 took part in radio, entertainment, and institutional programs, 75 helped during girls' week, 100 gave automobile service in connection with the traveling theater, 2 taught folk dancing groups, and 47 served on the Christmas committee. In another city more than a thousand individuals assisted in the recreation program of the park department during one year.

Junior Leaders.—Volunteer service is not restricted to adults, for boys and girls display a desire and capacity for leadership and service which express themselves in various ways, especially on the playground. Children are helpful in telling stories to younger children, guarding them at wading pools, assisting with first aid, preparing publications, giving instruction in simple crafts, caring for supplies and equipment, carrying responsibilities in athletic organizations, and instructing younger children in the use of apparatus. Safety patrols, junior police, junior leaders' corps, playground town governments, and junior towns give opportunity for voluntary leadership by boys and girls and also provide valuable training in leadership. Often these activities are considered parts of the playground program rather than as volunteer service.

Services of Organizations.—Local organizations or groups interested in leisure-time activities, as well as individuals, also render valuable assistance. Frequently the cooperation of an organization has made possible the starting of a new program feature such as a drama or nature club, the development of new facilities, or an increase in the department's budget. In a number of cities when the program has been threatened because of a drastic reduction in the budget, agencies like the parent-teacher association have enlisted from their membership a corps of volunteer workers to help carry on the playgrounds or centers. In other instances they have successfully demanded that budget cuts be restored. Local organizations have donated playgrounds, swimming pools, or other recreation facilities to the city, have met the expense of operating camps, or have provided leaders for specific program features such as storytelling, a nature museum, or an indoor center. The recreation council, on which local agencies interested in recreation have representation, is a means of stimulating volunteer service and securing support for the recreation program. This form of organization, which has proved a great asset to many recreation departments, will be discussed later in the chapter.

VALUES IN VOLUNTEER SERVICE

From the examples just cited it is clear that the active interest of unpaid lay men and women is vital to the larger success of the movement. There are so many tasks to be done that were it not for volunteers much work would remain unaccomplished. Among the chief advantages of volunteer service to the recreation department are these:

1. Volunteers bring a fresh point of view and an enthusiasm valuable alike to the professional staff and to the participants in the program. In some instances they also have a more intimate knowledge of the background, attitudes, and interests of the people served than the paid workers.
2. It mobilizes the skill, intelligence, enthusiasm, and support of persons interested in the development of a particular part of the program, such as nature study, chess, or puppetry.
3. Participation of volunteers in recreation work tends to make the program more democratic and contributes to the principle of self-direction.
4. The fact that people are willing to serve the department gladly without compensation gives the employed staff a renewed sense of the value of the work.
5. The trained volunteer, through his work on committees and in the conduct of activities, can make easier the acceptance of high standards.
6. By taking responsibility for performing specific functions or by helping with details the volunteer frees part of the paid worker's time and makes possible a larger or richer program.
7. Volunteers have an advantage as interpreters. In "speaking up" for recreation they cannot be accused of trying to preserve their jobs. They are in a position to help in clearing away misunderstandings and in educating the public to needed changes and advances in recreation. Frequently the layman has a more influential relationship with the public than does the professional worker.

As a superintendent of recreation has pointed out: "Volunteers of wealth and prestige have the power to safeguard, interpret, and promote any program for public good to which they may care to commit themselves." Realizing the truth of this statement, forward-looking recreation authorities are enlisting the interest and support of prominent men and women in their communities.

DIFFICULTIES IN THE USE OF VOLUNTEERS

It must not be taken for granted that because volunteers can and do render valuable service, no difficulties are experienced in using them. As a matter of fact, some recreation workers do not use volunteers extensively because they believe that it requires more time to secure, train, and supervise them than it does to do the work themselves. What are some of the difficulties experienced with volunteer service?

Except in rare instances, the volunteer's recreation interest is a secondary one which is likely to be sidetracked by others. It is more difficult to hold to strict account persons who are giving their services than paid workers. Unless volunteers accept a definite responsibility for reporting for duty promptly and performing the duties expected of them, they are not likely to sacrifice a social engagement in order to attend a club or committee meeting. The different basis upon which volunteers and paid workers serve has sometimes given rise to problems in their relationships. Programs dependent upon lay leaders have less assurance of being completed or maintained continuously than when paid workers are used. If the social status of the volunteer and the people served differ greatly, a lack of sympathetic understanding and confidence may result unless the volunteer is a person of good judgment. Sometimes a person willing to serve has had little or no specific training for the job. On the other hand, individuals who have had highly specialized training in some form of recreation are not acceptable if they do not understand leadership principles and methods, or share the ideals and standards of the department. Occasionally persons feel that after a period of volunteer service they should be employed. In spite of these difficulties, experience has shown that the intelligent use of volunteers has yielded exceedingly worth-while results.

PROCEDURES IN DEVELOPING VOLUNTEER SERVICE

The effective use of volunteers in municipal recreation service requires careful planning and administration on the part of the authorities in order that the maximum benefits may be secured. The principal procedures in the development and use of volunteer service are recruiting, training, assigning, supervising, and evaluating the workers. The following discussion of these factors relates primarily to volunteer service involving activity or group leadership or assistance with program projects. For the most part it does not apply directly to administrative or advisory service involving membership on boards, committees, or councils. The special problems and procedures in dealing with volunteers of this type will be considered separately.

Recruiting.—The recruiting of volunteers requires time and studied effort on the part of the recreation and staff. In times of crisis it has proved easier to recruit volunteer leaders than during normal conditions. When budgets were cut early in the depression, necessitating drastic reductions in the department staffs in some cities, the number of volunteers rapidly increased. In several cities where the playgrounds were about to be closed, relays of volunteers undertook to operate them and to conduct the daily program. However, when emergency workers were later assigned to recreation positions, thereby removing the urgent need for this type of service, the number of volunteers quickly declined.

Essential Qualifications.—In recruiting, recreation authorities keep in mind the general qualifications desirable in all volunteers and the particular requirements called for by the work to be done. Among the qualities which are considered essential in all individuals who are to be used by the recreation department, regardless of the type of service to be performed, are: (1) character and high standard of personal conduct, (2) dependability, (3) adaptability, (4) a conscientious workmanlike approach to their tasks, (5) a willingness to accept the department's methods, policies, and philosophy, (6) readiness to take and benefit by training, supervision, suggestions, and criticism, (7) ability and willingness to carry projects through to completion, and (8) emotional stability.

Additional qualifications for activity leadership are a knowledge of activities, a certain amount of personal skill in them, and ability to organize, teach, and deal with groups. Board membership, on the other hand, calls for a person with broad understanding, good judgment, standing in the community, forcefulness, and an enthusiastic belief in the recreation movement—to mention only a few desirable traits.

While the volunteer who comes to an organization equipped with skill, education, experience, and a sympathetic attitude finds readiest acceptance, this does not mean that the inexperienced youngster or adult whose only apparent asset is a desire to serve is useless. The recreation department has so many types of tasks covering so wide a range of responsibilities that there is certain to be a place where every intelligent individual can serve effectively.

Sources of Volunteers.—In view of the great variety of tasks performed by volunteers, they are recruited from widely different sources. Individuals who are often willing to help with leadership projects are former recreation workers, teachers, hobbyists of all kinds, experts in activities such as swimming, tennis, or birdlore, and young people who have been trained in leadership methods and have enjoyed their experience as participants in various forms of recreation. Adults and youth who have benefited from the department's program, parents of playground children, retired men and women, and young women with leisure are often willing to help. Older boys and girls taking part in playground or center activities can frequently be enlisted for some form of volunteer service.

If technical ability or special skills are required for a job, the sources of volunteers are thereby limited. A leader for an orchestra or choral group is sought among persons who are actively engaged in music or who have had experience in this field. For help in conducting a track meet or water sports carnival, the recreation department turns to individuals who have been members of college track or swimming teams or to athletic organizations promoting these sports. The ranks of the archery enthusiasts usually include a person who is ready to furnish instruction or take charge of a tournament in this sport. If a group of playground children need transportation to a swimming pool or museum, the best source of volunteers may be the parents of the playground children. Groups regularly attending a playground or center are sometimes called on to help care for game materials or apparatus, assist with registration or program features, or mark off game courts.

When a piece of work needs to be done, the recreation authorities often turn to local organizations which might be expected to have an interest in the project. The American Legion is asked to take charge of the Fourth-of-July celebration, the parent-teacher association to sponsor a back-yard playground contest, or one of the service clubs to help finance an overnight camp. A little-theater group may provide volunteer leadership for a children's drama club, the local garden club for a community garden project, or the women's club for a girls' activity. The resourceful recreation executive can usually find an organization which will assist with a worth-while project which requires volunteer service or support. Later chapters, especially Chaps. XXVII and XXXIV, contain numerous references to successful activities sponsored by or carried on with the help of local organizations.

Enlistment Methods.—Experience has indicated that it is usually necessary to ask people to help. Occasionally people apply on their own initiative or because of the urging of friends, but in most cases they will not volunteer unless they are asked to do so. The most successful means of enlisting volunteers are personal contacts with individuals who have special interests or hobbies and appeals to organizations known to be interested in recreation. Talks to parent-teacher associations, church groups, women's clubs, and colleges are often effective. Newspaper appeals, the use of letters and printed matter, and announcements at community gatherings sometimes lead to the discovery of good volunteers, although the applicants resulting from such methods sometimes lack proper qualifications. Persons participating in recreation institutes are especially good prospects as program volunteers. Student volunteers are sometimes secured through interviews arranged by local university authorities who often give credit for such service to students in recreation courses. Recreation departments also utilize volunteer service bureaus which have been established in large cities, usually by councils of social agencies. The presentation of special needs to groups taking part in the recreation program often results in offers of service.

Motives in Volunteer Service.—In looking for volunteers and in appealing to individuals for help, the recreation executive must keep in mind the motives that impel a person to serve. When individuals offer their services, he must attempt to discover their reason for doing so, because their motives may influence their effectiveness as workers. A desire to be of service in the community doubtless underlies most volunteer service in recreation. In every community there are individuals who consider part of the fun of living to consist of neighborliness, of generous helpfulness, of everyday human kindness. However, this dominant impulse is often combined with a great variety of other more or less selfish motives, which may—or may not— interfere with an individual's usefulness as a volunteer leader.

The student who is considering recreation as a profession realizes the value of practical knowledge and experience and also is interested in the credits received for practice teaching. The prosperous businessman who feels that he owes some return to his community makes it in the recreation field because his personal interests lie there or because of pressure from friends already engaged in volunteer recreation service. The young man or young woman who has benefited by participation in the recreation program is anxious to help others enjoy similar opportunities. Sometimes individuals who desire a position with the recreation department are willing to serve as volunteers in the hope that such service may ultimately lead to employment. The woman with increased leisure because her children have grown up wishes to be identified with some worth-while activity. The nature enthusiast is so passionately interested in birds, plants, and minerals that he is eager to have others learn about the things that have delighted him. Some individuals see in recreation service an opportunity to secure recognition, prestige, and possibly some business advantage; still others have been genuinely fired with a sense of the great human need for recreation and wish to have a part in meeting it. Volunteering for some kind of civic work has even become a tradition in some social circles. Many people who secure great enjoyment from participation in group activity find leadership of a recreation group a satisfying social experience. In fact, with the great increase in leisure, such volunteer service is itself becoming a distinct form of recreation activity.

Service Agreements.—In a few cities it has been found practicable to ask persons volunteering for activity or group leadership to fill out and sign a businesslike contract covering the nature and duration of their service. Among other things the signer agrees to send a substitute if prevented from keeping an appointment for service. The practice of using such contracts is not widespread; usually reliance is put on verbal agreements. The use of a formal agreement tends to discourage the well-intentioned individual who has not considered the obligation involved in undertaking service as a group or activity leader.

Training.—The importance of adequate training for recreation work, pointed out in the preceding chapter, applies also to volunteers, especially those who are serving as group or activity leaders. In selecting helpers the executive naturally seeks to enlist individuals who by training and experience are best qualified to perform the work to be done. Nevertheless, every volunteer leader in municipal recreation requires some training by the department, regardless of the skill and experience which he brings to his work. The amount and type of training depend upon the nature of the task and the extent to which the volunteer is prepared to perform it.

The department obviously cannot train an individual to be an orchestra conductor, a crafts instructor, or a naturalist. On the other hand, a person who has had special training in the field of music, crafts, or nature, needs to become familiar with the aims and ideals of the department, the objectives to be sought in the activity, the general procedure to be followed, and the specific duties he is expected to perform. He needs to know the nature of his relationships with, and his responsibilities to, the members of the group to be served and to the employed workers. Persons who are to serve the department in other ways than through leadership or program projects also need similar instruction. As with the paid workers, training does not consist merely of preliminary preparation for a job. It is a process which is continued throughout the period of service by means of staff meetings, conferences, advice from supervisors, directed reading, and observation of the work of others.

Institutes.—Recreation departments which use volunteers extensively conduct special institutes for them or permit them to share some of the training opportunities arranged for paid workers. In one city, a 10-session course was held for young married women who were eager to help with the summer playground program. An institute in another city was designed to train women as volunteer storytellers at the summer playgrounds. An annual feature of the training program in a third city is an institute designed primarily for men and women leaders of adult groups, covering such topics as social recreation, hobbies, handicraft, progressive game parties, music, and drama. Some volunteer institutes are primarily to train leaders, not for service in the recreation department, but with other agencies or with their own recreation groups. These institutes often prove a fertile ground for recruiting volunteers for the municipal recreation program, but their greatest value lies in the fact that they enable the recreation department to extend its influence far beyond its own facilities and program and they are a means of assisting community groups to expand and enrich their own recreation activities.

College Training for Volunteers.—Many of the most useful volunteers in recreation departments are drawn from the ranks of college students and graduates. Their educational background, usually supplemented by specialized training and participation in forms of recreation activity, has fitted them particularly for service in the recreation field. Recreation authorities, therefore, have a major interest and concern in the training opportunities offered in schools and colleges. The growing importance of recreation in modern life, the desirability of exposing students to various leisure-time activities, and the increasing opportunities for volunteer service which the recreation field affords have caused college authorities to consider the desirability of establishing nonprofessional courses in this field.

Such courses are not intended to develop experts in any particular form of recreation activity but they are built largely around the practice and demonstration of social recreation, music, crafts, nature, drama, and other activities. Discussions of such subjects as the responsibilities and qualifications of volunteers, recreation values, program planning, objectives, and leadership methods are also essential. It is desirable that such courses interpret the significance of leisure, the importance of recreation in modern life, and the relationship of the recreation department to other community agencies. Observation of representative programs and visits to recreation centers enable students to test the knowledge acquired through the classroom work and supplementary reading.[1]

Assignment of Duties.—If volunteers have been recruited with care and have completed satisfactorily a period of training, the recreation executive has a sufficient knowledge of their aptitudes and abilities to enable him to assign them successfully. If he has a clear and definite idea as to the task to be performed before he asks a volunteer to undertake it, he can define the responsibilities involved and make specific arrangements for meeting them. It is important that the volunteer understand the

---

[1] On request, the National Recreation Association has prepared suggested outlines for 30-hour courses for volunteers, one an elementary and the other a more advanced course.

place and time at which the service is to be performed, the duration of the assignment, the nature of the duties to be carried on, the individual to whom he is to report, the type of records to be kept, or the materials to be provided. As a rule it is preferable to limit the task to a definite period such as a month or a season, because volunteers like to have the satisfaction of completing a job they have undertaken. It is usually easier to recruit helpers for a specific period; in case a volunteer is not rendering satisfactory service it is easier to end the arrangement than if there is no definite date for terminating it. This problem does not arise in cases where the service merely involves work on a particular day or at a specific occasion. Assignments must be made with a full realization of the requirements of the work to be done and the abilities of the persons available for service.

Supervision and Evaluation.—Experience has shown that except in rare instances and for specific types of projects volunteer service is not likely to be successful in the recreation department unless there is a competent paid staff which supervises and guides the work of the volunteers. It has been truly said that "the key to the successful development in leisure-time activities through volunteer leadership is to be found in the existence of an adequate number of paid and trained leaders of organizing ability and inspirational power, who provide dynamic power and the sound guidance which is indispensable." If there is one capable paid worker on a playground, he can use to good advantage one or more volunteers. An experienced center director can likewise help volunteer leaders conduct a successful club program. Rarely, however, can such leaders assume full responsibility for directing an indoor or outdoor center. They need to have the suggestions, advice, and inspiration which the paid worker can give and the assurance that he is at hand to help them with difficult problems. The volunteer in a music, craft, or drama activity in the large city can call upon the supervisor of the particular activity for needed assistance and guidance. The executive and his assistants have a definite responsibility to the public to keep in close touch with the work of volunteers in order to assure the proper conduct of the activities and to protect and maintain the standards of the department.

Securing the Best Results.—The following are conditions which experience has shown to be conducive to successful and contented work on the part of volunteers:

1. When they feel there is a genuine need for the work they are asked to do
2. When the assigned tasks are adjusted to their abilities, are definite, and are preferably in writing
3. When their associates are sociable and congenial. (Occasional social events for volunteers are desirable.)

4. When they see the relationship of their task to the objectives and functions of the department

5. When reasonable attention is paid to the proper maintenance of the places in which they are asked to work

6. When they are not kept waiting long for assignments

7. When the department heads do not begrudge the time required to train and supervise them

8. When there is progression in service. Volunteers expect no money reward but they appreciate promotion in responsibility

9. When the paid workers are cooperative and helpful and do not expect them to do the work for which they themselves are paid

10. When opportunity is given them for initiative and creative activity

Appraising the Volunteer.—The success of a volunteer is evaluated by the executive, his supervisors, and the other paid workers who have an opportunity to observe him and his achievements. If he is an activity leader he may be judged primarily by the attitude, attendance, and accomplishments of his group. Other factors to be considered are his relationships with other paid and volunteer leaders, his punctuality, his sense of responsibility for carrying out assignments, and his attitude toward the department and its work. Much can be learned by the executive or supervisor through discussions with the volunteers and self-evaluation of their own work. Recreation departments are anxious to secure renewed offers of service from individuals whose work has been satisfactory, but kind though firm action is taken to discontinue service which does not contribute to the department's effectiveness. In order to have a complete and accurate record of volunteers for future reference the department usually keeps a special file of all who give service. Each individual has a card on which are entered personal data, a record of the work done, and an appraisal of its quality.

CITIZEN GROUPS

As stated early in this chapter, there are many committees, councils, associations, and other citizen groups which are lending effective support to local recreation departments. Such organizations are particularly useful in cities where the department is not administered by a recreation board or other lay group, because they make possible citizen participation in recreation planning. In some instances where the organization was formed to provide needed recreation service in the locality, after a recreation department was established it continued to conduct parts of the program or to supplement the work of the department in an advisory capacity. In other cases committees have been formed to make a study of local recreation problems and needs and to recommend a plan of action. Where severe cuts in the recreation budget have been threatened, groups of citizens have been organized to arouse the public to the need for preventing such action and to present to the appropriating body the importance of maintaining the recreation program. Advisory committees are especially useful in exploring the possibilities of expanding the department's program in some special field such as drama or nature and in guiding the development of activities in these fields. Several examples of the service rendered by such groups are cited in Chaps. XXVII, XXXIII, and XXXIV.

The Recreation Board.—No form of volunteer service has made a more valuable contribution to the recreation movement or is exerting a greater influence upon municipal recreation service than membership upon a recreation board or commission. In selecting persons for such service it is natural for the appointing authorities to turn to civic or community leaders of unusual ability who have demonstrated a sincere interest in recreation and a willingness to work for its advancement. Desirable qualifications for board membership include a genuine desire to serve the city, integrity of purpose, an open mind, an enthusiasm for and belief in the work of the department, keenness of judgment, ability to make some direct contribution to the work, willingness to devote time to it, and a readiness to give loyal support to the department staff and its program. In cities where board members have been selected with care they have rendered inestimable service. Unlike the other citizen groups mentioned in this chapter, this board is charged with the responsibility for administering the recreation department. Its duties, procedures, and relationships will be considered in Chap. XXX.

The Recreation Council.—The recreation council, one of the most useful and common of citizen groups, is usually created at the suggestion and with the help of the recreation authorities, and is composed of influential citizens selected because of their interest in recreation. The functions of a council are primarily to educate the public to the value and need for adequate recreation, arouse interest in specific projects, and serve as a nucleus of organized favorable opinion in times of crisis. It can be an effective medium, especially if the executive is alert to suggest specific ways in which it may serve and projects which it may support. A few of the activities of recreation councils are:

1. Making surveys of the recreation needs and services of the city and recommendations to the recreation department and the public. Surveys may involve a study of areas and facilities, leadership, salaries, budget, public relations, training, or other problems
2. Making addresses on recreation at meetings of civic clubs, women's organizations, and other groups
3. Visiting activities and facilities conducted by the recreation department
4. Sponsoring or conducting community-wide or holiday programs and securing the cooperation of all interested organizations
5. Interesting potential donors of land or money for recreation purposes

6. Raising money for specific projects
7. Cooperating with recreation agencies in initiating recreation projects
8. Supporting recreation budget requests before the city authorities

In addition to the city-wide recreation councils, similar neighborhood groups have been formed at individual playgrounds or indoor centers. They usually represent the people using the playground or center and also neighborhood agencies. Their objective is to further recreation interests in the neighborhood and support the center program.

The Significance of the Voluntary Organization.—Active membership in a body such as a recreation council is one of the most significant forms of volunteer service and one which offers promise of increasing effectiveness in the future. "The voluntary organization," stated George McAneny, president of the Regional Plan Association, Inc., of New York City at its annual meeting in May, 1926, "is a peculiarly American institution. Whatever may be the defects in our political institutions, we have devised in the voluntary organization an instrument which goes far to remedy these defects." He further stated:

Such organizations assure continuity of thought and action impossible in frequently changing political administrations; they attract and put at the disposal of the public a high order of civic and professional talent, often lacking in the public service; provide imagination, foresight, and initiative, which law and tradition at times combine to restrict in public office; and awaken potent resources of public sentiment and support for officials who undertake to do things somewhat ahead of popular understanding.

Citizen Groups in Cleveland.—Cleveland furnishes an excellent example of a city where citizen groups have rendered effective service to the cause of public recreation. In an address entitled, The Role of the Layman in the Recreation Movement,[1] Mayor Harold L. Burton described some of the accomplishments of such groups. Most important is the Mayor's Advisory Board on Playgrounds and Recreation, a group of 28 representative citizens, which after a comprehensive study has been instrumental in bringing about many needed improvements in the city's recreation system and has raised the standard of the recreation personnel and service. Its influence with the city council and other public and private agencies has been demonstrated on numerous occasions. Another group of 13 men, the Cleveland Baseball Federation, devote themselves throughout the year to procuring equipment and medical supplies, arranging schedules and caring for the welfare of boys' and men's baseball teams in the city, and meeting the expense of teams participating in national tournaments. The Municipal Basketball Association, the

[1] *Proceedings of the Twenty-third Recreation Congress*, National Recreation Association, 1938.

County Amateur Boxing Commission, and the Cleveland Tennis Federation are doing similar work in other branches of sport. An attempt is made to secure an advisory committee of competent, interested citizens to serve in every sport. As Mayor Burton says of these committees, "They keep the rackets out of sports."

In addition, around the recreation centers in the seven neighborhood districts, citizens' committees are formed who maintain contacts with neighborhood agencies, help with the centers' activities, investigate complaints, and advise with reference to policies, program, finance, and staff. Park protective committees formed in the schools have proved an effective means of preserving the beauty of the parks and preventing vandalism. The Advisory Committee on Music raises money for band concerts in the parks, and the Zoological Committee assists the city in a similar manner. Experience with these various groups led Mayor Burton to give the following advice to recreation authorities: "I urge you not to hesitate to invite the layman . . . He is anxious to help you, and you have a great opportunity for him."

PART III

AREAS AND FACILITIES

Recreation leaders can serve large numbers of people only if there are suitable areas, properly located, developed, and equipped, where recreation activities and programs can be carried on. Part III treats the importance of city planning for recreation, the types of areas needed for a well-balanced municipal recreation program, and some of the problems to be considered in securing such properties. Areas have only a limited recreation value and usefulness until they are designed and equipped for specific recreation uses. Essential principles and methods of developing different types of recreation properties and of constructing recreation facilities and buildings are discussed briefly in this part.

CHAPTER XI

CITY PLANNING FOR RECREATION

Land, which was "once the cheapest thing in the world," but today in congested centers of population is both scarce and costly, is indispensable to a well-balanced community recreation program. As the Urbanism Committee of the National Resources Committee pointed out, "the most obvious problem in urban recreation arises out of a lack of sufficient space for play and recreation in some cities and, still more, out of the poor distribution and consequent ineffectiveness of existing recreational areas in many more cities."[1] The relation of recreation areas to the city plan, the essential requirements of an adequate system of publicly owned recreation spaces, and the methods of acquiring such areas are subjects of primary importance to the recreation movement.

RECREATION A FACTOR IN CITY PLANNING

Before 1900 little thought was given to the acquisition of public open spaces according to a city-wide plan. Individual parks and play areas were acquired by purchase, gift, or otherwise, because they filled some local or neighborhood need. With the growth of the city planning movement after the turn of the century, cities began to study their park and recreation needs on a city-wide basis and to prepare plans for meeting them. An early example of such plans and also one of the first attempts to set up standards for recreation space was a plan prepared at the organization meeting of the Playground Association of America in 1906 and later adopted by the Board of Education of the District of Columbia. It sought to provide 30 square feet of school playground for each child enrolled, an outdoor playground of not less than 2 acres for each school district, and an athletic field for each of the four sections of the city of Washington.

The subsequent expansion in municipal recreation areas and the increasing demand for the development of varied recreation facilities have been factors in emphasizing the importance of city planning for recreation and in developing suitable standards. As late as 1923 George Ford, the noted city planner, urged recreation authorities at the Recreation Congress to help formulate standards which could be used as a

[1] *Our Cities: Their Role in the National Economy*, National Resources Committee, 1937.

guide by his profession. Today recreation spaces are recognized as a major factor to be considered in the city plan along with zoning, streets, public utilities, and building sites. The general requirements for parks and recreation areas are included as a part of the master plan. Only as it is intelligently integrated with other aspects of the city plan is a scheme for the acquisition of recreation areas likely to prove sound and effective. Important to the recreation movement is the fact that city planning does not concern itself only with physical development but also with the enrichment of life in our cities. According to one city planner its object is "to discover and prepare the road to human happiness. . . . This should lead us in planning to emphasize the fact that the pleasantness in living conditions and the elements concerned with even fuller enjoyment in the various forms of recreation are factors which should be most highly regarded."[1] At the National Recreation Congress in 1934, Jacob L. Crane, Jr., then president of the American City Planning Institute, in an address entitled Planning Our Cities for Abundant Living stated, "Our recreation planning, as a part of city planning for the abundant life, therefore involves . . . an imaginative appraisal of what people want to do, of the circumstances conditioning their choice of leisure-time activities, and of the things they would gladly do if opportunity offered."

Leaders welcome this recognition by city planners of their responsibility in the field of recreation and look to them as effective allies in the attainment of an adequate system of suitable areas. City planning can help bring to realization in our cities the priceless benefits which "land, open space, sunshine, parks, and playgrounds" yield to the people.

City Planning Affects Recreation Planning.—The growth of most American cities has been characterized by a lack of planning but city officials are now exercising a greater degree of guidance and control through zoning, subdivision regulation, and a definite program of public improvements. Future recreation space requirements of cities and neighborhoods can therefore be estimated more accurately than before. In view of the high cost of land and improvements recreation authorities have no excuse for ignoring the city plan when acquiring new areas. Additions to the recreation system should be made in conformance with the recommendations of the local city plan or should be related to them. The effect of zoning on recreation needs is significant because the space requirements of a neighborhood zoned for apartments will differ from those of one restricted to single family dwellings. In considering future needs, land for children's playgrounds will be required in areas zoned for residen-

---

[1] Richard Schermerhorn, "Monotony in Cities," *The Planners Journal*, November-December, 1936, p. 160.

tial development but not in areas zoned for manufacturing. In business districts small landscape parks are more likely to be needed than areas for active recreation use.

Proposed major highways, transportation systems, large-scale housing projects, and other public improvements affect materially the requirements for recreation areas in the vicinity of such contemplated developments. The plans of school authorities for the acquisition of school sites have a vital relation to the need for publicly owned neighborhood recreation areas. Just as recreation authorities must be guided by the city plan, planning authorities, as implied by Mr. Crane, require the advice and experience of recreation workers in determining the recreation needs of the people and the types of areas which enable these needs and desires to be satisfied.

TYPES OF RECREATION AREAS

Because of the widely divergent conditions and resources in different cities and neighborhoods, and because of the varied recreation interests, habits, and desires of people, present-day recreation systems comprise many different types of properties developed for a variety of uses. Experience has demonstrated that several of these types are essential to a well-balanced recreation system; others are less common but make possible valuable recreation services. The functions, size, and location of the more important types of areas will be considered briefly here. Their layout, equipment, and special features will be treated in the next two chapters.

The Play Lot or Block Playground.—Play lots are small areas intended for the use of children of preschool age. They serve as a substitute for the back yard and are rarely provided by the municipality except in large-scale housing projects or in underprivileged neighborhoods where back-yard play opportunities are not available. A space from 1,500 to 5,000 square feet is considered adequate. The play lot is usually located in the interior of a large city block or in or near the center of one or more units of a multiple-family housing development. It should not be necessary for small children to cross a busy street in order to reach a play lot.

The Neighborhood Playground.—This area is primarily intended to provide opportunities for children, especially between the ages of six and fifteen inclusive, to take part in a variety of fundamental and enjoyable play activities. Most playgrounds in addition provide facilities which may be used under certain conditions for the play of young people and adults, and a small section is often set aside for the exclusive use of the preschool group. The playground should be the most numerous of all types of municipal recreation areas. The size varies according to the number of children in the neighborhood to be served, but it is usually between 3 and 7 acres. Seldom is a smaller area satisfactory even in a sparsely settled neighborhood, and if a playground larger than 7 acres is required, more effective service will usually be given by two smaller areas. For most cities a reasonable standard for children's playground space is one acre for each 1,000 of the total population, with an adequate playground in every residential neighborhood.

Since the playground serves primarily children of grammar-school age, it is usually desirable for the children's playground to be located at or adjoining the elementary-school site. It can then be used during and after school hours and facilities in the school building can serve the purposes of a shelter house. In such a location the playground becomes an important part of the neighborhood's center of community activities. In congested neighborhoods, the most effective radius is a quarter mile or less, and under the most favorable conditions there should be a playground within one half mile of every home. The location of playgrounds along heavily trafficked streets or railroads is to be avoided, because children should be able to reach a playground without being exposed to special hazards. Industrial sites, cemeteries, institutions, and other nonresidential properties affect the need for playgrounds in a neighborhood and also the location of the recreation areas.

The Playfield.—This area provides varied forms of recreation activity for young people and adults, although a section is usually developed as a children's playground. From 10 to 20 acres are required for this type of area, and if more space is available it is often used for landscape development. A reasonable standard for playfield space in a city is one acre for each 800 of the total population.

There should be a playfield within a mile of every home and in congested or densely built-up districts one of these areas is needed in every square mile. Because many of the facilities provided by this type are used for junior and senior high-school physical education and sports programs, it is usually desirable that the neighborhood playfield be a part of or adjoin a high-school site. In general, a playfield serves an area comprising four or five neighborhoods in each of which there is a children's playground.

The Large "Recreation" Park.—This area is intended to provide the city dweller with an opportunity to get away from the noise and rush of city traffic and to bring him in contact with nature. It affords an opportunity for the restful contemplation of the out-of-doors and provides a pleasant environment for engaging in recreation activities. With the growing tendency for cities to acquire large, easily accessible areas of the reservation type outside the city limits, a greater percentage of the recreation park is being devoted to active recreation uses.

It is seldom possible to secure the desired park effect in an area of less than 100 acres, and it is not often possible to secure suitable areas of more than 300 acres within the city limits. Each city needs an area of this type, and it has been suggested that large cities provide one for every 40,000 inhabitants. There is an advantage in selecting an area the shape of which is related to the pattern of the city. For example, in a city where the main thoroughfares radiate out from a central axis, it is well, if possible, to acquire a wedge-shaped property with the point toward the center of the city. A park of this shape and location is less likely to interfere with normal traffic flow.

The Reservation.—The reservation is a large tract of land which is kept primarily in its natural state although it is made available for the recreational use of the people for such activities as hiking, camping, picnicking, nature study, and winter sports. Most municipal areas of this type are located either near the boundaries of the city or outside its limits. Many cities do not have this type of area but rely upon Federal, state, or county areas for such services. The reservation is usually 1,000 acres or more in extent.

Special Recreation Areas.—Other areas that primarily serve a particular active recreation use include the municipal golf course, municipal camp, bathing beach, swimming pool, athletic field, and stadium. Sometimes these facilities are established in the types of areas previously discussed, but there is a tendency for cities to acquire properties for these special uses.

The space requirements of these areas vary widely. Forty or fifty acres are needed for a 9-hole golf course and not less than 100 for an 18-hole course. The bathing beach may comprise only a small tract of land along a river, lake, or ocean; on the other hand, it may extend along a mile or more of waterfrontage. A space of one acre may suffice for a small artificial swimming pool, but several acres are needed for a major center, especially since a parking space for automobiles is generally provided on the site. The athletic field or stadium is a special type of center intended primarily for highly organized games and sports. At least 5 acres are required for an athletic field, and 20 acres or more may be needed for a large stadium where extensive parking facilities are essential. A minimum desirable site for a municipal camp is 20 acres; some camps occupy sites of several hundred acres.

Definite standards cannot be set for the location of special recreation areas because, unlike the playgrounds and playfields, they are not provided in each section of a city. The golf course, requiring a large acreage preferably with an uneven topography and some woodland, must be located where suitable land is available at reasonable cost. People will travel farther to play golf than to engage in some other forms of sport.

The location of the bathing beach is determined by the availability of property with suitable natural features. The athletic field or stadium is often established at a high-school site or on a special area that is readily accessible by various forms of transportation. The organized camp, for which a degree of isolation and seclusion is desirable, is almost always located outside the city limits.

The Intown or Neighborhood Park.—Properties of this type are much more numerous than any of the others included in city park systems. This area is primarily a landscape park with trees, shrubbery, and lawn, and is frequently of a more or less formal design. It is intended to provide an attractive neighborhood setting and to afford a place for quiet, informal recreation. It sometimes serves as a restful breathing spot in a business district or congested residential neighborhood or as a setting for a civic center. Because it is seldom used for active or organized recreation, it is not always considered as a recreation area. Several cities have found that by installing game facilities in these intown parks their usefulness has been enhanced with no resulting loss in appearance. The size of these parks varies widely. The small park at a street intersection may be only a fraction of an acre whereas some neighborhood parks, especially in outlying sections of the city, comprise 30 acres or more. It is suggested that there should be at least one of these parks in every square mile of the city. Uneven areas such as ravines or steep wooded slopes not suitable for building purposes often serve admirably as neighborhood parks.

The Parkway.—The parkway is essentially an elongated park with a road running through it, the use of which is restricted to pleasure traffic. As in the case of other park properties, abutting property owners have no rights of light, air, or access. The parkway often affords a connection between the center of a city and one or more outlying park areas, and sometimes several large units of a park system are connected by a circumferential parkway. Stream valleys often lend themselves to this type of development. Two hundred feet is considered the minimum desirable width for a parkway, and it is sometimes sufficiently wide along certain sections to permit the development of a playground, playfield, picnic area, or other special recreation facilities. The parkway is rarely found except in the larger cities, although it holds a place of growing importance in metropolitan, county, and regional park systems.

Other Types.—Among other types of recreation properties are the areas acquired as sites for museums, zoological gardens, botanical gardens, nurseries, bird sanctuaries, community gardens, outlooks, nature trails, and other special purposes. The location and space requirements of these different areas vary widely, and in some cases are not subject to definite standards.

HOW MUCH SPACE FOR RECREATION?

It has been shown that a well-balanced system of recreation areas consists of many types of properties and that their location can best be determined only in relation to the city plan. But the question arises, "How much permanent open recreation space is needed in a city in order to provide the people with adequate outdoor recreation opportunities?" Clearly the needs are affected by density of population, economic status, recreation opportunities in the surrounding region, climatic conditions, and other factors. No standard of publicly owned park and recreation space can be applied uniformly in all cities, but there is value in developing a standard that may serve as a sort of measuring stick.

Attempts have been made to determine the amount of recreation space needed in terms of a certain percentage of the city's total area. In 1902, George A. Parker, Sr., one of the most forward-looking park men of his day, urged that one-twentieth of a city's area should be reserved for parks and squares. More recently the suggestion has repeatedly been made that at least one-tenth of its area should be devoted to parks and other recreation uses. A standard of this type is not satisfactory, however, unless it provides a varying percentage dependent upon the density of population. It is obvious that a larger proportion of the city's total area is needed for recreation in a city with a high density than in one which is sparsely settled.

Present—or estimated future—population is a sounder basis for determining recreation standards. There is a rather general agreement on the part of recreation and city planning authorities that not less than one acre of permanent publicly owned open space is needed for each 100 population, and some cities may find it desirable and practicable to secure considerably more. This ratio applies only to park and recreation areas within or immediately adjoining the city and not to properties at a distance from the city. In most municipalities of less than 10,000 population, more than one acre of recreation area per 100 is needed in order to provide a well-balanced variety of facilities and uses. The National Park Service has suggested that in communities of less than 2,500 population it is desirable that an acre of park be provided for each 40 to 50 people.[1] Another proposed standard which is receiving recognition is that *in addition* to the parks within and adjoining the city limits, there should be for each 1,000 people in a whole region, 10 acres of park lands in such properties as stream valley parks and parkways and large

[1] *Recreational Use of Land in the United States*, prepared by the National Park Service for the Land Planning Committee of the National Resources Board, U. S. Government Printing Office, 1938, p. 103.

scenic recreation and forest parks under municipal, county, state, or other authorities.[1]

Sir Raymond Unwin, a leader in the city planning movement, has pointed out that in Letchworth, England, where communal open spaces and recreation grounds represent an area of 16¾ acres for each 1,000 of the population, this is not considered an overabundance of such areas. In urging the provision of adequate open space, he says, "There are needs for amenity and recreation which call for larger stretches of the open land background than any which have been included so far in our calculations."[2] This opinion confirms the belief based upon the conditions and trends pointed out in Chap. II, that the demand for recreation areas will increase rather than decrease. Present standards of recreation space should therefore be considered as minimum requirements which may well be supplemented by additional acreage in anticipation of future needs.

A Well-balanced Recreation System Essential.—Necessary as ample recreation space is, acreage alone does not assure a well-balanced municipal recreation system. A sufficient number of properties of different types, appropriate size, suitable location, and proper development are needed to serve the recreation needs of all the people. These needs cannot be met satisfactorily if the city's recreation area is in a single large property, even though it affords one acre for each 100 or less of the population. On the other hand, small properties alone do not make possible many popular forms of recreation that can be carried on only in a large area. The best results are attained when there is a proper relationship in number, type, and location between the various areas— children's playgrounds, neighborhood parks, playfields, large recreation parks, and others.

Various suggestions have been offered as to the percentage of a city's recreation area which should be in different types of properties. No rigid formula can be prescribed for use in all cities. Widely differing local conditions as well as changes in the standard of living and in the social and economic structure of our cities affect the requirements of a municipal recreation system. The size and location of landscape parks, for example, are often influenced by the availability of properties of uneven topography or unusual scenic value, which afford opportunities for varied, interesting development. These types naturally do not lend themselves to closely defined standards. On the other hand, because the need for playgrounds and playfields exists in all residential neighborhoods, and because the requirements of these areas can be determined

[1] *Nature's Plan for Parks and Parkways*, Regional Planning Federation of the Philadelphia Tri-State District, 1932.

[2] *The American City*, October, 1935, p. 42.

with some degree of accuracy, it is possible to estimate the space needed for these two types of areas.

A city which has an acre of playground for each 1,000 people and an acre of playfield for each 800, standards suggested earlier in the chapter, and which has one acre of open space for each 100 of its population, will have 10 per cent of this space in playgrounds and 12½ per cent in playfields. In addition to these two types of properties the city will probably have athletic fields, golf courses, bathing beaches, and other areas used for various active forms of physical recreation. It is gradually becoming recognized by planning authorities that approximately half of a city's total park and recreation acreage should be developed for active uses.

To What Extent Have These Standards Been Attained?—The standards that have been suggested for a city's recreation area are not ideal or theoretical objectives, but they are practicably attainable. A study of municipal parks in 1935[1] revealed the fact that 253 cities of varying sizes had acquired more than one acre of park for each 100 population. Most of these cities also have playgrounds on school property. It is true that some of the largest park properties owned by a number of these cities lie outside the city limits, but for the most part they are fairly accessible. An analysis of 268 selected cities varying in population from less than 3,000 to more than 1,000,000 showed that the average park provision in these cities was one acre for each 64 people. Further evidence that American cities have made marked progress toward attaining the standard for total park acreage is contained in a report[2] indicating that 471 Illinois communities in 1938 had an average of 9.6 acres of parks, playgrounds, and school grounds per 1,000 persons. However, only 31.5 per cent of these communities reported possessing the acreage required under "the minimum standard of 10 acres of urban park for every 1,000 inhabitants."

In spite of this advance there is a woeful lack of parks in hundreds of communities. In the 1935 park study, 209 reported they did not own a single park. The situation tends to substantiate the statement of Russell Van Nest Black, past president of the American City Planning Institute, that no part of city building has been treated more casually than that of the provision of places for outdoor recreation.[3]

Deficiency in Playgrounds and Playfields.—Available figures indicate that American cities have been more successful in acquiring park acreage than in developing well-balanced recreation systems.[4] More cities have

---

[1] *Municipal and County Parks in the United States*, 1935, National Park Service.

[2] *Municipal Parks and Playgrounds in Illinois*, Illinois State Planning Commission, 1938.

[3] *Planning for the Small American City*, Public Administration Service, 1933.

[4] Data from *Municipal and County Parks in the United States*, 1935.

acquired neighborhood parks than other types of areas, but often these parks are not located or designed so as to render effective service. Cities are most deficient in the number and acreage of playgrounds and playfields, which together comprise only 5 per cent of the total acreage reported as compared with the suggested standard of 22½ per cent. This deficiency would be reduced if acreage in school properties were included, but as Bassett and Williams have pointed out, "Perhaps the greatest lack in the modern city is the lack of sufficient park space for local playgrounds."[1] Unfortunately the shortage in recreation areas in our cities is most marked in the neighborhoods where the need for them is greatest.

The fact that in 1935 large parks and reservations comprised more than 70 per cent of the total acreage of city park systems indicates that cities have paid more attention to acquiring these large outlying properties than to providing smaller areas which would serve neighborhood needs. Jesse F. Steiner recognized this fact when he wrote, "In our enthusiastic acceptance of rapid and convenient means of travel, we have responded to the lure of distant places and have built up a pattern of recreation in which the values of neighborhood play have been largely forgotten."[2] The high cost of acquiring land in built-up neighborhoods is one of the reasons cities have turned to outlying areas where land was relatively cheap, but it does not justify the failure to acquire properties near the homes of the people.

The great lack of play areas and the maldistribution of existing parks were two of the significant facts disclosed in the Report on Regional Planning in the St. Louis Region, issued by the National Resources Committee in 1936. Only 18 per cent of the 833 elementary schools in the region had sites of 2 acres or more, and only 3 per cent had sites of the standard size of 5 acres. Several sections of the region were found to have no neighborhood parks, and no city had an adequate system of properties of this type. There was only .38 acre of park per 100 persons in the metropolitan district, according to the report, as compared with the suggested standard of 2 acres per 100, one within the city limits and the other in regional park areas. This situation unfortunately does not differ widely from that in some other metropolitan regions.

A number of cities, on the other hand, have a playground within a quarter of a mile of the homes of a majority of their children and within a half mile of practically all of them. Others are taking steps to correct their deficiencies, especially in children's playgrounds. Cities which find it impossible to attain the suggested standards for recreation space should not be deterred from attempting to approach them.

---

[1] Report by E. M. Bassett and F. B. Williams in *Model Laws for Planning Cities, Counties, and States*, Harvard University Press, 1935.

[2] "The New Recreational Era," *The New York Times Magazine*, July 21, 1933.

The current nationwide movement for large-scale public housing, involving as it does the planning of new neighborhoods and the rebuilding of slum areas, offers an exceptional opportunity for the acquisition of adequate neighborhood recreation space. The provision of recreation areas to serve people to be accommodated in housing projects is an important problem in city or neighborhood planning, and according to a report[1] prepared by a group of recreation, city planning, and housing authorities, it demands thoughtful attention by leaders in these fields. Specific suggestions as to the size, type, location, and development of these areas are presented in the report. There is evidence that many public housing authorities realize the need for providing recreation areas in the neighborhoods they are creating but other municipal agencies must share with them the responsibility and cost of providing, improving, and operating these areas.

CITY PARKS AND PLAYGROUNDS VS. SCHOOL AREAS

Earlier in the chapter it was pointed out that in general the best location for the children's playground is at or adjoining the elementary school, and that the playfield may well adjoin the high school. The problem of providing neighborhood areas for active recreation would be largely met if all schools attained the widely accepted minimum standard of 5 acres for elementary-school sites, 10 acres or more for junior high schools, and 20 acres for senior high schools. Still more extensive and elaborate school facilities are envisioned by educational leaders for the near future. For example, Prof. Arthur S. Mochlman, editor of *The Nation's Schools*, prophesies, "Twenty acres will be the minimum for elementary schools and forty acres for secondary buildings."[2] Unfortunately in most cities school properties fall far short even of present-day standards. Prof. George D. Strayer of Teachers College, Columbia University, made the very conservative estimate in 1935 that "at least one-fourth of all the children enrolled in our schools have no adequate play facilities provided for them."

Even though it is agreed that neighborhood recreation areas may be established most advantageously at or near public schools, the question arises whether or not they should be located on school property. In this connection it is well to note a distinction between the legal status of parks and school property. A park is a plot of land, permanently open space, which can be used only for recreation. It cannot be disposed of or used for any other purpose except by court or legislative action. The school ground, on the other hand, is essentially a building site which can be built upon or disposed of at the will of the local school board. Unlike the park

---

[1] *Play Space in New Neighborhoods*, National Recreation Association, 1939.

[2] "Schools of Tomorrow in the United States," *The Architectural Forum*, January, 1935, p. 22.

playground, it can be, and frequently is, restricted to use during school hours, and therefore does not serve as a public play area. If a city is relying upon its school authorities to provide neighborhood play opportunities in the form of playgrounds and playfields, it is essential that proper safeguards be taken to make sure that these will be permanent play areas and will be made available for public recreation use.

Cooperation between City and School Authorities.—Regardless of whether the responsibility for providing neighborhood recreation areas is assigned to the municipal or school authorities, close cooperation between city and schools in the acquisition and development of these areas is highly desirable. Only through such cooperation is it possible to give all neighborhoods equal consideration, to acquire adequate areas where they will render maximum service, to avoid duplication or overlapping of facilities, and to secure a maximum return from the money expended. There are comparatively few cities in which such cooperation exists today. That sufficient importance has not been attached to this relationship is indicated by recent study which has shown that city planning literature is "woefully inadequate" in its concern with school buildings, and that city plan reports give "insufficient attention" to the school program.[1]

The experience of a number of cities with cooperative planning by school and city authorities has demonstrated the possibilities and values of joint action. In Cincinnati, for example, through a pooling of resources and funds, several district athletic fields have been developed adjoining the high schools of the city. Land is owned by the School Board, but the improvements are made by the Recreation Commission which is given a long-term lease on the property for all use except during school hours. The School Board pays the Commission a stated amount each year toward the cost of maintenance and operation. In Detroit several areas have been acquired and developed on a school-playground-park plan. The site of the school building is controlled and maintained by the Department of Recreation, the school has full use of the outdoor recreation facilities, and the recreation department has the use of the indoor facilities after school hours. In other instances the department has acquired land adjacent to school buildings for playgrounds.

In Milwaukee new play areas are purchased by the City Council upon the joint recommendation of the playground engineer of the Department of Public Works and the superintendent of recreation of the Board of Education. These areas are not school properties, although in some instances they are adjacent to school sites. In some cases the school authorities have purchased adjoining land for school buildings. The play areas are developed by the city department according to plans worked out

[1] Russell A. Holy, *The Relationship of City Planning to School Plant Planning*, Teachers College, Columbia University, 1935.

in cooperation with the school authorities, and in some cases the old schoolyards and the new playgrounds have been designed and improved as a single unit. A policy of coordination approved by the School Department and the Playground and Recreation Department in Los Angeles, including a plan for cooperation in the acquisition of new play areas, is outlined in Chap. XXXIV.

In such cooperative action, especially if carried out in conformity with an effective city plan, lies the hope that cities may be able to acquire adequate neighborhood recreation areas.

METHODS OF ACQUIRING LAND FOR RECREATION

Consideration of the various ways by which land can be acquired for recreation use is appropriate in a discussion of city planning for recreation and is essential in the formulation of a plan of action. Most public recreation areas are obtained through purchase, gift, or transfer, and in most cities several methods of acquisition have been used. A city requiring additional land for recreation will do well to consider carefully the possibilities of using the various methods described briefly in the following paragraphs.

Purchase.—The most common method of acquiring areas is by direct purchase after negotiation between the owner and the governmental agency desiring the property. In case satisfactory terms of purchase cannot be arranged, condemnation proceedings may be resorted to, but they are avoided wherever possible as they are likely to be long, tedious, and expensive. In rare instances recreation areas have been acquired through excess purchase, but the constitutionality of this method is generally open to question. A special assessment plan, under which benefited property owners meet at least part of the cost, has been used extensively for the purchase of playgrounds and neighborhood parks in several cities, and for the acquisition of parkways. Under city planning legislation in certain states, a city may reserve for purchase within a stipulated period areas which are designated for recreation on subdivision plots submitted for approval. In rare instances areas have been purchased with the understanding that they would be paid for from revenues secured from their use.

Gifts.—Gifts of land for recreation purposes have played a large part in the development of many municipal park and recreation systems. A study of donated parks and playgrounds, made in 1928, revealed a total of 3,158 such areas in nearly 1,000 communities.[1] The estimated value of these properties was in excess of 100 million dollars, and their combined

[1] *Donated Parks and Play Areas in the United States*, National Recreation Association, 1929.

area equaled nearly one-third of the total municipal park acreage in the country. Many gifts of land and of money for the purchase of recreation areas have been reported since 1928. Land is usually given in fee simple and deeded directly to the municipality, or it is given in trust for recreation use, sometimes with the provision that if not used for recreation it shall revert to the donor or his heirs. Experience has shown that whereas gifts of land should be encouraged by city authorities it is wise to accept only areas which are suitable in location, size, and topography, adaptable for recreation, and free from narrow use restrictions.

Dedication.—Frequently a subdivider laying out a tract of land for residential use sets aside one or more areas and dedicates them in perpetuity for recreation use. He may continue to hold title to these areas, deed them to an organization of property owners, or give them outright to the city. The extent of this practice is indicated by the fact that in 1930 recreation areas dedicated and recorded in 278 real estate subdivisions totaled more than 8,000 acres, or an average of 7 per cent of the entire acreage of the subdivisions.[1] The practical value of dedicating land for recreation has made the practice common. As the Committee on Subdivision Layout of President Hoover's Conference on Home Building and Home Ownership pointed out, "No subdivision operation is complete until the subdivider has provided, or arranged for, adequate parks and play areas within or accessible to, the lots which he is selling." Realizing that land might be dedicated for recreation which was not suitable for that purpose, the Committee continued, "These areas, as with the subdivision itself, should be designed to fit into the whole recreation plan and program of the city and the neighborhood." Otherwise the city is unwise to accept title to such areas.

Transfer.—Many properties which were originally acquired by a governmental agency for some purpose other than recreation have become no longer needed for the original purpose and have been transferred to the city park or recreation agency. State and county lands have been turned over to cities for recreation purposes, but much more numerous are the cases where land under the jurisdiction of some other city department has been transferred to a park or recreation commission. Abandoned city reservoirs, old sewage-disposal areas, institution sites, cemeteries, commons, and waterfront properties have been added to city park systems. The opportunity which the development of these areas offered in using unemployed labor as well as for adding to the city's recreation resources prompted many such transfers during the depression. Reclamation has been the means of transforming marshes, swamps, and dilapidated waterfronts from unsightly, unhealthful areas into attractive recreation properties serving a useful purpose. Numerous tax-delinquent properties

[1] *Recreation Areas in Real Estate Subdivisions*, National Recreation Association, 1930.

have also been turned over to city recreation authorities to be developed for recreation use or to be exchanged for other more suitable areas.

THE VALUE OF PLANNING

American cities have been wasteful of their natural resources. Waterfronts are lined with ramshackle structures, streams are polluted, woodlands are destroyed, ravines are used for dumping grounds, and roadsides are disfigured. Frequently the most beautiful sections of our cities and the sites which offer the greatest opportunity for civic development are turned over to uses which not only fail to take advantage of, but actually destroy, their beauty. Fortunately cities have taken steps to correct their mistakes. Outstanding examples of such action are the recapture and rehabilitation of the lake fronts in Chicago and Milwaukee, and the remarkable progress which New York City has made toward restoring to the use of the people many of the natural advantages which its waterfrontage offers for various forms of recreation. Studies of the effect of recreation areas upon the value of property in the neighborhood have shown that properly located and well-designed recreation areas have so raised property values in the vicinity as to more than offset their original cost. The value of parks as investments has been repeatedly demonstrated, and many a realtor has learned the dollars-and-cents value of neighborhood play areas.

Small Communities Also Need Planning.—The advantages of planning are not restricted to the larger cities. Suburban communities, towns, and even rural areas often are more drab and lacking in opportunities for joyous, satisfying living than the cities. In an address before the National Appraisers Forum, John E. Burton, director of research of the New York State Mortgage Commission, pointed out how unsupervised suburban developments degenerate into a dreary shanty town and concluded, "All this might have been prevented by proper supervision providing recreation centers, playgrounds, swimming pools, the foci of community life."[1] One of the urgent problems today in improving living conditions in the small communities is to make the people aware of the profound values of recreation facilities in civic life. For as Prof. Phillips Bradley of Amherst College has said of them, "Here is one utility at least which the more intensively used becomes the more indispensable—and socially profitable."[2]

Only an awakened and insistent public opinion can demand that governmental agencies take immediate steps to secure adequate and suitable areas to care for present and future recreation needs, in our towns and villages as well as in the large population centers.

[1] *New York Herald Tribune*, November 28, 1937.
[2] "The Place of Planning in Local Government," *The Planners Journal*, September, October, 1937.

CHAPTER XII

THE DESIGN AND EQUIPMENT OF RECREATION AREAS

The usefulness of a city's recreation areas depends not alone upon their size and location but upon the way in which they are designed, developed, equipped, maintained, and operated for recreation use. Most of the activities that comprise the municipal recreation program are possible only when areas, buildings, facilities, and equipment are provided. The extent to which a city's recreation system furnishes such features determines largely the nature and scope of its recreation service.

Recreation leaders must utilize fully the possibilities offered by the areas under their control and must recognize the potentialities for recreation of other properties which might be acquired by the city. In the hands of competent recreation authorities a vacant lot, a city dump, or an abandoned farm may be transformed into a children's playground, an athletic field, or a golf course, respectively. A capable recreation leader with imagination and ingenuity can accomplish much with limited space and facilities, whereas the finest equipment will not assure a successful program under poor leadership. On the other hand, sustained interest in such games as tennis, handball, or bowling depends primarily upon conveniently located, properly constructed, and well-maintained courts. Many playgrounds fail to attract twelve- to fifteen-year-old boys because they are too small to provide a baseball or even a softball diamond; others offer only a physical program because they do not have suitable indoor or outdoor facilities for dramatics, arts and crafts, and other activities. Water sports, winter sports, camping, golf, and picnicking are possible for large numbers of people only as necessary facilities are provided through public funds. During much of the year recreation opportunities are very limited unless buildings are made available for indoor activities.

TYPES OF OUTDOOR RECREATION FACILITIES

Facilities for outdoor recreation include a great variety of features which serve men and women, youth and children. Some are used the year round; others during a single season. Many afford opportunities for highly organized, competitive sports; others provide recreation for individuals or family groups. They differ widely in the activities they make possible, in their construction and operation cost, space requirements, location, in the number of persons served, and in the amount of leadership or supervision required. These factors are important in evaluating the service that they render. The following list is not all-inclusive but in it appear most of the important and commonly provided outdoor facilities:[1]

GAME COURTS AND FIELDS

Badminton courts	Horseshoe courts
Baseball diamonds	Ice hockey rinks
Basketball courts	Paddle tennis courts
Boccie courts	Polo fields
Bowling greens	Quoits courts
Clock golf courts	Roque courts
Cricket fields	Shuffleboard courts
Croquet courts	Soccer fields
Curling rinks	Softball diamonds
Football fields	Tennis courts
Handball courts	Tether tennis
Hockey fields	Volley ball courts

SPORTS FACILITIES

Archery ranges	Roller skating tracks
Batting cages	Running tracks
Casting pools	Ski jumps
Ice skating tracks	Sled slides
Jumping pits	Toboggan slides
Pistol ranges	Trap shooting ranges
Rifle ranges	Vaulting pits

STRUCTURES

Bandstands and shells	Pavilions
Bleachers	Recreation piers
Boat docks	Shelters, open
Council rings	Shower baths
Dance pavilions	Stadiums
Diving pools	Stages
Fishing piers	Swimming pools
Grandstands	Wading pools
Outdoor theaters	

EQUIPMENT

Backstops for baseball and softball	Motion-picture screens, portable
Barbeque pits	Picnic facilities—benches, tables, ovens
Benches	Playground apparatus
Block building platforms	Playground showers
Drinking fountains	Playhouses, portable
Fireplaces	Sand courts and boxes
Flagpoles	Tables for games and crafts
Floodlights	

[1] For a list of recreation building types and of indoor facilities see Chap. XIII.

Arboretums	Hiking trails
Athletic fields	Ice skating areas
Bathing beaches	Model yacht ponds
Bicycle tracks	Motorboat basins
Boating areas	Nature trails
Bridle paths	Parking fields
Camps	Picnic areas
Coasting hills	Playgrounds for children
Concert areas	Putting greens
Farm plots	Skiing areas
Gardens	Tourist camps
Golf courses	Yacht harbors

PRINCIPLES IN PLANNING RECREATION AREAS

Each recreation area presents a distinct problem in landscape design, requiring individual analysis and treatment. The effectiveness and appearance of the area depend in large measure upon the understanding, skill, and imagination of the planner. Naturally the problem of design varies with the type of area being planned. In designing a landscape park, for example, full advantage is taken of the peculiar characteristics of the site such as uneven topography, existing trees, streams, and other natural features that contribute to the beauty of the park. In the case of an athletic field, however, the plan is evolved around certain essential sports facilities such as the football or baseball field and running track which are highly standardized in their space requirements and development. Interest and variety are desirable in the design of active recreation areas, but the facilities, space requirements, arrangement, and use of the recreation features demand primary consideration.

Planning Objectives.—Regardless of the type of recreation area, there are certain factors to be considered and objectives to be sought in planning it. Among them are the following:

1. *Effective Use of the Entire Area.*—Since public recreation areas are seldom larger than necessary, every part of the property should have a definite function and contribute to either its utility or its beauty, or both. The maximum possibilities for the multiple use of areas should be realized, where desirable.

2. *Location and Arrangement of the Areas and Facilities.*—Major or primary features are planned first; minor or incidental features receive secondary consideration.

3. *Adequate Space for the Facilities.*—To assure safety and satisfactory play, equipment, game courts, playing fields, and other features must be allowed ample space. In areas used for picnicking and camping, considerable space is desirable for privacy.

4. *Ease of Supervision or Operation.*—Some features require constant supervision; others, little. This fact is important in designing an area.

5. *Accessibility and Relationship of Various Features.*—Sections serving small children are located near the entrance or on the side nearest the children's homes.

6. *Utilization of Natural Features.*—A natural slope may be used to advantage for an outdoor theater or for winter sports, a grove of trees for a picnic area or music grove, and a large level open area for an athletic field.

7. *Safety.*—On the playground this may be secured by careful arrangement of apparatus and game courts; on the large park or reservation by a proper location of roads and paths in relation to major features.

8. *Economy in Construction.*—Through careful planning expensive operations like grading and drainage may be reduced to a minimum, multiple use of facilities may be secured, and plumbing, surfacing, and other costs may be kept low.

9. *Economy in Maintenance.*—Maintenance costs often bear a direct relation to construction costs; a small addition to the latter through the use of better materials may result in a considerable saving in maintenance. Careful planning simplifies such duties as grass cutting, hedge trimming, cleaning of pools and buildings, and the care of game courts. Features requiring much maintenance such as a bowling green should not be constructed unless adequate means of maintenance are assured.

10. *Convenience of People Using Area.*—Frequently an otherwise satisfactory area fails to provide adequately for the comfort and the convenience of the people using it. Toilet facilities, drinking fountains, seating accommodations, and parking space are essential service features. In the case of some areas transportation facilities are needed.

11. *Appearance.*—Every recreation area should present a pleasing appearance from within and without, even though little space can be made available for plantings. This is achieved through proper architectural and landscape design.

Achieving These Objectives.—The attainment of these objectives is achieved by a variety of methods and their importance varies with different types of properties. The problem of determining the most essential areas and facilities is comparatively simple in the case of the small children's playground, but complex when a plan for a large park is under consideration. Accessibility is less important in selecting the site for a golf clubhouse than it is in locating a shelter house to serve children on a neighborhood playfield. Other factors that influence design are the size and shape of the area, its topography, the type of neighborhood, needs to be served, special recreation interests of the people, funds available for development and maintenance, and probable amount and type of leadership. The effective solution of a particular problem demands, on the part of the designer, an understanding of the recreation needs and interests to be met by the area, a knowledge of the facilities which can meet these needs, their requirements as to space, location, and construction, and the ability to impose these features upon the area in such a way as to produce an effective and attractive plan.

ESSENTIAL FACTORS IN DEVELOPING RECREATION AREAS

Certain procedures and operations are involved in the proper development of every recreation area. Sometimes they are neglected, but they contribute directly to the usefulness of the area and therefore merit careful attention. A few of them are described briefly in the following paragraphs.

Survey and Plan.—It is unwise to start work on an area until a general plan has been prepared and approved by the proper authorities. Best results are likely to be attained if it is prepared by a competent landscape architect experienced in the design of recreation areas, in collaboration with the recreation executive. Frequently the authorities who are to be responsible for developing and operating the area secure the services of a recreation planner as consultant. The general plan indicates the location of the various features and affords a basis for orderly development in case the work cannot be completed at one time. Before preparing the plan, the designer needs to know the boundaries of the area, its topography, the location and size of trees and other natural features and of the sewers and water mains serving it, and the soil, water, and drainage conditions upon it.

Grading and Drainage.—Uneven properties may serve admirably for golf courses and camp sites, but comparatively level areas are needed for playgrounds, playfields, and athletic fields. It is frequently necessary to grade parts of a play area to provide level spaces for such games as tennis, handball, baseball, and football, but because grading is expensive it is avoided wherever possible. On large properties grading is usually limited to sections developed for roads, parking areas, building sites, and other special features.

The purpose of drainage is to remove excess surface and ground water which would otherwise interfere with the recreational use of an area. The former is usually carried off by inlets and catch basins which are connected with a storm sewer or near-by stream. Ground water, on the other hand, is collected and removed by tile drains laid under the surface of the area. The use of underground drainage systems is most common in the construction of athletic fields and special game areas such as tennis courts and bowling greens.

Surfacing.—Different forms of recreation activity require different kinds of surfaces and a great variety of surfacing materials is used in the development of a recreation system. Turf is the best surface for small children's play areas, for the golf course, the bowling green, and the croquet court, and for such games as football and baseball. On the other hand, courts requiring an accurate bounce and subjected to considerable use, such as handball and tennis, usually have a surface of asphalt, clay, or cement, although inexpensive native materials sometimes prove satisfactory. In large parks and reservations only such features as paths, roads, and areas of intensive use receive special surface treatment. Authorities have experimented widely with various surfacing materials for intensively used play areas, but the ideal surface has not yet been discovered. Excellent results have been secured from the use of cork asphalt on the children's playground, but the expense of this material makes its general use prohibitive. Valuable information on surfacing methods and materials has been compiled by a committee appointed by the National Recreation Association.[1]

Lighting.—Cities are extending the usefulness of recreation areas and facilities by lighting them for evening use. A study conducted by the National Recreation Association[2] revealed that of 112 recreation agencies reporting lighted facilities in 1937, 40 had none prior to 1934. Among the lighted facilities reported were 472 horseshoe courts, 422 tennis courts, 313 ice skating areas, 310 playgrounds, and 269 softball diamonds. The most widely lighted areas, however, were softball diamonds reported by 76 agencies, tennis courts and swimming pools by 59, horseshoe courts by 55, and football fields by 51. Bathing beaches, winter sports facilities, and various game courts are lighted in many cities. Baseball is played at night but with less success than the other sports. Lighting is a highly technical problem, the solution of which requires the advice of competent illumination engineers.

Paths and Roads.—On the smaller, intensively used properties the chief function of paths is to assist people in reaching directly and easily the various facilities and special features, and also to prevent interference with the play activities. In the larger outlying areas they may contribute directly to such forms of recreation as walking and hiking; they may lead to or through areas of special beauty or scenic interest, or may afford access to centers of activity. With the exception of service drives, roads have no place in the smaller recreation areas. In the larger properties, however, roads are often needed to make the various sections accessible. Roads and parking spaces for automobiles must be provided in connection with athletic fields, swimming pools, picnic centers, camps, and other features which attract or serve large numbers of people.

Fencing.—It is almost universally agreed that the playground should be fenced for safety and effective operation. The athletic field and stadium site are almost always enclosed in order to facilitate control and the collection of admission fees. A fence is essential around the outdoor swimming pool in order to restrict access to the pool to bathers alone. Tennis requires a fence for satisfactory play, and low fences are often erected on the playground around special features such as the wading pool and game courts, to protect plantings or to serve as a division between sections of the area. There are few recreation areas where some form of fencing is not necessary or desirable.

Water.—Water contributes to both the appearance and usefulness of recreation areas. It often enhances the beauty of the landscape, can be

---

[1] *Surfacing Playground Areas*, 1932, and *Supplement*, 1937.
[2] See "Lighting of Outdoor Recreation Facilities," *Recreation*, February, 1938, p. 665.

stocked for fishing, affords a habitat for water fowl, and makes possible bathing, boating, and other aquatic sports. In addition to water surfaces it serves many essential functions. Drinking fountains, sprinkling systems for use on the running track, athletic field, and planted areas, service rooms in field houses and other structures, swimming and wading pools, all require a large quantity of pure water.

Beauty.—Beauty, whether derived from existing natural features or resulting from human planning, has always been considered an essential and natural feature of the neighborhood park, the large park, and the reservation. It has often been sadly neglected, however, on such areas as the playground and athletic field. No matter how small an area may be or how intensively used, it is possible to provide pleasing landscape effects and at the same time secure the maximum use for play. This is achieved primarily through the wise selection, location, and maintenance of plant materials likely to thrive in the location, climate, soil, and conditions to which they are subjected. Often the boundary fence is set back a few feet and the area outside the fence is used for plantings. Large, uneven properties afford greater possibilities for more interesting and varied developments. Plant materials are not the only features to contribute beauty, attractiveness, and interest to a play area. Every building, structure, or piece of equipment can be so designed, constructed, and maintained as to add to the appearance of the property of which it is a part.

EQUIPMENT AND GAME FACILITIES

Before considering the design and equipment of the various types of recreation areas, it may be well to point out some of the features which are commonly found on these areas, especially on the playground and playfield. They include playground apparatus, facilities for games and sports, seating facilities, the wading pool, and other types of equipment.

Playground Apparatus.—Apparatus has an important place on the playground and is also used at the playfield, the bathing beach, and the picnic center. Children enjoy using it. It contributes to physical development, cares for many children, and provides a much needed opportunity for such age-old activities as climbing, swinging, balancing, and hanging by hands and feet. Less space is devoted to apparatus on the playground today than a generation ago, and only those types that have proved their value are favored by most authorities.

In 1929 a committee of recreation executives issued a report on apparatus standards in which a minimum list of apparatus was recommended.[1] This list was subsequently revised by the committee as follows:

[1] *Standards in Playground Apparatus*, National Recreation Association, 1929.

For preschool age children (under 6 years):
Chair swings (set of 6)
Sandbox
Small slide
Simple, low climbing device
For children of elementary-school age (6–12 years and older):
Swings—frame 12 ft. high (set of 6)
Slide—8 ft. high (approx. 16 ft. long)
Horizontal ladder
Giant stride
Horizontal bar
Balance beam
Optional, if available funds, space, and attendance justify:
Seesaws (set of 3–4)
Traveling rings
Low climbing device

Communities equipping playgrounds may well be guided by these suggestions. The use of three types included in the list—the giant stride, rings, and seesaws—is not favored by some executives. Experience has shown that it is wise to install only apparatus which is of moderate height and is well built of suitable materials to withstand the strenuous use to which it is subjected. Here again valuable advice may be secured from a report of a committee which made a study of the construction of playground apparatus.[1]

The Wading Pool.—The wading pool is perhaps the most popular feature of the playground during the summer months, and facilities for wading are often provided in the large park, the reservation, and the swimming center, as well. In the city it is seldom possible to use a stream for wading because of pollution of the water; most pools are therefore built of cement and are filled from the city water system. When not used for wading, pools may serve as basins for sailing model boats. Some are also used when empty for a variety of games and for roller skating and in the winter for ice skating rinks.

Wading pools vary in size, shape, and depth, depending upon the location and the requirements of the area. In planning and constructing a pool, special attention is given to drainage, water supply, outlet controls, and to the surrounding area. As a rule, the maximum depth does not exceed 15 inches, and the deep area is at or near the center. On some playgrounds, pools are constructed with a depth of water of 24 or even 36 inches, but such pools are for all practical purposes children's swimming pools. They are not recommended unless enclosed by a fence and unless the same measures are taken to assure safety and sanitation as at a swimming pool.

[1] *Standards in the Construction of Playground Apparatus*, National Recreation Association, 1933.

Areas and Facilities for Games and Sports.—Fields and facilities for games and sports are provided in practically all recreation areas with the exception of small landscape parks. They occupy a large percentage of most playfields, athletic fields, and playgrounds. Their importance is due to the strong appeal which games and sports make to people of all ages and of both sexes. They include facilities for horseshoes, lawn bowling, croquet, and shuffleboard which are enjoyed by old as well as young, handball and football in which young men find a keen interest, field hockey and field ball which are primarily for young women and girls, and tennis, softball, and volley ball which are played by men and women, boys and girls. Because these activities have such an important place in the program, recreation workers need to have a knowledge of the facilities and areas which are essential for conducting them.

The requirements of these games and sports in the way of space, surfacing, and equipment vary widely. Mention has already been made of the different types of surfacing needed for different games. Only as a suitable surface for play is provided can people thoroughly enjoy most games or attain a high degree of skill in them. Orientation is also important, because unless courts or fields are properly laid out, the sun is likely to interfere with some of the players. Since most of the play is lengthwise of the court in such games as tennis, volley ball, archery, and horseshoes, these courts are laid with the long axis in a general north and south direction. Since football is usually played in the fall, it is best for the field to lie northwest and southeast. There is no ideal orientation for baseball, but many favor placing the home plate in the southwest or northwest corner.

Permanent equipment is essential for most games. It generally consists of items (1) essential to the game itself, such as tennis nets and posts, goal posts for soccer and football, horseshoe stakes, handball walls and basketball goals, and (2) incidental but necessary to playing the game in a satisfactory manner, such as baseball backstops and tennis court enclosures. The proper development of a recreation field requires a knowledge of the essential materials, dimensions, location, and installation of this equipment.

Limited space in most public recreation areas generally necessitates use of the same area for different games at different seasons of the year, or even during the same season. Baseball and football fields often overlap; space used for field hockey is also used for softball, and the same court serves for both paddle tennis and volley ball. To get the maximum service from an area removable standards or goals are used whenever possible and permanent features are erected so as not to interfere with areas required for play.

SPACE REQUIREMENTS FOR GAME COURTS AND SPORTS FIELDS

Name	Dimensions of play areas, feet	Use dimensions, feet	Space required, square feet	Number of players
Badminton	17 × 44 (single)	25 × 60	1,500	2
	20 × 44 (double)	30 × 60	1,800	4
Baseball	90 ft. diamond	300 × 300 (min.)	90,000	18
		350 × 350 (av.)	122,500	
Basketball (men)	35 × 60 (min.)	60 × 100 (av.)	6,000	10
	50 × 94 (max.)			
Basketball (women)	45 × 90	55 × 100	5,500	12-18
Boccie	18 × 62	30 × 80	2,400	2- 4
Bowling green*	14 × 110 (1 alley)	120 × 120	14,400	32-64
Box hockey	4 × 10	16 × 20	320	2
Clock golf	Circle 20-24 ft. in diam.	30 ft. circle	706	Any number (4-8)
Cricket	Wickets 66 ft. apart	420 × 420	176,400	22
Croquet	30 × 60	30 × 60	1,800	Any number (4-8)
Deck tennis	12 × 40 (single)	20 × 50	1,000	2
	18 × 40 (double)	26 × 50	1,300	4
Field ball	180 × 300	210 × 340	71,400	22
Field hockey	150 × 270 (min.)	200 × 350 (av.)	70,000	22
	180 × 300 (max.)			
Football	160 × 360	180 × 420	75,600	22
Golf croquet	Variable	....	....	Any number
Handball	20 × 34	30 × 50	1,500	2 or 4
Hand tennis	16 × 40	25 × 60	1,500	2 or 4
Horseshoes (men)	Stakes 40 ft. apart	12 × 50	600	2 or 4
Horseshoes (women)	Stakes 30 ft. apart	12 × 40	480	2 or 4
Lacrosse	210 × 450 (min.)	260 × 500 (av.)	130,000	24
Paddle tennis	16 × 44 (single)	30 × 70	2,100	2
	20 × 44 (double)	35 × 70	2,450	4
Polo.	600 × 960 (max.)	600 × 960	576,000	8
Quoits	Stakes 54 ft. apart	25 × 80	2,000	2 or 4
Roque	30 × 60	30 × 60	1,800	4
Shuffleboard	6 × 52	10 × 64	640	2 or 4
Soccer (men)	150 × 300 (min.)	240 × 360 (av.)	86,400	22
	300 × 390 (max.)			
Soccer (women)	120 × 240 (min.)	200 × 320 (av.)	64,000	22
	180 × 300 (max.)			
Softball	60 ft. diamond	250 × 250 (min.)	62,500	20
	45 ft. diamond	200 × 200	40,000	
Speedball (men)	160 × 240 (min.)	180 × 300	54,000	22
	160 × 360 (max.)	180 × 420	75,600	
Speedball (women)	180 × 300	200 × 340	68,000	22
Table tennis	5 × 9	12 × 20	240	2 or 4
Tennis	27 × 78 (single)			
	36 × 78 (double	60 × 120	7,200	2 or 4
Tether tennis	Circle 6 ft. in diam.	20 × 20	400	2
Touch football	160 × 300	175 × 330	57,750	22
Volley ball	30 × 60	50 × 80	4,000	12-16

* Most bowling greens in public recreation areas are 120 by 120 ft., which provide 8 alleys. The amount of space required for a single alley would be 20 by 120 ft.

Space Requirements.—Official dimensions have been adopted for many game areas, but in the case of others, courts or fields of varying dimensions may be used. Games like shuffleboard and roque require very little space outside the actual game courts, whereas others such as tennis and baseball necessitate the setting aside of considerable space outside the boundaries of the court or field. The table shown on p. 165, taken from *The New Play Areas—Their Design and Equipment*,[1] indicates for most of the common games the court dimensions, the approximate space needed for the activity, and the number of players served. If designed primarily for children's use, courts or fields are made smaller in the case of such games as basketball, baseball, horseshoes, and soccer.

Facilities for Track and Field Events.—The running track, jumping pits, and other facilities for field events are essential features of the athletic field and are also found at many playfields and large parks. Playgrounds are rarely equipped with a running track, although they often have a straightaway for use in the dashes and a jumping pit. A quarter-mile track with an end radius between 100 and 125 feet is recommended for general use. Opinions differ as to the best materials to use in track construction, but a top dressing of screened cinders and clay or loam, thoroughly mixed, has given highly satisfactory results. Field events—running broad and high jumps, pole vault, hammer throw, shot put, javelin throw—are usually carried on within the track. Runways, pits, and areas for these events are arranged so as to minimize the danger of injury to participants, enable spectators to see them, and interfere as little as possible with the use of the field for other sports.

Seating Facilities.—Seating facilities, which contribute greatly to the comfort and convenience of people using recreation areas, vary in size and type from benches placed alongside the tennis court or wading pool to the stadium seating thousands of people. On the playground benches are provided for mothers in the small children's section, near the game courts, and at the other suitable locations. Occasionally, temporary bleachers are erected when a circus, playday, or other special event is to be held. On the playfield and large park benches are needed, especially near the game courts used by adults. In addition, bleachers, preferably of the knockdown or movable type, are erected for the convenience of spectators at ball games and other special events. Seating facilities are also desirable at outdoor areas where concerts, motion pictures, or dramatic productions are presented.

At the athletic field or stadium the seating of spectators is a major consideration, and permanent structures are usually erected for this purpose. Toilet, shower, locker, and storage rooms are often provided

[1] *The New Play Areas, Their Design and Equipment*, A. S. Barnes & Company, 1938.

under such structures. Other things being equal, the main seating facilities should be on the west side of the field so that afternoon sun will not shine in the spectators' eyes. In the neighborhood parks and at points of scenic interest in the large park or reservation, benches are frequently provided for the comfort of people who come to enjoy the beauty of the area.

Other Equipment.—Tables and benches are needed in connection with craft activities, for quiet games enjoyed by children and adults, and also for use at picnic centers. Other valuable playground features are a platform for folk dancing and block building, a bicycle rack, bulletin boards, and a shower spray. A fireplace and council ring on the playground or playfield serve playground, family, or scouting groups. Drinking fountains, receptacles for waste materials, boxes for storing supplies and equipment, a flagpole, and an American flag are important features. Other types of equipment will be mentioned in late sections.

THE DESIGN AND EQUIPMENT OF SPECIFIC TYPES OF AREAS

A few of the significant characteristics of the design, equipment, and general development of the chief types of recreation areas are described briefly in the following pages. Much excellent literature on the planning of recreation areas is available for those who desire to make a more thorough study of the subject.

The Play Lot.—This type of property is seldom provided by municipal agencies, but a section of the neighborhood playground is sometimes set aside for the use of preschool children. Their safety requires that it be entirely surrounded with a low fence or hedge. Desirable features are a row of shade trees around the borders and a central grass plot; play equipment placed under the trees, and possibly a wide concrete walk separating the apparatus area from the grass plot, to be used for kiddie cars and velocipedes. The equipment includes such items as sandboxes, block-building platform, blocks and sand tools, playhouses, low drinking fountain, small shallow wading pool, a few pieces of playground apparatus, benches and tables for mothers or nurses, an open shelter for baby carriages and for use in case of sudden showers, a flagpole, and a birdbath.

The Neighborhood Playground.—In order to care for the varying needs and interests of children of different ages, sections of the playground are developed for specific uses. No standardized pattern of playground design is desirable or practicable, but the definite divisions suggested here provide for the essential playground activities and services. Sometimes it is necessary to combine or eliminate one or more of the divisions. These are so planned and located as to facilitate circulation, simplify supervision, and enable the activities to be engaged in with a maximum of enjoyment. The following divisions are suggested:

1. *Small Area for the Exclusive Use of Children of Preschool Age.*—In crowded neighborhoods this section is essential; in high-class residential areas it may not be needed. Its layout and equipment correspond to those previously suggested for the play lot. Proximity to the entrance and to the shelter house are desirable factors in determining the location of this section which should be enclosed by a low fence or hedge.

2. *Apparatus Area for Older Children* (primarily for six- to eleven-year-olds).—As a rule it is preferable to have the apparatus for this age group concentrated in one section rather than scattered over the playground. One set usually serves the needs of both boys and girls. The location of the various apparatus units and the provision of ample safety zones require special care. This section is often near the shelter house and wading pool where it is under fairly continuous observation by the playground workers.

3. *Area for Free Play and Low Organized Games.*—Children six to eleven years of age require an open space for a great variety of running, circle, and low organized games, and for free play. The section set aside for these activities is frequently near the apparatus area which is used by children of the same age.

4. *Area for Older Boys.*—This section is developed largely for team games and individual sports. Other common features are a jumping pit, straightaway track, and one or more types of gymnastic apparatus. It requires a large level area and can be farther from the entrance and center of control than the features previously listed. Access to this section and to the toilets from it should not necessitate crossing the girls' area. If the playground is open to young men and adults, this is the section most likely to be used by them.

5. *Area for Older Girls.*[1]—This section is similar to the older boys' area. Many of the game courts such as volley ball, paddle tennis, and softball are identical; others serve the special interests of older girls. Tennis courts are sometimes located here or between the boys' and girls' areas.

6. *Shelter House and Wading Pool.*—The shelter house is an essential feature and its location is important since it serves as the center of control and also the chief architectural feature of the playground. A location fairly near the main entrance makes it accessible from the various divisions, and lends itself to an attractive landscape development. The building should not be so near the street, however, that it invites use as a public comfort station. Frequently the wading pool is constructed near the shelter house—an arrangement which is economical and effective.

[1] Where space is limited, divisions 4 and 5 may be combined and the use of the various courts and fields may be divided between the girls and boys.

7. *Shaded Area for Handicraft and Quiet Activities.*—Frequently crafts, storytelling, music, drama, and other quiet activities are carried on inside the playground building. Where possible, however, a shaded outdoor area equipped with tables and benches, a small stage or platform, and spaces for marbles, hopscotch, and other quiet games is preferable. A quiet corner of the playground adjoining the small children's area is a good location for this section.

8. *Landscape Area.*—This area is often confined largely to a planting strip outside the fence along the sides of the playground bordering on a street. Sometimes additional spaces such as the area in front of the playground shelter are set aside for plantings.

Total Space Requirements.—No definite space requirements can be prescribed for the various divisions of the children's playground but the following table suggests the amount of space which might normally be allotted to each. It will be noted that nearly 4 acres are required for this type of playground.

Name of Division	Suggested Space, Square Feet
Area for children of preschool age	10,000
Apparatus area	7,500
Open space for children's games	10,000
Older girls' area	37,500
Older boys' area	75,000
Shaded area for crafts	7,500
Shelter house and wading pool	7,500
Landscape area	10,000
Total	165,000 (3.79 acres)

In addition to the items mentioned the playground requires equipment for games and sports, an ample supply of game and play materials, and many of the facilities described earlier in the chapter.

The Playfield.—The design of the playfield is even less subject to standardization than that of the playground, but a few guiding principles are considered important. A section of the playfield comprising not more than three areas is usually developed as a children's playground. This is placed along the side which is most accessible from the children's homes so they will not have to cross sections of the field used for baseball and other adult activities. Separate sections consisting of large, comparatively level open areas and devoted primarily to games and sports are provided for men and for women. The men's section contains fields and courts for baseball, football, soccer, softball, volley ball, and some of the less strenuous sports such as roque, bowling, and horseshoes. The section for women and older girls is devoted largely to team games such as softball, soccer, field hockey, and volley ball, and also to individual sports. Its use is enhanced when it is enclosed by a hedge or fence.

The swimming pool is a frequent feature of the playfield, and the bathhouse in connection with it is sometimes planned as the service building for the entire area. In some instances a well-equipped recreation building is erected on the playfield, enabling it to serve as a year-round center. The pool and building are often placed near the street so people may reach them easily without crossing other sections. Features like an outdoor theater, bandstand, and fireplaces, benches, and tables for neighborhood picnics are best located in a section removed from the noisy, intensively used areas. Paths separate the various sections and lead people directly to the main features. If a part of the playfield is wooded and rugged, it may be developed as a landscape park.

The Large Park.—In designing this type of property two major objectives are sought. In the first place the planner seeks to utilize the natural features and advantages of the site in order to secure interesting and varied landscape effects through the effective use of woodland, open lawn, meadow, and valley. Vistas are created, sequestered sections are provided, and access to vantage points is afforded through the effective location of paths, roads, and hiking and bridle trails. Besides, he takes advantage of the opportunities which the area affords for various forms of recreation. Although many large parks were originally intended primarily for informal, passive recreation, they are being developed more and more for picnicking, games, and sports. Boating and bathing facilities are provided at water areas which also serve for skating in the winter. Park slopes are used for tobogganing, coasting, and skiing. Sections are set aside near the entrance for parking automobiles, which are used by large numbers of people in reaching these areas. Comfort stations or shelters are provided at places where people congregate in the largest numbers. A zoological garden, water fowl sanctuary, outdoor theater, botanical garden, nature trail, and nature museum are desirable features. In some instances a section of a large park has been developed for a day camp or golf course.

The Reservation.—In developing the reservation an attempt is made to keep it as nearly as possible in its natural state. Improvements and facilities are segregated and introduced in such a way as not to interfere with the informal, naturalistic condition of the remainder of the area. Water areas are utilized for water sports or are set aside as sanctuaries for water fowl, and camps and picnic centers are established at suitable locations. These facilities are made accessible by automobile roads, but large sections of the reservation can be reached only by bridle and hiking trails. Increasingly these areas are used for winter sports and for a variety of nature activities.

The Neighborhood Park.—The wide range in the size, topography, and location of these areas necessitates varied methods of development.

Some are distinctly formal in design; others, especially where there are interesting natural features, are treated in an informal, naturalistic manner. Sometimes they comprise a part of a neighborhood playfield-park. Much space is devoted to trees, shrubs, turf, and other plantings. A fountain, pool, band shell, statue, or ornamental flagpole is often an important feature in the design of the neighborhood park. Benches where people may sit and enjoy the beauty of the park and paths for pedestrians are sometimes the only facilities provided. Occasionally, however, pools are used for sailing toy boats, small sections are developed for little children's play, and shuffleboard, croquet, or other courts are provided for older people. These facilities add greatly to the usefulness of the parks and when properly designed and located do not detract from their beauty.

CHAPTER XIII

PLANNING SPECIAL AREAS AND STRUCTURES

It is impossible in this volume to discuss the design and construction of all the sports facilities, structures, and special areas listed at the beginning of Chap. XII. However, a few of these features which serve large numbers of people and are commonly provided by recreation authorities are described briefly. Likewise, consideration is given to the many types of buildings which are essential to a community recreation program.

SPECIAL RECREATION AREAS

Facilities for golf, swimming, picnicking, camping, and boating, as indicated in the preceding chapter, are sometimes included among the features of the playfield, the large park, or the reservation. There is an increasing tendency, however, for cities to acquire and develop special-use areas, such as a camp site, golf course, bathing beach, or athletic field. In either case, their design and equipment are influenced by certain definite use requirements. Several of the most important considerations in planning and constructing these areas and facilities are mentioned briefly.

The Bathing Beach.—Fortunate are cities with waterfronts suitable for bathing, which have been acquired and developed for such use. The ideal bathing beach combines deep water for the experienced swimmer and shallow water for the beginner, has a gradual slope free from obstructions or holes, and a sand surface extending into the water beyond the wadable area. In selecting a site for a beach, especially along a river, care is taken to make sure that the water is pure and free from swift currents. Jetties or groins are often required at ocean beaches to prevent the sand from being washed away or to help build up the beach. Fences are erected at many beaches to facilitate control and to restrict bathing to supervised, safe areas.

The bathhouse, a necessary feature, varies from a simple structure to one affording locker, shower, checking, toilet, suit, first-aid, refreshment, and office facilities. All these rooms are needed at an extensive beach attracting large numbers of people from a considerable distance. Ready access to the water from the building is desirable, but the limitations of the beach area usually justify a site which does not encroach upon the sand beach. Facilities for volley ball, horseshoes, handball, and shuffleboard, and an area for informal games conveniently located so

172

as not to interfere with bathers, add greatly to the popularity of a beach. A picnic area with tables, benches, and fireplaces is also a popular feature at many beaches. Necessary space is set aside for the parking of automobiles. Safety equipment is a factor of first importance. For nonswimmers a portion of the water area is often marked off or is enclosed on three sides by lines of rope supported by floats secured in place at the corners. The area to be used by swimmers is also plainly indicated. A float with diving boards or platform is generally provided and is anchored in at least 10 feet of water. One or more towers for lifeguards on the beach, life boats, ring buoys, ropes, first-aid supplies, and grappling irons comprise the equipment essential to adequate protection of bathers. Night lighting greatly increases the usefulness of the beach.

The Golf Course.—There are courses in parks previously designed for some other purpose, but best results are usually secured when land is acquired and developed primarily for golf. Uneven but not rugged topography, some woodland, a soil such as sandy loam, and good drainage are desirable characteristics of a site. The golf course presents an exceptional opportunity for harmonizing landscape beauty and active play. Expert advice is needed in the solution of the peculiar problems which arise in the planning and construction of a golf course. It is necessary to decide at the start whether the course is to be built for the expert, the average golfer, or the "dub." Some public courses are too difficult for the average golfer with the result that play is slowed up and satisfactory golf is possible for only a few. Courses are made interesting through variation in the length of holes, in the width of fairways, the introduction of hazards, and the utilization of varied topography and natural tree growth. Provision of water holes, "dog leg" fairways, traps, and hazards make the course more difficult.

Among the factors important in golf course design and construction are location and length of the holes, orientation of fairways, construction of tees and greens, provision of traps and hazards, drainage, seeding and fertilizing, installation of watering system, and the location and construction of the clubhouse, entrance road, and parking area. The clubhouse is placed near the first and the last greens where people start and finish play, and like the parking area is usually close to the entrance. Wherever possible roads bordering or passing through the course are eliminated. When facilities such as tennis courts, practice greens, croquet courts, and a playground for children are provided, preferably near the clubhouse, the area serves as a family recreation center. In the Northern states where little golf is played during the winter months, the course is often used for coasting, skiing, and tobogganing, and the clubhouse serves as a warming house and indoor recreation center.

The Camp.—In planning an organized camp for boys, girls, or family groups, an attempt is made to conserve or to create an environment in contrast to artificial city conditions. This is achieved through the use of native materials and through the selection of a site large enough to permit a considerable degree of isolation for the camp. Most municipal camps are therefore located in a large park or forest area or in a special site, usually at some distance from the city.

Many buildings are needed in the camp, among them cabins, floored tents, or other sleeping quarters, recreation hall or lodge, dining hall, administration building, boathouse, toilets, infirmary, washhouse, barn or stable, storage and pump house, craft building, and nature museum. Topography influences the layout of the camp although other factors are more important. The sleeping quarters are usually grouped in one or more units, the administration building is centrally located, and the kitchen is at a distance from both sleeping quarters and toilet buildings. Special care is taken to protect the water supply and to prevent the pollution of water used for drinking, washing, or water sports.

Most camps have access to a lake or stream where a bathing beach is developed and facilities for boating such as a dock and boathouse are constructed; otherwise a swimming pool is needed. A council ring, campfire circle, or outdoor amphitheater affords a center for evening activities, and the camp museum and nature trail serve the nature interests of the campers. These facilities are much more important to the camp program than game courts or a sports field, although these, too, are usually provided. Most municipal camps are primarily for summer use, but more and more they are being used throughout the year.

The Day Camp.—During the depression period many cities have set aside sections of their large parks or reservations to serve as day camps, and the success of these projects indicates that the day camp merits a place in the municipal camping program. Areas of a varied and rugged character with interesting natural features are well suited to such use. Day camp sites need to be readily accessible from the homes of the children, yet large enough to afford a degree of isolation for the campers. The few special facilities needed are outdoor cooking places, a supply of good drinking water, shade, a building with toilets, storage space, and room or shelter in case of sudden showers. A level area for games and play activities is desirable, as are tables and benches, council ring, nature trail, birdbaths, feeding station, and other aids to nature study.

The Athletic Field or Stadium.—This area, primarily a center for major games and sports, varies from a field with bleachers seating a few hundred people to a stadium accommodating many thousands. Its chief characteristics are one or more large open spaces including a running track and major sports areas, permanent seating facilities for spectators, a field house—unless lockers, toilets, showers, and storage spaces are provided under the stands or in a school building—parking spaces for automobiles, and a fence or wall around the entire area. The layout of the athletic field is determined largely by the activities to be carried on and the number of spectators to be accommodated. If the field is to be used primarily for football and track, as is often the case, the problem of layout is comparatively simple, for the football field can be laid out within the track and the same area used for both sports. On the other hand, because baseball cannot be played to the best advantage on a field designed for football and track, a separate diamond and bleachers are often provided for this sport when space and funds permit. Otherwise, the diamond must be laid out within the track enclosure which also affords the location for facilities used in the field events. Orientation is highly important from the point of view of both participants and spectators.

The efficient handling of crowds at athletic events requires that entrances be properly located, paths be of ample size, sections of the stands be clearly marked, and the parking area be convenient to the stands, large enough to serve the field adequately, and located so as to minimize the traffic problem. In recent years there has been a definite trend toward lighting athletic fields and stadiums to permit their use at night for games and sports and for other community events. Many athletic fields are still used primarily for exhibition games, but the tendency is growing to design them so that several games can be carried on simultaneously and also for a variety of activities.

The Swimming Pool.—Most outdoor pools are in playfields or large parks, but some occupy special sites developed as swimming centers. Perhaps no other recreation facility demands greater care in its planning and construction than the swimming pool. This is true because of the varied and complex problems involved and also because if it is not built properly the health and safety of the bathers are endangered. The problems confronted in pool construction relate to location, size, and shape of the pool, thickness and reinforcement of pool walls, drainage, water supply, waterproofing, heating, and recirculation. Authorities responsible for the development of a swimming pool should never proceed with the project until they have secured the advice of a competent engineer experienced in pool construction.

Swimming pools vary in size from the small playground pool to the large swimming center accommodating hundreds of people at one time. There are also many types and shapes of pools. The small pool is usually built in a single rectangular unit with shallow water at one end and a diving area at the other. Many large pools are elliptical or oval in shape, with shallow water at the edges and a platform for diving near the center. A number of rectangular pools have been built, 150 or more feet long and

60 or more feet wide, with shallow sections at each end and a deep section for diving across the center of the pool. Lines of buoys or floats strung across the pool define the three areas, which can be used simultaneously and advantageously for various activities. Several cities have built pools consisting of two or three distinct units: one used for general swimming, another for diving, and the third for children or nonswimmers. A multiple pool of this type has many advantages where the volume of use justifies its construction.

A few principles in planning and constructing the swimming pool follow: The slope of the bottom should be gradual—not more than 1 foot in 15; as much of the pool area as practicable should be wadable; depths should be clearly marked and the height of diving boards related to depth of water under them. Essential parts are overflow troughs, properly sloped runways around the pool, recessed steps or ladders, and water inlets and outlets adequate in size and located so as to assure proper circulation. Filters are installed to clean the water and a chlorinator or other device to disinfect it. Other items of equipment are pumps, heater, strainers, and cleaning equipment. Most pools are surrounded by a fence which serves as a safety measure and makes them accessible to bathers only, but bleachers for spectators are often erected outside the pool enclosure.

The bathhouse, a necessary feature, is located close to the pool, preferably near the shallow end. Bathhouse facilities include locker, shower, dressing, checking, and toilet rooms, office, laundry, and first-aid room. They are arranged so as to simplify the circulation of bathers and facilitate supervision of the building. Among the types of special equipment used at pools are diving boards and towers, floats, water slides, first-aid kits, and lifesaving equipment. Many pools are provided with underwater lights as well as floodlights which illuminate the entire pool area. Game courts, playground apparatus, and large sand areas are sometimes provided. Some of the larger pools are being equipped and used for a variety of games and play activities outside the swimming season, and a few serve as ice skating rinks during the winter.

Boating Facilities.—Communities in which there are opportunities for boating have a recreation asset of great value. Boating facilities vary according to the nature and extent of the water areas, which determine the types of boats used and their docking and storage requirements. At a small lake or stream where rowboats and canoes only are used, the facilities may consist of a landing dock, a boathouse for canoe storage, and a mooring place for the rowboats. Adjoining large water areas more elaborate facilities are often developed. Piers, protected boat basins with walks affording access to the berthing places, shipways, and hoists for removing boats from the water afford accommodations for owners of

motorboats, passenger launches, and sailing craft. Mooring posts are
provided for sailboats whereas berthing spaces are used by motor craft.
In case of large or exposed water areas it is sometimes necessary to construct a breakwater or sea wall to afford protection for the boat basin.
Where boating is restricted to small lakes or streams, a fleet of rowboats or canoes is generally available for rental by the public. Other
craft such as passenger launches, electric motorboats, or crew boats are
provided where conditions justify. On Lake Merritt in Oakland, California, the recreation department has 3 large passenger launches, 30
rowboats, 50 canoes, 7 motor canoes, 16 electric motorboats, and 20 crew
boats. The crew boats, averaging 30 feet in length and with a beam of 6
feet, accommodate a crew of 12, a pilot, a coxswain, and one adult passenger. Oars are furnished by the various organizations which participate
in the rowing program. In some cities the boats are owned by individuals, and the service rendered by the recreation authorities consists
primarily of providing mooring and storage facilities.

Boathouses afford such widely used facilities as storage racks for
small craft, repair shop, dining room, clubroom for model boat builders,
dressing room and showers, and storage room for oars and other
equipment.

Winter Sports Facilities.—Recreation areas afford many such facilities. Tennis courts, pools, and fields are turned into skating rinks; park
hills are set aside for coasting and skiing; toboggan slides and ski jumps
are being erected on golf courses and reservations; and ponds, kept clear of
snow, serve as skating and ice hockey centers. The use of these facilities
is of course dependent upon the weather, and disappointments are numerous. However, where climatic conditions permit winter sports the effort
to provide the necessary facilities yields large returns in healthful, enjoyable outdoor activity.

Slow-moving streams or ponds make the most satisfactory skating
areas, but where they are lacking rinks may be formed by either flooding or spraying. Experience has proved that unless the cold is extreme,
building an ice surface on the ground by spraying is more satisfactory
than attempting to flood an area. Artificial rinks require continuous
and careful maintenance. A section of the ice area is often set aside for
ice hockey, a popular winter sport which requires a rink approximately
85 by 190 feet. Curling is another ice game enjoyed by adults.

Where other coasting facilities are lacking small sled slides with platforms about 10 feet above the ground are sometimes erected on the playgrounds for children's use. Toboggan slides constructed of sections of
wooden troughs or of snow are built on natural slopes. In constructing
a toboggan slide, care must be taken that the trough is not too wide, that
the sections are strongly built and fitted together carefully, that the sides

are of sufficient height, that curves are avoided, and that there is a long, level outrun, free from obstructions. A northerly slope is desirable. In cities where winter sports are an important part of the program, ski jumps have been provided, but the use of this facility is restricted to expert jumpers. Warming shelters are commonly provided at winter sports centers for the comfort and convenience of the people using them.

Picnic Centers.—Picnicking has become so popular that most cities provide picnic opportunities and facilities. There are two types of picnic centers, (1) those designed for use by large organized groups and (2) areas intended primarily for families or other small groups. The same center may provide both types but better results are likely to be attained if an area is planned for a specific type of use. Desirable features of any picnic center, however, are a wooded area, preferably bordering a stream or lake, a location distant from sections used for other purposes, an attractive setting, and easy access from an automobile road.

The picnic center for large groups is equipped with several fireplaces, one or more large ovens where quantities of food may be prepared at one time, or a barbecue pit. Numerous picnic tables and benches, preferably the combination type, are erected near the fireplaces or ovens. Containers for rubbish, drinking fountains, and one or more faucets for drawing water are also provided. Toilets for both sexes are located at a distance from the other facilities. A useful feature at a group picnic center is a refreshment stand where fuel, food, and picnic supplies can be secured and equipment rented. Some type of shelter is necessary; it may consist merely of an open structure affording protection in case of sudden rains, or it may include toilet rooms, a stove, a caretaker's room, and other features. An open field for sports and for children's games makes possible activities which are commonly included in the picnic program, and a few types of playground apparatus appeal to the children.

Most families and other small picnic groups like seclusion, so it is customary for the facilities provided for them to be more widely distributed. Small, simply constructed fireplaces or open grates are most satisfactory; tables and benches are desirable but not necessary; toilets, water supply, and shelter are essential at most such centers. Large game areas are not needed, but a softball diamond and a few horseshoe courts are popular features.

Because picnic centers often cover a considerable area, it is helpful if each of the units has a name or number and if the center is well provided with signs indicating the location of the various features. Maps posted at the centers are also useful, and, parking spaces are set aside near large group areas. The individual picnic units are less readily accessible but they are sometimes built along a park road and include a space for an automobile; otherwise a central parking area is provided.

The Outdoor Theater.—The need for suitable places in which to hold outdoor plays, pageants, concerts, and meetings may be met by the construction of outdoor theaters. The simplest type is the playground theater which sometimes consists merely of a quiet corner of the playground, bordered by a fence or a hedge. A section of the turf serves as a stage and curtains are temporarily erected for dressing rooms and wings. On some playgrounds small naturalistic theaters have been developed; at others platforms have been erected on which plays are presented. The theater is sometimes built in combination with the playground shelter house. It seldom provides seating facilities although seats may be set up for special occasions.

Most municipal outdoor theaters are constructed in playfields or large parks and are designed in a naturalistic manner to conform to the character of their setting. A natural slope affords a desirable location for the amphitheater, especially if it is distant or well screened from noisy streets or play areas. Unless there is a natural wooded background trees and shrubs are often planted along the rear and on the wings of the stage for the sake of appearance and to serve as a sounding board. Sometimes walls are erected for this purpose. Provision is made for suitable stage entrances. At most theaters the stage is of turf and is sometimes built on two levels. Grassy slopes, sodded terraces, cement walls in the form of steps or terraces, or permanent or removable benches serve as seats for the spectators. Other essential or desirable features of the outdoor theater are dressing rooms for participants, amplifying equipment, orchestra pit, lighting equipment, and water basin between the stage and audience. Fountains or water curtains with colored lights are installed at some of the more elaborate theaters. A parking area for automobiles is generally provided at a sufficient distance to prevent disturbance from noise.

In a few cities elaborate outdoor theaters have been constructed, formal in design like the Greek Theater in Griffiths Park, Los Angeles, or they have been combined with a band shell as in the Zoological Park in Toledo.

Other Features.—The preceding pages indicate only a few of the diversified facilities which enable people to find outlets for their desire to engage in various forms of outdoor activities. Several others can merely be mentioned. Bridle, riding, and nature trails lure riders and hikers from congested sections of recreation areas; hurling, cricket, boccie, and pelota courts enable foreign-born groups to play games with which they are familiar; hunters and fishermen develop their skill at trap shooting ranges and fly-casting pools in anticipation of the open season for their respective sports. Gardeners and nature lovers find enjoyment and enduring interest and satisfaction in the rose garden, conservatory, or botanical garden. Through the development of their properties for such uses, recreation authorities have made a great contribution to the abundant life of the people. In most communities, however, only a beginning has been made in utilizing the possibilities afforded by existing areas.

FACILITIES FOR INDOOR RECREATION

Indoor facilities are needed for many forms of recreation, and during part of the year only a limited number of outdoor activities are possible for large numbers of people. Consequently, suitable indoor facilities must be provided if people are to have an opportunity to engage in recreation activities throughout the year.

Buildings of many types have been erected by municipal recreation authorities to meet the public demand for indoor activities. Most play areas have some kind of structure, varying from the simple open shelter on the park or playground to the elaborate building which serves as a center for the recreation life of a community or city neighborhood. Some recreation buildings occupy sites acquired especially for the purpose; others are located on areas which also provide outdoor facilities. Many schools, municipal auditoriums, libraries, and other public buildings not primarily intended for recreation have one or more rooms equipped and made available for community recreation use.

Types of Recreation Buildings.—Buildings used primarily or exclusively for recreation may be classified into three groups according to their primary functions as follows:

1. Buildings which have diversified facilities and are used for many types of activity
2. Buildings designed primarily for a single type of activity although they may be adapted for other uses
3. Buildings which provide essential service facilities in connection with the recreational use of areas. They sometimes have one or more rooms used for recreation activities

In the following list, buildings provided by recreation authorities are classified according to these three groups:

MULTIPLE-USE BUILDINGS	SINGLE-USE BUILDINGS	SERVICE BUILDINGS
Amphitheater	Aquarium	Administration building
Arena	Art museum	Boathouse
Arts center	Band shell	Bathhouse
Clubhouse	Botanical garden	Comfort station
Community house	Camp buildings	Golf course buildings
Field house[1]	Crafts center	Overlook shelter
Playhouse	Conservatory	Overnight cabin
Recreation building	Dance pavilion	Picnic shelter

[1] In many cities this term is applied to a service building, especially on the athletic field.

MULTIPLE-USE BUILDINGS	SINGLE-USE BUILDINGS	SERVICE BUILDINGS
	Historical museum	Playground shelter
	Natural history museum	Stables
	Nature museum	
	Observatory	
	Planetarium	
	Restaurant	
	Swimming pool	
	Theater	
	Yacht club	
	Zoo	

A fourth type which is not used directly for recreation but which is necessary in a recreation system is the service building such as the garage, blacksmith shop, greenhouse, carpenter shop, and storage building. Mention has already been made of buildings such as the school, city hall, and auditorium, which are not used primarily for recreation but in which recreation activities are sometimes carried on.

Facilities in Recreation Buildings.—A survey of the recreation facilities provided in the buildings previously listed would show that almost every type of recreation interest which can be met indoors is being served in one or more of them. The list which follows comprises the rooms and special features which are more or less commonly provided in recreation buildings. Some of them, like the gymnasium, clubroom, or auditorium, serve a variety of uses; others, like the rifle range, squash court, or bowling alley, can be used for only one activity:

Archery range
Art gallery
Auditorium
Banquet hall
Bowling alleys
Card room
Child welfare station
Clubroom
Craft room
Dance hall
Dining room
Drama workshop
Dressing room
Exhibition room
First-aid and physical examination room
Gymnasium
Indoor swimming pool
Indoor tennis court
Kitchen
Lecture hall
Library
Locker room
Lounge

Machine shop
Meeting rooms for the American Red Cross, American Legion, Women's Club, etc.
Moving-picture booth and projector
Music room
Nature museum
Office
Pistol or rifle range
Pool and billiards room
Reading room
Roller skating rink
Rooms for boxing, wrestling, etc.
Rooms for special handicrafts
Roughhouse room
Running track
Shower room
Social hall
Squash court
Stage with equipment
Table game room
Team room

PLANNING THE RECREATION BUILDING

There are no standard recreation buildings. Each project is planned to meet the requirements of the particular location and afford the facilities required by the recreation area, the neighborhood, or the community it is to serve. If a special site is to be acquired for a community building, the problem of location is most important; on the other hand, if the building is to be erected on an existing recreation area the problem is primarily one of relating its location to that of other features on the area. The economical and successful operation of a building depends to a great extent upon proper planning. Best results are obtained when the plan is prepared by a competent architect, experienced in the design and use of recreation buildings, in cooperation with the local recreation authorities who are familiar with the requirements to be met and are to be responsible for operating the building.

Essential factors to be considered before a building is planned are: the specific activities which it is intended to make possible; the number of people who need to be accommodated in these activities at one time; the extent to which multiple use can be made of various rooms; the special needs of children, women, and girls; the amount and types of leadership and maintenance service likely to be provided; the length of season the building will be in use; the desirability of heating only parts of the building; the relation of the rooms to outdoor facilities and to their use by outside groups; the amount of money available for construction and operation; the possibility of later expansion. The problem of acoustics is important but frequently neglected. Local building regulations must be studied and the limitations of the site taken into account. The collaboration of an experienced architect and a capable recreation worker helps to prevent costly mistakes and to assure a building which is attractive, in good taste, and suitable for its location, and which will function efficiently.

Essential Planning Objectives.—Several objectives which apply to all types, although they are relatively more important in the case of the larger, more elaborate buildings, are ease of supervision and circulation, flexibility of use, and minimum upkeep and operating budget. These objectives are realized when the building is so planned that it can be supervised by the smallest staff possible. Constructing the auditorium as a unit with separate entrances and exits and placing the director's office where it overlooks as many rooms as possible facilitate control. Corridors are reduced to a minimum and circulation is so arranged that groups using the building are not disturbed. To secure flexibility of use, facilities such as the pool and the gymnasium are arranged so that men can use one while women are using the other. Clubrooms are made available to many groups rather than assigned to the exclusive use of a single organization. A wise selection of building materials and careful planning of construction details enable yearly repairs, maintenance costs, and janitor service to be reduced to a minimum. Unneeded space in rooms and corridors means greater original cost and added insurance, daily janitor service, cost of heating and lighting, and periodic painting.

Some Important Construction Details.—Every building presents an individual problem in the selection of building materials, but experience has indicated that certain practices and methods merit general application. For example, stucco, brick, or stone are favored in many cities for exterior walls because of the low maintenance cost and because a rough surface is less easily defaced than a smooth one. In the toilet rooms glazed tile has been found most satisfactory, and translucent glass, generally reinforced, is used in the windows. Cement floors are favored for toilet, shower, and storage rooms. The use of wood on the interior of buildings which are closed for many months of the year is unwise because of dampness, and steel frames are recommended for windows. As far as possible all pipes, traps, valves, and other plumbing fixtures are placed in a corridor between the walls in order to facilitate the making of necessary repairs.

Experience has taught that a room to serve as a gymnasium will not prove satisfactory if its floor is less than 50 by 75 feet and its height less than 18 feet. At one time relegated to the basement, the gymnasium and swimming pool are now placed where an abundance of light and air is available. If funds and space are limited, folding or knockdown bleachers are preferable to permanent seating facilities. If a room is to be used as a gymnasium and auditorium, an elevated stage is needed for dramatic productions and other uses. Plays can be produced on smaller stages but the minimum desirable dimensions are: width 40 feet, depth 24 feet, height at least 4 feet above proscenium opening, which should be not less than 12 by 24 feet. Stage design involves not only the stage itself but also the location of the lights, entrances, dressing rooms, and doors for bringing in and taking out the scenery. The control of lights in an auditorium from several points such as the main entrance, stage, and motion-picture booth, is essential.

The importance of providing large, conveniently located storage rooms cannot be emphasized too strongly, especially in a building where the same facilities are to be used for different activities. Removable chairs are commonly used, since they can be piled on rubber-tired trucks and stored under the stage when the room is used as a gymnasium, for dancing, or social recreation. Special care needs to be taken in the arrangement of the toilet, locker, and shower rooms for the two sexes. When a building also serves people using outdoor facilities, separate convenient entrances to the shower and toilet rooms are often provided for them.

GENERAL RECREATION BUILDINGS

Many recreation buildings, as previously stated, provide diversified facilities and are used for a wide range of activities. This type of building is often found in the towns and smaller cities where it is known as a community house and serves as a center for the indoor recreational life of the community. Other examples of this type are the park field houses and recreation buildings located on playfields or large parks, especially in the larger cities.

The facilities commonly provided in this type of building are:

1. A social hall which can be used for dances, parties, dinners, or entertainments
2. An auditorium with stage and equipped with motion-picture projector, used for concerts, community sings, dramatic productions, lectures, movies, and debates
3. A gymnasium with removable or folding bleachers, used for gym classes. basketball, volley ball, boxing, wrestling, dancing, stunts, and exhibitions
4. Locker, shower, and toilet rooms for people using the gymnasium
5. Meeting rooms for clubs, organizations, music, and other groups
6. Workshops for handicrafts, arts, and hobbies
7. Game rooms with facilities for table games, Ping-pong, billiards, or bowling
8. Kitchen and serving pantry
9. Library and reading room—also used for storytelling
10. Indoor swimming pool with spectators' gallery
11. Service features such as heater and fuel rooms, storage, janitor's room, and general toilet rooms

All these features are seldom found in a single building. The number and kinds required depend upon existing facilities, local interests and needs, available funds, and the number of people to be served. In neighborhoods or communities where large numbers are likely to use the building daily, several rooms are provided in which different activities can be carried on at the same time. In a small community fewer rooms are needed, but they are planned for several uses. Some large-city buildings have a separate gymnasium and an auditorium as well as a social hall; occasionally two gymnasiums are provided, one for men and the other for women. More often, however, the building has only one large room equipped to serve as gymnasium, auditorium, and social hall, and one or two smaller rooms which are used as club, craft, meeting, and game rooms.

Because a gymnasium and its accessory features such as shower and locker rooms are expensive to build, are adapted to only a limited variety of uses, and are commonly provided in high schools, many cities have eliminated them from their recreation buildings. Less elaborate field houses, or clubhouses as they are sometimes called, have been constructed instead. They cannot be used for basketball and volley ball, but they serve for social recreation, informal dramatics, arts and crafts, and various neighborhood and club activities.

Three Typical Recreation Buildings.—The Community House at Dalton, Massachusetts, an example of the community type of recreation building, is situated on a site of 1½ acres near the center of this town of 4,000 people. Across the front of the first floor are the rooms available for general use, including a social hall, men's clubroom, ladies' parlor, offices, two clubrooms which may be combined, and rooms for the Red Cross and American Legion. To the rear is a well-equipped gymnasium with permanent and knockdown bleachers and a portable stage equipped with curtain, drops, and lights. In the basement is a swimming pool 20 by 60 feet, with adjoining rooms and lockers for men and for women. On the same floor are four bowling alleys, a clubroom, and pool tables. This building, erected in 1923 at a cost of $125,000, affords excellent opportunities for indoor recreation to the people of this small community.

Some of the largest and most fully equipped recreation buildings in the United States have been erected in the parks of Chicago. The field house in Calumet Park, erected at a cost of $380,000, is typical. It contains separate gymnasiums, lockers, and showers for men and women, library, lounge, lecture room, large assembly hall with stage, and clubrooms. In the basement are a kitchen and banquet room, workshops and craft rooms equipped with sewing machines, quilting looms, and other facilities. It is obvious that the construction of such a building is justifiable only where a large population is to be served and where a comprehensive program is to be carried on under competent leadership.

The field house at Elmwood Park in East Orange is typical of the buildings without a gymnasium-auditorium. It is a two-story structure on the second floor of which is a wide awning-covered terrace overlooking the playfield. On this floor is also a large playroom with stage used for plays, community gatherings, and many other activities. At the end opposite the stage is a large fireplace. Anterooms give entrance to the stage, connecting with two craft rooms and the office of the girls' supervisor. The ground floor is used for the service facilities—storage rooms, dressing rooms with lockers, showers, and toilets, public toilet rooms, heater room, and rooms for the boys' worker and field superintendent.

SPECIAL RECREATION BUILDINGS

Most buildings, like the ones previously described, serve many uses, but several cities have erected structures designed for experimentation and participation in one specific form of recreation activity. Typical of such buildings are the community drama center, the crafts workshop, the sports building, the swimming pool, or the nature museum. In some instances these buildings serve as a city-wide center for a particular activity. Here individuals who have developed interest or skill in the activity in their neighborhood centers can engage in it more intensively with others who have acquired similar skills. This type of center may attract fewer individuals than the general recreation building, but to a greater extent it fosters a continuing, progressive, and absorbing interest in the special field to which it is dedicated. For this reason it is likely to play a part of increasing importance in recreation programs of the future.

It is easier to work out a satisfactory plan for a building to be used for one special activity than for one to serve a variety of uses. In designing a theater, for example, to be used exclusively for the presentation of dramatic productions, the materials best suited for the particular purpose are selected and seats are placed to the best advantage for viewing productions. The special requirements of the stage with respect to space, equipment, lighting, and facilities for erecting and moving scenery receive careful consideration. Dressing, storage, and work rooms essential to carrying on a comprehensive drama program are not neglected. These various features cannot be arranged so effectively or provided so completely in a building where the auditorium must also serve as a gymnasium and social hall. The planning and construction of these special-use buildings necessitate a careful study of their particular requirements.

Two Special Recreation Buildings.—The Junior Museum established by the San Francisco Recreation Commission is an example of the building dedicated to a particular use. The Museum "seeks to help young people realize the beauties of nature, the important facts of history, and the achievements of man, to illustrate the principles of science, and to provide opportunities for creative education through various activities or hobbies." The building contains workshops and clubrooms for nature study and the preparation of collections, a darkroom with facilities for developing and printing photographs, rooms with tools for various forms of handicraft, especially those related to science and nature, and a gallery for art and other exhibitions. The drawing power of the museum is attested by the fact that the monthly attendance is reported to be about 3,500.

Palo Alto, California, is one of the few American cities that has a municipal Community Playhouse, a gift of one of its residents. The Playhouse serves as a center for artistic and cultural activities and is available for music and dance recitals, dramatic productions, lectures, and forums. The auditorium seats 428 people, and the stage, fully equipped with up-to-date devices, is larger than that of many commercial theaters. Other facilities are a two-story workshop, dressing rooms, costume room, greenroom, director's office, rest rooms, checkroom, and foyer which is designed to serve also as an art gallery. Several rooms are available for rehearsals and serve as classrooms for the School of the Theater. Citizens of Palo Alto and surrounding communities are finding in this building a center where they may spend their leisure hours in enjoyable relaxation or in creative participation.

RECREATION SERVICE BUILDINGS

These structures afford the facilities necessary to accommodate the people making use of recreation areas such as swimming pools, golf courses, and boating areas. They commonly contain dressing, locker, toilet, and shower rooms for both sexes, rooms for checking or storing sports and maintenance equipment, a shelter, lobby, or lounge, refectory, and repair shop. Each type has its special requirements. The bath-house, in addition to the usual service features, frequently has a first-aid room, a laundry, suit drying room, and space for the pump, filter, and purification equipment. The boathouse, on the other hand, requires rooms or racks for storing boats, docking facilities, shipways, and a carpenter shop where repairs can be made. Without service buildings the use of outdoor recreation areas by large numbers of people would not be possible.

In addition to their service features they frequently contain rooms or facilities for recreation use. In Portland, Oregon, for example, the bathhouse at a large swimming pool has a room 60 by 100 feet which is used the year round. Basketball and volley ball courts are laid out in it, and a portable stage at one end enables it to serve as an auditorium seating 1,000 people. Clubhouses at golf courses often contain rooms which are used for dances, banquets, parties, and many social functions. In Oakland a clubroom for model yacht enthusiasts is provided at one of the boat houses; another has facilities for the use of picnic groups in case inclement weather prevents the use of the near-by fireplaces and barbecue pit. In most playground shelter houses there is a room in which club meetings, crafts, and other activities may be carried on.

INDOOR RECREATION CENTERS

Indoor recreation activity is by no means restricted to buildings constructed exclusively for such use. Recreation departments conduct activities in many buildings intended primarily for some other purpose such as schools, churches, industrial plants, institutions, settlements, apartment houses, and municipal buildings. The facilities vary from elaborate school physical education plants including gymnasiums, swimming pool, and special game rooms, to a storytelling room in a library, or a city hall basement in which bowling alleys or horseshoe courts have been installed.

The same principles are followed in planning these facilities as in planning special recreation buildings, but additional factors must often be considered. In a school gymnasium, for example, a larger number of lockers is likely to be needed, owing to its use by both school and community groups, than in a gymnasium used by community groups only. Swimming pool and locker rooms in a school building should be placed not only where they are easily accessible from the gymnasium but where groups using them evenings or in the summer can reach them without passing through other parts of the building. Unfortunately, many school buildings are constructed in such a way as to make their recreation use by community groups exceedingly difficult.

ADAPTING OLD BUILDINGS FOR RECREATION USE

During the depression period the urgent demand for more indoor recreation facilities and the need for buildings in which emergency recreation leaders might be put to work resulted in the utilization for recreation of many buildings originally planned for some other use. In one city, a two-story bakery was transformed into a recreation center. An old three-story medical school building in another city was turned into a fully equipped center with large meeting room, library, clubrooms, music, card, and game rooms, and handball courts. A building once an armory now houses a large gymnasium, reading, club, and game rooms. An old county jail with its 13-acre site has been handed over to a recreation commission and adapted as an indoor and outdoor recreation center. Garages, stores, lodge halls, and abandoned school buildings have been utilized for social and recreation purposes.

Often the adaptation of old buildings presents serious problems, but ingenuity, imagination, and effort have accomplished remarkable results. Windows and lights have been screened where there was a room large enough for games like basketball and volley ball or suitable for a "roughhouse" room for strenuous low organized games. Unpromising rooms have been made attractive for club meetings, crafts, quiet games, and reading by whitewashing the walls, installing suitable lights, and hanging bright-colored curtains. In adapting old buildings care must be taken to make sure they are structurally sound, conform with building code requirements, and are provided with adequate stairways and fire escapes.

A SUGGESTION

In conclusion, the more knowledge the recreation worker has of the design and equipment of recreation areas and facilities—indoor and outdoor—the better able he will be to secure the maximum returns from the available properties and to meet the problems which confront him with reference to their development and expansion. He must remember, however, that many of these problems require technical advice which can best be secured from the architect, engineer, and landscape architect. And he must not forget that there is much excellent literature available which can help him in the solving of his design and equipment problems.

PART IV

ACTIVITIES AND PROGRAM PLANNING

Activities are the mediums through which individuals satisfy their recreation desires and interests. The recreation department performs its chief service by employing a staff who, utilizing areas and facilities, plan, organize, supervise, and conduct a program of attractive activities. In addition, it stimulates individuals and groups to develop recreation interests and to initiate recreation activities and assists people with their own leisure-time programs. Recreation workers therefore need to know the activities which are commonly considered as recreation, the satisfactions which they afford, and the basis on which they may be included in the municipal program. The use of activities in the recreation program is influenced by the age, skill, and sex of people, the type of community, the size of the group, the time element, and many other factors. Because of the diversity of activities in the recreation program, different methods must be used in initiating, conducting, and guiding various parts of the program. The significance of these activities and some of the problems involved in their use in municipal recreation programs are considered in this part.

CHAPTER XIV

RECREATION ACTIVITIES

Recreation activities cover the whole field of human interests. The forms of recreation in which people engage vary as widely as the interests of a single individual throughout his lifetime and are as diverse as people are different from each other. Beginning with the doll play of babyhood, and up through the active games and sports of youth to the quiet pastimes of old age, the variety of recreation activities in which an individual engages is almost limitless. Yet this diversity of an individual's interests is small in comparison with the difference in the recreation interests of a group of people.

One characteristic of all forms of recreation is that each provides an outlet for some basic urge or need. Each represents a medium through which personality achieves satisfying expression and which contributes to human happiness. This characteristic of recreation activity accounts for the great diversity of recreation forms. It explains the close relationship between the essential satisfactions which people seek in recreation activities and the ways in which the personality functions. Just as the individual personality expresses itself through the exercise of its physical, social, mental, and creative powers, so recreation activities in their varied forms bring physical, social, mental, and creative satisfactions to the individual engaging in them.

Recreation activities are frequently grouped according to these major types of personality expression, but such a grouping is not entirely satisfactory. In an activity like a modern dance, originated and executed by a group, the individual participants may find expression not only physically and socially, but mentally and creatively as well. A classification of activities under such headings as physical, dramatic, rhythmic, or social is convenient and useful for the recreation worker, especially in planning programs, but in considering recreation activities from the point of view of the individual participant, an entirely different approach is desirable.

SATISFACTIONS THE FUNDAMENTAL TEST

The satisfactions which people seek and find in various forms of recreation activity afford such an approach. Among these satisfactions which large numbers of people attain through forms of recreation are the opportunity to create, fellowship, adventure, a sense of achievement, the enjoyment of one's physical powers, the use of one's mental powers, emotional stimulation, beauty, relaxation, and opportunities for service. It is because some individuals find that certain forms of activity yield one or more of these satisfactions that these activities become for them recreation. The same activities are not recreation for other individuals who gain no satisfaction from them. In planning programs it is therefore important for the recreation worker to consider not only the types of activity but the motives which induce people to engage in them.

No hard and fast grouping of activities under the various types of satisfactions is possible or essential. In the first place, different individuals seek and find different kinds of pleasurable responses from the same activity. One person may sing in a chorus primarily for the sociability which it affords, another because it furnishes an outlet for using and developing his skill as a singer, and a third for the emotional satisfaction which comes to him while singing with a group. Another reason is that a single form of activity may yield several types of satisfaction to the same individual. The recreation value of an activity for a particular person depends upon the way in which he is affected by it and upon the richness of the experience which it brings to him.

The use of the term "higher recreations" which is sometimes applied to certain forms of activity, particularly the cultural arts, implies that this is the case. Yet this label carries a connotation which is not always justified. Other forms of recreation such as swimming, square dancing, or mountain climbing may have more meaning and offer more satisfying outlets of expression for a certain individual at a particular time than the so-called "higher recreations." No specific forms of recreation have an exclusive right to this title, but certain activities which serve a wide range of basic human needs and afford great possibilities for rich and satisfying experience have gained for themselves a high rank in recreation values. Thus an activity in which an individual can create, achieve, and find beauty, fellowship, and relaxation is more likely to have enduring value than one which yields only one or two types of satisfaction. The relationship between senses and satisfactions is implied by Harry A. Overstreet in his statement, "The more senses we lend to an experience, the more vivid and rich it becomes."[1]

SATISFACTIONS A BASIS FOR CLASSIFYING ACTIVITIES

Activities cannot be divided into groups according to the satisfactions which people seek from them in the same manner as they are classified according to types, as music, drama, arts and crafts, and physical activities. It is important for the recreation leader to be familiar with

[1] *A Guide to Civilized Leisure*, p. 51, W. W. Norton & Company, Inc., 1934.

the activities which are commonly grouped under these headings; it is still more important that he know in what ways they satisfy the fundamental desires of people. He may discover, for example, that certain people participate in a craft or music activity, not so much because of their interest in crafts or music, but because the activity affords an opportunity for fellowship, achievement, or relaxation which they cannot gain in any other way.

The following pages point out some of the satisfactions which people seek through recreation and indicate how different forms of recreation activity contribute to human happiness by supplying these satisfactions. At the close of the chapter is presented a comprehensive list of the activities commonly considered as recreation, grouped under the type headings by which these activities are frequently identified.

The Joy of Creation.—Civilization affords a striking illustration of the potency and universality of man's urge to make and to create. His desire and capacity for creative craftsmanship are two of man's precious possessions which have persisted "through the ages like a rainbow thread." The child building a castle in the sand, primitive man shaping and carving his canoe, and the artist painting on his canvas, are all giving expression to this desire. The effectiveness of creative ability as a means of self-expression is pointed out by Howard Braucher in the following quotation:

Culture is not a matter of words and sounds alone. The hands may speak also—may convey messages, may reveal thoughts and emotions too deep and too sacred for careless, easily uttered words.

Working with wood and clay and marble, fashioning images of dreams and emotions too real for tripping words, man becomes articulate, reveals himself even to himself, lives in another world, understands himself better, whence he has come, whither he is moving, adds another dimension to his world.[1]

He continues to point out its significance in the field of recreation as follows: "No recreation worker, seeking to give men and women everywhere the makings of an abundant life, can ignore what man hath wrought with his hands, what men do now in the crafts, what cravings lie deep inside men that will find satisfaction only in activity of the hands."

The most common forms of recreation activity in which this urge finds expression are the arts and crafts. These take such a wide variety of forms that every individual, regardless of age, sex, education, occupation, or skill, can find a suitable medium. Like the forms, the materials available for these activities are limitless. Among the most common are wood, clay, leather, metals, oils, cloth, and paper. The desire to create brings together young and old in the photography club, gives model air-

[1] "Make," *Recreation*, February, 1936, p. 525.

craft its strong appeal to young men long after they have lost their interest in many other activities, and attracts women to the needlework groups where clothing is designed and made, or to the weaving class where original patterns are worked into rugs or blankets. Among children it finds expression in the making of mud pies, the weaving of baskets, and the construction of realistic animals for the circus parade.

Important as arts and crafts are among the creative activities, there are other ways in which this desire finds expression. Some individuals achieve it through the composing of music, others through the writing of poetry, or the creation of characters in a story or play. In a sense the dancer, the actor, and the director of a dramatic production create the personality of the characters portrayed. The true gardener joins forces with the Creator in bringing into being a place of beauty.

Of special' significance to recreation workers is the extent to which these activities can be related to and integrated with other forms. The making of model boats, kites, or pushmobiles, for example, leads up to the actual use of the objects made. Important features of the drama program in which the creative interest predominates are the making of puppets, scenery, costumes, and stage equipment. In the field of nature are the building of birdhouses, the mounting of exihibits, and the construction of nature trails. A part of the music program often consists of making the instruments. Trips to museums, industries, and other centers of interest afford opportunities to observe the results of others' creative activity. These few illustrations make clear the important part which the desire for self-expression through creation plays in the recreation life of people. As a matter of fact, the degree to which the creative spirit is present in any activity determines to a large extent whether it is a dull or a vital experience.

Fellowship.—Man is essentially a gregarious being. No human desire is perhaps more fully met through recreation or is achieved in as many forms as the desire for fellowship. Because most forms of recreation are essentially group activities or may be carried on by individuals with others, they minister directly to man's need for companionship, social relationships, and cooperative activity. The importance of providing opportunities for fellowship through recreation is pointed out as follows in the chapter entitled Youth at Play in the survey of youth in the state of Maryland, conducted for the American Youth Commission: "Possibly the most significant revelation that has come out of this analysis is the need, and the demand for various types of social recreation."[1]

Activities which are commonly considered as meeting this particular need are community gatherings, parties, social dancing, dinners, and outings of various types. Such widely differing activities as a birthday

[1] Howard M. Bell, *Youth Tell Their Story*, American Council on Education, 1938.

party in the home, a holiday celebration in a large community center, or a Chamber of Commerce clambake, all belong within this group. Fellowship plays a part in team games, athletic contests, group singing, and clubs of all types. It is basic in such a simple but widespread activity as conversation. Canoeing, hiking, camping, and many other activities are enriched when they are done in company with others of similar interests. Frequently a discussion group is held together as much by the sociability of its members as by the topics discussed. Part of the value of membership in an orchestra, chorus, or baseball team is derived from the fact that these groups make cooperative activity possible.

Many people join groups as much because of their desire for the resulting sociability as because of their interest in the particular activity engaged in by the groups. Failures in the recreation program are often caused by the fact that the element of sociability has been lacking. The primary satisfactions which an individual gains from most forms of recreation activity are enhanced by the sociability, stimulation, and mutual helpfulness that result from group participation. The strong and widespread desire for fellowship is recognized by introducing regular or occasional social activities in the programs of groups primarily formed for some other purpose.

Adventure—The Desire for New Experience.—Children are living question marks, and the persisting desire on the part of man to extend his knowledge and to gain new experiences makes for continued growth and progress. Many forms of recreation owe their appeal to the fact that they contribute to this universal human desire. This is especially true of nature activities which afford unlimited opportunities for exploring the wonders of the world about us. Man's curiosity and his desire for new experience go far in explaining the tremendous popularity of travel. The drawing power of the zoo is different only in degree from that which induces man to track the animals in their native habitat, and the excitement which attends the nature lover's search for new birds, flowers, or marine life is not essentially different from the thrill of hunting big game.

Sailing, camping, mountain climbing, and photography alike open avenues of adventure to large numbers of people. Just as truly, though perhaps to a lesser degree, the musician finds it in playing a new composition for the first time, the craftsman in working in a new medium, or the actor in learning a new part. The new but expanding field of recreation through service offers limitless opportunities for pioneering and adventurous experience. The widespread appeal of many popular story and pictorial magazines and of the moving picture may be accounted for in part by the fact that they afford opportunities for new, though vicarious, experiences to large numbers of people, many of whom do not have the courage, opportunity, or ability to seek their own adventure.

The elements of variety, adventure, and surprise are important in planning and conducting children's play activities. Programs which are stereotyped, unchanged from day to day, unrelated to the varying interests of boys and girls, have little appeal. The bleak, unattractive playground, lacking in interest or beauty, fails to attract and hold children partly because it offers no opportunities for adventure. The imaginative leader, however, who recognizes the value of introducing new games, initiates novel, challenging activities, and encourages the children to adapt them and to work out new play forms and projects, is building a continuing interest in the program. Similarly with adults, the occasional introduction of a surprise feature, the undertaking of an experimental project, or the sponsoring of an untried activity yield an added element of satisfaction to the appeal of the regular activities.

Sense of Achievement.—Man craves some area in life where he can excel and feel a sense of achievement. Because, like adventure, this experience is denied to most people in their work, it is sought in forms of recreation. There are a few people who cannot achieve it in some form if they can only be helped to find the right medium. It is commonly associated with competitive activities, especially games and sports, but its fulfillment is possible in almost any form of recreation activity. Most people attain it by raising their own standard of performance rather than by surpassing others in competition. Only a favored few can achieve outstanding success, but everyone can gain the satisfaction which results from making progress and increasing his skill in some activity.

This desire for progress and achievement accounts in part for the widespread interest in games and sports. The boy willingly spends time and energy and undergoes strict training in order to make the school team and to help win. He practices diligently in preparation for the athletic contests, just as his father strives to improve his golf or bowling score. An individual feels a sense of accomplishment when he has mastered a difficult music score or dance step, has found a long-sought specimen for his nature collection, has solved a difficult problem in designing the scenery for a play, has completed a satisfactory piece of leadership service, or has even solved a knotty crossword puzzle.

Part of the fascination of many recreation activities is the opportunity which they offer for the utilization of existing skills and their challenge to greater attainment. Interest in an activity often dies when it no longer affords opportunity for further progress or presents a challenge to the participant. Much of the value of team games, choral groups, debating, and other group activities is due to the fact that the achievements of the group are shared by the individual members, some of whom may have no means of gaining individual success. The satisfaction which comes from achievement is most vital and enduring in the case of activities which require physical, mental, or creative effort on the part of the individual. It is comparatively lacking in the appeal of social recreation, reading, and spectator activities.

There is a close relationship between the satisfaction resulting from achievement in recreation activities and the recognition or prestige which these activities bring to individuals. In some cases the desire for recognition underlies the willingness of people to undertake volunteer recreation service. However, in seeking recognition through recreation, an individual is more likely to select an activity in which he has the greatest likelihood of achieving success and of excelling the performance of others. He chooses an activity not because it yields direct satisfaction but because the chance for achievement which it offers promises to bring him recognition. This, therefore, is a by-product and not an immediate satisfaction resulting directly from participation in the activity.

Physical Well-being.—Physical activity is a fundamental function of life. The play of the child is characterized by continuous bodily activity, and as he grows older he continues to gain satisfaction from the spontaneous use of his growing physical powers. Running, jumping, climbing, and wrestling are often engaged in for the pure joy of it. Later, team games and individual sports give the sense of well-being which comes from the full use of the body, although part of the satisfaction in these activities, as previously mentioned, is derived from the fellowship which accompanies them and from the opportunities for achievement which they provide. Through adult life such activities as skating, swimming, or skiing bring joy and a sense of well-being to the individual primarily because they are channels affording satisfying outlets for his physical energy. Certain forms of the dance also bring a sense of coordination, balance, and control of the body and its movements.

In many other forms of recreation the expenditure of physical energy plays a secondary though important role. Social recreation programs are enlivened by periods of active games, and much of the fun of camping, picnicking, and nature hiking lies in the exertion which these activities entail. Other activities such as playing certain musical instruments make strenuous demands upon the physical stamina of the participants, although this factor may detract from rather than contribute to the enjoyment afforded by the activities. Many people because of chronic fatigue or laziness do not enjoy any forms of strenous physical exercise. They are likely to seek other kinds of recreation which are essentially passive in nature and in which this element of satisfaction is entirely lacking. Others, however, seek strenuous activities primarily because they furnish outlets for their physical energy.

Use of Mental Powers.—Because of the common association of mental effort and work, the relationship of recreation to the exercise of one's mental powers may not be immediately apparent. Yet man engages in many forms of recreation primarily because they afford a stimulation to mental activity. This factor has a preponderant or highly important place in such activities as forums, debating, discussion group meetings, chess, nature study, music appreciation, and creative writing, to mention only a few. As a matter of fact, relatively few forms of recreation have a lasting or growing appeal which do not call for a considerable degree of intelligence and mental effort. Interest in an activity is likely to lag when it no longer makes demands upon the mental powers of the participant.

A few examples will illustrate the important place which mental alertness plays in activities in which some other factor is usually considered more dominating. Playing bridge is essentially a mental activity, although it is frequently classed as a form of social recreation. To sail a boat requires that one study carefully his boat and its equipment, wind, waves, charts, and weather, and that he be constantly alert in observing conditions along the course. The actor studies not only his lines but also the character he is portraying. Collecting, whether it be stamps, books, or fossils, involves much reading and careful research. Making or performing good music is a matter of intelligence as well as of spirit and technique. Most games call for keen judgment and mental alertness, and the challenge of volunteer service as a club leader lies partly in the resourcefulness required to keep ahead of the group. Because the interplay of minds is stimulating and revealing, many of the so-called mental activities are most successful when carried on within a group. Mental games are also likely to be enjoyed more if two or more individuals work out the solutions together.

True, there are widely popular forms of recreation such as reading the pulp magazines, certain types of conversation, and listening to certain radio programs in which this appeal is entirely lacking. Nevertheless, the challenge which many other types of recreation activity afford to the mental powers of the participant accounts for their extensive and enduring appeal.

Emotional Experience.—The significant part which emotional response plays in giving to activities the character of recreation makes it a factor of fundamental importance. Unless participation in an activity brings a favorable emotional response to the individual, it is not likely to become for him a form of recreation. The emotional satisfactions which are sought and achieved through recreation are as varied in quality and scope as humanity itself. In so far as they are wholesome, inspiring, or rich in association, they make a contribution of the utmost importance.

On the other hand, the danger of many forms of commercial recreation lies in the fact that they have a strong appeal which is directed toward the individual's baser emotions. The thrill of tobogganing, the mass hysteria at the championship fight, the suspense of the reader as he approaches the climax of the novel or the solution of the detective mystery, illustrate how in certain forms of activity emotion plays a large or predominating part. Emotional satisfactions are shared by participants and spectators alike, although in different ways and intensities. To an unusual degree they are achieved by persons who observe an activity as well as those who actively take part in it. The tense excitement of the ninth-inning rally thrills the crowd in the stands as well as the players, the soul-stirring majesty of the symphony is felt by both musicians and listeners, and the emotion with which the actor plays his part or the warmth with which important issues are threshed out in the forum is shared by the audience. The strong appeal to the emotions which characterizes many of the offerings of the motion-picture theaters, dance halls, and sex and adventure magazines explains much of their widespread popularity.

There are other forms of recreation in which the element of emotion is less important but in which the emotional experience may be heightened by the recreation leader. For instance, a simple game like horseshoes or jackstones may arouse considerable feeling if a tournament is organized. Arranging for public performances or demonstrations by music, drama, or hobby groups may be the means of stimulating added enthusiasm. The emotional appeal of a party, beach picnic, or moonlight sail is greatly enhanced when it is conducted as a co-recreational project. This factor is present to a greater or less degree in all activities engaged in jointly by young men and young women.

Enjoyment of Beauty.—The universal love of beauty, like the craving for emotional experience, underlies many forms of recreation activity. Man seeks not only to create beauty but to experience it in its various forms. The love of beauty is closely associated with the desire to create, a desire which finds its highest fulfillment in objects of beauty. Beauty of landscape, scenery of unusual grandeur, gardens, works of art, poetry, stage designs, and outstanding architecture are among the most commonly understood mediums through which man's yearning for beauty finds gratification. These are not, however, the only means at his disposal. The grace and rhythm of the athlete, the dancer, and the skater, the sheer beauty of certain passages in orchestral and vocal compositions, the possibilities afforded by collecting articles of unusual line, form, color, and texture, and the still greater satisfaction which comes from shaping these objects with one's own hand, are merely illustrative of the ways in which recreation activities are characterized by the beautiful. The lure of travel and the drawing power of the parkways and large park and forest areas are due in large measure to the opportunities which they afford for seeing and enjoying places of unusual beauty. The satisfaction of this love of beauty is one of the primary functions of the art museum and the botanical garden.

It was because he saw these endless possibilities which recreation affords that Lorado Taft, the great artist, had a passion to help people "find recreation in the love and study of beauty." The failure of many recreation agencies to appreciate and serve this universal human desire accounts in part for the fact that their programs have not elicited a more favorable response from the public. The motion-picture theater, on the other hand, has been alert to satisfy this desire by bringing to the people pictures portraying natural scenery of supreme beauty, handsome, well-dressed actors, buildings, gardens, and home interiors of quality and luxury, and other objects of beauty which their own world of reality denies them.

Sense of Service.—Service is seldom considered as contributing to recreation because it is commonly associated with self-sacrifice, moral duty, and a sense of obligation, all of which run counter to the essential nature of recreation. Yet the satisfaction which results from serving our fellow men brings service within the sphere of recreation. This was clearly pointed out by V. K. Brown in his address before the Recreation Congress in 1937. In his opinion, just as the concept of recreation has enlarged to embrace those activities growing out of our intellectual curiosities, so it now includes service to our fellows. "We must think of outlets for the benevolent impulses of people in recreation just as we think of affording outlets for creative impulses or the physical activity impulses."[1]

People have discovered that membership on a recreation board or playground committee, helping with a community chest drive, or leadership of a boys' club, junior choral group, or playground team, brings returns in satisfaction comparable to those resulting from participation in the more common forms of recreation activity. An individual can secure just as great joy and satisfaction watching the development of a group of children in a club under his guidance as he can watching the unfolding of the flowers in his garden. Other satisfactions which result from participation in service activities are the fellowship which results from working together with or leading a group, and there is no lack of mental stimulation or of adventure for those who wholeheartedly engage in such activities. The genuine desire of children to help is illustrated

[1] V. K. Brown, "The Capture of Leisure for Use in Volunteer Service to Government and the Community," *Proceedings of the Twenty-second Recreation Congress,* National Recreation Association, 1937.

by the junior leadership and service groups found on many playgrounds. Experience has shown that the enthusiasm of the volunteer who is enlisted to help a club or group desiring to engage in his particular hobby often exceeds that of a paid leader.

Relaxation.—Relaxation is what many people who approach their leisure hours fatigued in body, mind, or spirit, most desire from their recreation. Like the other satisfactions previously considered, relaxation is achieved by different people through different forms of recreation. For some, an evening spent with a good book affords the ideal antidote for a hectic day. Others find relaxation in listening to the radio, attending the movies or theater, listening to a concert, or taking a brisk hike with an agreeable companion. Individuals whose work taxes their mental rather than their physical energy may relax in a game of volley ball, tennis, or bowling. Gardening, caring for pets, conversation, the enjoyment of nature, a social game, or just loafing are ways in which this desired end is attained by large numbers of people. Children rarely seek relaxation; it has a minor place among the satisfactions desired by young people, but it is a factor of primary importance in the recreation life of adults. The significance of the various forms of recreation activity cannot be fully appreciated except as their possibilities for relaxation are understood.

NINETEEN RECREATION PRINCIPLES

The recreation leader must have a knowledge of what people seek and find in various forms of recreation activity, but in addition he must know the kinds of recreation that are most popular and best meet the needs of large numbers of people. Some forms of recreation are so fundamental and have such a wide appeal that they are immediately recognized as deserving a place in every recreation program. The National Recreation Association has prepared a statement entitled Nineteen Recreation Principles which sets forth the fundamental needs of individuals in terms of specific recreation activities. This statement, based upon the association's long experience and approved by hundreds of leaders in American life, affords a foundation for the building of a recreation program for the individual or the community. The major desires and interests of individuals outlined in the preceding pages are given opportunity for fulfillment when the principles which follow are put into practice:

Every child needs to be exposed to the growth-giving activities that have brought satisfaction through the ages—to climbing, chasing, tumbling; to tramping, swimming, dancing, skating, ball games; to singing, playing musical instruments, dramatizing; to making things with his hands, to working with sticks and stones and sand and water, to building and modeling; to caring for pets; to gardening, to nature; to trying simple scientific experiments; to learning team play, group activity and adventure, comradeship in doing things with others.

Every child needs to discover which activities give him personal satisfaction. In these activities he should be helped to develop the essential skills. Several of these activities should be of such a nature that he can keep them up in adult life.

Every man should have certain forms of recreation which require little space and which can be fitted into small fragments of time.

Every man needs to know well a certain limited number of indoor and outdoor games which he himself likes so that there will never be an occasion when he cannot think of anything to do.

Every man should be helped to form the habit of finding pleasure in reading.

Most men should know at least a few songs with good music so that they may sing when they feel like it.

Every man should be helped to learn how to make something of beauty in line, form, color, sound, or graceful use of his own body. At least he should find pleasure in what others do in painting, woodworking, sculpture, photography, if he cannot himself use these forms of expression.

Every man should be helped to form habits of being active, of breathing deeply in the sunlit outdoor air. Man thrives best in the sunlight. Since living, not business, is the end of life, our cities should be planned for living as well as for business and industry. Sunlight, air, open spaces, parks, playgrounds, in abundant measure are essentials to any living that is to give permanent satisfaction.

Every man should be encouraged to find one or more hobbies.

It is of the greatest importance that every person be exposed to rhythm because without rhythm man is incomplete.

About one year in every ten of a man's life is spent in eating. It is of fundamental importance that this one-tenth of a man's life shall be so lit up by play of mind upon mind that eating shall not be a hurried chore but an opportunity for comradeship and for growth for the whole man. Eating should be a social occasion, in the home something of a ceremony.

Rest, repose, reflection, contemplation are in themselves forms of recreation and ought never to be crowded out by more active play.

Those recreation activities are most important which most completely command the individual so that he loses himself in them and gives all that he has and is to them.

Ultimate satisfaction in recreation comes only through one's own achievement, of some kind.

The form of one's recreation as an adult, often though not always, should be such as to use in part powers unused in the rest of one's life.

A man is successful in his recreation life in so far as the forms of activity he chooses create a play spirit, a humor, which to some extent pervades all his working hours, helping him to find enjoyment constantly in the little events of life.

The happy play of childhood is essential to normal growth. Normal men are most likely to grow from the children who have played well and happily. Normal men more easily continue normal as they keep up childhood habits of play. Participation as a citizen in the cooperative building of a better way of life in which all may share is one of the most permanently satisfying forms of recreation. That children and men and women may be more likely to live this kind of life, experience shows there is need for community action. Every community should provide opportunity for its children when they leave school to continue the musical and dramatic and other specialized recreation activities which they have enjoyed during school days. Community recreation programs should allow for a broad range of tastes and interests and varying degrees of mental and physical energy. Satisfying recreation, whether for the individual or for the community, involves careful planning.

A CLASSIFIED LIST OF RECREATION ACTIVITIES

There are many ways of classifying recreation activities. They are commonly grouped according to types, such as games and sports, crafts, or nature activities. Or they are classified by the age or sex of the persons participating, by space requirements, skill, cost, seasons, members taking part, or forms of organization. Indoor activities are segregated from outdoor, or individual activities from those in which formal or informal groups participate. Few recreation activities lend themselves to classification under exclusive categories. Therefore, although these groupings are useful to the recreation leader, their limitations as well as their values must be recognized.

There is considerable value, however, in listing the many forms of activity which are considered as recreation and in grouping them according to the general headings under which such activities are commonly classified. Such a list indicates the diversity and extent of the activities encompassed within the field of recreation; it brings together the many forms under the major types such as music, drama, and athletics; it is useful to the recreation worker in planning programs and in considering the forms of recreation which might appeal to a particular community or group. The following pages are therefore devoted to a list of the more or less common types of recreation, a majority of which are carried on by one or more departments. Certain characteristics which the activities under each type have in common afford a basis for grouping them. Many activities are of such varied nature that they might be classified under two or more types. Furthermore, some of the activities listed under a heading such as music may have more in common with the crafts or drama group than with the other music activities.

In studying the list which follows it should be kept in mind that some of the activities are primarily for children, others are particularly for youth or adults, while many of them appeal to people of all ages. Some of the activities are essentially for men and boys, others for women and girls. Large spaces and elaborate equipment are necessary for some kinds; others may be carried on in the home. Solitude is essential for the fullest enjoyment of some activities, while other forms yield their greatest satisfaction when engaged in by a group. Certain activities have an almost universal appeal, whereas others are enjoyed by comparatively few. Some are engaged in informally; others require a high degree of organization. Some are competitive in nature; others are not. Some require active participation for fullest enjoyment; others give equal satisfaction to the spectator and the participant.

It is clear that a list of activities, helpful as it is, does not alone provide a sufficient basis for planning a recreation program. In addition to being familiar with the range of activities, their forms, and adaptions, and to having an understanding of how the activities serve the fundamental interests and needs of individuals, a person must have a knowledge of the facilities which are necessary in order to carry them on and of the forms of organization under which the activities are likely to prove successful.

I. Active Games and Sports

Low organized games:

Bull in the ring	Poison
Cat and mouse	Prisoner's base
Club snatch	Relays
Fox and geese	Snow games
Hare and hounds	Tag games
Hide-and-seek	Three deep
Hill dill	

Individual and dual games and activities:

Athletic tests	Horseshoes
Badminton	Indoor bowling
Baseball fundamentals	Marbles
Baseball pitching	O'leary
Billiards	Paddle tennis
Boccie	Pool
Bowling-on-the-green	Quoits
Box hockey	Ring tennis
Clock golf	Roque
Croquet	Scooter racing
Curling	Squash
Golf	Stilt walking
Golf croquet	Table tennis
Handball	Tennis
Hand tennis	Tetherball
Hopscotch	Top spinning

Gymnastics and stunts:
  Apparatus work
  Bag punching
  Baton twirling
  Calisthenics
  Cartwheels
Group or team games:
  Baseball
  Basketball
  Batball
  Bicycle polo
  Broom hockey
  Cage ball
  Captain ball
  Crew rowing
  Cricket
  Dodge ball
  End ball
  Football
  Field hockey
  Hit pin baseball
  Ice hockey
  Kickball
  Lacrosse
Sports:
  Aquaplaning
  Archery
  Aviation
  Bicycle riding
  Boating
  Bob sledding
  Boxing
  Canoeing
  Coasting
  Crew racing
  Cross-country running
  Diving
  Dog sledding
  Fencing
  Field events
    Jumping
    Pole vaulting
    Throwing discus, etc.
  Figure skating
  Fly casting
  Hiking
  Horseback riding
  Horsemanship
  Ice boating

Gymnastic marching
Lariat throwing
Pyramid building
Rope jumping
Tumbling

Longball
Mass athletics
Net ball
Newcomb
Nine court basketball
Polo
Roller-skate hockey
Schlag ball
Shinny
Soccer
Soccer baseball
Softball
Speedball
Touch football
Tug-o'-war
Volley ball
Water polo

Ice sailing
Ice skating
Junior Olympics
Kite flying
Lifesaving
Model boat sailing
Motorboating
Motorcycling
Pistol shooting
Rifle shooting
Roller skating
Sailing
Ski hiking
Skiing
Skijoring
Ski jumping
Snowshoeing
Swimming
Tobogganing
Track events
Trap shooting
Wrestling
Yachting

II. Social Activities

Banquets
Barbecues
Barn dances
Basket suppers
Beach parties
Candy pulls
Card games
  Bridge
  Hearts
  Pinochle
  Pit
Clambakes
Community social evenings
Corn roasts
Conversation
Entertaining
Family or club reunions
Father and son dinners
Fun nights
Get-acquainted stunts
Grand march
Lodge and club meetings
Marshmallow roasts
Mother and daughter dinners
Old home weeks
Parties
  Barn warming
  Birthday
  Block
  College
  Costume
  Hard times
  Holiday
    Christmas
    Halloween
    New Year's
    St. Patrick's
    Twelfth night

Valentine
Washington's birthday
Masquerade
Progressive contest
Progressive games
Quilting
Sailing
Splash
Tacky
Pencil and paper games
Playing house
Pot-luck suppers
Scavenger hunts
Social dancing
Social games
  Buzz
  Crambo
  Going to Jerusalem
  I have a face
  Murder
Socials
Square dancing
Straw rides
  . Table games
  Anagrams
  Backgammon
  Camelot
  Caroms
  Checkers
  Chess
  Crokinole
  Dominoes
  Monopoly
  Parchesi
Treasure hunts
Visiting
Wiener roasts

III. Music Activities

Vocal:
  A cappella choirs
  Action songs
  Choruses
    Men's
    Women's
    Mixed
  Christmas caroling
  Community singing

Glee clubs
Informal singing groups
Mother singers
Opera groups
Quartets
Singing games
Whistling groups

Instrumental:
- Bands
- Bugle corps
- Chamber music groups
- Cigar box fiddlers
- Fife-and-drum corps
- Harmonica bands
- Instrumental choruses
- Kazoo bands
- Mandolin and guitar groups
- Ocarina choirs
- Orchestras
- Rhythm bands
- Saxophone ensembles
- String quartets or ensembles
- Symphony orchestras
- Ukulele orchestras

Performances:
- Band concerts
- Cantatas
- Glee club concerts
- Incidental music at pageants, festivals, etc.
- Music competitions
- Music festivals
- Old fiddler's contests
- Operas
- Operettas
- Oratorios
- Orchestral concerts
- Original song contests
- Radio concerts
- Victrola concerts

Miscellaneous:
- Composing music
- Listening groups
- Making musical instruments
- Music appreciation courses
- Music study clubs
- Music weeks

IV. ARTS AND CRAFTS

- Basketry
- Bead craft
- Block printing
- Bookbinding
- Cabinetmaking
- Cardboard construction
- Carving—soap, wood, bone
- Cellophane craft
- Cement craft
- Cookery
- Costume design
- Crayonexing
- Drawing
- Dyeing and coloring
- Electrical work
- Embossing
- Embroidery
- Etching
- Fabric decoration
- Home decoration
- Jewelry making
- Knitting
- Leather craft
- Making scrapbooks
- Making sports equipment
- Map making
- Mechanics
- Metal craft
- Millinery
- Modeling
- Model aircraft
- Model making
- Needlework
- Painting
- Paper craft
- Paper folding and cutting
- Photography
- Poster making
- Pottery
- Printing
- Quilting
- Radio
- Reed and raffia
- Rug making
- Sand craft
- Sculpture
- Sewing
- Ship model building
- Sketching
- Snow sculpture
- Stagecraft
- Tin craft
- Toy making
- Visiting art museums
- Weaving
- Woodworking

V. Drama Activities

Carnivals
Charades
Costume design
Costume dyeing
Doll fashion shows
Dramatic stunts
Fairs
Fashion shows
Feast of lanterns
Festivals
Follies
Impersonations
Informal dramatizations
Making scenery
Marionettes
Mask making
Masquerades
Mimetic exercises
Minstrel shows
Mock trials
Movie making
Movie shows
Musical dramas and comedies
One-act plays

Pageants
Pantomimes
Parades
Peep shows
Play exchange circuit
Play reading
Play tournaments
Playwriting
Playwriting contests
Punch-and-Judy shows
Puppetry
Radio dramas
Shadowgraphs
Song impersonations
Stagecraft
Stage lighting
Story dramatization
Story plays
Storytelling
Three-act plays
Traveling theater
Vaudeville acts
Water pageants
Workshop

VI. Dancing

Acrobatic
Ballet
Classic
Clog
Folk
Gymnastic

Eurhythmics
Interpretive
Natural
Social
Square
Tap

VII. Nature and Outing Activities

Astronomy
Auto riding for pleasure
Bee culture
Birdhouse building
Bird walks
Camping
   Auto
   Day
   Family
   Group
   Overnight
Caring for home grounds
Caring for pets
Exploration

Excursions or trips to
   Art galleries
   Industrial plants
   Museums
   Parks
   Places of historic interest
   Places of scenic interest
   Public buildings
Fishing
Flower arrangement
Fruit raising
Hiking
Hunting

Gardening
  Flower
  Miniature
  Vegetable
Log rolling
Making nature trails
Microscope study
Mountain climbing
Nature games
Nature hikes
Nature museum projects
Nature study, collection and identification
  Animals
  Birds
  Flowers
  Fossils
  Insects
  Marine life
  Minerals

Mosses
Reptiles
Trees
Nature tours
Pet shows
Picnicking
Pigeon clubs
Plant exchange days
Playground zoo or aquarium
Raising poultry
Sand play
Snow tracking
Travel
Traveling zoo, garden, or barnyard
Treasure hunts
Visiting zoos
Wading
Zoo contests

VIII. Mental and Linguistic Activities

Book clubs
Charm school
Creative writing
Debates
Diction
Discussion clubs
Foreign language study groups
Fortunetelling
Forums
Guessing games
Lectures
Listening to radio
Magic
Mathemagic
Mental games
Paper and pencil games
Poetry groups

Public speaking
Puzzles
  Crossword
  Jigsaw
  Others
Radio programs
Reading
Reading aloud
Reciting
Riddles
Spelling bees
Study groups
Storytelling
Tricks
Verse speaking choir
Writing letters

IX. Collecting

Antiques
Armor
Autographs
Bookplates
Books
  Almanacs
  Autographed
  By a particular author
  Cookbooks
  Early printing
  First editions

Manuscripts
Miniatures
  On specific subjects
Bottles
Buttons
China
Clocks
Coins
Dime novels
Dolls
Etchings

Firearms
Furniture
Glassware
Indian arrowheads
Lamps
Medals
Music instruments
Natural objects
  Antlers
  Butterflies
  Fossils
  Sea shells

Paintings
Pictures
Post cards
Pottery
Ship models
Silver
Stamps
Tapestries
Toys
Weapons
Woodcuts

X. Service Activities

Group leadership in settlement, boys' club, or playground
Membership on park, school, or recreation board
Service as scoutmaster or troop committeeman
Service as coach, official, or other assistant at playground or recreation center
Directing glee club, orchestra, dramatic group
Helping conduct a hobby. craft. or nature project
Assisting in organizing a holiday celebration, city beautiful week, or a campaign for a civic improvement
Assisting with publicity, money raising, or public relations program of a recreation or other agency
Forms of church activity

CHAPTER XV

PROGRAM PLANNING PRINCIPLES AND METHODS

The statement of recreation principles in Chap. XIV outlines the fundamental human needs in the field of recreation. Local governments, as previously pointed out, cannot assume the entire responsibility for meeting these needs but the municipality has a responsibility for providing recreation opportunities which will enable all its people to have a satisfying, abundant life. This does not mean that community recreation programs should be standardized. Widely differing conditions, urban and rural, climatic, racial, social, and economic, make variations in such programs necessary and desirable.

THE MUNICIPAL RECREATION PROGRAM

Factors determining the responsibility of the municipality in the field of recreation were mentioned briefly in Chap. IV. Joseph Lee defined the basic requirements of a community recreation program in the following words:

A community program for recreation must include the discovery of potential interests, talents, and skills, training and education in the creative use of leisure, and a wide variety of opportunities to serve the multitudinous interests—physical, social, musical, dramatic, nature, etc.—of different individuals.

Government, the collective agency of the people, is responsible for fostering and administering such a rich program of leisure-time opportunity.[1]

Cities are increasingly accepting this definition as a basis for building their programs. Typical of this tendency is the statement of a local recreation commission that its "basic policy is that of extending to the greatest possible number of people in all parts of the city, the most desirable and the most varied activities which it is practical to originate and sponsor." In spite of the fact that communities, like individuals, differ in their recreation interests and needs, it is nevertheless possible to set forth certain essential characteristics of a community recreation program. Some of these apply particularly to the recreation program of the municipal department; others relate to the program of any agency.

Criteria for a Community Recreation Program.—The following may be considered as essential criteria for an adequate community recreation

[1] "Certain Basic Assumptions Underlying the Work of the National Recreation Association," *Recreation*, October, 1934.

program regardless of the size or type of community. These criteria are based upon the principle that all such programs should minister to individual and social needs, afford outlets for creative expression, and contribute to the abundant life of all the people. Activities which all people need and which have a universal appeal as well as the individual differences in recreation tastes and interests are taken into account by the criteria which follow:

Every community recreation program should:

1. *Provide equality of opportunity for all.*—This democratic principle applies particularly in the field of recreation. For example, as far as possible all neighborhoods should have adequate playgrounds, not just a favored few. Facilities and programs should be sufficiently broad and well distributed to enable all the people to be served.

2. *Provide a wide range of individual choices in different types of activities.*—It should not be devoted primarily to a single type of activity such as athletic games and sports to the neglect of other interests, but should include games, music, arts and crafts, nature, drama, social recreation, and other activities.

3. *Continue throughout the year.*—People need recreation twelve months of the year and a responsibility rests upon the city to provide a year-round program. Activities are especially needed during seasons when other recreation opportunities are very limited.

4. *Serve all ages.*—It should provide for children of all ages, young people and adults, including the old folks. Facilities for golf should not be expanded if children's play needs are thereby neglected, and in meeting the demand for youth programs, the older people's needs should not be overlooked.

5. *Provide equally for both sexes.*—Until recently men and boys received a lion's share of consideration in the program, but women and girls are taking advantage of the increasing opportunities which are rightfully being provided for them. The promotion of recreation activities in which both sexes may participate together is also important.

6. *Encourage family recreation.*—Many forms of recreation tend to divide or separate the family. Occasions should be provided when the family can play together, either as a separate unit or with other family groups.

7. *Utilize fully all existing facilities.*—Facilities which are idle or restricted to one or two activities when they might afford many types of recreation use represent an economic loss as well as a failure to realize their potentialities for service. Their use should be planned to yield the maximum returns.

8. *Include passive as well as active forms of recreation.*—There are times when people do not desire strenuous activity. Some people find

their greatest satisfaction in quiet or passive forms. Programs should provide not only for vigorous participation but for the enjoyment that comes from watching, listening, or contemplation.

9. *Provide activities for different periods of free time.*—Noon hours, afterschool periods, week ends, holidays, twilight hours, recess periods, vacations—all afford opportunities for recreation which require consideration in the program. Unless these periods are utilized, the needs of many people are likely to be neglected and valuable opportunities for service lost. The recreation needs of men who work nights or who have unusual free-time periods must not be overlooked.

10. *Be related to other programs in the city.*—The service to be rendered by the recreation department is so great that it cannot afford to duplicate or overlap the recreation services of other agencies in the city nor to ignore them in its planning. Cooperation with other recreation agencies is essential in planning the program.

11. *Carry over the leisure-time skills and interests developed in the schools.*—It should make it possible and easy for young people who in school have played on athletic teams or taken part in drama activities to join groups in which their abilities may continue to find satisfactory expression.

12. *Provide activities of a progressive nature.*—Few people keep a long continuing interest in an activity unless it affords goals or objectives to be attained. Music, drama, or craft groups which function on different levels of skill or ability offer incentives for individuals to advance to higher achievement.

13. *Include activities that will persist at the adult level.*—So many activities—physical and others—can be carried on into adult life that they should have an important part in community recreation programs. Swimming, tennis, and volley ball, for example, satisfy this criterion, whereas track events and football do not.

14. *Offer possibilities for varying degrees of skill, aptitudes, and capacities.*—Some measure of success is necessary if the activity is to contribute to the individual's personality development and afford satisfaction. The person of average skill and the "dub," who represents a large majority of the people, must be provided for as well as the "stars," and they need even greater encouragement.

15. *Encourage individuals and groups to provide their own activities.*— If the program merely entertains people or provides activity at the playgrounds and centers, it is not serving its full purpose. It should stimulate interests and develop self-leadership so that individuals and groups can better provide for their own recreation life.

16. *Furnish outlets for the satisfaction of the desire for social relationships.*—Through the recreation program people should have opportunities

for developing the social qualities and for experiencing the fellowship which results from membership in a group.

17. *Recognize the different tastes and interests of the individual.*— Important as group activity and interest are, there should be phases of the program in which the needs and personal development of the individual receive consideration.

18. *Give people who participate a share in the planning and control.*— "Handing out" programs which can be taken or rejected is not a sound democratic process, nor does it contribute greatly to personal development. People desire and are entitled to share in determining the program. Only in this way does it truly reflect their desires and yield the greatest benefits.

19. *Place recreation opportunities within the financial abilities of all the people.*—Facilities and activities, no matter how great their potential value, render limited service if they are available only on payment of fees or charges which a large part of the population cannot afford. Many essential services must be free and easily accessible to all.

20. *Make possible the wisest use of available funds.*—In spending money for leadership, facilities, supplies, or other purposes, the best interest of the largest number of people should be considered. Unwise or extravagant expenditures for limited services deprive people who may need them most of essential recreation opportunities.

21. *Provide outlets for creative expression.*—Important as it is that large numbers of people be served in activities in which the creative factor has little significance, the needs of the group who desire outlets for their creative ability should not be neglected. The possibilities of creative expression in physical activities as well as in the cultural arts should also be recognized.

22. *Assure safe and healthful conditions for recreation activity.*—The contribution which outdoor bathing makes to health is widely accepted, but unless proper precautions are taken to assure safety and the purity of the water in which people swim, bathing may become a menace. Vigorous physical activity is essential to the growth of children and young people, but their health may be jeopardized by unwise participation or overexertion.

23. *Afford opportunities for developing good citizenship.*—There should be in the program activities in which team play is featured rather than individual achievement; where cooperation is stressed rather than competition; and where leadership and service opportunities are presented. Through the program people should learn by experience the values of cooperative effort and community service.

24. *Be based upon the specific interests and needs of the people in different parts of the city.*—It should not be patterned upon the desires of the

authorities or include their "pet" projects but rather should be adapted to different neighborhoods and reflect the genuine recreation requirements of the people.

25. *Be sensitive to changing conditions and needs.*—Flexibility is an essential quality in the recreation program. Though advance planning is necessary, programs should be subject to revision as experience proves change to be desirable.

IMPORTANT FACTORS IN PROGRAM PLANNING

The preceding criteria relate primarily to community recreation programs as a whole, but in varying degrees they apply also to individual program features. Program planning involves the setting up of a comprehensive, city-wide plan of recreation service, the selection of activities in the individual neighborhoods, playgrounds, and centers, and preparations for conducting activities such as music or athletics on a community-wide basis. Several factors play a large part in determining the success or failure of program planning. The significance of these factors and the principles which experience has proved practical in dealing with them are briefly presented here. Detailed suggestions for putting some of these principles into effect will be found in later chapters.

Interest.—Recreation programs must be built around the desires and interests of the people to be served. Many play interests of children are so universal that there is no doubt as to the appeal of fundamental play activities. The interests of young people and adults are more diverse, but even so, certain activities are known to be widely popular. Games and sports, for example, are greatly desired by most young men, social dancing is enjoyed by large numbers of people, a community Christmas celebration appeals to old and young, and the popularity of swimming among people of all ages has been demonstrated repeatedly. Numerous studies of the recreation interests and desires of children, youth, and adults provide data which is of great value in program planning, but a knowledge of neighborhood conditions is essential in planning the program for a particular play area or recreation center. This is especially true if adults are to be served. The use of check lists on which people may indicate their choice of activities is sometimes a helpful means of determining recreation interests. Neighborhood leaders can often advise as to projects which are most desired or which would bring the greatest satisfaction to and response from the people.

Common interests afford a sound basis for organizing recreation groups. After discovering what people would like to do, the recreation department helps those with similar interests to get together and to form groups centering around these common interests. Children are often eager for any new recreation experience but most adults are attracted to the program only when the first approach is through an activity which they already know and enjoy. Starting with this activity, the skillful leader can expand and enrich the individual's recreation life by creating opportunities for him to engage in other forms of activity which yield a pleasurable experience. In this way new interests are revealed and developed. Programs sometimes fail because the leaders stress activities which reflect their own interests and experience rather than those of the people to be served. The leader must obviously be familiar with and interested in whatever activity he is conducting if his leadership is to be inspiring and helpful to the group, but it is the interest of the group and not that of the leader which should determine the activities to be carried on.

Age.—The variation in recreation interests at different ages is another factor to be considered. The young child's favorite activities lose their appeal as he grows older and develops new desires and interests. Some activities have a brief interest span; others persist throughout life. Sports and activities involving strenuous physical exertion have an important part in the play life of children and youth. On the other hand, recreational reading, social activities, hobbies, social service, and home activities such as gardening assume places of greater importance in the leisure time of adults.

Programs must take into account the characteristics of the particular age groups to be served. Recognition of the differences in play interests at different age levels as recorded by thoughtful observers of children's play activities is fundamental in successful playground program planning. The playground program which attracts and holds the interest of large numbers of boys and girls of varying ages is one which provides a variety of activities selected from those that strongly appeal to various age groups. The length of play periods as well as the activities themselves must be adapted to the ages of the players, and the age factor is also important in arranging the conditions of play. Differences in the function and methods of recreation leadership in dealing with various age groups were pointed out in Chap. VI.

Planning recreation for children and youth is comparatively easy because they have so many vital common interests at the various age levels. Planning for adults is more difficult because until recently "education was not concerned with the development of individual skills and interests," and the recreation of the individual is influenced largely by the activities he engages in before he is eighteen. Even though many people acquire new skills and interests after reaching maturity, adults as a rule have fewer recreation interests than children. Age differences, however, are less significant among adults than children. Still most people like to play with persons of their own age because endurance, skill, and understanding are likely to be similar in the same age group, especially in the case of active games and sports. However, a person skilled in dramatics, crafts, or nature may be a most acceptable member of a group composed of persons interested in one of these activities, even though he is much older or younger than a majority of the members.

Sex.—Differences in the two sexes influence their interest and participation in many forms of recreation activity. Differences in the playground activities of boys and girls, largely the result of social attitudes, environment, education, and tradition, have been decreased markedly during the past generation. Boys and girls under ten years of age are much alike in their ability and interest in physical activity, and it is generally believed desirable for them to play together. After puberty is reached, however, boys usually excel in games and sports to a degree which makes competition between the sexes unsatisfactory. Programs for older girls feature activities in which form and skill are emphasized rather than strength and speed. Competition between older boys and girls in games involving bodily contact is avoided, but in the interest of social education the two sexes are brought together as much as possible in the nonphysical types of recreation such as dramatics, music, handicraft, social dancing, and outing activities, and in such games as tennis, bowling, volley ball, or badminton. After maturity there is a tendency for men and women to engage in common activities although differences in the interests of the sexes are still apparent. Games and sports play an important role in recreation programs for men, whereas social and more sedentary activities have a larger place in women's programs. Men enjoy crafts utilizing wood or metal, whereas needlework and interior decorating appeal more strongly to women. On the whole, however, individual skills, habits, tastes, and interests exert a greater influence than sex in determining the activities in which adults take part.

Place.—The places required for different forms of recreation vary from the quiet corner in which one reads a book to the extensive properties needed for hunting, horseback riding, or mountain climbing. Effective program planning involves a knowledge of the space requirements of various activities and a familiarity with the types which may be introduced successfully in available indoor and outdoor spaces. Small playgrounds do not make possible a program which appeals to the twelve- to fourteen-year-old boys although they may be adequate for younger children. The popularity of such games as softball and paddle tennis has been partly due to the fact that they require less space than baseball and tennis, activities which could not be provided on many playgrounds. Recreation programs are limited not only by the space available but by the facilities which it affords. An old-fashioned school offers few possibilities for recreation compared with a modern building designed for community use.

The suitability of a particular place for the activities carried on is an important factor in determining their success. In a gymnasium where the ceiling is low, where projecting walls create a hazard, and where shower and locker facilities are lacking or inadequate, a basketball tournament is conducted under a severe handicap. A play night is highly successful in the large clubroom or auditorium with attractive furnishings and a congenial atmosphere, but it is a failure when held in a drab and badly ventilated gymnasium. The easy chairs, flowers, piano, and fireplace in the community house lobby present a more hospitable appearance and create a more friendly atmosphere than the entrance hall of many a school center. More people attend a band concert if they can sit on the grass, or if seating facilities are provided, than if they are obliged to stand throughout the program. When events designed to attract only a small number of people are held in a large auditorium, the psychological effect is likely to be worse than when overcrowding occurs. These few illustrations indicate the importance of place and space in planning recreation programs.

Skill.—Successful planning involves the selection or adaptation of activities to the skill or ability of the people who are to take part in them. In starting a choral group of untrained singers it is unwise to introduce the same types of music as in a group composed of experienced musicians. People are likely to be discouraged if they undertake craft or other projects which are too difficult for them and in which they have little likelihood of achievement or success. Matching the beginner and the expert in tennis, golf, or handball brings satisfaction to neither player. Activities must be provided which call for varying degrees of skill in order that all who are interested may find a level at which they can participate successfully. As individuals acquire greater skill they can join groups engaging in the activity at a more advanced level. Careful classifications of participants in activities involving competition is especially important.

The successful recreation program lays special emphasis upon activities like coasting, hiking, community singing, and bathing in which large numbers may take part and in which no special skill is required. It also utilizes the possibilities of the ski jump, *a cappella* choir, and diving pool which serve a limited group with special skills. The desire of people to improve existing skills and to acquire new ones is satisfied by the provision of instructors in such widely different activities such as golf and puppetry, folk dancing and ceramics, boxing and debating. The teaching of fundamental skills involved in the individual and highly organized team games contributes to successful participation in these activities.

Time.—The significance of time in program planning is demonstrated by the well-balanced program in which activities follow in a reasonable progressive sequence without overcrowding of schedules or long periods of inactivity. Special events are arranged from time to time to provide occasions toward which groups may direct their efforts and demonstrate their achievements. Full advantage is taken of brief seasons when water and winter sports may be carried on, and of the opportunities which holidays and special days offer for developing novel and attractive features.

The dates for opening the season at the golf course, the indoor center, or the municipal camp are determined only after careful study of local conditions. In some neighborhoods playgrounds or centers need to be open for a longer season or more hours each day than in others. Some activities have a brief interest span whereas others can be carried on indefinitely. The recreation worker needs to know how much time is required for developing an activity to a point where it may be carried on successfully. He does not attempt to organize a symphony orchestra in a short summer playground season although he might develop one as a feature of the longer indoor center program. In arranging league schedules, games must be played often enough to sustain the players' interest and to permit completion of a satisfactory schedule within a reasonable period, but overcrowding must be avoided and time allowed for postponed games.

The time factor is especially important in arranging meetings and events. In an industrial community where people work near their homes, evening affairs may be scheduled at 7:30, but in a suburban community with many commuters it is difficult to start programs before 8:30. The working and living conditions and habits of the groups served must also be considered in selecting the time of day and day of the week for regular program features and for special events. Failure to realize that activities must begin and end on time has resulted in the failure of many otherwise excellent programs.

Timeliness in program planning is also taken into account by alert recreation workers who capitalize on widespread public interest in an event of unusual importance. An international yacht race, the arrival of a circus, a new scientific discovery, or an event of local or international significance may prove an incentive for developing some new phase of the recreation program or lend added interest to existing activities.

Size of Group.—Program planning involves a knowledge of the numbers of people who are needed to carry on different activities in a satisfactory manner. A few stamp or chess enthusiasts may form a highly successful stamp or chess club, but a community chorus or a play festival cannot be carried on unless a considerable number of people wish to take part. The size of the group is also a factor in scheduling the use of indoor or outdoor facilities, for a large organization or meeting will require an auditorium, whereas a small group may be accommodated in a clubroom. The use of large picnic center units is sometimes restricted to church, lodge, industrial, or other groups. Provided a certain number of individuals express a desire to engage in an activity, some recreation departments will furnish a leader and a regular meeting place.

The interests of the largest possible number of people deserve primary consideration, and emphasis is laid on activities and events which have a wide appeal and benefit many. Still, the interests of relatively small groups must not be overlooked. If a genuine and enduring interest in nature study can be developed in even a small number of children, or if a limited group can be given a satisfying experience through a craft class, the resulting benefit justifies the expense and effort involved. On the other hand, thoughtful recreation workers believe that a community or interplayground playday in which large numbers can take part has more value than a city-wide track and field meet in which only the best players participate.

The size of the group frequently influences the method of conducting an activity. A volley ball league may be organized on a large city playground, but on one serving a small neighborhood it may be possible to have only one team of a particular age group, in which case games must be arranged with outside teams.

Type of Organization.—The purpose of organization is to enable people to secure the greatest values and enjoyment from recreation activities. Some activities, such as reading, listening to the radio, playing cards, or creative writing require no special organization or promotion. Others like gardening or hiking are primarily self-operating, yet through organization their recreation possibilities are greatly enlarged. When the recreation department helps hiking enthusiasts form a club the activity takes on a new element of sociability, and when it organizes a horseshoe league or tournament, the game acquires an added incentive in the form of friendly rivalry. The skillful leader knows how to use organization as a means of bringing out these added values without causing the individual to lose any of the satisfaction which he gained from participation in the activity on an informal basis.

Many recreation activities, some of which involve competition, are most successful when carried on by highly organized groups. Baseball may be played informally but it yields the greatest satisfaction to most individuals when they play on a team enrolled in a league and competing on a regular schedule. An orchestra is likely to succeed only if its membership is restricted to persons who have suitable qualifications and who are willing to attend rehearsals regularly. Other group activities such as nature hikes, dances, parties, and fun nights do not require formal group organization. Many interests are best served through the organization of clubs, either around a specific activity such as bird study or puppetry or around a common age, neighborhood, or other interest. Individuals can carry on a hobby without any organization, but its possibilities for enjoyment are enlarged when it becomes a common center of interest of a hobby group.

The planning and conducting of special performances, exhibitions, or community celebrations, especially if they involve cooperation between different groups, require another type of organization. The drama group prepares zestfully for and awaits eagerly its public productions, the music group its concerts, the arts and crafts group its exhibits, and the sports group its carnival. The playground circus and festival require long and careful preparations but they afford opportunities for demonstrating many of the regular playground activities. The Christmas celebration, an occasion for combining the interests of many groups, likewise requires a high degree of organization.

Type of Community.—Nationality, race, occupation, education, economic status, and standard of living are factors which must be known in planning a recreation program for the people of a city or neighborhood. A program which appeals to a cultured, well-to-do community may fail in an industrial town with a high percentage of underprivileged foreign-born. Differences are less marked among children than adults, but a knowledge of home conditions is essential even in the planning of playground programs. Factory workers usually desire and require different forms of recreation than office workers. A program designed for a junior league may not meet the needs of a group of industrial girls. Lighted tennis courts are of limited value in a low-income neighborhood if equipment is not provided and a charge is made for their use. Foreign-born adults are reluctant to go outside their immediate neighborhood for recreation, so programs must be provided near their homes. On the other hand, in neighborhoods where most families own automobiles, people will drive a considerable distance to take part in a craft, dance, drama, or other group activity. The recreation worker in rural communities learns that most of the people prefer to create their own forms of recreation than to have talent brought in from the city.

Neighborhoods with many foreign-born afford a chance for featuring in their recreation program arts, crafts, games, music, and folk dances which are related to the former play life of the people. Rhythmic activities are stressed in planning for colored groups; debating, dramatics, and club activity appeal strongly to Jewish people; competitive athletics are popular with the Italians, and singing with the Welsh. Special aptitudes of national and racial groups are particularly valuable in initiating recreation programs for their benefit although an attempt should be made to broaden the interests of these groups and to draw them increasingly into community-wide activities.

Purpose.—The primary purpose of recreation program planning—to help individuals gain the greatest satisfaction, joy, and benefit from their leisure time—is achieved in many different ways. The recreation worker must know how to utilize activities to contribute to the attainment of this objective and also to serve other secondary purposes. The same form of recreation may serve different ends. For example, a band concert may be designed to give a large audience the enjoyment of listening to a professional band or to culminate a long period of effort by an amateur music group which has gained its greatest value from playing together. Arts, crafts, and nature activities are valuable not only because they furnish immediate satisfactions but because they may be the means of arousing interests which contribute richly to the life of the individual over a long period. Holiday celebrations serve to develop community solidarity and enthusiasm in addition to yielding direct satisfaction to the individuals taking part. Demonstrations of recreation activities may be arranged to interest others in the activities demonstrated or to helping convince the community of their value. Many activities offer possibilities for achieving objectives in addition to their primary purpose, but recreation leaders must be alert to prevent recreation from being exploited for unjustifiable or questionable ends.

Leadership and Funds Available.—Leaders should be selected because they have certain qualifications for the job, but naturally the particular qualifications of the leaders employed influence the type of program. A worker specially trained in music, for example, is likely to develop music activities to a greater extent than nature study or athletics. Where several workers are employed by a city, the selection of persons with varying abilities, training, and experience makes possible a well-rounded program. Because competent leadership discovers the capacities and skills of people in the community and enlists them for volunteer service, the availability of such persons in the locality is a factor in program planning.

The available funds often determine whether or not a particular project can be carried out. Program planning also involves a consideration of the unit costs of different activities. The number of people a particular activity will serve, the extent to which it may lead to continuing self-activity, its contribution to individuals and the community in happiness, safety, health, or civic value, and its possibilities of becoming self-sustaining must be considered in relation to its cost. In attempting to secure the maximum benefit from the funds available, it is necessary to determine the activities to be carried on, the centers to be operated, the length of season, the leadership to be provided, and other factors. Wise planning also recognizes that certain types of programs which appeal to influential groups in the community serve as foundations for increased financial support.

Other Local Recreation Programs.—Since municipal recreation budgets are never adequate for all local recreation needs, consideration must be given to the recreation programs of other agencies. If a boys' club is conducting a satisfactory indoor athletic program for boys, if a Y.W.C.A. is effectively serving industrial girls, if the schools are offering an adult education program which includes recreation activities, or if a community committee is sponsoring an annual Christmas celebration, the municipal department does not duplicate these services. It lends support to these projects and directs its major efforts into other channels. Cooperative planning among local agencies sometimes results in a redistribution of service in the interests of the entire community. If in a particular city swimming facilities provided by commercial agencies are satisfactorily serving a large part of the population but picnic facilities are lacking, it is obvious that the recreation department should attempt to secure areas suitable for picnicking rather than launch a campaign for swimming pools. Recreation needs and opportunities are so great that no recreation department is justified in ignoring the service already being rendered by other agencies.

A FEW PLANNING SUGGESTIONS

Thus far consideration has been given to the essential principles underlying the planning of community recreation programs and to the factors which influence planning. This chapter ends with a few comments on the problems and difficulties encountered in the practical application of these principles, and with a brief statement on the responsibility for program planning in the recreation department.

Responsibility for Program Planning.—The general planning of the municipal recreation program is essentially a responsibility of the recreation executive. Final approval of all phases of the program rests with the authorities to whom he is responsible, whether a recreation board, school board, city manager, or other official. Control over the program does not consist merely of approval of specific recreation activities and projects, but it is exercised through the assignment of personnel, the distribution of the department's funds, and the development of areas and facilities. Responsibility for the program as a whole must be fixed and centralized, but the advice and recommendations of the entire employed staff are sought, especially on parts of the program with which the workers are familiar and for which they have special responsibility. Supervisors in charge of a particular division such as athletics or drama usually submit for approval a tentative program for their respective divisions. Workers at the individual playgrounds and centers can make a valuable contribution to program planning because they are closer to the people than the executive and supervisors and therefore are likely to be more familiar with the desires and needs of the neighborhoods which they serve.

Giving the people of a community or neighborhood a share in planning the programs intended for their benefit is not only a democratic process but a means of assuring their active participation in the activities. Various methods of securing information as to people's interests and desires have already been mentioned. The formation of committees in the neighborhoods where playgrounds and indoor centers are located provides an effective means of giving the people a voice in program planning. These committees assist the employed staff in determining the interests and desires of the people in the neighborhood and in selecting the projects to be undertaken at the playground or center.

Administering the Program.—After the department's general program for the year has been prepared by the executive and approved by the board or other managing authority, it becomes the basic plan which the leadership staff is responsible for carrying out. No essential features can be changed without proper approval, although a considerable degree of flexibility in selecting and conducting the activities is essential in order to allow for varying neighborhood conditions or for unexpected developments. The workers must be thoroughly instructed as to the program, the methods to be followed in carrying it out, and the conditions under which variations are authorized. The degree of freedom allowed workers within the general limits of the program adopted depends largely upon their competence and experience and upon the amount of general supervision available. In a few cities where workers at large are employed, they are left comparatively free to work out their own methods and programs. As a rule, minimum program requirements are set up to which each unit must conform but within which workers may determine the particular activities that will best serve the people with whom they are working. Personal observation, regular reports, and the visits of supervisors are means used by the executive to keep him informed on the results attained at each center and to assure the proper conduct of the program.

A Definite Progressive Plan.—The word "planning" implies looking toward the future. Every progressive recreation department is considering plans not merely for the current year but for the years ahead. It is anticipating the future needs of the community and is taking steps to secure additional areas and facilities, is building up public support for an enlarged program, and is interpreting the significance of new recreation developments. Because the work of the department is largely dependent upon governmental funds for its support, plans must be related to the city's financial resources.   They must have flexibility in order that they may be readily revised to meet changing conditions and unexpected needs.   The depression revealed that many cities had given little consideration to ways of serving the greatly expanded leisure time of their people.   They were consequently unprepared to take advantage of the opportunity presented to them of utilizing Federal funds in the development of recreation areas and programs.   Today no city is justified in ignoring the present recreation needs of its people or in failing to give serious thought to the expanding programs which will be demanded in the years ahead.

Extremes to Be Avoided.—A study of municipal recreation programs indicates two common failures in program planning.   Perhaps the more frequent is revealed by the meagerness, drabness, and monotony of programs which include only a few activities covering a narrow range of recreation interests.   Such programs lack a varied, rich, creative, challenging quality.   Usually they provide outdoor activities at the summer playgrounds and a limited range of indoor center projects, but the cultural arts, nature, hobbies, forums, and community-wide features are largely or entirely neglected.   Such programs obviously fail to meet the criteria suggested early in this chapter and they indicate a lack of initiative, training, or understanding on the part of the recreation authorities, executive, and staff.

The other tendency is to schedule more events and to start more projects than can possibly be carried to a successful conclusion.   When this is done, many parts of the program are likely to suffer, and some activities are doomed to failure.   The result is disappointment, loss of interest, and a setback to the work as a whole.   Desirable as it is that the program afford a great variety of recreation opportunities, it is unwise to initiate activities and organize groups unless there is sufficient leadership, time, and interest to ensure the likelihood of their success.

Types of Programs.—Planning a municipal recreation program, as has been indicated, is not a simple problem.   The program itself has many aspects, each of which involves special procedures.   One phase of the program is the scheduling of the major city-wide events in which the department as a whole participates.   This type of program is often arranged on a month-by-month basis.   The planning of events to be carried on by each of the major divisions is another problem.   The athletic division, for example, determines the various leagues that are to be formed, and prepares a detailed schedule for each team in each league in each sport, determines the tournaments, special events, and championships to be held, and selects the dates for each.   Separate programs must be prepared for the playgrounds and indoor centers, indicating the dates of opening and closing and the special events to be carried on.   In addition, each playground and center requires some kind of daily, weekly, or seasonal schedule.   Each club or organization served by the department's staff and facilities prepares its own program more or less subject to the department's approval.   If there are swimming pools, golf courses, or other such facilities, definite plans must be made for their operation and use.

It is clear that program planning is a most important phase of the recreation department's work.   Knowledge of the criteria and factors discussed in this chapter and of the special requirements of various activities and groups is necessary to successful planning.   Obviously no specific rules can be laid down for the preparation of all types of programs.   The chapters that follow indicate some of the ways in which the principles suggested can be put into effect.

CHAPTER XVI

ORGANIZING AND CONDUCTING RECREATION ACTIVITIES

In the organization and conduct of activities the recreation leader reveals his knowledge of activities, his understanding of program planning principles, and his ability to apply them in the situation confronting him. The diversified content of the municipal recreation program necessitates the use of widely different organization and leadership methods.

WHY METHODS DIFFER

A few illustrations indicate why organization methods vary. A glee club may be started with a small group at a single center, but a community Fourth-of-July celebration involves a city-wide organization in which many groups cooperate and a large number of individuals take part. Teaching a game on the playground is a relatively simple process compared with the promotion of the same game on a city-wide basis or the organization of a municipal athletic association. Different methods are used in developing a miniature garden project for shut-ins and in building a nature trail. The techniques which make a charm school a successful girls' club project do not necessarily apply in setting up a sports program for industrial girls.

Even on a single playground the storytelling hour, the folk dancing period, the safety club, and the closing festival present widely differing problems of organization. Swimming places and band concerts are designed to serve large numbers of people, while the playground team and the club at the indoor center are small-group projects. Preparation for an opera or a community pageant extends over a period of weeks or even months; other events require little advance planning. Some involve a high degree of organization whereas others are more or less self-operating. Personal relationships and individual guidance by the leader play an important role in club programs, while in mass activities they are unimportant factors. These few illustrations indicate why the recreation department requires a staff with diversified training, resourcefulness, and ability in order to carry on successfully the various parts of the program.

STARTING A PROGRAM IN A CITY

Before describing how specific recreation activities are started and carried on, it may be well to consider a few essentials in establishing a municipal recreation program. In most cities a year-round recreation program is a gradual development. The first step is usually the operation of summer playgrounds. Indoor center activities, winter sports, swimming and picnic facilities, and perhaps hobby, craft, or music activities are added from time to time in response to demands from local groups. Finally, when the city recognizes the value and need of recreation opportunities under continuous leadership throughout the year, a recreation department is established under a full-time executive.

Guiding Principles.—One of the first duties of the agency or department responsible for developing a recreation program, whether for a single season or for the entire year, is to determine what activities and special projects should be carried on. Responsibility for recommending the features to be developed rests primarily with the recreation executive. Local conditions and requirements alone afford the basis for selecting them and they differ for every city, but there are a few principles which serve as guides.

1. The program should start with the activities that have been carried on before in the city and that have proved successful. Activities with which the people are familiar and which have proved popular in a given city serve as a nucleus around which to build the program. They assure participation in and support of these program features.

2. The program should be expanded in fields of universal or well-known interest. Observation and experience have demonstrated that children will respond to familiar playground activities; that young men want to play softball or baseball; that young people are eager to dance; that family groups enjoy picnicking; that swimming is a most popular activity. Well-planned and well-conducted programs run no risk of failure when built upon such activities.

3. New activities should be organized as the special interests or desires of the people are discovered and as new wants develop. In working with people the recreation leaders make it a point to discover what they want to do, encourage them to make their wishes known, and use every opportunity to draw out suggestions for new projects. Thus the growth of the program expresses the evolving desires and expanding interests of the people.

4. When the executive has had an opportunity to study the community, its resources, people, and needs, he should attempt consciously to develop new activities which will enrich the life of the community. Experience has shown that large numbers of people desire to participate in a particular activity only after they have had an opportunity to observe it or to experience the joy and satisfaction which it can bring them. The agency should therefore gradually introduce into the program activities for which there may be no popular demand but which are likely to be successful once their value has been demonstrated.

Considerable time is required for the worker to know his community, gain its confidence, and establish a well-balanced program of recreation activities. This is particularly true if the worker is employed only during the summer months or on a part-time basis. An adequate year-round recreation program is rarely possible except as a trained man or woman gives full time to thinking, planning, and working toward this end. In building the program the executive will seek and be guided by the advice of local leaders, of the people participating in the program, and of the community at large. He will, of course, be restricted by factors more or less beyond his control such as limitations of his budget, the areas and facilities at his disposal, and the qualifications of his workers.

Although the general planning of the program is primarily a responsibility of the executive, the work of forming the participating groups, of furnishing direct leadership and guidance, and of caring for the details involved in carrying on the activities, rests largely upon the rank and file of the recreation staff. Some aspects of their work will now be considered.

CONDUCTING ACTIVITIES ON THE PLAYGROUND

The playground is a most important feature of the municipal recreation system and even though it serves primarily a limited age group—from six to fifteen years—its operation calls for a variety of organization methods and leadership techniques. Every playground worker must determine the particular activities to be encouraged on his playground, the degree to which each should be organized, and the manner in which they should be conducted. Successful playground leadership requires an understanding of child psychology, children's play interests, and the techniques of organizing activities. In addition, the leader must recognize the limitations which the peculiar conditions found on most playgrounds place upon him in conducting a program.

Conditions Affecting Playground Operation.—In the first place, attendance is entirely voluntary; if the boy and girl do not enjoy the activities presented or like the way in which they are carried on, they do not attend. Child interest is at the heart of all successful playground activity, for unless the program appeals to the children, it is doomed to failure. Playground programs must compete with a great variety of home duties, other attractions, and distractions. As a result, attendance is seldom regular or continuous, especially during the summer months when family outings and vacations interrupt the playground schedule. For this reason, organization must be comparatively informal and groups must be more or less flexible. Eligibility requirements must be less strict in the case of playground teams than in school or indoor center leagues, and a more generous use of substitutes must be permitted. Otherwise teams would often find it impossible to meet league schedules.

The playground worker carries a greater responsibility than the leader of most other types of groups. He must consider the happiness and safety of a large number of boys and girls of different ages taking part in a variety of activities and scattered about a large outdoor area equipped with many types of facilities. In a situation of this kind the leader cannot give his undivided attention to a single group except for short periods because he must "keep an eye" on the other children and supervise the use of other facilities. He must develop skill in starting one group after another in different activities, and in giving intermittent leadership or supervision to these groups as need arises. Naturally, some forms of activity such as apparatus stunts require considerable guidance but others like apparatus play are largely self-operating.

Playground programs are also influenced by the hours the playground is open. Children are not likely to attend regularly nor spend many hours on the playground unless the program has variety and includes projects which sustain interest over a long period. Scheduling specific activities at a fairly definite hour encourages children to come for that period. Yet, because so many children drop in at the playground at different times of the day and for varying intervals, the program must be flexible enough so these children can fit into it readily. It must be made easy for children attracted to the playground by curiosity to be drawn into group activity. Otherwise they will not return. Children come to the playground bursting with energy and the leader must find suitable outlets for it. Because of the space limitations at most playgrounds it requires skillful planning to assure all groups a fair opportunity to engage in strenuous activity without jeopardizing the safety or enjoyment of the others.

Weather, too, is very important. Few playgrounds have ample indoor facilities for accommodating large playground groups, and in many cases the program must stop entirely whenever it rains. In planning for special events and in arranging schedules the possibility of rain makes it necessary to allow ample time for preparations and for playing postponed games. The leader is often obliged to make quick substitutions in the announced program when weather conditions make such action necessary or advisable. This applies not only to rainy days, but to periods when excessive heat makes it wise to postpone events calling for strenuous physical activity. Such adjustments are seldom necessary in the indoor center program.

These limiting factors should be kept in mind in reading the following statements describing some of the methods used in conducting forms of playground activity. For a detailed discussion of playground operation, see Chap. XVII.

Methods of Conducting Playground Activities.—Many activities such as play on the apparatus, in the sandbox, or in the wading pool are informal, individual, unorganized, and more or less continuous. They require occasional attention on the part of the leader in order to assure safety and fair opportunity for all the children, but primarily, they are free play activities. Even so, they may be made more interesting or purposeful if the leader teaches stunts on the apparatus, helps plan sand modeling projects, or organizes a wading pool carnival. Doll play requires no special organization, but it is likely to take on added significance if a group of children undertake a dollhouse-building project or form a group to make dresses for their dolls.

Team games for the older boys and girls are played informally by pick-up teams or unorganized groups but they are usually conducted on an organized basis, with the participants classified to assure fair, keen competition. Teams in the various sports compete in inter- or intraplayground or city-wide leagues. Crafts are usually carried on through informal, unrestricted groups which meet at regularly scheduled periods, although they are also engaged in by individual members of these groups at other times. Interest in a particular activity such as nature study or chess is sometimes stimulated or perpetuated through the organization of a club with officers, although participation in the activity is rarely limited to club members. Active games like paddle tennis and horseshoes, and quiet games like checkers and crokinole are played more or less continuously, but occasional instruction periods and ladder, kings, and ranking tournaments encourage participation and the improvement of the players' skill.

Special Events.—Unlike the activities previously mentioned, most of which are carried on throughout the season, are the special events which are arranged from time to time and which afford the highlights of the playground program. Some, such as the wiener roast, the treasure hunt, and the playground picnic are unrelated to the regular playground activities. Others, like the circus, closing festival, folk dance demonstration, and hobby show are built around them. The special events provide an objective toward which activities may be directed and afford an opportunity for demonstrating the results accomplished through the playground program. Typical of another type of special event is the music festival, playground dance, or father and son party, in which the parents of the children and neighborhood groups have an opportunity to participate.

The extent of preparation, kinds of organization, and leadership techniques used in conducting a few of these regular and special playground activities will be considered in the pages which follow.

Teams and Leagues.—Due to the popularity of team games and individual sports, facilities for these activities are likely to receive intensive use even though no special form of organization is provided. On the other hand, participation in team games is more interesting, satisfactory, and is sustained over longer periods when play is organized on a team and league basis. If at a playground the attendance and interest in a game are sufficient to enable several teams to be formed into an intramural league, the game can be made largely self-operating. However, unless at least four teams of fairly equal ability can be organized in a particular game, it is usually not practicable to form such a league, but one or more teams may be organized and entered in a district league.

In forming an intraplayground league the director estimates the number of teams that can be formed on his playground. Sometimes he chooses the boys to serve as captains and permits them to form their teams by selecting the members in turn from the group desiring to play. This method helps assure teams that are fairly matched. If, however, the boys have already formed their own teams, these are entered in the league along with others organized with the help of the director. After the teams are selected, the playground director assists the team managers or captains in arranging a schedule of games and in adopting a few simple rules to govern the play. Sometimes a board of arbitration consisting of the captain and elected representatives from each team is formed to hear disputes and to settle league questions that may arise from time to time. The idea of such a board appeals to the boys, provides valuable experience in cooperative action, and releases some of the director's time for additional projects. Officials such as umpires may be selected by the director or appointed by the teams themselves, subject to his approval. Well-marked fields, competent officials, the posting of individual and team standings, and strict adherence to schedules contribute to a league's success. An occasional game with an outside team or a baseball playday affords interesting variations in the league program. At the end of the season a short series of games is often arranged between the winning teams on the individual playgrounds for the purpose of determining the city playground championship.

Informal Group Activities.—Competition provides the chief incentive for team games and individual sports, but there are many play activities in which this element is relatively unimportant. Some of these are most enjoyable when organized on a club basis; others are equally successful when conducted as informal group activities. Folk dancing, tumbling, and crafts such as beadwork, knitting, or soap carving, are typical of activities usually carried on with informal groups rather than organized on a club basis. When interest in a particular activity is discovered or expressed, the playground leader forms a group, announces it as widely as possible, and encourages all boys or girls interested in the activity to join it. The leader sets aside definite periods each week when he can devote his time and attention to the activity, finds a suitable place on the playground for conducting it, and secures the necessary equipment or supplies. He discusses with the group projects which might be undertaken during the regular activity periods or between meetings. In some cases he helps set up definite goals to be accomplished or specific activities to be carried on.

The activities are conducted in an informal manner so that new children can join the group from day to day or week to week just as they would a low organized game. Under such conditions it is impossible to expect as high a standard of achievement from all members of the group as is attained in a small, restricted class, but on the summer playground regular attendance throughout the season, which formal group organization requires, is impossible for many children. Furthermore, boys and girls feel more free to attend meetings of informal groups and to try out the activities which are being conducted than they do to join formal classes. Usually one or more occasions such as a craft exhibit, folk dance exhibition, or tumbling demonstration are arranged during the season by members of the groups. Participation in these special events is usually restricted to members who have attained a certain degree of skill or who are willing to rehearse regularly in preparation for them.

Playground Clubs.—Nature study, puppetry, and gardening are activities which are often organized on a club basis. When a leader finds that several children have a great interest in nature, for example, he knows that this will take on added significance for the individual children if it is shared in a nature club. He also knows that the organization of the club will tend to arouse the curiosity of other children. So a nature club is formed, officers are elected, and tentative plans are considered for the season's activities. These plans must be elastic but the program becomes more purposeful when it is decided that the club will conduct nature hikes, make collections, label the trees on the playground, conduct a pet show, or sponsor a birdhouse-building contest. These activities are generally open to club members and others alike, but the members feel a greater sense of responsibility for the success of the projects. The playground leader attends the regular meetings of the club and supervises its various activities. He also encourages the members to continue their study of nature between meetings and away from the playground.

The procedure is very similar in the case of other playground clubs. Interest is the only qualification for membership, and as a rule all playground children are free to participate in most of the activities. Organization must be very informal on the summer playground with its short season, shifting child attendance, and limited leadership staff. Formal club organization is more feasible at the year-round playground or indoor center where the longer season permits the undertaking of more challenging club projects and where the leader has a better opportunity to know and to work closely with the members.

The Circus or Festival.—Unlike the playground activities previously mentioned, which are carried on with more or less regularity throughout the playground season, are the special events which are arranged from time to time. Outstanding examples are the circus, festival, or playday, which often provide the climax to the playground season. Sometimes these are city-wide events, but there is a growing tendency for each playground to conduct its own closing program. This type of feature involves cooperative planning on the part of the leaders and many playground groups and since a period of careful preparation is required, plans must be made weeks in advance. A city-wide event necessitates a more complex organization because many playgrounds must be assigned their part in the program, transportation must be provided, and arrangements made to care for large numbers of children at the place where the event is held. In any case, preparations involve the planning of the program and the selection and training of the participating groups. Additional items of importance are the preparing of posters and other announcements, providing the necessary equipment, costumes, and properties, securing a permit for the parade, and arranging for seating facilities, lights, ushers, programs, and police protection.

Responsibility for the circus preparations is often shared by a committee of playground children, with subcommittees made responsible for specific features. The arts group prepare posters announcing the event; animals for the parade are constructed in a handicraft class, and costumes in a sewing group. Tumbling and acrobatic stunts, folk dances, dramatic skits, music, and other features demonstrate regular playground activities. Because the circus affects so many children and includes so many events, there is some danger that it will be permitted to dominate the regular play activities, that undue emphasis will be laid upon circus preparations, and that children will be urged to participate in circus projects when they prefer to take part in other play activities. These undesirable results can be avoided by intelligent advance planning.

Few features in the municipal recreation program furnish greater enjoyment to participants and spectators alike than does the playground circus or festival. Not only do many children take part, but they enjoy the opportunity which the occasion affords for dressing up and performing before their parents and friends. The circus or festival is an effective and integrating project which serves as a culmination of the normal summer activities and gives the public a review of the playground program. Many adults enjoy assisting the leaders and children in staging events of this kind. For these reasons it is essential to make plans carefully, prepare a schedule for the completion of the various preliminary arrangements, check all details thoroughly, and conduct the circus in a manner which brings satisfaction to participants and spectators alike and credit to the playground authorities.

CONDUCTING INDOOR CENTER ACTIVITIES

In some respects the methods of organizing and conducting activities on the playground also apply in the indoor center but in many ways the problems of the center are very different. Most of the individuals using the center are young people and adults, whereas the playground is attended largely by children. Many adults have definite recreation interests, but they do not make them known as easily as children do, and they tend to be less ready and willing to mingle with strangers. Children, on the other hand, are much more anxious to try out new activities and to join play groups.

Because the playground is an open, out-of-door area where the activities are visible to all who pass by, there is a much greater inducement and tendency for children to "drop in" at the playground than for adults to visit the indoor center where the activities are carried on within a building. In the center there is less overlapping in the types of activities carried on in the various rooms than on the playground areas; often rooms are devoted to a single specific use. Activities tend to be more highly specialized in the center than on the playground because the indoor center season extends over a much longer period. It is therefore possible to organize more elaborate projects and more specialized groups, which can prove successful only if carried on over a considerable period.

Many adults come to a center after a hard day's work feeling somewhat fatigued and desiring relaxation, while most children come to the playground to engage in strenuous play activities. The weather is a less important factor in center programs inasmuch as the activities are carried on indoors. Another difference affecting program planning at many centers is the fact that most of the leaders are part-time workers responsible only for a specific phase of the program, whereas most playground workers, at least during the summer months, give all of their time to the general play program. Some of these differences between conditions on the playground and at the center help to explain the differences in organization methods.

TYPES OF CENTER ACTIVITIES

Most community center activities can be classified according to the way in which they are organized and carried on. Informal, continuous, self-directing activities are provided in the rooms devoted to reading or quiet games. Activities such as drama, chess, nature study, or hobbies are conducted on a club basis although some clubs have a wide range of interests. Class organization is used for activities involving instruction such as tap dancing, millinery, public speaking, or certain kinds of crafts. Athletics are carried on by various center groups or by teams formed outside but permitted to use the center's facilities. The center program also includes activities which are scheduled from time to time and to which the entire neighborhood is invited, such as holiday celebrations, parties, social dances, and demonstrations. Methods of organizing a few of these activities will be considered briefly. A detailed discussion of indoor center operation is found in Chap. XVIII.

Informal Activities.—Organization of informal activities consists primarily of providing the facilities and equipment, of maintaining a hospitable and attractive atmosphere, and of assuring to all who visit the center a cordial welcome and a pleasurable recreation experience. Through the game room, reading room, or lobby, many individuals get their first impression of the center. If they enjoy their experience and meet congenial people, they are likely to return and ultimately to participate in other features of the center program. The leader therefore encourages visitors to use the equipment, provides instruction in its use when necessary, helps the newcomers to make the acquaintance of others and to join in activities with them, finds out their interests and desires, and encourages them to join congenial groups and to take part in other center activities.

Clubs.—Clubs play an important role in the center program. They differ from many other center groups in that they usually have officers and a constitution, keep attendance records, charge dues, and set up qualifications for membership. Most center clubs meet weekly, and a suitable room is assigned for their exclusive use during these meeting periods. Some clubs devote themselves to a particular interest which provides the basis for the organization; others consist of neighborhood groups who just want to do things together and to belong to some group. Different leadership methods are used in organizing and conducting these two types of clubs.

The Special Interest Club.—The special interest club is often started by the center director because several individuals have expressed a desire for a particular activity, whether it be bird study, model aircraft, or photography. Sometimes a special program or lecture at the center or an event of local or national significance gives rise to a desire to form a club, to study a particular subject, or to engage in an activity. Before organizing the club announcements are posted conspicuously in the center and are made at meetings of center groups and at neighborhood gatherings. Recruits are enlisted from individuals taking part in the informal activities or belonging to the general interest groups. When a club is being organized it is customary for a member of the center staff to be assigned as leader or counselor, depending upon the type of group and the age of its members. Application forms which have been devised for use at many centers supply the director with information about the constituency of the group that is useful in preliminary organization plans.

The degree of organization desirable varies with the size of the group, its primary purpose, and the ages and abilities of its members. Formal organization procedure is less important in the special interest club than in the club formed around a natural neighborhood group. Details are worked out by the group in consultation with the leader, subject to modification as the club develops. The success of the club program depends in large measure upon the extent to which it reflects the genuine interests and desires of the members and affords them opportunity for active participation in the particular activity around which interest centers. A leader skilled in this particular field is necessary; in an adult club he may be chosen from within the group. A fairly definite program with specific objectives can often be worked out for this type of club.

The General Interest Club.—The club formed around some natural motivation or group consciousness usually has a different origin from the special interest club. The group is often formed outside the center by the members themselves and its first contact with the center director is when it seeks the use of center facilities. On the other hand, the suggestion that a group of boys, girls, or young people in the neighborhood form a club and make use of the center may originate with the director or with individuals taking part in the center program. In any case a leader is assigned to assist the group in developing its club organization and membership and to help the members plan and carry on a program based upon their common interests. Young people like this type of club; adults are more likely to join a group formed to engage in a specific activity.

The members of such a club are usually brought together by common factors of age, nationality, class, or neighborhood, and they are held together by a strong sense of group interest and loyalty. They are anxious to do things together; the particular activity in which they engage is of secondary importance. Unlike the special activity club where the chief interest of the members centers about a specific activity, whether it is bowling or debating, checkers or boat building, the desires of its members often must be discovered or stimulated by the club leader. Skilled leadership is required in selecting activities which will enlist the continuing interest of club members and in developing projects which afford progressively satisfying participation.

The objectives in organizing such a club are to preserve the natural group relationships and to afford opportunities for the individual members to participate in constructive, joyous recreation activities with the group.

The club leader has a real responsibility, however, not only for maintaining the group, but also for guiding its members into activities outside the club which may have special value for them. A boy who shows a special aptitude for music is therefore encouraged to join one of the music groups, and a girl who has unusual artistic ability is helped to find an opportunity for developing it. In some instances it may even be advisable to suggest that an individual drop out of the club entirely if it is clear that he will gain more from some other activity or group. In any case, the club leader needs to recognize the limitations of the small, exclusive club and to bring its members into contact with a variety of personalities, interests, and group activities afforded by the center. One means of accomplishing this is by arranging events in which a number of clubs cooperate, such as a father and son dinner.

Community Nights.—In marked contrast to the indoor center's clubs and classes, which are composed of comparatively small groups, are the events conducted for the entire community. In many centers a social recreation evening is held regularly every week or two for the persons attending the center and also for the people of the neighborhood. Some community nights take the form of a music festival, Christmas pageant, hobby show, or a gymnasium demonstration presented by center groups; others, such as a dance or play night, are designed to secure participation by all who attend. Some programs include both features. The special events are usually arranged by center groups such as drama clubs, athletic teams, or music organizations; sometimes they are sponsored by an inter-club or center council. The preparation for these events is a factor in planning the programs of the individual clubs and affords occasions for cooperation between the various center groups. If properly planned and well conducted, these features serve to inform the neighborhood about the center and to enlist recruits for the center activities.

In planning and publicizing these special programs as well as the regular community night features such as dances and parties, the most effective means of informing the people in the particular neighborhood are utilized. In selecting the best time for holding them, other neighborhood events and the habits of the people are considered. Besides preparing an attractive, well-presented program, the director must make sure that the people receive a cordial welcome, that facilities are provided for checking wraps, that the room where the event is held has a suitable temperature and adequate seating facilities, that the program starts and stops at a reasonable hour, and that the people are given some opportunity to participate. In some neighborhoods where parents cannot attend these programs unless they bring their young children, a leader conducts play activities for the children in another room while the community programs are being carried on in the auditorium or gymnasium.

ORGANIZING SPORTS PROGRAMS

In most cities sports attract a larger number of individuals of all ages and of both sexes than any other type of recreation activity. For this reason and also because sports require special areas and facilities, include so many widely differing types of activities, and involve many forms of competition, the organization of the sports program is an important and complicated procedure. It must provide for the varying ages and skills of the players, furnish opportunity for those who wish to participate informally and those who desire highly organized competition, assure the maximum use of areas and facilities, take into account not only the programs at the individual centers and areas but the promotion of city-wide activities, and include individual and group sports as well as team games. Much has been written on the problems involved in organizing and conducting athletic games and sports so only two aspects of sports organization will be mentioned here—city-wide league organization and the promotion of individual sports. Several municipal sports programs are described in Chap. XXI.

Adult City-wide League Organization.—In initiating a city-wide organization in a particular team game, a meeting is usually called by the recreation department to which all groups interested in it and all existing teams are invited to send representatives. At the meeting the advisability of organizing one or more leagues is discussed and, if the interest warrants, plans are made for the setting up of such leagues on some basis which will assure keen interest and satisfactory play. Teams may be classified according to a common factor such as by industries, churches, clubs, or neighborhoods, or they may be grouped on the basis of skill in order to assure keener competition. League organization involves the creation of a more or less formal association, council, or committee to assume responsibility for working out the many details and for conducting the leagues. This group is comprised largely of representatives of the various teams, with a member of the department staff serving as secretary and adviser.

Among the details for which this body is responsible are the grouping of teams into leagues, adoption of rules governing eligibility and other conditions of play, determination of the length of the playing season, arrangement of team schedules, provision for the making and consideration of protests, selection of capable officials, fixing and collection of entry fees, disposition of funds, and the conduct of a post-season inter-league championship series. Since a large degree of democratic control within the leagues is desirable, major responsibility for determining their policies and administering their activities rests with the representatives of the teams participating. However, since the leagues are a part of the municipal recreation program and use the recreation department's facilities, it is necessary that their actions be subject to department approval.

Responsibility for initiating athletic leagues and for guiding them throughout their season of play is assigned to a particular member of the recreation department staff, usually the supervisor of athletics. He calls together the team representatives at the beginning of the season, helps them form their organization, and meets with the league committees and officers as they make plans and determine policies. He advises the group as to the department's policies, puts into effect the plans adopted by the group, and assigns the use of fields, courts, or indoor facilities to the various teams at specified times throughout the season. One of his important functions is to arrange training courses for league officials where such action seems necessary. He encourages widespread participation in the sport and assures all teams which desire to play an opportunity to enroll in a league and share the use of the department's facilities.

Individual Sports.—The program of individual sports carried on at the playgrounds and centers consists primarily of informal participation and of contests and tournaments arranged by the directors. It doubtless accommodates more people than any other phase of the department's sports program. The specific activities engaged in vary from one center to another, depending primarily upon the available facilities and the sports which are popular in the neighborhood. Participation in the activities is limited largely to people living in the vicinity.

Another way in which the recreation department encourages and facilitates participation in individual sports is through the development of special centers or areas devoted to a particular activity. A centrally located, well-lighted battery of horseshoe courts, for example, attracts players from all over the city, is used for important local and intercity matches, and stimulates interest in the sport. Classes are formed for group instruction in golf, tennis, archery, or some other sport, either free or at a nominal charge. Such classes are welcomed by people who have been deterred from playing a game because of their lack of skill. The rental of equipment such as golf clubs by the recreation department has encouraged many individuals to try the game who otherwise would have hesitated to do so because they lacked the equipment.

One of the most effective methods of stimulating public interest in a particular sport such as badminton, shuffleboard, or skiing is through the organization of a city-wide club or association which undertakes to promote a particular activity. The recreation department cooperates by helping form the organization, by encouraging groups at the public play centers to be represented in it, by clearing schedules and policies, by placing its facilities at the association's disposal for championship and other tournaments, and by utilizing new ideas for instruction in and conduct of the activity. Frequently a city-wide group of this type can revive a sport, the popularity of which has waned due to lack of adequate promotion. As an example, canoeing in the lakes of a New Jersey county park system was given a new and expanding interest through the formation of canoe clubs which organized regattas and conducted water carnivals. In many cities the recreation department has helped form local organizations patterned after and affiliated with such national bodies as the National Public Parks Tennis Association.

HIKING

Hiking represents a type of outdoor activity which differs from most forms of sport in that the element of competition is very small and it requires no special equipment, expense, or skill on the part of the participant. The membership in hiking clubs is therefore likely to be more representative of different sections of the city's population and to include persons with a wider range of ages than many other recreation groups. Most municipal hiking clubs are recruited from all parts of the city and are composed of both men and women. Unlike most of the activities previously described, hiking is not dependent upon facilities provided by the recreation department although it sometimes makes use of them. It is one of the few outdoor activities that may be engaged in the year round. A few aspects of its organization are illustrated by the experience of local hiking clubs.

One of the best known municipal hiking groups is the Minnehikers, affiliated with the Minneapolis Park Board. It was organized in 1920 when a group of park officials and others interested in the out-of-doors began a series of Sunday afternoon hikes, each of which included some part of the city park system. The original idea was to acquaint the people of the city with the beauties which lay within its boundaries. Out of this small beginning grew the club. As the demand for more hikes increased, several Sunday hikes a month were held and Wednesday night hikes were added to the schedule. At first all programs were arranged and led by a representative of the Park Board, but gradually a share of the responsibility for planning and conducting them was turned over to the members of the group, and finally a committee was appointed to take charge of the schedule. The club has grown in membership and in the scope of its activities so that now it has a board of directors and several standing and special committees. Hikes are conducted throughout the year and the club program is varied with skating and sleigh-ride parties, canoe trips, week-end outings, Friday night dinners, dances, and other social occasions.

There are several reasons for the success of certain municipal hiking clubs. Although they are organized on a democratic basis and the planning is in the hands of the club members, continuous leadership and guidance are provided by a worker on the recreation department staff. The department office usually serves as the club's headquarters. The activity is inexpensive, membership fees are low, and even in the case of the special outings costs are kept at a minimum. Among the methods used to maintain interest and to encourage sociability between hikes are the arranging for social events and the publication of a club yearbook. The fact that most hikes average only about six miles makes it possible for all who desire, to take part; occasionally more strenuous outings are arranged for members who prefer them. It has been observed that even in the case of older clubs which have attempted to enlarge their membership there is a tendency of the group to remain at about the same size. This is perhaps due to the fact that when a hiking group becomes much larger than forty it becomes unwieldy, cannot be accommodated in a single bus or served meals quickly. The hiking club is an excellent example of the type of organization which crosses neighborhood, age, and natural group lines, and which draws together people with an enthusiastic interest in a simple form of recreation.

SPECIAL COMMUNITY EVENTS

Most recreation department activities are carried on with more or less regularity throughout a season or the entire year. Just as feature events are scheduled from time to time at the playgrounds and centers, however, special community programs are also arranged which serve the entire city. In some cases these programs, which usually attract large numbers of participants and spectators, are organized entirely by the recreation department; in others they are projects in which many agencies cooperate. Because they present unusual problems of organization, and the methods of conducting them are different from others mentioned in this chapter, a few of these activities are described briefly.

The Halloween Celebration.—Typical of the projects which attract large numbers of people is the community-wide Halloween celebration. In the smaller cities it may be organized as a single unit; in larger ones the celebration is conducted on a district basis. The methods and activities used differ widely, but important features include a parade in costume for boys and girls of all ages, with appropriate prizes for costumes of various types, a huge bonfire, which may provide the incentive for a clean-up campaign, stunts, and singing around the bonfire. Following the parade the participants may assemble in a large auditorium for moving pictures, games, music, and refreshments. Such a celebration furnishes the thrills and excitement which the children desire and consumes the energy which otherwise might be spent in the destruction of property. It is at once a joy for the participants, a spectacle for spectators, and a civic asset. Its success requires effective advance publicity, a wisely selected route for the parade, adequate policing, careful planning of the events following the parade, preparation for providing and serving refreshments, and competent leadership. Most important of all, the entire celebration must be carried on in a spirit of hilarity appropriate to the holiday.

Outdoor Dances.—A very different form of outdoor activity affording recreation for large numbers of participants and spectators is the program of outdoor social dancing. Special pavilions have been constructed for this purpose, although roadways, tennis courts, or other cement surfaces are often used. Essential for this type of popular event are a suitable well-lighted location where the groups can be accommodated both on and off the dance area, a good orchestra which plays carefully selected music, a sufficient number of well-trained leaders to supervise the dancing, and the presence of one or more policemen. It is necessary to formulate and strictly enforce a few simple rules of conduct covering such points as cutting in, the wearing of coats by men, and clearing the dance area at the end of every dance. Outdoor dancing has been highly successful in many cities where it has become a regular feature of the summer program.

Christmas Caroling.—In several cities the recreation department organizes and conducts a community Christmas caroling campaign; in others it cooperates with local agencies in the project. Unlike the outdoor dances, preparations for a Christmas caroling program bring into play the active cooperation of large numbers of people. For this reason it is often jointly undertaken by a group of community agencies even though the recreation department assumes the major responsibility for the project. The great care required in preparing adequately for such an event is apparent from the following list of steps which need to be taken: enlisting the participation of vocal groups, especially church choirs, or forming groups in the various community agencies or neighborhoods; securing leaders and meeting places for rehearsals; dividing the city into districts; listing the names and addresses of shut-ins and institutions and preparing lists by districts; assigning choral groups to districts near their homes, if possible; selecting carols to be learned and sung; providing music and song sheets; furnishing transportation for certain caroling groups; arranging for publicity and preparing costumes for the carolers. It is clear that a caroling campaign calls for cooperation on the part of many organizations and individuals. Paid workers with the recreation department and other agencies usually carry the major responsibility for the campaign, but many of the tasks are performed by volunteers.

Nationality Programs.—The racial and cultural programs sponsored by the Hartford Park Department illustrate how the recreation department serves large numbers of people by encouraging the use of its facilities for programs presented by community groups. Incidentally they also show how a current event of wide public interest—in this instance the State Tercentenary celebration—may be used as an occasion for introducing unusual features in the recreation schedule. At a meeting of representative leaders of the various local racial groups, called together by the recreation supervisor, it was arranged that each group would prepare and present an evening program representing the folklore, music, traditions, and costumes of its particular nation or race. The park department agreed to make available for these programs its open-air dance pavilion with large, well-equipped stage and platform, and to furnish lighting, adequate policing, seating facilities, and its own personnel to serve as ushers and attendants. Selection of the programs was left entirely in the hands of the various racial groups—an arrangement which added zest to the preparations, enabled the groups to enlist their own leaders and directors, and afforded variety in the productions. The enthusiasm with which the groups rehearsed and the enjoyment which they received from the opportunity to present in public the dances, songs, and costumes of their native lands exceeded even the wide acclaim which the series received.

Through this type of program the recreation department can draw out hidden talents, develop public respect for the various racial groups, enlist participation on the part of many who otherwise have no share in the recreation program, encourage foreign-born groups to perpetuate their native recreation heritage, and afford entertainment to large numbers of spectators—all at a comparatively small expense to the public.

THE INCIDENTAL USE OF RECREATION ACTIVITIES

Thus far in this chapter it has been assumed that the activities described were organized to meet a major interest of the individuals taking part in them. Thus baseball leagues are arranged for the baseball teams; archery is organized for the archery enthusiasts; the hiking club affords recreation opportunity to persons interested in hiking. Most of the recreation department's activities are organized to serve directly particular interests of individuals and groups. At the same time, the recreation leader needs to appreciate the extent to which and the ways in which one form of recreation may contribute to activities of a totally different type. This is especially true of certain simple music and drama forms which may be introduced into a great variety of other recreation projects.

There are many possibilities for introducing music in a community center, for example, apart from the special music groups and projects. Gymnasium activities such as mass gymnastics, marching, or dancing are enlivened by the use of a piano or by singing on the part of the participants. Community singing and solo or group numbers between the acts of a play in the auditorium tend to bind the audience together and to make the intervals pass quickly and pleasantly. Singing at dinners or club meetings and victrola or radio concerts in craft or quiet game rooms are other examples of the informal use of music to enrich recreation activities. The skillful leader is continually alert to take advantage of such opportunities. Often the results from the incidental use of such activities in the program are more successful than when efforts are made to introduce the activities on an organized basis. Group singing may be more spontaneous and enjoyable on a boat ride, on a hike, or around a campfire, than if the group were brought together for a period of singing. Such occasions may prove the means of arousing interest in activities of a more formal type.

The few illustrations presented in this chapter suggest the variety of problems faced by recreation departments in organizing and conducting different phases of the municipal recreation program and describe organization methods which have proved successful in presenting several forms of recreation activity. Additional detailed information on the organization of major types of service will be presented in later chapters.

PART V

THE OPERATION OF AREAS AND FACILITIES

Leadership, areas and facilities, and activities are the principal elements of the municipal recreation program. The program in most cities consists largely of activities furnished at playgrounds, recreation buildings, indoor centers, golf courses, bathing beaches, swimming pools, and other facilities operated under the leadership staff. The operation of these properties gives rise to many complex problems, the solution of which involves the use of divergent methods and procedures. Part V deals briefly with some of these problems, particularly as they relate to function, personnel, length of season, protection of persons served, finance, organization, program, and maintenance, and with methods of dealing with them.

A great variety of activities is included in the programs at these areas and facilities, especially the playgrounds and recreation buildings, but they are merely mentioned in the three chapters which follow. Detailed descriptions of these activities are contained in Part VI, which deals with special program features and city-wide services.

CHAPTER XVII

THE OPERATION OF PLAYGROUNDS

The playground, as indicated in Chap. XI, is the type of area designed to afford a wide range of enjoyable and desirable activities primarily for children between the ages of six and fifteen, although many large playgrounds are opened for use by youth, adults, and family groups during certain periods or for specific activities. It was noted that between three and five acres are required for a playground which provides a wading pool, shelter house, apparatus area, section for outdoor crafts, drama, and quiet games, small children's area, space for low organized games, team games, and such games as tennis, handball, and horseshoes. A playground is needed in every neighborhood and it is often advisable to have it located at or adjoining the elementary-school site. The operation of playgrounds is a major feature of most community recreation programs.

THE FUNCTION OF THE PLAYGROUND

The ideal playground is a place where children have a chance to enjoy themselves completely, where they may take part in the many activities which appeal to them and which, for the most part, cannot be carried on elsewhere. It affords not only fun but safety—an important factor in modern city life. On the playground children build up healthy bodies and physical vigor by spending hours in the air and sunlight in varied forms of active play. Right habits and attitudes are developed under the guidance of able leaders, and sportsmanship and cooperation are put into practice through participation in team games. Well-equipped, ample, and properly located playgrounds under competent leadership encourage wholesome, constructive activity and thereby tend to reduce juvenile delinquency.

It must be admitted that many playgrounds make only a limited contribution in fun, safety, health, and character because they fail to meet certain conditions which are essential if a playground is to yield definite and lasting satisfactions to children. A few of the characteristics of the ideal playground are:

1. It is large enough to afford opportunities for all the children in the neighborhood to engage in their favorite play activities.
2. It is attractive, well designed, and affords a pleasant setting for play.
3. Boys and girls can let off steam there and play without repression.
4. Every age has a fair chance, and girls are given equal consideration with boys.

5. A variety of skills is developed and children with all degrees of ability have an equal chance to play.

6. Varied interests are considered—music, crafts, nature, athletics.

7. It gives an opportunity for making new acquaintances.

8. There is always something interesting for all to do.

9. Fair play is the rule—all have equal opportunity.

10. Safety and healthful participation are assured.

11. Children are given opportunities for service.

12. As far as practicable, family play is encouraged.

According to Howard Braucher, the task of the playground is "helping the individual child to do well and happily what he most wants to do now and will want to do later." The function of playground administration is to accomplish this task—to bring into reality the limitless possibilities which the playground affords for fun and good citizenship.

CITY-WIDE PLAYGROUND ORGANIZATION

Playground organization involves such procedures as selecting the playgrounds at which programs are to be conducted under leadership; fixing the length of season, hours per day, and days per week when leadership is to be provided at each; determining the personnel required, selecting the staff, and distributing it among the different grounds; providing equipment, supplies, and play materials; arranging for the maintenance of the grounds and buildings; and developing a general program and a plan for administering and supervising it. The various aspects of playground organization are closely interrelated inasmuch as programs are dependent upon the facilities, funds, and leadership available. The form of staff organization is influenced by the qualifications of the workers and the type of program desired. Uniform methods cannot be used in all localities or for all types of playgrounds, but the local plan of organization must be worked out in such a way as to secure the maximum service and benefits from the facilities, personnel, and funds available.

Selection of Playgrounds.—In selecting the playgrounds at which programs are to be provided, an attempt is made to serve each section of the city. If this is not possible, the neighborhoods in greatest need of a play program receive first consideration. Normally the larger, well-equipped playgrounds are selected first because they afford more play opportunities and serve more children. Sometimes, however, small inadequate areas are used in order that play opportunities may be provided within walking distance of the younger children. In some neighborhoods it is necessary to operate two playgrounds, one of which may be suitable only for small children's play, the other affording facilities used only by older children.

Among the questions to be answered in determining the number of playgrounds to be conducted are: Is it better to open a few large playgrounds with a staff which will enable a well-balanced program to be provided at each, or to open many playgrounds even though the program provided will be limited? Is it better to open a few playgrounds during a long season or to open more playgrounds and reduce the period of operation? If funds are inadequate, is it better to develop a good program at a few centers, even though some neighborhoods are neglected, than to spread out the work so that results are unsatisfactory? Local conditions alone can provide the answers.

Length of Season.—In many cities playgrounds are conducted under leadership only during the summer months; in others they are also open under leadership for several weeks during the spring and fall, but in most large cities play programs are conducted throughout the year. Year-round operation is especially desirable where weather conditions permit outdoor play during most of the year, where recreation opportunities in the homes or other neighborhood agencies are lacking, and where the playground affords suitable indoor facilities. Most playgrounds are conducted during the summer when children have the greatest amount of free time. The length of the summer season is influenced by that of the school vacation; in general, the playgrounds open on a full schedule soon after the schools close and remain open until the end of vacation.

Playground Hours.—The hours during which playgrounds are open under leadership vary from season to season. During the school year they are usually open only during the afternoon, but if on or adjoining the playground there is a building used as an indoor center, leadership is sometimes provided both afternoon and evening. Limited leadership is occasionally provided in the morning when very young children or people beyond school age are accommodated. During the summer months most playgrounds are conducted morning, afternoon, and evening.

The playground hours vary not only from season to season but from one playground to another. In some neighborhoods the needs of the children can be met adequately if the playground is open only a few hours a day. In congested, underprivileged neighborhoods, however, there is need for playgrounds to be open continuously from early morning until late in the evening. Occasionally, due to the fact that families seek recreation elsewhere, playgrounds are closed or operated with a limited staff on Saturdays. Regular programs are carried on in few cities on Sunday, though most playgrounds are open for informal play.

THE PLAYGROUND STAFF

Because leadership is the most important factor in successful playground operation, the selection of the staff is a major responsibility of the recreation authorities. Types of workers who have a share in the playground program are the recreation superintendent, supervisor of playgrounds, supervisors of special activities such as arts and crafts, nature, or drama, playground directors and assistants, play leaders, and specialists. In addition, the personnel required for a large playground system includes office and maintenance workers. The number and kinds of personnel required on the playground staff vary according to the type of playground organization, the number of playgrounds operated, their facilities, the nature of the program, the length of the season, and other local factors.

The duties and qualifications of persons serving in the leadership positions listed above and methods of selecting and training them were pointed out in preceding chapters. In most cities the playground staff consists largely of persons employed for the summer months only, or on a part-time basis during the school year. In a few cities personnel serves on a full-time, year-round basis.

Requirements of a Small City.—Every playground system requires some degree of overhead supervision in addition to the leaders employed to serve at the individual grounds. The superintendent of recreation or, if there is no year-round system, the supervisor of playgrounds who is employed on a seasonal basis, organizes the playground staff, maps out a general program, and supervises the work of all the playgrounds. In the small city the only other essential leaders are the playground directors and their assistants or play leaders, but as a rule one or more special supervisors or specialists are employed, sometimes on a part-time basis, to help with particular phases of the program. Provisions must also be made for the maintenance of the playgrounds and an office worker is usually needed, at least part of the time, to serve as supply clerk and keep the playground records.

The Staff in a Larger City.—Since in a large city with many playgrounds the executive is unable to supervise personally the work at all centers, the city is often divided into geographical districts and one general supervisor is assigned to each. He serves ten or more playgrounds, visiting them frequently to observe the work being done, to help the directors with their programs, special problems, and reports, to ensure compliance with department policies, and to arrange interplayground and city-wide projects.

One or more supervisors of special activities are also employed, the number depending upon the kinds of activity to be featured and the ability and experience of the workers in the system. If, for example, a nature program is to be promoted and if the workers know little about nature activities, a nature supervisor is essential. To serve the increasing popular interest in the acquisition of recreation skills, the city playground staff often includes one or more specialists such as a tennis instructor or a teacher of some particular form of craft or music activity, who organize and instruct groups on the different playgrounds. In addition to the leadership staff, maintenance personnel are required and one or more clerical workers to care for playground supplies, reports, and office records.

The Staff on the Individual Playground.—Most playgrounds have a director who has full responsibility for the playground and its operation. This position is generally open to both men and women; if the director is a man, the assistant is a woman, and vice versa. Where three workers are employed it is possible to arrange their schedules so that two of them are on the playground during each morning, afternoon, and evening session. In assigning workers to a playground, their training and abilities are taken into consideration. Thus, if the man is experienced in conducting games and athletics, an attempt is made to assign to the same ground a woman who is skilled in arts, crafts, drama, or some other form of activity. Since the more competent directors are usually assigned to the larger playgrounds which require more workers, assistants and play leaders have an opportunity to secure valuable training by working under their direction. The special skills, aptitudes, and personalities of workers and the characteristics and requirements of different neighborhoods are taken into account in making assignments in order to assure a maximum degree of success.

There is no hard or fast rule as to the division of work on a playground but usually the man conducts most of the activities for the older boys and the woman works with the small children and the older girls. Special activities such as nature, drama, or crafts are cared for by the individual worker who is best qualified to conduct them, and feature events are jointly planned and conducted by all the workers. Responsibilities are fairly divided and determined by the director who takes into account the qualifications of each worker. As a rule, he personally assumes responsibility for inspecting the apparatus, for handling problems of discipline, for preparing the reports, for community relationships, and for approving programs and special program features. Time schedules of the workers are arranged so that either the director or the assistant director is present at the playground during all periods.

Junior Leaders.—Children constantly practice leadership on the playground and capable playground workers are alert to the opportunities which play activities afford them for developing qualities of leadership and for directing them into proper channels. Few playgrounds have an adequate staff, and where junior leaders are used part of the workers' time is released for other service. At the same time boys and girls secure valuable training and experience through performing duties, making decisions, exercising judgment and control, and leading other children in play activities. Many problems arise in the enlistment and use of junior leaders but if they are faced fairly and intelligently, the children, the workers, and the playground program are likely to benefit.

Types of Junior Service.—Many children assist with the playground activities. An older boy helps in coaching or managing a team or league; a girl who is skillful in some form of crafts conducts a group of younger girls; a child who has a special interest in storytelling or nature helps with the storytelling hour or serves as leader of a nature club. A more common type of junior service consists of collecting game materials, guarding children in the wading pool, marking game courts, or taking the attendance.

The service is sometimes rendered informally by children whose desire to help has been recognized and used by the playground worker, but frequently junior organizations such as a safety patrol, junior police, or junior leaders' club are organized. Such formal groups require expert handling. Otherwise, they may require too much of the workers' time, limit service opportunities to only a few children, benefit those children who need them least, and interfere with the members' own play life. Under wise leadership these groups render valuable playground service, provide excellent leadership training, encourage self-government, and win an important place in the playground program.

PROGRAM PLANNING

In outlining the general playground program for a city, the executive keeps in mind the abilities and qualifications of the workers who are to conduct it, the previous experience of the city with playground programs, the amount and type of supervision to be provided, the facilities available, and the emphasis to be laid on interplayground and city-wide activities. With the assistance of the staff he develops a general plan for the entire playground system. This provides a framework upon which the individual playground programs are built, each of them being designed to meet the special interests and needs of the neighborhood served.

Instructions governing programs and program planning issued to all workers at the beginning of the playground season usually indicate the chief objectives to be sought by the program and general methods of attaining them. They point out the types of activities which directors are expected to carry on regularly from day to day, or from week to week. They list a number of special events, tournaments, and activities which are to be conducted at all playgrounds or from which the directors may select the ones best suited to their individual grounds. They indicate the times when the special supervisors and specialists are to visit the playgrounds, the special features to be arranged by every playground, such as a weekly community program or a closing festival, and the interplayground or city-wide events. These instructions enable the directors of the individual playgrounds to plan their programs in such a way that they conform with the general pattern followed by all the playgrounds of the city, even though they are adapted to meet the needs of the individual neighborhoods.

Advance Planning Essential.—At first glance the idea of a program prepared in advance might seem out of place on the playground to which people come voluntarily to do only what they want to do. Yet only by planning can the playground's facilities be fully utilized, the children's varied play interests be served, and the leadership staff render the maximum service. The fullest use of popular facilities such as softball diamonds is secured only if they are set aside for the use of teams or informal groups during definite periods. Without a program interests like nature or music are likely to be neglected. Special events such as a picnic or festival are looked forward to eagerly by the children but unless arrangements are made well in advance, the leaders are "swamped" with last minute preparations with the result that the children do not get as much fun out of the occasions as they would otherwise.

In interpreting and supervising programs, the executive encourages each worker to use his resourcefulness in adapting old forms of play and in devising new ones. He insists that the worker provide a variety of activities to meet the needs of all the children, but does not require the same projects to be carried on at all playgrounds. He expects that program schedules will be adjusted when desirable. For example, if the nature period is scheduled for Wednesday afternoon but on Tuesday a rare bird is seen or a locust emerges from its shell, the wise leader will consider the children's nature interest of greater importance than the prearranged program. Through the reports of supervisors' visits, staff meetings, and weekly playground reports, he supplements his own observations as to how the program is progressing. In several cities questionnaires submitted to the playground workers at the close of the playground season have yielded many practical suggestions which have proved useful in planning the program for the following year.

Factors Affecting Planning.—Uniform playground programs or play projects cannot be developed at all units of a playground system even if this were advisable. Many activities which are possible on a 5-acre playground cannot be considered on a small schoolyard. The playground with three or more workers offers greater possibilities for a varied program than one with a single worker. Several general planning factors mentioned in Chap. XV influence the operation of the individual playground and the type of program it makes possible.

The Leaders.—If only one worker is present on a playground which serves children of a wide range of ages, he gives most of his time to general supervision of the area. He suggests activities, helps start games, and assures safety and fair opportunity for all, but he cannot spend much time in working with small groups. Where two or more leaders are present, however, one can initiate and give intensive guidance or instruction to groups engaged in such activities as arts and crafts or nature, while the other is helping with the general operation of the playground. The qualifications of the workers also influence the type of program because leaders are likely to emphasize those activities with which they are most familiar. Where there are special supervisors and specialists who visit the playground regularly they can develop major projects which otherwise would not be possible.

The Playgrounds.—Small playgrounds afford few opportunities for team games which appeal strongly to the boys over twelve, but they may meet admirably the interests of the younger children. Large playgrounds, on the other hand, make possible a varied program and attract the older boys and girls who take part not only in sports but in other features as well. Unless facilities for activities like drama, music, and arts and crafts, are available on a playground it is difficult to carry on such projects successfully. A playground with limited facilities is handicapped for participation in interplayground or city-wide activities. Where space and equipment are inadequate, the leaders need greater resourcefulness in adapting games and in discovering activities which can be carried on satisfactorily.

The Children.—Playground programs are built around the interests of children—are "child centered" and not "activity centered." Leaders are justified in stressing activities which have a wide appeal and in which a large number of children can be served, but the special interests of the individual child must not be neglected. Small-group activities requiring considerable guidance are conspicuous in the program where adequate leadership is available.

The ages of the children attending a playground affect not only the activities provided but the length of the play periods. Fewer children of preschool age attend playgrounds in neighborhoods with single-family houses than in tenement sections where special attention is paid to the play of young children. The type of neighborhood also influences the playground program. In high-class residential neighborhoods, activities involving expensive materials or game equipment may be carried on, but in the poorer sections children cannot afford to take part in such activities. Trips or outings are a regular playground feature in some neighborhoods but due to their cost are not practicable in others.

A Few Planning Methods.—Certain principles and methods described in an earlier chapter have been found useful in planning programs of all kinds, but a few of them are especially applicable to playgrounds.

Variety of Play Interests.—The successful playground leader realizes that children like variety, that different activities have interest spans which vary widely, that all children do not like the same activities, that some forms of play have a much wider appeal than others, and that strenuous and quiet activities should be interspersed in the program. Variety is essential in order to attract a large number of different children and to sustain their interest after they come to the playground. More major projects are not started than the leaders have reason to believe can be carried through successfully, but those selected include several types of play activities and furnish outlets for a variety of play interests.

Various Organization Methods.—One effective device for introducing variety into the program is to utilize different methods of organizing activities. Thus a desire to increase one's skill in horeseshoes or paddle tennis may be stimulated by organizing tournaments with participants classified according to age, ability, or sex. Competition between mixed teams or teams composed of brothers and sisters arouses unusual interest. Groups with a common interest are helped to organize clubs or teams, and apparatus play is stimulated through the teaching of stunts. Playground leaders make the program more purposeful by relating playground activities to a definite objective or event. A pushmobile or kite contest affords an incentive for boys to make pushmobiles or kites and serves as a valuable craft project during the weeks preceding the event. Activities that require little preparation are arranged for young children, but older boys and girls will spend weeks getting ready for a special event.

In planning and conducting the program, a balance is sought between individual and group projects, competitive and cooperative activities, free and organized play, informal sports and tournaments, clubs and open groups, pick-up games and league play, routine and special feature events.

Interrelating Activities.—Many activities are unrelated to one another. Handball played by fifteen-year-old boys admittedly has no relation to the little tots' story hour. Yet other playground projects involve the cooperation of different groups and bring together diversified interests. Birdhouse construction, for example, is not only related to the study of nature, but it involves craft and service interests. Play production offers opportunity for creative writing, the designing of costumes, scenery, and posters, the construction of scenery, properties, and lighting equipment, acting, and the study of speech and color. Program features such as the festival not only have value to the children who participate but they encourage mutual understanding and cooperation on the part of the workers on the individual playground.

PLAYGROUND PROGRAMS

There are three general types of playground programs. One consists of the schedule of special feature events which are proposed for all playgrounds during the season, whether spring, summer, fall, or winter. The others are the weekly and daily programs which are arranged for each individual playground.   In the following pages, which contain a description of typical playground programs, special consideration is given to summer activities since this is the season when most playgrounds are in operation.   The same principles apply, however, in the planning of playgrounds for other seasons.

The Summer Program.—In every city there are certain events which stand out as the high lights of the summer program.   These vary with local traditions, interests, and resources but they often include such events as a water sports day, pageant, hobby exhibit, track and field meet, circus, or festival.   Some are related to and focus attention upon day-by-day activities; others may take the form of an outing or motion-picture show.   The well-planned summer program furnishes objectives for the regular activities, includes events which appeal to all ages, and distributes these events throughout the summer in such a way as to prevent overcrowding of the schedule and permit adequate preparation for them.

Occasionally a special theme is selected for the program which is carried throughout the entire playground season.   Programs have been built, for example, around the American Indian or the colonial period, with games, crafts, ceremonials, dances, plays, and other activities related to the particular subject.   In one city the theme "America, the Beautiful" was chosen and each playground represented an American country or a section of the United States, and built its program around the play life and traditions of the country chosen.

A Typical Summer Program.—The following list of special events sponsored by the Playground and Recreation Commission of Alton, Illinois, during the summer of 1939 is typical of the program in many cities:

Date	Day	Special events	Time	Place
June 30	Friday......	On Wheels Day	P.M.	Playground
July 3	Monday....	Boys' Baseball League Opens	9 A.M.	East End
July 7	Friday......	Doll Show	P.M.	Playground
July 14	Friday......	Open Date	P.M.	Playground
July 20	Thursday...	(Colored) Playday and Picnic	10 A.M.	Rock Spring Park
July 21	Friday......	(White) Playday and Picnic	10 A.M.	Rock Spring Park
July 28	Friday	Radio Track and Field Meet	2 P.M.	East End
Aug. 4	Friday......	Hobby Show	P.M.	Playground
Aug. 8	Tuesday....	Girls' Swimming Meet	10 A.M.	Y.W.C.A.
Aug. 11	Friday......	Alton Day	P.M.	Playground
Aug. 17	Thursday...	Championship Day	9 A.M.	Hellrung
Aug. 18	Friday......	Handicraft Display	7 P.M.	Playground

The Dayton Program.—In preparing for the summer, some playground authorities, besides outlining special events to be carried out

Week	Designation	Feature event	Special activities	Preparation
1st, May 23.....	Know Your Community Week	Organize community committee	Organize safety patrol Teach low organized games Organize clubs—camera, sewing, woodcraft, nature, hobby, knothole, etc.	Start safety posters Prepare for community night Teach hopscotch
2d, May 30.....	Safety Week	Safety posters displayed Community night programs Marble tournaments	Baseball field day Marble tournament for boys Hopscotch tournament for girls	Teach track and field activities Organize softball teams
3d, June 6.......	Track and Field Week	Start day camp program Track and field meet	Start softball leagues Start volley ball leagues Jacks tournament for girls Mumble peg tournament for boys	Prepare health posters Make lanterns
4th, June 13....	Health Week	Lantern parade Health posters displayed	Horseshoe tournament Finish making lanterns	Start nature collections Teach hand tennis
5th, June 20.....	Nature Week	Nature displays Treasure hunts on all grounds	Hand tennis tournaments, boys and girls	Prepare for parents' week
6th, June 27....	Parents' Week	Father and son day Mother and daughter day	Rope jumping tournament for girls Knife baseball tournament for boys	Prepare dolls Organize for play-day
7th, July 4......	Patriotic Week	Playdays on all grounds	Doll shows Paddle tennis tournaments	Teach halma, 9-man morris, etc. Prepare puppets
8th, July 11.....	Music and Drama Week	Community night Puppet shows Community sings	Quiet games tournament Sand modeling contest	Organize for vehicle races
9th, July 18.....	On Wheels Week	Parade of vehicles Vehicle races	Races on coasters, bicycles, roller skates, and scooters	Make quiet games Contact visiting nurses to learn of shut-ins Prepare for pet shows
10th, July 25....	Shut-in Week Pet Show	Contact all shut-ins Pet shows on all grounds	Progressive games parties	Prepare for horseshoe and deck tennis tournaments
11th, Aug. 1....	Golf and Tennis Week	Golf tournament at Community Tennis tournament at Walnut Hills	Second horseshoe tournament Deck tennis tournament	Collect craft materials for display Prepare for pageant
12th, Aug. 8.....	Handicraft and Hobby Week	Handicraft and hobby displays on all grounds Softball finals at Kottering Field	Ring-o-let tournament	Prepare for pageant
13th, Aug. 15....	Pageant Week	Pageant at Barney Community		

during the season, select a theme or special designation for each week, suggest the special activities to be carried on, and outline the projects which should be initiated each week in preparation for future events. Such a program helps to focus attention upon desired objectives, to secure balance in the program, and to assure adequate preparation for special events. It is not intended as a pattern which each playground must follow regardless of its peculiar conditions, but rather as a plan which the playground staff has set up as likely to yield a satisfying and interesting summer for the people of the city. The outline shown on p. 261 issued by the Bureau of Recreation, Dayton, Ohio, for the 1938 summer season illustrates a typical playground program of this type.

The Daily Program.—The playground day is divided into periods set aside for different kinds of activities for the various age groups, for boys, and for girls. By following the same general schedule day after day children learn the times when the activities of special interest to them are carried on. The opening period in the morning is usually one of preparation and informal activity. The midmorning hours are well suited to strenuous activities. The periods before and after lunch are usually devoted to relatively quiet forms of play and to group activities such as crafts and drama. Tournaments, special events, and league games are often scheduled in the middle of the afternoon. The early evening hours are among the busiest and events are frequently planned in which young people and adults participate.

Classes, clubs, and other groups meeting regularly are scheduled at the hour when most members can be present. At least two, and frequently more, activities are being carried on at all times; while one worker is with a group requiring continuous attention, the other is helping with less formal activities. Brief intervals between periods encourage informal play, give leaders an opportunity to prepare for scheduled activities, and avoid crowding of the program. As a rule, activity periods for small children are short; craft classes and team games, on the other hand, require considerable time.

A Suggested Daily Program.—The program which follows has been set up for a playground at which three leaders are employed—one man and two women. Two workers are on duty during each morning, afternoon, and evening session. The asterisks (*) indicate the activities to which the leaders give more or less direct and continuous supervision. In cases where more than two activities are so indicated in a given period, all the activities are not conducted each day. Thus at 10:00 on Monday, Wednesday, and Friday a worker may conduct group and team games for the boys and girls over eleven; on other days he conducts low organized games for the younger group at this hour. The age classification indicated in the program is merely suggestive. Groups formed in such

SUGGESTED DAILY SUMMER PLAYGROUND PROGRAM

	Children under 8	Children 8 to 11	Boys and girls over 11
9:30–10:00	Flag raising. Getting out equipment; inspecting apparatus and grounds; marking courts; distributing game supplies; posting announcements; organizing groups for morning play		
10:00–10:45	Group and singing games.* Apparatus play	Low organized games.* Apparatus play Sandbox play	Group and team games.* Practice for contests and tournaments
10:45–11:00	No special activity scheduled; free play; attendance taken; playground clean-up		
11:00–11:30	Sandbox play Block building	Handicraft.* Music.* Badge test events, stunts, etc.* Quiet games. Nature activities*	Folk dancing (girls).* Badge test events, stunts, etc.* Handicraft.* Music.* Nature activities*
11:30–12:00	Storytelling.* Quiet games		
12:00– 1:30	No scheduled activity; one leader present; occasional "picnics" or weiner roasts; quiet games		
1:30– 2:00	Storytelling and story acting* Apparatus play	Group games and relays* Apparatus play	Group games and relays* Individual games and athletic stunts
2:00– 2:30	Sandbox play. Free play activities Quiet games	Quiet games. Free play activities Preparation for future events	Organization of team games.* Practice for league games. Preparation for special or feature events*
2:30– 2:45	No special activity scheduled; free play; attendance taken; preparation for special events and contests		
2:45– 4:15	Apparatus play. Singing games. Taking part in or watching special events	Contests, tournaments or special features.* Handicraft. Watching league games	Special features, contests, tournaments or outings.* League games.* Handicraft. Preparation for future events
4:15– 5:15	Sandbox play Quiet games	Storytelling.* Dramatics.* Quiet games Meetings of clubs and committees	Storytelling.*. Dramatics.* Quiet games. Completion of special features.* Meetings of clubs and committees. Preparation for community night events*
5:15– 5:30	Collecting game materials and playground supplies; check-up on playground		

SUGGESTED DAILY SUMMER PLAYGROUND PROGRAM—(*Continued*)

	Children under 8	Children 8 to 11	Boys and girls over 11
5:30– 6:30	No scheduled activity—one leader present. Playground used by young people or adults for team games and for informal play		
6:30– 8:30	Free play on apparatus and self-organized games. Watching special events. Quiet games		Twilight leagues for young people and adults. Informal individual and team games. Special neighborhood programs and demonstrations**

activities as music, drama, and nature commonly include children from eight years of age upwards, and children from the two younger groups often join in the same activities.

The Weekly Program.—The diversity of interests and activities on the playground makes it impossible with a limited staff to conduct all activities each day. A weekly schedule is therefore needed to supplement the daily program. It indicates the days on which periods will be devoted to crafts, drama, nature, and other activities which require fairly continuous guidance and are usually scheduled two or three times a week. It notes the time when safety or leaders' clubs will meet, and when tournaments or special events will be held. There is an advantage in scheduling the special weekly events at the same day each week, and it is common practice to hold all community evening programs on a certain day of the week so people will tend to reserve that time for them. Adjustments in the daily schedule are needed for the weekly staff meeting, the occasional playground outing, and interplayground activities; but in preparing the weekly schedule an attempt is made to fit the activities as closely as possible into the regular daily program.

Programs for Other Seasons.—The same general principles apply in planning playground programs for other seasons, but in actual practice the problems differ from those during the summer months. While school is in session most of the children served by playgrounds are busy until midafternoon, and outdoor activities are limited largely to a two- or three-hour session daily. Because children have been in school most of the day, and because climatic conditions are usually suitable for them, vigorous activities play a large part in the programs carried on in the fall, winter, and spring. Events which require long periods of preparation are less satisfactory than intraplayground leagues, contests, tournaments, hiking, low organized games, and seasonal activities such as marbles, skating, and snow games. Programs are frequently hindered by inclement weather, especially where suitable indoor facilities are lacking. Consequently, during the school year more diversified programs are practicable in the Southern and Pacific Coast cities and at playgrounds with indoor facilities. Where playgrounds are operated in connection with buildings or indoor centers young people and adults usually have a large part in the program during the evening hours.

OTHER ASPECTS OF PLAYGROUND OPERATION

Playgrounds must be suitably developed, a competent staff selected, trained, and assigned, and a program of activities planned in order to assure successful playground operation. But still other steps need to be taken, some of which involve preliminary preparation, others continuous attention throughout the entire playground season.

Safety.—Safety is a basic consideration in playground operation and the well-managed playground is a safe place for children to play. This does not mean that all opportunity for adventure has been eliminated, but continual care is exercised to prevent accidents on play areas where large numbers of children are taking part in a variety of activities. The following are some of the most effective means of assuring safety on the playground:

1. Lay out the playground wisely, with proper locations for the various sections and features, with adequate space for each, with fences, entrances, and paths so placed as to reduce hazards. If these conditions do not obtain, the playground needs to be redesigned.

2. Install only equipment and apparatus that is well constructed and safe for use by the children. High apparatus and deep wading pools are not desirable on the playground because of the hazards arising from their use.

3. Assure proper use of the apparatus by teaching correct methods of use and insisting that they be followed. Prohibit all misuse of equipment.

4. Inspect regularly and thoroughly all apparatus and equipment and withdraw it from use immediately when it gives evidence of needing repairs.

5. Prepare and enforce simple rules for the use of game areas. Restrict the playing of games such as horseshoes or the batting of balls to areas set aside for them.

6. Eliminate all hazards such as poor surfacing, especially under the apparatus, exposed pipes, and unprotected window wells.

7. Be vigilant in enforcing safety rules and in preventing dangerous practices, and enlist the cooperation of the children, perhaps through the organization of a junior safety corps.

Playground authorities also have a responsibility for safeguarding and promoting health and for eliminating conditions which might undermine it. To this end they check carefully the condition of the water in the wading pool, maintain buildings and grounds in a sanitary condition, supervise participation in games involving extreme exertion, and are on the watch to prevent children with infections or contagious diseases from taking part in the playground program.

Playground Accidents.—No matter how carefully they are guarded against, accidents are bound to occur and playground workers must be prepared to act promptly and intelligently whenever there is one. Requirements for such action are:

1. A first-aid kit, easily accessible and adequate for all ordinary situations. This essential feature of every playground should be available at all times and supplies should be replenished regularly and used only for first-aid purposes.

2. A knowledge of first-aid methods on the part of all playground workers. Often the playground is in charge of a single worker and he must know what action to take and how to perform it.

3. A knowledge of the procedure to be followed in the case of serious accidents. Local practices differ, but each worker must receive explicit instructions as to what to do in case of an accident requiring more than first-aid treatment. Failure to know and act promptly and to submit accident reports may prove serious.

Problems of Conduct.—On the playground all are permitted the greatest possible freedom in the use of facilities and in the choice of activities, provided such freedom does not interfere with the best interests of the entire group. Discipline is essential on the playground, but the need for enforcing it is least evident when there is the greatest amount of interesting activity. Among children who attend the playground regularly it is seldom necessary to do more than call attention to their misconduct or infraction of a rule. Occasionally they must be denied for brief periods the privilege of using certain facilities or of taking part in an activity, but disciplinary cases requiring severe penalties are rare. On the other hand, in problem neighborhoods rowdies sometimes come to the playground to disrupt the program and to destroy property. In such cases exceptional tact and firmness on the part of the director are needed if trouble is to be averted, and prompt, decisive action is essential.

The playground worker who understands child nature and gives the children a sense of reality in the program is not likely to have great difficulty in handling them. Proper conduct is encouraged by having a few concise rules and enforcing them, by anticipating trouble before it gets under way, by encouraging self-government, by dealing fairly, by investigating before punishing, and by making few threats and promises. Penalties vary with the nature and seriousness of the offense and, if possible, are linked up with it. Suspension or expulsion is used only as a last resort after consultation with the supervisor. Close cooperation between the playground workers, parents, and the neighborhood police help reduce the problem of discipline on the playground.

Supplies.—Supplies of many kinds are needed on every playground. Game courts and fields, playground buildings, and other features can be used to advantage only as suitable materials and supplies are available. Crafts, drama, nature, social, and most other playground activities cannot be carried on successfully without them. The requirements of a playground vary according to its size, attendance, facilities, and the program to be carried on. Essential supplies are provided by the authorities but children often bring additional materials to the playground. Care in the use and conservation of supplies is a responsibility of playground workers. The following are the types commonly used:

1. *Game Supplies.*—These include handballs, horseshoes and stakes, softballs, bats and bases, volley balls and nets, play balls, soccer balls, rainy-day materials, and paddle tennis outfits. As a rule, children provide their own tennis racquets. If the playground includes a baseball diamond or running track, additional supplies are needed. Quiet game materials such as bean bags, peg boards and pegs, ring toss, checkers, caroms, and dominoes are of great value and can be made by the children as a craft project. Materials used in conducting social games and parties are needed at playgrounds having buildings serving as indoor centers.

2. *Craft Supplies.*—These consist primarily of tools and equipment such as hammer and nails, knives, scissors, pliers, files, sandpaper, paste, crayons, and paints; and crafts materials such as clay, cloth, wood, leather, magazines, and yarn. Materials supplied by the department are often supplemented by those brought by the children or obtained by the leaders from neighborhood stores or local factories.

3. *Accessories.*—Many types of supplies are needed for the music, nature, or drama program. A victrola and records are useful for folk dancing. Equipment is also needed for the office. Every playground needs a flag, bulletin board, repair kit, and first-aid kit.

4. *The Playground Library.*—A set of publications on playground operation and activities is a part of the essential equipment of the director's office. Books containing rules for games, publications on program features, manuals and other instructions issued by the department office, and standard publications on playground work have a place in the playground library.

5. *General Supplies.*—Necessary maintenance supplies include materials for marking courts, dust binders, sawdust, grease, and janitor's supplies. Office forms and other materials are also needed.

6. *Tools.*—Regardless of the system used for maintaining playgrounds, at least a few tools are required at every area.

Maintenance.—The playground, like every other part of the recreation system, represents a considerable public investment and playground authorities have a definite responsibility for keeping it in the best possible condition. Otherwise it cannot render the maximum service and is likely to become a liability in the neighborhood. Continuous care and proper use of the grounds and buildings minimize the amount of maintenance work that must be done. Enlistment of the cooperation of the children, sometimes through the organization of junior service groups, has been found helpful in developing a respect for playground property and preventing damage to it.

School playgrounds are generally kept in condition by the school janitorial staff, park playgrounds by the caretakers serving the entire park area. On large, well-equipped playgrounds with recreation build-ings used the year round, a worker is employed full time as caretaker and janitor. Since most playgrounds do not require the services of a care-taker more than a few hours daily, a single worker sometimes cares for two or more areas. In several cities a specially trained traveling main-tenance crew is used. It eliminates the need for buying a complete set of maintenance equipment for each area, performs certain duties which the individual caretaker may not be able to perform, and eliminates the need for maintenance workers at most playgrounds. A certain amount of cleaning, marking, and other tasks must be performed regularly each day, but most of the maintenance service can be performed by the traveling crew on its periodic visits. In case of emergency the director calls the central office or workshop.

Among the usual maintenance duties are keeping a satisfactory sur-face, cleaning the building and grounds, caring for plantings, marking game courts, cutting grass and hedges, changing water in the wading pool and cleaning it, inspecting apparatus, bringing in and setting up equip-ment, keeping tools and equipment in good condition, and making minor repairs.

These activities have a definite relationship to the playground pro-gram. Game courts which are marked accurately and distinctly not only look well but facilitate the teaching of obedience to the rules of the game. Satisfactory play is impossible on a poorly surfaced court or field. A thoroughly cleaned wading pool makes for safe, healthful, and enjoyable play. Game materials last longer and give more satis-factory service when children are taught to use them properly, when they are stored away carefully while not in use, and when they are repaired promptly. The attitude of the playground workers toward the appearance and condition of the playground goes far in determining the degree to which it is respected by the children and the entire neighborhood.

Regulating the Use of the Playground.—Few rules are needed on the playground where spontaneous, free play should be encouraged and where there should be a minimum of suppression and regulation. Some depart-ments, however, have adopted simple rules setting forth the conditions under which the playgrounds can be used and the responsibility of the department and of the persons using them. If the playground building serves as a center for activities, regulations are usually adopted governing its use by playground and community groups. Because in most cities the demand for tennis courts and softball diamonds exceeds the supply, definite rules are needed governing the conditions and periods of play, the making of reservations, the collection of fees, or the restriction as to the people who can use them. The purpose of such rules is to assure to all equal, convenient, safe, and satisfactory use of the areas and facilities.

Playground Records and Reports.—The primary job of playground workers is to conduct and promote play programs. Hence they should be asked to keep only records which have real value and require little time. In most cities a weekly report is required of each director (a list of the kinds of information commonly included in such a report is given in Chap. XXXII). A few departments require their workers also to prepare a report for the playground at the end of the year or season. In it unusual events, relationships, successes, and failures are recorded, as well as attendance, activities of various types, volunteer service, club projects, and suggestions for the future. Such a report is valuable as a historical record and is exceedingly helpful to a new director coming to the playground.

It is advantageous for playground workers to know and record the children who attend their playground. Most recreation executives who have used a registration system at their playgrounds believe it fully merits the time and effort required to maintain it. Where it is used, an attempt is made to enroll as many children as possible, especially during the first week or two of the season. Each child coming to the playground is asked to fill out a card with spaces for name, address, age, parents' names, grade in school, telephone number, etc. In this way the workers gain information which is valuable in program planning, in securing financial support, and in their relationships with the individual children.

Other records on file at the playground are rosters of playground teams, membership lists of playground clubs, junior leaders, winners of special events and tournaments, and the names of children entered in competitive and interplayground activities. In some cities playground merit point systems have been established under which the individual children receive points for participation or achievement in a wide range of activities. Such a system requires the keeping of a careful record for each child. Since the use of standard forms makes for simplification and uniformity in record keeping, such forms as registration cards, entry forms for special events, team rosters, permits for courts and other facilities, time sheets, accident report forms, weekly report forms, requisition blanks, receipts, and membership cards are in common use. The subject of records and reports, including a discussion of attendance taking on the playground, is treated more fully in Chap. XXXII.

Other Aspects of Playground Operation.—Among the many other types of problems that arise in the operation of a playground system or of a single playground is the question of budgets and the responsibility of workers for handling playground funds. Awards are an important factor in the playgrounds in many cities, and their use gives rise to many problems. Interplayground and city-wide projects, which have a considerable place in many programs, require special planning. Trips by groups to points at a distance from the playground necessitate precautions to assure health and safety. Regulations are needed governing rainy-day procedure, the type of costume to be worn by workers on duty, relationships with neighborhood agencies, the opening and closing of the playground, and the promotion of activities by outside groups, and many other questions. Some of these problems are considered later in this volume, but for a detailed treatment of these and related subjects readers are referred to *Playgrounds, Their Administration and Operation.*[1]

---

[1] Edited by George D. Butler for the National Recreation Association and published by A. S. Barnes & Company, 1936.

CHAPTER XVIII

THE OPERATION OF RECREATION BUILDINGS AND INDOOR CENTERS

Recreation buildings and indoor centers play an important part in the service of the municipal recreation department because they make possible certain indoor activities, and in most cities a continuous, year-round program cannot be carried on without them. The different types of recreation buildings and the great variety of facilities provided in them were described in Chap. XII. Some of the problems involved in operating such buildings are common to all types but others are peculiar to special-use buildings. Because of the importance of the general recreation buildings and the school recreation center and because they are most numerous, major consideration will be given to them.

Operation of a building or center involves selection and organization of a staff, expenditure of funds for operation and maintenance, planning and conducting a program, scheduling activities, determining the conditions under which facilities may be used, and establishing relationships with the people in the city or neighborhood. Local conditions and the facilities provided at the building naturally affect both the plan of operation and the program carried on, in the case of the general recreation building and the school center.

CITY-WIDE ADMINISTRATION

Where the recreation building is a major feature of a playground, playfield, or other recreation area, and at school centers where the grounds are used for neighborhood play activities, the outdoor and indoor facilities are usually administered as a single unit. The general plan of overhead playground organization described in Chap. XVII therefore often applies to the indoor centers as well. However, there is less uniformity in the methods used to supervise the operation of buildings and centers because, unlike playgrounds, they are seldom widely or evenly distributed throughout a city. General responsibility for the indoor facilities, staff, and program rests with the recreation executive, although in a large city system it may be assigned to a supervisor of recreation centers or divided among several district supervisors. Supervisors of special activities assist in planning building and center programs for the entire city, in organizing city-wide groups which use these facilities, and in promoting intercenter events in their respective fields.

Special-use buildings, on the other hand, such as the museum, craft shop, or theater, are usually administered as units more or less independently of other centers. The peculiar problems and programs at these special-use buildings will be considered in later chapters dealing with particular phases of the recreation program.

THE GENERAL RECREATION BUILDING

As previously indicated, this title is applied to buildings frequently called field houses, clubhouses, community center buildings, and community houses, which are generally owned and operated by a municipal department and which are devoted exclusively or primarily to a diversified program of recreation activities. This type of building includes several of the following facilities: gymnasium, clubrooms, social hall, craft room, kitchen, assembly hall or auditorium with stage, lobby, swimming pool, and service features.

In Chap. V reference was made to the Chicago field houses erected early in the century and to the action taken by other cities in constructing similar buildings. For many years such buildings were confined mostly to the large cities and to play areas that were operated the year round. Reasons for this were the difficulty in securing money for constructing the buildings, the fact that the expenditure was not justified unless ample funds were available for operating the building throughout the year, and the rather widespread opinion that indoor community recreation needs could be served by existing school buildings. Since 1930, however, due to the increasing demand for year-round recreation programs and to the availability of emergency funds for construction and operating personnel, a great number of cities, large and small, have erected recreation buildings. In spite of this, most city neighborhoods still lack suitable recreation facilities.

Why the Recreation Building?—The question is frequently raised as to why a city should incur the expense of constructing and maintaining a special recreation building when the schools contain many suitable recreation facilities. Several reasons are suggested. One is that during many hours of the day the school facilities are not available for community use, especially in the junior and senior high schools which are best equipped with facilities for recreation. Even outside school hours these facilities are frequently reserved for the use of school groups engaged in extracurricular activities, inter- and intraschool athletics, socials, dances, music, or drama productions. As a result, the public has only limited access to them, and the periods of community use are determined by the interest of the schools rather than of the public. School buildings are never available in the morning hours when many women are most free to engage in recreation activities. A recreation building, on the other hand, can be used morning, afternoon, and evening. This makes possible full-time employment of trained leadership which is likely to prove much more satisfactory than leaders engaged on a part-time, interrupted basis. The problems of fixing responsibility when nonschool agencies conduct a program on school property, and the difficulties presented by dual use of such facilities as locker rooms, have hindered the wider use of schools in many cities.

These reasons apply in neighborhoods where there are modern, attractive school buildings planned for community use and where school authorities are favorable to such use. Unfortunately in many neighborhoods schools lack suitable well-designed facilities; school authorities are not sympathetic toward the community use of school buildings; the schools are unattractive and their atmosphere is not conducive to recreation activity; and the restrictions set up by the school authorities, such as the prohibition of smoking, discourage community use. Where such conditions exist it is little wonder that steps have been taken to provide buildings that are designed especially for recreation, are available at all times, are administered by a staff of recreation workers, and make possible a well-balanced indoor program.

Recreation buildings are usually erected at a playground or playfield, an arrangement which has many advantages. It makes possible economies in construction, maintenance, and operation because the same facilities can serve groups taking part in outdoor and indoor activities. During the winter months lockers, showers, and dressing rooms are used primarily in connection with the gymnasium. In other seasons when outside activity predominates, they serve individuals and groups engaging in outdoor sports. If there is an outdoor swimming pool on the area, the building serves as a bathhouse. The operation of the building and recreation area as a single unit permits the full-time employment and effective utilization of maintenance personnel to care for both outdoor and indoor facilities. Even more important, it makes possible the development of a year-round community recreation center which serves all the people of the neighborhood.

The Staff.—Leadership is as vital an element in determining the success of the recreation building as of the playground. It is the function of the director and his assistants to attract people to the building and help them get the maximum benefit and enjoyment from participation in its activities and from their use of its facilities. To accomplish this requires expertness as recreation leaders and an understanding of the neighborhood and of the desires and needs of the people living in it.

The leadership requirements of a building vary according to its facilities and the program to be carried on, but every building, like every playground, needs a director. He is responsible for the operation of the building and of the outside area which has a direct relationship to, it, and is usually employed on a full-time, year-round basis. Other members of the leadership staff are a full-time assistant, one or more specialists, also employed the year round, and part-time leaders who assist with various parts of the building program such as dancing, music, or drama. If the building has a gymnasium, an instructor is needed for men and boys, and another for women and girls. In centers where an activity like arts and crafts is featured, one or more workers are employed on either a full-time or a part-time basis. The staff not only conducts the indoor program but is in charge of the outdoor activities on the adjoining play area.

In addition to the leadership staff, one or more janitors, caretakers, or attendants are needed to maintain the building and grounds, and a full-time secretary or office clerk may be required. Part-time assistants are employed to care for checking, taking tickets, helping in the locker room, or for various other duties.

Finance.—Municipal recreation buildings are operated through funds provided in the department budget. At some buildings all activities are free; sometimes a fee is charged for admission to special events, for enrollment in a particular class, or for the use of a facility such as a swimming pool or bowling alley. Such charges give persons served a chance to pay part of the cost and provide funds for extending needed services. On the whole, however, these buildings are open for use by the public without charge, and no attempt is made to help meet the cost of operation by charging admission or by use or rental fees. Recreation authorities are therefore free to plan the program and conduct the building so as to serve the best interests of the people rather than to yield the maximum revenue. In some buildings facilities or rooms are rented to organizations at nominal rates when they are not needed for general use by the community.

Items in the operating budget of a recreation building are salaries and wages of leadership and maintenance personnel, fuel, light, water, recreation and office supplies, telephone, insurance, janitorial supplies, repairs, and miscellaneous expenses. Salaries and wages for leadership, the largest expenditure item, sometimes represents as much as one half the total current building budget.

Hours Open.—Many recreation buildings are open morning, afternoon, and evening except Sundays, although in some instances, where conditions warrant, buildings serve effectively seven days a week. The hours depend somewhat upon the nature of the facilities, the type of neighborhood, and the available funds and personnel. The greatest activity is in the late afternoon and evening hours but due to the large number of unemployed and to the growing participation of women in the recreation program, buildings are opened increasingly for morning use, sometimes with a limited staff. In some buildings morning play periods are arranged for children of preschool age. Long evening periods enable at least two groups to be accommodated at each of the major units during the evening. Sometimes, where the demand for a facility such as a gymnasium is very great, it is in continuous use until eleven o'clock, and during the afternoon and evening several groups are assigned a period of one to two hours each.

Use of Building Facilities.—Careful organization is essential to assure maximum use of the building facilities, satisfactory conduct of the various program features, and equal opportunity to all who desire to participate in the activities. To this end, gymnasium periods are divided between basketball teams organized in leagues and playing on a carefully worked out schedule and informal groups who meet for low organized games, gymnasium classes, or individual sports. Club and social rooms are allotted for definite periods to classes in arts, crafts, or dancing, and to clubs formed by individuals interested in such activities as gardening, radio, stamps, or chess. Most clubs which meet in recreation buildings are organized around one of these particular recreation interests although neighborhood groups formed into "general interest" clubs are fairly common. Table game rooms and reading rooms are usually open at all times and without restriction as to age or sex, although children are sometimes excluded during the evening. If the building contains an auditorium with stage, its use is divided between drama and music groups and community affairs such as entertainments, moving-picture shows, lectures, or dances. Sometimes a clubroom or assembly hall is made available at stated times for meetings of organizations like the American Legion or Red Cross.

In preparing a schedule for the use of the building facilities, an attempt is made to give equal consideration to young and old, boys and girls, men and women, to serve varied interests, and to prevent any particular group from securing special privileges. Periods are made of sufficient length to assure satisfactory participation in the particular activity. Periods for strenuous activities such as handball may be short, but for craft projects they should be comparatively long. Activities for children are seldom scheduled in the evening except on Friday or Saturday when family activities are often arranged. It is usually advantageous to assign a gymnasium and related facilities such as showers and locker rooms to either men's or women's groups on a single evening, rather than to alternate the sexes at successive periods on the same evening.

Program.—The activities carried on in recreation buildings depend primarily upon the facilities in the building and the resourcefulness of the leaders in putting them to varied recreation uses. Where the gymnasium is the chief feature, sports and games are likely to receive major emphasis. Social, cultural, and small-group activities of various types are predominant in the programs at many smaller buildings. Buildings with ample and diversified facilities make possible a great variety of indoor recreation activities.

Recreation building programs are built around several general types of activities which involve different organization methods. Use of the rooms set aside for reading, table games, low organized games, and billiards does not involve enrollment in a group or participation in any formal way. Other activities are carried on through clubs, classes, or selective groups. Boxing, tap dancing, choral or instrumental music, dramatics, arts and crafts are usually conducted as group projects with regular meetings and with special instruction or guidance. Social clubs, married couples' clubs, chess or photography clubs, and other similar membership groups meet regularly but do not require continuous leadership. Parties, dances, concerts, and dinners are sometimes open to the entire neighborhood. The athletic program is built around teams and leagues, although in some centers intracenter activities and informal use of the gymnasium receive more emphasis than intercenter competition. The methods commonly used in organizing and conducting several typical indoor activities were discussed in some detail in Chap. XVI.

The following statements describing the activities at three typical recreation buildings illustrate the nature of the programs carried on at different types of buildings and indicate the policies governing their operation. The program at Two Rivers, Wisconsin, described in detail in Chap. XXVII centers largely around the city's recreation building.

Douglas Park Community House, Racine, Wisconsin.—This building, erected at a cost of $58,000 and opened for use early in 1937, adjoins and serves a park playground. The total attendance of persons who took part in various parts of the building program during 1937 was reported to be more than 67,000. The following statement by B. A. Solbraa, Racine's director of recreation, describes the activities carried on during the first year the building was in operation and indicates the contribution which it is making to the recreation life of the city:

Practically all of the activities that center in the building are free and open to the public. Basketball plays the major part, with some of the games being played cross court. A total of 70 basketball teams play many of their games in the new center, six different periods during the week being given over to that sport. On Monday, Wednesday, Thursday, and Sunday nights, as well as on Saturday and Sunday afternoons, basketball is scheduled there. All games are free and open to the public and are well attended.

On Tuesday nights municipal indoor baseball is played there, and here too spectators are treated with the best type of indoor ball. On Friday nights, old-time dances are held. The low admission of ten cents is popular with the adults and square dances and circle two-steps are mostly in demand. Saturday nights the building can be rented for a fee of twenty-five dollars. That takes care of seven nights each week.

The new community center is busy every supper hour. On Monday, Tuesday, and Wednesday between 5:30 and 7:00 the popular game of badminton is played by mixed groups. The department furnishes rackets and shuttlecocks. On Thursday during the supper hour the indoor archery club uses the gym, and on Friday a girls' volley ball team holds its games.

On Saturday mornings and each day after school boys' and girls' after-school clubs meet. Here the program includes floor games, tap dancing, handicraft, music, storytelling, model boat building, athletic sports, singing, some amateur drama, and other activities. Three periods each week are given to boys of grammar-school age, and a like number to the little girls.

Free play for the older unemployed boys is enjoyed from 10:00 to 12:00 each morning and from 1:30 to 3:30 each afternoon except on some occasions when a departmental activity is in the gym. Large numbers of these older boys and young men utilize the gym floor and game rooms during their idle hours. Dressing rooms and shower baths are in the basement.

The small library is open at all hours, and free books and magazines can be had. The game rooms are open during the afternoons and some evenings, and table tennis, chess and checkers, caroms, cards, small billiard tables, and other table games make the day enjoyable for the unemployed youths.

The game rooms with accordian doors are used for larger club meetings, and once weekly for a community card club. The kitchen off the game room, though small, is sufficiently large to serve the needs of meetings held in the lower game rooms. Besides the small custodians' rooms, office and small storage space, there are two upstairs clubrooms which are used almost every night of the week. Archery construction classes, drama meetings, boy and girl scout troops, and several women's sewing and knitting clubs use these clubrooms. All the activities are sponsored by or closely allied with the recreation department.[1]

Green Lake Field House, Seattle, Washington.—This building, one of several built and operated by the Seattle Park Board, is located on the shore of Green Lake and adjacent to it is a 12-acre playfield. Its facilities include a large gymnasium with fully equipped stage, two social rooms each with fireplace, piano, and appropriate furnishings, and locker and dressing rooms which enable the building to serve as a bathhouse during the summer months. The building was erected in 1929 at a cost of $125,000, and during its first 14 months of operation the attendance in its organized activities alone totaled 130,000. Its activities and program are described as follows by Ben Evans, superintendent of recreation with the Park Board:

A good idea of the scope of the field house may be gained by following through a week's activity. The building opens at 2:00 P.M. Monday, and the pupils

[1] "Racine's New Community House," *The Municipality*, April, 1938, p. 77.

from neighboring grade schools soon gather at the building.   A gymnasium class for small girls, six to nine years, is the first group to use the gymnasium, followed by a class of girls from nine to twelve years, another from twelve to fourteen, and a fourth of girls from fourteen to sixteen. From 6:00 until 7:00 P.M. the gymnasium is open to outside organized groups for practice sessions. From 7:00 to 8:00 o'clock a group of high-school boys has the gymnasium followed during the next hour by a class of businessmen for calisthenics. The last class of the day is for men's sports. During the afternoon and evening the clubrooms are used by community groups, while at various times youngsters play games in the large upstairs game halls or on the stage. This program is duplicated on Wednesday.

Tuesday afternoon's first class is for senior women's gymnasium during the period between the opening of the building and the dismissal of school. Then for the remainder of the afternoon, boys play in their gymnasium classes, grouped according to age and size much the same as the girls were. The first evening class is for high-school girls, with senior women using the floor for the final two hours. This program is followed again on Thursday.

Friday afternoon the boys and girls gather in the gymnasium for a general mixer, a party—possibly an entertainment program on the stage. They play in separate classes for the first four days of the week, hence the general mixer each Friday. In the evening, Boy Scouts, Girl Scouts, Camp Fire Girls, and similar junior organizations hold their meetings in the building. Older boys' and men's interfield house athletic games, principally basketball, are played on Friday evenings, after which the building is open for general adult recreation.

Saturday morning sees the boys engage in their interfield house sports competition, sometimes playing in their home gymnasium and at other times visiting another field house. Dancing classes are held Saturday afternoon with separate classes for girls of different ages. These are exceptionally popular and attract 500 or more junior girls each Saturday to Green Lake alone. Saturday evening is devoted to adult recreation. The supervisors cooperate with parents, guardians, and school officials by not scheduling activities for juniors in the evenings of schooldays, except on special occasions.

The social rooms are used free of charge by any community group simply by applying and reserving the date desired. They serve for meetings, dramatics, musicals, institutes, civic welfare meetings, lectures, dances, and a variety of social gatherings. Either an organized club or an unorganized group in the community may use the facilities. Card playing is prohibited, as are meetings of a religious or political nature.

The aim of the Park Board is to make the field house a family recreation center as well as a civic gathering place. Activities are designed to provide every member of a family with his or her favorite sport or hobby, while all civic groups are urged to make full use of the clubrooms and auditorium. Each field house is the hub of civic, social, and recreational activities of the community it serves.[1]

Kenah Community House, Elizabeth, New Jersey.—Most recreation buildings which are open the year round, as in the case of the two pre-

[1] "A Center That Knows No Depression," *Recreation*, October, 1932, p. 319.

viously described, have at least one large room which serves as a gymnasium-auditorium and one or more smaller rooms used for group activities. Kenah Community House located on a small neighborhood playground in Elizabeth, however, illustrates how a small building with only limited facilities can serve as a year-round recreation center. The only room available for recreation is one approximately 20 feet square, but an interesting and varied program is carried on. Among the groups which hold their meetings at the building are a Chess Club, Fencing Club, Radio Club, Art Club, Dancing Club, and a Dramatic Club which has presented plays at several schools and centers. Of special interest to the older boys is the Athletic Club which participates in football, soccer, handball, Ping-pong, and basketball, and a baseball league comprising six teams. These athletic groups meet in the building although most of their activities are carried on out of doors or at other centers with suitable facilities. A Ping-pong Club arranges occasional parties and includes social dancing as a feature of its meetings. Other groups organized at the center are Boy Scout and Girl Scout Troops and Cub Pack. In addition to these organized groups, parties are held at the building in connection with such holidays as Halloween, Christmas, St. Valentine's, and Thanksgiving. The program carried on at the Kenah building illustrates not only the possibilities of usefulness of a small building with few facilities but also its limitations.

THE COMMUNITY HOUSE

The subject of recreation buildings cannot be concluded without a brief consideration of the community house which is a type of building used primarily or exclusively for recreation. Unlike the buildings previously described, most community houses are owned and operated by a private group or organization rather than by municipal recreation authorities, and are located on sites which do not afford facilities for outdoor recreation. Many of them are in towns or small cities and serve as the center of the recreation life of the entire community. The facilities in the community house are similar to those in other general recreation buildings, but in addition they frequently include such features as the office of the Red Cross or visiting nurse, and quarters for the community library. It usually has a central location.

Most of such houses have been built with funds raised by community effort or contributed by an individual or family. Sometimes part of the funds are set aside to provide income to help meet the cost of operation. Occasionally the local government appropriates money toward the operating budget of a community house although in most cases the income is secured through a community chest, local contributions, membership dues, and fees and charges. Management usually rests with a board of trustees appointed by the donor in case the building is a gift, or with a house council elected by members of the association owning or controlling the building. Some community houses are operated entirely through volunteer leaders, but most well-equipped buildings have a full-time director and one or more assistants.

Reference was made in Chap. V to the fact that following the World War there was a nationwide movement for the erection of community houses as memorials and that many such buildings were constructed. Unfortunately, due to lack of competent leadership or to the failure to provide adequate funds for operation, a number of these buildings have failed. The most successful ones are those which have had partial support through endowment funds, which have had trained leaders, and which truly represented a desire on the part of the community for a meeting place and recreation center. In several cities responsibility for operation has been turned over to the municipality even though in some instances title has remained in the hands of a private group. In other instances funds have been appropriated to the community house organization in return for the use of its recreation facilities by school or municipal agencies. Community buildings have been given directly to several cities with the understanding that support be provided from municipal funds.

This tendency to relate the community house to the municipal recreation department has resulted in the coordination of "house" activities with those at other centers throughout the city. This has been effected either through the appointment of the recreation executive as community house director or through the extension of the director's duties to include the operation of playgrounds and other public facilities. The program in Two Rivers, Wisconsin, described in Chap. XXVII, is an example of such coordination. The community house, privately financed and operated, has contributed richly to community life in many small cities and rural communities. However, the advantages of relating its program to other local recreation services and of securing municipal support for the building suggest the desirability of incorporating it in the municipal recreation system where there is one. When administered and financed by the municipality, the community house does not differ essentially from the recreation buildings considered earlier in this chapter.

The Community House at Moorestown, New Jersey.—This town of 7,500 people has a building which in many ways is a typical community house and which illustrates a number of the features mentioned in the preceding statement. Erected at a cost of $200,000 as a gift of a local citizen to the community, the building contains the usual recreation features and in addition a swimming pool, an apartment for the nurses employed by the Visiting Nurses' Organization, a clinic room, a library, and a suite of rooms for the Church Federation. One of the conditions of the gift was that a fund be raised to assure adequate maintenance of the building and a total of $110,000 was secured by public subscription for this purpose. The operation of the building is financed from this fund, from room rentals and activities fees, and from a town appropriation.

By request of the Board of Trustees of the Community House, the management has been assumed by the Township Recreation Commission which is also responsible for the operation of the town's playground and other recreation services. In this way a cooperative recreation program at the building and throughout the community is made possible. Some 25 clubs and organizations meet regularly in the building which is also used for a variety of informal and community activities.

THE SCHOOL CENTER

The term "indoor recreation center" is commonly applied to a building which is *not* used primarily or exclusively for recreation but in which recreation activities are regularly provided under leadership for community groups. Indoor recreation centers are sometimes provided in city halls, churches, libraries, and other types of buildings, but most frequently in school buildings. In hundreds of communities schools are opened for community recreation use, and there is a growing tendency to plan and construct new school buildings in such a manner as to facilitate their use for recreation by nonschool groups. One of the significant developments growing out of the depression has been the realization by local school authorities of the fact, recognized many years ago by the National Education Association, that they should provide facilities suitable for community recreation use. The important place which the school center plays in the recreation life of many cities necessitates special consideration of this type of indoor center.

A number of reasons have been given why a special building is more satisfactory than a school building for use as a community recreation center, but the advocates of school centers can marshal strong arguments for the community use of such buildings. The modern school with its gymnasiums, auditorium, music room, workshops, stage, library, art room, and other features is admirably equipped for recreation. To use these facilities only a few hours each day and to permit them to be idle during long periods when citizens desire to use them is an unjustifiable economic waste. A small addition to the school budget for operating the centers adds greatly to the service rendered by the school plant. In one city it was found that by adding only $10,000 for community recreation to the school budget of $500,000, the total use of the school plant was increased 30 per cent. Citizens are more likely to support a school-building program if they realize that the plant is to serve young people and adults as well as the school population. Even though many adults today hesitate about going to a school for their recreation, the modern school offers such an attractive program that the former attitude toward it is changing, and it is not difficult to consider it as a recreation center. The fact that a well-located school occupies a focal point in the neighborhood, from a geographical standpoint, is another item in its favor. The general opinion prevails that the school building, supported by tax funds and representing a place where all can meet without political or religious bias, affords a logical center for the civic and recreation life of the people of a community or neighborhood.

Types of School Centers.—Many and varied are the community uses of school buildings for recreation and the methods under which they are conducted. In some instances local organizations such as a scout troop, orchestra, or woman's club are permitted to use schoolrooms for their regular meetings; in others groups of young men or women use the school gymnasium one evening a week for basketball and other games. In such cases responsibility for conducting the activity and for caring for school property rests entirely with the organization or group, since the school provides no leadership but requires that the activity be carried on under the guidance of a responsible adult. School authorities frequently grant organizations free use of the auditorium for lectures, concerts, and other events which are open to the public without cost. The practice of renting school facilities to organizations or groups for meetings, recreation activities, or occasional special functions is a common one. The type of use to be considered here, however, is that in which a program of recreation activities is regularly carried on at a school building under the leadership of a recreation agency serving all the people. In some instances the agency provides a diversified program utilizing many facilities in the building which consequently serves as a genuine neighborhood center, but in others it merely uses one or two facilities to furnish specialized activities for unrelated community groups.

Agencies Conducting Centers.—Many school centers are operated by the school authorities themselves through a recreation department, an extension division, an adult education department, a department of community centers, or the physical education department. Frequently a city recreation department is responsible for the school centers; sometimes they are conducted by the park department or some other municipal agency. They are occasionally sponsored by a private group or organization. In some states legislation indicates the manner in which centers are to be established and financed; in others the method to be followed is left to the discretion of the local authorities. In the final analysis, authority and responsibility for the centers and their operation rest with the local school board. When the centers are conducted by a nonschool agency it is essential that it establish and maintain cooperative and satisfactory working relationships with the school board, the school superintendent, and the regular school staff serving in the buildings used as centers.

School Center Hours.—Most school centers are open only two or three evenings a week although in a few instances a program is carried on from Monday through Friday. The evening periods are usually from two to four hours in length, although they vary from city to city and sometimes when a special event such as a dance is held, the center is kept open later than usual. As a rule, the center season extends from early in the fall until well into the spring, but in a very few cities, especially where the center is operated in connection with an outdoor play area, the program extends throughout the year. Activities at such centers are carried on continuously from midafternoon throughout the evening. Because of its use by regular school groups the school center obviously cannot be made available for as long a period daily as the building used exclusively for recreation purposes.

The Staff.—Each individual center has a director who is in full charge and who sometimes also serves as director of the school playground. Among his assistants are one or more recreation leaders serving on a full-time basis, a doorman, a host or hostess, an instructor or leader for each of several activities such as athletics, dramatics, swimming, or instrumental music, club leaders, checkroom and locker room attendants, and a clerk. Regardless of the auspices under which the centers are conducted, the principal of the school usually has full authority over his building and grounds at all times, and the center director must work closely with him. Cooperation between day school and evening center workers is assured in one large city by appointing the school principal center director and by paying him $500 additional per year because of his added duties. He is required to spend two evenings each week at the center, but the chief responsibility for its operation is carried by the assistant director who is a full-time recreation worker.

Most of the workers at the individual centers are employed on a part-time basis for service one or more evenings each week. This arrangement is highly satisfactory in the case of specialists such as dancing instructors, teachers of special crafts, choral directors, or fencing instructors who serve one or a few groups. It is highly desirable, however, that the director and one or more of his assistants be employed on a full-time, year-round basis, for only then is it possible to secure trained workers who devote their full time to the center, become acquainted with the people in the neighborhood, and work with several center groups. Unless the center staff is built around one or more such workers, the individual leaders tend to be interested only in their particular activities and groups, and the potentialities of the school for becoming a genuine center of neighborhood life are not likely to be realized. The employment of full-time, year-round workers makes possible a continuous, coordinated indoor and outdoor program, closely related to neighborhood interests and needs. In one large successful school center conducted five evenings each week, the total staff numbers approximately forty workers. Four of them are full-time, year-round workers, several work on a full-time per diem basis, and the others are employed part-time to teach classes, conduct activities, or supervise game rooms.

No consideration of the school center staff can fail to take into account the janitor or custodian. Recreation executives have repeatedly been brought face to face with the fact that the smooth, harmonious, and effective operation of a school center program depends in no small measure upon the cooperation of the janitorial staff. In some cities the recreation use of the schools has been seriously retarded by the lack of such cooperation. Center workers who insist upon proper care in the use of school property and recognize the responsibility of janitors for its protection and maintenance find that their difficulties on this score are minimized.

The Use of School Facilities.—Operation of a school center is facilitated in a building that has been designed for community use. If such facilities as the gymnasium, auditorium, art and craft rooms, library, locker and shower rooms, and a few classrooms are arranged in separate units or are located in one section of the building, it is unnecessary to open and heat the entire building when the center is in operation. Ample storage space for tables, chairs, game equipment, craft supplies, and other accessories is essential. Removable seats in classrooms and in the auditorium permit multiple use. An attractive lounge or social room and a reading room bring many people to the center. Special rooms are needed for billiards or the rougher kinds of games; classrooms may be used for quiet, table, or the less strenuous games such as box bowling, indoor quoits, or table tennis.

The dual use of school facilities gives rise to many problems. When desks are moved from a classroom to make space for center activities, they must be replaced before school opens the following morning. The tables, chairs, and equipment used for these activities must be safely stored until they are next needed, when they must be brought out and set up again. The use of a drama or craft workshop or art rooms by adult groups raises problems as to the care and use of tools and equipment, the storage of materials, and the protection of articles in process of construction. Additional locker facilities are usually needed in a school where the gymnasium is to be used by groups in the evening. Unless a building has been designed for dual use there will be some difficulty in conducting activities and in providing and caring for equipment. In one city where many classrooms are used for games, crafts, and other activities equipment for which must be set up daily, two men are employed for a couple of hours each evening after the centers close to assist the school janitor in preparing the rooms for the opening of school the following morning.

In a Newark Center.—The wide range of activities for which various schoolrooms may be used is suggested by the list which follows, taken from a bulletin issued by the Central Avenue Community Center of Newark, New Jersey:

Auditorium:
  Dramatic presentations
  Symphony orchestra rehearsals
  Forums and lectures
  Band concerts
  Choral group rehearsals
  Motion pictures
  Dance band rehearsals
  Minstrels
  Recitals
Large gymnasium:
  Exhibitions and demonstrations
  Club activity program
  Leagues in all sports
  Special holiday dances
  Reducing classes
  Game tournaments
  Apparatus groups
Medical room:
  Home nursing instruction
  First-aid classes
  Hygiene classes
Cooking room:
  Nutrition classes
  Preparation of party refreshments
Class rooms:
  Club meetings
  Dressing rooms
  Check rooms
  Literary club meetings
  Civic group meetings

Kindergarten:
  Club parties and socials
  Social dancing classes
  Social club meetings
  Tap dancing groups
  Lectures to small groups
  Bridge games
  Scout programs
  Toy band
  Dance band rehearsals
Small gymnasium:
  Fencing groups
  Social dances
  Special meetings
  Scout programs
  Boxing classes
  Lectures
  Calisthenics
Music room:
  Choral group rehearsals
  Club meetings
  Dance band rehearsals
School courts:
  Ping-pong tournaments
  Active games rooms
Sewing room:
  Handicraft groups
  Parties and socials
  Council meetings
  Club meetings
  Health lectures

Finance.—School centers operated by school authorities, like other parts of the school program, are financed primarily through budget appropriations. In a few cities a special mill tax is levied by the school board for recreation purposes. School tax funds usually cover heat, light, janitor service, and leadership. Most center activities are free to all, but nominal charges are sometimes made for enrollment in classes requiring special leadership or equipment to defray the cost of this special service. In one city this enrollment fee of $1 is returned to individuals who attend 75 per cent of the class or group sessions. Where the centers are not conducted by the school authorities, costs are met in various ways. In several cities where the recreation department or other group conducting the centers provides the program leadership and meets other expenses, heat, light, and supplementary janitor service are paid out of school funds. In others the schools provide heat and light only, whereas in a few cities the schools meet none of the expense of center operation. In such cases the department conducting the centers is charged for the use of the building and must include in its budget an item for school rentals as well as for leadership and other necessary services. As a result, the program is likely to be limited and participants may be called upon to meet part of the expense.

The Program.—Indoor center programs are similar in many respects to those at recreation buildings, and the same principles govern program planning at the school center and the playground. Evening center activities, however, are often restricted to young people who have left school and to adults. The limited evening periods necessitate careful planning to accommodate all groups, especially where centers are open only a couple of evenings each week. In one city, the school gymnasiums are in such demand for basketball that three evening periods of one hour and fifteen minutes each are arranged. In general, activities must be conducted in an informal manner, be adapted to the varying interests of adults, and be appropriate to the neighborhood. The character of the program is sometimes influenced by the participation of foreign-born groups who have their peculiar social and cultural interests. Leadership personnel, facilities, other community resources, and available funds also influence program planning. Methods of conducting many types of indoor center activities will be considered in subsequent chapters.

The Program in Milwaukee.—The school centers in Milwaukee, as well as the city's major municipal recreation service, are provided by the Board of Education through its Department of Municipal Recreation and Adult Education. Its program is presented here because it contains a comprehensive list of activities from which other communities may select the particular subjects best suited to their special needs. The following activities were offered in the Milwaukee centers during the season beginning September, 1937:

ARTS AND CRAFTS

Applied arts: Art novelties, gift articles, home decorations, household novelties
Crocheting: Laces, gloves, neckwear, dresses, sweaters, scarfs, neckties, purses, luncheon sets, etc.
Flower making: Woodfiber paper, silk, organdie
Food preparation and service

Garment remodeling: Ripping, sponging, washing, dyeing—from old to new
Interior decorating
Knitting: Suits, dresses, sweaters, scarfs, berets, hats, mittens, golf socks, etc.
Lamp shades
Leather tooling: Coin purses, handbags, book covers, novelties
Life sketching
Metal work: Bowls, dishes, jewelry, book ends, candlesticks, sconces, etc.
Needle craft: Embroidery, needlepoint, cross-stitch, smocking, hardanger, Italian cutwork
Painting: Water color and oil
Patchwork quilts: Historic and modern designs
Pottery and clay modeling
Rugs: Hooked, braided, knit, crochet
Sculpturing
Sewing and dressmaking: Use and adaptation of commercial patterns
Tin craft
Toys: Dolls, stuffed animals, games, doll houses, toy furniture, wagons, etc.
Weaving: Card weaving and loom weaving
Wood carving and whittling
Woodwork: Furniture, boats, model boats, ship models

HOME CARE OF THE SICK

Care of invalid's bed, changing linen with patient in bed, bathing patient, care of fever patient, poultices and compresses, sickbed comforts, care of convalescents, invalid cookery, etc.

BEAUTY CULTURE AND PERSONAL CARE

Care of hair, skin, fingernails, teeth, eyes, feet

ATHLETICS AND SPORTS

Badminton: Informal play and tournaments
Boxing: Organized scientific instruction—pulleys, platform bag, striking bag, shadow boxing, rope skipping, calisthenics, limited bouts
Gymnasium classes: Keeping-fit classes for men, reducing classes, and general gymnasium classes for men and women
Low organized games: For boys who do not care to participate in the highly organized team games, an informal active game room is provided
Table tennis: Informal play, instruction, municipal leagues and tournaments
Team games: The social center gymnasiums offer opportunity for informal games of basketball, indoor baseball, and volley ball for both boys and girls and men and women. Those who desire membership in formally organized teams for local or city-wide league play will find opportunity for such participation in the neighborhood or the municipal leagues. The regularly scheduled league games provide the general public with an opportunity to witness high-grade play in the various sports

DANCING

Creative dancing
Dances of foreign lands: Taught and interpreted by native-born with special study of national costumes, customs, music, and racial backgrounds
Married people's dance clubs
Old-time dance clubs

Saturday evening informals
Social dancing: Special classes for high-school groups
Tap dancing

GAMES

Billiards: Pocket billiards
Checkers: Informal play, instruction, intersocial center league, municipal checker
  league for adults
Chess: Informal play, instruction in beginners' and advanced chess at all social cen-
  ters, municipal tournaments and leagues, simultaneous exhibitions by masters
Contract bridge: Classes in bidding and play of the hand, Culbertson system
Municipal chess room, park social center: Open afternoons and evenings
Skat: Courses of ten lessons
Table games: Caroms, miniature bowling, parchesi, dominoes, rook, flinch, etc.

LITERARY ORGANIZATIONS

Debating clubs   Parliamentary law classes
English for foreign-born   Public speaking
English study classes   Reading groups

CITIZENSHIP TRAINING FOR FOREIGN-BORN

American literature and history classes for new Americans
Citizenship classes for preparation for naturalization
Classes in advanced English
Classes in beginners' English
Free help in filling out first and second papers

DRAMATICS

Milwaukee Players: (Experimental group—members elected from the Social Center
  Drama Guild upon ability and merit) Weekly studio night for voice, diction,
  rhythmic exercises, dancing, stage technique; workshop for designing and building
  scenery, designing and making costumes and properties, stage lighting; periodic
  public production; annual Shakespeare festival
Milwaukee Social Center Drama Guild: (Composed of members of social center drama
  clubs) Monthly drama tea, lectures, demonstrations, theater parties, annual one-
  act play tournament
Play reading groups: Informal reading and discussion of classical and modern plays
Social center drama clubs: Open to anyone above elementary-school age

MUSIC

Bands   Novelty bands
Glee clubs—men   Opera clubs
Glee clubs—women   Orchestras
Mandolin and string ensembles   Ukulele clubs
Mixed choruses   Vocal training classes

CAMERA CLASSES AND CLUBS

Advanced course: Chemistry of photography; filters and filter factors; enlargements;
  homemade equipment and darkrooms

Beginners' course: Parts, construction, and manipulation of the camera; physics and chemistry of photography; developing and printing
Photographic art clubs
Photographic clinic: A consultation hour to which amateurs are invited to bring their pictures for analysis, criticism, and suggestion. Special attention paid to cinema photography

AERONAUTICS AND MODEL PLANES

Instruction in building and flying of model planes of various types, with lectures on theory and history of aviation
Model plane contests

CIVIC AND SOCIAL ORGANIZATIONS

Boy scouts	Married people's social clubs
Civic associations	Mothers' clubs
Clubs for all ages	Neighborhood card parties
Community clubs	Parent training classes
Girl scouts	Parent-teacher associations
Guardian clubs	Social, study, and hobby clubs
Junior Optimist club	

COMMUNITY FEATURES

Weekly entertainments: Motion pictures, recitals, concerts, lectures, plays, etc.
Saturday afternoon children's entertainments
Saturday night informals: Dancing and, for those who do not care to dance, table tennis, cards, social games, and visiting

FORUMS

Lectures and discussion of topics of local and national interest. Special youth forums

Additional special features are expert instruction in beginning and advanced handloom weaving, swimming and Red Cross lifesaving classes for men and women, a children's theater with Saturday afternoon productions, reading rooms, children's rooms where parents attending centers may leave their children in charge of a trained play leader, and afterschool children's activities at nine centers.

The Weekly Program—Sioux City.—The indoor center program carried on at four junior high schools in Sioux City, Iowa, is typical of that in many American cities. The centers, open three evenings each week from 7:15 to 9:45, afford a varied program. Each center has a director, a gym instructor, and locker room attendant for men, and a game room attendant. By scheduling on alternate evenings special activities such as tap dancing, ladies' gymnasium, and art and craft classes, the additional workers in charge of these activities are able to serve two centers. Two groups are served in the gymnasium each evening, but most of the other activities are carried on throughout the entire evening. The schedule of activities conducted each evening at one of the centers and the rooms in which they are held are indicated in the following outline:

NORTH JUNIOR HIGH SCHOOL CENTER PROGRAM

Rooms used	Monday	Wednesday	Thursday
Girls' gymnasium	Ladies' gymnasium class Athletic leagues	Badminton	Tap dance class Badminton
Boys' gymnasium	Game and reading room	Men's gymnasium class Athletic leagues	Men's gymnasium class Athletic leagues
Auditorium	Table tennis	Table tennis	Table tennis
Corridor	Dart baseball	Dart baseball	Dart baseball
Room 1	Art and craft class		
Room 2	Game and reading room	Game and reading room	Game and reading room
Room 3		Dramatic club meeting	

Special Events.—Regular meetings of the many groups that come to the center to engage in activities of their own choice and to enjoy the sociability of others with similar interests constitute the bulk of the indoor center program.   Many groups, however, enjoy an opportunity to demonstrate to their friends and to the neighborhood the prowess they have achieved in their respective activities or to cooperate with other groups in special projects.   The program, therefore, includes a number of feature events, some of them in the nature of demonstrations, others utilizing the interest in a holiday or special season.   The following list of the feature activities at the Central Avenue Community Center in Newark, New Jersey, illustrates the nature of such events:

Dedication of Christmas Tree	Church Choir Festival
Playground Springtime Revue	Senior Chorus Concert
Negro History Week Program	Joint Council Meeting
Symphony Orchestra Concert	Mothers' Club Rally
Negro Health Week Program	Youth Week Program
Sewing Club Fashion Show	Annual Club Plays
Junior Chorus Operetta	Holiday Festivals

A FEW SUGGESTIONS

Many other aspects of school center operation merit careful study, but only a few can be mentioned briefly here:

1. A brightly lighted entrance to the building helps advertise the center, serves as a welcome, and reduces discipline problems.

2. Registration of regular attendants at the center creates a sense of belonging to the center, facilitates record keeping, and reduces problems of conduct.

3. Making visitors to the center welcome is an important function of the doorman, host, or director. An attractive lobby helps to create a favorable impression.

4. A room for checking wraps encourages a person to prolong his visit to the center, facilitates control, and improves the appearance of the center.

5. A center council organized from representatives of neighborhood agencies, from representatives of groups using the center, or both, gives expression to neighborhood opinion. It is also helpful in planning the program, in determining policies, in conducting special activities, in interpreting the center to the public, and in enlisting volunteer service.

6. Attractive posters, printed or mimeographed program schedules, newspaper announcements, and talks to neighborhood groups help build center attendance.

7. Carefully kept attendance and cost records facilitate the evaluation of services and costs and are an aid in planning.

8. A feeling of pride in the center is developed when proper conduct, dress, care of rooms, and relationships are recognized by the neighborhood as essential.

9. The board of education should be kept informed of the program and interested in it through regular reports and invitations to attend special events. In one city the board members arranged a tour of the centers and news photographers took pictures of the activities with board members taking part.

The preceding discussion has related primarily to the school center which is opened several evenings a week for a widely varied program. It must be kept in mind that in many cities or neighborhoods centers are open only one or two evenings a week and for a limited range of activities. The problems involved in operating such centers are less complex than those at the major centers. In general, however, the same principles apply to all types of school centers and to other buildings which are not intended primarily for recreation but which are used in connection with the recreation program.

CHAPTER XIX

THE OPERATION OF RECREATION FACILITIES

The great variety of areas and facilities comprising a modern municipal recreation system were described in Chaps. XI and XII. The effectiveness of the service which they can render is dependent upon the manner in which they are administered as well as upon their design, development, and equipment. Some of the methods and factors important in the operation of recreation buildings and centers apply equally in the case of recreation facilities. Yet the successful operation of these facilities calls for a knowledge of the peculiar problems which must be met and of the procedures for solving them.

The city which merely develops, protects, and maintains its recreation facilities and leaves it to the public to use them or not, fails to realize fully on its investment and to meet its entire responsibility. It is true that where new facilities have been provided because of an urgent demand for them, they have been used to capacity as soon as they were opened. Sometimes, however, lack of skill, inability to purchase the necessary personal equipment, inadequate publicity concerning the facilities, excessive fees, and unwise use regulations deter large numbers of people from using facilities furnished by recreation authorities. Many people have never had an opportunity to play golf, to go camping, or to engage in water sports, and therefore do not realize the satisfaction which these activities afford. Only when recreation facilities are placed under the direction of qualified personnel familiar with recreation leadership methods and techniques are the fullest utilization of the facilities and maximum service to the public assured.

Major objectives of recreation authorities in operating recreation facilities are to extend their use to the greatest possible number of people, to assure equal opportunity to all, to maintain the facilities in the best possible condition, and to make their use as safe, convenient, pleasant, and satisfying as possible. To achieve these objectives the authorities adopt general policies under which the facilities are to be operated and issue detailed instructions governing their use by the public. Successful operation necessitates the employment of a well-trained manager or director and an adequate, competent staff of assistants and maintenance workers.

Principles and methods of leadership in recreation activities have long been applied to the municipal camp program, but they have been considered less important at other recreation facilities. Progressive recreation authorities are now extending recreation leadership to such facilities as the golf course, swimming pool, bathing beach, and athletic field. The promotion of a varied, interesting program of activities is being regarded as of even greater importance than the essential function of maintaining the facilities.

THE BATHING BEACH AND SWIMMING POOL

Swimming is an activity which appeals to people of all ages; it is an ideal form of recreation for the family and for mixed groups. Considered by many authorities as the finest all-round type of exercise, it also affords an excellent means of social activity. No other municipal recreation facilities except the playgrounds have as high an attendance each year as the pools and beaches. In 1938 more than 200 million visits were recorded at the 1,070 swimming centers for which attendance was reported.[1] Most studies of the popularity of different forms of recreation have indicated that swimming heads the list. Therefore the operation of pools and beaches has become a major phase of municipal recreation service and one which demands intelligent planning in order that the people may realize to the fullest possible extent the recreational possibilities of the water sports program.

In many respects the problems of operating the beach and the pool are similar, but in others they differ widely, especially in the case of the indoor pool which is usually operated as a part of a recreation building or school plant. Three factors that require major attention at both types of water areas are (1) the purity of the water, (2) the safety of the bathers, and (3) the promotion of swimming and other activities. To assure that these conditions are met, a trained and competent staff is needed at the beach or pool whenever it is open for public use.

The Staff.—The manager has full authority and responsibility for the operation of the beach or pool. One or more lifeguards are on duty during all bathing hours, the number required varying with the size of the beach or pool, the depth of the water, the number of people served, and the hours it is open each day. One recreation department requires a lifeguard to be on duty for every 200 bathers in its pools. An attendant stationed at the shower room or pool entrance inspects the bathers and ensures their taking a thorough cleansing bath before entering the water. Additional workers usually needed are a cashier, suit attendants, and a caretaker. Generally speaking, the minimum staff at a beach or outdoor pool includes a manager, a cashier, two lifeguards, a man and a woman attendant, and a caretaker. All employees at a pool or beach should be

[1] *Recreation*, June, 1939, p. 129.

capable swimmers and competent in lifesaving methods. To assure adequate preparation on the part of workers at pools and beaches, special schools or training institutes are held in several cities prior to the swimming season.

Sanitation.—Recreation authorities have a serious obligation to the public for maintaining a high standard of cleanliness at pools and beaches. Purification and recirculation systems are installed at artificial pools to assure a sanitary condition of the water, but they require careful and continuous supervision. In many states the sanitary control of pools and beaches rests with the public health authorities, and local health departments render valuable assistance to the recreation agencies in testing the water and in checking the purification methods and equipment. Because at most bathing beaches it is not feasible to treat or to control the water supply and thereby assure its purity, it is not customary to require so high a standard of bacterial quality at a beach as at a pool. Nevertheless, at some beaches the water is treated satisfactorily with liquid chlorine released from a perforated pipe laid at the bottom or applied from a boat. In all pools daily tests of the water are essential and care is also taken to assure the sanitary condition of bathhouses, dressing rooms, toilet facilities, suits, and towels. Before entering a pool, persons are generally required to take a cleansing bath, using warm water and soap. Persons with open wounds or with communicable or skin diseases are not permitted to enter.

Safety.—Constant vigilance is required on the part of the lifeguards to prevent accidents and to render prompt assistance to bathers who need it. To assure safety, rules are adopted and posted at the beach or pool indicating the water areas which may be used, the conditions of use, and the practices which are not permitted. Running and playing games are usually prohibited on the pool runways although a section of the beach is often set aside for games and sports. The diving area and other deep parts of the pool require special attention, and swimming near rip tides, piers, and other obstructions is prohibited at beaches. In one city with many municipal pools nonswimmers are required to wear white bathing caps, thereby enabling the lifeguards to watch them more closely and prevent them from entering deep water. Rules must be strictly enforced, lifesaving and first-aid equipment must be constantly available and in good condition, and workers must be given definite instructions as to the procedure to be followed in case of serious accidents. At some of the ocean beaches, lifesaving methods include the use of fast patrol boats and two-way radios in the lifeguard ambulance and high-speed rescue cars. Junior lifeguard corps have been organized in several cities. The efficiency of the accident prevention and rescue work of municipal lifeguards is strikingly illustrated in the case of the Los Angeles municipal beaches which in the summer of 1938 served 6,364,691 visitors without a single drowning.

The Program.—The chief activities at municipal pools and beaches are (1) general swimming and diving, (2) swimming instruction, (3) competitive swimming, and (4) feature events such as carnivals, pageants, or playdays. The popularity of the pool or beach depends not only upon the facilities and their maintenance but upon the promotional and leadership ability of the manager and his assistants. Learn-to-swim campaigns, the formation of swimming clubs, the use of progressive tests for proficiency in the water, and the organization of meets and special events are effective methods of expanding the service of pools and beaches and of developing more widespread interest and participation in the water sports program. The outdoor swimming season extends for about three months in most parts of the country.

General Swimming.—Most people come to the pool or beach to engage in informal swimming, diving, and sun bathing, and to enjoy the relaxation and invigoration which come from participation in these activities. Nonorganized swimming is the chief feature of the program, and most of the time during which the pool or beach is open is devoted to it. The sociability which swimming and informal water sports afford attracts more people to the beach and pool than competitive activity. Care must therefore be taken not to schedule too many special events which would interfere with the general swimming periods. In the multiple-unit pools the largest unit is usually used for general swimming which is conducted as a co-recreational activity. Most indoor pools are used primarily by gymnasium classes for swimming instruction or by special groups, usually of one sex, rather than for general swimming. Increasingly, however, mixed adult swimming is encouraged, as in one city where the pools are reserved for Party Club Swims on certain evenings.

Swimming Instruction.—People cannot secure the fullest enjoyment from bathing unless they know how to swim. Because opportunities for learning are otherwise denied to large numbers of children and adults, swimming instruction is a valuable feature of the program at most municipal pools and beaches. Thousands of children are taught to swim each summer, and others are helped to attain greater proficiency in swimming, diving, and lifesaving. Definite periods are set aside for instruction, demonstration, and practice. Many cities encourage boys and girls to improve their skill in the water through the use of graded tests worked out locally, the Red Cross events, or the swimming badge tests prepared by the National Recreation Association. Emblems are awarded to all who succeed in passing these tests. As a rule, swimming classes are free to children although a nominal charge is frequently made for adult instruction.

Competition.—Swimming and diving are also conducted on a competitive basis. Teams are sometimes formed at the different playgrounds, and interplayground or interpool swimming leagues are features of the programs in several cities. Occasional swimming meets provide an incentive for enrollment in the instruction classes or for improving one's proficiency in the water. A city-wide tournament is commonly held at the end of the season to determine the champions in the various events.

Special Features.—Aquatic carnivals including a variety of water games, stunts, and special events, pageants in which large numbers of people take part, a water circus, exhibitions of swimming and diving, and lifesaving contests afford variety in the program. In announcing its schedule of summer aquatic carnivals and fun frolics, one recreation department stated: "Everything from lantern parades, pattern swimming, and paddle board jousting, to comedy diving, mock lifesaving, and a 'world's championship night shirt relay,' will be included in the free programs, to be enacted by swimmers and divers before average audiences expected to exceed five thousand at each pool." At beaches it is often possible to permit general swimming while a part of the beach is reserved for special events, but most pools are closed to public use during these feature programs.

Events featuring canoes, rowboats, and sailboats, and distance swims are possible at ocean or lake beaches. General pleasure boating, crew racing, sea scouting, and a variety of boating activities are sometimes included in the beach program. Boats are excluded, however, from the areas used by bathers. At bathing beaches, and to a lesser extent at swimming pools, there is a growing tendency to introduce facilities for games such as volley ball, table tennis, paddle tennis, and shuffleboard, which have increased attendance and have proved very popular. Refreshment facilities are provided at most beaches, sometimes beach chairs and umbrellas are rented, and areas are set aside for picnicking. An unusual feature at Cabrillo Beach, Los Angeles, is a Marine Museum which contains a collection of interesting shells, fish, plant life, coral, birds, and other marine life of the Pacific Coast.

Costs.—Most cities charge admission to their swimming pools. In some instances the charge includes special services such as locker, suit, soap, and towel; in other cases an additional amount is charged for them. One or more sessions each week are usually set aside as free swimming periods for children. Fees for services rendered at bathing beaches are also fairly common. Few cities attempt to make a profit on their swimming facilities, but as a rule the income approximates the operating cost. In 1935 the average reported income at 229 pools was $2,538.18 as compared with an average operating cost at 295 pools of $2,573.50. The average income at 110 bathing beaches in 1935 was $1,422.36; the average operating cost at 170 beaches was $2,663.96. Except in the cities of over one million, however, the average cost of beach operation was not much greater than the average income.

GOLF COURSES

The remarkable development of municipal golf during the past two decades has been one of the outstanding features of the public recreation movement. The insistent demand by golfers for additional facilities and the belief that these could be made self-sustaining have resulted in some cities in a more adequate provision for golf than for children's play or other types of recreation service. The golf course has become an important feature of the recreation system and its operation presents many special problems to the administrator.

The Staff.—The golf course, like the beach or pool, is usually in charge of a manager who in many cities is employed on a 12-month basis. In practice there is a great variety in the functions and duties of the manager but many believe that he should be given entire responsibility for the maintenance and operation of the course and clubhouse. Other workers are a professional, head greenkeeper, starter, caddie master, janitor, locker room attendants, rangers, cashier, refectory clerks, cook, and maintenance crew. The number and duties of the different types of workers vary widely, depending upon the intensity of play, the facilities and services afforded at the clubhouse, and the general plan of operation. Frequently two or more functions are cared for by a single individual, as for example the professional and manager or the starter and caddie master. The average number of employees at an 18-hole course during the active playing season varies from 10 to 20.

On many courses play continues the year round, although in some Northern cities the season is only about eight months. As a rule, a few workers are employed on a year-round basis and others are used only during the busy summer season. The maintenance staff at the municipal golf course is exceedingly important because only through the employment of a sufficient number of competent workers can a course which receives intensive use be kept in a satisfactory playing condition.

Controlling the Play.—Only a limited number of persons can use a golf course at one time, so methods must be devised to assure to all who desire to play a fair opportunity to use the course. It is common practice to operate municipal courses on the "first come, first served" basis. People desiring to play wait their turn if there are others ahead of them waiting for a chance to tee off. Unless there are four individuals waiting who can be started off together, "foursomes" are given the preference. In some cities a dual system of assigning periods of golf is in use, especially over week ends. Half of the starting periods may be reserved in advance, the alternate periods being kept free for persons who have not made reservations.   Advantages of the reservation system are that it is convenient for golfers because they do not have to wait in line for a chance to play, and it relieves congestion at the first tee.   At courses where special privileges or reduced rates are granted to holders of season tickets or to local residents, registration cards are issued, sometimes containing the holder's photograph, which are used for identification purposes.

As a rule "foursomes" are run off every five minutes, which means that 48 people can leave the first tee each hour.   Because inexperienced players slow up the play, there is an advantage in providing a comparatively easy course for beginners and in restricting play on the more difficult courses, at least during periods of intensive use such as over the week ends, to individuals who have passed certain qualifying tests.   Such an arrangement is advantageous to both beginners and experienced golfers.   Rangers are employed at the busy courses to regulate the play, to settle difficulties, to protect the course, and to encourage players to observe the common courtesies associated with the sport.

Costs.—Perhaps no other municipal sport has offered greater promise of being self-supporting than golf.   In constructing their courses many cities have assumed that income would equal operating costs, and in a few instances arrangements have been made for the cost of acquiring the land and building the course to be met from the profits.   During the depression receipts fell off and many courses failed to secure sufficient income to meet even the cost of operation.   The average reported income at 75 municipal 9-hole courses in 1935 was $4,085.69, as compared with an average operating cost of $4,888.41.   In the same year, 126 18-hole courses yielded an average income of $10,239.30, and 121 courses reported an average operating cost of $11,898.62.   The fee charged for a round of 18 holes is usually between 50 and 75 cents with a somewhat higher rate on week ends.   The annual or seasonal fee in most cities is between $10 and $20.   The rates at 9-hole courses are somewhat lower, and a special rate is sometimes fixed for children.   At a few courses an additional fee is charged for making reservations.

Promoting an Interest in Golf.—The success of golf is measured in some cities by the receipts at the courses, but in most cities the game is considered, like other parts of the recreation program, an activity to be made available at a minimum cost to the greatest number of people.   The Cincinnati Recreation Commission has promoted golf through offering lessons to beginners, organizing classes, promoting golf in high schools and business concerns, renting equipment at a low fee, reducing green fees, and fixing low rates for school pupils.   The growing interest of high-school students in golf has been noted and stimulated in several cities.   Family golf also is being encouraged by arranging classes for women, special periods for play at a reduced rate, and golf playdays for women, with stroke competition, putting, and other events. Golf clubs and associations at municipal courses have proved a means of sustaining a year-round interest in golf, of elevating standards of play, and of enforcing the rules. Exhibitions, demonstrations, and tournaments are arranged from time to time, but they should not be so frequent as to interfere seriously with play by the general public. Interest in the game has been stimulated in some cities by special events such as father and son, professional and caddie, or intercity caddie tournaments.

Other Activities at the Golf Course.—The desirability of encouraging family recreation and the demand for the maximum year-round use of all public recreation facilities have turned the attention of recreation executives to the possibilities of introducing at the golf course activities which appeal to all members of the family and which are carried on throughout the year. To this end play programs are being provided at courses for children whose parents are playing golf. Archery, tennis, bowling, and other game courts have been constructed near the clubhouse, and in some instances clubs have been formed in these games and sports. Courses are often used for tobogganing, coasting, skating, and skiing during the winter months. In one city 16 driving tees have been laid out near the start of the course so that persons waiting to play may have an opportunity to practice driving. Golf clubhouses with their beautiful dance floors, cozy clubrooms, and attractive dining rooms are used by many community groups for social events, especially during the winter months, and also serve as centers of winter sports activities. Under competent recreation leadership, the golf course is becoming a genuine recreation center rather than an area used only for a highly specialized activity by a relatively small percentage of the community.

WINTER SPORTS FACILITIES

As a result of the remarkable growth of public interest in winter sports, facilities for skating, tobogganing, skiing, and other outdoor winter activities have become common features of the municipal recreation system in parts of the country where such activities are possible. Winter sports afford healthful and stimulating activity to large numbers of people at a relatively low cost.

The Skating Rink.—Natural, quiet, shallow water areas make excellent skating rinks. Care must be taken to prevent people from skating on the ice until it is sufficiently thick to assure safety, and if the water is deep, lifesaving equipment must be conspicuously provided near by for use in case of emergencies. Except in neighborhoods with natural water areas, artificial rinks are provided as described in Chap. XIII. The preparation of areas for skating requires advance planning as equipment must be ready and workers must be carefully instructed as to the methods of constructing the rinks so that no time will be lost when cold weather arrives. As a rule, rinks are constructed at night when the temperature is lowest, and at both natural and artificial skating areas the maintenance work is often done after the rink is closed in the evening. Proper and continuous care of the ice is essential to secure the maximum number of skating days and satisfactory ice conditions. Because of the shortness of the season it is desirable to light the facilities to permit evening use.

In general, a worker is stationed at each skating rink to maintain order, care for the ice, and have general supervision of the rink while it is in use. One or more additional workers may be employed for a few hours each day after the rink closes to scrape, clean, and resurface it for the following day. In one city three-man crews clean and flood several rinks each night. There is much to be said in favor of employing a recreation leader to take charge of a large rink, for in addition to serving as a general supervisor, he can help children learn to skate, organize hockey teams, and promote a program of special events.

The size of the area naturally influences the activities that can be carried on. On large areas a section approximately 100 by 200 feet may be set aside for a hockey rink, preferably at one side, although it is sometimes located in the center. Where competitive skating is popular a track may be marked off, possibly around the hockey rink, for the use of expert skaters and for races. Most people use the section set aside for general skating, located so as not to interfere with the specialized activities. In case a building near the rink is used as a warming shelter and has facilities for checking skates, a worker is generally needed to care for it. Skating rinks are free to the public, although a small charge is sometimes made for checking or other special service.

The Toboggan Slide.—Tobogganing is a thrilling sport which requires a well-constructed and carefully operated slide. At least two persons are employed at a slide to operate it and keep it in good condition. One is the starter at the top of the slide who sees that persons are properly seated on the toboggan and that the toboggan does not start down the slide until the preceding group is clear of it. The other worker, usually stationed near the bottom, is the signal man who indicates when the toboggan may start down the slide and who prevents persons from crossing the course. When the attendance is large it may be necessary to employ one or more workers to keep people away from the outrun. There is seldom a charge for the use of a toboggan slide if a group has its own toboggan, but if toboggans are rented, as is usually the case, a third worker is needed to care for them.

Coasting.—The great popularity of coasting among children has caused recreation authorities to utilize for this sport park hillsides free from obstructions, golf courses, and other large areas with natural slopes. These areas as well as the low sled slides often erected on playgrounds require some supervision but their operation and maintenance are relatively easy. In spite of traffic hazards, the street is still the most popular sliding place, and where other suitable places are not available, recreation authorities set aside certain streets for coasting. With the cooperation of the police, barriers are placed at these streets during the periods when coasting is permitted and supervised. Access is not denied to vehicles, but traffic is reduced to a minimum. Sometimes police are stationed at coasting streets; usually, however, these are supervised by the recreation department which is also responsible for placing barricades at the top and bottom of the hills, and for filling, cleaning, and lighting the lanterns placed on the barricades. In one city information as to the condition of the coasting hills is furnished the newspapers and is telephoned daily to each of the schools.

THE STADIUM

Some stadiums are large structures; others seat only a few thousand people and might better be classed as grandstands. In proportion to their cost many large stadiums contribute little to the recreation life of the cities in which they are located; others are operated in such a manner as to make them valuable recreation assets   Experience has demonstrated the truth of the statement: "It is not easy to justify such an expensive project as a municipal stadium unless it is built and managed with the general recreational needs of the community in mind."[1] The most useful and successful stadiums are those which have been erected to meet a definite community need rather than as a means of attracting major sporting events to the city. Some of the largest stadiums are administered by special commissions; others are among the facilities controlled by the recreation authorities.

The problems and policies of stadium operation differ with the type of structure and the major function it is expected to fulfill. The stadium seating 50,000 people and upwards, for example, is rarely required for league games, athletic contests, or other community events organized and conducted by the local recreation authorities. In order to produce revenue which will help meet the cost of its maintenance and operation, the use of such a stadium is therefore granted to institutions, organizations, or commercial agencies for football or baseball games and other events that attract large crowds. The preference is naturally given to the group that will promise the greatest revenue, a policy which has some justification in that it enables the largest number of spectators

[1] Randolph O. Huus and Dorothy I. Cline, *Municipal, School, and University Stadia*, Public Administration Service, 1931.

to be served. Local groups benefit more, however, from the policy adopted by the Park Department in a Pacific Coast city where the city schools, the recreation department, and local colleges are given priority in the making of reservations rather than outside groups that may promise a greater attendance and larger gate receipts. In this city community organizations and activites are not charged a rental fee, but they pay the expenses of caretakers and janitor services for preparing and cleaning up the stadium.

Soldier Field, Chicago.—Soldier Field in Chicago, under the management of the Chicago Park District, is one of the most successful of the large municipal stadiums. Its normal seating capacity is 85,000 but as many as 110,000 have attended a football game in it. The policy established by the Chicago Park Commissioners has been

. . . to permit the use of Soldier Field for any sort of civic, sports, musical, or other form of entertainment or event which does not entail its use as a forum for propaganda on political or economic subjects of a controversial nature. Organizations using this institution are charged a fee either on a percentage basis of the gate receipts or on a rental basis in addition to a guarantee of all expenses incurred by the Chicago Park District in the preparation of the Field before the event and the restoration of the grounds to the proper condition following the events.[1]

Attractions at Soldier Field in 1935 and 1936 included Easter Sunrise Services, Fourth-of-July celebrations, music festivals, Ringling Brothers' Circus, professional, college, and high-school football games, track meets, ski jump tournament, softball tournament, and amateur nights. In spite of these diversified events, the comparatively limited use of this well-constructed and efficiently managed stadium is illustrated by the fact that the total attendance at all events at the field in 1935 and 1936 was only 417,000 and 615,500 respectively. It suggests that authorities will do well to study their local situation carefully before investing the huge sum necessary to erect and maintain a large stadium which will rarely be filled to capacity.

Smaller Stadiums.—A stadium seating 10,000 to 15,000 people is adequate for the normal needs of most cities, and a smaller one may be ample. If properly designed it can be used for a variety of recreation activities such as city-wide championship games in various sports, major track and field meets, pageants, festivals, playground demonstrations, special music events, opera, civic meetings, and mass gatherings. Toboggan slides have been erected at stadiums in some cities, enabling the area to serve as a winter sports center. Under competent leadership a well-rounded municipal recreation program is likely to include a sufficient number of special outdoor events to assure a fairly continuous diversified

[1] *First Annual Report*, Chicago Park District, 1935.

use of such a stadium during many months of the year.   When not required for use by the recreation authorities, it can be rented to organizations for suitable purposes; such use, however, should be secondary.

Rancho Cienega Stadium, Los Angeles.—This new stadium seating 6,000 is the only area controlled by the Playground and Recreation Commission which is well fenced and provided with adequate bleachers, where crowds can be controlled, and where admission can be conveniently charged.   The policy adopted for its operation was designed not only to protect the department's program but to avoid competition with commercially managed stadiums in the city.   The following excerpts from the regulations governing its use indicate the basis on which the stadium is operated and a few important operation details:

> The main purpose of the Stadium is to provide a place for recreation activities that are an outgrowth of the city-wide program conducted by the Department and which require accommodations for a large number of spectators or unusual control of spectators.
>
> The Stadium is not intended primarily as a place for the raising of revenue or for the accommodation of professional and semiprofessional events from which profit is made.
>
> The recreation program of the Department will tax the capacity of the Stadium, consuming all available periods.
>
> Contests will be confined primarily to Saturday afternoons and Sundays. High-school contests, however, will be held usually on Friday afternoons.
>
> Practice of teams in various sports will have to be curtailed and will be the exception rather than the rule in order to preserve the grass for the week ends.
>
> Interdistrict school contests, contests of parochial schools and of private schools will be considered suitable for the Stadium.
>
> Generally speaking and probably for all Department activities, admission will be general without reserved seats.
>
> Applications for special uses of the Stadium outside of the Department's regular program will be considered on their individual merit and permits will be granted on satisfactory terms only by action in each case of the Board of Commissioners.   Such outside uses will be governed by a standard form of contract to be developed.
>
> The standard of maintenance and condition of facilities will be a little higher than that which would apply to playgrounds generally.
>
> When and if any non-Department events are held, the management of the spectators will be under control of the Department, but the cost thereof including ushers will be borne by the lessee.   The lessee will also pay a reasonable charge for clean-up.
>
> Concession rights will be reserved by the Playground and Recreation Commission, but no concession for more than a single event will be granted until use of the Stadium indicates the advisability of such concession.
>
> The director of the Rancho Cienega Playground will act as manager or director of the Stadium and will report to the Superintendent.

Operating Factors.—A number of important and distinctive aspects of stadium operation referred to in the preceding statement merit special comment. The leasing of the stadium to outside agencies—an important feature in many cities—is a minor consideration. Because the stadium, unlike most recreation facilities, is primarily a place where spectators are accommodated at events of unusual interest rather than where large numbers actively participate, an admission fee is commonly charged. The large stadium has a manager whose chief function is booking attractions and supervising operations, but at the small stadium, which is a feature of a general recreation area, the director of the area is usually in charge, although special events may be scheduled through the central office of the department.

The operation of a large stadium involves such problems as the handling of crowds, plans for controlling motor and pedestrian traffic, and the recruiting and training of a corps of workers to serve as ticket sellers and takers, guards, ushers, and parking field attendants. All of these problems are faced to a lesser degree at the smaller stadiums. A small maintenance crew is needed to keep the grounds in condition; this must be supplemented before and after events at which large crowds are accommodated.

THE MUNICIPAL CAMP

Camping affords an unexcelled opportunity for adventure, for discovery, for developing social relationships, and for a change from routine activities and the normal environment. There is a growing belief among leaders in the fields of education and recreation that all citizens, young and old, should have the benefit of a camping experience. The lack of suitable camp sites and the cost of providing camp service have deterred recreation authorities in most cities from including camping as a feature of their program. The greatest development of organized municipal camping has taken place on the Pacific Coast where several cities have established camps, many of them in National Forest areas. With the pronounced trend toward the acquisition of extraurban properties, cities are giving greater attention to the camp problem and are attempting to provide many of the values of a camping experience through the operation of overnight or day camps which involve little expense. Exceptional opportunities for municipal camping are afforded by the recreation demonstration areas developed by the National Park Service. One city has established an auto tourist camp for the use of its citizens, similar to the camping centers provided in many of the state parks. Another city operates, in a large outlying park, camping facilities serving individual guests, a center where large groups can be accommodated in a former CCC camp, a conference camp unit consisting of farm cottages grouped about a main building, and family cabins which can be rented by the week. The operation of the various types of camps naturally involves different personnel, regulations, rates, and services.

The Organized Municipal Camp.—In this type of camp[1] the recreation agency, besides providing the facilities, feeds the campers, conducts a program of activities, and in some instances furnishes transportation to and from the camp. In practically every instance these camps are at a considerable distance from the city; one such camp is 335 miles away. Reservations which are made in advance at the department office are usually on a weekly basis, but campers may stay for more than one week. One- and two-week outings are featured at some of the family camps. Many accommodate families; some are for boys or girls. A nominal fee is charged which helps considerably in meeting the expense of operation, but arrangements are sometimes made for children without funds to attend the camp. A few municipal camps are for underprivileged or undernourished children selected by the social agencies of the city, although most camps are open to everyone. As a rule, camps are operated during the summer months only, although they are sometimes available for week-end or vacation use during other seasons; in a few cases they serve as centers for winter sports.

Staff.—Every camp is in charge of a manager who has full responsibility for its operation and who acts as host. In many instances his wife serves as camp hostess. The recreation program at the camp is conducted by a director, and in some camps a naturalist is also employed. A most important member of the staff is the cook, who has one or more assistants in addition to dishwashers and kitchen helpers. Other employees are a dining-room manager, waitresses, office clerk, general utility man, lifeguard, nurse, and one or more caretakers. These are seasonal workers with the exception of the caretaker, who is often employed to care for the camp throughout the year. If a city operates several camps, a general supervisor is needed, and since many camps are used continuously, this person is usually a year-round worker.

Programs.—Programs are planned to take advantage of the camp environment and afford a change from the activities regularly engaged in at home. Swimming, boating, and fishing are popular camp activities, and nature hikes are conducted regularly by the naturalist, who also helps campers in nature study and in making nature collections. Horseback riding, picnics, overnight hikes, moonlight rides, and pack-train trips into the mountains are featured, especially at the Western camps. Courts are provided for tennis, badminton, horseshoes, archery, and a variety of sports. Social activities, dances, and parties are arranged from time to

---

[1] A description of the vacation camps conducted by the Oakland Recreation Department, a pioneer in this field, will be found in Chap. XXVII.

time. The center of interest in the evening is the campfire where amateur theatricals, impromptu musical numbers, storytelling, stunts, community singing, "weenie" and marshmallow roasts round out the camp
day.

Camp programs have often been criticized on the grounds they were
too highly organized, that too many activities were crowded into the day,
and that the campers have not had an opportunity for sufficient rest and
relaxation.   Municipal camp programs are rarely open to this criticism.
They provide varied, attractive activities, many of which utilize the
special advantages afforded by the camp environment, but they are informal in nature and campers are free to choose the activities in which they
desire to take part.   As one camp folder states, the sole duty of the
campers is "to make the most of their time in the enjoyment of their
vacation."

Protection of the Campers.—Recreation authorities have a greater
responsibility in operating a camp than they do in conducting a center
located near the homes of the people served.   In the summer camp,
which is usually many miles from the city in which the campers live, the
people must be cared for 24 hours a day for periods of a week or more.
Special precautions must be taken to protect the health and safety of all
the campers and in some camps individuals are required to submit
health certificates before they are permitted to register.   A nurse is an
essential member of every camp staff.   People who handle the food are
required to have a clean bill of health, and purity of the water supply is
assured not only for drinking purposes but also for swimming.   Provision
must be made for the proper disposal of waste and continuous care taken
to assure the sanitary condition of the entire camp site.   The regulations
governing boating and swimming, which are required at camps with water
areas, and other rules are designed to assure safe and enjoyable vacations
for all.

Overnight Camps.—The overnight camp makes it possible for boys
and girls who are unable to attend camps for a longer period to experience
the joys of camping.   Several cities have established camping centers
where groups of boys or girls are accommodated during a 24-hour period.
These camps are usually in an outlying park, but in one city overnight
camps were set up on the city playgrounds.   Various methods are used
to reach camp—hiking, trolley or bus lines, private cars, or chartered
busses.   As a rule, children arrive in camp in the early afternoon and
leave after lunch the following day.   Boys and girls sometimes bring their
own food, but it is often more satisfactory for the camp to supply the food
even though the children are charged a moderate fee to defray the cost.
In the larger cities, the camp is conducted continuously throughout the
summer with groups attending from the various playgrounds and boys and

girls alternating. In some small cities the camp is operated only two nights a week.

At a camp which has been operated successfully for several years the staff consists of a director, a caretaker, a cook, and a lifeguard. The groups are usually accompanied by a leader on their way to and from camp. Programs are designed to give the children "a good time" and an experience which they will remember with pleasure. Hikes, nature activities, swimming, boating, campfire programs, and games are featured. At one camp there is a horse which every child has an opportunity to ride. Consideration of others, self-reliance, and cooperative activity are by-products of the overnight camp, as well as of the other types.

Day Camps.—The day camp has had a more rapid growth than any other type operated by municipal recreation authorities. It affords much of the appeal and joy of camping, without the expense and responsibility involved in providing overnight accommodations for the campers. Most day camps are conducted in large parks, although they have been established on playgrounds and even in indoor centers. They are usually accessible by bus or street car, but in some instances special transportation is provided for the children who are brought from playgrounds, settlements, institutions, or schools to spend the day at camp. Milk is generally furnished by the camp agency; lunch, too, is sometimes provided at a small charge, or children bring their own lunch, frequently cooking it at the camp. In addition to the director and one or more assistants, the staff often includes a naturalist and a nurse.

Day camp programs are designed to take fullest advantage of the opportunities offered by the camp site and to satisfy the child's craving for adventure. In one large city explorers' clubs have been organized at the day camps to encourage development of the nature interest. Nature collections are made, nature games are played, weather signs are noted, campfire methods are demonstrated, treasure hunts are held, and Indian crafts, dances, and ceremonials are enjoyed. For many city children wading in the brook, running on the grass, and climbing trees are new and thrilling experiences.

As a rule, the camp day closes in the late afternoon. In one city, however, the program of the day camp for boys, which was conducted only once a week, extended from 1:00 till 9:00 p.m. The boys were divided into groups of ten, each under an adult leader, and each group took the name of an Indian tribe. Afternoon activities included a visit to the park museum and zoo, a nature hunt, crafts, and games with competition on an intertribal basis. After supper dual contests were held until time for the evening fire, when a program of songs, games, stunts, stories, and competitive cheering was finally ended with the playing of "Taps."

PART VI

PROGRAM FEATURES AND SERVICES

The service rendered by the recreation department may be analyzed in several ways. One is to consider the programs carried on at the various units in the recreation system—the playground, the recreation building, or the golf course—as was done in the preceding section. Another is to appraise the service of the department in various forms of recreation —music, athletics, nature, crafts, and others. The following chapters deal with the contribution which the recreation department is making in several of these major forms, whether rendered at its centers or on a city-wide basis, to groups participating in its own programs or to other community agencies. They describe the specific activities carried on and the many different methods used in conducting them. Because of its nature and significance, the service to special groups such as homes, industries, and institutions is recorded in a separate chapter. Part VI concludes with a description of the recreation facilities, activities, and services of five representative recreation departments.

CHAPTER XX

ARTS AND CRAFTS

Dr. L. P. Jacks, the noted English educator, has said, "Recreation includes all the beautiful skills, crafts, and hobbies that human beings can practice, on and up to the finest arts." Few other activities yield as direct, immediate, and lasting satisfactions to the individual as arts and crafts. Seeing an object take shape in one's own hands or transforming an idea into tangible form gives a person a satisfying sense of achievement. Through arts and crafts people may develop skills and hobbies which they can enjoy in their homes and apart from any group throughout their entire lives. They can make objects of usefulness and beauty, find outlets for their creative abilities, and relieve the nervous tensions of present-day living. Many kinds of craft activity are closely related to some other form of recreation such as music, drama, games, and nature. It is not surprising, therefore, that arts and crafts have an important place in the program of the recreation department. Some of the specific ways in which the possibilities of these activities are being realized on the playgrounds, in the centers, and through community-wide activities will be considered briefly in the pages which follow.

SOME CHARACTERISTICS OF THE ARTS AND CRAFTS PROGRAM

Municipal recreation programs in different cities vary widely in the nature, scope, and quality of their arts and crafts activities. Recreation authorities are realizing more and more, however, that these activities have great potential value and that in conducting them high standards are essential. Increasingly projects are selected according to the abilities, interests, and capacities of the members of the group; individuals are encouraged to create their own designs rather than to follow patterns worked out by others. A spirit of informality characterizes the groups, the members of which are usually free to select the particular medium or project to which they wish to devote their effort. In a needlework group in an indoor center one may find women engaged in a great variety of activities including embroidering, knitting, dressmaking, or crocheting, while in a community workshop men may be busily occupied with such varied projects as a model sailboat, a desk lamp, or a piece of fine furniture.

311

Usefulness and lasting value are emphasized in the arts and crafts program.   For example, a girl on a playground may make for herself a bright-colored necklace which she wants very much and which she will prize more highly than one that had been purchased for her.   The use of simple hand tools is encouraged—sometimes the need for implements may itself furnish the basis for a craft project as where a group constructs its own simple tools for leather craft, looms for weaving, or a kiln for firing objects to be made in a pottery class.   The use of local materials is fostered, often for reasons of economy, but also because it is desirable to use resources furnished by the community in which the people are living, and because it offers the possibility of developing local folk arts and crafts.   In sections where honeysuckle is abundant it is widely used for basketry and other crafts, and in cities with a tannery leather craft is popular.   Sea shells, pine cones, and other native materials are used in a variety of ways.

More and more, recreation departments are employing skilled craftsmen to serve as teachers, who under the guidance of trained recreation leaders are helping both children and adults to attain greater skills and to secure more satisfaction from their participation in the arts and crafts program.

ON THE PLAYGROUND

Since the early days of the playground movement, arts and crafts in various forms have had a place in the program.   The term "industrial work" which was formerly applied to these activities suggests the restricted, practical, and formal nature of such projects.   Today, however, playground crafts are almost limitless in variety, using widely different mediums and producing an equally varied list of objects.   Among the most common crafts are sketching, modeling, woodwork, weaving, basketry, carving, leather craft, beadwork, papier-mâché, needlework, and poster making.   The character of the workmanship, the specific types of projects, and the time required for completing them vary according to the age and skill of the individual children, but most crafts appeal to both boys and girls of varying ages.

The activities are usually carried on within the playground building or on the porch, although often benches and tables are set up out of doors, preferably in the shade.   Tools and supplies are provided as a part of the equipment of every playground, their number and types varying with the funds available, the number of children to be served, and the projects to be undertaken.   They are stored carefully in cabinets in the building or in a strong box kept near the place where the activities are carried on.

Because of limited funds in most cities, inexpensive and salvaged materials are widely used.   Rags are made into woven and hooked rugs, patchwork quilts, pot holders, and table mats; cardboard boxes are transformed into wastepaper baskets and letter files; wooden boxes become door stops, cutout animals, looms, dollhouses, furniture, and pushmobiles; and inner tubes are used for block printing, toys, and musical instruments. Boys and girls on many playgrounds construct checkerboards, ringtoss games, softball bases, paddles, quoits, puzzles, and card games, which contribute to the joy of the playground children and which in some instances are more appreciated and better cared for than game materials purchased by the playground authorities.

Art activities on the playground are less common than crafts and are usually of an elementary nature. A more serious art project was the outdoor sketching class offered one day a week on a park playground in a Western city. A lecture course on the fundamentals of composition, color, and technique started at 10 A.M. after which members of the class painted until 2:30. The sketches were then studied and criticized by the group under the guidance of the instructor.

Relating Crafts to Other Activities.—On most playgrounds, especially during the short summer season, arts and crafts are conducted in a relatively informal manner. Many of the projects are related to other phases of the program or to activities or special events in which the objects made are either displayed or utilized. The construction of bird and ant houses and spatter printing combine both the craft and nature interest, and flower and leaf arrangements, colors, and prints furnish motifs for art projects. The program posters, costumes, properties, and stage equipment needed for simple plays or an elaborate playground pageant are made by arts or crafts groups. Music and crafts are often related through the construction of tom-toms, tambourines, snare drums, pipes of Pan, shepherd's pipes, transverse flutes, and simple stringed instruments which have later been used in developing music activities. Puppetry combines both the craft and drama interests.

The announcement of a pushmobile derby is an incentive for boys to construct all kinds of vehicles, just as the opportunity to test kites and model boats in a contest gives added zest to these constructive activities, stimulates resourcefulness, and encourages expert workmanship. An unusual example of this kind of project occurred in one city where the boys in the radio clubs developed installations in the short-wave bands and placed portable radio outfits on floats entered in a water carnival. During the carnival the floats kept in orderly procession, responding instantly to the calls sent from the shore by the members of the radio clubs.

Indian Crafts in Louisville.—Occasionally a recreation department builds its summer playground program around a particular theme such as colonial or Indian life and when this is done, crafts, like other activities, are directly related to this theme.　In Louisville, Kentucky, the annual playground play contest was based on Indian themes and the need of properties furnished the incentive for many craft projects some of which are described as follows:

Tepees were fashioned from burlap bags sewn together, brown wrapping paper, and old sheets painted in approved Indian style and color. Macaroni, painted and broken into short lengths and then strung, made necklaces. Melon seeds colored with crepe-paper dye, and bits of colored magazine advertisements rolled into cylinders also made effective beads, while polished tin provided material for jewelry making. War bonnets and other headdresses were made from crepe paper, feathers, and painted tag board. Twisted strands of black crepe paper and old stockings became long, realistic braids of hair for the Indian maidens. Moccasins were created from old tennis slippers and sneakers painted with appropriate designs. Tin cans filled with pebbles served for rattles. The "boom-boom" of the Indian drums came from wooden cheese boxes and large lard cans covered with stretched canvas and decorated with mystic symbols. A local pottery furnished slightly chipped jars and bowls at give-away prices, and four-hour enamel was used to give them a permanent decoration. Snowshoes were woven from willows gathered near the Ohio River which also furnished shells for other projects. Burlap bags, expertly cut and decorated, supplied the basis for most of the costumes, and so well done was the work that these costumes belied their humble origin. One playground made a beautiful canoe of light wood and strips of paper mounted on a coaster wagon which supplied the necessary power for the canoe to glide majestically on its way.[1]

This brief account indicates the great variety of interesting activities undertaken in preparing for a playground contest in one city.　It also suggests the infinite possibilities which the playground program offers to the resourceful recreation leader.　Similar experiences in many other cities in preparing for the playground circus, festival, pageant, or other feature event could be recorded.

IN THE INDOOR RECREATION CENTER

The informality and flexibility of playground programs and the short season make it difficult to conduct elaborate arts and crafts activities on the summer playground.　Conditions are quite different at the indoor center which serves primarily youth and adults and is open during a longer season.　The center program is more highly specialized, many people attend to take part in a particular activity, and special leaders are often provided to serve groups interested in arts and crafts.　In some cities instruction is offered to women and girls during the morning and afternoon, to children after school, and to men and women in evening groups and classes.　The range of arts and crafts included in a com-

[1] "On the Summer Playgrounds of 1934," *Recreation*, June, 1935, p. 147.

prehensive indoor center program is indicated by the list of such activities in the Milwaukee School Centers, which begins on page 286. The seriousness with which boys voluntarily undertake difficult craft projects is recorded in the 1937 report of the Chicago Park District. The members of the model airplane clubs, it is pointed out, "must cultivate patience and application. Their workmanship is unbelievably delicate. They make completed planes weighing less than half an ounce." Other boys' groups are talking overseas with fellow enthusiasts abroad by means of short-wave radio sets which they have engineered and put together. In one of the park shops boys are fabricating from solid blocks of steel vest-pocket engines, operated by an eye dropper full of gasoline, to drive their miniature powered planes. Inspired by the adult yachting fraternity which generously furnishes materials, a score of junior yachting clubs are building their passenger dinghies of solid mahogany. The boats must be accurate to within one-quarter of an inch. In these activities boys are meeting and overcoming difficult and challenging problems.

Facilities for Arts and Crafts.—In many recreation buildings there are special craft rooms such as a woodworking shop, a weaving room equipped with looms, or a room devoted entirely to model aircraft construction. Such facilities make possible the development of a more highly specialized crafts program, facilitate the storing of tools and materials, and enable the rooms to be reserved for individual or group use during considerable periods of time. A few recreation buildings contain a room set aside for art instruction or for the exhibition of paintings and other art objects. In many cases, however, the arts and crafts program is handicapped by the fact that it must share the use of facilities with other activities. At most school centers classrooms are used for sewing, leather craft, modeling, art classes, and other crafts which require no fixed equipment. In an increasing number of school buildings manual training and domestic science rooms are opened in the evening for woodworking, metal craft, or hobby groups, sewing or cooking classes, and other activities. The employment of day-school instructors to take charge of the evening activities in these rooms simplifies the problems arising from the use of tools and equipment by community groups.

In a number of instances arts and crafts groups have themselves undertaken to make the facilities at the centers more attractive. An outstanding example of such cooperation occurred in a large city where 36 parks entered a contest for the renovating and decoration of the clubhouse quarters. Walls were treated, seats and cabinets built, wall hangings installed, furniture redecorated, and unused basement rooms transformed into attractive meeting places for clubs and other groups.

In one park a group of young artists who call themselves The Portfolio Club painted a mural which they presented to the park officials for the field house in which they held their meetings.

Center Craft Clubs.—Most of the groups engaged in arts and crafts activities at indoor centers are informal in organization and are open to all who wish to enroll. There are many examples, however, of groups which have developed a continuing interest in a particular activity— often one which involves progressively higher degrees of skill—and which have been organized on a formal club basis, sometimes with definite membership requirements. Examples—in addition to the two described here—are model boat building clubs, photography clubs, and puppetry clubs.

A Quilting Club.—For a number of years one of the most successful groups at a Chicago park center has been a quilting club which meets one day each week from ten until four. It has the use of a well-lighted room which accommodates four quilting frames. Each of the forty members makes her own quilt top and in turn the quilt is put on a frame and all help in the quilting. Provision is made for storing the frames and quilts between meetings. Ideas for patterns are gathered from all available sources and much originality is shown in adapting them or in developing the members' own patterns. Quilting is accompanied by singing and conversation. Occasionally dances and other social occasions are arranged for husbands and other members of the family and each year an exhibit of the quilts made by the group is held. A waiting list attests the popularity of this club and the excellence of its handiwork.

Aircraft Clubs.—A different but equally successful activity is carried on by the model airplane clubs in a number of cities. Detroit has been one of the leaders in this field, having organized a club of forty boys in one of its recreation centers in 1926. By 1938 there were 28 clubs with an enrollment of over 1,700 members, which met each week. The importance of this project has necessitated the employment of a full-time aircraft director who has the assistance of emergency workers. Several work-rooms, including a small experimental laboratory, are made available for the use of the division in charge of model airplane clubs. Materials are purchased by the city and sold at cost to club members. On the roster of the Recreation Aircraft Clubs are boys as young as ten years old, many high-school boys studying aero courses, and men interested in aeronautical engineering or in model aircraft as a hobby. A graded series of tests has been devised, and after club members have successfully passed one of them, they may advance to a more experienced group. The final or ace test requires a well-rounded knowledge of all phases of aircraft construction and flight and is rarely achieved by anyone with less than six years of model-building experience. The contests for various types of model aircraft arranged from time to time are sanctioned by the National Aeronautics Association. The challenging and progressively difficult activities in the program of these clubs explains in part their success in holding the interest of boys over a much longer period than most other forms of activity.

SPECIAL ARTS AND CRAFTS CENTERS

Although many arts and crafts activities are carried on as a part of the playground or indoor center program and are more or less related to other parts of the program, several cities have special arts and crafts centers. The scope of their facilities and programs and the emphasis placed upon formal instruction vary widely. In one small community the Board of Education has opened its manual training shop as a boys' craft center during the summer months with a trained worker in charge. The boys are allowed to enter and leave at will, there is no formal program, and no effort is made to control their activity other than by visual suggestion. Around the shop are various pieces of equipment such as electric bells and buzzers, telephones, magnetic coils, and motors which the boys were free to manipulate. Opportunities are available for making windmills, gliders, letter holders, scooters, and model boats. A more typical example is in another city where the manual training shops of the junior high schools are opened during the vacation months under the supervision of the instructor in charge during the school year. Boys are taught the use of tools and materials and make many articles especially of wood, tin cans, and wrought iron.

A Junior Museum.—The children of San Francisco have an exceptional opportunity "to learn to discover themselves in a rich and satisfying manner" at the Junior Museum in that city. Arts and crafts share with nature study the program at this true activity center. Opportunities are provided for making model airplanes, boats, and railroads as well as birdhouses and feeding stations, relief maps, and equipment used in nature study. Some of the unusual projects which such a center makes possible have been described as follows by Miss Josephine D. Randall, the city superintendent of recreation:

Scale models of old and historic ships are being constructed from blueprints made by the boys themselves; a model of Fort Union has just been finished in complete and accurate detail by a group of boys particularly interested in the early cross-country treks to California.

A model of Fort Ross is being constructed by this same group in connection with their interest in the history of the days of Russian occupancy of the Northern California Coast. A kayak that would please an eskimo seal hunter is nearing completion; a picture of the historical development of gardens is being portrayed in perfect scale models, the earliest of which shows the Hanging Gardens of

Babylon. Beautiful and exquisitely finished models of small musical instruments used in early times in many countries are being made and carved with great interest and precision on the part of the workers.

A well-equipped darkroom provides adequate facilities for developing and finishing photographs. Instruction in the art of photography is given, and results of the efforts of our amateurs have received wide recognition.[1]

Multiple Use of a Center.—During the early depression period workshops were established in several cities to provide a place where mechanics, carpenters, and others out of employment could carry on constructive work in their respective fields and also where the unemployed could spend some of their unwanted leisure. One community workshop of this kind, established early in the depression, is being used by the recreation department for a purpose different from that originally intended. Until 4 P.M. the power machinery and tools in the shop are used by the department's maintenance staff for the making and repairing of equipment. After that time the shop is open to boys between the ages of ten and fifteen who may build airplanes, model boats, kites, and all kinds of articles. In the evening the shop affords a place where adults who enjoy working with wood or machinery may do so to their heart's content, or may engage in such practical projects as the making or repairing of furniture. The shop is open throughout the year at all times under competent leadership. In addition to the informal activities at the center drawing, sketching, coloring, and modeling classes are conducted for children, and sketching and marionette classes for adults.

The Westchester Workshop.—An outstanding arts and crafts center is the Westchester County, New York, Workshop, the facilities of which include a lecture hall, exhibit room, large basement workshop, and exhibition hall. In addition, a handicraft workshop is maintained in another building. The activity program is planned to meet the needs of all types of people, young and old, and is carried on under a staff of competent teachers. Classes in several crafts such as basketry, dressmaking, jewelry, metal, weaving, and woodwork are free of charge. Instruction fees varying from 50 cents to $1 or more per session are charged for classes in ceramics, marionettes, painting, pottery, and sculpture.

In addition to the activities at the workshop, assistance is given to clubs, schools, and institutions throughout the county, and with the help of the director arts and crafts programs and workshops have been established in several localities. A County Arts and Crafts Guild affiliated with the workshop has been organized "to afford opportunities for creative work and to further interest in arts and crafts as recreational, inspirational, and educational activities." Among the guild's activities are exhibitions, lectures, and classes. As a recreation worker who made a careful study of the activities at the center stated, "Ambitious

[1] "A Recreation Museum for Juniors," *Recreation*, April, 1938, p. 27.

children and adults, art and beauty lovers, teachers seeking new material and practice, artists gaining inspiration and companionship—all find relaxation, companionship, and real joy in the Westchester Workshop."

OTHER FEATURES

Supplementing the activities regularly carried on at the playgrounds and centers, the recreation department fosters an interest in arts and crafts in many ways, some of them conducted on a community-wide basis.

Arts and Crafts Exhibits.—The arts and crafts exhibit is an annual feature in many cities. Sometimes exhibits of the articles made at the individual playgrounds or centers are shown in the neighborhood stores, but more often the exhibition is city-wide and housed in a centrally located building with suitable display facilities. Greater interest is stimulated when the display of articles already made is accompanied by demonstrations of arts and crafts activities by playground and center groups. In one large city where the exhibit was on display for an entire week several booths were devoted to such demonstrations. In one booth labeled "For the Home" leather craft, metal craft, rug hooking, loom weaving, raffia, pottery, and other crafts were demonstrated on succeeding days. In the "To Wear" booth weaving, sewing, crocheting, knitting, and jewelry making were demonstrated. In the workshop groups constructed model airplanes, games, model yachts, musical instruments and archery tackle, while model airplanes were flown in the hall. Puppetry shows were held as well as group musical and dramatic performances.

Such exhibits and demonstrations are exceedingly valuable in interpreting to the public this phase of the department's program. They afford an occasion for informing people as to the time, place, and nature of the various clubs and classes and for recruiting new members. They furnish a special incentive to the individuals in the arts and crafts groups to put forth their best efforts and an opportunity for them to show their friends and the public objects which in varying degrees express their own personality. Closely related to the crafts exhibits are the exhibitions of photographs which are arranged by photography clubs or which follow photographic contests.

Training Opportunities.—The recreation department helps train people in recreation skills and leadership methods, who in turn share their knowledge with other groups they are serving either as paid or volunteer leaders. To this end the recreation department often conducts training courses in arts and crafts activities, either utilizing its own personnel or bringing to the city experts in special crafts. The recreation institutes conducted in many cities by the National Recreation Association under the sponsorship of local recreation agencies have afforded practical training in arts and crafts.

Community Arts and Crafts Groups.—The recreation department also serves to bring together into a community-wide organization individuals with a common interest in some form of arts or crafts activity. An example of such a group is the Municipal Sketch Club in Long Beach, California, which has been active for several years under the leadership of a local artist and teacher. This club with a membership of 65 men and women interested in art as a means of self-expression was organized "for the purpose of encouraging a better appreciation of art both for individual members and for the public at large." There are no membership fees, officers, or organization. Each member provides his own materials, but the director's salary and other incidental expenses are met by the Recreation Commission. Meetings of the club are held weekly, occasionally at the homes of the members. Club excursions to art galleries, exhibits, and other centers of interest are arranged, and frequent trips are made to near-by scenic spots affording interesting subjects for sketching. Prominent artists are sometimes invited to these outdoor meetings.

The Sketch Club has provided an outlet for self-expression to many people who have been anxious to pursue the study of art but have lacked the opportunity or funds to do so. The mediums used are pencil, crayon, pastel, pen and ink, and water colors. The variety of work done assures a welcome for the novice as well as for the experienced artist. The club has also rendered service to the community through the arrangement and hanging of exhibits in the recreation clubhouses and municipal buildings. Several thousand paintings of outstanding artists have been hung and the work of several local artists has also been included. Another phase of the club program is the Mornings in Art at which speakers on costume and dress design, arts and crafts, and general art address the group.

In another Western city a series of sketching picnics has been arranged at various picturesque points in the vicinity. Individuals bring their own drawing equipment on these excursions, but free instruction in the fundamentals of sketching is provided for beginners.

Publications.—The recreation department is also encouraging activity in this field through the preparation of bulletins and manuals dealing with arts and crafts. Perhaps the most comprehensive of such publications is the series issued by the Chicago Park District which includes such titles as "Whittling," "Wood Inlay," "Hooked Rugs," "Leathercraft," "Simple Weaving," "Games and Gameboards," "Animated Toys," and several others. These booklets prepared by expert craftsmen are profusely illustrated with diagrams and contain practical instructions for the respective projects. Supplementing as they do the activities at the park centers, these publications comprise a valuable part of the department's extension service.

CHAPTER XXI

ATHLETICS AND SPORTS

The strong appeal made by athletics and sports to both participants and spectators at outdoor recreation areas and indoor centers has already been indicated. There was a time when most recreation programs provided only a few forms of highly competitive games and sports, primarily for men and boys. During the past two decades, however, a great variety of athletic activities appealing to a wide range of ages has been introduced, and an effort has been made to encourage participation by large numbers of individuals rather than by a few highly skilled players. Special attention has also been given to the development of programs for women and girls.

The Carnegie Foundation for the Advancement of Teaching[1] has pointed out that athletics have come to be regarded as an important part of the educational process at practically all levels but especially for youth, and that athletic directors are regarded as highly important teachers of youth. The overwhelming popularity of the recreation department's athletic program for youth is largely explained by the fact that "the true incentives for youth's playing basketball or football or tennis, or for running or throwing a hammer, include the primal need for physical activity, the joy of overcoming, the individual or communal rewards of victory, and the aspiration to do something well before the eyes of one's fellows, young or old."[2] These incentives apply not only to youth but to people of all ages. In later life, however, physical activity tends to become less strenuous and social relationships play a more conspicuous part in the sports program. The athletic program is especially valuable in offsetting the unsatisfactory environment and the unfavorable working conditions to which a large part of our population is exposed, particularly in the industrial centers.

No other agency is doing so much as the recreation department to promote and provide athletics for children, young people, and adults. On the playgrounds it helps boys and girls develop interest and skills in games and sports and gives them training in sportsmanship and experience in competition. It furnishes facilities such as tennis, handball,

[1] See "The Literature of American School and College Athletics," *Bulletin* 24.

[2] "Current Developments in American College Sport," The Carnegie Foundation for the Advancement of Teaching, *Bulletin* 26.

horseshoe, and badminton courts, swimming pools, and skating rinks where individuals may engage in informal, self-directed activity. It also encourages advancement in skill through the organization of contests and tournaments in these activities and offers individual or group instruction in fundamental game skills. Through the organization of teams and leagues in baseball, volley ball, soccer and other team games it affords opportunity for large numbers of individuals to play regularly with others of similar ability, whether they are "dubs" or players of high rank. It helps people interested in a particular sport to find means of enjoying it and of enlisting others in the activity. It cooperates with local, state, or national bodies in the promotion of special events, some of which involve intercity competition.

A MUNICIPAL SPORTS PROGRAM

The well-rounded program of games and athletics conducted in Minneapolis by the Recreation Division of the Board of Park Commissioners may be considered representative of the municipal sports programs in other cities. Especially noteworthy are the popularity of softball (called locally diamond ball), the extent of the winter sports program, and the wide participation by women and girls. Some of the activities are promoted chiefly at the individual playgrounds, playfields, indoor centers, and special recreation areas; others are organized on a city-wide basis.

The summary (p. 323) of the athletic activities carried on in Minneapolis in 1937 indicates the scope of the program, the number of different individuals and groups participating, and the extent to which people were served as either participants or spectators. The large registration in such sports as diamond ball, football, ice hockey, and volley ball reflects unusual local interest in, and effective promotion of, these sports. Many of the city-wide activities are controlled by a municipal athletic association which operates under a special permit given by the park board.

In addition to the activities and attendance figures listed, 132,861 rounds of golf were played on the five municipal courses; the attendance at the 201 tennis courts totaled 321,600 during "free play" periods; 54 ice skating rinks provided more than 2 million individual skating periods, and the total attendance at the four park beaches was 647,000 during the year. The importance of the contribution which recreation departments make to the physical well-being of the people and to their joyous participation in a sports program is amply demonstrated by the Minneapolis record.

An Expanding Sports Program.—The marked expansion in the scope of city-wide municipal sports programs and the resulting trends are

GAMES AND SPORTS PROMOTED BY THE DIVISION OF RECREATION, BOARD OF PARK
COMMISSIONERS, MINNEAPOLIS, DURING 1937

	Number of groups	Number of persons registered	Estimated participants	Estimated spectators
I. Spring and summer activities:				
Bait and fly casting*	1	150	750	2,000
Baseball	239	2,925	22,770	82,425
Diamond ball—men's	932	5,660	54,900	292,300
Diamond ball—women's	226	2,542	14,818	19,787
Golf—women's clubs*	7	188	2,009	
Golf—women's tournaments*	2	115	115	50
Golf—men's commercial*	16	80.	800	150
Golf—men's tournaments†	4	490	1,128	2,550
Horseshoe*	1	130	250	150
Roque†	1	30	1,960	6,000
Tennis—men's tournament—exhibition*	...	1,150	2,900	7,500
Tennis—men's commercial*	18	90	450	150
Tennis—women's lessons*	2	93	299	
Tennis—women's tournaments*.	9	363	726	700
Water festival†	1	.....	175	10,000
Bicycle finals†	...	350	350	3,500
Swimming meet†	1	105	105	
Volley ball—playground†	514	3,598	18,895	10,700
Touchball—playground†	165	2,475	9,900	1,250
Basketball—playground†	108	560	2,800	1,500
II. Fall and winter activities:				
Badminton*	1	50	359	260
Basketball—men*	97	1,164	11,640	2,400
Basketball—women*	18	216	2,540	6,536
Bowling—women*	80	336	9,408	5,000
Bowling—tournaments*	5	48	853	575
Bowling banquet*	1	275	275	
Football—men	363	4,985	31,415	176,330
Hockey	434	3,676	19,738	74,100
Speed skating*	8	250	1,125	24,380
Table tennis*	1	158	500	2,000
Billiards—women*	2	27	293	10
Billiards—tournaments*	3	26	52	10
Volley ball—women*	25	135	1,849	376
Glenwood Arlberg Ski Club*	1	57	650	250
Men's skiing*	1	82	483	5,940
Golf lessons and caddie school	7	250	1,336	
Dog derby*	1	41	41	5,000

* This activity is organized on a city-wide basis only.
† This activity is not conducted on a city-wide basis.

illustrated by the following chart describing the activities in Milwaukee. In 1919 the program consisted of three highly organized competitive team sports in which participation was restricted primarily to young men. Nineteen years later it comprised 29 activities several of which appeal to old and young alike, are widely used in co-recreation programs, require little organization and equipment, involve informal participation rather than a high degree of competition, and afford lifelong recreation interests.

MUNICIPAL SPORTS ACTIVITIES IN MILWAUKEE, 1938

Conducted in 1919	Started, 1920–1925	Started, 1926–1931	Started, 1932–1938
Baseball	Canoeing	Curling	Archery
Basketball	Cross country	Hiking	Badminton
Football	Cycling	Lawn bowling	Dartball
	Horseshoe pitching	Roller skating	Fencing
	Indoor baseball	Skiing	Fistball
	Ice skating		Handball
	Soccer		Table tennis
	Softball		Tobogganing
	Swimming (outdoor and indoor)		Touch football
	Tennis (outdoor)		
	Track and field (outdoor and indoor)		
	Volley ball		

The number of teams participating in this program in 1938 was 1,861; the total number of team members or tournament entrants, 29,175. As in Minneapolis, softball led in the number of enrolled players, followed by basketball, table tennis, and baseball in the order named.

CITY-WIDE SPORTS ORGANIZATION

The organization and supervision of a comprehensive municipal sports program involve relationships with hundreds of individuals and teams engaged in a variety of sports, the arrangement of league and tournament schedules, the allocation of playing facilities, the selection of officials, the handling of entry fees, and many other procedures. In most larger cities a division of athletics is created within the recreation department to care for this part of the program. The major objectives of this division and the methods which it uses in initiating and conducting leagues and in promoting individual sports were discussed in some detail in Chap. XVI. The following pages describe the experience of several cities in dealing with various aspects of sports organization on a city-wide basis.

The Municipal Athletic Federation.—Many recreation departments have been instrumental in forming a city-wide sports body, usually designated as the municipal athletic federation or association, which assists the athletic division in conducting the sports program. Membership is usually composed of local associations which have been organized among the participants in the various games and sports sponsored by the department. The objects of such an organization are clearly indicated in the constitution of the Los Angeles Federation as follows:

1. To extend, foster, and promote ideals in ethics and conduct, of all amateur athletic activities under the jurisdiction of the Playground and Recreation Department.

2. To endeavor to bring together all municipal associations for the purpose of raising the standard of individual and team athletics played throughout the city.

3. To promote only high ideals in sportsmanship, fair play, and good conduct.

4. To provide a clearinghouse for athletic information, dates of competition and schedules, and as a final court of appeals for the arbitration of disputes in reference to the interpretation of rules, to bring together the municipal associations under one organization in order to control and regulate matters pertaining to all sports in general and to none in particular.

5. To encourage organization and promotion by officiating and assisting in conducting all city-wide sanctioned athletic activities, tournaments, meets, and conferences.

The federation has proved to be an effective means of coordinating activities in the field of sports and of eliminating the difficulties often encountered in cities with many local sports-governing bodies and a wide variation in their standards and practices. As a rule, a representative of the recreation department, usually the director of municipal athletics, serves as executive officer for the federation, thereby assuring a close relationship with the municipal authorities. The programs in Minneapolis and Milwaukee described earlier in the chapter are largely administered by city-wide municipal athletic organizations.

Organizing Players in a Particular Sport.—The common method of administering a city-wide program in a particular game or sport is through an association representing the teams and individuals participating in the activity. The groups interested in baseball, for example, form a baseball association which, in cooperation with the recreation department, adopts rules and regulations for the conduct of the game on an organized basis. In the same way, a municipal tennis association fosters the game of tennis, develops rules and policies, and arranges and conducts tournaments. These city-wide organizations are designed to permit a democratic control by the teams, clubs, and individuals primarily interested in the respective sports. Policies and methods must conform to basic principles laid down by the recreation department which is responsible for the areas and facilities used and for the general conduct of the program, but they are largely determined by the member groups. The magnitude of the sports organization in many cities would make it impossible, even though it were desirable, for the department staff to arrange the many details involved in league organization, schedule making, officiating, handling protests, and conducting tournaments. Valuable assistance in taking care of such matters is rendered by the officers and committees of the sports associations.

Promoting Interest in a Sport.—In addition to meeting the demand for facilities and league organization by sports enthusiasts, the department has a responsibility for promoting public interest in sports and encouraging people to take part in them. Promotion, demonstration, and instruction are essential features of such a program. In an earlier chapter reference was made to the remarkable stimulus given to playing golf in Cincinnati after instruction classes were organized and sets of golf clubs provided on a loan basis. Sometimes exhibition games or matches are arranged for the purpose of demonstrating to the public the possibilities of a game which is little known in the locality. Participation and interest in sports have increased many fold when the authorities have promoted the activity effectively and have provided suitable facilities and leadership. The lighting of areas for night play has greatly extended their usefulness.

Archery.—The thorough preparation underlying a campaign for the promotion of a sport with a relatively small following is illustrated by this statement describing a cooperative plan carried out by the Chicago Park District:

Archery has been a hobby of a few devoted enthusiasts in the city for many years. When these enthusiasts appealed to us to further the development of interest in this activity, our Physical Activities Section attacked the problem of effecting city-wide organization, developing an archery association to cover the entire city, and federated the volunteer efforts of the exponents of the sport for greater effectiveness. Our experts in crafts made a study of the making of bows, arrows, targets, gantlets and other equipment, involving the woodworkers in the study of how to make high quality bows and arrow shafts, experts in leather tooling in the fabrication of gantlets and quivers, and miscellaneous skills in preparing bow strings, fabricating and painting targets, designing and building target supports and the other miscellaneous properties needed. Our Indian craftsman, Chief Whirling Thunder, contributed his store of information on the American Indian practices in this highly specialized field. Artists and engineers lent their aid in essential elements of design and pattern. Institutes were held to acquaint all of our crafts workers with the processes involved, the sessions continuing until every crafts worker had actually made a full set of equipment and could direct beginners not from a mere theoretical knowledge of the subject only but based rather on practical experience.

When we were thus prepared, the various section directors, in their supervisory administrative capacities, stimulated a campaign of promotional publicity in the six districts of the city. The local park directors, in turn, began to suggest this new field in which people might find a fascinating new sport to engage their attention. Sunday hours were set aside in some of the indoor gymnasiums, and a tremendous revival of public interest in archery was the result—classes ranging in age from juvenile enthusiasts under ten years of age to adult groups, many of advanced years, all of whom were encouraged to make their own equipment and all having equal representative voice in a self-governing archery association.[1]

Although many recreation departments are not prepared to promote an activity to the extent described in the preceding paragraphs, comparable results have been attained elsewhere. In one city the year after table tennis was introduced into the program, 149 men and women participated in the local tournament which included singles and doubles events for novices and advanced players, men, women, and mixed teams. In another city shortly after fencing was first introduced, regular time for lessons and practice was set aside for the sport in ten centers, so great was the interest developed in it. More than thirty married couples were devoting at least one night a week to fencing, according to a report from another city.

Bowling.—The value of leadership in promoting a sports program is illustrated by the experience in a town of 8,500. When the recreation department was established there were no bowling alleys in the town, and the people had had little experience in any form of league organization. A five-man team which bowled in an intercity league was used by the recreation executive as a nucleus for a bowling program and 18 teams were formed. It was not long before the novices were demanding a league of their own. An instruction class was later started for the women, and they, too, were organized in a league. So popular did the game become that within little more than a year after the program started two bowling establishments were opened in the community and 240 individuals had become enthusiastic members of bowling teams.

WATER AND WINTER SPORTS

The rapidly growing public interest in these seasonal activities is pointed out in Chap. XIX, which also describes the operation of facilities for water and winter sports. Responsibility for the water sports program is sometimes assigned to a division of aquatics or of pools and beaches but winter sports are more commonly promoted by the department's sports division. In most of the country the season for these activities is shorter

[1] *Second Annual Report*, Chicago Park District, 1936, p. 178.

than for other team games and individual sports, and unlike much of the athletic program which is conducted on a city-wide basis, water and winter sports are restricted largely to a few special centers.

An Aquatic Program.—Long Beach, California, is outstanding in its program of aquatics largely because of its various excellent water areas which make boating possible in addition to swimming, diving, lifesaving, and water carnivals. Classes in sailing, seamanship, and crew rowing are carried on, and junior sailing clubs conduct frequent sailing races. Boys' and girls' canoeing classes are held at one of the centers. The model boat shop where boys—and a few girls—make many kinds of boats which are later tested in the water is an unusual feature. Motor-boating, rowing, yachting, and canoeing attract great throngs, and the department cooperates with yachting and motorboat clubs in promoting regattas and other racing events.

Winter Sports Activities.—Snow and ice sports afford thrilling and healthful features in the winter athletic program. Common activities are skiing, skating, coasting, tobogganing, ice hockey, and snow and ice games, which are carried on chiefly at the large parks and in the neighborhood recreation areas. The high light of the season is the city-wide winter carnival in which a variety of special features is introduced. Where facilities are available and conditions favorable the program includes skate sailing, skijoring, snowshoeing, *slalom* racing, cross-country skiing, dog racing, winter camping, and other activities. To a greater degree than most athletic activities, winter sports appeal to people of a wide range of ages and attract many family groups. In general, the expense of providing them is comparatively low; on the other hand, unfavorable weather conditions such as thaws, rain, heavy snows, or excessive cold often interfere with carefully prepared programs or necessitate their cancellation.

SPECTATORS AT ATHLETIC EVENTS

"Spectatoritis," in the opinion of some writers, is an indication that people have lost their initiative and vigor and marks the beginning of a decline in vitality and achievement. Fortunately there is little danger in it as long as it accompanies the effective promotion of a sports-for-all program. As a matter of fact, the ranks of the spectators at major athletic events are naturally swelled as increasing numbers of individuals become interested in playing the game themselves. In neighborhoods where softball and other leagues have been organized, the families and neighbors of the players turn out in large numbers to watch and "root" for their favorite teams.

Recreation departments, through their athletic and sports programs, are performing an outstanding service in providing opportunities for large numbers of people to watch others engage in strenuous play. The number of spectators at the organized games of baseball and softball sponsored by one recreation department in 1937 was conservatively estimated at 4½ times the city's total population. Another city reports that attendance at its softball games has exceeded the one million mark for several years. The municipal sports program cannot be fairly appraised without taking into account the thousands who watch city-wide skating or ski-jumping tournaments, track and field meets, regattas, and aquatic contests, as well as the countless number of people whose leisure hours are enjoyably spent in watching others playing games at the individual playgrounds and recreation centers.

WOMEN'S AND GIRLS' ATHLETICS

As a result of the major emphasis formerly given to athletic programs for men and boys, activities for older girls and women were not always carried on under conditions, or in a manner, conductive to the best interests of the players or the sport. With the increased consideration given to women and girls in the municipal athletic program, standards of play have been materially improved. Today large numbers of women and girls have opportunity to participate in a variety of games and sports in a favorable environment, under competent leadership of their own sex, and with adequate precautions taken to protect their health and safety. Enjoyment of the sport and sociability, rather than winning championships, are stressed as primary objectives of this part of the program.

Several factors which have brought about this change have been the employment of women supervisors and athletic instructors on the recreation department staff, recognition by the authorities that women and girls are entitled to a larger share of leadership, facilities, and funds, an educational program for the adoption of suitable standards governing women's and girls' athletics, and a growing emphasis upon large-group participation rather than upon the development of star athletes or teams. The widespread introduction of games and sports in school and college programs has given large numbers of girls and young women an interest and skill in these activities, which can be continued through the recreation department program after they leave school.

Team games such as volley ball, basketball, and softball are highly popular with women and girls but the interest in them is primarily among the younger groups and does not extend over so long a period as it does among men. There is a growing trend toward participation in individual activities such as archery, badminton, tennis, golf, and swimming. Reasons for this trend are that these activities do not tax the player's stamina as much as some of the team games, and therefore their appeal continues into later life; they do not require the presence of a team or group, but can be played by two or more individuals; and they have co-recreational value because men and women can play them together. Gymnasium classes in which weight reducing often replaces recreation as the major objective are a popular feature of the women's program in a number of cities.

Games and sports are sometimes organized and conducted for women, as they are for men, on a city-wide basis with league schedules and championship tournaments. This was indicated by the Minneapolis athletic program outlined earlier in the chapter. Enrollment is often arranged through the industries and commercial organizations where the girls and women are employed. Housewives, too, are encouraged to take part in the program, as in one city where 50 women's volley ball teams were organized at the playgrounds. There is a growing tendency in some cities to stress the informal "playday" type of organization in conducting the women's sports program rather than formal competition between teams representing a particular agency or group. Both forms have their place in a comprehensive community-wide program.

ATHLETICS ON THE PLAYGROUND

The extent to which the playground furnishes opportunities for large numbers of people to take part in athletic games and sports and the methods used on the playground in conducting athletic activities have already been mentioned. In line with the growing emphasis upon "sports for all," leagues are usually organized on an intraplayground or district basis rather than for interplayground or city-wide play. Round-robin or perpetual tournaments are used when practicable for tennis, handball, horseshoes, and similar sports rather than the elimination type which does not encourage continuing play. Where facilities permit, a diversified athletic program is arranged to attract a greater number of boys and girls. Enjoyment in the activity, the development of sportsmanship, and the acquisition of game skills are major objectives rather than the winning of championships.

A Typical Summer Program.—The following list, prepared by the games committee in Washington, D. C., represents the activities which it was agreed should be organized and carried on during the summer of 1938. The playgrounds were grouped into units composed of from four to eight grounds each, and the activities were developed on an intraunit basis. Gang, street, and neighborhood groupings were followed whenever possible in organizing the activities.

ACTIVITIES

For boys	For girls
Archery	Archery
Badminton	Badminton

For boys	For girls
Baseball	Croquet
Basketball (goal shooting)	Dodge ball
Croquet	Paddle tennis
Dodge ball	Quoits
Handball	Shuffleboard
Horseshoes	Softball
Paddle tennis	Swimming
Quoits	Table tennis
Shuffleboard	Tennis
Softball	Tetherball
Swimming	Volley ball
Table tennis	
Tennis	
Tetherball	
Track	
Volley ball	

Supplementing the activities arranged for the individual playgrounds and also for playgrounds within the same unit, a limited program of sectional or city-wide tournaments and leagues was carried on. For boys this program was limited to softball, swimming, tennis, and track, and for girls to swimming, tennis, and sectional field days. These events provided an added incentive to the regular playground activities by enabling winners in intraunit competition to match their ability with individuals or teams from other parts of the city.

Teaching Game Skills.—Instruction in athletic games and sports has not been universally recognized as an essential part of the playground program but experience has fully demonstrated its value. Many individuals who have never taken part in a particular form of athletics are reluctant to engage in it with a group which already has considerable skill, but they welcome an opportunity to join a beginner's class. Some playground instruction groups are designed to initiate the members in the fundamental skills of the game and to prepare them for satisfactory participation in it. Others aim to teach players the fine points of the game and to help them achieve greater skill in it.

Events or tests involving the essential elements of a major game or sport have proved successful in developing game skills, especially on the part of young children. On many playgrounds games requiring a single basketball goal have been used in developing skill in such fundamentals as throwing, passing, and dribbling. Baseball pitching and throwing contests are a common feature of the playground program. Several cities have worked out football tests consisting of passing and kicking events of various types. Boys receive group instruction in these activities involving game skills, and tournaments are held in which large numbers participate.

There are few municipal pools and beaches in which some form of swimming instruction is not provided, at least for children. Twenty thousand people in one large city alone were taught to swim in 1937. Instructors in such sports as baseball, tennis, boxing, or archery help people of all ages gain greater enjoyment from their participation in these activities. In one city where an attempt was made to interest school children in the game of tennis 30 classes were organized with a total enrollment of 705, the members drawn largely from the fifth, sixth, seventh, and eighth grades.

Baseball Schools.—More formal in nature are the schools through which recreation departments are helping bring back baseball as the great American game. Nearly 4,000 youngsters attended the weekly indoor sessions held in four social centers in one city. The faculty was composed of big-league players, local residents who contributed their services and who were repaid by the eagerness of their pupils and the thrill with which they listened to every word. Later came eight weeks of outdoor sessions under the direction of a former league player, in which the boys were taught as they played. On rainy days the field house was used for "skull" talks and blackboard illustration. Following the close of school in June 100 boys' teams swung into action on the city's regulation diamonds.

"Knothole" Organizations.—An interesting feature of many playground sports programs is the formation of "knothole" clubs consisting primarily of boys interested in baseball. Often membership is restricted to boys enrolled on playground teams, but sometimes it embraces children in schools, orphanages, and other institutions. Arrangements are made for members to be admitted free to certain games at the local baseball parks. In one large city in 1937, 116,000 boys and girls between the ages of nine and fourteen were admitted free in supervised groups to games in the major league ball parks. The cost of providing baseballs has been reduced in one department since it arranged for the members of the "Knothole" organization to retrieve balls lost during the city league games and to turn them over to the recreation commission for use by boys' baseball teams. In this city the Knothole League is composed of 775 teams with a total enrollment of more than 11,000 boys.

Sportsmanship.—One of the recreation department's chief objectives in its athletic program is the development of the spirit and attitude of good sportsmanship. Scoring systems which allow more points for good sportsmanship than for attaining first place are used in some cities to teach children and young people that sportsmanship pays. Other recreation authorities feel that rather than offering rewards for sportsmanship it should be encouraged by the example of the leader, by appealing to the sporting qualities of the players, and by encouraging the participating groups to establish and maintain their own codes of conduct.

Informal Activities.—In considering games and athletics on the playground, as on other recreation areas, it is important to remember that even though organized activities receive considerable attention, the game courts and facilities are used more or less continuously for informal or individual play. Tennis, handball, or horseshoe tournaments represent only a small percentage of total participation in these activities, and on most playgrounds ball diamonds and game courts are used much more for "pick-up" or practice games than for league schedules. In the opinion of many recreation leaders the playday, featuring participation by informal groups in a spirit of play, and the playground festival have much greater value than interplayground contests engaged in by organized teams determined to win or the highly competitive track and field meet. In all probability, the recreation department makes its most valuable contribution in the field of athletics by encouraging and enabling large numbers of people to engage in enjoyable sports of lifelong interest.

DEVELOPING CHAMPIONS

The development of champions is not a major objective in municipal recreation, but public playgrounds and recreation facilities have given a start to many athletes who have gained wide renown. Four players in the 1938 World Series played as boys in the baseball leagues sponsored by the recreation department in a Western city. Many leading tennis players have come up through the municipal ranks. A recent report of the Chicago Park District cites many champions who used the park facilities before they won fame. Among them were Knute Rockne and Ralph Metcalfe, who played on park teams before they went to college, "Chick" Evans, who learned to play golf in Jackson Park, Johnny Weissmuller, who was "the product of a park beach," and "Bobby" McLean, who started skating in one of the parks. In this city young men who give promise of becoming big-league players are brought to the attention of the league authorities and are encouraged to advance in the field of sport.

CHAPTER XXII

DRAMA

Drama, like music and dancing, has always belonged to the people. As Barrett Clark reminded a Recreation Congress group, the plays of all primitive peoples arise out of a superabundance of the joy of life. In commenting on the extraordinary interest manifested in late years in dramatics in this country, he pointed out that it "is not a fad; it is no more than a natural and inevitable development of a deeply rooted instinct almost as old as man himself. It can no more go out of style than blue eyes or an autumn sunset." One of the functions of the recreation department is to enable children, young people, and adults to enjoy, as participants or spectators, various forms of drama. The department's drama activities, like other phases of its program, are not confined to its playgrounds and indoor centers, but include diversified services to groups throughout the community.

ON THE PLAYGROUNDS

Simple, spontaneous forms of drama such as dressing up, playing house, or acting out stories are a fundamental part of children's play life which find expression on the playground. Drama activities of a more formal nature are often carried on, the most common being puppetry and the production of one-act plays. The latter have been produced successfully at areas where the stage consisted merely of cretonne hung on the playground fence to serve as backdrop, and with portable screens used for wings. In one city the screen frames, constructed as a handicraft project, were made with grooves to permit the insertion of panels of composition board. These panels can be decorated and changed easily as the scenes in the plays presented may require. On many a playground, boys or girls holding sheets in front of them with their extended arms have served as a living curtain to shut off the stage while properties were being put in place. Sometimes audiences are called upon to imagine there is a curtain while the scenery is being changed before their eyes. Many simple, attractive playground theaters have been constructed with background and wings of growing trees and shrubbery, and in a few cities elaborately equipped outdoor theaters affording seats for a large number of spectators serve as centers for children's playground drama activities.

In a Small Community.—The possibilities of developing playground drama in communities where leadership and facilities are limited are

334

illustrated by the experience of one small city. The director of the summer playground in this community had only one assistant and therefore was able to give only part of her time to drama activities. Yet, because of her belief that the presentation of plays offered great possibilities for creative recreation and also for correlation with other activities, she decided to stress children's drama in the playground program. Each Monday morning the cast for the week's play was selected from the children present. Any child who desired to have a part in the cast was given one, but care was taken to make sure that no child repeatedly played a leading part. Rehearsals were held each morning with occasional but interrupted guidance on the part of the playground leader, and on Friday morning the play was performed. Three large screens set up among the trees furnished the background and provided ample facilities for stage entrances. The audience was seated on the grass. Additional stage preparations were made for the final pageant which was the only evening production. With floodlights, gay costumes, dancing, and music, it afforded a gala affair for the closing week of the playground season.

Other playground activities were correlated with drama and contributed to its success. For the storytelling hour, stories were selected which related to the play being presented during the current week. A rhythm band sometimes furnished incidental music, and occasionally dancing groups took part in the production. Costumes and properties were made during the handicraft period; miniature stages were constructed; and posters and invitations were prepared for the closing pageant. All these activities added to the effectiveness of the weekly plays and made possible greater unity and interest in the entire playground program.

In Larger Cities.—In larger cities with specialized leadership and more adequate facilities a greater variety of projects is possible, and the drama activities regularly carried on at the individual playgrounds are supplemented by special features. In one city where these activities are guided by a supervisor of drama and pageantry, several well-distributed playgrounds have been designated as matinee centers. Weekly programs are presented at each of these centers by boys and girls from various playgrounds of the district, each playground having an opportunity to present at least one performance during the summer. The programs include not only a one-act play but children's choruses, instrumental and dancing groups, and participation of the audiences in community singing. The popularity of these matinees is evidenced by the fact that the attendance exceeds that of any other activity at the grounds where they are presented.

In cities with a number of playgrounds at which plays are presented during the summer months, it is not uncommon for the season to close with a tournament or festival in which children's drama groups from all the playgrounds participate.   As many as 1,000 children from 16 playgrounds have taken part in the event in one city where a children's drama tournament has been held for several years.   Thirteen playgrounds participating in a closing interplayground tournament in another city each selected a Grimm's fairy tale and arranged a pantomime of the story.

In Oak Park.—In Oak Park, Illinois, where for many years drama has been an important feature of the playground program, the activities have centered about the children's drama clubs.   In a recent summer 37 different plays were given by the children who presented 52 performances at the playgrounds and before many community organizations.   Children who do not have playing parts are encouraged to help in making costumes and designing sets.   One group of boys wrote a play and directed it.   As in other cities, the summer season usually culminates in a special production such as a pageant, festival, or pantomime.   Because the playgrounds in this city are provided with buildings which are equipped for dramatic activities, the program is carried on throughout the year.   One-act plays and skits are produced from time to time, with special attention paid to holidays and with themes ranging from fairy tales to religious and modern realistic plays.   Interest has been keen and some unusual talent has been developed among the children.

The Pageant.—The pageant is not only the culmination of the playground season for groups interested in drama, but it frequently is the major event in the entire playground program.   The production of a pageant affords opportunity for a great variety of playground groups to participate, because music, dancing, and games usually share a place with drama in the pageant program.   Fairy tales are a most popular theme, and in many a city the pageant has been built around the story of Cinderella, Snow White, Alice in Wonderland, Hansel and Gretel, and the Pied Piper.   Historical pageants also have a strong appeal, particularly if they are related to local history, and where the entire playground program is related to an idea such as Indian or colonial life, this also affords the subject for the closing pageant.   Play itself often furnishes the theme, enabling playground groups to demonstrate present forms of play and to depict the various sports, music, dances, and games of other peoples and other times.

Pageants of this type enlist the participation of large numbers and also help demonstrate to the large audiences which usually attend them the significance of the playground program.   Sometimes the pageant is a city-wide project with all the playgrounds taking part but there is a tendency, especially in the larger cities, for each playground—or group of playgrounds in a district—to present its own pageant.   Such a plan enables more children to take part and eliminates some of the difficulties of a city-wide production.

Other Activities.—A series of nationality programs arranged in one city afforded opportunity for a variety of playground activities. Eight foreign countries were selected for study during one summer and scores of folk tales of each country were told and dramatized. The following year drama activity centered around a number of other countries; among the forms of drama included in the program at the various playgrounds were the puppet show, pantomime, shadowgraph, opera, one-act play, and story dramatization.

In recent years hand puppetry and the marionette theater have become popular playground features. Stage, puppets, and costumes are made by the children who frequently write the plays which are presented and construct and operate the theater. Remarkable skill and ingenuity have been developed in the making and use of marionettes, activities which appeal especially to the older boys and girls. In some cities marionette theaters constructed and operated by playground groups travel from playground to playground. In this way many children have an opportunity to see the plays which have been worked out on the different grounds and the troupes gain added experience.

IN THE INDOOR CENTERS

"From one end of the country to another there has been a great revival of interest in amateur drama; groups of old and young hungry for drama and self-expression are engaging in dramatic activities."[1] This observation by the National Commission on the Enrichment of Adult Life is borne out by the popularity of drama in community centers. Unlike playground drama which is primarily for children, drama in the indoor center serves large numbers of young people and adults as well. Men and women of various ages use the center's facilities for play production, occasionally under the guidance of an expert director, but frequently under leadership drawn from their own groups. Classes are conducted in such subjects as stagecraft, play reading, casting, diction, lighting, and directing. Indoor center activity in the field of drama is limited largely to members of participating groups, although from time to time public performances are arranged. In some cities where drama clubs have been organized at several centers, an exchange of plays is arranged between them, thus giving groups an opportunity to present their plays several times and also to observe the work done by other drama organizations.

Play Tournaments.—The one-act play contest or tournament, a common feature of the drama program, affords a special incentive and

[1] *Suggestions in Community Drama for the Enrichment of Adult Life,* National Education Association, 1935.

objective for center groups and other local drama organizations. Its popularity is illustrated by the experience in Rock Island, Illinois, where for more than ten years an annual drama tournament has been held which has aroused great public interest. In most tournaments, entries are limited to amateur groups, each of which presents a one-act play. Usually four plays are presented each evening and participation is limited to 16 groups. In this way the preliminaries extend over a period of four evenings, and the winner in each of the evening programs competes in the finals, thus enabling the tournament to be completed within a week. Each play is judged according to a number of factors such as presentation, acting, diction, and choice of play. In one city participating groups are classified into junior-high-school, senior-high-school, and adult divisions, and winners are selected in each division. Great care needs to be taken in conducting tournaments to assure fair consideration and equal opportunity to all participating groups and to avoid the difficulties and misunderstandings frequently associated with such tournaments.

Many leaders believe that a play festival in which the element of competition is eliminated and at which no awards are made offers the benefits, and avoids the disadvantages, of a tournament. Drama festivals have replaced tournaments in several cities. The contest or festival, in addition to affording opportunities for public performances and an incentive for attaining a high standard of production, often serves as an educational medium. An outstanding drama authority is sometimes engaged as a critic and adviser. Each evening he meets with the groups presenting plays, criticizes their productions, and for the benefit of the audience gives a brief résumé of the evening's presentations at the close of each program.

CITY-WIDE SERVICES AND ORGANIZATIONS

Recreation departments, especially those with full-time drama supervisors, provide many additional special services to groups participating in the department's drama program and to other individuals and community agencies interested in drama. The type of service rendered ranges from assisting with the selection of a play to assuming full responsibility for the production and staging of a pageant. It sometimes includes the maintenance of a play library from which local groups may borrow plays for study or use in productions. Institutes are conducted which are open to representatives of drama groups and to individuals responsible for drama activity in churches, clubs, and other local agencies. The courses afford practical training in play production and other forms of drama activity, often culminating in the presentation of plays by the institute members. In a number of cities the recreation department has been the means of organizing city-wide drama groups.

All-city Drama Groups.—An all-city players' organization is some-times formed as a by-product of the play tournament or festival. It affords an opportunity for players with unusual talent and ability to pursue this special interest in a selected group and serves as an incentive or goal toward which the members of the small groups aspire. One or more outstanding players from each tournament production are generally chosen for membership in the all-city players organization. In one city any member of an indoor center drama group who has attended 75 per cent of its meetings is eligible for a "tryout" with the selected group. Membership in one city-wide organization known as The Players is limited to persons who belong to social center drama clubs and who agree to share with the members of these clubs the knowledge and experience they gain through the meetings of The Players. The all-city players groups serve the same function in the field of drama as the all-city orches-tra drawn from members of the orchestras organized at the individual centers.

Little Theater Groups.—Somewhat similar in purpose to the all-city players groups are the little theater organizations which have been established in many cities under the sponsorship of the recreation depart-ment. Frequently, however, these organizations do not draw their members from the indoor center groups, nor are they necessarily related to other parts of the department's drama program. Their primary pur-pose is to give individuals interested in the theater as a hobby an oppor-tunity to enjoy dramatics under trained supervision and to produce and see a variety of plays and other forms of drama, many of which are not presented on the commercial stage. Primarily for amateurs, they fre-quently include in their membership persons who have had professional drama experience. In one local group with 118 active members, eight had played in summer stock or road companies, five had attended schools of painting and design, 38 had taken courses in dramatics in college or drama schools, a few were students of period furniture, two were costume experts, and the others had only an amateur drama experience or were taking an interest in the activity for the first time.

The program of these organizations is not limited to play production but it frequently includes classes in diction, playwriting, scenic design, rhythms, and make-up. The workshop is an important feature. In one city the program of the community players organized under the recreation department includes two major productions each year, four monthly theater nights, eight workshop nights, weekly radio plays over the local radio station, and weekly lectures on acting. An annual playwriting contest, a drama tournament, and a civic Christmas pageant are among the activities of another similar group, the major productions of which combine the allied arts of the theater—music, dancing, and drama.

Little theater groups vary widely in the methods by which they are organized, directed, and financed, and in the type of facilities which are at their disposal.   In one city 700 individuals are enrolled as members of the local Players and pay $1 a year membership fee.   The director receives part of his salary from the funds of The Players but a major portion from the Board of Education which employs him as a teacher of high-school English classes.   The Board of Education also gives the use of rooms in school buildings for rehearsals, tryouts, the building of scenery, and the storing of costumes.   School auditoriums are open for lectures and major productions.   In another city the civic theater sponsored by the recreation commission was originally an amalgamation of several purely producing groups.   It uses the facilities in the local high school.   A professional director is employed and funds are secured through sponsorships at $5 each, the sale of season tickets, and admissions to single productions.   In a third city the little theater group meets in one of the park field houses fully equipped for dramatic productions, and the director is a WPA worker who gives his entire time to this project.

Costume and Service Bureau.—The costume bureau, a feature of the drama service of many departments, sometimes consists merely of a collection of costumes kept in the department office or storeroom, but in a number of cities special buildings have been equipped for the manufacture, storage, and collection of costumes.   They are furnished with cupboards where costumes of all types are stored, ironing boards, wash-tubs, gas plates, sewing machines, and other facilities for making, dyeing, and washing the costumes.   Spaces are provided for storing properties, lighting equipment, scenery, curtains, and other accessories which are also loaned by the department.   In one city masks, jewelry, and other materials used in plays are also available; in another, stage lighting equipment is constructed and loaned to drama groups.

The costume service is provided in some cities exclusively for groups affiliated with the department for use in connection with playground and center plays, community pageants, festivals, and other special events.   In others, local community groups may avail themselves of the service, sometimes at a nominal charge.   In one year Pasadena's recreation department wardrobe served nine dramatic club centers with 1,889 costumes, and furnished nearly 11,000 costumes for use in school programs and more than 2,000 to private schools, churches, clubs, and individuals.   In this city costumes, stage properties, and equipment are also furnished, and a large number of wigs have been made for use in dramatic productions.

Other Activities.—Other drama activities, which can only be mentioned, are the promotion of playwriting contests, the organization and production of city-wide holiday pageants which will be described in a later section, the sponsoring of professional artists, and the arrangement of series of matinees for children. In one city such a series is promoted by the recreation department in a downtown theater, with weekly performances during the school season. Radio programs not only provide entertainment features on the air but afford opportunities for playground and center groups to perform for the benefit of a large public and incidentally inform the public concerning the drama activities in the department's program.

TRAVELING THEATERS

In a few cities where drama has received major attention, the recreation department has established a traveling theater. This has enabled various types of drama productions to be presented at the parks and playgrounds and in the neighborhoods throughout the city. Under the sponsorship of the Federal WPA Drama Project the number of traveling theater groups has increased rapidly. Several traveling troupes have been organized which throughout the summer season present one-act plays, vaudeville shows, minstrels, and operettas before large and enthusiastic audiences comprising many individuals who have never previously seen a dramatic performance.

In Minneapolis a dramatic troupe sponsored by the Board of Park Commissioners in one year staged 151 performances before nearly 150,000 spectators. During the summer months the troupe appeared for from 1- to 4-week stands at the larger parks where there were bandstands that could be transformed into stages. During the winter season they played for 1-week stands at the centers which had halls or gymnasiums of sufficient size to accommodate a temporary stage and an audience of at least 300. An enjoyable feature of this program has been the community singing in which the audiences have had an enthusiastic part. In addition to its productions at the indoor and outdoor centers, the troupe has performed at the old soldiers' home, veterans' hospital, settlement houses, and various other private agencies, and has participated in the radio broadcasting program.

Another type of traveling theater which has made its appearance in several cities is the marionette theater. Hartford, Connecticut, is one of the cities where this type of project has been carried on most successfully under a director of marionettes, an expert wood carver, and a troupe of operators, all of whom were paid from emergency funds. An interesting group of puppets has been made with great care and expert workmanship, and their costumes have been executed with greatest attention paid to modes, color, and design. An old Ford chassis was used as a base for the foundation on which the theater's superstructure was erected. In a single year the marionette troupe gave 157 performances. Schools, parks, playgrounds, and institutions comprised the regular circuit at which each of the shows was presented during the summer. Auditoriums were used during the winter months. So popular was this feature and so widespread was interest in it, that at the close of the summer playground season it was taken on a tour of the state and county fairs. The usefulness of the marionette troupe was further extended by the setting up of a course of instruction in puppetry for children and adults.

CHAPTER XXIII

MUSIC

"There is no country today where so many people are listening to music, practising the art, and engaging in music composition," according to the report of a study of music in adult and community life.[1] In this brief record tribute is paid to the contribution which municipal recreation agencies are making to the musical life of America. Although in many cities only a beginning has been made in the utilization and development of the community's music resources, recreation departments are giving music an important place in their programs. They are recognizing that it has a universal appeal, that more and more people are seeking recreation through it, that people may engage in music activity in many forms and on various levels, and that music may contribute richly to other forms of recreation activity. The municipal recreation program is furnishing opportunities for people to enjoy a rich music experience.

TYPES OF MUSIC SERVICE

Music activities sponsored or conducted by recreation departments, some of which were listed in Chap. XIV, vary widely in type, in the numbers and ages of the people participating, in purpose, and in value. In considering the department's music service it may be helpful to group its activities as follows: (1) conducting recreational music activities for children, supplementing music instruction in the schools, and integrating it with life outside the schools; (2) organizing and furnishing leadership for groups of young people and adults, thus making it possible for them to participate in various forms of music activity; (3) affording opportunities for people to listen to and enjoy music provided by others; (4) cooperating with other community agencies in organizing and conducting community-wide activities such as festivals or caroling projects, and coordinating or bringing together existing music groups; (5) serving individuals and community groups through training institutes, certain kinds of music instruction, and the provision of music leaders; (6) providing community music groups with auditoriums, concert halls, and clubrooms to be used for concerts, rehearsals, meetings, and other activities.

[1] Willem Van de Wall, *The Music of the People*, American Association for Adult Education, 1938.

MUSIC FOR CHILDREN

Music instruction is a part of the regular elementary- and high-school program in most cities.   The schools are making a valuable contribution by arousing children's interest in music and by developing skills which can be used in later life and which contribute to the child's life outside the school.   Much music instruction, however, is formal in character and affords little opportunity for participation growing out of the child's own desires and interests.   The music program of the recreation department supplements that of the schools in two ways.   It gives the child an opportunity to use, outside the schools, interests and skills developed inside them, and it also provides additional forms of recreational music in which children have much freedom of choice.   During the long school vacation periods these music activities are the only outlet for music expression for a large number of boys and girls.

The activities provided by the recreation department of the Board of Education in a large Eastern city illustrate this phase of the municipal music program.   Toy and rhythm bands are organized for the small children who are taught the fundamental rhythms through the use of cymbals, tambourines, drums, sticks, and triangles.   As they grow older and progress, the children become interested in and join one of the 32 harmonica bands which have been organized in the schools.   As many as 1,500 boys and girls have attended the weekly harmonica classes.   For the more advanced students a city harmonica band has been formed comprising 75 boys and girls selected from the various school harmonica bands, and this also practices one evening each week.   This experience, in turn, frequently leads to participation in school orchestras and bands.   According to the harmonica instructor, almost 60 per cent of the children who have been under his supervision over a period of years, after discovering their music talents in the harmonica bands, were stimulated to a study of the orchestral and other standard instruments.

The value of relating their children's music program to that in the schools has been recognized by several recreation departments who have employed school music supervisors to take charge of the music activities at playgrounds and indoor centers.   This arrangement resulted in the enrollment of 540 boys and girls in 14 different bands and orchestras at one city's summer playgrounds.   These groups enjoyed the experience of presenting concerts during the season which closed with a final musical program in which they all participated.   In another city where three part-time music directors were employed to help with the summer playground program, activities consisted of rhythm orchestras, children's chorus, glee clubs, group and community singing, singing games, and folk dancing.

Typical Playground Activities.—Music played a conspicuous part in one summer program which centered around the theme of early American life. Each playground organized a glee club for boys and girls and a music week was scheduled in August when all grounds gave a community concert. The songs which received special attention were Appalachian ballads, Southern melodies, sea chanties, and folk songs of the surrounding countryside. Other features of the music program in this city were a band composed of young children and one for children of high-school age. The possibilities of playground music have been demonstrated in a large Western city in which the recreation department employed a supervisor of music. She first made a survey to determine what activities were practicable and best suited to the interests and needs of the children. Within a few years there were 16 groups of small children who met regularly for singing, 12 toy symphonies, 5 harmonica bands, several small orchestras, and a city-wide boys' choir which has sung during several opera seasons.

In cities with a large foreign population neighborhood bands, orchestras, and choral groups have been formed to take advantage of their special skills and interests. Typical of such groups is a tamborica orchestra composed of young Croatian musicians which has represented its playground on many occasions. The possibilities of making musical instruments on the playground were mentioned in the section relating to the arts and crafts program. Rhythms, singing, and various forms of dancing are featured on many playgrounds. A few playground groups have been formed for the presentation of light operas, but projects of this type are rarely attempted except at playgrounds conducted the year round.

Informal music activities at the playground and indoor center can be conducted successfully even though specially trained music leaders are not employed. Many playground and center directors who lack professional expertness in music but who have interest and some natural ability serve effectively as song leaders, conduct children's rhythm bands, and instruct folk dance groups.

Competitive Activities.—Much of the music activity on the summer playgrounds is in a lighter vein and is occasionally conducted in the typical American spirit of competition. One department holds an annual musical jamboree with preliminary contests at the various playgrounds. Among the activities are harmonica contests, ukulele contests with song accompaniments, solo or group whistlers, fiddling contests, barbershop quartets, glee clubs, and community group singing. A city-wide barbershop contest in another city attracts many participants, young and old. Preliminary contests are held, and the winners, dressed in costume, participate in the finals. The judging is done by noted musicians, and the mayor and other city officials lend an air of importance to the informal and often amusing occasion by serving as honorary judges.

Music in the Indoor Centers.—The music interests of children are also served in community centers where the longer season permits the introduction of more ambitious projects. The means by which this is accomplished is illustrated by the experience in a small Illinois city. Here the initial effort to develop music activities for children was a series of tryouts at each of the centers during the first two weeks of the season. Children were permitted to try various band and orchestral instruments to determine their fitness or aptitude for a definite type. Small instrumental classes were subsequently formed at each of the centers and as the groups advanced in skill and began making public appearances, interest and participation increased and orchestras were organized. The study of new music and the thrill of playing with a group have stimulated membership in the orchestras. When the desire to play more ambitious music was expressed by children of unusual ability, a recreation department orchestra was organized whose members include a number of children who began their music career in groups organized by the department.

Biweekly instruction is also given to beginners who look forward to membership in an orchestra, and children of kindergarten and primary age are organized into rhythm and melody bands. The instrumental music program continues throughout the summer when instruction is given in the park pavilions, and the children occasionally take part in the family and community night programs.

MUSIC FOR YOUNG PEOPLE AND ADULTS

It is equally important that this interest in music which recreation departments are helping children develop be maintained in later years and that boys and girls continue to use their music skills. Recreation departments are therefore affording music opportunities for young people and adults. The program, especially at the indoor centers, includes such features as choruses, glee clubs, orchestras, small instrumental and vocal groups, opera clubs, music appreciation groups, and community singing. Occasionally one of the center's instrumental groups furnishes accompaniments for its weekly sings.

A nationally known music leader, after a visit to the school centers in a Midwestern city, reported enthusiastically on the music groups which he observed, as follows:

We saw young people's opera groups practicing the *Nautical Knot*, an Italian young people's group practicing *Lucia;* two fretted instrument organizations, one Hawaiian and elementary, the other mostly German and just about perfect; a barn dance group entertained us; a splendid adult woman's chorus sang for us;

a colored band played; a Jewish women's group sang its old world pieces for us. Twelve hundred people are participating in the public recreation music programs.

In the same city, a number of other music groups are flourishing which had their beginnings in the social centers.

Instrumental Groups.—Instrumental groups organized and conducted by recreation departments vary from harmonica bands to symphony orchestras. Following the development of harmonica bands among the school children in one city many schoolteachers who wished either to help their pupils or to play the instrument for pleasure likewise demanded instruction. Consequently, an adult group was formed including members of the board of education as well as school principals. At the request of a group of patrolmen, a police harmonica band was also organized.

Orchestras primarily afford their members the joy of playing together, but they also contribute to special events and programs at the social centers. Members of orchestras frequently represent many nationalities and occupations and a wide range of ages. Playing under the guidance of competent directors, these orchestras afford immense satisfaction through progress in musical ability and appreciation. Special instrumental groups are often formed from individuals of a particular nationality or background. Typical of such groups are a Czechoslovakian Tamburas Club, numbering 23 native Czechoslovakians who play folk music on their native instruments and a band of old troupers, all of them veterans of professional circus or troupers' bands.

Orchestras.—Recreation departments have often taken the leadership in organizing and sponsoring a civic orchestra. Most members are amateurs and the membership usually includes both men and women, although a number of successful orchestras are composed entirely of women and girls. A civic orchestra which has been in existence for twelve years presents outstanding performances during the year including one or more summer concerts in the parks, an outdoor summer production in the form of an operetta, and concerts during the indoor season.

The 120 members of one women's symphony orchestra have been organized into several small instrumental groups, which include a violin choir of twenty, a flute choir of ten, and a trumpet ensemble. These groups appeal strongly to the younger members of the orchestra many of whom are high-school students and there is a great demand for their services. Requests for appearances at dinners, meetings, and entertainments are handled by the recreation department which also arranges for transportation, compensation, and other details.

Besides being invited to join community music organizations, recent high-school graduates are encouraged to continue their interest in orchestral music through the organization of orchestras recruited from former members of high-school orchestras. In some instances instrumental teachers in the high schools are paid to take charge of these orchestras, thus assuring leadership accustomed to deal with young people and familiar with the school music program. The success of these so-called alumni groups is partly due to the fact that their members are of comparatively one age, they enjoy being and playing together, and many social activities are arranged in connection with their meetings.

Choral Groups.—Typical of the choral groups sponsored by recreation departments is the Civic Opera Company in one city of less than 100,000. It is the direct outgrowth of a woman's municipal chorus of some 65 members who regarded their membership in the chorus as a means of securing further vocal training and enjoyment from singing together. During its three years of existence the chorus took part in regional folk festivals and presented light operas and special programs. The enlistment of a number of men to sing in the operas proved such a successful and enjoyable experience that it was decided to form an opera company. The women's chorus was merged in the larger organization which has a mixed membership of nearly one hundred.

Of four choruses sponsored by one recreation department, one, known as the Civic Chorus, is composed of 300 men and women, and the other three are alumni groups of young people. These groups meet weekly for rehearsals of operas, concerts, and other programs. Dances and other social get-togethers help in maintaining a unity among them and in recruiting new singers. The caliber of music sung by such choral groups is usually very high, and occasionally they join with orchestral groups in producing programs of city-wide interest, as in one city where the civic chorus with the cooperation of the women's symphony orchestra presented Handel's *Messiah*. The organization of music festivals, holiday programs, and special musical events enable the instrumental and choral groups to produce music that brings satisfaction to the participants and enjoyment to large numbers of listeners.

Alumni choruses in several cities afford opportunities for young people to continue singing after they leave school. Among the widely different vocal groups organized at municipal recreation centers are glee clubs formed among mothers of playground children, groups of young men who meet regularly to sing together, madrigal groups of high-school students, and men's and women's choruses developed among Negro groups.

OPPORTUNITIES FOR LISTENING TO MUSIC

Participation is of primary importance, but opportunities for listening to good music are not neglected. The concerts regularly provided in many cities serve large audiences and frequent opportunities for hearing good music are furnished by groups organized within the department. One department's music committee arranged 54 concerts in a single year for its various music groups, and a total attendance of nearly 24,000 was reported at these concerts, many of which were held in outlying districts of the city. A Western city reports that a series of 48 Sunday afternoon concerts presented by orchestras, bands, chorus groups, string ensembles, readers, and lecturers was attended by more than 29,000. In the same city a successful series of 24 programs was given two evenings a week during the summer, with audiences totaling more than 35,500.

Band concerts, often accompanied by community singing, are common features of the program especially during the summer months, and occasionally symphony concerts are presented. Such concerts are not usually sponsored by the recreation department but are given by a local music organization or by professional music groups paid by the city. In 1937 one Park District, in cooperation with the Federation of Musicians, presented the Civic Opera Orchestra in its 36th annual series of open-air concerts, the total attendance at which was 2,650,000. In a few cities the recreation authorities or a civic body sponsor outdoor opera programs that attract large audiences.

In order that people may enjoy and understand better the programs which are presented, music appreciation classes are sometimes organized. In more than one city groups meet weekly to study the works to be presented by the local symphony orchestra. A lecturer describes the numbers, and electrical recordings of them are played. In this way people come to appreciate and enjoy more fully the orchestral works played by the local music groups.

The radio is being used more and more as a means of carrying good music to a large audience and at the same time of demonstrating to the public what it is doing through the department's music program. One department has an hour's broadcast each week devoted to symphonies by the masters, with recorded music. Various music groups sponsored by local departments take part in their regular broadcasts. In one city harmonica lessons were given over the radio, and music appreciation was encouraged through a series of music stories, illustrated by musical compositions.

A CLEARINGHOUSE FOR MUSIC PROJECTS

The department serves as a cooperative agency in planning local music activities and fostering music projects. A municipal advisory music council has been organized by the recreation commission in one city for the purpose of advising the commission on matters of policy, programs, and relationships with other music agencies. Members of this council include representatives of the local public schools, conservatory, university, and music organizations. This council has proved of great help to the commission, particularly in fostering the development of neighborhood music groups and in making studies and surveys of community music resources and needs.

Music festivals have proved an effective means for bringing together local music groups in a joint project. These festivals have frequently centered around the music of the various racial groups in the city, as in the program described in Chap. XVI. A regional folk festival which has become a tradition with the local recreation body in another city enlists the cooperation of such groups as the girls' municipal orchestra, the Synagogue choir, women's municipal chorus, college glee club, Negro choir, and dancers from several racial groups. Holiday celebrations on a community-wide scale are often promoted with the cooperation of local agencies. Typical are a Christmas "tree of light" program with several hundred participants, which attracts thousands of spectators, and a caroling program which, with the cooperation of neighborhood groups, brings Christmas cheer to hospitals, orphans' homes, hotels, railway stations, and even the local jails.

Other Services.—Recreation departments also conduct institutes for the training of socially minded music leaders who are so essential to the success of music groups. Sixty-one community singing directors completed a local course in song leading, the purpose of which was not only to give instruction in proper methods but also to encourage the development of community singing groups within the organizations by the members of the class. In another city a song leaders' association, an auxiliary of the recreation commission, is in charge of the training of volunteer leaders and conducts institutes for them from time to time. The commission also serves as a clearinghouse for these volunteer song leaders. Members of the department staff frequently lead singing at local conventions, banquets, and special occasions.

Because the lack of available music has hindered the success of music groups in many cities, music libraries have been established for the purpose of furnishing suitable music of many types to groups who need and will make effective use of it. A house-to-house canvass and several special parties arranged by one department proved successful methods of accumulating a large amount of music which was later sorted and catalogued for the municipal music library.

The recreation department also has a part in arranging programs for community groups, assisting individuals or organizations in securing music instruments, organizing conferences for a discussion of music problems, advising organizations on the selection of appropriate music for particular occasions, serving as adviser to the Federally supported music programs, and conducting special music studies. It helps local music groups, whether organized by the department or not, to secure competent leaders and to find suitable meeting places for their rehearsals. In many cities rooms in recreation buildings and indoor centers are made available for the regular meetings of local music organizations. In brief, the recreation department is helping people find opportunities to make and enjoy good music. It is cooperating with all agencies working toward this end and is promoting music activities on all fronts, frequently coordinating music with other activities in the department's program.

CHAPTER XXIV

NATURE, GARDENING, AND OUTING ACTIVITIES

Luther Burbank once said:

Every child should have mud pies, grasshoppers, waterbugs, tadpoles, frogs, mud turtles, elderberries, wild strawberries, acorns, chestnuts, trees to climb, brooks to wade in, water lilies, woodchucks, bats, bees, butterflies, various animals to pet, hay fields, pine cones, rocks to roll, sand, snakes, huckleberries, and hornets; and any child who has been deprived of these has been deprived of the best part of his education.

Unfortunately large numbers of city children have been deprived of the opportunities which Mr. Burbank felt were so essential in the life of every child. School authorities through their natural science courses and nature projects are giving many city children opportunities to become acquainted with the wonders and beauty of nature. Recreation departments, however, are particularly well fitted to carry on an extensive nature program because their freedom in developing programs enables them to place emphasis upon out-of-door activities and their access to large parks and reservations affords exceptional opportunities for studying various forms of plant and animal life. During the past few years there has been greater emphasis upon nature activities in the recreation program, and through the help of trained workers the wonders of the out-of-doors are being interpreted to growing numbers of children, youth, and adults.

NATURE ACTIVITIES FOR CHILDREN

No phase of the recreation department's nature program is of greater importance or reaches a larger number of individuals than the nature activities carried on as a part of the playground program. These activities foster in the children a love of natural beauty and a respect for growing things, while the experience furnishes valuable training in observation. Incidentally, children are taught the importance of conservation, and by developing their interest in trees, shrubs, flowers, and other growing things on the play areas they are stimulated to learn more about the world in which they are living. Any playground director can initiate simple nature activities, but the most worth-while results are accomplished in cities where there is at least one nature specialist on the staff of the recreation department. Such a worker trains the playground lead-

ers, initiates special nature projects, and helps with the nature clubs and
activities on the individual playgrounds.

Playground Nature Projects.—Unusual opportunities which the playgrounds offer for nature activities are not overlooked. Children attending a playground near the seashore in one city have made a careful study
of the water birds, and have also made and recorded observations of
weather conditions. The labeling of all playground trees and shrubs is
an instructive and interesting project. In localities where the playgrounds afford meager opportunities to study and observe nature at first
hand, hikes to city parks or near-by reservations are an important feature
of the program. These hikes enable children to observe nature in its
many forms, secure specimens for their collections and museums, gather
information which is useful in planning club programs, play nature games,
and cook out of doors.

Nature interest is stimulated and turned into constructive channels
through the observance of bird days, when birdbaths or birdhouses are
built and set up on the playgrounds. The care and maintenance of these
facilities furnish valuable nature experiences as do pet shows, a common
playground feature. Arbor and tree days have been the occasion for
planting shrubs and trees on many playgrounds. .Children cooperate
in the winter by feeding birds near their homes and in large outlying
areas. They also assist in eradicating pests such as hay fever weeds or
tussock moths.

Miniature Museum.—The miniature natural history museum is one
of the most interesting and valuable features of playground nature
programs. Some of these museums are very simple, consisting merely
of one or more cases and posters set up in a corner of the playground
shelter. Living exhibits have a strong appeal, and aquariums are especially successful. Frogs, ants, mosquitoes, and other insects are reared
through all life stages. Collections showing the natural bark of trees
and the color and grain of the wood, wild flower seeds, flowers dried
and mounted, and insect collections find a place in many of these
museums.

The Junior Nature Museum.—The establishment of a junior nature
museum has resulted in the stimulation of greater interest in nature
activities than any other project and has furnished a center where groups
can pursue this interest throughout the year. Reference was made in
Chap. XX to the Junior Museum in San Francisco where nature activities
comprise a large part of its program. Under the heading of biology,
groups study insects, reptiles, amphibia, and fish. The children also
receive instruction in methods of collecting, mounting, and classifying
biological material and in the care and feeding of specimens. Interest in
geology is stimulated through a study of rocks, minerals, volcanoes,

glaciers, and erosions, and by instruction in collecting and classifying specimens. Museum members have the use of a laboratory for analyses, stories, charts, maps, and pictures. Regular field trips for observation and collecting are a most important part of the program. A junior Audubon Club holds weekly meetings and bird hikes. The study of botany is encouraged through instruction in collecting, pressing, mounting, and classifying flowers and leaves, and casting them in wax. Its monthly bulletin, *The Junior Naturalist*, prepared by the children is a valuable educational medium.

Not only is the center well equipped for indoor activities but the development of nature trails and outdoor gardens and the planting of shrubs and wild flowers on the building site make it unique and fascinating. One phase of the museum's service is to assist the city's playgrounds in their nature activities. Through its extension service terrariums, aquariums, and wall chart exhibits are loaned to the playgrounds, and, if desired, an assistant is periodically assigned for special work on the individual grounds.

Portable Barnyard.—Playground directors in one large city reported that many of their children had never seen such farm animals as cows, goats, pigs, ducks, or turkeys. So the park department made a collection of such animals and constructed a barn on wheels with a runway to convey them from one playground to another. A section of the playground was enclosed with portable fencing during the visits, which were usually for a period of three days. Many children saw domestic animals for the first time, and interesting experiences were related in connection with the farmyard. It was found that children were not the only ones who took a keen interest in the animals and their care, but a large number of adults, particularly those brought up in the country, spent a great deal of time watching the animals.

Zoo Trips.—Instead of bringing the animals to the children, several cities have made special arrangements for taking groups of children to the city zoo. These trips, as well as zoological contests, furnish the incentive for study into the interesting ways of animals and attracted to the zoo large numbers of playground children. Special zoo days incidentally afford an opportunity for educational publicity concerning animals, their native habitats and peculiarities, which demonstrates to citizens the value of a zoo and the wisdom of public appropriations for its support.

Other public facilities and agencies serving the city's nature interest, such as the natural history museum or the planetarium, are made available for the use of playground groups in a number of cities. Special arrangements are made for groups of playground children to visit these centers, and such trips afford the basis for interesting playground discussions, activities, and projects.

In a Western City.—The typical weekly program of a well-qualified nature expert employed as nature supervisor during the summer playground season consisted of leading two or three all-day hikes and collecting trips and visiting five or six other playgrounds each day for the remainder of the week. On these visits he gave lectures, taught crafts, initiated projects, played games, and conducted other activities, all related to nature. As a means of arousing interest at the time of his first visit, he brought with him to the playground live snakes, lizards, spiders, and other animals and a collection of handicraft projects and materials related to a nature program. Playground nature clubs, natural history museums, weekly nature meetings, hikes, and nature handicraft projects proved highly successful in promoting the program.

In an Eastern County.—Two nature specialists employed during the summer by a county recreation department for the guidance of playground children, initiated and stimulated many interesting activities. In one community there was a nature walk every day, nature motives were used in the arts and crafts program, and the nature theme was also stressed in the interpretive dancing. Another town boasted a volunteer speaker's bureau which provided authorities on nature subjects each week. Leaf identification, tree maps, the construction of nature trails, and the making of scrapbooks were features in another community. Nature treasure hunts, visits to nature museums, and a club for the study of marine life were also on the county's nature program.

NATURE ACTIVITIES FOR COMMUNITY GROUPS

Nature interest is by no means limited to children, and recreation departments are more and more providing nature activities which appeal to young people and adults. It has been truly said that nature study meets all the requirements of a good hobby because it deals with life itself and is therefore intensely interesting. It can be carried on practically without cost anywhere, alone or with a group. Furthermore, it takes people out of doors and brings them in contact with the natural world in which they live and from which they have been shut out by urban living conditions.

Its growing popularity is indicated as follows in a recreation department bulletin announcing nature study courses: "Plants and animals of the mountains, the fields and the seashore . . . birds and butterflies, snakes, insects, shellfish, seaweeds, wild flowers, and a host of other creations of prodigal nature are being collected and studied by people seeking constructive uses for their leisure." Bird clubs, marine study groups, astronomy clubs and other groups organized for the study of nature in various forms are meeting in the recreation centers in scores of cities.

In the Cleveland Metropolitan Parks.—The construction of nature trails, the employment of naturalists, and the operation of trailside museums are among the most valuable services rendered to nature lovers by park and recreation departments. The Cleveland Metropolitan Park District has been a leader in this field and for a number of years, in cooperation with the Cleveland Museum of Natural History, has employed a park naturalist who devotes his time to developing a program designed to interest people of the Cleveland region in the natural history of the district. Pre-eminently an outdoor program, it encourages groups and individuals to visit the parks and seeks to interpret to them the many interesting natural exhibits contained in them.

Popular features of the program are the trailside museums which contain exhibits and collections. Near each one is a labeled nature trail, a wild flower trail, and an area where outdoor lectures are given. The wild flower trails are particularly interesting and attract large numbers of visitors. In the early spring, plants along the trail, most of them close to the paths, are labeled for easy identification. As different species come into bloom new labels are added and these are changed continuously to keep pace with the developing vegetation. During the wild flower season the park naturalist is in attendance every Saturday and Sunday afternoon to answer questions and to give informal talks on the wild flowers.

In summer the trailside museums are open daily with a resident naturalist in charge whose duty it is to explain and interpret the exhibits, answer questions about the natural history of the park areas, and give informal talks to visiting groups. Guided trips throughout the park are arranged from time to time during which talks are given on the trees, birds, geology, and other features encountered along the way. Bird walks are sponsored during the spring months. Valuable cooperation in the building and maintenance of the nature trails is received from the Cleveland Natural Science Club which has recently completed a new lodge in one of the parks.

Saturday and Sunday nature tours or caravan trips to outlying parks or reservations where naturalists explain the geology, forestry, wild life, and other natural resources are arranged in a number of cities. One park naturalist conducts weekly campfire programs every Friday evening throughout the summer months, featuring world-wide travelers and explorers who give illustrated talks about their experiences. An annual outing in the form of an early spring maple "sugaring-off" party is one of the most popular events in one nature program.

A Marine Museum.—The marine museum established by the Playground and Recreation Department in Los Angeles is a unique institution. Originally started in a small room on a municipal pier, the museum has expanded until it now occupies a special building at one of the city beaches. Not a single specimen has been purchased although the collection now contains more than 13,000 items. Shells, crabs, sea urchins, starfish, marine birds, fish, and a giant turtle are included among the specimens on display, as well as a small aquarium and a group of seals. Several ship models, an Eskimo canoe, and fishing equipment represent a start toward a maritime museum. Several natural history hobby groups whose interests center about the museum have been formed in the city. In a recent year the museum was visited by approximately 150,000 people and its services and facilities were extended to many school, scouting, and other community groups.

An Exceptional Nature Program.—An outstanding example of a nature program is the one which for a number of years has been conducted at Oglebay Park near Wheeling, West Virginia, under the sponsorship of the Nature Association of that state. Its success has been due in large measure to the fact that an experienced naturalist has been in charge and in part to the unusual facilities in the park. A regular schedule of early Sunday morning field trips is conducted from April to October; when the weather permits an outdoor breakfast is served at the conclusion of the walk. The Oglebay Plant Club, the Brooks Bird Club, and the Nature Sketching Club are three park hobby groups. The monthly meetings and frequent field trips of these organizations have resulted in the development of a remarkable degree of scientific interest in their respective fields. The Astronomy Club counts as its chief accomplishment the construction of an 8-inch telescope which is in use on the average of three nights a week. Members of the club serve as volunteers on Saturday nights when the public is invited to make use of it.

Campfire programs including motion pictures with reels devoted to outdoor features are held every Saturday night during the summer at the council circle in the park camp. A nature training school is conducted each year with a 2-week session at the park and 2 weeks in a mountain camp. Through this school a large number of teachers, camp leaders, club workers, and individuals interested in nature study as a hobby have received valuable training. Field trips conducted in connection with the playground and family day camps have been a means of awakening interest in nature on the part of large numbers of children. For several years field trips were arranged for school children with transportation provided by local school boards in the region.

A trailside museum has been established, made up largely of material collected by children and adults on field trips in the park, and a nature library serves the hobby club members, bird walk patrons, and campers in the park. A sound movie projector has proved a great asset to the nature teaching program and has been used at the playground and family day camps for daily shows related to exhibits in the nature museum. The influence of the nature study program centering at the park has also been extended widely through its publications which include 4-H Club nature study projects.

GARDENING

"Happiness grows with radishes and roses in a children's garden. . . . The child gardener finds a primitive and deeply satisfying field for self-expression. With his hands in the earth he touches, comes to know and appreciate the basic things of life, the simple things, the beautiful things."[1] The joy of gardening is no less real for adults than for children. In many municipal recreation programs the emphasis has been on children's gardens, but gardening as a wholesome form of leisure-time activity for adults merits, and is receiving, increased attention. Recognition must be given to the fine work in gardening carried on by many schools as a phase of their nature education or vocational training programs. In the following pages reference will be made only to those gardening projects which are carried on outside of school hours or as a form of adult leisure-time activity.

Gardening in New York City.—In view of the limited opportunity for home gardens in New York City it is not surprising that the Park Department has set aside areas for children's gardens. The first of these was established in 1902, and from this beginning has developed a Bureau of School Farms which is operated as a part of the public recreation program. It consists of eleven gardens under a staff which includes a director, several assistants employed on a 6-month basis, and permanent attendants.

The children's plots are formally arranged and uniformly planted, and the gardens are bordered with flower beds and ornamental shade trees so that the whole is in harmony with the park landscape. Each garden center is provided with benches, drinking fountains, and rural dipping wells, and near the gate stands a small garden house which serves as a tool shed and office.

Early in the spring children in the neighborhood, either individually or in school groups, are assigned space in the gardens for the planting and care of early maturing crops. During the summer children may come to the garden every day if they choose. They not only care for their individual plots but cultivate and water the flower and observation gardens that are planted with peanuts, sweet potatoes, wheat, herbs, and other crops. From time to time interesting stories are told about plants, garden insects, and bird visitors. In these gardens the children find a new world of living things amidst the brick and stone of the city streets and buildings.

[1] "Radishes and Roses," *Recreation*, May, 1936, p. 74.

Following the first harvest in early July the gardens are again planted with crops which mature in October, when the final harvest day is made the occasion of a festival and the presentation of awards. Boys and girls are encouraged to show their products at the Junior Garden Club Show conducted by one of the city newspapers. The popularity of the gardens is indicated by the fact that more than 200,000 visits by children varying in age from eight to fourteen years were reported during a single season.

In Cedar Rapids, Iowa.—The promotion of gardening is by no means limited to recreation departments in the large cities. For many years children's gardens have been an outstanding project of the Playground Commission in Cedar Rapids, Iowa. Home gardens are encouraged for boys and girls who can have a plot of ground at home, and playground gardens are designed for children who wish to have their gardens in a large plot. Many of these plots are loaned to the commission which pays for plowing and harrowing them in the spring and for cleaning them in the fall. Every young gardener has his own individual garden which he prepares, plants, and cultivates.

The program is under the guidance of a garden director who in the spring visits the elementary schools for the purpose of interesting children in the project. During the summer she makes weekly visits to each playground garden, conducts simple lessons in gardening, and assists children in keeping notebook records. The home gardeners often attend the sessions at the nearest playground garden, but each of the home gardens is visited at least twice during the summer by a member of the department staff. Features of the season are an August picnic and the display of garden products. Through the cooperation of the local garden club awards are given for fine gardens and for the best notebooks. The fact that in a recent season nearly 500 boys and girls applied for playground gardens and more than 1,400 cared for home gardens indicates the popularity of this activity in Cedar Rapids.

Cooperative Garden Projects.—Gardening is one phase of the municipal recreation program in which an unusual amount of cooperation has been received from local agencies. School cooperation is particularly important in arousing the interest of the children before the gardening season, in enrolling them for gardening groups, and in distributing seeds, bulbs, and other materials. Women's groups and garden clubs have been especially ready to help with such programs. An example of a cooperative project is the Woburn Garden operated by the Boston Park Commission. The school department furnishes instructors, seed, and equipment for 400 children who are transported to the garden by busses three days each week during the summer. The Women's Municipal League has helped make the project possible by supplying lunches for the children. All products harvested in the gardens are taken home by the children who grow them. The supervisor of the project has developed an elaborate program including games and nature walks which supplement the gardening activities.

Another cooperative gardening project is carried on in Hastings on Hudson, New York, where a Junior Gardeners' Council appointed from members of the local garden club and the garden section of the woman's club sponsors the project with the cooperation of the schools. Interested citizens serve as inspectors of the children's gardens during the summer, visiting each garden at least twice a month, keeping records, and giving suggestions and advice to the young gardeners. Through the Recreation Division arrangements are made for the county nature specialist to meet with the club members several times during the summer. Hikes to near-by woods for wild flower study are conducted, and in the fall the garden club members make a number of all-day trips in the school bus to nature trails and other points of interest in the vicinity. The experience in this community shows the value of conducting a junior garden club as a community project for which the schools, garden clubs, and recreation authorities share the responsibility.

Garden Centers.—Advice and information on various horticultural problems are furnished to home gardeners by a number of park and recreation departments. In Buffalo, New York, a garden center institute has been set up in the clubhouse of a city park for the purpose of encouraging the art of gardening and related subjects. Among its various services, this institute helps garden clubs in the district plan programs and correlate their activities. It furnishes home gardeners the knowlege needed for everyday gardening activity. A majority of the questions answered by the institute staff come from persons having only a small garden plot and who need advice in improving poor soil, in utilizing the space to the best advantage, in securing a successful lawn, or in eliminating garden pests. Particularly helpful to beginning gardeners are a landscape consultation service and a garden maintenance service bureau conducted by persons interested in the work of the center. Classes in gardening supply the amateur with information needed for everyday dirt gardening. Instruction is not limited to lectures alone but includes actual practice and experience in gardening and in the observation of a test garden. The institute has gradually developed an excellent library of books, magazines, and pamphlets available for the guidance of the gardener. Other features of the program have been a series of horticultural lectures by outstanding authorities in the field and a junior gardening club.

Park Department Services.—Park departments reach a greater number of people through their floral and horticultural exhibits than through any other service in the field of gardening. In addition to their floral displays and plant collections, park authorities conduct educational activities including gardening lectures at the conservatories and field houses to organizations, groups, and classes from public and private schools, radio lectures, assistance in judging flower and garden contests, the dissemination of horticultural information, and the promotion of garden club and neighborhood improvement programs. Guides are provided in the conservatories to conduct groups of grammar-school and high-school children, garden clubs, and other organizations through the exhibits. The floral displays at two park conservatories attracted more than 1,000,000 visitors in 1937, and in the same city nearly 600,000 people passed through the flower, rose, and perennial gardens throughout the season on Sunday afternoons alone. The chrysanthemum show, Christmas flower show, Easter and spring shows attract more and more visitors each year.

A recent development which promises to yield valuable results both in the landscape development of parks and in neighborhood interest is the tendency of park designers to consult garden clubs and other interested neighborhood groups with reference to the planning of park landscape features, particularly the gardens. The development of indoor gardens, both in homes and in recreation centers, offers possibilities which have only begun to be realized, and the soilless growth of plants gives promise of becoming a popular hobby.

OUTING ACTIVITIES

Some people go to the country to study nature; others seek the woods and open spaces primarily for exercise, relaxation, or to get away from the city environment. The recreation department serves the interest of such people by organizing hiking and outing clubs and providing areas, facilities, and equipment for picnicking, camping, and other related activities. Equally important, however, are the informal enjoyment and use of the larger parks and reservations by individuals and small groups. By offering opportunity for strolling along park paths or trails, lying on the grass or under the trees, or enjoying the beauty of the landscape while sitting on a park bench, park and recreation departments furnish delightful leisure-time activities for hundreds of thousands of individuals who do not engage in the organized forms of outing activity. As a matter of fact, the number of individuals who make such informal use of parks generally exceeds the number participating in organized activities.

Hiking Clubs.—Chapter XVI contained a brief description of the Minnehikers, a group which for many years has furnished hiking and outing opportunities for large numbers of Minneapolis citizens. Walking is one of the first activities of childhood and is enjoyed until old age. Most clubs find that it helps to have a regular membership with nominal dues, a schedule extending throughout the year, and a definite plan for leadership, often furnished by members of the organization.   Week-end hikes—usually to an outlying park, beach, reservation, or museum—are most popular.   Outdoor cooking is enjoyed by most hikers so the hike often includes a "cook-out" and it frequently ends at a park shelter or farmhouse where dancing or games are enjoyed by the group.

Youth hostels which have been established with the cooperation of recreation authorities are used by hiking groups which they sponsor. Many state parks also afford facilities for overnight and week-end outings by local hiking clubs.   In one state park an old barn was remodeled and now serves as the week-end objective for hikes and bicycle trips arranged by the recreation department in a near-by city.

Horseback Riding.—Automobiles have largely replaced horses for commercial uses, but horseback riding as a sport is gaining in popularity. The Union County, New Jersey, Park Commission is outstanding among recreation authorities in its provision of riding trails, conduct of horse shows, and organization of groups for equestrian sport.   It maintains a large stable located in its 2,000-acre reservation and 25 miles of carefully prepared bridle trails.   Horses may be boarded at the stable and there are horses available for rental by the hour.   Competent riding instructors are provided and class instruction is furnished for school children.   Special programs such as moonlight rides and paper chases are held from time to time.   A riding and driving club promotes an annual horse show in the riding ring which has an attractive setting.   The facilities and program conducted by the commission have stimulated the development of riding stables and clubs in near-by communities.

Another successful group is the Wyoming Valley Equestrian Club, sponsored by the Playground and Recreation Association.   Its representative membership includes people with widely diversified interests— schoolteachers, college students, business and professional men and women.   When first organized in 1933 only weekly horseback rides were undertaken, but with the development of interest and ability varied features have been initiated.   Overnight rides have become an annual feature.   Breakfast and moonlight rides wind up at the clubhouse. Several "drag" and "paper" hunts have been held and polo has become one of the club's activities.   Although the club is an adult organization it makes its facilites available to children at certain times during the week, and several of the members have given instruction to members of local high-school riding clubs.

Bicycling.—Recreation dpeartments have been alert in responding to the revival of public interest in bicycle riding.   Suitable park areas have been set aside and paths built for cyclists, bicycle clubs have been formed, and outings have been arranged for lovers of the sport.   In one city where a large area was set aside for bicycling, a quantity of bicycles was acquired by the recreation commission and these are loaned to children who do not own one.

In the case of most bicycle clubs for boys and girls organized among playground children, officers are elected and regular trips are scheduled. Special costumes for club members were made in the playground sewing classes in one city. To promote safety, members of bicycle clubs are sometimes required to sign a safety pledge, weekly bicycle inspections are held to make sure that lights, brakes, tires, pedals, and other parts are in good condition, and lectures and moving pictures on highway safety travel are presented. In selecting routes for the weekly outings care is taken to avoid roads with heavy traffic. In one city an automobile equipped with a large sign, "Motorists please drive with care; bicycle club ahead," accompanies the club on all field trips. The car carries a complete first-aid kit, repair kit, and other tools, and is available for the transportation of any club member whose bicycle breaks down on the journey.

Like other outing groups, bicycle clubs vary their program by introducing special features such as breakfast rides, "splash" rides, picnic rides, and overnight camping trips. On one trip in a series sponsored by a recreation department boys, girls, and adults with their bicycles and lunches boarded a train which carried them into the country, and the remainder of the day was spent in riding back to the city. As a safety precaution, roads used by the group were patrolled by the state police during the rides.

Day Outings.—The recent widespread development of the day camp has furnished day outing for a great number of children, especially in the larger cities. Groups of children are transported by subway or bus lines to wooded sections of large parks or to reservations or waterfront areas where they enjoy the experiences of nature which city life denies them. Through the day camp program children are taught to know and love the out-of-doors; they become conservationists and develop interests which will afford satisfying use of their leisure hours in later life.

An Explorer's Club, planned to supply the children's craving for adventure and at the same time to expose the children to nature interests, was a most successful part of one city's day camp program. The hikes were real explorations and resulted in collections of rocks, shells, bugs, salamanders, and all kinds of plant life. Games were played, with competition in observance of nature sounds, forestry, birds, fish, insects, and rocks; time was read by the sun; weather signs were noted; and treasure hunts created a new interest in geography, history, and nature lore. Trail making, compass hikes, and measuring distances all had a place on the club program.

Camping.—In an earlier chapter reference was made to the various types of camps conducted by recreation departments throughout the country. Naturally the camp programs vary greatly between the intown day camp, the overnight or week-end camp, and the vacation camp where groups of children or adults spend a week or more. Nature and outing interests play an important part in all of these camp programs, but particularly in the camps where naturalists are employed. More and more the camps are being used throughout the entire year, especially in sections of the country where winter sports may be enjoyed.

Fishing.—Few outdoor activities engage the enthusiastic interest of a greater number of children and adults than fishing. Recreation authorities are only beginning to recognize the extent of this interest and to render a special service to anglers. A unique example of such service is a series of bulletins issued by at least two recreation departments listing the streams in the vicinity which have been stocked with various kinds of fish, and including directions for reaching these streams. The bulletins also tell where other kinds of fish may be found, list names of the game wardens, and suggest that fishermen would do well to get acquainted with these officials.

Suitable water areas have been stocked for the benefit of local fishermen in several cities, sometimes with the cooperation of state conservation departments. Fish hatcheries have been established to supply fish for municipally owned and controlled waters and to supplement the supply obtained from the state hatcheries. A fisherman's paradise was developed at one park lake by planting water lilies and native moss for fish cover and feed, and constructing a fishing pier 800 feet long for the convenience of the anglers. In some instances only children are permitted to try their luck in the well-stocked park lakes.

Anglers' clubs are among the groups organized by the recreation department or using its facilities. Fly-casting tournaments with events calling for distance and accuracy are conducted annually in a number of cities, in some instances at special casting pools. For eleven years an ardent angler has voluntarily conducted a class in fly casting in a municipal gymnasium for groups of boys and girls ranging in age from six to sixteen. Recently three youthful members of this class were taken to the national sportsman's show, and the boys outcast the national champion in both plain and trick casting. A Tackle Buster's Club whose membership consists of young fishing enthusiasts meets weekly under an adviser in a Western city. Members go on a fishing trip each Friday and meetings are often addressed by state or county conservation officials or by deep-sea fishermen who relate their experiences. This club receives much help from the adult Fly and Bait Casting Club which is also sponsored by the local recreation department. Fly-tying groups, like the casting clubs, are recruited largely from fishing enthusiasts.

It is seldom possible for local recreation agencies to serve the interests of hunters in a comparable manner, but in a number of cities indoor or outdoor rifle ranges have been erected and rifle tournaments are conducted. In a few instances trapshooting ranges have been installed for the benefit of hunters preparing for the open season.

Picnics.—The picnic bureau, a division of the recreation department in many cities, offers a medium for building good will for the department by serving many community groups. In some instances it offers local organizations a complete picnic service, including the furnishing of equipment and leadership. It helps in selecting picnic sites, gives advice in organizing a program of games and entertainment, lends game equipment, and reserves sports facilities adjoining the picnic grounds. Sometimes the bureau assigns a worker to conduct the entire picnic program upon payment of a nominal fee to cover the cost of this service. Usually a deposit fee is required for equipment, but most picnic services are given without cost.

Picnic kits consisting of such articles as tug-of-war rope, sacks for races, Indian clubs, horseshoe pegs and horseshoes, soccer ball, volley ball and net, and first-aid kit are furnished by many departments on a loan or rental basis. In some cases a special kit of equipment is assembled on request to meet the needs of the particular group which is to use it. In one city where a picnic supervisor is employed throughout the summer the picnic bureau in 1937 assisted more than 225 churches, business firms, lodges, clubs, and other groups in preparing for and conducting picnic programs.

CHAPTER XXV

OTHER PROGRAM FEATURES

Several of the most important aspects of the recreation department program have been described in the five preceding chapters, but there are other program features that merit consideration. Some of these, such as forums or discussion groups, are less generally or extensively conducted by recreation authorities than the ones previously mentioned. Holiday celebrations or hobby groups represent a combination of activities or include a cross section of several major groupings. Social recreation and dancing are often introduced to supplement the activities of groups whose primary interest is in some other form of recreation. A separate division is rarely set up in the recreation department to administer these activities, as is done in the case of the other program features, although specialists are sometimes employed to conduct them.

SOCIAL RECREATION

One of the objectives of the recreation department is to encourage happier relationships among individuals by enabling them to take part in recreation activities with their friends or others who have similar interests. The importance of sociability and fellowship is continually emphasized throughout the entire recreation program. There are several kinds of activity, however, such as dinners, dances, parties, and play nights, in which the element of sociability is uppermost. They are sometimes conducted as distinct program features. But they often supplement the routine activities carried on by groups formed to take part in music, nature, drama, or crafts. In fact, there are few groups which do not include in their schedule occasional functions intended to develop a better acquaintance and feeling of fellowship between the individual members.

The recreation department often renders its greatest service in the field of social recreation to individuals and agencies not directly related to its program. It assists local organizations with their parties, picnics, and socials by furnishing suggestions, equipment, or leadership and by issuing and distributing party bulletins. One department has described its service of this type during a 12-month period as follows:

Programs were planned and directed for nineteen organizations; picnic or game kits loaned to seventy-five groups, principally churches, lodges, industries, and social clubs. Suggestions for holiday socials were published in the newspapers and distributed through our office. A Social Recreation Leader's Course, enrolling fifty-two members, presented techniques and material which could be carried back for use in their own group.

Holidays are occasions when social features receive special emphasis, particularly by groups meeting in recreation buildings and indoor centers. Valentine's Day, Halloween, Thanksgiving, Christmas, and other holidays are celebrated by parties at which games, dramatic stunts, dancing, refreshments, and music are the chief attractions. The programs of boys' and girls' clubs include special parties and dances which are arranged from time to time, and in many cities father and son or mother and daughter dinners are high lights of the programs of such groups. An "army bean feed," a sports night featuring outstanding athletic stars, or a talk by a noted traveler, are typical events making for good fellowship in a boys' or men's club.

Table Games.—The quiet game room where individuals may spend a social hour or an evening playing cards, chess, or checkers with their friends, is one of the most popular and most informal rooms in the recreation center. Interest in these games is so keen that classes are organized for both beginners and advanced players and checker and chess clubs have been formed which meet regularly for tournaments and informal play. A municipal chess association has been organized in one city where enthusiasm runs high. Players are classified according to their ability, and a schedule of intercenter matches is carried on throughout the season. A room has been set aside as headquarters for the organization in one of the park centers where on an average of 150 players meet every Monday evening during the league season. The association takes great pride in its home which the members have redecorated and furnished with chess tables, furniture, and chess pictures for the walls. The chess association is primarily for adults but the game has caught the interest of the older boys in the evening centers, and is also being taught to children of elementary-school age in several of the afternoon centers and on the playgrounds.

Friendly Clubs.—To meet the needs of strangers, lonely people, and others who have not had an opportunity to make friends, "Friendly" or "Meet a Body" clubs have been organized by several recreation departments. An invitation is usually issued through the local press, announcing the organization of the group and inviting to its membership any adult who wishes to spend an evening a week singing, playing games, visiting, or taking part in discussions or other activities. In one small city where a club of this type has been particularly successful the attendance averages 125 each week and the total membership exceeds 200. The club programs offer a splendid opportunity for the members of the group not only to become acquainted and to participate in recreation activities but also to express talents which otherwise might remain hidden. In some cases the members have gradually been induced to join regular groups sponsored by the department, with the result that the club for strangers has been abandoned as a distinct activity.

Training Courses.—Leadership training courses are one of the most effective means used by recreation departments for encouraging social recreation programs. Probably more cities offer training courses for social recreation leaders than for any other volunteer group. Leaders receive instruction in game selection and leadership, party planning methods, game supplies, and related subjects. Occasionally at the conclusion of a training course the group forms a social recreation club for the purpose of continuing its training in leadership methods and materials and of assisting the department in meeting calls from local organizations for help in planning and conducting parties and other social functions. Institutes have sometimes resulted in the formation of party-a-month clubs which meet monthly to enjoy a social evening, to exchange ideas, and to learn new activities.

Party Kits.—Many departments have found it helpful to prepare game or party kits which, like the picnic kits, are lent to local organizations. These kits usually contain game equipment, supplies, and materials which can be used in conducting an evening's program of social games. Indian clubs, two sets of alphabet cards, chalk, rubber balls, song sheets, hoops, wooden blocks, number cards, relay batons, tape measures, and blinders are a few of the items usually included in a party kit.

The popularity of progressive game parties has created a special demand for progressive game kits. One recreation department has built ten such kits which are in frequent use. Each one contains enough equipment for 18 games, and provides a full 3-hour period of entertainment if all the games are used simultaneously. The kit will keep 72 people busy if four people play each game; additional game materials are added if a larger group is to be served. A dart board, ringtoss board, muffin pan, checker-flipping board, set of pick-up sticks, box of anagrams, marble game, bean bag board, set of indoor horseshoes, pencils, score cards, and many others comprise the kit. The varying requirements of groups calling for assistance in planning their socials often make it desirable to assemble kits to meet the needs of a particular group rather than to use standard kits.

Social Activites for Mixed Groups.—The provision of co-recreational activities is a normal and growing tendency in recreation programs. In addition to the small mixed groups interested in specific activities, young men and women need opportunities for a wider acquaintance with persons of the opposite sex. Perhaps the best functions for this purpose are the game party and social dance, which enable strangers to get acquainted without a formal introduction and are frequently the only means of introducing mixed activities to a group which apparently has no other common recreation interest. They may be the means of inducing young men and women to form their own social groups or to join organizations already participating in the program. Games such as table tennis, darts, and checkers are widely played by mixed groups. In several of the Chicago parks co-recreational teams composed of older boys and girls have been organized for informal interpark play and have proved highly successful. Teams arrange matches involving several kinds of games, which are followed by a social hour during which the home team furnishes simple refreshments.

Dancing has an important place in the program of the sixteen young people's social clubs which have been organized at the centers operated by the Recreation Bureau in St. Paul. Evenings are set aside regularly for social games and dancing, and instruction is provided in ballroom dancing, old-time square dancing, ice breakers, and some of the popular dance forms. Occasional parties are arranged to which members of the social clubs in other centers are invited. Several clubs sometimes join in arranging picnics and steamboat excursions which are held during the summer. Tournaments in volley ball, Ping-pong, and other games are held at various centers, followed by intercenter competition. In addition to enjoying the companionship and fun which the activities afford, club members are cultivating skills and courtesy in their social relationships through the guidance of sympathetic and understanding leaders who assist the young people in planning and conducting their own program.

DANCING

"No art is more popular with youth than dancing," and the rhythm and beauty of the dance have a strong appeal for children and adults as well. The membership of dance groups sponsored by the recreation department includes a large number of individuals whose favorite form of recreation is dancing. The social dance is a major feature of the weekly program but in many recreation centers other forms of dancing also have an important place. Dancing contributes to other parts of the program such as pageants, parties, or neighborhood nights at a recreation center.

Community Dances in Lancaster.—In Lancaster, Pennsylvania, for many years a Saturday evening dance has been an outstandingly successful part of the winter program of the local recreation association. These dances are held at the Y.W.C.A. under the direction of a community dance board consisting of young people from sixteen to twenty-five years of age who represent the various youth organizations of the city.

The dances give the boys and girls what they desire—a rendezvous where they can spend their Saturday evenings in an agreeable manner; they encourage social dancing as a highly desirable form of recreation, and incidentally, they give peace of mind to the parents of young people. The democratic leadership furnished by the board of governors with the guidance of the recreation superintendent has been largely responsible for the success of this project. Each weekly dance is sponsored by the representatives of one of the cooperating organizations, this group being responsible for the decorations and program features in addition to serving as hosts and hostesses of the evening. At least two feature dances such as elimination dances, prize waltzes, spot dances, and other original numbers are introduced in each program. Behavior problems have been exceedingly few. An admission charge of 25 cents a person has provided sufficient income to meet the expense of renting the hall, engaging an orchestra, buying decorations, providing a fund for emergencies, and making possible an end-of-the-season complimentary dinner and theater party for the board members in recognition of their services.

Dancing Out of Doors.—Social dancing is by no means limited to indoor centers but has attained great popularity as an outdoor activity. Reference was made in Chap. XVI to the various methods which have proved successful in conducting outdoor dances. Cities have constructed outdoor platforms or pavilions where hundreds of people dance in the open air on summer evenings. If such facilities are not available, paved parking areas are utilized or streets temporarily closed to traffic serve as dance floors. Gaily colored lights suspended around the area used for dancing add a festive air to the street dances. If an orchestra is not available, a public address system is used either with a radio or with phonograph records. In one city where nine such dances were held during the summer season, the average attendance was 2,500.

Dance Classes.—Where the need of furnishing instruction in social dancing has become apparent, classes for boys and girls have been organized and evening groups have been formed for adults. Members are helped to develop poise and social graces as well as acquire dance skills. More than 500 high-school boys and girls in one city attended the Saturday afternoon classes which were conducted as social parties, with good music and with games interspersed throughout the periods in order to make the sessions as interesting and enjoyable as possible.

In Oak Park, Illinois, dancing is the most popular fall and winter playground activity. As many as 700 children have beeen enrolled in the classes in ballet, ballroom, tap, old-fashioned square dancing, acrobatic, character, and folk dancing. Preschool children are taught singing and dramatic games, in addition to folk dances, and simple tap work. In some groups children have frequently arranged their own dances, and the high-school festival, circus, stunt day, and other occasions have furnished opportunities for demonstrating their ability.   In addition to the classes, social dances, barn dances, and old-fashioned square dances are also popular features of the program for both children and adults.

Adult Dance Groups.—Many adult groups have been formed with the help of local recreation departments, primarily to engage in social dancing or in old-fashioned square country dances.   Four dance clubs comprising more than 150 couples, for the most part business and professional men and their wives, regularly use facilities furnished by the department in one small city.   The number of square dance groups is growing rapidly. Square dances have seldom competed successfully with social dancing for the interest of the young people although several cities report them to be very popular with their youth.   Contests for square dance sets and callers to determine champions of the city or district often attract people living in near-by small communities where the square dances have continued to maintain their popularity.

Folk Dancing.—The varied and colorful folk dances, many of them introduced in this country from different nations of Europe, have a strong appeal and a conspicuous place in playground and center programs. "A thing of beauty and joy, with inviting warmth of melody and rhythm," folk dancing is one of the activities commonly carried on throughout the playground season and has an important part in the pageant or festival. It contains the "very essence of social group play," and in neighborhoods with a large foreign-born population who delight to take part in their familiar native dances, it has a conspicuous place in indoor center programs.   Twenty-five folk dance groups, authentically costumed, have been organized in one large Midwestern city where the park authorities, in sponsoring folk dance festivals, use every means to encourage a reviving interest in folk dancing among the different nationalities.

An International Dance Group sponsored by a local recreation commission brings together people of many nationalities interested in folk dancing.   Members attend the monthly meetings dressed in national costumes—a custom which helps greatly in creating an atmosphere favorable to dancing.   Usually a nationality group demonstrates a difficult dance of its own and then the entire gathering learns one or two simpler dances taught by a member of the demonstrating group, after which there is a review of old favorites.   Once a year a festival is held with many groups dancing in native costume.

Folk dancing, long popular in Reading, Pennsylvania, received unusual attention in the 1937 summer program which was built around the theme, "Pennsylvania Folklore."   Dances of the early pioneers were revived and playground leaders were trained intensively in square dances, quadrilles, and the Virginia reel.   Each Tuesday evening throughout the summer was "square dance night" in City Park, and approximately one thousand children from all parts of the city attended weekly. After the playground children had danced for an hour to the music of a professional orchestra, the adults folk-danced for an hour. The old-fashioned dances attracted the middle-aged citizens and they "had the time of their lives." The carry-over value of these events was demonstrated by the number of parents who were seen square-dancing on their neighborhood playgrounds to the tunes of a jug orchestra or an informal music group.

HOBBIES

Hobbies have been described as of three fundamental types, the acquiring of knowledge, the acquiring of things, and the creation of things. The term is commonly applied to a wide range of activities, but there are those who hold the opinion that "a true hobby is a personal, intimate matter, capable of enjoyment by one's self, to be shared only with a few kindred souls." Because of the significance of hobbies in the leisure time of large numbers of individuals, the recreation department is concerned with helping people acquire hobbies and find opportunities of enjoying them with others who have similar interests. Hobbies have a definite place in the program at most playgrounds, and the long season and special facilities of the indoor center are conducive to the formation of hobby groups.

Photography.—Photography is an example of a hobby that appeals to old and young alike. Camera clubs are sponsored by recreation departments as a means of enabling enthusiasts to acquire greater skill in the activity, exchange experiences, and enjoy the association with other camera hobbyists. A small juvenile camera club started in a park field house in one city met with such success that by the end of 1938, 21 similar clubs had been established in several other centers. These groups, which include adult as well as youthful photographers, hold weekly meetings. One meeting each month is called "studio night" and is devoted to demonstration and experimentation on lighting and composition, and some picture taking. Other meetings are devoted to business, talks, demonstrations, and lectures by outside speakers. Group instruction is given in such subjects as developing, printing, enlarging, and toning, and the work of club members is submitted and criticized at their meetings. A "picture of the month" contest is carried on among the camera clubs to choose the picture for the frontispiece of the department's monthly report. The park authorities provide merely a sink, water, and electric connections, all other equipment being furnished by the clubs.

Some camera clubs have been organized as an outgrowth of amateur photography contests sponsored by the recreation authorities. A

County Camera Club started in this way proved so successful that at least half a dozen other clubs were organized in the county during the following year. One recreation department which sponsors a number of camera clubs arranged a photographic holiday in the form of a week-end outing for club members at one of the city's mountain camps. Members of the camera club in another city, in addition to the usual activities of such a group, manage the motion-picture shows that are held regularly at the center. They often combine with the Mountaineers' Club at the same center in its week-end and annual pack trips, and have produced some exceptionally fine photographs and motion pictures of these outings. Exhibits are an annual event on most camera club programs.

Stamp Collecting.—Stamp collecting is another hobby which in spite of its popularity has been often overlooked in the recreation program. The cultivation of this hobby is highly desirable since it embraces history, art, geography, civics, printing, design, and social relationships. Interest in stamps may readily be fostered through club organization, and such clubs have met with an enthusiastic response. In one city where the activity was introduced with the help of emergency leaders in 1936, more than 3,000 children were enrolled in stamp clubs in a period of less than 60 days, and at the end of the year more than 120 clubs were meeting regularly. Groups of boys in ten different community centers in another city were organized into clubs with the help of an outstanding local stamp authority. During the part of the meetings devoted to educational activities, the leader tells stories about the stamps of the various countries, illustrating them with displays, and describes the historical significance of stamps, their design, color, and perforations. The later and exciting part of the meetings is devoted to trading. Club programs in a third city are made interesting by a series of "trips around the world" with stamps, during which competitions are held among the members in supplying information concerning stamps issued by the countries "visited." An annual exhibit is an important part of many club programs. During the First International Recreation Congress at Los Angeles in 1932 the local stamp club not only maintained an exhibit but made available to the delegates a special cover commemorating the Congress.

A Hobby League.—In Philadelphia, the Playground and Recreation Association was instrumental in forming a hobby league, the purposes of which are

1. To encourage the practice of hobbies in general, and to assist in securing leadership and a place of meeting for those who wish to work or join with others of similar interests in clubs or classes, rather for recreative than scholastic instruction.

2. To serve as a clearinghouse and bureau of information for those who wish only information. This includes the provision of lists of schools, groups and

organizations that would more fully meet their needs than the Hobby League, and the arrangement of personal contacts where that is permissible or desirable.

3. To organize and promote a yearly Hobby Show for the exhibition of hobbies by those of noncommercial interests and the presentation of cultural programs of the strictly hobby type.

At the beginning it was intended that the league should serve primarily as a clearinghouse for information and should refer inquirers to groups and agencies throughout the city conducting activities in which the individuals were interested. It soon became apparent, however, that more facilities were needed and that large numbers could not be accommodated in existing groups. Consequently, a number of clubs were organized, and soon the league sought larger quarters in one of the city's school buildings. Two years after its organization, 30 groups, each representing a different hobby, with a registration of more than 1,500 active members, were affiliated with the league and held regular meetings at the hobby center. The league's activities include an annual hobby show and the publication of a monthly magazine, *The Hobbyist*. The association is assisted in carrying on the work of the league by a council composed of one representative from each of the participating groups.

Hobby Shows.—Hobbies are also promoted by means of shows in which individuals and organizations throughout the city exhibit the articles they have made or collected. Demonstrations by members of the hobby groups usually attract great attention and interest. The second show of the Philadelphia Hobby League included demonstrations by members of the fencing, chorus, public speaking, orchestra, writers, and tap, ballroom, and rhythmic dance groups. They were also presented in the studios of the photographic, art, handicraft, short-wave radio, and marionette groups. Such demonstrations, which enable visitors to observe the hobbyists in action, arouse even greater interest than exhibits of the work accomplished by the various clubs.

STUDY GROUPS AND FORUMS

Current public interest in national and world problems has stimulated the formation of discussion groups, forums, and similar "informal education" activities at many indoor recreation centers. Forensic and study groups afford outlets for self-expression and personal development to large numbers of people and are a means for generating active interest in civic affairs. Typical of such groups is the Thursday Night Club which meets in the library of a community house in a New England college town. Intended to stimulate interest in current events of local, state, national, and international importance, the club has been called a "place where everything is argued, debated, and discussed, but where nothing is settled."

The Milwaukee indoor center program, outlined in Chap. XVIII, includes among its many varied offerings forums—some of which are arranged especially for youth—civic associations, lectures, debating clubs, parliamentary law and public speaking classes, citizenship training courses for the foreign-born, and play-reading groups. Throughout the country, however, such activities are not commonly provided as distinct units of the recreation program. Meetings to discuss problems affecting the welfare of the neighborhood or city are arranged from time to time but, in general, study and discussion are related to some specific form of recreation activity. For example, stamp clubs explore a wide variety of fields and arts and crafts groups make intensive studies of such widely different subjects as the history and development of forms, color, craft materials and their sources of production, the life of primitive peoples, and local arts and crafts resources. Music activities become more meaningful if the groups study the composers of the music used, or trace the development of musical instruments or of music as a form of expression. Groups interested in a game or sport such as tennis or baseball welcome an opportunity to hear a lecture by an expert, see a technical sports film, or join a discussion of proposed changes in the rules governing play. In fact, study and discussion play an important, though secondary, role in the activities of most groups sponsored by the recreation department.

Interest in travel has been used in some cities as a basis for meetings arranged throughout the winter season. Local citizens who have visited foreign countries or taken unusually interesting trips share their experiences with their fellow citizens. Such talks, usually illustrated with lantern slides or moving pictures, not only inform people about life in distant places but furnish the listeners an incentive for travel. The entertainment and educational value of motion pictures produced by the travel agencies or showing scenes in the national parks and forests gives them a place in many indoor center programs.

HOLIDAY CELEBRATIONS

There is perhaps no project in which so many different forms of recreation are introduced or in which so large a number of community groups participate as the celebrations organized in connection with some of the more important holidays. Reference was made on page 244 to the ways in which Halloween enthusiasm is directed into festive but wholesome channels. Independence Day is the occasion for parades, patriotic festivals, athletic events, and fireworks, often provided by the recreation authorities. Valentine Day and St. Patrick's Day are celebrated by parties and other appropriate social activities in the indoor centers.

Christmas.—Many recreation departments have a leading part in making Christmas the foremost holiday season. Centers for repairing and distributing toys to needy children are conducted with the help of children or volunteer leaders. Scrapbooks and gifts for shut-ins and inmates of charitable institutions are made by recreation center groups. Craft classes are organized in which individuals make their Christmas gifts. City-wide campaigns are organized for the decoration of homes, playgrounds, streets, and public buildings, with the decorations sometimes made in the handicraft groups. Christmas caroling is arranged in the various centers or on a city-wide basis, with caroling groups singing on the streets, and in hotels, radio stations, hospitals, and other institutions. Many cities erect a tree of light in their parks or decorate growing trees at which carol and other services are held. Christmas parties are arranged for playground or center groups, sometimes for underprivileged children who receive toys made or repaired in the department's toy centers. Drama is represented in the Christmas activities through the production of plays, tableaux, and operettas appropriate to the season, or of elaborate Christmas pageants. There is perhaps no other type of project sponsored by the municipal recreation department in which the cooperation of so many individuals and organizations is enlisted as the city-wide community Christmas celebration.

Christmas in Hartford.—Among the outstanding public observances of Christmas in 1938 was the open-air reproduction in Hartford, Connecticut, of the Nativity of Christ. Set in the hillside of a park located near the center of the city, it consisted of 22 life-size figures grouped around a replica of the Bethlehem stable. The scene, designed by artists assigned from the Federal Art Project and effectively lighted by hidden colored spotlights, was nearly 100 feet long and 20 feet high.

Inside the stable which was the focal point of the spectacle sat the Virgin Mary with the Christ Child on her lap, Joseph standing slightly in the rear, and at her side was the little wooden manger with her white cape draped across it. Kneeling in adoration before her was the figure of a shepherd boy, while opposite, a sedate donkey, gazing stolidly at the scene, stood near an ox whose head and shoulders protruded from a stall.

Approaching from the right, past a row of evergreens and cedars, were three brightly caparisoned camels bearing on their backs the Wise Men of the East. Coming from the other direction were shepherds and a flock of sheep passing three open archways that revealed a panorama of the town of Bethlehem in the distance. In front of the stable other shepherds knelt, while high overhead a huge electric star shone on the setting.[1]

COMMUNITY FESTIVALS

Festivals in which a great number of community groups participate have become annual events of major significance in several cities. The

[1] John M. Hurley, "Hartford Celebrates Christmas," *Recreation*, February, 1939.

May Day Festival in Central Park, New York City, in which thousands of children trained at the city's playgrounds participate in May pole dances and other festivities, has become a traditional event. Across the country in Palo Alto, California, the May Day Festival conducted by the recreation department with the help of a festival committee is attended by practically the entire city. The program comprises a huge parade, the coronation of the May Queen, a spring pageant, hobby exhibits, variety show, social dancing, and many other features.

Miami, Florida, is one of the cities where the recreation department plays a leading part in organizing a municipal birthday anniversary celebration. Events in the 1937 program included a "Gay Nineties" costume party, a day-long gathering of Miami pioneers in one of the community houses, and an outdoor stage show depicting the high lights of the city's history. Each year the recreation department also utilizes its resources and personnel in arranging a Pan-American Day celebration consisting of a parade, review, or pageant in which music and dances typical of South American countries are introduced.

The Pennsylvania Folk Festival sponsored by the Allentown Recreation Commission is helping preserve the state's rich folklore, especially the unique contribution of the anthracite coal miners and the Pennsylvania Germans. Santa Claus parades, with enormous floats and figures representing storybook characters and other children's favorites, have been a feature of the program in Lincoln, Nebraska, for a number of years and have also been inaugurated on a large scale in other cities.

Often the recreation authorities assist local festival organizations in conducting community celebrations. One of the major events in the cotton carnival at Memphis is the Children's Court and Ball arranged and directed by the recreation department of the local Park Commission. The annual winter carnival in St. Paul, Minnesota, including an enormous parade, outdoor winter sports events, and indoor ice shows, makes use of the municipal winter sports facilities and receives effective cooperation from the local recreation authorities.

These community-wide events which afford festive occasions not only for the cities conducting them but also for neighboring communities, play a large part in the recreational life of the people. They furnish opportunities for groups participating in the recreation department program to take part and also focus the attention of the citizens upon the city's recreation facilities and activities. To an exceptional degree they help to foster community pride and a consciousness of local resources and furnish an outlet for artistic, creative, and civic service.

CHAPTER XXVI

SERVICE TO SPECIAL GROUPS

Homes, industries, churches, institutions, and many other community agencies offer channels through which the recreation department may serve the leisure-time interests of large numbers of people. In general, the facilities and activities of the department are available for everyone, regardless of occupation, age, race, income, or any other factor. People participate in the program as members of the community, not as employees in a certain factory or members of a particular church or nationality group. Nevertheless, many recreation authorities realize that one of their most important functions is to assist existing agencies and groups with their own recreation activities and programs. By furnishing leadership, facilities, and guidance to such groups the recreation department supplements its own program and greatly extends its influence and service.

HOME AND FAMILY RECREATION

Howard Braucher once said, "The first responsibility of recreation board, school board, church, with reference to play and recreation is to create a play spirit that carries back to the home to make and keep family life vital."[1] Recreation departments have been criticized because they tend to draw children, youth, and adults away from their homes and because their programs separate families rather than influencing them to play together. Many of their activities, however, emphasize the importance of home and family play, and recreation departments are doing much to encourage play in the home. Games learned on the playground are later played in the back yard; forms of social recreation enjoyed at the indoor centers are introduced at family and neighborhood gatherings. Mothers' clubs are taught games that can be played in the home. Craft skills and hobby interests resulting from the department's program occupy many of the leisure hours spent at home. Picnic facilities, camps, and beaches serve family groups, and increasingly recreation areas are being developed as centers for the entire family. Mother and daughter dinners induce better relations in the home, family nights at playground or center inspire the family to play together, and many of the special events and tournaments invite participation by married couples, fathers and sons, or other related groups.

[1] *Recreation*, March, 1931, p. 641.

Back-yard Playground Contests.—Among the more direct means by which recreation departments foster play in the home is the back-yard playground contest which has been promoted successfully in both large and small cities. One recreation department, working through the local parent-teacher groups, enlisted the interest of the Fathers' Councils in the project of making attractive home playgrounds out of waste areas in their back yards. The department prepared and distributed bulletins giving valuable hints and advice as to exactly how to proceed. Printed folders were also sent out containing working drawings and plans for the construction of simple apparatus. The improved back yards were rated on their suitability for use by all members of the family and on the design and construction of the play facilities. Consideration was given to workmanship, practical use, appearance, safety, cost, and originality. Entrants in the contest were classified according to the amount expended in constructing the playgrounds.

Judges representing the parent-teacher associations, municipal playgrounds, and city schools visited every back yard entered in the competition and selected the best one in each neighborhood. These local winners were then judged by a city-wide committee which made the final awards, the winners receiving certificates presented with due ceremony. The remarkable success of the first contest and the effect which it had upon the development of back-yard play throughout the city encouraged the parent-teacher federation and the recreation department to make the contest an annual spring event.

Home Play Bulletins.—Publications containing suggestions for home play activities and for the construction of back-yard playgrounds have been issued in conection with intensive home play campaigns and also as a part of the routine service offered to parents. Sometimes these publications are fairly comprehensive booklets, but more often they are merely bulletins relating to some form of play adapted to home or family use. The following is a list of the publications of interest to parents which may be obtained upon request from the Recreation Commission in Berkeley, California:

Games for Families to Play Together	Nature Games and Hikes
Home Workshops	Flowers of California
Back-yard Playgrounds	Christmas Games and Handicraft
Picnic Suggestions	Hallowe'en Games
Dramatics for the Home	Patriotic Week Games
Storytelling in the Home	Valentine's Day Games
Hikes in and around the East Bay	Thanksgiving Games
Places of Interest to Take Children	Cut-Outs and Handicraft Projects
Handicraft	Places of Interest to Children in East Bay
Games for Rainy Days	Scrap Craft

Home Play Campaigns.—A distinctive feature of one recreation department's plan for the city-wide promotion of home play activities was the enrollment of fathers and mothers in a "Parents' Home Play Group," the members of which agreed to endeavor to devote at least three hours each week to play activity with their children. The organization of special home play weeks has focused attention upon the importance of home play. During this week parents are encouraged to devote special time to play with their children; the press, pulpit, and radio proclaim the values of play in the home; store windows display equipment and materials; and demonstrations of home play activities are arranged. In cities conducting a special recreation week one of the days is sometimes designated as "home play day."

Training Courses.—Successful home play programs require a sympathetic attitude on the part of parents and an understanding of play leadership methods and activities. For this reason, courses in home recreation have been conducted in several cities for the benefit of parents. In one case the recreation department arranged a series of demonstrations presented largely as parties, which included material and suggestions for mixers with or without music, crafts, active, quiet, and table games, stunts, simple dramatics, storytelling, singing games, music, story play, hobbies, and magic suitable for use in the home. Hiking, back-yard play, home play equipment, sand modeling, and social recreation were also considered. Another course, arranged in cooperation with a local university and attended by 130 parents, was initiated primarily to arouse interest in the local back-yard playground contest.

An unusual training course in home play was conducted by the Playground and Recreation Association of Philadelphia. Its purpose was to teach boys and girls from eleven to thirteen years old to direct an indoor play program in the home not only for themselves but more particularly for their younger brothers and sisters. Boys and girls were taught simple rules for conducting activities and afterward were given opportunities to participate in them and to demonstrate their ability in conducting them. They were also taught to use inexpensive materials and games which can be carried on with limited space and equipment. Mothers were invited to one of the meetings in order that they might know the nature of the program and the purpose of the course. Portable kits of home play materials were prepared and members of the class were taught how to use the equipment. Following the course, an association representative made visits to neighborhood homes where demonstrations of play programs were presented.

Service to Shut-ins.—Many individuals because of physical handicaps or illness are unable to participate in the recreation program, but the special needs of this group are now being met through the organization of a service for shut-ins. In East Orange, New Jersey, one of the pioneers in this field, the work is carried on by the Board of Recreation Commissioners through a council formed by a group of women in 1928. Ten years later the council with representatives from 23 different organizations provided a program for an average of 135 shut-ins. Fresh flowers from local gardens are delivered twice each month during the outdoor growing season and once a month during the winter to each of the individuals. Magazines, novels, picture puzzles, and games are also provided. Persons traveling are asked to send letters or postcards to certain shut-ins. A monthly letter is sent out from the recreation office, sweaters and bed jackets are distributed to needy individuals, the shut-ins receive free handicraft instruction, and exhibits and sales of handmade articles are arranged.

The Kenosha, Wisconsin, recreation department has also developed a successful "home bound" program. Leaders visit shut-ins who are placed on a weekly calling list, giving them instruction in handicraft, helping them in retarded studies, and furnishing library, book, or magazine service. Older members of the group are assisted in making articles which are sold through a central handicraft exhibition for disabled craftsmen. Friends of the movement provide automobiles to take the shut-ins to monthly socials, and the department publishes and distributes a bulletin, *An Open Window*, which is greatly enjoyed by the members of the group.

In other cities the program for shut-ins consists primarily of visits to homes where leaders tell stories, play games with the children, read to them, help them in making scrapbooks, and teach them simple games and crafts. In times of epidemics when schools or playgrounds are closed and all children are confined to their homes, recreation departments have proved a boon to parents by distributing bulletins suggesting suitable home play activities for those who are confined but are not actually ill. Closely related to the service to shut-ins is that furnished to physically handicapped groups. Typical of such service are glee clubs, swimming, and dancing classes for the blind, and special activities arranged for the hard of hearing.

Toy Loan Centers.—Play opportunities are limited in many homes because of the lack of toys and other play materials. Realizing that there are children who have no toys, recreation departments have established toy loan centers which have proved a delight to children in the surrounding neighborhoods. Appeals through the press and local organizations have brought in toys and games of all kinds. These are repaired, disinfected, and circulated through the centers in much the same way as library books. Toys are usually lent for a period of one week. In several cities toy centers are operated as a cooperative project by a number of community agencies.

Other Services.—The radio is being used more and more as a means of bringing to parents suggestions for home games, rainy-day activities, music, and dramatics. Through plant exchange days, home beautification campaigns, and lectures before neighborhood groups and garden clubs, many departments are fostering home gardens and the improvement of home grounds. By promoting attractive co-recreational activities, they are encouraging young men and women to play together and to develop common leisure-time interests which are considered so important in a happy, successful married life.

INDUSTRIES

At a recent anniversary celebration of one of America's leading retail and wholesale houses rules drawn up by the company for its first employees eighty years before were read. Among these rules were the following which relate to the "abundant life" and "the wise use of leisure":[1]

The employee who is in the habit of smoking Spanish cigars, being shaved at the barber's, going to dances and other places of amusement, will surely give his employer reason to be suspicious of his integrity and honesty.

Men employees are given one evening a week for courting and two if they go to prayer meeting.

After 14 hours of work in the store, the leisure hours should be spent mostly in reading.

Such rules sound strange indeed today, yet employers are still concerned with the way their workers spend their leisure time.

Many employers, realizing that leisure-time activities create a spirit of mutual understanding, confidence, and joy, have established recreation facilities and are promoting suitable programs for their employees. Frequently they have turned to the local recreation department for help in establishing and conducting such services. Today, however, most employers believe that it is better for their workers to spend their leisure hours away from their places of employment and to participate in recreation activities as members of the community rather than as employees of a particular company. They are therefore supporting municipal recreation programs which serve their employees rather than furnishing activities directly to their workers. Since in most cities industrial and commercial workers with their families comprise a large percentage of the total population, participants in the municipal recreation program are drawn largely from these groups.

The most common form of special service furnished by recreation departments to industrial groups is the operation of leagues in baseball,

[1] *Journal of Adult Education*, January, 1935.

softball, basketball, and other sports. These leagues, formed of teams representing factories, banks, stores, and other business concerns, comprise a large part of the municipal sports program in many cities. In Minneapolis, for example, approximately 60 per cent of the team participation in organized city-wide activities for men and women is made up from industrial and commercial concerns. Factory groups are also assisted in initiating noon hour activities and in planning picnics, parties, and special events. City-wide industrial athletic organizations have been formed to facilitate competitive play and to provide recreation among employees.

Activities in Chicago.—Chicago's experience in softball demonstrates the value of assistance given by municipal recreation authorities in promoting a sports program among employees. Before 1935 there were only six softball diamonds in and about Grant Park, located near the central business district, and they were not overtaxed. To establish a closer relation between the park department and companies employing large numbers of workers, two supervisors were assigned that year to give special attention to developing contacts with men and women in industry. Through the personnel departments of downtown establishments teams were organized into leagues, and the demand for accommodations immediately took on new volume. During the first part of the summer more than 20 diamonds were in such heavy demand as to necessitate close scheduling, and were still inadequate. By 1937, 41 diamonds were in use in the park, and nearly 9,000 individuals took part in the games sponsored by the Grant Park Softball Association which was organized to serve the growing interest in the sport among the men employed in the district.

Other projects undertaken for employed women were an indoor bowling league, week-end hikes, instruction in tennis, basketball, and folk dancing, field days, picnics, golf, and other activities. The Grant Park Softball Association expanded its interest to include bowling, tennis, volley ball, horseshoes, chess, checkers, and pinochle. The industries themselves have been assisted in managing their own activities and also in relating them to the entire community program. Much of the increased attendance in the local parks is attributed by the authorities to these contacts in places of employment where the employees were urged to take advantage of their home and neighborhood park activities.

An Industrial Division.—Comprehensive programs involving direct service to industrial groups have been developed in several Pacific Coast cities where special industrial divisions have been established as a part of recreation department program.[1] The objectives of such a division,

---

[1] The program in Oakland, California, a pioneer in the industrial recreation field, is described in Chap. XXVII.

according to the constitution of the organization in San Francisco, are as follows:

1. To foster and promote athletic activities for employees of industrial firms in the City and County of San Francisco
2. To encourage employees to participate in recreational activities
3. To promote recreation within the firms
4. To promote athletic meets and tournaments between member firms in all seasonal activities
5. To further the social activities of those firms

All industrial firms operating within the city and county are eligible for membership and individuals employed by these member firms are entitled to participate in the activities. In 1938, 7 years after the division was established, 86 firms were members.

The activities are managed by the department's supervisor of athletics and supervisor of girls and women's activities with the assistance of another worker. Plans and policies of the division are established by a board of representatives, board of directors, and executive committee. Participation in the division's program is limited to athletes who do not receive remuneration directly or indirectly for participating in the games held under its auspices. School gymnasiums and recreation buildings are made available for evening use by employees. Special events on the sports calendar for the year 1937–1938 included softball, basketball, volley ball, tennis, golf, swimming, table tennis, and putting tourney for men and women; also horseshoes, baseball, and bowling for men.

The highly developed program for industrial workers in Los Angeles includes morning activities for employees whose irregular working hours do not enable them to take part in the afternoon and evening groups. Noon hour activities include gymnastics, games, folk dancing, and dramatics. Industrial firms are given assistance in organizing and conducting interdepartmental leagues and tournaments, in establishing a recreation association for their own employees, or in planning any feature of their recreation program. Often, however, employees find it more convenient to take part in activities at the neighborhood centers where programs are provided for employees from several firms.

The program promoted by the Division of Industrial Recreation includes basketball, classes in clogging, dancing (folk, natural, and social), gymnasium classes, horseback riding, hiking, sketching, camping (weekend, winter, and summer), ice skating, tennis, archery, and social recreation. It especially emphasizes playdays for girls in which the idea of playing with each other rather than against each other predominates. In fact, the program for employed girls is comparatively free from highly competitive activities. In other cities competition plays an important part, as in Minneapolis where 48 girls' softball teams all attired in athletic uniforms play simultaneously on a large field which has been set aside for their exclusive use one evening a week.

Special Groups.—Workers whose hours or conditions of employment do not enable them to take part in the regular recreation program have not been forgotten by recreation departments. Newsboy clubs and caddie clubs have been organized and activities have been provided for bakers, milkmen, hotel employees, and policemen. An earlier chapter mentions the midnight baseball league organized in one city for theater workers who were employed during the late afternoon and evening. Gymnasium classes and other activities have been organized for nurses whose schedules often make it difficult for them to join in the normal schedule of activities. Recreation departments strengthen their relations with the employees of other city departments by organizing outings, parties, and other special events for workers in the local city government.

CHURCHES

Institutes to which churches send representatives for training in social recreation leadership are perhaps the most common form of special service rendered to churches by recreation departments. At the first play institute held in one city, 85 per cent of the group were delegates sent by the churches. In another city the interest in social recreation on the part of the local church groups resulted in an annual training institute for leaders in young people's group activities. In a third city a gathering was arranged in cooperation with church educational leaders for the purpose of demonstrating methods of leading community singing, conducting folk dancing and folk games, and planning stunt programs.

Churches avail themselves of the department's picnic and party kits and service, song sheets, costumes, and other materials. Recreation executives meet from time to time with representatives of the local churches and assist them in working out a recreation program. Churches are also helped in forming their own church and Sunday school leagues or by enrolling their groups in the department's athletic program. Parks and other recreation facilities are made available to churches for Easter sunrise or special community services. In one city a religious drama festival in which a total of 18 church groups presented plays did much to promote good-fellowship among the churches. An annual song festival for choirs representing the colored churches, held at one of the community centers in another city, has helped arouse greater interest in good church music.

Daily vacation Bible schools are seldom held at municipal playgrounds, but in Greensboro, North Carolina, the recreation authorities cooperate with the churches in conducting them. During 1937, Bible school programs were arranged at four playgrounds for a period of two weeks, the playground leaders assisting with the recreation features. The recreation authorities have found that many children who attend the Bible school form the habit of coming to the playground, that the program brings the playground activities to the attention of many people, and that the department benefits from the cooperation with and service to the local church leaders.

INSTITUTIONS

Hospitals, orphanages, and similar institutions often lack recreation facilities or leadership, although their occupants are in special need of play opportunities. Comparatively few recreation departments provide regular service to institutions, but the results which have been accomplished fully justify the efforts expended in behalf of these unfortunate groups.

In Reading, Pennsylvania, the recreation department for a number of years has supervised a program serving several local institutions. The trained worker, who is financed by the Junior League, visits the institutions and conducts such activities as storytelling, handicraft, games, holiday programs, and pageants. The total attendance at the programs carried on at the orphanages and sanitarium, and in the children's ward of three hospitals, each year exceeds 10,000.

Christmas is a special occasion for the children in the orphanages and correctional institutions as well as for the needy children in Reading, because each year the recreation department conducts a Christmas party for them in the city hall auditorium which is gaily decorated for the occasion. The program includes the singing of Christmas carols, words of greeting from the Mayor, a special entertainment, and a visit from Santa Claus, who distributes oranges and candy. This annual party is a red-letter day for these children, who look forward eagerly to the Christmas season.

Other ways in which recreation departments serve institutions are: Service bureaus furnish leadership and equipment for picnics and parties; institution workers are enrolled in training courses; groups are transported to swimming pools for free swimming periods or are invited to attend or participate in unusual playground events; and roving storytellers make the rounds of hospitals and other institutions. It is customary for special programs such as Christmas plays, the playground circus, and folk dance festivals to be taken to homes, orphanages, and hospitals. A splendid example of combining a handicraft and service project occurred in Minneapolis where before Christmas children at 19 playgrounds constructed miniature circuses. The greatest ingenuity was shown by the boys and girls in building these circuses which really functioned as they should.

After being displayed in the City Hall they were distributed to orphanages and hospitals, one of them being presented to the Georgia Warm Springs Foundation at the request of the children.

Hospital Service.—Into the children's ward of several Detroit hospitals and institutions there is wheeled every morning a toy cart from which patients are allowed to choose bright-colored game blocks, storybooks, magazines, toys, and other articles made by the local WPA Toy Project. Conducted under the supervision of the Department of Recreation and with the financial aid of the Children's Foundation of Michigan, this project has served a real community need by making special types of toys to fit the needs of the hospitalized child. Hand puppets induce children to develop coordination and to bring afflicted arms or hands into use; interesting educational toys help keep minds alert, and wheelbarrows loaded with colored blocks increase confidence in walking. Volunteer leaders assist the children in making their own toys, scrapbooks, and puzzles. They plan parties and musical programs, thereby speeding the time for the sick children and keeping them interested and happy. The program has subsequently been extended to young people and adults with the result that crafts, games, and recreational hobbies have become popular. The success of this project has led to a request from other hospitals for similar services.

NATIONALITY GROUPS

The community recreation program is one of the most powerful agencies for absorbing the various nationality groups into American life. Foreign-born people are encouraged to participate in the program, not as members of a particular race but as neighbors and potential citizens. Racial prejudices, ignorance, and timidity have often discouraged persons of different nationalities from taking part, but through the efforts of competent leaders, often recruited from the racial groups themselves, they are gradually being eliminated. The special interests, skills, and customs of people from other nationalities sometimes influence the planning of facilities and programs. Boccie and pelota courts, bowling greens, and cricket fields, are often provided in neighborhoods of national groups among whom these games are traditional. Native festivals and holiday programs are built around the games, music, and dances of the various national groups. Reference has already been made to the nationality programs presented in Hartford and to the international folk festival and the folk dance groups which are typical of activities among the foreign-born. Nationality nights, where publicized by radio announcements, foreign-language newspapers, and presentations before the clubs and lodges serving the nationality groups, have attracted large and enthusiastic audiences.

Although the foreign-born are encouraged to participate in the department's activities as members of the community rather than of a nationality group, they are sometimes more willing to take part if they are allowed to do so with their own people. Twelve teams representing different nationalities participated in the fourth annual all-nation's basketball tournament in a Wisconsin city, with the Poles taking the title. In a small Rocky Mountain city the basketball season was climaxed with a similar tournament in which nine teams were entered and the German group was victorious. The softball season closed with an all-nation's tournament in which the Slovakians won the nationality title.

The Recreation Commission in Highland Park, Michigan, maintains as a part of its service an American Citizenship Bureau which combines four specific programs—naturalization, immigration, adult education, and social activity. Forty different nationalities are served by the bureau and receptions are arranged for new citizens when their naturalization papers are presented. Choral groups of English, Scotch, Irish, Rumanian, Italian, and American people have been organized, and a Citizenship School Association composed of graduates of the bureau's citizenship classes fosters friendship among nationality groups and arranges many social occasions in which recreation plays an important part.

RECREATION FOR NEGROES

Colored people, like other racial groups, are entitled to share in the recreation programs provided by the municipality. In many sections of the country recreation authorities provide facilities in colored neighborhoods much as they do in other parts of the city, and often the same facilities are used jointly by white and colored people. However, where under legislation there is a dual system of education for the two racial groups, dual provision for recreation is necessary if the needs of Negroes are to be served. In many Southern cities separate programs and certain special facilities are therefore made available for the use of colored people.

Extent and Nature of Service.—Before the World War comparatively little was done by municipalities to meet the recreation needs of colored people, but since that time interest in furnishing wholesome recreation opportunities for Negroes has grown rapidly. Reports for 1938[1] reaching the National Recreation Association indicated that 196 cities furnished leadership for a total of 623 outdoor playgrounds serving colored people, in addition to facilities used by both white and colored groups. One hundred and seven cities reported a total of 156 special recreation buildings for colored people. The total participation at 107 of these buildings during 1937 was more than 4 million. These figures, which for the most part relate to facilities developed in Southern communities, bear testi-

[1] *Recreation*, June, 1939, p. 127.

mony to the progress which has been made in serving the recreation needs of this group.

Where special facilities and leadership have been provided for Negroes the programs are similar in most respects to those for white people. Because of their great love for music, vocal and instrumental groups have been particularly successful. The pageants, festivals, and other outdoor and indoor celebrations which have been presented by colored groups rank high in artistic merit. Drama, too, is very popular, and in the Cincinnati annual drama contest a play presented by a colored group was in two consecutive years awarded the prize for the most outstanding production. In cities where recreation buildings have been erected in colored neighborhoods, "domestic science has crept in under 'household hobbies,' physical recreation absorbs a medical clinic, and reading rooms approaching a branch library were often the initial provision."[1]

In Greensboro, North Carolina.—The Recreation Commission in Greensboro has been outstanding in its concern for the recreation interests of its colored people. A Negro Division has been established in the recreation department, with a director and supervisor of girls' and women's activities, both employed full time the year around. Assistants in crafts and dramatics and music, a corps of emergency leaders, and a large group of volunteers assist in conducting the activities of the division. Advice and guidance in the planning and operation of the program for Negro citizens is furnished by a Negro Advisory Committee appointed by the chairman of the commission.

Windsor Community Center, a well-equipped recreation building located in a city park and erected in 1937 at a cost of $60,000, is the most important of the facilities available for the use of the colored people. Adjoining the building is an outdoor swimming pool, 100 feet wide and 175 feet long, and on the grounds surrounding the center are tennis and paddle tennis courts, a baseball diamond, a playground, and a picnic center. Two other playgrounds are conducted under leadership during the summer months. Operation of the center and outside facilities in the best interests of the Negro group is assured by the organization of an executive committee, community center council, and women's recreation committee.

The activities at the center have been described by the director as follows:

Every available period between the hours of 10:00 A.M. and 10:00 P.M. is used for hobbies, handicraft, music, physical, social, dramatic, and educational activities. Committee and club meetings, civic gatherings, and citizenship classes, as well as programs of a musical and dramatic nature are held at the center.

[1] E. T. Attwell, "Recreation for Colored Citizens in the New Democracy," *Recreation*, January, 1937, p. 491.

Special events include monthly community nights, a choir festival, a public school sing, checker tournaments, community music recitals, and lectures by outstanding speakers. Badminton, checkers, Ping-pong, handball, dominoes, and jig-saw puzzles are to be found on the program. Recreation clubs for professional workers, girls' clubs, men's clubs, a mothers' chorus, a community glee club, sewing, woodwork, and flower-making classes, indoor baseball, volley ball, and games are all proving popular. Of special interest is the kindergarten held daily at the center between the hours of nine and twelve.

During the year 1937–1938 the total attendance of participants and spectators at the activities sponsored by the Negro Division in Greensboro was 147,000. This figure, which includes the summer playgrounds, swimming pool, picnic facilities, community center, city-wide events, and hospital recreation service, indicates the appreciation of the colored people for the recreation service provided by the city authorities.

In Northern Cities.—Large colored communities in a number of Northern cities enjoy the use of splendid recreation facilities. Linden Center in Dayton, Ohio, for example, a successful recreation building serving the needs of Negroes, was constructed through special tax funds approved by the people in a general referendum vote. Its original operating budget of $5,000, which has been increased to some $25,000, provides for a recreation, social, and health program and is met from municipal and chest funds. The combined auditorium-gymnasium, clubrooms, and indoor swimming pool make the building an all-round indoor center, and its "extension division" operates an excellent nine-hole golf course. One of the finest recreation buildings in America was constructed by the Recreation Department of Detroit at a cost of nearly $400,000 to serve a section of the city occupied chiefly by Negroes. The Public Recreation Commission in Cincinnati, Ohio, has established a Department of Work with Colored Citizens which, with the help of a Citizens' Recreation Council operates five year-round centers at which programs comprising a great variety of activities are conducted for children, youth, and adults.

OTHER SERVICES

Space permits only a brief mention of several other ways in which recreation departments render unusual service or provide special activities for restricted groups.

Preschool Children.—With the expansion of the recreation program, and especially with the availability of emergency leadership, greater attention has been given to the special needs of preschool children who previously did not share to any great extent in the municipality's provision for recreation. In many public playgrounds sections had been set aside for the exclusive use of very small children, and in a few cities special nursery playgrounds had been established. On the whole, however, the playground facilities and programs were primarily for children of school age. Among the exceptions were the tiny tots' play areas in several of the parks in Hartford, the Children's Playhouse in Fairmount Park, Philadelphia, and the Mothers' Hall in Fleishhacker Playground in San Francisco. The Board of Education in New York City for many years has conducted "mothers' and babies'" playgrounds during the summer months, and has provided leadership for summer play schools. The Tot-Lot Playground established in Philadelphia for the benefit of small children living in the immediate neighborhood has been widely publicized, and a number of its features have been copied in other cities.

Supplementing the special facilities for the preschool group have been the kindergarten classes conducted in playground and park buildings during the morning hours when the facilities are otherwise little used. A program of this type established for the first time at two of the park centers in Miami in 1938 was patronized by nearly 5,000 boys and girls, indicating the need for and appreciation of such a service. Among the activities commonly carried on at these preschool centers are simple crafts, storytelling, singing and running games, rhythm bands, and apparatus play. In one city where nine of these "playschools" are conducted, a visiting nurse calls on each of them twice a week to assure the maintenance of proper health standards. It has been demonstrated that these programs for preschool children meet a real need, and incidentally assure a greater return on the investment in the areas and facilities used by the children.

Tourists.—Furnishing recreation for tourists and visitors is an important business in cities which thrive largely on the tourist trade. Recreation programs are looked upon by the city authorities primarily as a means of attracting and serving visitors rather than as a service to community groups. Special emphasis is therefore given to the provision of game courts, particularly badminton, bowling-on-the-green, shuffleboard, croquet, and others in which individuals rather than teams participate, also to facilities for aquatics and fishing, indoor centers for dining, dancing, cards and other quiet games, picnic facilities, and opportunities for music, arts, and dramatics. Many resort cities have daily organ recitals, frequent band and orchestra concerts, and community sings, and maintain reading rooms and library service. Recreation authorities organize social recreation clubs for their winter visitors, and conduct frequent dances, card parties, and socials for the benefit of this group. Unfortunately, in some resort cities the needs of local citizens are overlooked in the attempt to furnish facilities that will appeal to the tourists.

The community service program held one evening each week in the municipal auditorium of a California city illustrates a special type of entertainment which appeals primarily to tourists although it also serves many local citizens. These weekly programs, which attract an average attendance of 3,000 a night, are usually divided into three parts. The first half hour is devoted to community singing, the next part to a stage presentation consisting of music, drama, dancing, and novelty performances, and the evening is concluded with two hours of old-time square dancing.

Servicemen.—Cities with army posts or naval stations cannot overlook the special needs of the servicemen who are assigned to duty within their borders. In Long Beach, California, the recreation authorities have made special provision for men in the naval and military service by maintaining a men's club which is open every day of the year with a director in charge. Its facilities include reading and writing materials, pool tables, games, lounges, and checking facilities, all of which are free to servicemen. Attendance at the club averages 2,500 per week. The regular social program includes Saturday night dances, Friday night bridge parties for single men, Thursday night dinners, and vespers on Sunday. Special events such as bridge parties, mountain trips, and holiday dances are arranged from time to time. Members of the girls' auxiliary plan the social affairs and act as hostesses.

The servicemen's families are also provided for through special groups organized by the department. A Navy Wives' Club, members of which meet weekly for bridge with their husbands, has its own meetings and does welfare work for enlisted men's families. A Navy Mothers' Club for mothers of enlisted men living in the district arranges special parties for the men, supplementing the program carried on by the servicemen's club. Enlisted men in large numbers avail themselves of the other facilities and activities provided by the department, especially in the athletic and aquatic divisions.

Transients.—The many transients who came to cities seeking employment opportunities or relief, especially during the early depression years, presented an acute problem. A few cities opened special centers for unemployed men, but an attempt was generally made to draw them into the normal activities at the centers serving community groups. Cincinnati is one of the cities where a special program for transients was inaugurated in 1933 and has been continued as a feature of the recreation department's program. Some twenty different centers are used to care for the needs of these unattached men who range in age from fifteen to eighty years and upward. The program, which is under the direction of one of the department's supervisors, is otherwise carried on by emergency leaders. In 1937, 58,000 different individuals were served and 32 activities were provided. Among the most popular have been bolo-ball, checkers, dart ball, team games, listening to the radio, using the reading rooms, shuffleboard, table games, and table tennis. One of the most unusual and interesting developments has been the handicraft activity for handicapped men who have made Christmas toys for the city's needy children. In a section of one of the intown city parks, the bandstand and sidewalks surrounding it, as well as a limited area under the trees, are thronged with members of this group. It has become the checker center of the city, patronized not only by the homeless men but by some of the best checker players in Cincinnati. During the winter the players move into the small shelter house which serves the park playground during the summer months.

Emergency Service.—In a number of instances when disaster has befallen a community the city officials have turned to the recreation department for emergency service. Splendid assistance was rendered the flood victims in several cities along the Ohio River early in 1937. In Cincinnati, for example, when thousands of the people were driven from their homes, recreation programs were carried on continuously from 8 A.M. into the evening hours at a number of centers. In planning the program an attempt was made to divert the attention of adults from their worries and anxieties. To this end, the services of orchestral, dramatic, and vaudeville units were enlisted and in the larger centers entertainments were given three times a day. Volunteers presented or assisted with vaudeville shows, symphony concerts, band concerts, exhibitions of magic, motion-picture performances, and dance programs. Recreation leaders also helped the refugees provide their own entertainment by organizing spelling bees, tap dancing contests, checker tournaments, and choruses. Athletic games were arranged out of doors when weather permitted. Activities were also conducted for the children. In Louisville the knowledge and experience of the recreation staff were utilized not only for organizing recreation programs but for a variety of tasks ranging from typing to rowing boats, and from cooking to organizing relief centers. Salvaged material in Evansville was utilized for a variety of craft projects in the centers established by the recreation department.

Following the earthquake at Long Beach, California, the staff of the Recreation Commission was likewise marshaled for emergency service. Refugee camps were established and entertainment programs were arranged. Radio and newspaper requests for volunteers brought a splendid response from amateur and professional music leaders, entertainers, orchestras, bands, and church choirs. During the two weeks following the earthquake 85 community programs arranged and presented in the city parks were attended by approximately 200,000. As the period of excitement wore off, entertainment features were supplemented by organized programs including activities in which people of all ages had an opportunity to participate. The program for children was especially appreciated by children and parents alike because for a time the schools were closed.

Through these emergency programs recreation authorities have demonstrated their readiness to serve in time of disaster. They have proved to the people the value of a recreation program under leadership in times of crisis as well as under normal conditions.

CHAPTER XXVII

TYPICAL MUNICIPAL RECREATION PROGRAMS

Desirable as it is to know what kinds of facilities, activities, and services are furnished by recreation authorities in different cities, it is equally important to know to what extent these are included within the program of a single department. In order that the reader may have a knowledge of the nature and scope of the services rendered by a progressive recreation department, a summarized description of the facilities, programs, and services in five cities is presented in the following pages.

The programs selected are in cities which vary widely in population and geographic location and are conducted under different forms of managing authority. Because of the complexity and extent of the recreation work in the large metropolitan cities, they are not represented here. The cities selected vary in size from Oakland, California, with 300,000 people to Hastings on Hudson, New York, with a population of 7,500. Various sections of the country are represented in the following statement which describes the work carried on by park, school, and recreation boards and a community service council.

The programs are not presented as necessarily representing the best in their respective groups. There are doubtless many cities which in some respects are doing more effective recreation work than the departments used as examples. However, the programs described are representative of the city-wide service carried on by well-administered recreation departments of similar size, type, and management. Space does not permit a full account of all activities, but sufficient detail is given for the reader to gain a fair appreciation of what each department is doing in furnishing opportunities for the enjoyable and constructive use of the people's leisure. Special mention is made of unusual projects and services. It should be borne in mind that most recreation departments are using emergency personnel, and that some of the activities described would not have been carried on had it not been for the assistance of WPA and NYA workers.

In the following pages are described the programs in Oakland, California; Hartford, Connecticut; Sioux City, Iowa; Hastings on Hudson, New York; and Two Rivers, Wisconsin.

OAKLAND, CALIFORNIA

Oakland, a city of 300,000, was a pioneer in the field of public recreation, its first Playground Commission having been appointed in 1908. Since that time it has been widely known for the quality and diversity of its program which is administered by a Board of Playground Directors of five members. This board cooperates closely with the school authorities and under a provision of the city charter is responsible for the operation of all recreation areas and facilities in the city parks. A superintendent of recreation, who also serves as supervisor of physical education in the public schools, heads the department's staff of supervisors, directors, and other workers.

Because of climatic conditions, the diversified program in Oakland, like that in many other California cities, consists primarily of outdoor activities which can be carried on throughout the year. Among the facilities and areas operated by the department are:[1]

12 municipal playgrounds	85 horseshoe pits
64 school playgrounds	3 clubhouses
3 community centers	2 garden theaters
2 family mountain camps	2 boat houses
3 supervised camps	1 swimming pool
43 tennis courts (10 lighted)	7 picnic areas
1 18-hole golf course	2 recreation centers
12 official baseball diamonds	3 bowling greens
4 lighted softball diamonds	1 bowling-billiards court
12 evening gymnasiums	

Playgrounds.—"The core of municipal recreation in Oakland is its playgrounds," at which the attendance during the year totaled 2,175,980 children-visits and 649,701 adult-visits. The 64 school playgrounds are operated after school hours and on Saturdays, Sundays, holidays, and during vacation periods. Sports and games comprise a large part of the program, and the boys and girls who participate are carefully classified according to age, height, and weight. Culminating each girls' sport season, district playdays in which participation varies from 2,000 to 3,500 girls are held in each neighborhood throughout the city. Batball, kick ball, netball, bowl club ball, softball, paddle handball, tennis, relays, and crew rowing are among the scheduled athletic activities for girls. Sports days for boys are also arranged, and the more popular boys' activities are softball, basketball, soccer, track, crew rowing, and handball.

The large municipal playgrounds with their greater area and more diversified facilities are open longer than the school playgrounds. Their

---

[1] The statistics used in describing the work in Oakland are taken from its report for the year ending June 30, 1938.

program is richer and more varied, especially in summer when the playgrounds are open all day and in the early evening. In addition to games and sports, playground groups are organized for dramatics, handicraft, nature lore, rhythmics, and storytelling. A number of recreation specialists assist the playground directors in planning and conducting these activities. Clubs organized upon the basis of common interests include junior playground leaders, hobby groups, dramatic clubs, and tennis and swimming units. Such activities as doll shows, soap bubble contests, treasure hunts, pet shows, kite flying tournaments, parades, and excursions away from the playground add variety to the program. During the summer, in each district of the city, the children and playground directors join in observing a special day of games and stunts, with refreshments.

Recreation for Adults.—Adult activities play a large part in the Oakland program. The 18-hole golf course, Lake Merritt, the family camps, community centers, softball and baseball diamonds, and game courts serve large numbers of men and women. Organization for adult sports includes leagues and tournaments in golf, tennis, boating, swimming, baseball, softball, archery, bowling, horseshoes, basketball, and badminton. Softball is the outstanding sport with 471 adult teams and 9,420 players served during the year. The Alameda County Softball Committee has been organized to help coordinate play in Oakland and neighboring cities and to conduct the annual county championships. The lighting of tennis courts and softball diamonds has greatly increased the adult use of these facilities.

Golf Course.—The department operates an 18-hole golf course of spectacular beauty where people may enjoy the game at a minimum cost. Two golf clubs, one for men and one for women, have been organized to popularize the sport and to encourage tournament play. A special effort to interest high-school students and other youth in the game is meeting with unusual success. In response to public demand the department has arranged for a monthly play ticket including Saturdays as well as weekdays at a charge of only $3. The 15 leading tournaments held on the course during the year attracted a total of 1,099 entries.

Industrial Recreation.—An organized program for employees of industrial and mercantile establishments is carried on through the Industrial Athletic Association of Metropolitan Oakland. More than 80 firms with some 32,000 employees are members of the association, which is directly sponsored by the recreation department. Among the activities for both men and women are tennis, softball, crew, bridge, bowling, basketball, volley ball, badminton, and swimming. Interfirm games are also scheduled in leagues for men in handball, baseball, golf, track, horseshoes, and ice hockey. The outstanding annual event of the association's program is a spectacular sports carnival held at the municipal auditorium, in which more than 1,300 men and women employees of member firms participate. Following the colorful parade with many floats depicting sports comes a series of demonstration games, stunts, and contests.

Community Centers.—In addition to its playground facilities, Oakland operates three community center buildings in highly industrial areas. Around these centers are coordinated and centralized the recreation activities and facilities of the districts in which they are located. Each has a gymnasium and two also have outdoor playgrounds one of which is lighted. Persons of all ages are served at each center through programs organized on the club plan. Homogeneous groups take part in dramatics, handicraft, tap and folk dancing, music, sewing, cooking, hobbies, forums, bridge, and social activities.

At one of the centers in a neighborhood with many Portuguese people, puppetry, sewing, and cooking are most popular. The lighted playground adjoining this center has a large evening attendance and furnishes facilities for a boys' 29-team league in softball. At another center an interesting development is the library service using worn books contributed by the city library. Community nights are held semimonthly in each center, and special celebrations are outstanding. Not a holiday or special occasion passes without fitting festivities. A carnival is the outstanding annual feature at one center; at another it is an international spring festival. The community house in a Mexican neighborhood celebrates Mexican Independence Day in September and conducts a typical Mexican piñata party and a special Mother's Day fiesta.

At a number of other areas combined indoor and outdoor centers are being developed, in some instances utilizing the recreation facilities in school buildings for indoor activities.

Drama.—Dramatics and pageantry reach their climax in Oakland in the annual performance of the "Light of the World," a Christmas pageant produced by the department in cooperation with the public schools. In 1937 groups from 60 schools and playgrounds with a total of 1,507 participants had a part in the pageant. The Oakland Council of Dads' Clubs acted as sponsors, and members of a woman's group served as patronesses at the two performances. The costumes used in the pageant, as well as in the department's other drama activities, are made in its costume room in which more than 9,000 costumes are stored, catalogued, and arranged according to styles, periods, and sizes.

Other drama activities include a summer playground pageant and the programs presented each week during the summer at the Mosswood Garden Theater by children from playgrounds throughout the city.

Special drama workers give playground children opportunity for creative activity through storytelling, puppetry, pantomimes, and plays carried on by members of the drama clubs.

Aquatics.—Lake Merritt, in the heart of the city, is a popular year-round recreation center. On the lake the department maintains a boat house and canoe house from which are operated a fleet of rowboats, canoes, passenger launches, electric motorboats, and other craft. The boat house unit includes a designing room, yacht club meeting rooms, and crew quarters. Many private craft are cared for at the lake in addition to the boats maintained by the department. The Lake Merritt Sail Club holds regular meetings and sailing events for boat club members and visiting boats. A crew program is culminated in the summer playground regatta and special regattas for elementary boys and girls. The girls' regatta included crews from 39 school playgrounds. The lake is used for the annual maneuvers of the Sea Scouts and for special celebrations with motorboat races on Independence Day, Admission Day, and Columbus Day. Interest in aquatic activities among children and adults is stimulated through the Lake Merritt Model Yacht Club which arranges races and regattas and the Model Power Boat Club whose members build and race their own craft.

Supplementing the aquatic sports at Lake Merritt is Oakland's municipal swimming pool with bathhouse and sandy beach, where life-saving classes and interplayground swimming meets are scheduled throughout the season. During 121 swimming days in 1937 the total attendances at the pool was 38,182.

Vacation Camps.—Oakland was one of the pioneers in providing vacation camps for its people on a cost-covering basis. Through the cooperation of the U. S. Forest Service the department maintains two family camps in the High Sierras and in conjunction with these it operates a supervised camp for boys and one for girls. Among the attractions which the camps offer are a beautiful setting, rustic buildings, trails for hiking and horseback riding, and streams for fishing and swimming. Food is provided by the camp staff. Overnight trips, games of various kinds, fishing, riding, hiking, swimming, and evening campfire programs help to make life in camp interesting. At the two family camps 1,887 persons were served in 1937 for a total of 15,775 camper-days. During the fishing season the camps are kept open for the convenience of people who wish to make use of the equipment and facilities. Adjoining the family camp sites are a camp for boys and another for girls. Here capable leaders, taking advantage of the opportunities afforded by the camp setting, carry on a program in which nature lore and campcraft receive special emphasis. Short overnight trips with opportunities for cooking out are enjoyed by both boys and girls.

A fifth camp is an intown camp located near the municipal golf course and operated during the summer vacation. It accommodates groups of girls from the city playgrounds who arrive in camp on Monday morning and remain until the following Saturday noon. Over week ends throughout the year the camp is generally used by groups affiliated with local organizations, especially character-building agencies.

Special Services.—The Oakland Recreation Department supplements its own program of activities under leadership by furnishing services to individuals and groups throughout the city. Staff members are available for consultation regarding plans and equipment for back-yard playgrounds and home play activities. The department grants permits for groups wishing to use school gymnasiums for evening sports, and also furnishes a recreation leader. It has issued instructions for party games, picnic suggestions, and social recreation stunts in bulletin form, assists local groups in planning and organizing programs, and lends them outing kits and social recreation equipment. The costume department maintains not only costumes but properties and scenery which may be borrowed at a nominal service charge by groups sponsoring children's educational dramatics. Reservations of picnic areas for use by small or large groups, and permits for the use of tennis courts and other facilities for tournaments or league games, are also issued by the department. Its library facilities consisting of some 500 volumes are available for consultation, and motion pictures of the department's activities are shown on request to local organizations.

Training.—Recognizing the importance of adequately trained leadership, the department's supervisory staff provides training courses, conferences, group discussions, and regular staff meetings for workers. Committees of staff workers have a large part in planning and conducting the annual training course for playground directors and recreation leaders which is held prior to the beginning of the summer vacation period. Supplementary meetings and conferences continue the leadership training program throughout the year, and special institutes are planned and conducted from time to time to meet the needs of parent-teacher associations, churches, clubs, and other groups. In 1938 the annual training course was replaced by one of the recreation institutes conducted by workers from the National Recreation Association and sponsored jointly by the University of California. Of the 343 individuals who were enrolled in the institute, 67 were members of the department staff.

HARTFORD, CONNECTICUT

Hartford was one of the first American cities to establish a Board of Park Commissioners and to develop a system of city parks. Since the appointment of the Park Board in 1860 the system has grown until it now comprises more than 2,700 acres. The outdoor facilities which have been developed in Hartford, and the activities carried on in this city of 180,000 people, are fairly representative of the service rendered by progressive park departments. The program is administered by a recreation division in charge of a supervisor with a corps of full-time and seasonal assistants.

Outdoor Facilities.—The Hartford parks have been designed and constructed to furnish the people with a great variety of outdoor recreation activities. In addition to the twenty playgrounds, there are three outdoor pools and a lake beach which furnish opportunities for swimming. Informal picnic centers in many of the parks serve individuals, families, and large groups, and the department furnishes a recreation leader for the benefit of picnic parties in the large parks. A 27-hole and an 18-hole golf course are in constant use. Four bowling greens are popular with the older citizens, while the tennis courts, baseball diamonds, soccer, lacrosse, and football fields and running tracks appeal primarily to a younger group. An outdoor dancing pavilion in use every evening except Sundays from May to September attracts large numbers of dancers and also provides hundreds of seats for those who come to enjoy the music played by the orchestra. Quoits and horseshoes, shuffleboard, handball, badminton, and archery are carried on at one or more centers. Boating and fishing, horseback riding, and overnight camping are among other activities which the park facilities make possible.

City-wide Activities.—Supplementing the individual and informal use of the park facilities is a comprehensive municipal sports organization sponsored by the department. More than 540 baseball teams used the baseball diamonds in 1937. Sixteen weekly bicycle races at a track in one of the parks had a total of 560 entries and attracted more than 50,000 spectators. Championship contests are held in baseball, golf, bicycling, archery, croquet, paddle tennis, handball, track and field, and swimming. In addition to the football teams promoted by the department, semiprofessional and high-school teams make use of the municipal stadium. When conditions permit, park facilities are used for skating, curling, skate sailing and ice boating, coasting, skiing, and other winter sports. A model yacht regatta, baseball school, boy's baseball radio league, and tournaments in bolo and "Filipino Twirler" supplemented the usual activities at the department's twenty playgrounds.

Special Outdoor Features.—During the summer months the music shell in one of the parks in the center of the city is used two evenings a week for concerts by a 60-piece WPA symphony orchestra, and one evening a week for a vaudeville show by talent recruited from the centers and playgrounds. The department is entrusted with the supervision of the Fourth-of-July and Labor Day observances, and in 1937 staged an outdoor pageant which climaxed the Constitution anniversary celebration. Reference has already been made to the remarkable Nativity presentation arranged for the 1938 Christmas season and to the outdoor Nationality Nights.

Indoor Center Activities.—Hartford is one of the cities where the park authorities use school buildings for community recreation programs. Following the close of the outdoor playgrounds, activities in Hartford are transferred to 21 centers located in park and school buildings. Every day except Sunday these centers are open from 3:30 to 9:00 P.M. for crafts, quiet games, athletics, dancing, dramatics, and social recreation. Before 1937 the program was restricted largely to children's activities, but since that time the service has been extended to adults. Among the most popular adult activities have been the women's classes in art, needlecraft, home planning and decoration, handloom weaving, knitting, dressmaking, leather craft, puppetry, and tap dancing. Another successful innovation has been the social dances for young men and women. During the winter of 1937–1938, 57 such dances were attended by more than 17,595 people.

Drama.—A marionette troupe, originated in Hartford as a WPA project to produce entertainments for school children, has proved so successful that its service has been extended to public and private institutions in and around the city, and it has been called upon to make a tour of the state and county fairs. Three plays, "Hansel and Gretel," "Rip Van Winkle," and "Snow White and the Seven Dwarfs" were presented 152 times during one year. The puppetry program has been expanded to include several children's groups who receive instruction in the construction, clothing, and operation of puppets and the presentation of puppet shows.

Another feature of the drama program is the children's drama group which in 1937 staged eleven different productions, two outdoor pageants, four outdoor variety programs, and two musical shows. The group which presents these programs is composed of children who are selected from the drama classes and also from the singing and dancing groups conducted at the centers. An offspring of the children's drama program is a radio group of community center children who assist the "Story Lady" with a weekly radio broadcast featuring children's tales, folklore, and fairy stories. At Christmas the department conducts the Mayor's annual theater party for the children of the city as well as other parties for crippled children and orphans.

Use of Emergency Funds.—The Hartford Park Department has been particularly resourceful in developing improvement projects involving the use of emergency funds, in salvaging discarded materials for the construction of recreation facilities, and in initiating activity projects that utilize the talents of emergency personnel. Particularly worthwhile service has been rendered by a dance ensemble sponsored by the Federal Music Project. This group assisted the department throughout the year with its dances and other activities and also furnished a series of musical entertainments for shut-ins in hospitals and institutions in Hartford and vicinity. Many of the activities in the following attendance report were made possible through the use of emergency leadership.

List of Activities.—The 1937–1938 attendance at activities under supervision in the parks, playgrounds, and community centers was 2,334,479, two-thirds of which was recorded for summer activities. The following table lists the activities carried on during the year:

Applied art	Dramatics, classes	Radio broadcasts (28)
Archery	Dramatics, plays (11)	Ringtoss and ring-o-lett
Badminton	Dressmaking	Sewing
Band concerts .	Fireplaces	Shell programs (4)
Baseball	Football	Shuffleboard
Basketball	Golf	Singing
Beachfront	Gymnastics (indoor and outdoor)	Skating
Bicycle races	Handball	Social parties
Bicycling	Horseshoes and quoits	Softball
Boating	Knitting	Stamp clubs
Camping	Marionettes	Storytelling
Caroms	Model airplane classes	Swimming
Checkers	Needlecraft	Swimming lessons
Coasting	Paddle tennis	Table games
Croquet	Pageants (2)	Table tennis
Dance instruction	Picnics	Tennis
Dances, social	Pinochle pool	Track and field
Dodge ball	Pool	Volley ball

SIOUX CITY, IOWA

The Board of Education is responsible for the program of the Department of Public Recreation in Sioux City. An extension committee of four members follows directly the work of the department, which is carried on under the leadership of a director of recreation, a woman assistant director, an office secretary, and a staff of part-time workers. Started in 1913 with a program of summer playground activities for children, the work now embraces all age groups and is carried on throughout the year. Supplementing the activities of the school authorities, the Park Department maintains five bathing beaches, a 9-hole golf course, three outdoor swimming pools, picnic centers, a large outdoor amphitheater, 31 tennis courts, and other facilities. Unlike the recreation authorities in Oakland and Hartford, the recreation department in this city of 80,000 does not have the responsibility for maintaining and operating large outdoor areas and facilities.

The nature and scope of the program in Sioux City are briefly described in the following statement which is based largely upon the department's reports for 1937 and 1938. In several respects the work in Sioux City is comparable to that provided by a number of other school authorities.

School Year Activities.—The recreation department conducts many diversified activities for boys and girls throughout the school year as an afterschool activity program. Opportunities are given them to attend classes in creative drama, marionettes and puppets, model aircraft, and tap dancing at 25 schools. A total of 69 different clubs have been organized, with more than 2,000 children taking part in the program. As a follow-up to the drama, marionette, and puppet classes, Saturday morning programs for the children are conducted during the winter months, at which children present plays and shows planned during the afterschool activity periods. As a climax to the tap dancing classes is a tap dance festival in which more than 900 girls have participated.

Fall and spring playgrounds are conducted from 3:30·to 7:00 P.M. at eight different playgrounds, and in addition, a program of intraschool competition is carried on, featuring soccer as a fall activity for the boys and soccer-kick ball for the girls. In the spring the boys play softball, and bat ball is the major girls' activity. Individual tournaments in marbles, jackstones, and rope skipping are also conducted. An average of 500 boys attend the Saturday morning recreation program of sports, table games, and quiet activities at the four junior high schools. With the cooperation of the school mothers' clubs, a program of art and craft activities has been organized for a group of deaf children.

Evening Recreation Centers.—During the winter months the department conducts a program of adult recreation at four school buildings for twenty weeks. More than 3,000 individuals participate in the social dancing classes, old-fashioned dancing, tap dancing, art and craft classes, archery, quiet games, reading rooms, dart baseball, gymnasium classes for men and women, and drama clubs. Social recreation nights attract a large attendance. The enthusiasm over table tennis and badminton is reflected in the large number of entries in the tournaments conducted in these sports, with competition arranged for various groups. The weekly program at the centers is described in Chap. XVIII.

Summer Playground Activities.—Following a training institute for playground leaders, 21 play centers are conducted for a 9-week period. A playground supervisor, a music instructor, and a folk dance director supplement the workers at the individual playgrounds. The program includes the usual summer activities for children, special weekly features, and a community night once a week on each of the playgrounds. One of the most popular events is the folk dance festival and feast of lanterns which in 1938 was witnessed by 10,000 people. The 400 girls who participated in the folk dancing included a group from each playground, and 1,800 lanterns of varied and intricate design constructed in the handicraft classes were used in the parade. An all-activity day in which the winners of various contests on individual playgrounds come together in one of the city parks for a day of competitive activities ranging from checkers and hopscotch to sand modeling and track events is another major event.

Free swimming classes conducted each morning during the summer at the three park pools enable hundreds of boys and girls to learn to swim. The summer movie program is presented each week at twelve different play areas, the sound pictures being carefully selected to appeal to family groups. As many as 6,000 people have attended the movie program at one playground on a single evening. The total swimming attendance for the 1938 season reached 10,923, the movie attendance was 157,185, and the grand total for the entire playground program was 427,340.

An honor award system sponsored by the local Quota Club is used on the playgrounds in Sioux City to encourage participation and achievement. Playground and honor certificates are given to children earning a certain number of points, and the highest scoring boy and girl on each playground receive bronze medals. Silver medals are awarded to the boy and girl receiving the highest number of points for the entire city. Awards are presented at a banquet given in honor of the recipients.

Nature Tours.—With the assistance of an Advisory Nature Committee and the cooperation of the National Park Service a series of conducted nature tours was arranged at a large outlying park. Approximately 240 people in six different groups took part in the first tour during which park specialists stationed along the route described the geology, forestry, wild life, and historical significance of the park. Similar tours were conducted each Sunday afternoon throughout the summer, with leadership recruited from the local Hiking Club, Bird Club, Garden Club, and CCC camp.

Because of the keen interest shown by the community in the nature tours which were conducted for two summers as indicated above, in 1938 the State Conservation Commission and Iowa State College employed a full-time naturalist throughout the summer months. This worker served under the supervision of the Recreation Department and tours were conducted in the park under his leadership with a total attendance of 3,000.

Community-wide Activities.—The Department of Recreation conducts a program of athletic league competition for men and women in softball, basketball, and volley ball, and organizes city-wide tournaments in archery, table tennis, and badminton.

One of its newer activities is the planning of a program celebrating National Music Week. A Music Week Association consisting of leaders from all local music organizations was organized which planned a well-rounded Music Week observance. The afternoon and evening programs were presented by different groups of performers including local organists, combined church choirs, public-school choruses and orchestras, the Sioux City Symphony Orchestra, and other choral and instrumental groups. Children's recitals were held in the afternoons and many radio programs were presented during the week. Practically every local music organization cooperated in the Music Week observance and more than 3,000 persons actively participated in the program.

A Winter Sports Festival, conducted annually by the department in conjunction with the Junior Chamber of Commerce, extends over a 4-day period. The carnival, which is conducted against the setting of a shining ice palace, offers competition in figure skating, costuming, and ice basketball, reaching its climax with the selection of the King and Queen. Speed skating for children, tri-state speed skating events for men and women, ice hockey, and a dog derby are other features. Thousands of children and adults actively participate in the various activities and approximately 7,500 spectators witnessed the latest carnival.

Special Year-round Services.—The Sioux City department has been one of the leaders in providing a special service for people who because of old age, sickness, or physical handicaps are unable to take part in the regular program. Its Shut-In Club has 103 active members. A recreation leader delivers a monthly letter called *Cheerio* to club members and helps them with handicraft suggestions. Copies of the magazine are also taken into the four city hospitals each month. Recreation leaders conduct activities at institutions caring for boys and girls and at the Home for Homeless Men.

Other typical services are the loan of picnic equipment, assistance in the planning of picnic and social programs, the showing of colored moving pictures of the department's activities before local groups, and advice to local organizations in planning and conducting recreation projects. The department assists one newspaper in conducting an annual swimming meet and another paper with the annual soap box derby. Arrangements for an annual children's concert conducted by the Junior League are made with the help of the department.

HASTINGS ON HUDSON, NEW YORK

The recreation program in Hastings illustrates the possibilities of municipal recreation service in a village of 7,500 people. Working with a budget of less than $6,000 a year, most of which has been spent for recreation leadership, and with limited facilities the authorities have been unusually successful in marshaling community interest, participation, and support. The recreation work in Hastings, which was established on a year-round basis in 1935, is under the Recreation Division of the Community Service Council and is financed by a village appropriation. A committee of 11 citizens is in charge of the division and its program is carried on by a director, an athletic supervisor, and a girls' supervisor, all employed full time the year round, and a number of seasonal workers.

The facilities in Hastings suitable for recreation use are rather typical of those found in many communities of equal size. They are an athletic field with baseball diamond, three children's playgrounds, three tennis courts, two gymnasiums—one in the elementary school and the other in the high school—and quarters for a boys' club on the second floor of the Hook and Ladder Station. Several schoolrooms are also used for group activities.

Activities Report.—The statistical report (p. 408) of the division's work in the year ending February 28, 1938, indicates the scope of its activities, the number of people served, and the range of groups participating in the program. It illustrates how in a small city paid and volunteer leaders can utilize a modest budget to make possible a comprehensive leisure-time service. The total attendance at the activities during the year was nearly ten times the total population of the village. Approximately 1,800 different individuals participated in the program, not including such activities as block dances, concerts, parties, and skating. The child enrollment at the summer playgrounds totaled about one-half the child population, a percentage attained in very few communities.

Trips and Outings.—Some of the methods and program features in Hastings show the influence of conditions found in small communities. Because of the limited possibilities of conducting an interplayground program, children are given opportunities to take part in many activities involving trips away from the village. Playground groups competed in the county Olympics and the annual district track meet; others were taken to New York City to see ball games at the Yankee Stadium and Polo Grounds and to inspect an ocean liner. Outings in 1937 included playdays in neighboring communities, picnics, and all-day outings at a near-by county park. In the summer children were transported to a county park swimming pool where classes were conducted, and during the indoor season they used the Y.W.C.A. and Y.M.C.A. pools in a near-by city. To provide ice skating, a school bus transported children each Saturday morning during the winter to an indoor rink in one of the county parks. These various outings supplemented the regular activi-

SUMMARY OF ACTIVITIES AND ATTENDANCE

Activity	Number of sessions	Different participants	Age or sex of group	Total attendance
Aeroplane club................	9	20	10–15	75
Badminton—recreation.........	37	38	Adults	327
Badminton—club..............	41	40	Adults	557
Badminton—Sunday...........	8	35	Adults	147
Band.......................	47	45	Boys and men	913
Baseball				
Playground league...........	41	170	Boys	1,623
Rotary.....................	24	50	12–16	713
Twilight...................	34	95	18–30	1,954
Basketball...................	158	380	Mixed group	6,955
Basketry....................	10	30	Girls, 10–14	210
Boys' center.................	Daily	150	6–18	7,841
Boxing bouts................	1	20	Mixed group	650
Boxing instruction............	8	15	Boys, 14–18	58
Camps......................	3 weeks period	26	Girls and boys	26
Checker club.................	4	15	Adults	44
Chess......................	12	16	Adults	126
Christmas club...............	4	25	Girls	84
Concerts....................	3	500	Mixed group	1,350
Dances (block)..............	1	600	Mixed group	1,500
First aid....................	2	14	Adults	20
Folk dancing.................	14	60	Girls, 9–14	255
Girls' center.................	Daily	185	6–18	2,351
Girls' softball...............	10	25	14–19	180
Holiday celebrations...........	2	700	Mixed group	950
Knitting and crocheting........	12	15	Girls, 16–19	88
Marionette club..............	47	15	Girls, 15–19	391
Metal craft..................	62	25	11–15	378
Nature study................	6	25	Boys and girls	100
Outings.....................	11	75	Mixed group	338
Playgrounds.................	20 weeks (daily)	790	Mixed group	29,163
Rhythmic group..............	20	15	Adults	114
Showers....................	25	125	Boys and girls	1,250
Skating....................	24	400	Mixed group	2,023
Social dancing instruction				
Adults....................	7	24	Adults	133
Children..................	40	75	12–15	869
Social recreation group........	16	200	Mixed group	1,060
Softball leagues..............	14	70	Adults	543
Special features..............	12	200	Mixed group	775
Storytelling..................	30	80	Boys and girls	800
Table tennis league				
Girls.....................	3	40	15–18	120
Boys.....................	15	50	Mixed	800
Tennis instruction............	17	30	Boys and girls	272
Touch football..............	6	60	Young men	1,050
Tournaments................	24	300	Mixed group	870

ties, tournaments, and feature events at the local playgrounds which are open under leadership from early May into October.

Activities for Various Groups.—One of the most worth-while projects is the boys' center where every afternoon and evening boys play table tennis, pool, table and quiet games, listen to the radio, and read magazines. Two afternoons a week the center is used for the making of model airplanes and ships and metal craft, and each Monday evening for a moving-picture show. Special events include tournaments in table tennis, pool, caroms, and bowling, Halloween, Valentine, and Christmas parties, and educational trips. Since the center does not have a gymnasium, the boys use a school gymnasium for athletics twice each week.

A room in one of the elementary-school buildings is used as a center for girls' activities which include weekly storytelling hours for small children, marionette club, acrobatic class, groups for sewing, knitting, and crocheting, and tap dancing classes. Socials, parties, and dances are arranged from time to time and two gymnasium periods are held weekly.

In addition to the customary major sports program, a touch football league has been organized for the young men and boxing instruction is provided for boys over eighteen years of age. Several dances which have been held in connection with the basketball league games have proved very successful. Badminton is one of the most popular co-recreational activities, and the division has had difficulty in finding space to meet the demands of all the players. Chess and checker clubs and a women's class in rhythmics meet regularly. A band organized in 1937 provides opportunity for local musicians to play together for their own enjoyment and it has also presented a number of concerts for the benefit of the community.

Instruction Emphasized.—Opportunities for instruction have been stressed in Hastings. Lessons in tennis were conducted twice weekly for boys and girls during the summer, and approximately 145 children were registered in the swimming and lifesaving classes. Before the annual boxing program, a two months' period of instruction assisted young men in training for the event. Social dancing classes have been arranged, one for junior-high-school students, another for high-school students, and a third for adults. In some cases a moderate fee has been charged to help meet the cost of furnishing instruction.

Use of School Buildings.—Hastings furnishes an outstanding example of the community use of school buildings under the guidance of a municipal recreation body. The elementary- and high-school buildings are used every evening except when school functions are held. As previously mentioned, boys' and girls' clubs use the school gymnasiums afternoons for their athletic activities and the girls' center is in a school building.

Basketball leagues for young people and adults use the gymnasiums for their games and dances and the chess and checker clubs meet regularly in classrooms. The badminton club has two weekly sessions in the high-school gymnasium, which is also reserved two additional evenings and Sunday afternoon each week for informal badminton groups. A boys' basketball league plays in the high-school gymnasium on Saturday mornings, while a Scout league is in the elementary gymnasium. The community band meets each Sunday morning in the high-school band room.

Volunteers.—The widespread use of volunteer leaders in Hastings is one of the reasons why three full-time workers are able to supervise such a varied program. Five women who were trained in the art of story-telling at a local institute told stories on the summer playgrounds, and another conducted a weekly story hour at the girls' center during the indoor season. A volunteer gave his time to train the young men preparing for the boxing program, and another served as manager of the table tennis league. The success of the band is largely due to the efforts of its unpaid director. Valuable volunteer assistance has also been rendered in dancing, knitting, tennis, swimming, chess, baseball, and badminton.

Cooperation.—To an unusual degree the program in Hastings includes activities carried on in cooperation with other agencies. The County Recreation Commission sponsors the county Olympics, entertains the playground baseball champions at its camp, assists with the nature study program, and furnishes the instructor for the volunteer storytellers' institute. Several awards in the pet show are made by the local S.P.C.A. chapter. An intercommunity track meet is sponsored each summer by the Rotary Club. Children are selected for free periods at the county recreation camp after consultation with local agencies who also help in financing the project. An industry furnishes facilities for the annual boxing bouts. In an earlier chapter reference was made to the cooperation of the Women's Club and the School Board in conducting the nature activities. The Mayor's Relief Committee, Junior Red Cross Club, and high-school officials assist in collecting toys which are repaired and distributed among needy children at Christmas. The local theater manager dedicates the use of the theater and shows an appropriate picture for the annual Christmas party to which a number of local agencies contribute funds, and a men's social club donates the eggs and prizes for the Annual Easter Hunt.[1]

[1] The report for 1938 indicates additional service extended to many local organizations, a new day camp for boys, and more trips to points of interest. A few activities were discontinued but many others were added, including dramatics, wrestling, home hygiene course, field hockey, archery, soccer, forum, and six-man football.

TWO RIVERS, WISCONSIN

Recreation activities in this city of 10,000 people center about a fully equipped community house representing an investment of more than $150,000. This center, which was presented to the city, is operated by a Department of Recreation which under a Recreation Board also conducts activities at three playgrounds, an indoor municipal swimming pool, a bathing beach, and two school gymnasiums. The department was first established in 1927 and four years later the community house was opened. The facilities in the building include a gymnasium with bleachers which when used as an auditorium seats 1,000 people, a large stage, several clubrooms, banquet room, kitchen, game room, billiard room, bowling alley, and handball court, in addition to the usual service features. This recreation plant makes possible an indoor program of unusual variety and interest. Approximately $25,000 was spent for operating the building and carrying on the community program in 1937, but of this amount less than $10,000 was appropriated by the city, the balance being secured through receipts and earnings at the community house.

Program of Activities.—The following is a list of the activities sponsored by the Two Rivers Recreation Department through its staff of three full-time and several part-time workers. It is to be observed that several of the activities listed under the heading "Community Functions" can be carried on only in a city where suitable indoor facilities are available. Little is done with adults in drama, music, and crafts because these activities are sponsored through the local Board of Vocational Education which receives state funds for leadership.

RECREATION ACTIVITIES IN TWO RIVERS, WISCONSIN

Indoors

Department Activities		Community Functions
Archery	Motion pictures	Safety school
Basketball	Girls' club programs	Home show
Badminton	Boys' club programs	Cooking school
Bowling	Tap dancing	Auto show
Billiards	Social dancing	Conventions
Handball	Game parties	Political meetings
Table tennis	Boys' and girls' jamborees	Forum
Boxing	Holiday programs	Miscellaneous meetings
Tumbling	Shower service	Dramatic productions
Wrestling	Hobby show	Boxing shows
Volley ball	Pet show	Public dances
Athletic carnival	Miscellaneous tournaments	Music festival
Game rooms	Puppetry	Card parties
Craft shoppe	Swimming classes	Banquet service

	Department Activities	Community Functions
Stamp club	Model airplane club	Concert series
Gun club	Tourist information bureau	Homemakers' meetings
Flying club	Art classes	Farmers' institute
		Health clinics
		Art exhibits
		Health exhibits

Outdoors

	Summer	Fall, Winter, and Spring
Overnight camping	Shuffleboard	Fall playground program
Hiking	Badminton	Touch football
Horseshoes	Volley ball	Skating
Tennis	Bathing beaches	Hockey
Archery	Wading pools	Sliding
Picnic service	Park concerts	Hiking
Baseball	Tourist service	Snow modeling
Softball	Tournaments and exhibits	Spring playground program
	Playground theater	

A Community Meeting Place.—The intensive use made of the Two Rivers Community House is indicated by a few facts relating to the groups served in 1937. The building was open to the public 365 days during the year. A total of 1,233 meetings were held in the meeting rooms, the auditorium was used 590 times, and the kitchen facilities on 112 occasions. Ninety-one different organizations held meetings in the building and 38 dances were conducted in it. The shower baths were open to the public 110 days. The total attendance at the building during the year, not including persons using shower rooms, handball court, lounge, bowling alley, and billiard room was 116,831 or more than eleven times the total population of the city. Since the city appropriation toward its operation was $3,300, the average cost to the city per unit of attendance in 1937 was less than 3 cents.

The following comment from a local newspaper editorial indicates how the people of Two Rivers feel toward the community house:

As a public utility the building is unique. It extends its hospitality to sport fans, dancers, theater groups, businessmen, committees, diners, boxers, bowlers, billiard players, church folk—to every one. In the few years since its erection it has become Every Man's Club and Every Woman's, too. Its atmosphere is thoroughly democratic and unpretentious, but it is clean and wholesome. . . . We all feel at home in it, and we can all find there something that we like. . . . The nature of the building plus the wise policies laid down by the recreation board for its operation, have proved their worth over and over.

Other Activities.—Special projects which make leisure hours enjoyable to the young people of this small city are four girls' clubs with a membership of more than 160, and an equal number of boys' clubs which carry on a year-round program for 120 members. Other groups are two social clubs, one for boys and girls from fifteen to seventeen years of age, and the other for boys and girls from thirteen to fifteen, with a combined membership of 160. There is also a touch football league for boys. Twenty-seven men's softball teams and 24 basketball teams attracted an average of 200 spectators to each of their games. Indicative of the quality of leadership is the fact that in all the games played in 1937 not a single protest was submitted to the Board of Governors. The department conducts swimming classes for children and adults at the indoor pool and operates the park beach which is exceedingly popular. A feature of the summer playgrounds is an achievement club for boys and girls, the members of which participate in a program including 43 competitive play activities.

PART VII

ORGANIZATION AND ADMINISTRATION PROBLEMS

Governmental organization for municipal recreation service is essential. It is not important of itself, but it affects materially the extent and quality of the recreation program. The forms of organization for recreation and the powers and duties of the authorities charged with responsibility for this function are dependent upon state and local legislative enactments. The internal organization of recreation departments, on the other hand, is determined largely by the recreation authorities themselves, as are other administrative questions relating to records, reports, and public relations. Part VII deals with these questions and with legislation, types of recreation governing authorities, and the organization of the recreation department. The final chapter deals with the subject of cooperation and relationships, which play such an important part in the service of every recreation department.

CHAPTER XXVIII

THE LEGAL ASPECTS OF MUNICIPAL RECREATION

A municipality or school board must have legal authorization from the state and local governments in order to conduct recreation activities as a part of local municipal or school functions. Legal powers are needed for the acquisition, development, and maintenance of recreation areas, the construction and operation of buildings and facilities, the purchase of supplies, and the employment of personnel for leadership and other services.

HOW RECREATION LEGISLATION DEVELOPED

The establishment of children's playgrounds in the larger metropolitan centers, one of the first steps in the development of the municipal recreation movement, did not require enabling legislation by the state. Authority was based on the general welfare or police powers in state constitutions and local home-rule charters, and on broad interpretations of existing park and school legislation. In some cases the cities secured the enactment of special laws by the state legislature applicable to themselves alone and not to other cities in the state.

As the necessity for local public action became evident in other cities, local authorities in some states were reluctant to act without having more specific legal powers. Consequently, park authorities made efforts to secure broader park legislation and school authorities to enlarge the powers of school boards. Other local officials and many recreation leaders worked for the passage of general recreation enabling acts. These acts permitted any locality in the state to conduct recreation programs under the type of administrative arrangement considered most effective or advantageous in the particular locality.

Powers of Park Authorities.—The broadening of park legislation in a number of states enabled park authorities to add to the traditional park areas and services already being provided the many facilities and activities essential to a comprehensive recreation program. In many states the powers of park authorities under existing legislation were enlarged through court decisions giving broad interpretations of the terms "park" and "park purposes." Minnesota and Kansas are two examples of states where outstanding liberal park decisions were handed down. These decisions, together with the broadening of park laws themselves,

417

made possible the development of recreation service in many localities but were ineffective in communities where local park leadership refused to take advantage of them.

School Legislation.—For many years the greatest uncertainty existed as to the legal authority of local school boards to conduct community-wide activities for all ages and in all types of centers. Indiana passed legislation authorizing the community use of school facilities as early as 1859, and by 1897, 23 states had laws permitting the use of school buildings as civic or social centers. Recreation was one of the approved uses in most states but no expenditure of school funds was authorized for community purposes except in New York and Massachusetts. The intent of the laws was primarily to make school buildings available to groups for meeting purposes and to permit school authorities to provide heat, light, and janitor service and charge for them if advisable. At present, most states have laws permitting the community use of school buildings and areas.

As the children's playground movement developed, some states passed laws permitting schools to operate children's playgrounds, but only a few states have special laws authorizing school authorities to conduct and finance a broad recreation program for the whole community. In most cases where school boards are providing extensive recreation services, their authority for doing so is found either in general enabling acts which include schools in their provisions, or in broad interpretations of their powers to provide civic centers, physical education, or adult education.

Use of Constitutional Powers.—California and Texas are good examples of states where broad home-rule powers granted by the state constitution to municipal governments are the basis for many local recreation systems. Since no special state legislation was necessary, recreation systems have been established through amendments to the local city charter. General police and welfare powers in state constitutions usually furnish states the authority to enact recreation laws, although in some states parks and playgrounds are specifically mentioned in the constitutions themselves. On the other hand, the constitution may actually prove to be a limiting factor in the development of a recreation program, as in Missouri where the educational provision of the state constitution restricts the public educational program of the state to persons between the ages of six and twenty.

Special Laws.—In addition to legislation relating to playgrounds and community recreation programs, there are many special state laws covering specific forms of recreation such as band concerts, municipal music and opera, public baths, auditoriums, community buildings, stadiums, swimming pools, golf courses, and Sunday recreation. Most of these laws were passed many years ago. In general, they represent piecemeal approaches to the recreation problem rather than intelligent consideration of local recreation needs. Frequently they have resulted from the pressure of special interest groups or the desire of local governing bodies to retain direct control of some special, particularly revenue-producing, facilities. The power to acquire, construct, and operate these facilities and to conduct these activities is included in general enabling acts of the type described in the following paragraphs.

STATE RECREATION ENABLING ACTS

The modern type of recreation legislation is the state enabling act which in one law gives every municipality in the state general powers to conduct a broad recreation program under any form of organization of the local government which the municipality may consider most effective. It provides for recreation home rule. It obviates the necessity for separate recreation laws applicable only to school, park, or separate recreation boards, or to other city departments. It takes the place of special legislation authorizing joint or cooperative action on the part of different municipal departments, of municipalities with school boards, or any other desirable combination of local government units.

The first enabling act of this type was passed in New Jersey in 1915. By 1939 the following 26 states had such laws:

State	Year first passed	State	Year first passed
Arkansas...................	1940	Minnesota..................	1937
California.................	1939	New Hampshire.....:........	1917
Colorado...................	1935	New Jersey.................	1915
Connecticut...............	1919	New York..................	1917
Florida...................	1925	North Carolina.............	1923
Georgia...................	1923	Ohio......................	1921
Illinois...................	1923	Pennsylvania...............	1919
Indiana...................	1925	Rhode Island..............	1924
Iowa.....................	1915	South Dakota..............	1917
Kentucky.................	1924	Utah.....................	1923
Louisiana.................	1924	Vermont..................	1925
Massachusetts.............	1919	Virginia..................	1924
Michigan.................	1917	West Virginia..............	1925

Essential Features.—These state enabling laws differ in many aspects and none of them is entirely satisfactory. Most of the laws, however, contain certain provisions which are characteristic of such legislation and which are necessary in order that it may accomplish the purpose it is intended to serve.   Because of widely differing conditions in the various states, no standard form of law is practicable but, in general, enabling legislation should

Permit the municipality (or school board) to provide for the establishment and maintenance of playgrounds, recreation centers, or other areas and facilities, conduct play and recreation activities for all ages, and meet the cost from general or special tax funds of the municipality (or school board).

Authorize any two or more municipalities, counties, and school districts to combine in the operation of a program.

Authorize any two or more departments (including the school board) in a municipality to cooperate in conducting the program.

Permit the governing authority to acquire lands, buildings, or other properties for recreation by gift, bequest, dedication, purchase, condemnation, or transfer, within or without the boundaries of the local governing unit, and to spend current funds and to issue bonds for such.

Permit the governing authority to designate the school board, park board or department, or any other municipal department, or a special recreation board or department as the managing authority for recreation.

Permit the designated recreation managing authority to use the facilities and areas of other departments (including the schools) with the approval of such departments, and to conduct activities on private property with the consent of the owner.

Assign to the designated managing authority the power to equip and maintain recreation areas, buildings, and other facilities, to conduct play and recreation activities of all kinds for all the people of the community, and to employ such personnel for these purposes as the managing authority may deem proper.

Permit the recreation managing authority to use areas and facilities outside the limits of the municipality.

Empower the recreation managing authority to accept any grant or devise of real estate or any gift or bequest of money or other personal properties or donation, to be applied, principle or income, for either temporary or permanent use for recreation purposes, provided that the approval of the governing body of the municipality is secured where such loan or gift would subject the municipality as a whole to additional expense.

In authorizing recreation boards or commissions, the enabling act should designate the manner of appointment, number of officers, term of office, and the manner of filling vacancies.   In addition, many believe that state enabling legislation should include the following provisions to permit local referenda and special taxes in those communities within the state where local leadership considers them advisable or necessary:

Require the local governing body to conduct a referendum vote at a regular or general election, upon petition of a stated number of qualified or registered voters that a proposition be submitted calling for the establishment and conduct of a recreation program and the levying of a stated millage tax.

Require a special tax levy for the establishment and maintenance of a recreation program upon the adoption of a referendum proposal by a majority vote of those voting on the proposition.

Authorize the local governing body to appropriate additional general tax funds where the governing body considers this necessary and desirable.

The Michigan Law.—One of the earliest examples of state enabling legislation, and one of the shortest, is the Michigan Act passed in 1917. In spite of its brevity it includes many of the essential features previously listed but does not provide for a local referendum or special millage tax. The Michigan Act, granting broad general powers to local governmental units, follows:

The People of the State of Michigan enact:

SECTION 1. Any city, village, county, or township may operate a system of public recreation and playgrounds; acquire, equip, and maintain land, buildings or other recreational facilities; employ a superintendent of recreation and assistants; vote and expend funds for the operation of such system.

SECTION 2. Any school district may operate a system of public recreation and playgrounds, may vote a tax to provide funds for operation of same, and may exercise all other powers enumerated in Section 1.

SECTION 3. Any city, village, county, township, or school district may operate such a system independently or they may cooperate in its conduct in any manner in which they may mutually agree; or they may delegate the operation of the system to a recreation board created by any or all of them, and appropriate money, voted for this purpose, to such board.

SECTION 4. Any municipal corporation or board given charge of the recreation system is authorized to conduct its activities on (1) property, under its custody and management; (2) other public property, under the custody of other municipal corporations or boards, with the consent of such corporations or boards; (3) private property, with the consent of the owners.

In several states the enabling acts are much more specific as to the methods to be followed and treat the various features in greater detail than the Michigan law.

Laws with a Referendum and Special Tax Feature.—Many cities have been denied adequate recreation service because reactionary local authorities have hesitated to incur the expense of establishing such service without previous endorsement by the community. Therefore, in a number of states a provision for local referendum elections has been included in the enabling acts. Such a provision enables the voters to express their desire for a recreation system and to authorize the levying of a special tax to finance it. The enabling acts in the following states contain referendum and special tax provisions:

Florida	Iowa	Ohio
Georgia	New Jersey	Vermont
Illinois	New York	Virginia
Indiana	North Carolina	West Virginia

The following sections from the Florida recreation law are typical of special mill tax provisions in state enabling legislation:

SECTION 8.   Whenever a petition signed by at least five (5) per cent of the qualified and registered voters in such municipality or county requesting the governing body of such municipality or county to provide, establish, maintain and conduct a supervised recreation system and to levy an annual tax for the conduct and maintenance thereof of not less than one-half of one mill nor more than one mill on each dollar of assessed valuation of all taxable property within the corporate limits or boundaries of such municipality or county, it shall be the duty of the governing body of such municipality or county to cause the question of the establishment, maintenance, and conduct of such supervised recreation system to be submitted to the qualified voters who are freeholders to be voted upon at the next general or special election of such municipality or county; Provided, however, that such question shall not be voted upon at the next general or special election unless such petition shall have been filed at least thirty days prior to the date of such election.

SECTION 9.   Upon the adoption of such proposition by a majority of those voting on it at an election, the governing body of such municipality or county shall, by appropriate resolution or ordinance, provide for the establishment, maintenance, and conduct of such supervised recreation system as they may deem advisable and practicable to provide and maintain out of the tax money thus voted.   And the said governing body may designate, by appropriate resolution or ordinance, the board or commission to be vested with the powers, duties, and obligations necessary for the establishment, maintenance, and conduct of such recreation system as provided for in this Act.

SECTION 10.   The governing body of such municipality or county adopting the provisions of this Act at an election and until revoked at an election by a majority of the qualified voters who are freeholders, shall thereafter annually levy and collect a tax of not less than the minimum nor more than the maximum amount set out in the said petition for such election, which tax shall be designated as "Playground and recreation tax" and shall be levied and collected in like manner as the general tax for such municipality or county.

The recreation mill tax is further considered in Chap. XXXI.

LOCAL RECREATION LEGISLATION

It is well for any locality planning to establish or reorganize a recreation program to consult the city attorney or some other competent legal adviser as to the nature and extent of its existing powers.   It may be necessary through proper channels to secure the opinion of the state attorney general in cases where doubt exists in the minds of local legal authorities as to the locality's authorization to carry on recreation service.   In most states, however, as pointed out earlier in the chapter, such power is either specifically granted in enabling acts or is included under general home-rule powers.

After analyzing the existing local powers to establish a recreation program and determining the form of organization under which it may best be established, some kind of local legislation is necessary.   This takes the form of a charter amendment in localities where general home-rule powers are used; where action is based upon specific powers granted by state enabling legislation, an ordinance is passed by the local city council.

Local Charter Provisions.—City charter amendments vary in length, depending upon the extent to which they prescribe in detail the powers and procedures of recreation managing authorities. The following charter amendment, adopted by the city of Cincinnati in November, 1926, provides for the appointment of a Public Recreation Commission. It is an example of a brief charter amendment which grants general authority and which needs to be supplemented by city council ordinances.

ARTICLE VII—Boards and Commissions
SECTION 14: Public Recreation Commission—Term—Appointments—Power—Funds, etc.

There shall be a Public Recreation Commission consisting of one member of the Board of Education appointed by said Board, one member of the Board of Park Commissioners appointed by said Board, and three citizens appointed by the Mayor, to serve without compensation. The term of office of said members and the powers and duties of said Commission shall be fixed by ordinance of the Council, but all funds obtained from levies for recreational purposes, appropriated by other public bodies, or donated for such purposes to the City of Cincinnati or the Public Recreation Commission, shall be expended by said Commission.

Suggested Local Ordinance.—The provisions of local ordinances differ according to the type of recreation managing authority they establish and the extent of administrative authority delegated to it. Where ordinances are based upon state laws and local charters which outline powers and duties specifically, they must conform to the authority on which they are based. The following suggested ordinance for the creation of a Recreation Commission indicates the powers which are granted by most state enabling acts and which should be generally incorporated in a local ordinance:

An Ordinance Creating a Recreation Board
Prescribing Terms of Members, Organization,
Powers, and Duties
Be it Ordained by _____
     of the City of _____:
1. Under the provisions of Section ___ of Chapter ___ of the General Laws of ___, there is hereby established a RECREATION COMMISSION. This Commission shall consist of five (5) persons serving without pay who shall be appointed by the Mayor.[1] The term of office shall be for five (5) years or until their successors are appointed and qualified, except that the members of such Commission first

[1] It is often desirable that one member of the Recreation Commission be a member of the School Board, and one a member of the Park Board or Commission, if there be one.

appointed shall be appointed for such terms that the term of one member shall expire annually thereafter. Vacancies in such Commission occurring otherwise than by expiration of term shall be filled by the Mayor for the unexpired term.

2. Immediately after their appointment, they shall meet and organize by electing one of their members President and such other officers as may be necessary. The Commission shall have the power to adopt bylaws, rules, and regulations for the proper conduct of public recreation for the city.

3. The Recreation Commission shall provide, conduct, and supervise public playgrounds, athletic fields, recreation centers, and other recreation facilities and activities on any of the properties owned or controlled by the city, or on other properties with the consent of the owners and authorities thereof. It shall have the power to conduct any form of recreation or cultural activity that will employ the leisure time of the people in a constructive and wholesome manner.

4. The Recreation Commission shall have the power to appoint or designate some one to act as Superintendent who is trained and properly qualified for the work and such other personnel as the Commission deems proper.

5. Annually the Recreation Commission shall submit a budget to the city Governing Body for its approval. The Commission may also solicit or receive any gifts or bequests of money or other personal property or any donation to be applied, principal or income, for either temporary or permanent use for playgrounds or other recreational purposes.

6. The Recreation Commission shall make full and complete monthly and annual reports to the Governing Body of the city and other reports from time to time as requested.

7. All ordinances, resolutions, or parts thereof, in conflict with the provisions and intent of this Ordinance are hereby repealed.

PASSED AND ADOPTED this _____ day of _____ 19____
ATTEST:

LEGAL LIABILITY OF MUNICIPALITIES

In establishing new municipal functions local government authorities are concerned with their financial liability for injuries sustained by individuals because of the exercise of these functions. The knowledge or fear that they would be liable has furnished local authorities an excuse for not establishing a recreation program. In general, the extent of liability is based upon the decision of the state courts as to whether the conduct of recreation is a governmental or proprietary function.

Governmental vs. Proprietary Functions.—The following extract from a decision of the United States Supreme Court[1] is frequently quoted in discussing the difference between a proprietary and a governmental function:

The distinction between the municipality as an agent of the state for governmental purposes and as an organization to care for local needs in a private or proprietary capacity has been applied in various branches of the law of municipal corporations. The most numerous illustrations are found in cases involving the question of liability for negligent acts or omissions of its officers and agents.

[1] *City of Trenton v. State of New Jersey*, 262 U. S. 182, handed down in 1923.

. . . It has been held that municipalities are not liable for such acts and omissions in the exercise of the police power, or in the performance of such municipal faculties as the erection and maintenance of a city hall and courthouse, the protection of the city's inhabitants against disease and insanitary conditions, the care of the sick, the operation of fire departments, the inspection of steam boilers, the promotion of education, and the administration of public charities. On the other hand, they have been held liable when such acts or omissions occur in the exercise of the power to build and maintain bridges, streets and highways, and waterworks, construct sewers, collect refuse, and care for the dump where it is deposited. Recovery is denied where the act or omission occurs in the exercise of what are deemed to be governmental powers, and is permitted if it occurs in a proprietary capacity. The basis of the distinction is difficult to state, and there is no established rule for the determination of what belongs to the one or the other class. It originated with the courts.

A basic reason for relieving local governments of liability for those activities which are considered governmental is to remove a deterrent to the proper provision of such essential services. This is brought out in a decision of the Kentucky Court as follows:

The reason for exempting a municipality from damages for injuries inflicted in the performance of its governmental functions is one of public policy, to protect public funds and public property. Taxes are raised for certain specific governmental purposes; and, if they could be diverted to the payment of damage claims, the more important work of the government, which every municipality must perform regardless of its other relations, would be seriously impaired, if not totally destroyed.[1]

Park Decisions.—Many of the court decisions relating to this problem are generally considered "park" decisions, but they can reasonably be assumed to apply to all the more general types of park and recreation areas, structures, and activities. In Minnesota, for example, a playground is considered legally as a park area, the term "playground" being embraced in the term "park."[2] The Kansas Court outlined a broad definition of the term "park purposes"

. . . to include, a race track, a tourist camp, bridle trails, boating, bathing, refreshment and lunch stands, providing bathing suits, towels, and rooms for bathers, dressing pavilion, waiting room for streetcars, refreshment room and shelter for the public, grandstand, baseball diamond, race meets, tennis courts, croquet grounds, children's playgrounds, hotels, restaurants, museums, art galleries, zoological and botanical gardens, conservatories, and many other recreational and educational facilities.[3]

[1] *O'Connell v. Merchants and Police District Telephone Company (Ky.)*, 180 SW.845, L.R.A. 1915 D. 508.
[2] *Horn v. Minneapolis*, 152 Minn. 175.
[3] *Wichita v. Clapp et al.*, 125 Kan. 100 (1928), 263 Pac. 12.

"Nuisance" Decisions.—Court decisions in some states hold that even though the work is accepted by the courts to be a governmental function, there is a liability for maintenance of an attractive nuisance. The Wisconsin court has stated: "Negligence in the performance of a governmental function by the officers or agents of a municipality does not give a right of action, except that a municipality may not maintain a public nuisance even where it is performing a governmental duty."[1] Likewise, the Connecticut Supreme Court of Errors held:

Where a municipal corporation creates and maintains a nuisance, it is liable for damages to any person suffering special injury therefrom, irrespective of whether the misfeasance or non-feasance causing the nuisance also constituted negligence. This liability cannot be avoided on the ground that the municipality was exercising governmental functions or powers, even in jurisdictions where, as here, immunity is afforded from liability for negligence in the performance of such functions.[2]

These nuisance decisions have real significance to recreation authorities because they indicate that even in states where recreation is held to be a governmental function, reasonable precautions must be taken to protect the public. In the Connecticut case just cited, the authorities failed to do so in that they erected a diving board over shallow water at the municipal bathing beach without properly warning bathers of the danger.

RECREATION—A GOVERNMENTAL FUNCTION

In 1932 a study of court decisions in 36 states revealed that in 21 of them park and recreation service was considered a governmental function; in 14 it appeared to be proprietary, whereas one was doubtful.[3] Since that time several decisions of the higher courts have supported the claim of governmental status for parks and recreation. In one of these the U. S. Court of Appeals for the First Circuit, in an opinion handed down March 14, 1934, affirmed a decision of the Board of Tax Appeals that a park employee was exempt from Federal income tax. It stated:

Whatever may have been the early tendency of the courts in this respect, we think that the modern view, supported by the weight of authority, is that the creation and maintenance of public parks is a governmental function of the state and its exercise is essential to the health and general welfare of all the citizens of a state.[4]

---

[1] *Bernstein v. City of Milwaukee (Wis.)*, 149 N.W. 362.

[2] *Hoffman v. City of Bristol (Conn.)*, 155 Atl. 499.

[3] See *Is Park and Recreation Service a Governmental or Proprietary Function?* National Recreation Association, 1932.

[4] *Commissioner of Internal Revenue v. Jessie P. Sherman, Executrix*, October Term, 1933, No. 2863.

A decision handed down by the Supreme Court of North Carolina in 1936 is held to have far-reaching significance in establishing park and recreation service as an essential governmental function. In this case an attempt was made to prevent the city from putting into effect an ordinance authorizing the issuing of bonds for the acquisition of land for parks and playgrounds and for their development and also the levying of a tax to pay the principal and interest on the bonds. The court held that in enacting the ordinance the city was "performing a governmental function, useful and necessary in the preservation and promotion of the health, safety, and morals of the people," and that the issuance of the bonds and levying of the tax were a "necessary expense."[1]

How Fees and Charges Affect the Type of Function.—Practically all of the "governmental function" decisions include references to health, recreation, and other contributions which parks and playgrounds make to the public welfare, and some of them touch upon the public duty of the municipality to maintain such services. Many decisions refer to the free character of park services and to the assumption that no special benefit or pecuniary profit accrues to the municipal corporation or residents of the municipality. The growing tendency to charge for the use of park and recreation facilities therefore gives rise to the question as to the effect of such charges on the attitude of the courts in cases calling for a decision on the function of such services. The effects of charging have varied in different states. It would appear, however, that, in general, in the states where recreation is a governmental function incidental charges do not affect the nature of the function; that charges which result in operating profits tend to change the function; and that charges imposed for the purpose of making a profit change the function in practically all states.

Because of the difference in court decisions in different states and because of the changing attitude of the courts with reference to the recreation function and liability, it is important that each locality study its own liability in the light of decisions of its own state courts and of subsequent decisions in the higher courts. In states where liability exists, many cities have secured protection through insurance.

[1] *John L. Atkins v. City of Durham*, Spring Term, 1936, No. 762.

CHAPTER XXIX

MUNICIPAL ORGANIZATION FOR RECREATION

There is no one pattern by which local government meets its responsibility for recreation service, nor should there necessarily be one. Further experimentation with various methods may well be carried on before attempting to standardize the form of municipal organization for this relatively new and rapidly expanding function. The governmental machinery for providing recreation service in any locality must be worked out in the light of the local situation and of experience under similar conditions. The consideration of any plan for the organization of public recreation must take account of the following factors:

The existing legal powers of the municipality, park, or school district
The legal and extralegal relationships of the local school corporation to the local municipal corporation
The type of local municipal government
The ownership and control of properties available for recreation use
The attitude toward recreation of individuals in authoritative positions in the local government and school board
The ability of city or school district to finance recreation services adequately
The weight of local public opinion with reference to recreation and the local governmental agencies

However fine and idealistic a concept of local recreation administration might be developed, a recreation program can actually be achieved only if plans for its organization are worked out on a realistic basis.

SUGGESTED ORGANIZATION METHODS

Educators, park authorities, recreation workers, and leaders in organizations promoting good government have from time to time advanced "ideal" plans for the organization of municipal recreation work. These plans, designed to provide a logical, simple, uniform procedure, usually reflect the major interest of the individuals or groups advancing them. Educators have considered the organization of recreation from the point of view of the schools as the central controlling authority. Park officials have regarded the park department as the logical agency for providing and administering recreation service. Experts in municipal government have approached the problem with a view to the simplification of government and centralized control of all municipal services. Recreation workers, on the other hand, usually advocate the type of administration under which they have served or which in practice they have observed to be most successful.   In general, these various proposals have not been based on comprehensive studies of existing recreation services or on careful analyses of the factors which have resulted in success or failure in different communities.

For the reason stated at the beginning of the chapter, no single specific plan of organization for recreation is advocated here.   Examples of successful recreation administration may be found in cities where the program is under a board of education, a park department, a recreation commission, a separate recreation department without a commission, or under other public authorities.   Examples of mediocre and poor service may likewise be found under these various administrative agencies.   Any attempt to urge the general adoption of a uniform plan of organization should be the result of a more comprehensive study and more critical analysis of accumulated experience than have been made thus far.   It is worth while, however, to consider carefully the advantages and disadvantages commonly associated with the different forms of organization for municipal recreation service.

School Administration of Recreation.—Educators and other advocates of the board of education as the proper administrative authority advance the following arguments:

1. Play is largely educational and therefore should be controlled by those who administer the city's public education system.
2. The schools already have charge of a majority of the children during most of the day.
3. Parents and the public have confidence in the board of education and respect the work which it is doing for their children.
4. Large numbers of teachers with their knowledge of educational methods and experience in handling children are available for recreation leadership.   The character, education, and ideals of the teaching staff are generally on the high plane desirable for such service.
5. School authorities control buildings and grounds needed and suitable for community recreation use, and geographically located near centers of population. Increasingly, school facilities are being planned so as to render more adequate and effective recreation service for school and community groups.
6. Schools today are adopting curricula which involve the development of leisure-time interests, and the teaching of skills that have a definite recreation value.   The community program should be related to this work in the schools.
7. The schools already administer physical education, music, arts, nature, and other programs for school children—programs in which play is a motivating factor and which include many play activities.
8. Adult education programs offered by school systems include arts and crafts, music, discussion groups, dramatics, and other forms of recreation.

The following objections have been raised to the administration of the community recreation program by the school board:

1. Although play for children is largely educational, the recreation program includes activities for all age groups.   Recreation for adults is broadly educational in the sense that many other aspects of life are educational, but it embraces a much wider range of activities than are included in the term "education," used in the restricted sense of the formal school program or as commonly understood by school authorities.

2. The school board is not the only public agency that controls recreation facilities. Park, recreation, and other city departments provide facilities such as golf courses, picnic areas, and bathing beaches, in addition to the kinds also furnished by the schools.   School buildings and grounds are often unattractive, particularly the space made available for community use.   Besides, many school authorities have denied community groups access to these facilities.

3. In many communities, school budgets are inadequate to finance the formal educational program, to say nothing of a community recreation service.   Experience has shown that where recreation has been included in the school budget, it has been one of the first items to suffer in times of financial stress.

4. The school board thinks largely in terms of the use of the school plant, seldom operates the facilities of other departments, and conducts most of its activities on school property.   The legality of spending school funds for recreation on properties not controlled by the school board is open to question in some states.

5. School authorities tend to carry over classroom disciplines and methods into the recreation program.   This tendency discourages participation on the part of many children, nonschool youth, and adults.   A rather widespread unfavorable psychological attitude toward the schools handicaps their use for recreation in some communities.

6. Most school boards that have undertaken to provide a seasonal or year-round recreation service have placed such work under the department of physical education. This reflects a lack of understanding of the nature and scope of recreation, or an unwillingness to give it the place of importance that it deserves.

7. Many schoolteachers are successful recreation leaders, but the fact that a teacher is well trained for her primary job is not in itself evidence of ability as a recreation leader.   A different form of leadership and control than is usually found in the classroom is needed to encourage voluntary participation in recreation.

8. Many boards fail to accept their responsibility for making school facilities available for community recreation use and many administrators of individual schools assume a proprietary attitude toward their building which makes its use by community groups difficult if not impossible.

Park Administration of Recreation.—Advocates of the control of recreation by park boards or departments point out that

1. Most of the publicly owned properties suitable for recreation use are under the control of park departments.

2. Many of the facilities essential for organized recreation service, such as playgrounds, playfields, baseball diamonds, swimming pools, tennis courts, and golf courses, are on park property.

3. Recreation is the chief function of all park service.   The enjoyment of beauty, motoring for pleasure on the parkways, and watching the animals at the zoo are as truly forms of recreation as participation in organized activities.

4. The construction and maintenance of these properties have been and are important services of the park department.   Their operation can never be divorced success-

fully from these functions in which park authorities have had special training and experience.

5. The park department is accustomed to serving large numbers of people and maintaining relationships with the public.

6. Park budgets are comparatively large and therefore will generally provide funds for securing and operating needed outdoor recreation facilities.

Reasons why park authorities should not administer the municipal recreation program have been advanced as follows:

1. The work of the park department involves a wide variety of functions in which primary consideration is given to engineering and maintenance problems, such as the construction of roads, bridges, and other park facilities, the maintenance of street trees, flower gardens, and landscape properties, the operation of zoological and botanical gardens, refectories and similar facilities, in addition to furnishing areas and facilities for active recreation use. Organization for the human use of facilities usually is considered of secondary importance by park authorities.

2. Because of the major emphasis upon construction and maintenance rather than program service, there is a tendency for park authorities to underestimate the importance of outstanding recreation leadership ability.

3. In selecting an executive, park authorities generally seek a man trained in horticulture or engineering rather than in recreation and human relationships. Thus recreation is given a subordinate place in park administration.

4. Park boards, like school boards, are primarily concerned with the operation of properties under their control, rather than with the problem of serving the various recreation needs of all the people in the community.

5. Most park boards have inadequate facilities for indoor recreation, and yet in relatively few cities do they use school buildings. With notable exceptions, the park program consists largely of physical activities carried on out of doors.

6. In case of budget cuts, recreation leadership suffers to a greater extent than other park services.

Administration of Recreation as a Separate Function.—Many recreation leaders believe that recreation can best be administered as a distinct function of local government with a separate department preferably under a citizen board or commission. Those who favor this plan of organization believe that

1. Recreation is of sufficient importance to justify the establishment of a separate department concerned with recreation alone. It requires the continuous, intelligent guidance of a group of citizens chosen because of their ability and interest in recreation. The function of recreation cannot be served adequately by a department that has some other function as its major responsibility.

2. A recreation board that includes in its membership representatives of school, park, or other public departments which control recreation facilities, provides effective unified cooperative machinery for the harmonious use of all of these facilities. Providing cooperative use of city and school facilities is a major problem of organization. As the municipality and school district are separate local government corporations and as neither has administrative control over the other, cooperation between the two can best be secured through a judicially minded policy-making board on which both are represented, as well as the community at large.

3. More adequate funds can be secured and assured for recreation if it is not combined with some other service or subordinated to some other function.

4. A separate recreation board with a capable executive can best sense the needs and interests of the people, interpret recreation to the public, and conduct a program for all the people, using all available facilities, public and private.

5. Where recreation is a separate function it has been easier to secure volunteer service for it, thus increasing the returns from each tax dollar expended.

6. Recreation requires leadership and control by individuals primarily trained in problems of human engineering and concerned with human services. Without recreation boards or commissions recreation executives are directly responsible to municipal authorities whose training and interests are in other fields, particularly engineering and the techniques of government.

Those who object to the creation of a separate recreation board or department say that

1. It is unnecessary to add to the complexity of local governmental machinery by setting up another city department.

2. The creation of a new department results in duplication of work and unnecessary additional expense.

3. It is inadvisable to create a department with little, if any, property, to conduct a program involving use of properties maintained and controlled by other departments.

4. All boards and commissions should be eliminated from local government to provide for centralized responsibility and control on the part of the chief executive of the city.

5. The appointment of a recreation commission, even though it includes representatives of the park and school boards, is an indication that these boards have no major responsibility for the recreation function. By emphasizing their primary functions as park maintenance and formal education, respectively, it may defeat its purpose of securing better cooperation on the part of park and school boards in furnishing recreation service.

Some who object to the recreation board favor a separate recreation department with an executive responsible directly to the mayor, city manager, or other city authority. They claim that under such a department an advisory recreation commission can perform the significant lay services to which advocates of the administrative board attach such great importance.

Other Methods.—Other theories have been advanced from time to time but have received less widespread support. Certain city managers have suggested that recreation should be under the local department of public welfare.[1] Neither theory nor practice, however, justifies the opinion that the function of public recreation can be dealt with effectively along with public relief, unemployment insurance, old age pensions, the operation of hospitals and jails, and similar services. The *Recreation*

[1] *How to Reduce Municipal Expenditures*, International City Managers' Association, Chicago, Illinois.

Year Book for 1938 indicates that of a total of 935 public recreation authorities reporting, only 12 were departments of public welfare.

In 1931 a committee of the National Municipal League recommended that the schools should provide recreation for children of school age on a year-round basis and that the municipal government should be wholly responsible for providing recreation for the adult group.[1] There is no record of a city where the responsibility for furnishing recreation has been divided between the schools and the municipality solely on the basis of age. It has been found impracticable to make such a division, for fully half the use of park areas and facilities is by children, and adults represent a large part of the community use of school athletic fields and evening recreation centers.

HOW MUNICIPAL RECREATION IS CONDUCTED

Political considerations and unusual local conditions naturally play an important part in determining the form of organization under which recreation service is set up in a particular city, but a study of present practice throughout the country and of organization trends over a period of years furnishes some indication of the relative validity of the arguments presented in the preceding pages. Available figures for 1938 have been analyzed to determine how cities are using the various major forms of organization in utilizing local resources to furnish recreation for their people, and the extent of certain services rendered under each of these forms.

The findings summarized in the following tables are based entirely upon *Recreation Year Book*[2] reports submitted by 935 municipal agencies administering recreation in 1938. Some of these authorities operate only a single playground for a short summer season; others conduct a diversified program of activities the year round. Since authorities employing at least one full-time, year-round recreation worker furnish the significant and comprehensive community recreation programs of the country and provide more than half of the total services, separate figures have been compiled for them. The figures used in preparing the tables in this chapter relate only to recreation programs financed in whole or in part by local tax funds.

Managing Authorities.—The following summary indicates the total number of municipal agencies of various types administering recreation in 1938, and the number providing full-time, year-round recreation leadership:

---

[1] *Standards of Play and Recreation Administration*, prepared by Jay B. Nash for the National Municipal League, New York, 1931.

[2] *Recreation*, June, 1939.

Type of managing authority*	Number of authorities	
	Total	With year-round leadership
Authorities administering recreation as a separate function	315	163
Authorities administering recreation in conjunction with park service	278	95
Authorities administering recreation in conjunction with school services	172	29
Other municipal authorities	170	39
Total	935	326

* For brevity, in subsequent tables in this chapter, authorities administering recreation as a separate function are called "Separate recreation authorities"; authorities administering recreation in conjunction with park service are called "Park authorities"; authorities administering recreation in conjunction with school services are called "School authorities"; and all othei municipal authorities administering recreation service are called "Other municipal authorities."

The preceding table indicates that separate recreation boards and departments are most numerous, representing nearly 34 per cent of the total agencies. They furnish as many programs under year-round leadership as all other types of authorities combined. More than half of the separate recreation authorities furnish year-round service; relatively few of the school and "other" authorities employ full-time recreation leaders.

By Regions.—An analysis of the managing authorities by regions reveals that 60 per cent are in the New England, Middle Atlantic, and East North Central States. Less than 15 per cent are in the three Southern districts. Park authorities lead in New England and the Central regions; in the others, separate recreation authorities are most numerous. The schools are relatively more prominent in the Middle Atlantic states than elsewhere. The failure of school boards in Southern states to accept responsibility for recreation is no doubt due primarily to the inadequacy of their educational budgets. This situation should be taken into consideration in judging any general proposal that all community recreation should be placed under the management of school authorities.

Trends in Organization.—Important as it is to know how cities are now conducting their municipal recreation service, it is also of interest to observe trends in the forms of local recreation organization. In 1928 for the first time, agencies submitting *Recreation Year Book* reports were classified in a way that makes possible comparisons with present conditions. The following table indicates the number of authorities of the four major types administering recreation in 1928 and in 1938, and the number of each with full-time, year-round leadership.

AGENCIES ADMINISTERING RECREATION

Type of managing authority	Total				With full-time leadership			
	Number		Percentage		Number		Percentage	
	1928	1938	1928	1938	1928	1938	1928	1938
Separate recreation authorities....	209	315	30	34	116	163	48	50
Park authorities.................	231	278	33	30	74	95	30	29
School authorities...............	158	172	23	18	25	29	10	9
Other municipal authorities.......	99	170	14	18	30	39	12	12
Totals......................	697	935	100	100	245	326	100	100

The preceding table indicates that during the decade ending with 1938 the park and school authorities did not keep pace with the separate recreation departments and that many "other" municipal authorities primarily responsible for some other function initiated recreation as an incidental or secondary service. The figures seem to indicate that a majority of the cities which established recreation programs on a year-round basis during this decade adopted the separate recreation department as the form of organization under which to administer them.

This table supports the findings in two previous analyses of trends in local governmental control of year-round recreation, one covering the period 1923 to 1933 and the other covering the period of 1928 to 1936.[1] These analyses showed that cities were increasingly considering year-round recreation service as a distinct municipal function and for its administration were establishing separate recreation departments, in most cases under a recreation board or commission. This tendency, which was especially marked previous to 1929, has been less evident during the depression, when comparatively few cities have established year-round recreation programs.

A COMPARISON OF SERVICES RENDERED BY DIFFERENT AUTHORITIES

Mere numbers do not afford a valid basis for judging the extent of the services rendered by managing authorities of different types. While the recreation service of some agencies consists merely of conducting a single playground or operating an outdoor swimming pool for a short summer season, others provide a diversified program for the entire community throughout the year. Some indication of the extent of the services rendered by the four types of managing authorities has been

[1] See *Recent Trends in Local Government of Year-round Recreation*, National Recreation Association, 1938.

obtained from an analysis of their leadership and of the facilities which they control and operate.   Complete figures concerning their facilities, services, and leadership are not available but the study based upon *Recreation Year Book* reports for 1938 provides some illuminating data. Only a few of the most significant findings can be recorded here.

Facilities.—Park and recreation departments operate a large percentage of all municipal recreation facilities.   Park departments lead in the number of special recreation buildings, baseball diamonds, swimming pools, tennis courts, beaches, and golf courses.   Recreation departments conduct more than half of the indoor centers other than special recreation buildings and more playgrounds than any other authority.   School officials operate 44 per cent of the indoor swimming pools and also conduct many playgrounds and indoor centers.

Because special problems in governmental organization arise in large metropolitan centers, a special study was made of the facilities in the ten largest cities.   This study revealed that nearly half of the playgrounds and indoor pools conducted under school leadership are in those cities, as well as approximately one-third of the playgrounds, baseball diamonds, and tennis courts under park auspices.   In the smaller cities more than half of all the year-round playgrounds and other indoor centers are under recreation department leadership.

It should be pointed out that full credit for furnishing recreation service does not belong entirely to the agency operating the facilities. In many instances the properties used are owned by another department which may also furnish maintenance costs.   A study of school facilities used for community recreation and reported in the 1937 *Recreation Year Book* revealed the fact that nearly 43 per cent of all the playgrounds reported under leadership that year were on school property.   On the other hand, only 24 per cent of the playgrounds were conducted under school auspices.   Seven out of eight indoor swimming pools were in schools but only 39 per cent were open under school auspices.   It is significant that less than half of the school outdoor facilities and less than one-fourth of the school buildings used for community recreation were conducted under school auspices.   This suggests that to a large degree school properties are made available for community use only where some other department undertakes to furnish the necessary leadership.

Leadership.—School departments are shown to employ the largest number of leaders but nearly half of them are in the ten largest cities and only one out of twenty-two is a full-time year-round recreation worker.   Park departments lead in the number of full-time workers but 65 per cent of them are employed in the large cities.   On the other hand, four out of five of the full-time leaders employed by separate recreation authorities are serving in the smaller cities.   In fact, nearly half of all the leaders working on a full-time, year-round basis in the smaller cities are employed by separate recreation departments.

SERVICES OF YEAR-ROUND MUNICIPAL RECREATION AGENCIES

In this volume it has been emphasized repeatedly that year-round leadership is essential to an adequate recreation program. Any consideration of the organization of municipal recreation should therefore take into account the part which agencies employing full-time year-round workers play in the total national picture. An indication of what 304 year-round municipal agencies accomplished in 1938 as compared with the total service reported by all agencies, numbering 1,107, is given in the following table. The figures in the column headed "All agencies" include those appearing in the last column.

WORK OF RECREATION AUTHORITIES, 1938

	All agencies	Agencies with full-time year-round workers
Number of playgrounds...........	9,712	6,047
Number of recreation buildings....	1,553	1,218
Number of indoor centers.........	4,059	2,531
Number of employed leaders.......	23,975	16,694
Amount spent for leadership*......	$7,884,882	$6,517,239
Number of volunteers.............	24,978	16,842

* Expenditures for leadership alone are used because they are the only available expenditure figures reliable for comparative purposes.

Even though the figures concerning the "year-round" recreation agencies are incomplete, the table shows that they operate a large percentage of the indoor and outdoor centers under leadership, employ two-thirds of the leaders, and spend 83 per cent of the money paid for leadership. This being the case, it may be well at this point to refer to the table on page 434 indicating the extent to which the four types of managing authorities employ full-time, year-round leadership. The willingness of authorities of different types to employ leaders on this basis is a factor to be considered in appraising forms of municipal recreation organization.

COOPERATION

The assertion has sometimes been made that the lack of uniformity in methods of organizing local recreation service has resulted in confusion, conflicts over jurisdiction, overlapping programs, and duplication of areas and facilities. Unquestionably, in cities where recreation properties are owned and recreation programs are provided by two or more agencies genuine cooperation between the authorities is essential for the best results. A study conducted by the National Recreation Association in 1937 to determine the nature and extent of cooperative relationships in cities with public agencies maintaining year-round recreation service revealed[1] that in a majority of these cities considerable cooperation has already been achieved. Although the possibilities of cooperative action have not been fully realized there is much more cooperation than duplication and competition between the agencies in the cities reporting.

The need for more consultation between city and school authorities on the acquisition of new areas and buildings to be used for recreation is clearly indicated but cooperation in the use of facilities once acquired is much more prevalent. Of the 135 nonschool agencies reporting on the use of school facilities in their programs, 80 per cent use facilities in school buildings and 85 per cent use outdoor school areas. Outdoor park facilities are used by 85 per cent of the 127 nonpark agencies which reported, but their use of park indoor facilities is much less common. The use of facilities of other departments is most widespread in the case of separate recreation departments, especially recreation boards. Examples of specific cooperation between city recreation agencies and the schools are given in Chaps. XI and XXXIV.

GENERAL ORGANIZATION PRINCIPLES

Experience indicates that, regardless of the form of organization which a city adopts for handling its recreation service, the following principles should be followed:

1. All publicly owned property suitable for recreation should be made available for the use of the department responsible for conducting the program, under conditions worked out between the recreation authority and the departments controlling the property.

2. A commission, committee, or some other organized group of citizens should be appointed to give continuous and collective thought to the leisure-time problems of the entire city and to work out effective means of solving them. It is advisable for both the school board and the park board to have representation on this group, because the use of school and park property is so essential to a successful recreation program. Making the terms of office of the members overlap, so that not more than one or two expire each year, facilitates continuity of planning.

3. A full-time trained recreation executive should be employed to direct the program. This task will require all of his time and attention. Rarely can an executive do full justice to community recreation work if he must give part of his time to some other position.

---

[1] See *The Organization of Municipal Recreation Programs*, National Recreation Association, 1938.

4. A definite segregated recreation budget is generally desirable. Many cities have voted a mill tax for recreation purposes, thus assuring the availability of a comparatively definite amount of money each year. In some states, cities may vote that a certain percentage of their park or school budget shall be used for recreation.

5. The program should serve all the recreation interests of the people, include physical activities, music, drama, arts and crafts, nature activities and social recreation, and provide for all groups without restriction as to race, religion, age, or sex.

6. Definite provision should be made for cooperative planning in the acquisition of new recreation areas and facilities, particularly between the city and schools.

7. Finally, vital, intelligent, efficient, progressive service of the public function, *recreation*, should be the primary consideration rather than control of property or administrative convenience. These latter are incidental and are subject to adjustment; the former is essential to successful accomplishment of the purpose. The important thing in the organization of public recreation is not so much the exact form of administration—in the last analysis local conditions must determine which is the best agency to administer the system—but the degree of cooperation which the governing body and the superintendent of recreation can secure from all city departments having facilities that should be utilized. Problems based on the joint use and control of facilities are bound to arise under any form of centralized administrative control yet devised. Wholehearted cooperation between the different departments is essential to success regardless of the form adopted; with such cooperation and under competent leadership, success is practically assured.

CHAPTER XXX

ORGANIZATION OF THE RECREATION DEPARTMENT

An organization is a living and dynamic entity. Each activity is born, has its periods of experimental development, of vigorous and stable activity, and, in some cases, of decline . . . It will therefore be found that not all of the activities of any government may be universally departmentalized neatly on the basis of a single universal plan.[1]

This quotation is especially applicable to the pioneering function of municipal recreation. It merits consideration in determining the specific authority under which to administer recreation in a city and also in developing an organization to carry out the function. Just as for good reason different cities have entrusted recreation to different agencies in the local government, so the methods of departmental organization used by these agencies vary from city to city.

In many respects the same organization principles apply equally to school, park, and separate recreation departments. Both park and school authorities, however, in organizing their recreation service are somewhat influenced by other considerations and functions to which recreation is often subordinated. For this reason, the organization of the separate recreation department, which is concerned exclusively or primarily with the function of recreation, will receive major attention in this chapter.

Further justification for devoting special attention to separate recreation departments is the fact that in 1938 they represented half of all the public agencies employing full-time recreation leadership. The importance of this department as the outstanding agency furnishing community-wide, year-round recreation is further indicated by the fact that whereas a number of the other authorities furnish a restricted recreation service most separate recreation departments offer a comprehensive program.

The powers and functions of a municipal recreation agency, some of which were indicated in Chap. XXVIII, depend upon state and local legislation. The nature and scope of the organization required to serve the purpose of the legislation depend largely upon the functions to be carried out. If the legislation merely provides for the conducting of school playgrounds or indoor centers or the furnishing of facilities for

[1] Luther Gulick and L. Urwick, *Papers on the Science of Administration*, Institute of Public Administration, 1937.

golf or swimming, a complex organization is not necessary. On the other hand, the broad powers granted under an enabling act call for a department with a comprehensive plan.

THE RECREATION BOARD OR COMMISSION

A recreation board or commission is the managing authority in the case of most separate recreation departments. Usually appointed by the mayor, in some instances with the council's approval, the official recreation board has full responsibility for the operation of the department. Advisory boards have been appointed in a number of cities, in most instances where the recreation executive is directly responsible to a city manager, but they have no direct authority and must not be confused with the official boards discussed here. Boards of five members are most numerous, although many have seven members, whose terms generally overlap and run for five years, seldom for a longer period. In most cities one or more members are women and sometimes the school board and the park board or city council are represented. Almost without exception, members receive no compensation for their services.

Functions of the Recreation Board.—In general the board is responsible for determining every fundamental policy of the department not otherwise prescribed. Among the essential recognized functions of the recreation board, in the opinion of a chairman, are the following:

The interpretation of the community recreation program to public officials and to the general citizenship in terms of adequate moral and financial support

The maintenance of high standards in recreation leadership and in quality of program service

The selection of the recreation executive or superintendent and the defining of the scope of his powers and duties

The appointment, upon recommendation of the recreation executive, of all employees, and the determination of their functions and duties

The determination and establishment of the general policies to be followed in carrying out the purpose for which the department was established

The consideration of and passing judgment upon the recommendations coming from any source outside the department, especially if such suggestions involve matters of general policy

Approval of the budget and the securing of the required funds

The authorization of expenditures within the budget granted and the careful examination of expenditures

A strict accounting to the people of the community through the proper fiscal authorities of the use of all funds

A full report to the public of all the activities of the department during the year[1]

[1] Clyde Doyle, "The Duties of a Recreation Board Member," *Recreation*, April, 1937, p. 12.

To this list might be added the responsibility for considering the future recreation needs of the city in terms of programs, areas, facilities, and services, and for developing plans to meet these needs.

Service Rendered by Board Members.—Advocates of the recreation board as the best form of organization for administering recreation in a locality feel that board members can accomplish certain things more effectively than professional workers. The extent to which the Recreation Commission in one city is carrying out its functions and serving the interests of the people is described as follows by the chairman:

The Commission takes its work seriously. The regularity of attendance at the weekly meetings has been unusual; members are thoroughly familiar with every one of the properties controlled by the Department; financial reports and preliminary budgets are taken home and studied; program plans of the executive and staff are submitted and discussed; the life-long acquaintance of the members of the Commission with the city and its growth is brought to the aid of the directors; the director of recreation is supported in his plans and activities after full understanding and approval by the Commission. Attendance by members at activities of the Department is frequent. These and other duties which go to make up an interested and business like administration are taken for granted.

The members of the Commission, however, have never felt that their duties ended there. They have studied the needs of their city for additional facilities and program items. They have kept themselves informed of the progress of the national movement for a wise use of leisure time, and they know much of the philosophy of the movement. They have also considered it their function to interpret the movement as occasions have arisen.

By joint meetings with other public boards, by appearances before city council committees, by talks at civic meetings, by interviews in newspapers, and by individual conversations, the Commission, as a body and through its individual members, has shown its conviction of the vital importance of recreation to the city. Especially during the past three years has it answered those few critics who would have cut its support or curbed its activities. It has in general relieved the employed staff from the burden of meeting such criticism and left their full energies for the increased program among the unemployed and the growing variety of activities for all groups.

The acceptance of this twofold responsibility by the Commission, first, for an efficient administration, and second, for an intelligent interpretation, is largely responsible for the place recreation now holds in Cincinnati as an accepted and necessary function of government on a par with any other department.[1]

Board Organization.—In order to function effectively, the board is formally organized and rules and regulations governing its procedure are adopted. They specify the officers to be elected and their duties, the time of regular meetings, the order of business at meetings, and the com-

---

[1] *Responsibility of Members of the Public Recreation Commission in Cincinnati,* **Bulletin** 2870, National Recreation Association, April, 1933.

mittees to be appointed. Rules are also adopted relative to the budget, the handling of finances, and the preparation of reports. Regular meetings as a rule are held at least monthly. Practices differ as to the appointment of committees, but many boards favor the use of committees because they give board members specific responsibilities, expedite the handling of board business, and save time at meetings. Typical of the committees are the following: Finance, Personnel, Properties, and Relationships. Sometimes a member of the board serves as secretary, although this duty may be assigned to the executive or another employee.

The rules and regulations adopted by the board are in a sense the constitution and bylaws under which the department is operated, and determine the relationships and respective responsibilities of the board and the executive who is employed to administer the department. In the well-organized department the board members recognize that their job is to determine policies, not to administer them. They do not assume the functions of the executive by attempting to dictate how details shall be carried out, by interfering with employment procedures, or by dealing directly in an executive capacity with subordinate workers. A sound principle in board-executive relationships is for the board to give the executive a free hand, within the limits of the policies laid down by it, to organize and carry on the affairs of the department as long as his efforts produce the results desired and meet with the general approval of the public.

THE RECREATION EXECUTIVE

The executive officer of the department, usually called the superintendent of recreation, has the duty of carrying out the policies of the board and of administering the work of the department in accordance with these policies. He also serves as technical adviser to the board, in which capacity he submits plans, furnishes data, and recommends policies for their consideration and action. Within the limitations of these major functions his responsibilities and activities in the field of recreation are restricted only by his vision and resourcefulness.

Administrative Duties.—The most important duties and responsibilities of the executive in his function of administrative officer, many of which are delegated to, or shared with, his assistants, may be grouped as follows:

Staff.—To organize, train, and supervise the staff, including volunteers, assign duties, and to maintain good relationships between the workers.

Program.—To select or approve the activities to be carried on, the special features to be presented, the services to be provided, and the new projects to be initiated, and to supervise the organization and conduct of the entire program.

Finance.—To direct the expenditure of department funds in accordance with budget appropriations, to prepare annual estimate of the department's financial needs, and to supervise the keeping of complete records of receipts and expenditures.

Areas and Facilities.—To arrange for proper maintenance and operation of the areas and facilities under the control of the department, to determine the season during which they are to be open, and to recommend new improvements or extensions of the recreation system.

Records and Reports.—To keep careful and complete records of department activities and services, personnel, and property, and to prepare regular reports.

Research.—To conduct studies of local conditions and needs affecting recreation in the city, to check the effectiveness of the various department services, and to keep informed as to developments in the recreation field.

Publicity and Relationships.—To interpret recreation to board members and the general public, to arrange for publicity, to keep in close touch with other city officials and local agencies concerned with recreation, to participate in city organizations and activities in which recreation has a vital interest, and to organize neighborhood or city-wide recreation councils or other groups.

The relative time and attention which executives spend on these varied functions differ widely, depending upon the type of managing authority which they serve, the extent of the facilities controlled, the scope of the program, the number and ability of supervisors, and other factors. In a small city where the executive must perform many of the duties himself rather than delegate them to assistants, he usually spends much time on the supervision of workers and programs, whereas in a large city he is free to devote more attention to research, interpretation, and relationships.

The Executive and the Board.—Perhaps the most important of all the executive's relationships are those with the members of his board, to whom he is directly responsible. Much of the success of the department depends upon his ability to take full advantage of their knowledge, ability, and interest in recreation. He treats the members impartially and with respect, and arranges for each one to have some special responsibility. He keeps the members informed as to the work of the department, stimulates discussion of recreation problems, suggests to them plans for future action, encourages expression of their own opinions, sends them literature on the recreation movement, and encourages them to attend meetings at which recreation is to be discussed. The wise executive always welcomes fair and honest criticisms of his plans and recommendations because the board can often evaluate their strong and weak points and see them more nearly as they will appear to the community. Once he has convinced the board of the soundness of his proposals, he can count on their wholehearted support against public criticism. It is highly important that in advance of board meetings the executive send each member an agenda indicating in some detail the specific items which are to be presented or considered at the meeting.

OTHER MANAGING AUTHORITIES

The preceding discussion of the organization of the recreation board and its relation to the executive applies only to a limited extent in the case of other forms of recreation organization. The executive of a separate recreation department without a board has much the same duties as previously indicated, but his responsibility is directly to a mayor, city council, city manager, or other official. The policies and methods to be followed by the executive in administering his department are subject to this official's approval. It is obvious that some of the services rendered by recreation board members cannot be expected from city employees or other public officials.

The situation is still different in the case of the recreation executive who is a part of a school or park organization. He is directly responsible to the superintendent of schools or of parks and does not have direct relations with the school or park board. Major recommendations submitted by the recreation executive to his superior may be passed on for consideration to the board, who approve all policies relative to recreation as well as other activities of their department. In this way some of the benefits of the recreation board are attained under a school or park board, particularly where a committee of school or park board members is appointed to pay special attention to recreation problems or to deal directly with the recreation executive. Such committees exist in Hartford and Sioux City, the recreation services of which were described in Chap. XXVII.

DEPARTMENTAL ORGANIZATION

Organizing the recreation department staff and functions so as to secure the maximum results from available personnel, funds, and facilities is one of the major tasks of the recreation executive. A relatively simple problem in the small community, it increases in complexity and importance with the size of the city and the comprehensiveness of the recreation system. In order to secure effective operation, organization is necessary but most important is "the development of the desire and will to work together for a purpose." Obviously this is most easily attained when the department is so organized as definitely to fix responsibility, prevent overlapping of authority, and facilitate supervision and the smooth and effective operation of every part of the program.

There is no uniformity in the organization of recreation departments, even under the same type of managing authority, but all organization plans are designed to facilitate the performance of their common functions. Regardless of the specific arrangements for handling these functions, they usually provide the following major divisions of work:

Recreation Activities and Program Services.—This division, the largest and most important, furnishes most of the activities and programs carried on under leadership. It is responsible for the operation of playgrounds, recreation buildings, and other indoor centers, for special activities such as athletics, music, nature, crafts, and hobbies, for community and holiday celebrations, and special services to industry and institutions.

Special Recreation Facilities.—The work of this division consists of operating golf courses, bathing beaches, boating centers, stadiums, camps, and other major facilities. Its function of assuring the maximum satisfactory public use of these facilities calls primarily for managerial, rather than activity leadership, ability.

Business and Accounting.—This division involves two primary functions. One is keeping the financial records and accounts; the other handling the many business details and keeping personnel, property, service, and other departmental records.

Construction and Maintenance.—The planning, construction, and maintenance of the areas, facilities, and equipment controlled or used by the department is the special responsibility of this division.

It is obvious that the first two divisions furnish the primary, essential services for which the department is established. The other two divisions serve secondary functions which are, however, necessary to its effective operation. In considering the specific forms of departmental organization, major emphasis will be given to the methods devised for conducting the work of the two primary divisions. The executive is responsible for the work of all four divisions.

Division of Recreation Activities.—This division is called by different names and sometimes its functions are divided between two or more divisions. In smaller cities the superintendent supervises it directly, often with the help of an assistant of the opposite sex. In large cities the worker in charge of the division, because of its importance, is sometimes given the title of assistant superintendent. The personnel assigned to this division include general supervisors, supervisors of special activities, directors, play leaders, and specialists, whose duties were described in Chap. VII. Widely different methods are used in organizing the staff of the activities division.

The work of this division may be divided roughly into three functions, which are closely interrelated. One consists of the operation of playgrounds and indoor facilities where diversified programs are carried on more or less continuously under the leadership of directors, play leaders, and specialists. Another involves the promotion of special program features—music, drama, athletics—on a city-wide basis, including the organization of groups and the conduct of special events which often necessitate the use of playgrounds and indoor centers. The third furnishes special service to community agencies and groups, such as homes, industries, and institutions. This function of the division is performed largely by supervisors of special activities and specialists.

The Organization of Playgrounds and Indoor Centers.—As pointed out in Chap. XVII, the superintendent of recreation often personally supervises the playground and center directors, but in a large city a special supervisor of playgrounds is usually employed, at least during the summer months, to take charge of the entire playground program and its operation. In other cases a supervisor of playgrounds and centers, employed on a year-round basis, performs this important function. In cities where it is impossible for a single supervisor to keep in close touch with playground and center operations, district organization is proving effective. The city is divided into districts each of which is placed in charge of a general supervisor to whom all playground and indoor center workers in the area are made responsible. A modification of this plan is in effect in a few cities where the chief director of a year-round center in each district is given general responsibility for the work at the other playgrounds and centers in the area.

In organizing the staff, little difficulty is experienced in the case of so-called "line" workers responsible for the operation of playgrounds and centers. It is relatively simple to fix the responsibility and authority of such workers, who comprise the largest leadership group. The flow of authority is from the superintendent to the supervisor of playgrounds or district supervisor, to the playground or center director, and finally to his assistants, the play leaders and special instructors. Each employee is responsible to just one official in the rank above his own, thus minimizing problems as to jurisdictional authority. Each playground or indoor center unit is in the charge of one person, the director, who has full authority and responsibility for its operation. All other workers at the playground or center are responsible to the director for the work which they perform there, including the specialist who comes for one or more periods weekly to conduct a class, club, or special activity and the maintenance workers, even though they are attached to another division.

The Organization of Special Activities and Services.—In the small city where only a few workers are employed to direct or conduct special activities, the recreation superintendent or supervisor of playgrounds can easily work out a plan by which their service is effectively related to that of the other workers. A supervisor of crafts, for example, employed for only the summer months, outlines a program which is approved by the executive and is carried out primarily through activity periods at the various playgrounds. He is responsible to the superintendent for the work done but while at a particular playground is generally subject to the jurisdiction of the director.

Some of the difficulties encountered in organizing the special activities staff in large cities are due to the fact that many of its workers combine both "line" and "staff" functions.   In carrying out strictly supervisory duties such as training workers, demonstrating leadership methods and activities, planning special projects, and advising on the selection of materials, supervisors of special activities serve as "staff" workers.   As such they have no administrative authority.   When, however, these workers are directly responsible for the work of specialists or when they themselves conduct activities at playgrounds or centers or organize city-wide events in which they have the assistance of directors and play leaders, they are serving as "line" workers.

In general, the responsibilities of this group of workers are handled in one of two ways.   In several cities with a well-trained, year-round staff, each supervisor of special activities serves primarily as an adviser, teacher, and planner.   He is directly responsible to the superintendent or the head of the activities division and his suggestions relative to the program are put into effect chiefly by the "line" workers—the general supervisors, directors, and leaders, over whom he has no authority. In addition, the special supervisor may personally direct special program features such as a municipal orchestra, drama tournament, crafts workshop, or municipal sports program or may be directly responsible for the workers who conduct them.   Under this arrangement, much of the actual work in the fields of music, drama, nature, and other special fields is performed by the regular workers at the playgrounds and centers, who benefit from the technical advice and guidance of the supervisors of special activities but are not directly responsible to them.   This plan encourages the all-round development of district supervisors and of playground and center directors by placing upon them responsibility for the organization and promotion of special activities, with the advice and technical assistance of the supervisors in the special fields.

In other cities the special supervisors are given more authority and freedom in promoting their particular activity.   There is consequently a tendency for them to build up independent subdivisions devoted to the specific activities under their control.   They have a group of subordinate workers whom they assign for service at playgrounds and centers or to help with community-wide activities and they initiate projects which call for the cooperation of playground directors, who are also urged to include specific activities in their programs.   As a result, directors are likely to be subject to pressure from several special supervisors each of whom is primarily concerned about the promotion and success of his particular activity.

In addition to the supervisors of special activities previously mentioned, some large departments employ one or more persons who are in charge of a special program feature such as industrial recreation or service to institutions.   These workers, like the supervisors of special activities, are usually responsible directly to the superintendent or to the head of the activities division.   They may call upon the special supervisors to help with their programs and may arrange with the general or district supervisors for the use of playground and indoor center facilities.

Trends in Supervision.—In spite of the wide variation in the methods of supervising the activities division and its program, a few trends in current practice may be noted, especially in large cities.   One is the tendency to divide the city into geographical divisions or districts and, as previously mentioned, to assign a district supervisor in charge of each. This worker acts for the superintendent in all matters relating to personnel, program, equipment, or interpretation of policies that may arise within the district.   In addition, his duties include the general promotion of recreation and the fostering of community relationships throughout the district.   Under this plan there is a tendency to make the supervisors of special activities primarily "staff" workers who function chiefly through the general supervisors, directors, and other line workers.   One of the duties of the district supervisor is to see that the playground and center directors cooperate with the special supervisors in carrying on activities in their respective fields.

Special supervisors in most cities still have specific titles indicating a responsibility for a specific field such as drama or athletics, but there is some indication of a tendency away from too much specialization in functions and titles.   Instead, workers with exceptional training and experience are assigned responsibility for duties usually assumed by special supervisors, but they are also used for other tasks.   For example, instead of creating the position of supervisor of music, a qualified worker is assigned to perform this function but is also called upon to help with other projects.   Such a plan makes for flexibility, avoids a top-heavy overspecialized staff, and permits a more effective use of the special supervisory workers.

An adaptation of the two preceding plans is for supervisors to give half of their time to some particular phase of the program and the other half to general supervision.[1]   In this way the ability of the worker in a particular field is utilized, and by serving as a district supervisor, he gains an understanding of, and contact with, the entire program.   Somewhat similar is the arrangement whereby one of the supervisors responsible for a special activity is also assigned to help with home play, industrial recreation, or some other program feature.   In small cities where it is not practicable to have a large supervisory staff, it is common for a single supervisor to care for two or more different parts of the program.

Division of Special Recreation Facilities.—This division includes the personnel responsible for the operation of golf courses, stadiums,

[1] See the Milwaukee organization chart on p. 456.

swimming pools, and other special facilities. Recreation departments under school auspices seldom have such a division because these facilities are not generally provided by the authorities. In many park departments its functions are a responsibility of the recreation division, although sometimes a special division is created to administer them. Most separate recreation departments operate one or more of these facilities but in practice these are not generally administered under the supervision of a single divisional head. As a rule the managers of the camps, golf courses, and swimming pools report directly to the superintendent, but where there are several facilities of one kind there may be a special supervisor for this particular type, such as a supervisor of camps, golf, or aquatics.

Since these special operating units are becoming more varied and numerous, since there are many common problems of operation, and since most of these facilities involve the collection of fees, it seems advisable to consider setting up a separate division for all of them, in charge of a supervisor responsible to the superintendent. In any case, it is commonly agreed that each major facility should have a manager who is in complete charge of the personnel required for its operation and maintenance. Close cooperation is required with the maintenance division which assigns caretaking personnel for work at the facilities and with the accounting division to which are submitted financial and service reports of the division's operations.

Division of Business and Accounting.—In a small department the work of this division may be done by a bookkeeper with the assistance of a stenographer-clerk who also answers the telephone and serves as secretary to the superintendent. In a large system, however, a number of workers are required. In addition to an accountant, chief clerk, typists, and clerical assistants, the employees of this division include the telephone operator, reception room clerk, and in some instances the workers in charge of permits and the supply room. Where the size of the staff warrants, an office manager is employed. A worker whose duty it is to keep the official records and handle the correspondence of the board is sometimes employed as secretary to the board. In a few cities workers in this division are assigned as cashiers at golf courses or pools, but when this is done, these workers should report directly to the director or manager who is responsible for seeing that they perform the duties expected of them.

Division of Construction and Maintenance.—Recreation departments which own or control recreation areas and facilities require a group of workers to develop them and keep them in good condition. In some instances these workers maintain not only the department's own properties but also park and school areas and facilities on which it conducts activities. Separate recreation departments conducting a program involving the use of park and school areas only do not require a construction and maintenance division, the functions of which are performed by the park and school authorities. In cities where the recreation program is under park or school auspices, maintenance is usually provided by the regular park or school maintenance organization.

The staff of this division depends upon the nature and extent of the recreation system and also upon the degree to which it is expanding. A department that is acquiring new areas and developing new facilities requires a planning, engineering, and construction staff if it is to design and develop the properties with its own workers. On the other hand, if the system is comparatively adequate to the city's needs, the task of the division is primarily one of maintenance. In either case a supervisor, engineer, or foreman is necessary, and his assistants will include repair and maintenance mechanics, gardeners, caretakers, and laborers. Specialists such as filter operators and greenkeepers may be added as required. One or more clerical workers to keep the essential records of work projects, labor, and materials are needed where the volume of work demands such personnel.

Part of the employees in this division will work at or out of the department's storehouse and workshops; others will be assigned for regular duty at the various areas and facilities. At each major recreation area and at playgrounds and playfields with recreation buildings, the full-time service of at least one caretaker-janitor is required. Sometimes a worker cares for the maintenance of two or more playgrounds in the same district. Traveling maintenance crews, each under a foreman, have proved economical and satisfactory. They are assigned to a group of areas in a district and either care for all upkeep and repairs or supplement the services of the maintenance workers regularly assigned to the areas. Caretakers, like greenkeepers, filter operators, and other maintenance workers, when assigned to a particular area or facility, report directly to the director or manager in charge.

DEPARTMENTAL ORGANIZATION IN SEVERAL CITIES

A study of the ways in which recreation departments are actually organized is helpful in considering the various problems involved in carrying on the work of a department. In the following pages are presented charts illustrating various organization methods used by different types of managing authorities in several cities. It is well to remember that the success or failure of specific methods depends more upon the "will to work together" than upon the method itself. What is more, if a recreation department does not make some changes in its organization plan over a period of years, in all probability it is not keeping abreast of

the times.   In progressive departments adjustments are made from
year to year as experience reveals the strength or weakness of various
units or relationships and as new activities and services are added to
the program.

Austin, Texas.—The Recreation Department in this city of 80,000
people is administered by a superintendent of recreation who is directly
responsible to the city manager.   There is no park department in Austin,
the parks of the city being maintained and operated by the Recreation
Department.   An advisory park and recreation board of eleven members
appointed by the mayor assists the city officials in planning and developing the recreation program.   The personnel of the department in 1939
consisted of the following year-round staff, in addition to caretakers and
laborers:

Superintendent	Manager of pools
Athletic director	Negro director
Two supervisors	Manager of golf course
Secretary	Foremen
Assistant athletic director	

Supplementing these workers was a corps of part-time and seasonal
playground leaders, athletic officials, and lifeguards as well as maintenance employees.   Because the department is responsible for park
maintenance, a larger percentage of its workers consists of nonleadership
personnel than is usually the case.

As the accompanying chart indicates, in 1939 there were no "staff"
workers.   All of the supervisory personnel assisting the superintendent
were directly responsible for the operation of major facilities or program
features.   In Austin most of the organized activities with the exception
of athletics are conducted under the joint direction of two supervisors,
one a man, the other a woman, but the titles indicate that the man is in
charge and that the woman gives special attention to women's and girls'
activities.   There is a supervisor of athletics who also serves in the
capacity of administrative assistant to the superintendent.

In a small city like Austin there is no need for district supervisors.
All supervisors and managers are directly responsible to the executive, an
arrangement which makes for centralized authority and responsibility.
The chart on page 453 indicates the division of functions and the services
for which the more important workers are responsible.

Detroit, Michigan.—The Department of Parks and Recreation in
Detroit was established in 1940 by a referendum authorizing the consolidation of the Department of Parks and the Department of Recreation.
The new department is administered by a park and recreation commission
of four members appointed by the mayor.   It controls many properties
with a great variety of indoor and outdoor recreation facilities, operates a

large number of school playgrounds and indoor centers, and uses other private and public properties for recreation purposes.

A general superintendent is in charge of the entire work of the department, which is carried on through five divisions. One of these is the Recreation Division under an executive with the title of assistant general superintendent. The Recreation Division is responsible for the entire recreation program of the department including the operation of certain services such as canoeing, bathing, golf, orchestra and band concerts in public parks. All the recreation activities of the Recreation Division are in charge of a director of recreation.

RECREATION DEPARTMENT ORGANIZATION,
AUSTIN, TEXAS

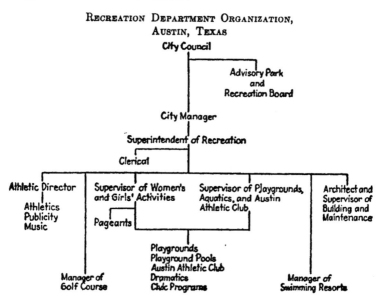

The chart on page 454 indicates the five divisions of the Detroit Department of Parks and Recreation and outlines in some detail the staff organization of the Recreation Division. For purposes of supervision and administration of the division the city is divided into four districts, and the four district supervisors, called assistant directors, are responsible for all recreation activities in their respective districts. They are also called upon to perform special duties such as the conducting of a city-wide championship swimming meet. The supervisor of athletics has charge of competitive athletics. A number of special instructors for specific activities like aircraft, handicraft, drama, etc., supplement the regular leadership staff at the playgrounds and centers. In Detroit the present plan, which calls for concentration of responsibility for program operation in a single major division organized on a district basis, was adopted after experimentation with other types of organization. It is proving more successful than divisions according to major activities or to sexes—plans that required more personnel, involved multiple responsibility, and made city-wide supervision more difficult.

Cincinnati, Ohio.—The Public Recreation Commission in Cincinnati has five members, three appointed by the mayor, one from the Board of Education, and another from the Park Board. It operates many facilities on school and park property as well as areas for which it is directly responsible. The recreation service of the department is furnished by a number of divisions each in charge of a supervisor who is directly responsible to the recreation executive, in this city, called director. Each supervisor has full responsibility for the conduct of the activities, the operation of the facilities, and the supervision and training of the workers assigned to his division. The work is divided according to special functions rather than by districts, the form of departmental organization being in marked contrast to that in Detroit, where the individuals in

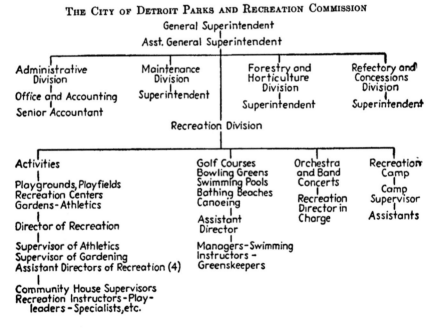

THE CITY OF DETROIT PARKS AND RECREATION COMMISSION

General Superintendent

Asst. General Superintendent

Administrative Division	Maintenance Division	Forestry and Horticulture Division	Refectory and Concessions Division
Office and Accounting	Superintendent		
Senior Accountant		Superintendent	Superintendent

Recreation Division

Activities	Golf Courses Bowling Greens Swimming Pools Bathing Beaches Canoeing	Orchestra and Band Concerts	Recreation Camp
Playgrounds, Playfields Recreation Centers Gardens-Athletics		Recreation Director in Charge	Camp Supervisor
Director of Recreation	Assistant Director		Assistants
Supervisor of Athletics Supervisor of Gardening Assistant Directors of Recreation (4)	Managers-Swimming Instructors – Greenskeepers		
Community House Supervisors Recreation Instructors-Play- leaders-Specialists,etc.			

charge of special activities do not have the status of division heads. Outdoor playgrounds, centers for colored groups, and community centers are operated independently in three separate divisions instead of under a single division, as is often the case. Although most of the division heads in Cincinnati are responsible for a specific function, some of them have been assigned additional duties, in line with a trend noted earlier in the chapter. Thus, the supervisor of golf also administers the nature program and the supervisor of music is in charge of special activities, in addition to his music program.

The Commission's Extension Division is an unusual feature, providing recreation service in communities throughout the county, but the salaries of the supervisor and all other workers are paid from emergency funds. Cincinnati is also perhaps the only city in which a special division has been set up for tennis, an activity which is usually under the supervisor of playgrounds or of athletics, and for centers provided for unattached men. The separate divisions for maintenance and for construction are more characteristic of park department organization than of a recreation department setup. In Cincinnati the large number of construction projects carried on during the depression period necessitated the creation of a separate construction division. The accompanying chart illustrates the recreation organization in Cincinnati and summarizes the type of personnel in each division.

RECREATION DEPARTMENT ORGANIZATION,
CINCINNATI, OHIO, 1937

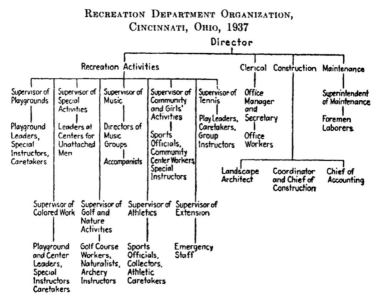

Milwaukee, Wisconsin.—The major recreation program in this city is provided by the Department of Municipal Recreation and Adult Education of the local School Board, under the direction of a worker who has the rank of assistant superintendent of schools. Many of the playgrounds and other recreation areas are acquired by the city and are constructed by the Department of Public Works, but after completion are turned over to the Department of Municipal Recreation for maintenance and operation. A supervisor who has the title of general field assistant is in charge of property maintenance and also serves in a supervisory capacity.

Five activity supervisors—who in Milwaukee have the title of director—are in charge of the recreation program. One of them gives his entire time to municipal athletics, another to citizenship training of foreign-born and newsboys' clubs. The other three have both "line" and "staff" functions and serve in the dual capacity of supervisors of special activities and general district supervisors. In addition to their city-wide responsibility for the promotion and supervision of one or more activities such as drama and clubs, each of the three directors supervises the playgrounds and indoor centers in a district.

As in other cities operating under different organization plans, all workers at a center or playground are responsible to its director for the performance of their duties. Special workers, however, such as a crafts

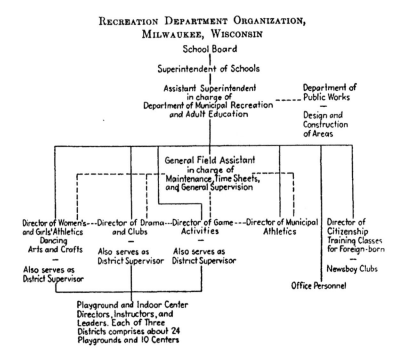

RECREATION DEPARTMENT ORGANIZATION, MILWAUKEE, WISCONSIN

instructor or club leader, receive advice and suggestions on methods of conducting their groups from the central office "director" in charge of the particular activity.

Oakland, California.—Municipal recreation in Oakland is administered by a Board of Playground Directors, the members of which are appointed by the Council upon nomination by the mayor and serve for

6-year terms. Broad powers are given the board under the city charter. The Board of Playground Directors and the Board of Education jointly employ a man who serves as municipal superintendent of recreation and supervisor of physical education in the schools. This arrangement makes possible a coordinated recreation program and facilitates the recreational use of school properties by community groups.

As the accompanying chart indicates, the recreation activities program is under the immediate direction of a general supervisor of recreation. Several special supervisors assist him in organizing and guiding the city-wide recreation services and the programs carried on under leadership at the playgrounds, centers, and camps, and two supervisors handle the comprehensive industrial recreation program. The workers in charge of most of the special facilities such as the camps,

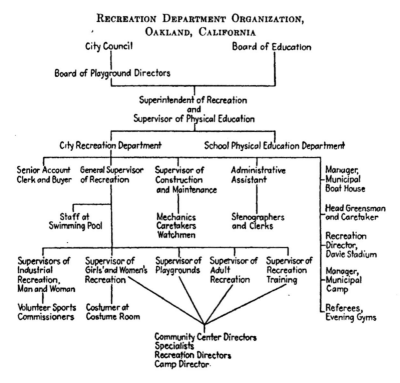

golf course, and boat house are responsible directly to the superintendent although, since they are revenue-producing facilities, the senior account clerk is concerned with their fiscal operations.

Reading, Pennsylvania.—The organization of the Department of Public Playgrounds and Recreation in Reading, Pennsylvania, is fairly representative of that in many smaller cities with a recreation board.

In Reading, the board is appointed by the mayor, but under the Pennsylvania law two of the five persons on the board must be members of the local Board of Education. The year-round program is largely administered by the superintendent and two supervisors who have broad responsibilities, primarily to each of the sex groups. One of them gives much of his time to the athletic program for men and boys; the other supervises girls' and women's athletics, social recreation, drama, and other activities. This is a common arrangement in smaller cities which have only a limited year-round supervisory staff. During the summer months additional supervisors are employed to conduct special program features and services, and from October 1 until the middle of May a Negro supervisor directs a Negro center. All supervisors are directly responsible to the superintendent.

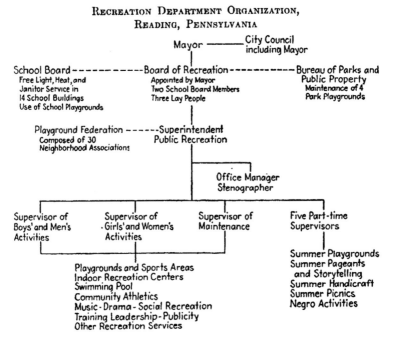

RECREATION DEPARTMENT ORGANIZATION,
READING, PENNSYLVANIA

POLICIES, RULES, AND REGULATIONS

The selection and organization of the department staff in such a way as to yield the maximum returns in service and the most harmonious working relationships are perhaps the most important aspects of the organization. Yet efficient operation requires, in addition, the adoption of many policies and procedures with reference to personnel, program, properties, and the public. Personal and professional qualifications of workers, salaries, promotions, vacations, sick leave, hours of service, and workmen's compensation are a few of the items concerning which policies are often adopted, not by the recreation department but by the city governing authorities, and they apply to all city workers. The recreation authorities, however, usually determine the policies and draw up the regulations covering such subjects as the objectives of the department's program, cooperation with other agencies, accidents, competition, publicity, awards, Sunday activities, and the transportation of children or adults in connection with activities sponsored by the department. Rules are often officially adopted relative to the hours, safety, sanitation, permits, and conditions and use of areas and facilities, and the charging of fees for their use. When these various aspects of the department's organization and operation are carefully considered by the authorities and suitable regulations have been adopted with reference to them, the executive and the other members of the staff have definite objectives and policies which guide them in the performance of their duties.

CHAPTER XXXI

FINANCING RECREATION

The power which has been granted to municipal and school authorities to appropriate and expend tax funds for recreation is basic to the
municipal recreation movement, and the development of local recreation
programs has been made possible in large measure by the laws authorizing
the expenditure of public funds for recreation purposes. The financing of
municipal recreation by taxation is commonly regarded as the only
practicable method of furnishing these facilities and activities for all
the people.

In Chap. V it was pointed out that private funds and initiative made
possible the beginning and early growth of the recreation movement
through the conducting of demonstration playgrounds and the stimulation of public interest in children's need for play. It soon became evident, however, that private philanthropy could not finance the purchase,
equipment, and operation of the many areas that were needed and that
public funds and credit would have to be made available. The prompt
acceptance of this responsibility by public authorities is indicated by the
first municipal recreation survey conducted by the Playground Association of America, for the year 1907. Only about 5 per cent of the money
reported spent during the year by 44 large cities came from private
funds. Thirty years later, in 1937, private sources furnished only 4 per
cent of the total expenditures reported in the *Recreation Year Book* by
more than 1,200 communities. Thus it is clear that since the early years
of the movement, funds for community recreation leadership, facilities,
and services have been derived almost entirely from public sources.

SOURCES OF FUNDS FOR LAND AND IMPROVEMENTS

Municipal funds for recreation have come from the usual sources of
local government revenue. Capital expenditures—for the purchase of
land and for buildings, facilities, and improvements—have been made
largely from funds raised through bond issues. To a lesser degree land
acquisition, construction, and improvements have been financed from
special tax levies, appropriations from general city and school tax
revenues, and from special funds. In purchasing new areas a relatively
small number of cities use the special assessment method by which
owners of property benefited by the area are assessed part or all of the

land and development cost. In one city the cost of constructing four swimming pools on municipally owned areas has been met by this method.

The extent to which bond issues have furnished the funds for financing the cost of land, buildings, and improvements is strikingly indicated by the fact that in 1930, when capital expenditures for parks and recreation in 721 cities exceeded $27,500,000, bond issues yielded $27,315,752. This represented 28 per cent of the total amount spent for all park purposes that year. Since 1933, however, few bonds have been voted and the cost of capital improvements in park and recreation areas has been met largely from emergency or relief funds. Thus in 1935, when $3,500,-000, or only 6 per cent of the total park expenditure in 1,071 cities, was for land, buildings, and improvements, bond issues yielded only one million dollars.

SOURCES OF FUNDS FOR CURRENT OPERATION

Current operating costs of recreation, on the other hand, have been met largely through annual appropriations from general city, park, and school tax funds. Some cities, however, support their program through special municipal and school recreation millage tax levies, or by allocating funds from special park taxes or special school taxes for extension activities.

City Appropriations.—Opinions differ as to the most acceptable way of allocating funds for current recreation activities and services. Experts in municipal government believe that recreation departments, like other city departments, should be financed by appropriations from the general city funds, as is the case in most cities. They hold that the recreation budget should be subject to the review and approval of the appropriating body along with the budgets of the other departments, and that the amount to be made available for recreation in a given year should be determined in the light of the total city funds available and in relation to the recreation needs as compared with the needs of other departments. This method of financing makes it necessary for recreation authorities to demonstrate to the city officials and to the public the value and effectiveness of their service, but on the other hand it offers the possibility of increased appropriations as the need for them is demonstrated. In cities where recreation is subordinated to the chief function of a park, school, public welfare, or other department, not only do budget requests for this work require the approval of the city appropriating authorities but the recreation division must compete with other parts of the department for its share of the department's budget.

The Recreation Mill Tax.—The special recreation tax levy is favored by many who believe that the department requires assured financial support until it has established itself in the eyes of the city governing authorities as an essential municipal service.   They feel that a new function like recreation is not likely to secure the funds it needs to meet the public demand for expanding service if it must compete with other larger and strongly entrenched departments which wield a greater influence with the appropriating body.   In cities with a special mill tax for recreation, the amount is usually fixed at a certain number of mills on each dollar of assessed valuation, varying in most instances from 0.1 mill to one mill (equivalent to from 1 cent to 10 cents per $100).   The amount of the tax is sometimes indicated in terms of the number of cents on each hundred dollars of assessed valuation, the usual range being from 2 to 7 cents.   In cases where a maximum and a minimum levy are specified the exact amount to be made available in a given year is determined by the city authorities.   The fact that a special mill tax can be put into effect and maintained only if a majority of the taxpayers are willing to support it, in the opinion of many recreation leaders, justifies its use. The special tax safeguards the recreation department against marked budget reductions, assuring a relatively steady annual income which can be spent as the recreation authorities deem best, without dictation from the city council.   Supplementary appropriations are authorized, but are not commonly granted.   Hence the tax may actually retard rather than assist the growth of the recreation department by yielding a smaller amount than might be appropriated by a sympathetic city council, and other city departments may resent the special privilege which it affords the recreation authorities.   The special mill tax is objected to by some because it deprives the city governing authorities of the power to determine the amount of tax money to be used for recreation and to control the specific uses for which it is to be spent.

Successful Referendum Campaigns.—It is significant that during the depression years when pressure for lowering taxes was unusually great, several cities in which referendum campaigns were carried on voted to establish such a tax or to increase the previous millage rate.   Canton, Ohio, which had completed a 5-year period under a 0.1 mill levy and which under the state law was obliged to resubmit the question to the voters if it wished to continue the tax, in 1932 secured a favorable vote on a 0.2 mill levy for its recreation department.   Decatur, Illinois, where a recreation program had been carried on by a private association, in 1936 approved by a more than two to one vote a minimum levy of $\frac{2}{3}$ mill. In Los Angeles the annual tax allocation to the Playground and Recreation Department of 4 cents on each $100 assessed value was increased in 1937 to 6 cents per $100, by a favorable vote of the people.   Milwaukee many years ago authorized a tax of 0.2 mill, which was increased in 1919 to 0.4 mill.   Following a referendum campaign in 1937, the citizens voted additional funds through the School Department of Municipal Recreation and Adult Education by increasing the tax as follows: not to exceed 0.6 mill in 1938; 0.7 mill in 1939, and 0.8 mill in 1940 and thereafter. It is worth noting that referendum campaigns are generally successful in cities where competent recreation leadership has carried on an effective program, the value of which had been demonstrated to the citizens.

Fees and Charges.—For many years certain recreation facilities have been financed in part from income received from fees and charges levied on persons using them. Since 1930, recreation authorities have given increased attention to fees and charges as a possible means of supplementing tax appropriations as a method of financing certain types of recreation.[1] Some authorities have considered them an easy source of revenue and have advocated a rather general application of a policy of charging wherever possible. Others have felt that such a policy is unsound socially and financially. There is a wide difference of opinion on many questions relating to fees and charges but it is generally agreed that if the application of a fee tends to reduce participation in an activity, there is something wrong with the fee.

Arguments Pro and Con.—Several reasons advanced by advocates of a general application of charges and fees are:

1. People appreciate things more if they are required to pay for them.
2. Charging simplifies control and discipline and tends to prevent the abuse of monopoly.
3. Persons benefiting from the use of a facility or from participation in an activity should share the expense of furnishing such service.
4. Unless the individuals directly benefiting from them help meet the cost of recreation facilities and services, the city cannot afford to serve the recreation needs of all the people.
5. The willingness of the public to pay for certain forms of recreation furnishes the authorities a guide in planning its program.
6. A small charge may increase the service rendered or make possible the enrichment of the program.

Those who feel that there should be no fees and charges offer the following:

1. Many of the people who need municipal recreation most do not have the money to pay for it.
2. Recreation is an essential public service and should be provided free of charge on the same basis of financial support as education and health.
3. Where charges are made, there is a tendency to judge and develop the work of the recreation department according to commercial standards rather than on the basis of maximum service to the people.

[1] For a comprehensive report of policies and practices see *Fees and Charges for Public Recreation*, National Park Service, 1939.

4. Charging stimulates the development of services and facilities which bring in revenue, with the resulting neglect of other parts of the program which are of greater value and importance.

5. The tendency to charge fees and the attempt to make recreation self-supporting increase the difficulty of securing adequate municipal appropriations for recreation.

6. Charging fees amounts to double taxation.

Local Practices.—The extent to which charges are made, the objectives sought in making them, and the policies and practices followed with reference to fees and charges, vary from city to city. However, in view of the recognized importance of play for children it is almost universally agreed that children of elementary-school age or younger should not be charged for recreation. Also, because of the large initial investment in golf courses, municipal camps for adults, and boating facilities, and because of the limited numbers of people they accommodate, the practice of charging for the use of such facilities is almost universal. At swimming pools and beaches charges are also common, but with few exceptions children are permitted the free use of these facilities during certain periods. Local practices vary more widely in the case of tennis, dancing, membership in special interest groups, handicraft materials, and instruction in various activities. Entry fees for adult teams enrolled in leagues or for individuals playing in tournaments conducted by the recreation department are common.

The objectives sought and the relationship of the charges to the people's ability to pay are major considerations in determining the results of any policy relating to fees. Reference was made in an earlier chapter to the remarkable impetus given to the playing of golf in one city by lowering the rates and furnishing facilities and equipment within the means of people who wished to play but previously had been unable to afford it. In certain other cities there is evidence that existing high rates are restricting public use of the courses. Establishing a charge merely for income sometimes fails to accomplish this and also defeats the very purpose for which the facility was established. An excellent example is furnished by a large city where, after a fee for the use of tennis courts was instituted, play fell off 70 per cent, and "the amount of money collected was just sufficient to pay the man who sat around to see that the people did not play." Very different was the experience in another city where week-end congestion on the courts was so great that the authorities decided to have a referendum among the tennis players to determine whether they were willing to pay a nominal fee for installing a week-end reservation system. In this instance the object of the fee was to enable the department to furnish better service, and the suggestion met a hearty response from the players.

Revenue from Fees and Charges.—Since 1929 the *Recreation Year Books* have shown that in general income from fees and charges, like income from tax sources, fluctuates with changing economic conditions. Although the number of agencies reporting receipts from fees and charges has increased considerably, there has been little change in the ratio of receipts from these sources to the total amounts made available for recreation. In 1930, $3,836,686, or 15 per cent of all operating costs, came from fees and charges, 222 cities reporting some income from this source. In 1937 the amount reported was $3,776,559, or 17 per cent of the total operating expenditures, with 430 cities reporting income from fees and charges. Between these two years the amount received from fees and charges fluctuated little, in all cases being less than $3,000,000, the average about $2,500,000. Total expenditures and income from fees and charges both reached a low point in 1934. Similar results are obtained by comparing the income from fees and charges reported by park departments for the years 1930 and 1935.

Experience during the years of changing economic conditions since 1929 seems to indicate clearly that, although charges and fees are desirable for some forms of municipal recreation service, in general they have not proved successful when applied on a money-raising basis. A comparison of the average cost of operation and the average income at golf courses, swimming pools, and bathing beaches in a number of cities was given in Chap. XIX.

Other Sources.—Income from concessions, gifts, contributions from community chests or private recreation associations, and sale of materials supplement the amount received from municipal sources in many cities. The total amount of such income is comparatively small and in some cases it must be used for specific purposes.

RECREATION EXPENDITURES

The best guide to the trend of expenditures for organized community recreation service is the *Recreation Year Book*, which although not complete includes reports from most cities conducting recreation during the year. It should be kept in mind, however, that in many cases the figures submitted by the agency which administers the program do not represent the entire capital and current expenditures for municipal recreation in the city. Items most often omitted are the cost of acquiring parks and other areas to be used at least in part for active recreation, expenditures for the construction of school buildings and other facilities which are utilized in the recreation program, and funds spent for maintaining areas and facilities. Park departments do not always charge the maintenance of recreation areas to the recreation budget, and school departments often furnish janitor service, light, and heat for community recreation centers, meeting the costs from their regular school funds. If the total amount of all such costs were obtainable, the actual figure for recreation expenditures would far exceed the amount which cities include in their recreation budgets and report in the *Recreation Year Book*.

A Summary of Expenditures.—The following table shows the annual expenditures as reported in the *Recreation Year Book* since 1917, by 5-year periods. Instead of 1932 data, figures are used for 1930 when the peak of expenditures was reached and for 1934, the lowest depression year. The table also shows the relation of the various amounts to the 1930 figures. Expenditures for recreation from emergency or relief funds are *not* included in the table.

EXPENDITURES FOR MUNICIPAL RECREATION, 1917–1937

Year	Total expenditures*		Expenditures for land, buildings, and permanent equipment		Expenditures for leadership		
	Amount	Per cent of 1930	Amount	Per cent of 1930	Amount	Per cent of 1930	Per cent of total current expenditure for same year
1917	$ 6,659,600	17.3	$ 2,551,027	20.2	(Not reported)		
1922	9,317,048	24.2	1,680,383	13.3	(Not reported)		
1927	32,191,763	83.6	15,184,035	120.4	(Not reported)		
1930	38,518,194	100.0	12,610,862	100.0	$8,135,656	100.0	31.4
1934	20,668,459	53.7	2,314,294	18.4	6,406,896	78.7	34.9
1937	25,794,537	67.0	3,403,191	27.0	7,469,427	91.8	33.4

* Each year many agencies report only total expenditures, furnishing no information as to the amounts spent for capital and for current items. Thus of the 1937 total of $25,794,537 approximately $5,000,000 was not classified as to type of expenditure.

The accompanying table indicates that capital expenditures increased strikingly during the decade ending in 1930 and fell off sharply during the depression. (This decrease has been more than offset, however, by the construction of new facilities and the improvement of existing properties through the Federal emergency work programs.) Although total expenditures in 1937 were far below the 1927 level, considerable improvement is noted as compared with 1934. During the depression expenditures for leadership were reduced proportionately less than other items and by 1937 were not far below the 1930 peak. Leadership accounts for approximately one-third of the current operating and maintenance expenditures for all cities. A special analysis of agencies providing year-round recreation service indicates that nearly 45 per cent of their 1937 expenditures was for leadership.

The proportion of current operating expenditures chargeable to the various types of organized recreation service cannot be determined with accuracy from available information. In general, however, it may be roughly estimated that the amount spent annually for playgrounds, recreation buildings, and other indoor centers equals that spent for all the other services reported in the *Recreation Year Book*. Approximately one-third of the total is spent for the operation and maintenance of recreation facilities such as pools. beaches, golf courses, camps, and athletic fields.

How Much Should a City Spend?—No definite and universally applicable standard for municipal recreation expenditures is practicable because communities differ widely in their municipal recreation needs and in their capacity to finance such a program. A well-to-do suburb with many private resources for individual, family, and group recreation may not need to spend so much per capita for community recreation as an industrial community of the same size, but on the other hand, it may be better able to meet the cost of needed services. Costs for the same facilities and services vary in different parts of the country and in communities of different sizes. Easy and cheap access to facilities furnished by county, state, or Federal agencies may relieve a city of the expense of providing similar facilities.

In spite of the local factors affecting the amount of money a city should spend annually to provide an adequate recreation service, experience affords a basis for arriving at a suggested standard. This presupposes that a city has adequate park and recreation acreage properly distributed and developed for recreation use, and modern school facilities fully utilized for community recreation. It is estimated that in order to provide adequate recreation opportunities for its citizens, any city should spend annually $1 per capita for its program under leadership, plus the maintenance costs. Of this amount approximately 75 cents is required for recreation leadership; the balance for supplies, supplementary personnel, and incidental expenses. An additional expenditure of 50 cents per capita should meet the cost of maintaining areas, buildings, and facilities used in connection with the recreation program. Therefore, a standard expenditure of $1.50 per capita provides for organized recreation activities and leadership and for maintaining and operating facilities, such as golf courses, swimming pools, and tennis courts, as well as playgrounds, playfields, and indoor centers. Of this $1.50, one-half is needed for recreation leadership.

For maintaining general park areas not used for active or organized recreation, operating special features such as a zoo, botanical gardens, and museums, and for miscellaneous recreation services such as band concerts and holiday celebrations, an additional $1.50 per capita is probably required. Three dollars per capita is therefore suggested as the desirable annual standard of expenditure for all forms of municipal recreation service in an American city. The various figures presented here relate to current expenditures only, and do not include amounts which may be spent by state or Federal agencies in furnishing recreation to people in the city.

These figures are presented not as scientific or inflexible standards but as a general indication of what would be required to provide adequate municipal recreation service. Although recreation expenditures in most cities have been far below this standard, figures issued by the Bureau of the Census show that the amount suggested is possible of attainment. According to the bureau,[1] in 1929 three cities over 30,000 population spent more than $3 per capita for operating and maintaining all forms of recreation, and several cities spent more than $2.50. The average current recreation expenditure by all cities over 30,000 population in 1929 was $1.56 per capita. In view of the rapid expansion in municipal recreation areas and facilities, most of which can be utilized effectively only as funds are made available for their operation and maintenance, it is reasonable to expect that cities will spend more for recreation in the years ahead than they have in the past.

RECREATION BUDGETS AND FINANCIAL REPORTS

The accounting systems adopted by cities, park districts, or school boards generally determine the primary financial procedures and reporting methods used by recreation departments operating under their jurisdiction. The governing authority also determines the type of budget and maintains most of the financial records which are usually kept according to the object classification set up in the budget, such as salaries, wages, and contractual services. It seldom maintains or requires the departments to maintain financial records under which their major functions are subdivided according to the activities carried on. Consequently, any desired financial reports on the costs of recreation activities, facilities, or services must be based upon records maintained in the recreation office. Owing to the lack of adequate office personnel in most

---

[1] See *Financial Statistics of Cities*, Bureau of the Census, U. S. Department of Commerce. Recreation expenditures in this report include money spent for parks, recreation programs, art galleries, museums, concerts, public celebrations, and all other recreation services, *not* including school expenditures for recreation.

recreation departments, the keeping of financial records and reports has been sadly neglected and few cost records of this type are available. This situation will not be corrected until recreation and park boards, city managers, mayors, and school authorities insist upon complete financial information and support budget requests for funds to provide the necessary bookkeeping and clerical service.

The Recreation Department Budget.—Each year the local recreation agency prepares a detailed estimate of its needs for the following year and of the amounts necessary to carry on the work. In case the recreation program is administered by park or school authorities, the park or school superintendent passes upon the statement before it is submitted to the proper board for approval. In the case of a recreation board, the recreation executive prepares the statement for the board's approval. In cities where the recreation funds come from general tax sources, the recreation authority, after taking favorable action upon the tentative budget, as the estimate statement is called, submits it to the municipal appropriating authorities. They consider it along with the estimates of other city departments, make any changes they deem essential or desirable, and determine the amount to be appropriated for recreation and the purposes for which it is to be used. The budget document setting forth these items then becomes the controlling financial plan of the department during the year or period which it covers. A tentative budget for a recreation commission appears on page 470.

Methods of Recording Expenditures.—The standard object classification recommended for use by municipal departments in budgeting and in recording current operating and maintenance costs is applicable to even the smallest recreation department.[1] However, records kept according to this classification, which includes personal services, contractual services, commodities, etc., do not furnish all the information essential to the intelligent preparation of a recreation budget. Records of expenditures by functions or types of service are also desirable.

The three major types of records recommended under a functional classification relate to administration, facilities, and special services. Under "administration" are recorded all expenditures necessary to the proper running of the department *as a whole*, such as the recreation executive's salary and the expenses of the department office. Under "facilities" separate accounts are set up for each major type of facility operated, such as playgrounds, swimming pools, camps, or stadiums. The term "special services" refers to special phases of the program such as music, drama, or athletics which are largely conducted by specialists,

---

[1] See *Recreation Cost Records*, a committee report issued by the National Recreation Association in 1938, for this classification and for a detailed discussion of financial record-keeping methods for recreation departments.

RECREATION BUDGET FOR 1939, BOARD OF RECREATION COMMISSIONERS, ELIZABETH, NEW JERSEY

Object classification	Administration and community relations	Office	Athletics	Community centers	Swimming pools	General	Playgrounds Spring	Playgrounds Summer	Playgrounds Fall	Playgrounds Total	Social arts	Winter sports	Totals
710—A—Salaries and Wages—Regular	$5,100	$2,580	$1,872	2,004.00			$600	$1,804	$600	$3,004			$14,560.00
Professional	5,100		1,872	600.00			600	400	600	1,600			9,172.00
Other		2,580		1,404.00				1,404		1,404			5,388.00
710—B—Salaries and Wages—Temporary				11,890.00	3,709‡		600	10,800	600	12,000			27,599.00
Professional				8,630.00	1,364*		600	8,784	600	9,984			19,978.00
Other				3,260.00	2,345†			2,016		2,016			7,621.00
710—C—Services—Contractual	250	1,275		2,217.00	1,266	767		400		1,167		$200	6,375.00
Communication and transportation	250	1,075		50.00	50	50							1,475.00
Substance													200.00
Printing, binding, advertising				67.00	66	67				67			200.00
Heat, light, power, water				1,500.00	1,150	650				650		100	3,400.00
Repairs		200		500.00				300		300			800.00
Others				100.00				100		100		100	300.00
710—D—Supplies and Materials		500	750	950.00	1,700*		100	1,175	100	1,375	$400		5,675.00
Supplies		500	450	550.00	1,700*		100	875	100	1,075	400		4,675.00
Materials			100					100		100			200.00
Repairs			200	400.00				200		200			800.00
710—E—Rental and Insurance		150	100	3,460.25	238	85		350		435			4,383.25
Rental		50		3,120.00				350		350			3,520.00
Insurance		50		340.25	238	85				85			713.25
Subscriptions and memberships		50	100										150.00
710—G—Properties		250		175.00		875				875			1,300.00
Equipment		250		75.00		775				775			1,100.00
Areas													
Buildings and improvements				100.00		100				100			200.00
Totals	$5,350	$4,755	$2,722	$20,696.25	$6,913§	$1,727	$1,300	$14,529	$1,300	$18,856	$400‖	$200‖	$59,892.25

* To be met from swimming pool receipts.
† $1,665 to be met from swimming pool receipts.
‡ $3,029 to be met from swimming pool receipts
§ $4,729 to be met from swimming pool receipts.
‖ This amount is allocated as follows: Arts and Crafts, $100; Dramatics, $125; Music, $125; Social Recreation, $50.

are city-wide in scope, and are seldom confined to the department's facilities.

Difficulties arise in securing complete and accurate cost records on a functional basis, no matter how efficient the system or the personnel maintaining it. Yet the value of such records cannot be questioned as they provide the information which the executive needs in order to secure the most effective use of the department's funds and economical conduct of the program in each center.

OPERATING STATEMENT FOR THE YEARS 1935–1936 AND 1936–1937
OF LOS ANGELES PLAYGROUND AND RECREATION DEPARTMENT

	1935–1936	1936–1937	Per cent increase or *decrease* over 1935–1936
Income:			
Appropriations from taxes.....	$526,398.83	$519,640.42	*1.28*
Gifts......................	2,057.51	2,919.89	41.91
Interest....................			
Direct departmental income ...			
Playgrounds...............	$ 28,505.21	$ 23,725.33	*16.77*
Local camps..............	882.22	1,198.08	35.80
Mountain camps..........	26,899.23	34,982.95	30.05
Men's club...............	670.00	2,201.00	228.51
Swimming pool............	33,795.72	28,017.74	*17.10*
Beaches..................	8,433.83	8,223.77	*2.49*
Promotional activities......	2,042.23	2,417.63	18.38
	$101,228.44	$100,766.50	*.46*
Total operating income........	$629,684.78	$623,326.81	*1.01*
Expenses:			
Playgrounds...............	$368,067.00	$370,594.99	.69
Local camps..............	4,398.84	3,727.53	*15.26*
Mountain camps............	33,939.22	43,550.67	28.32
Men's club................	843.66	1,470.35	74.28
Swimming pools............	63,675.09	61,369.17	*3.62*
Beaches...................	71,281.38	72,485.48	1.69
Promotional activities........	15,611.25	16,555.47	6.05
	$557,816.44	$569,753.66	2.14
Administrative..............	44,040.12	46,687.46	6.01
	$601,856.56	$616,441.12	2.42
Net operating income........	$ 27,828.22	$ 6,885.69	*75.26*

A Functional Budget.—The budget shown on page 470, based on the actual anticipated expenditures of the recreation department of Elizabeth, New Jersey, a city of 115,000 population, is set up according to the usual objects of expenditure, such as salaries, services, and supplies. In addition, however, it segregates items by functions as far as possible, thus giving a much better picture of the proposed program and costs than budgets which are broken down only by objects of expenditure.

A Departmental Operating Statement.—The Department of Playground and Recreation of the City of Los Angeles maintains a complete set of cost records and financial reports which furnish all detailed information as to costs and sources of income necessary for intelligent analysis and administration of the program. The statement on page 471, from the department's report for the year ending June 30, 1937, summarizes departmental income and expenditures during a 2-year period.

CONCLUSION

The foregoing examples represent the best practice in municipal recreation budget making and financial reporting. There is room for a great deal of improvement in most cities. Clarification of recreation costs is especially needed where recreation is a subdivision of a public department and receives its money from that department's budget, with no special segregation of recreation costs. Several cities are experimenting with the system of recreation cost records recommended by the committee of recreation executives referred to in the footnote on page 469.

CHAPTER XXXII

RECORDS, REPORTS, AND RESEARCH

The function of the recreation department is to help make available to all the people of the city satisfying constructive leisure-time activities. The essential records of that department should therefore indicate the amount of happiness that has resulted from its program, and its contribution to higher standards of life and to abundant living in the community. Obviously such factors cannot be measured with accuracy, so it is necessary to rely upon other types of information. Records of the number of people served and the types of activities and facilities provided and their comparative costs furnish the best basis now available for recording the extent and quality of the department's service.

Records are designed to serve various uses. A complete accounting for all department receipts and expenditures is essential not only because it is generally required by law, but also because recreation authorities owe it to the public to give a report of their stewardship over the funds entrusted to them. Only as a department gives evidence of having rendered a worth-while service can it merit or expect continued public support. Carefully kept records are essential to the preparation of departmental reports. Moreover, recreation authorities cannot appraise or evaluate their various activities, centers, or services unless they have full information concerning them and their costs. Intelligent planning for the future must be based upon an analysis of existing conditions and needs, which can be determined only as adequate data are available. Operation of a recreation department, like any other enterprise, requires current as well as accumulated records of personnel, facilities, programs, and business transactions. Because the records and reports of the recreation department are so numerous and important, a separate division is usually created to handle them.

TYPES OF RECORDS

Among the types of information which it is desirable or essential for the recreation department to have in its official records are

Reports of Recreation Service.—Daily, weekly, monthly, seasonal, or annual reports of individual playgrounds, centers, and special facilities; reports of district and special supervisors; departmental reports of the superintendent; programs of special events, institutes, and other features.

Legal Authority, Actions, and Policies.—Legislation relating to the department, rules and regulations adopted, minutes of board meetings, official correspondence, department policies, legal actions and court decisions affecting the department, and the departmental organization plan.

Description of Properties.—List of all departmental areas, their location, acreage, cost, assessed valuation, date and method of acquisition, facilities, and equipment; blueprints and drawings for all areas, buildings, facilities, and equipment; surveys and city maps; cost estimates and construction costs; specifications and inventories.

Personnel Records.—Lists of all employees with their personnel and service records; volunteer activity leaders and their service records; members of advisory councils, committees, and neighborhood recreation groups; individuals with permits for golf, tennis, skating, and other activities; membership lists of all teams, clubs, associations, and groups affiliated with the department and their officers; playground and indoor center registration lists; graduates of recreation institutes; winners in department activities, events, and tournaments; persons desiring special bulletins.

Business and Financial Records.—Budget work sheets, estimates, requests, appropriations, expenditures, and balances; accounting records including sources, amounts, and disposition of department funds, and detailed statement of expenditures; records of income and operating costs of areas and facilities such as golf courses or swimming pools; records of capital expenditures; time sheets, pay rolls, absences, workmen's liability cases and funds; purchase orders, quotations, deliveries, contracts, concessions, bids, agreements, and reports; insurance policies.

Administrative Records.—Permits and reservations for department properties; copies of publicity issued; instructions and suggestions for department workers; attendance reports; schedules of athletic leagues, interplayground programs, club activities, and city-wide projects; reports of complaints, property damage, and accidents resulting from department activities; program forecasts.

The preceding list is not inclusive but it indicates the variety of official records for which recreation authorities are responsible. In each department, the number and types of records kept depend upon its individual needs.

Record Forms.—In order to simplify record keeping, to secure uniform procedure throughout the department, and to reduce costs to a minimum, a variety of forms and blanks is used. Some of them, particularly the ones for keeping financial, personnel, and other business data, have been rather highly standardized, and sometimes they are prescribed by the municipal authorities for use in all city departments. There is a wide diversity, however, in the types of forms used for recording recreation service and for administrative purposes. Large cities with a comprehensive program use scores of such forms but only a few types can be mentioned here:

Activity Reports.—Daily, weekly, monthly, or seasonal. Separate forms are required for the playground, the recreation building or indoor center, golf course, camp, beach, and other facilities. Special forms are also needed for the supervisors, the specialists, and the executive.

Attendance Reports.—Daily, weekly, monthly, or seasonal. These are sometimes combined with activity report forms.

Permits and Reservations.—Applications for permits to use a building, facility, or area; individual registration cards; permit blanks for teams; etc.

Program Forms.—Typical of the many forms used in conducting the program are the following athletic forms: team roster blanks, individual registration and entry forms, applications for affiliation, report forms for athletic officials, team reservation blanks, individual contracts and releases, receipt blanks for entry fees, financial reports, certificates of award, score sheets, schedule blanks, etc.

Administrative Forms.—Accident and property damage reports including follow-up, requisitions, work plan, registration, achievement records, physicians' certification, parents' permission, and individual attendance record.

Special care must be taken in preparing the forms to make sure that they may be filled out easily and quickly, yield the essential data desired, and facilitate tabulation of the data in summary form. Careful instructions as to the methods and conditions of using the forms are also essential.

Financial Records.—Major responsibility for department accounting rests with the central office, but specific instructions in handling and recording funds must be given all employees who are in any way concerned with the receiving or paying out of money. This applies especially at facilities where charges are made or fees are collected, such as golf courses or boat houses, or where refreshments are sold. Accurate daily reports of receipts, tickets sold, or goods disposed of are submitted to the department office on specially prepared forms. The specific information requested corresponds in general to financial data required in business establishments. Chapter XXXI contains a brief discussion of the basic methods used in keeping such financial records.

Record-keeping Procedures.—Some of the specific procedures with reference to such records are described in the following statement taken from the 1937 report of the Detroit Recreation Department and describing the work of its Administrative Division:

Records are kept of the receipts, expenditures, requisitions, purchase orders, vouchers, payments, and all financial transactions in connection with the Department's appropriations. At the beginning of the fiscal year the annual budget appropriation is divided into four quarterly allotments. A division cannot exceed its quarterly allotment without first securing a transfer of funds which must be approved by the Common Council.

All financial records are kept in this division; receipts are deposited daily by the community house supervisors; and deposit slips and daily reports are turned in to the main office three times a week and are recorded and deposited with the City Treasurer.

In making purchases of supplies, materials, and equipment, division heads submit their requisitions to the office, prices are estimated by the storekeeper, the requisitions are certified by the office as to funds being available and the proper account numbers placed thereon; they are signed by the head clerk and commissioner and the purchases are then handled through the Department of

Purchases and Supplies after the approval of the Budget Bureau and the Controller's office.

Payment of petty cash bills, employees' automobile maintenance, Board of Education pay rolls, and other items not involving a purchase requisition are certified on a department voucher and forwarded for payment through the City Treasurer's office after being approved by the City Controller and the Common Council.

Recreation Service Records.—Unlike financial records, which conform to usual business procedures, records of recreation service are directly related to the peculiar functions and objectives of the recreation department. For this reason and because of the special problems and difficulties encountered in adequately recording recreation services, special consideration is given to such records. Accurate reports of recreation service are essential for two reasons: (1) They indicate the nature and scope of the activities provided by the department and the extent to which the people have taken advantage of the opportunities extended to them; (2) they enable authorities to evaluate the units in the recreation system and the various program features, and to determine the relationship between their costs and the services rendered. Without such records it is impossible to budget funds intelligently or to plan wisely for the future. There is considerable agreement among recreation authorities as to the kinds of information which should be assembled, but there is much divergence in the methods employed to gather it, and in the extent to which the records kept make this information available.

Basic Service Reports.—The periodic reports submitted by directors of indoor and outdoor centers, by managers of major facilities, and by supervisors of special activities, furnish the basic records of the department's service, and they are drawn upon largely for the facts presented in the annual report of the department. It is therefore exceedingly important that the forms used for these reports be designed to facilitate the recording of all essential data. The periods covered by them vary, but the weekly report is perhaps the most common. It usually contains not only a record of service rendered but also information of administrative value to the department, such as reports of property damage or repairs, time records, or requisitions for supplies.

The Weekly Playground Report.[1]—In spite of wide variations in the report forms used at playgrounds in different cities, the following types of information are commonly requested, many of them for each day of the week or for each period of the day: total attendance, generally broken down according to participants and spectators, and often by boys, girls,

[1] For a suggested weekly playground report form and a detailed discussion of playground records see *Playgrounds—Their Administration and Operation*, National Recreation Association, 1936.

and adults; weather conditions; participation in special activities; number using special facilities such as tennis courts, wading pools, or fireplaces; visits by supervisors or specialists; volunteer service; special events conducted and proposed; interplayground, city-wide, or extraplayground activities; neighborhood contacts or relationships; cash receipts and sources; needed repairs, supplies, or services; playground accidents; complaints or property damage; registration figures; workers' time records, and report on condition of playground equipment.

Few, if any, playground report forms provide for all the items listed, although they all have value. The figures relative to attendance, registration, and participation, especially if classified according to age and sex, are useful in planning programs, assigning workers, determining the need for additional facilities, and analyzing playground service. The reports of special events and activities and community relationships indicate the initiative shown by the workers on the playground. Data relating to working hours, accidents, requisitions, and conditions of property are requested for the protection of the authorities or to facilitate administration.

Other Service Reports.—Directors of recreation buildings and indoor centers are required to submit reports covering much the same information as that gathered on playgrounds. Center reports stress group enrollment, attendance at special rooms, and participation in specific program features. Reports of special supervisors indicate the projects planned and initiated, the groups served directly, cooperation extended department workers and outside agencies, training courses conducted, appraisals of workers, and accomplishments in the fields for which they have responsibility. Managers of facilities such as swimming pools are usually expected to submit reports covering three major items: (1) service to the public, (2) financial transactions, (3) maintenance of property.

MEASURING RECREATION SERVICE

Two questions commonly asked concerning the volume and extent of a recreation department's service are, "How many different individuals were served during the year?" and "What was the total attendance at all its activities and facilities?" A thoughtful questioner would also want to know how these figures were distributed among the various parts of the program and the different sections of the city's population. As Ridley and Simon have pointed out:

The record of attendance must be considered a measure both of performance and to a certain extent of results. For one of the objectives that recreation strives for is the very relaxation and enjoyment implied by participation. And the fact that adults prefer the municipal recreation program to alternative uses of leisure time is presumptive evidence that the recreational program is fulfilling its purposes.[1]

Registration.—According to a recent estimate, the parks of Chicago touch almost every resident of the city, and, conservatively, one-third of Chicago's population use them frequently and habitually.[2] Few recreation departments can even estimate the number of different individuals served, because the very nature of many recreation activities makes it difficult to obtain satisfactory attendance records. The recording of individual participation in some parts of the program is not possible although registration forms used at playgrounds and centers and for certain city-wide activities furnish authorities a definite record of the individuals reached by these services. Since registration forms give information as to age, sex, place of residence, and other factors, they furnish valuable data for use in studying and evaluating the services rendered different community groups.

Most recreation authorities believe the practical difficulties of keeping complete registration records outweigh their potential value, owing to the variety of facilities operated and to the fact that many programs do not lend themselves to records of this type. It is more important to know that a bathing beach, for example, is used to capacity and affords a certain number of swims than to know how many different persons used it during the season. Records of the total enrollment in drama groups, craft classes, and athletic leagues, on the other hand, which are relatively easy to obtain and indicate the degree of balance in the department's program, are being kept by an increasing number of departments, and registration at playgrounds and indoor centers is fairly common.

Attendance.—All recreation authorities attempt to count or estimate the attendance at their facilities and programs. Unfortunately, attendance figures often have little comparative value because different methods of recording attendance are used, because they are based upon estimates rather than actual counts, and because standard units of measurement are lacking. On the playground the most accurate unit is the "participant-hour," but there is scarcely a playground where the available staff is sufficient to permit the keeping of attendance records on this basis. In all probability the most practicable unit of playground attendance is the "visit." Test studies would furnish a basis for estimating the average length of visit, if this information is desired. At the indoor center where most activities are conducted on a highly organized basis and where many of the groups have a definite membership and meet regularly

---

[1] Clarence E. Ridley and Herbert A. Simon, *Measuring Municipal Activities*, Chap. VII, International City Managers' Association, 1938.
[2] V. K. Brown, "How Many Are Served," *Recreation*, November, 1938, p. 457.

with the same leader the problem of determining attendance is relatively simple. Attendance at pools, dance pavilions, picnic centers, toboggan slides, and other facilities can be determined with considerable accuracy, especially if a system of permits or fees is in effect.

Recording Summer Playground Attendance.—In 1938 a committee of recreation executives sponsored a study conducted by the National Recreation Association for the purpose of developing a more accurate, uniform method of recording attendance at summer playgrounds. Based on its study of 83 playgrounds in 43 cities, the committee recommended the following formula which playground authorities have subsequently used in many cities. Experience has proved it to be sound, and its widespread use in reporting summer playground attendance is anticipated. Adaptations in the formula may be advisable at individual playgrounds with unusual conditions, but they should be based upon records secured by test counts.

The Committee recommends that in determining playground attendance a careful count be taken at the peak of attendance during each morning, afternoon, or evening period during which the playground is open under leadership. (The afternoon session is considered as the period between the noon and evening meal, and the evening session the period between the evening meal and dark, or closing time.) This peak count furnishes the basis for recording attendance as follows: the morning count has an index value of 50; the afternoon count an index value of 40; and the evening count an index value of $66\frac{2}{3}$. *In order to determine the actual attendance, the morning count is multiplied by two, the afternoon count by 2.5, and the evening count by 1.5. The sum of these attendances represents the total for the day.* For example, if the peak count at a given playground is 50 in the morning, 100 in the afternoon, and 120 in the evening, the morning attendance will be 100, the afternoon attendance 250, and the evening attendance 180, making a total attendance for the day of 530.[1]

A breakdown of total playground attendance figures by special activities—dramatics, nature, art, etc.—would be desirable but is not practicable in most departments under present conditions. One of the values of such records, as of the other types previously mentioned, is to enable the authorities to estimate the unit costs of different types of service.

THE ANNUAL DEPARTMENT REPORT

The annual report of the recreation department, required by law in most cities, is based in large measure upon the records submitted by its workers throughout the year. Some of its characteristics are mentioned in Chap. XXXIII, but the essential qualities of a good municipal report,

[1] See *A New Formula for Determining Summer Playground Attendance,* National Recreation Association, 1938.

as indicated by the International City Managers' Association, merit mention here:

Specifically it explains the purpose and method of operation of the department; it describes major steps which have been taken to improve and modernize departmental operations; it attempts to measure the results attained, using the best statistical indices available, but not confining the evaluation to quantitative devices; it works the statistics into the text, relating them in proper perspective to the situation as a whole. Finally, it discusses the major problems of policy facing the department, attempting to give the reader information which will help him exercise intelligent citizenship.[1]

An analysis of recreation department reports shows that a large percentage of the space is devoted to accounts of activities carried on, and that in many cases little ingenuity has been used in presenting the facts graphically. Few departments make use of the annual report to interpret their objectives, to describe important progress in attaining them, or to stimulate desired action on major problems. There are striking exceptions, but, on the whole, recreation reports resemble technical statements prepared for study by the authorities rather than popular presentations of the accomplishments and needs of the department.

INFORMATION FILES

In addition to the records relating specifically to the department's official procedures and program there is need for a general information file. Such a file contains suggestions and rules for conducting all forms of recreation activities, descriptions and plans of recreation programs and facilities, and accounts of such services in other cities. Much of this information is mimeographed or printed matter in the form of books, bulletins, circulars, magazine articles, reports, charts, or blueprints. Data as to the city, its agencies, facilities, resources, finances, and programs, belong in the information files, along with material on the values of recreation, developments throughout the nation, and other pertinent data relative to the movement. The information in these files is available for study by the workers and is used by the staff in planning activities and programs, in the preparation of speeches and publicity, and in serving the public in various ways.

COMPETENT OFFICE WORKERS ESSENTIAL

It is perfectly clear that a record system, no matter how adequate, will fall into disuse and fail to serve its purpose unless trained, competent personnel are employed for the department office. Many recreation

---

[1] "What Annual Municipal Reports Contain," *Public Management*, January, 1939, p. 5.

departments are losing much in efficiency because their budgets do not provide needed clerical and accounting workers. In some instances a highly trained recreation executive devotes time to record keeping which might better be spent in developing the program. In order to do their work satisfactorily office workers require carefully selected, properly arranged, and well-maintained office space and equipment. The ability to supply prompt and accurate information makes for effectiveness within the department and also gives city officials and the public a favorable impression of the department's efficiency and service.

A WORK SCHEDULE

A work schedule or calendar for each division greatly facilitates the carrying out of essential tasks on scheduled time. Many of the duties of the executive, for example, must be done each year at a given time, others fall regularly each month, whereas some are seasonal responsibilities. The preparation of a calendar for each month or season of the year listing the projects to be carried out or planned for during the period is a great aid to administration.[1] The office manager also has reports of different types which are due from time to time, and the supervisor of maintenance and construction must plan ahead in order to accomplish the many duties that otherwise would be crowded into the outdoor season and to make the best use of his workers.

RESEARCH IN THE RECREATION DEPARTMENT

Up to this point consideration has been limited to the current, continuous, routine records and reports. They furnish the necessary data for conducting the normal work of the department but they do not afford all of the information required by progressive authorities. The increasing complexity of the recreation field, the growing insistence upon supporting data, the conflicting opinions on the place of recreation in modern life, and the need for revising policies and procedures, have forced authorities to assemble facts on which to base their claims, develop policies and programs, and lend weight to their demands. Many problems and questions that arise in conducting the work of a recreation department cannot be answered satisfactorily without special study.

Because of the variable human factors underlying recreation service, it is easier to gather factual data than it is to draw definite conclusions from them. As Joseph Lee once said, "It is difficult, for instance, to know what games a thousand or so of these boys would really like if they had tried them, and to find out the real reasons that cause them to come

---

[1] Charles K. Brightbill, "Calendar for Public Recreation Administration," *Recreation*, November, 1938, p. 462.

to the playgrounds or to stay away."[1] Nevertheless, studies of local conditions affecting recreation and of the leisure-time needs and interests of people have proved useful in the planning of programs and the development of recreation policies, and the number of local studies has increased greatly in recent years.

Types of Research.—The careful analysis of playground and indoor center reports for the purpose of determining unit costs, relation of registration to attendance, range of program, use of supplies, ratio of size and facilities to attendance and other factors, is a most important and continuous type of research. It is an essential part of the job of every superintendent and general supervisor. Special studies of leisure-time interests, neighborhood conditions, future playground sites, or juvenile delinquency in relation to playgrounds are required only from time to time. A type of study that is becoming fairly common is the appraisal of the recreation department in comparison with generally accepted criteria of service. The most ambitious form of local recreation research is the city-wide survey which usually includes a study of many community agencies and factors as well as of the services of the recreation department.

Studies of Recreation Interests.—Attempts by authorities to ascertain the desires and recreation interests of people eliminate the criticism sometimes made that recreation programs reflect the wishes of the workers rather than of the individuals to be served. A comprehensive inquiry into the desires of children, conducted by the Board of Education in Chicago, was a study of this type. The children of the sixth, seventh, and eighth grades in seven elementary schools were asked to answer the following questions:

Suppose I am a fairy or wealthy citizen, and I am going to give you a bar of gold to make a playground:
1. What kind of a playground would you have built?
2. What kind of playthings would you have installed?
3. What kind of play teacher would you have on the playground?

The replies which several thousand children made to these questions were most revealing and furnished valuable data for the guidance of the Recreation Bureau in program planning, the selection of leaders, and the development of play areas.

Studies of the recreation interests of adults vary from the informal inquiry as to the desires of persons attending an individual center to community-wide surveys. It is rather common for persons enrolling at indoor centers to be asked in what activities they would care to participate. More extensive studies involve the widespread distribution of forms on which people are asked to indicate their present leisure-time activities, their group affiliations, unmet recreation interests, and other

[1] "A Possible Justification of Research," *The Survey*, March 15, 1931.

pertinent data. Several recreation departments cooperated with the National Recreation Associaton in studying the leisure activities and desires of young people and adults.[1] The information gathered in this study revealed the extent to which people engaged in a long list of home and outside activities, recent changes in their participation, the activities in which they would enjoy taking part, and the organizations joined or dropped out of during the preceding two years. Studies of this type, especially if they contain questions designed to secure opinions as to local facilities, programs, or needs, prove exceedingly useful to local recreation authorities.

Playground Studies.—Many different types of studies have centered about playground subjects. Various attempts have been made, for example, to determine the effect of playgrounds upon the valuation of property in the neighborhood. A careful analysis of the cost of playground supplies is reported to have reduced by one-half the amount spent for such supplies in one city. A 3-year study of playground accidents sponsored by a committee of recreation workers in Southern California cities resulted in the elimination of apparatus presenting the greatest accident hazards and pointed out the need for protecting players in organized games through better supervision and more instruction. Attempts to trace the influence of playgrounds upon juvenile delinquency by comparing the number of arrests in neighborhoods without playgrounds and in the vicinity of play areas are so numerous as to require no further mention. Exceedingly valuable studies have been made of the relative drawing power of playgrounds of different sizes, leadership, and facilities. The study of playground attendance referred to earlier in this chapter yielded valuable data on the keeping of records.

Recommendations for new playground sites must be made only after a careful study of neighborhood conditions, population trends, land values, and other factors. The high cost of land in built-up sections and the difficulty of securing funds for the purchase of land in open areas make it doubly important that only suitable sites be urged for purchase. A memorandum entitled *Playground Sites Program* submitted to the Common Council of Milwaukee in 1936 and containing a revision of an earlier program illustrates the research involved in anticipating a city's playground needs. The city was divided into three sections and a thorough analysis was made of existing playgrounds in each. The report, recommending the purchase of new properties, the enlargement of existing areas, and the improvements needed at each, contained an estimate of capital costs over a period of years and a proposed expenditures program for an 11-year period. It indicated the name of each property, its location by streets and ward, assessed and market value, proposed develop-

---

[1] See *The Leisure Hours of 5,000 People*, National Recreation Association, 1934.

ment, and estimated costs. The various projects were ranked in order of urgency and importance to conform to the proposed expenditures program. In the introduction to the report were listed the principles underlying the location of playgrounds, upon which the recommendations were based, and in the conclusion was suggested the specific action to be taken in adopting the program. A report of this type, based upon careful research, furnishes a basis for intelligent action by the city authorities.

Other Research Problems.—Other subjects that merit more thoughtful study are the basis for making fees and charges and the effects of such charges upon participation,[1] the carry-overs of recreation activities into the home, ways in which the recreation department may serve problem children, causes of failure and success in recreation programs, the optimum size of different types of recreation groups, the relation of size and design to effectiveness of a playground or playfield, better methods of determining and serving recreation interests, the possibilities of volunteer recreation leadership as a form of leisure-time activity, more accurate ways of recording recreation service, and sounder criteria for judging its effectiveness.

Securing Suggestions from Workers.—Workers in the recreation department are particularly well fitted because of their training and intimate relationship to the people served to observe the shortcomings of its program and administration. Executives who realize this encourage their workers to submit constructive criticism and from time to time attempt to secure specific suggestions from all of them. At the end of the summer playground or indoor center season, for example, they submit a questionnaire to all directors and supervisors asking for comments on the program and its operation. The information gathered in this way, while recollections of the past season are fresh in mind, presents a record of mistakes and successes and suggests desirable changes which may prove exceedingly useful in evaluating policies, procedures, and programs. Such a questionnaire yields results only if workers are convinced that their frank opinions are really desired, will receive consideration, and will be treated as confidential.

In Reading, Pennsylvania, the recreation department has made effective use of this type of inquiry for many years. Typical of the questions asked the summer play leaders and directors are the following:

Did you like the idea of the overhead theme on "Pennsylvania Folk Lore" to motivate the program?

What helpful suggestions can you make relative to storytelling, or radio programs, nature study, etc.?

[1] A comprehensive study of this subject recently completed by the American Institute of Park Executives with the cooperation of the National Park Service is reported in *Fees and Charges for Public Recreation*, 1939.

What didn't you get at the institute which you would like to have?

Name several disciplinary problems you have encountered and tell how you have solved them.

What new improvements can you suggest for your playground?

What constructive criticism do you have to offer about the supervisors?

What are your reactions to the track meet? Did the children enjoy the relays, etc.?

Did the children like to act in simple plays? If not, did the fault lie with the leader, with the children, or with the playground environment? Why?

What is your reaction regarding the merit system of awards? How can we improve the system?

Has the lack of city-wide competition decreased participation or interest in local tournaments? If so, in what way?

It is clear that the replies to such questions not only furnish the superintendent with valuable information but are useful in appraising the intelligence and interest of the workers.

THE RECREATION SURVEY

The diversified studies described in the preceding pages relate primarily to the work of the recreation department, but other types are concerned with such subjects as the leisure time of the people, the recreation services of public agencies, or the functions, relationships, and needs of public and private agencies. These studies, which are often comprehensive in nature and are commonly known as surveys, are seldom initiated or conducted by the recreation department. However, since the recreation survey involves an analysis and appraisal of its services, a consideration of its relationship to other community agencies, and specific recommendations affecting its work, the recreation department has a vital interest in it and often benefits greatly from it. The survey has as its goals the gathering of accurate social data, the scientific analysis and interpretation of the findings, including attitudes and points of view, the formulation of recommendations for action, and a plan for putting them into effect. Funds for conducting such community surveys are usually provided by local foundations, civic organizations, or committees of citizens concerned about recreation conditions in the city.

Before a Survey.—Because of the expense, time, and effort involved in conducting a recreation survey, it is of the highest importance that needs, objectives, and procedures be clearly defined and accepted by the parties involved in the project. The essential considerations have been outlined as follows in a preliminary outline prepared by a Committee on Community Problems and Relationships of the National Social Work Council:

As early as possible before a survey is actually undertaken, there should be genuine discussion and agreement among all the parties concerned as to the key problems to be met; careful analysis of previous studies of the same or similar local problems, and the extent to which the findings of such studies have been acted upon; careful consideration of the alternatives to a survey; if a survey is finally desired, a clear understanding as to who wants it and how that question is determined; advance planning of the survey itself, perhaps in consultation with the prospective survey staff, considering the various types of surveys or studies designed to meet different needs.[1]

A Method of Procedure.—Once a survey has been decided upon, a specific procedure of conducting it must be decided upon by the sponsoring group in consultation with the individual selected as director or consultant. The brief outline prepared for use in a study of public recreation in Baltimore is illustrative. In this city, where for many years the major recreation service had been provided by a quasi-public agency, a group of citizens arranged for the study which was conducted under the direction of a member of the National Recreation Association staff. The following outline served as the basis for the Baltimore survey:

I. Purpose
    To work out a basis of administration and control of public recreation activities that will be sound and businesslike, well coordinated, and consistent with good governmental practice
II. Scope
    No exhaustive analysis of needed facilities and areas is necessary. The inquiry will center principally on management, finance, personnel, activities, relationships, the maintenance of facilities, and public information
III. Method
    The procedure will be:
    A. To analyze each of the governmental and private agencies now involved in public recreation with respect to:
        1. Management
        2. Finance
        3. Personnel
        4. Activities
        5. Relationships
        6. Maintenance of facilities
        7. Public information
    B. To digest the administration of recreation in comparable cities
    C. To arrive at a conclusion as to what is best for Baltimore in the light of the above findings

The restricted, clear-cut purpose of that survey called for a careful analysis of facts which were for the most part readily available from the records of public and private agencies.

In other, more comprehensive surveys the task of gathering the information desired involves the use of questionnaires, personal observation,

[1] *Community Social Surveys,* National Social Work Council, 1937.

special studies, and various research methods. For such surveys the director requires the assistance of paid or volunteer workers, and in some cases committees have been organized to supervise the gathering of data on special subjects. In the recreation survey conducted in Indianapolis, for example, under the sponsorship of the Indianapolis Foundation and the Council of Social Agencies, special consideration was given to recreation in the homes, churches, and industrial plants, and questionnaires were used in gathering much of the data concerning these agencies. School children supplied information as to where and how they played and commercial dance hall proprietors filled out blanks relating to their establishments. The facts assembled in this manner supplemented the data secured from the various public and private agencies serving the leisure of the people.

Content of Survey Reports.—The nature of the facts gathered and presented in recreation survey reports varies according to the purpose of the study, its scope, and the method by which it is carried on. As a rule, the data relate to general community facts, existing public recreation facilities and service, recreation provided by private and semipublic groups, and commercial recreation.[1] The tables of contents of the Baltimore and the Indianapolis surveys give an indication of the subject matter contained in the publications issued at the conclusion of a community recreation survey. The difference in the scope and the purpose of these two surveys is reflected in the varying nature of the reports.

In *Public Recreation in Baltimore*,[2] a summary of the study conducted in that city in 1937, the material is presented under the following headings:

I. *The Present Situation*
   Facilities; Employed Leaders; Activities; Numbers Reached by Private Agencies; Expenditures; Total Cost of Organized Public Recreation; Relationships
II. *Public Recreation in Other Cities*
   Administration; Facilities; Employed Leaders; Activities; Expenditures for Leadership; Relationships
III. *Recommendations for Baltimore*
   Reasons for a Separate Municipal Department; Recreation Board; Advisory Boards; Facilities; Employed Leaders; Activities; Budget

The Leisure of a People,[3] the report of the Indianapolis survey, which was more comprehensive in scope, contains the following sections:

[1] A suggested outline for a community recreation survey, listing the types of information which may well be covered and specific questions which should be answered is available from the National Recreation Association.

[2] Issued by the National Recreation Association, 1937.

[3] Published by the Indianapolis Council of Social Agencies, 1930.

I. What Manner of City Is This Indianapolis?
II. Leisure
III. Play and Recreation
IV. Agencies Related to the Leisure Needs of the People
    The Home and Leisure
    The Church and Recreation
    Public Agencies—Parks and Playgrounds, The Recreation Department,
        The Board of Education, Public Library, County and State Parks
    Semi-Public Agencies—Y.M.C.A., Y.W.C.A., Scouts, etc.
    Art Association of Indianapolis
    The Children's Museum
    Recreation by Private Groups
    Industrial or Vocational Recreation
    Commercial Recreation
V. Special Chapters
    A Modern Movement for Securing Lands for Public Recreation
    Opportunity for Adult Leisure-time Studies
    Social Work and Recreation
    Municipal Camps

Sixteen major recommendations growing out of the survey were presented in the introduction.

After the Survey—What?—The purpose of the survey is to secure data upon which to develop a sound plan of action. Wide publicity interpreting the findings and the recommendations is essential to secure public understanding and support. Some particular group, usually the one responsible for initiating and conducting the study, is assigned responsibility for securing definite action on the recommendations in the report. Such action usually involves acquisition or improvement of areas, revision of the form of local recreation organization, appointment of an official or advisory citizen group, staff reorganization, coordination of recreation services, redistribution of recreation functions, or changes in financial support. Only as the desired results are attained—in whole or in part—does the recreation survey achieve the purpose for which it was carried on. A specific plan of action, intelligently and persistently promoted, is essential to success.

Community Surveys of Social Welfare.—No consideration of recreation surveys can fail to include the local studies, many of which have been conducted by the Community Chests and Councils, Inc., relating to the various phases of social work in the cities studied. Recreation is one of the fields often included in such reports, along with public health, organized care of the sick, child care, family service, relief, and other problems. In many instances the recreation section of the survey has been conducted and reported by a member of the National Recreation Association staff. The subject is treated in much the same manner as in surveys dealing with community recreation alone, but, as a rule, the studies are less intensive, and greater emphasis is given in the report to the relationship of the leisure-time agencies to community welfare organizations.

EVALUATING RECREATION SERVICE

Recreation authorities today recognize the need for evaluating the work which they are doing and for strengthening the shortcomings of their service. They have been stimulated in this self-analysis by the preparation and distribution of an appraisal form for rating a city's recreation facilities and program.[1] In attempting to score their city on its provision for recreation they have been brought face to face with the necessity for keeping complete and accurate records without which an appraisal cannot be made. Although present criteria are open to question in many respects, the process of checking facilities, areas, personnel, participation, program, and finances against a standard affords a valuable research project. Advisory committees, recreation councils, and other citizens' groups, as well as efficiency experts and bureaus, have undertaken to evaluate recreation departments in a number of cities, and on the basis of their findings have recommended specific changes in departmental procedures or extensions of its facilities, staff, or program. When the recreation department itself takes the initiative in such studies, it gives evidence of its willingness to face criticism and of its desire to improve the quality of its service.

[1] *Schedule for the Appraisal of Community Recreation*, National Recreation Association, 1933.

CHAPTER XXXIII

PUBLICITY FOR RECREATION

"The greatest recreational problem is the education of the adult community as to the need for and philosophy of play."[1] Many who have worked closely with the recreation movement would agree with this conclusion reached by the Recreation Study Class at the 1938 national conference of the Association for Childhood Education. Lack of public understanding of the significance of play and recreation is retarding the progress of the movement and accounts for the inadequate recreation personnel, programs, and appropriations in many cities. Recreation leaders are beginning to realize this fact and are giving more consideration to interpreting their work and objectives. The enlarged function of recreation publicity was summarized in the following words at the Recreation Congress in 1935: "The very purpose of publicity is widening out beyond increasing attendance at a particular event or series of events. Publicity in recreation now proposes to make the citizens recreation-conscious; to show them the importance of recreation; to secure their support for recreation."[2]

IMPORTANCE

Public opinion favorable to recreation must be systematically cultivated in order to make sure that the people are fully informed as to local recreation services, know its values to the community, and realize the possibilities of an expanded program. This is true for a number of reasons. Efficient recreation service goes far in establishing good will, but alone it does not bring appropriations, votes, and widespread moral support. The relation of recreation to the public good is not so obvious as that of police and fire departments, public education, and other long-established functions of government. The lack of public appreciation of recreation values affects the program, especially in times when economic problems hold the center of the stage and the task of caring for the unemployed and the hungry is formidable. An expanding recreation department inevitably affects the program of some semipublic and private agencies and frequently arouses their concern. Commercial interests have a big stake in the way people use their spare time and employ high-pressure methods to advance their own interests, sometimes in direct

[1] Ivah Deering, "Recreation Comes Alive," *Recreation*, August, 1938, p. 292.
[2] "Summaries of Discussion Group Meetings," *Recreation*, November, 1935, p. 392.

opposition to new municipal developments. Perhaps the most important reason for effective publicity is the fact that the cardinal element of municipal recreation, leadership, is not easy to interpret.

Recreation publicity ranges in scope from intermittent newspaper notices on activities to a carefully planned program of interpretation designed to create favorable public relations for the recreation department. Systematic publicity requires just as thorough advance planning as budgets and activity programs. It is effective in so far as it has clearly visualized purposes, is directed toward definite groups, consists of wisely selected material, is timed appropriately, and utilizes all suitable mediums and available channels. The following pages contain a discussion of some of these planning factors, as applied to recreation department publicity.

PURPOSES

The objectives may briefly be summarized as follows:

1. To give the public an accounting of the work accomplished
2. To encourage people to participate in the activities and to use the facilities offered by the department
3. To impress the public with the extent, variety, and accomplishments of the city's services in recreation
4. To prepare the minds of citizens for proposed changes or expansion in the recreation system, such as the acquisition of needed areas, increased appropriations, or a new method of reserving tennis courts
5. To interpret the significance of recreation and its importance in the life of the people
6. To secure specific action in support of the department, such as signing a petition, speaking favorably of a measure, or voting in approval of a referendum
7. To enlist individuals to give volunteer service in some specific form
8. To give people information or suggestions on how to conduct recreation activities or construct facilities. Examples are radio talks on the conducting of picnics or a series of newspaper articles on homemade play equipment

AT WHOM IS PUBLICITY AIMED?

The community is not just one great public, identical in outlook, interests, and responsiveness, but a number of publics. Consequently, recreation publicity to be effective must be directed toward one or more of these groups. Often it is appropriately of the blunderbuss variety, directed to practically everybody at one time, but there are other occasions when the information is for particular groups and has a limited appeal. Analysis of systematic publicity programs shows the attempt to focus on these different publics.

Summer playgrounds are of primary interest to children and their parents, so recreation executives arrange to have folders describing them distributed through the schools and carried home by the children. Posters in places of employment, articles in company publications, and shop committees are effective means of informing workers of plans for an industrial recreation program. Addresses before civic and luncheon clubs afford opportunities for presenting special recreation needs to groups of influential citizens. To arouse interest in a neighborhood recreation center, posters in local stores and agencies, talks before neighborhood groups, the distribution of folders, and statements by local clergymen and other leaders have proved effective. Accounts of athletic activities, if published on the sports page, reach the group most interested in them.

CONTENT

The familiar formula for a news story may be applied to recreation publicity. That is, it should answer the following questions: who, what, when, where, how, and why? Answers to these questions are required not simply for given events or projects but for the program of the department as a whole. In practice, since recreation is something people want and touches so many of them, it has proved easy for any live department to answer these fundamental questions except for the final one, "Why?" An analysis based on replies to a questionnaire sent to representative cities showed that only a minority paid much attention to this question.

Except during financial crises, publicity centers chiefly about past or projected activities rather than the plans and objectives of the department or the needs and social values of recreation. Nevertheless, an invitation to "come have a good time" is a common note in publicity announcing forthcoming events. Department reports increasingly contain quotations from local or national leaders on the value and philosophy of recreation, statements of local recreation needs, and recommendations for future expansion of facilities or programs. It is always easier to explain the "why" of recreation in publicity which the department can fully control, such as printed reports, radio talks, or posters, than in newspapers.

Most departments take advantage of staff changes, the construction of new facilities, the addition of areas, the inauguration of new activities, and special program features to secure publicity, especially in the daily press. Without exception they stress the numbers using their facilities or taking part in their programs and the variety of activities offered the public. The inexpensiveness of municipal recreation in terms of low per capita costs or small percentages of the tax dollar is often emphasized. The effect of this emphasis, unaccompanied by statements of standard or desirable expenditures, has quite possibly conditioned some communities to accept inadequate recreation budgets.

Major Values Emphasized.—Many people have come to recognize recreation as essential to normal living and as having sufficient value in itself to require no further justification. Communities as a whole, however, are more ready to support a recreation program if they are convinced that it contributes to health, safety, and character, particularly if it can be shown that it also results in financial savings. Consequently, the values most frequently advanced for municipal recreation are crime prevention, safety to children, health building, and character growth.

A statement *Children and Crime* sent by the recreation department to board members, city officials, recreation council officials, and local papers inspired an editorial in the Houston, Texas, *Post* which among other things stated, "An adequate appropriation for Houston's recreation department may be considered an insurance premium against crime." In a New York city fliers distributed in a referendum campaign on the establishment of a recreation department declared that it would "keep our children off the streets, save children's lives, build children's health, guard children's character, and prevent juvenile delinquency."

A campaign in Milwaukee to increase the tax levy for recreation stressed these same values. The publicity included a table showing Milwaukee's good crime record as compared with that of other cities, and appealed to citizens to interest themselves in boys and their future. An exhibit in a Decatur, Illinois, campaign displayed a miniature baseball diamond and beside it by contrast a miniature jail. Children of the playgrounds carried posters in a street parade reading

> NEGLECT IN 1936
> MEANS TROUBLE IN 1946

and

> RECREATION ISN'T A FRILL
> IT'S A PART OF US

Training for citizenship and the problem of leisure receive considerable attention in recreation publicity, but its relationship to social hygiene and to the prevention of mental ill-health, which has ample scientific foundations, is seldom discussed. The opportunity which the recreation program offers for applying the methods and principles of democracy has largely been overlooked. The idea that a good recreation system attracts industries to a town because life in such a community is relished by employees and recreation is a stabilizing influence on the labor supply are less frequently mentioned than they were before the depression.

TIMING

The timing of publicity effort depends on the nature of its objectives and the skill of the recreation executive. The more statesmanlike executives begin to educate their boards, advisory committees, and other influential persons as to needed major improvements involving large sums of money, months or even years before they hope to have them put into effect. Attempts to secure favorable action on such projects suddenly are likely to end in defeat. The foundations of referendum campaigns are usually laid three to six months before election day, with a gradual intensification of effort on all fronts, reaching a climax one or two days before the vote. Advance publicity on special events, institutes, and other projects involving recruiting of personnel starts several weeks prior to the event.

Publicity on activities is usually in direct proportion to the frequency of the activities. In relatively slack periods the executive arranges news-creating conferences and discussions or brings out materials he has been putting aside for special feature articles and makes them available to newspaper reporters. The general principle followed in timing is that steady publicity the year around is much more valuable than splurges of copious publicity infrequently, with little or nothing in between. Local happenings of wide public interest, such as a public housing project or a new city plan, can often be turned to the advantage of the recreation department through furnishing an opportunity for publicity concerning some phase of its work. A drowning in an unprotected stream may serve as the basis for a campaign for a swimming pool. A report on street accidents either testifies to the effectiveness of playgrounds as a safety measure or indicates the need for more such service. Chapter XXXIV tells how one recreation department capitalized upon a local centennial celebration to expand its recreation facilities.

MEDIUMS

The familiar mediums and devices for publicity generally employed in American communities have been used to a greater or lesser extent by all recreation departments. Some cities have experimented with new and less well-known methods.

Newspapers.—The newspaper has been the principal stand-by of the recreation department. A good recreation program directly affects and interests so many newspaper readers that the press inevitably gives it good coverage. In large cities this extends to regular calls at the recreation department office by reporters. The preparation of live news copy requires reasonable skill in news writing on the part of the recreation executive or some member of his staff. There is a great deal of truth in the statement, "Playing, like eating and sleeping, is a fundamental instinct, but in print it is likely to sound dull and uninteresting unless it is treated with skill." The recreation program affords much material in the form of dramatic human-interest stories and illustrations which are welcomed by the papers if presented effectively. The importance of utilizing the foreign-language newspapers must not be overlooked.

Alert leaders secure an interpretation of recreation needs and values in the local newspapers by arranging for feature articles, furnishing material periodically as a basis for editorials, making suggestions to the cartoonist, writing letters to the editor, and setting up meetings at which prominent persons expound the philosophy of recreation. They also create news of the interpretive sort through inspired interviews with educators, clergymen, jurists, police officials, and others whose opinions carry weight with the press and the public. The preponderance of sports news in the scrapbooks of some departments not only reflects wide public interest in sports but usually indicates an overamphasis on this phase of the program. Recreation .workers who cultivate the acquaintance of editors, explain their objectives and activities, and cooperate with reporters are usually rewarded by the assignment of able reporters, generous news space, favorable editorials, and other evidences of newspaper good will.

A striking illustration of the value of newspaper cooperation is reported from a city in which the council had approved plans and estimates for two much-needed parks totaling 1,790 acres. They were intended as country retreats for city workers, and cost nearly a million dollars. Before submitting the plan to the voters of the city, the president of the council came to an influential local newspaper for its support. The editor, who found the plan sound and the measure progressive, was delighted. Promptly and vigorously he presented the advantages of these parks to the public, and energetically his paper concentrated the full force of its columns on the passage of this bill. And the entire program went through exactly as planned. The public was ready for it and knew the facts about it through a newspaper that had already established a reputation for fair dealing.

Radio.—The radio, like the newspaper, is a means of addressing the public at large, but it is much less generally used by recreation departments. Nevertheless, of 43 departments replying to a request for information sent out by the National Recreation Association in 1937, all but four made some use of the radio.[1] Thirty-one had regular programs of one type or another, while eight had occasional broadcasts. Little difficulty was reported in securing free radio time from local stations, but the time and effort involved in preparing good programs deter many departments from using this publicity medium. Regular broadcasts, weekly or twice a week, have been found more effective than occasional periods on the air. An appropriate title such as Messages from the

---

[1] See "Use of Radio in the Local Recreation Program," *Recreation*, February, 1938, p. 657.

Lighted Schoolhouse or Invested Leisure have been found helpful in attracting interest. Even with regular broadcasts it is important to have spot announcements, newspaper notices, circulars, and announcements at meetings and on bulletin boards if large numbers of listeners are to be reached. Recreation department news is welcomed by radio commentators conducting Round the Town programs featuring local happenings.

Common among the types of broadcasts found successful by recreation departments are these:

Descriptions of special events such as playground opening days, pageants, festivals, holiday celebrations, and city-wide athletic contests

Imaginary or actual trips through playgrounds and indoor centers; programs by playground, center, or community-wide musical groups

Talks or interviews by influential persons on recreation objectives, values, or local needs

Informative talks on such subjects as hobbies, holidays, or home play

Dramatizations by players' groups

Variety programs, in some cases conducted as an amateur hour

Suggestions or directions for games, crafts, or social recreation activities

Stories about the history of the recreation department and its activities

The first half of the weekly half-hour period conducted by one local recreation department and known as For Boys and Girls Only is under the direction of its music supervisor. Numbers are presented by the many music groups sponsored by the department, including girls' glee clubs, small children's choruses, young Italian men's choral group, toy symphony orchestras, harmonica bands, and other instrumental ensembles. The second half of the broadcasts consists of playground activities and special features. Spelling bees, dramatic plays, sports interviews, and impromptu dramatizations of stories told by the playground director have been popular. There is evidence that these broadcasts have attracted many children to the playgrounds.

Meetings.—Talks to service clubs, Bible classes, young people's groups, labor unions, parent-teacher associations, recreation councils, and other groups require much time of every recreation executive. Sometimes he is asked to address an organization which wishes to know more about the work of the department or desires assistance with some recreation project. In other cases he requests the opportunity of speaking in order that he may present the need for volunteers, arouse interest in a new department project, or enlist support for some recreation measure. Every such meeting can be used for interpreting recreation and creating new friends for the department. Talks are often supplemented by discussion and question periods, displays of recreation materials, or demonstrations by recreation groups. In cities where board members, other volunteers, and staff workers are developed as a speaker's group, the burden on the executive is lightened and a more extensive speaking program is possible. Such a group is especially useful in connection with campaigns.

Exhibits and Demonstrations.—Exhibits of crafts, photographs, models, charts, and other display materials are another common publicity medium. Models of playgrounds or recreation facilities, and city maps showing graphically the drawing power of the individual playgrounds or the unserved neighborhoods are especially effective. Handicraft displays in department store windows or at playgrounds are customary near the end of the season. Traveling exhibits of the work of the recreation department are sometimes sent from one section of the community to another. Silent lecturers displaying illuminated scenes of department activities with appropriate titles have been used effectively at conventions and in public buildings.

No publicity medium interprets the work of the department more strikingly or effectively than a demonstration of recreation activities. The playground circus, pageant, or festival, the community Halloween or Christmas celebration, the aquatic or sports carnival, presenting as they do various recreation activities, reach large numbers of people some of whom gain their chief impression of the department from watching them. Programs in the form of a recreation review have been arranged at recreation centers to acquaint the general public with the types of indoor activities conducted by the department. Group demonstrations add interest to exhibits and hobby shows. Much of the publicity value of such events lies in the joy and enthusiasm exhibited by the persons taking part in them.

Model-home exhibits, county and state fairs, and other exhibitions attracting large numbers of people are used by recreation departments to display and demonstrate their activities and services. The Recreation Department has had an important place in Pasadena's Municipal Exhibit, a highly popular and successful event which is held each year in the civic auditorium. Features of the department's exhibit include a miniature playground model complete with apparatus, game courts, wading pool, and other facilities, a marionette theater, periodic showings of slides portraying program activities, demonstrations of crafts, make-up, dancing, costume making, and hobbies. Signs and pictures tell of the department's service, folders are distributed, and paid and volunteer leaders in costume, stationed at the various booths, furnish special information as requested.

Motion Pictures.—Motion-picture films recording recreation activities, if made of carefully selected subjects and accompanied by appropriate captions, are useful in interpreting the work of the department to small neighborhood audiences or other special groups. The appearance of color film and its successful use in depicting recreation scenes and activities have awakened added interest among recreation executives in the educational values of motion pictures. A number of recreation departments have made excellent films portraying features of their programs.

Publications.—The most common publication is the annual report, but directories listing the outdoor areas and indoor centers and giving their location, the facilities in each, the hours during which they are open, charges for their use, and other similar data are published in many cities. An unusually attractive folder of this type, "Enjoy Health and Happiness at Dayton's Recreational Centers This Summer," profusely illustrated with varied recreation scenes, contains a map of the city, on which the parks, play centers, libraries, and other recreation resources are indicated. Accompanying the map and keyed to it is a list of the places and their locations, and also a list of recreation activities with indications as to the places where they may be enjoyed. Bulletins announcing seasonal programs with schedules for classes, groups, and special events are sometimes combined with the directory. A folder entitled "Outside Working Hours" issued in one city lists the special recreation opportunities for employed men and women. To answer the many questions raised concerning its organization, policies, program, finances, and facilities, one department has issued a comprehensive bulletin in question and answer form entitled "You Asked for It."

In addition to the publications dealing with the general work of the department are the many types relating to some specific activity or function. Announcements of institute courses or of the opening of playgrounds or centers, booklets on home-play or picnic activities, folders on the municipal athletic organization, or programs of special productions by the music or drama groups are typical. Yearbooks are issued by affiliated organizations such as a hiking or outing club, and many playgounds and centers issue a bulletin either regularly or on special occasions. In many of its publications the recreation department includes some material interpreting the significance of the work it is performing.

The Recreation Trial.—A novel way of acquainting the people of the city with its leisure-time services and needs is through a mock trial or public hearing. Such an event enlists the active participation of influential citizens, brings to light important facts concerning recreation in the city, arouses the curiosity of the citizens, and creates desirable newspaper publicity. Kalamazoo, Michigan, one of the cities to use this method, held in the municipal courtroom a trial of the case of the young men and women of the city against the citizens. A prominent clergyman acted as judge of the court; five witnesses presented the results of a recreation survey; the jury asked questions and deliberated; and summonses were issued to people whose attendance was important. The general public was invited to attend the trial. Severe indictments were offered because of the lack or inadequacy of certain recreation facilities and services. Among the judgments of the court were that more beneficial results would be attained under a revised plan and that a committee be organized to formulate and execute a plan to increase recreation opportunities for young men and women. The trial yielded a number of specific results, but "best of all, there is a more intelligent and widespread interest in the need of recreation facilities than ever before, with an assurance of decided development in the community center neighborhood program for next winter."[1]

A mock trial, *The People of Houston v. Public Recreation*, featured the annual meeting of the Houston, Texas, Board of Recreation, which often presents its work to the public in a novel way. Invitations to the 1936 meeting took the form of a subpoena to appear at the trial when citizens brought charges of laxity, misappropriation of funds, and extravagance against the recreation department. Immediately upon the close of the trial, newsboys entered the auditorium calling "Extra" and distributed copies of a pink newspaper which read in part as follows:

Case Against Public Recreation Dismissed

A surprise ending of the case *People of Houston v. Public Recreation* came when the State's Attorney moved to dismiss the case as the Defense continued to pile up evidence so that it became obvious there could be only one verdict, Not Guilty!!

One of the outcomes of the trial, as at Kalamazoo, was that the court granted a request of the state that a body of citizens be appointed or elected to guide the defendant's acts for the period of one year.

Tours.—"Come and see" tours of the parks and playgrounds, usually by automobile, have proved effective in giving city officials, parents, and other selected groups of citizens a firsthand view of recreation service in operation. Open nights at the indoor centers have also been arranged to show the people what is being done during the indoor season. A sense of reality as to conditions and services is thus obtained by people who might not be impressed by speeches or the printed word. The saying "seeing is believing" has been borne out by the results of a number of these trips. Those participating have not only been convinced of the value of the program but have translated their convictions into favorable action. Sometimes tours are conducted for the purpose of demonstrating unmet recreation needs or to show the advantages of acquiring a particular area.

[1] William G. Robinson, "Citizens on Trial," *Recreation*, October, 1934, p. 318.

Other Mediums.—Parades of children in special campaigns, the constant use of bulletin boards at playgrounds and community centers, public address systems, discussion groups, and conferences on problems such as safety and delinquency in relation to recreation are other familiar mediums of publicity. Several cities have an annual recreation week through which it is sought to impress large numbers of people with the work of the department and to enlist their participation in the program. In one city the mayor issues a proclamation officially designating Recreation Week which coincides with the closing of the schools for the summer. The celebration of Joseph Lee Day in 1938 gave recreation departments an opportunity to use many mediums for securing helpful publicity. These celebrations and, to an even greater extent, referendum campaigns and other general efforts calling for action by the voters call into play all major publicity methods. Special instances of cooperation by commercial groups in publicizing recreation are the enclosure of printed matter in pay envelopes, in store packages, on milk bottles, and in monthly bills.

No factor is more influential in gaining support for the recreation department than the good will of the people who benefit from its facilities and program. Recreation executives have not overlooked this in time of attacks upon the department or of campaigns requiring public support and action. As one worker wrote, "A newspaperman who came to our school basketball banquet where there were a hundred young men, said, 'Why do you worry about the center? If you should send these young men around to the polls on election day they would swing the election.'" The saying that a satisfied customer is the best advertisement applies particularly to the recreation department. By mobilizing those who are genuinely interested in and enjoy the services of the department, the recreation executive has a force of inestimable value at his disposal.

METHODS IN SPECIAL CAMPAIGNS

Attempts to reach the entire electorate for favorable action on recreation measures usually involve as intensive planning and effort as political campaigns or community chest drives. In such campaigns no method or medium of reaching the public effectively and favorably is overlooked. Campaigns are sometimes sponsored by voluntary associations as in Los Angeles where the parent-teacher associations of the city took the lead in the successful campaign referred to in Chap. XXXI. Elsewhere departments openly engineer the effort, as in the tax levy campaign in Canton, Ohio, a city of 105,000, in 1932. The following brief outline of that campaign serves to illustrate the methods commonly used.

The Canton Campaign.—A small group consisting of a recreation board of five, the mayor and the clerk of the council, directed this campaign for a recreation tax of 0.2 mill. Starting in midsummer, about four months ahead of election day, cards were passed out at all department activities stating that these activities were made possible by the city's department of recreation. One month prior to election day, posters, signs, and cards were placed on recreation facilities, in stores and busses, inviting votes for the recreation tax levy. Three weeks before election clergymen of all faiths were called together to discuss the recreation levy as a moral and religious issue. Out of this came the presentation of the levy to many congregations on the last two Sundays before the election, as a nonpolitical measure. A resolution favoring the levy, written and signed by officers of the Men's Federated Bible Classes, was read before all those groups. Sample ballots marked with red crayon were distributed to churches and Sunday schools. Small meetings of committee and club members, sponsors, players, and other participants in the department's activities, were held. The measure was brought to the attention of bridge clubs and other social groups. A recreation chairman was appointed for each parent-teacher association which heard about the measure from an influential person of its own neighborhood.

The central committee of a new political organization of foreign-born groups decided to favor the levy, thus ensuring a nearly 100 per cent favorable vote from foreign groups. The levy was brought up at all political rallies, Republican and Democratic, and was favored by all candidates. Public-school teachers and parochial-school Sisters explained to pupils the importance of the tax levy and had them take home a sample ballot the Monday noon before the election. As a final climax of the campaign, a truck with a police escort was driven through the business section of the city from 3:00 to 6:00 P.M. the day before election. It carried signs and a group of vociferous children who blew horns, rang bells, and sang a parody on a popular song to the effect of "Vote for the Recreation Levy."

While other forms of publicity such as outdoor advertising, newspaper stories, speeches, and cleverly arranged radio programs were not neglected, individual-to-individual contact was the heart of this campaign. The voter was approached through some political organization or particular friend or parent-teacher association canvasser or his own children. Throughout the campaign, emphasis was laid upon the moral, spiritual, and financial benefits of a city-wide, year-round recreation program. This highly integrated campaign brought a favorable vote on the measure, in the face of all the negative influences set up by unfavorable economic conditions.

CHAPTER XXXIV

COOPERATION AND RELATIONSHIPS

Affecting as it does the lives of people of all ages, types, and interests, and rendering such a variety of services, it is inevitable that the recreation department should be called upon to cooperate with community agencies and have close relationships with many public and private groups. It is likewise in a position to utilize the facilities and services of many other agencies. The preceding chapters, especially Chap. XXVII describing municipal recreation programs in several cities, contain numerous accounts of cooperation in conducting recreation activities and of recreation projects jointly sponsored by recreation departments and other authorities. Resourceful recreation leaders seek opportunities of this type which extend the influence and service of the department, help build up an understanding and appreciation of its work, and make possible a wider and more effective service than can be rendered by the department alone. They are also alert in taking advantage of community resources that may contribute to the recreation life of the people. There are few community agencies and groups with which cooperative relationships cannot be established and maintained to mutual advantage.

COOPERATION WITH PUBLIC DEPARTMENTS

The recreation department, as a unit in the local city government, is brought into close touch with many other departments and must rely on them for assistance in carrying on many of its services. In some cases the recreation authorities cannot avoid relationships with these departments; in others they have much to gain by enlisting their cooperation.

School Relationships.—Education and recreation are closely interrelated; school properties include many facilities suited to community recreation use; the same children are served by school and recreation leaders; training for leisure by the schools affects community recreation programs, and there are many common activities in the programs carried on in the schools and on the playgrounds. It is therefore essential that there be the closest understanding and cooperation between the two authorities. Fortunately, much progress has been made in this direction during the past decade, although in many cities there is little evidence of cooperation between these two groups. The following are a few of the specific ways in which school and recreation authorities are working together:

1. *Joint Employment of the Recreation Executive.*—Under this arrangement the person employed by the recreation department as executive also serves the school board in a related capacity. The conditions of employment of such workers differ from city to city. In Oakland, the recreation authorities employ the person who serves the schools as supervisor of physical education; in Long Beach, the Recreation Commission must employ this school official as recreation executive; and in San Diego, the two boards agree to elect jointly a recreation superintendent and an assistant. In Pittsburgh, the School Board helps meet the salary of the superintendent of the city bureau of recreation, who in return assists in the supervision of the schools' recreation program. Joint employment of this sort unifies planning and administration and eliminates conflicts in policies and programs. Executives of exceptional understanding and ability are required to assure the success of such a plan.

2. *School Board Representation on Recreation Board.*—As suggested in a previous chapter, it is often advisable for the recreation board to include a member of the school board. Such representation enables the school officials to be fully informed as to recreation plans and programs, keeps the recreation board in touch with the opinion of the school authorities on recreation matters, and facilitates cooperation in the use of school properties and joint action on problems of common interest and concern. Cincinnati and Reading are cities in which school boards are represented on the recreation commissions by one and two members, respectively.

3. *Cooperation in Acquisition and Development of Areas.*—School authorities need large play areas for use in the regular school program, and recreation departments also require such areas for serving children, youth, and adults, chiefly during nonschool hours. Economy and efficiency result when there is joint planning in the acquisition of such areas, and yet in 1938, only 57 out of 124 recreation agencies reporting on this question indicated any such cooperation.[1] Several outstanding examples of cooperative action between school and city authorities in acquiring recreation areas were cited in Chap. XI. Dallas, Texas, furnishes an instance of cooperation in the improvement of recreation areas designed for school and community use. Wading pools and tennis courts have been built on several school grounds in Dallas by the Park Board, which was authorized by a School Board resolution to build, operate, and maintain recreation facilities on school property.

4. *Joint Use of School and City Recreation Properties.*—In Reading, Pennsylvania, there is an understanding between the two boards that no

[1] *See The Organization of Municipal Recreation Programs*, National Recreation Association, 1938.

school site is to be sold until the Recreation Board has had a chance to consider its use as a playground, and if needed, it is to be leased to the city for $1 per year. The use of city-owned properties by school groups and of school properties by community groups is so common as to need only a brief mention. In Detroit, for example, during school hours the school authorities have full use of the city-owned outdoor areas and facilities; after school the Recreation Department uses the gymnasiums, pools, and community center facilities in the school buildings.

In Pittsburgh the Board of Education grants the City Bureau of Recreation the use of 43 properties for playground purposes and in return is granted permits for the use of 41 municipal playgrounds and athletic fields. A large majority of the year-round recreation departments make use of both indoor and outdoor school facilities, with maintenance costs resulting from such use generally met by the schools. School authorities are rarely obliged to pay for the maintenance of municipal areas during periods when they are using these properties.

5. *Cooperation in Program Planning and Policies.*—Because the two departments serve the same children and because the authorities provide recreation for young people after they leave school, a mutual understanding concerning program methods, objectives, and standards is highly desirable. Successful results have been achieved in this respect, especially in cities where recreation is administered under school auspices or under a coordinated plan, but much still needs to be done. Typical of the understandings that have been reached is an agreement in one city that school children may not play on recreation teams in evening basketball leagues, nor attend its games. Uniformity in rules and standards of athletic competition between school and recreation department teams has proved advantageous. Attempts to enlist high-school graduates in music and drama groups formed to meet their special needs and the employment of school music leaders to assist with the recreation music program are other examples of coordination in school and recreation department programs.

6. *Voluntary Coordination of Recreation Services.*—In most cities where a recreation commission has been established, as in Oakland, Reading, and Cincinnati, or where there is an independent recreation department without a board as in Detroit, the school authorities do not conduct a community recreation program. In Los Angeles, however, even though there is a playground and recreation commission, the School Board carries on a playground and indoor center program. Such a dual system presents opportunities for misunderstandings, conflicts, duplication, and jealousy between the two authorities but, in this instance, a series of steps has led to increasingly close cooperation between the recreation and the school departments. Informal conferences between

the executives were followed by the appointment of a joint committee which in turn resulted in the official approval by both boards of the following principles of correlation in providing recreation for children and adults:

1. Providing recreational areas, facilities, and supervision
2. Making school facilities available for the use of the general public through city-wide recreation programs
3. Securing additional play facilities, since even if all Board of Education areas were opened to general public use, there still would not be enough for the needs of the city
4. Avoiding overlapping of service, the Playground and Recreation Commission to put no new areas in neighborhoods that can be served by school grounds
5. Offering recreation service, no afterschool supervision to be given to school grounds in districts adequately served by municipal playgrounds
6. Approving existing cooperative methods, including the teaching of school classes at municipal plunges, the use of school gymnasiums for municipal recreation activities, the use of the municipal boys' and girls' camps by organized school groups and the provision of nature study features at municipal camps by the school department
7. Giving preference to each other's activities in granting the use of facilities
8. Formulating uniform rules, regulations, and practices wherever possible in conducting the recreation work of the two departments

Park Relationships.—In a majority of the cities with a separate recreation department, the operation of park playgrounds and the supervision of many other recreation facilities on park property are functions of this department, even though maintenance of such areas and facilities is provided by the park authorities. The furnishing of leadership on park properties and the organization of groups for the recreational use of park facilities are sometimes specifically designated by law as responsibilities of the recreation department. As a result of this arrangement, the function of some park authorities has become essentially that of acquiring, improving, and maintaining areas, the recreational use of which is controlled by the recreation department. On the other hand, it is common practice for park authorities to keep control of golf courses, boating facilities, and other services, especially those which produce revenue. In Cincinnati, however, the Recreation Commission furnishes the maintenance at both park and school areas transferred to it for operation, in addition to operating the municipal golf courses. There are a number of cities where the park and recreation functions have been combined in a single department with a recreation executive in charge.

Library Cooperation.—Library and recreation officials are alike interested in the promotion of reading as a popular and enjoyable leisure-time activity. In furthering this objective, many forms of cooperation have been developed. Branch libraries in field houses and recreation buildings are serving many people who do not make use of library buildings. On the other hand, clubrooms, auditoriums, and other library facilities are used by recreation departments for music, drama, crafts, and other activities. Some city libraries have a music division which maintains a large collection of opera and orchestral scores and various choral works, which are often borrowed by recreation department groups. Children's libraries cooperate with playground workers in the selection of stories to tell children, and in some instances furnish storytellers. One librarian prepared a special container with ten suitable books of stories for each of the local playgrounds. In several cities library trucks make weekly trips to the summer playgrounds taking books to the children.

Special displays of books on seasonal recreation activities have helped recruit participants for department programs, and literature on recreation subjects has been set aside in a number of libraries for use by persons attending recreation institutes. An excellent example of library cooperation is the annual amateur sports calendar issued by the Milwaukee Public Library. This calendar contains the dates for the opening of the leagues in the various sports promoted by the Municipal Athletic Association, and under the heading for each sport is a brief bibliography with the library number of each book. Recreation departments extend their cooperation to librarians in the promotion of Book Week and in posting on their bulletin boards announcements of activities sponsored by the library.

Housing Authorities.—The development of large-scale public housing projects has presented to housing and recreation authorities alike the problem of furnishing recreation service to the people occupying the new dwellings. Cooperation by the recreation department has been primarily of two types: (1) providing leadership at indoor and outdoor facilities within the housing development and (2) establishing recreation areas in close proximity to the housing units. The first type of cooperation has been fairly common and since, with the exception of play lots, recreation areas in public housing projects are usually open to persons in the surrounding neighborhood, it seems reasonable to expect that housing authorities will look to the recreation department to provide leadership at these areas, as at other properties open to public use.

The development of a large-scale housing project involves many problems related to city planning, in the solution of which other branches of the local government besides the recreation department have a vital share. In several cities recreation authorities have succeeded in working out a cooperative plan with the housing agency to furnish suitable outdoor recreation space, but in other cities a satisfactory solution has not been achieved. The importance of joint planning and action to the end that adequate space may be set aside permanently for recreation within or near all housing projects—public and private—and suggested procedures for attaining this end are presented in a report, *Play Space in New Neighborhoods*,[1] prepared at the request of the Society of Recreation Workers of America. Among the instances of successful cooperation cited in the report is the following:

In Pittsburgh, Pennsylvania, two large public housing projects being constructed in adjoining neighborhoods have afforded a basis for effective cooperation in neighborhood replanning. Through an arrangement between the city and housing authorities, part of a municipal playground of 5.8 acres on three levels lying between the two sites will be used for housing and in return the city will receive a new 12-acre area on one level. Among the recreation features to be provided on this area, which will be operated by the city Bureau of Recreation, is an outdoor swimming pool. The school authorities have acquired a site immediately adjoining the field on which they are to erect an elementary school which will contain an indoor swimming pool. Thus through cooperative planning, the people will have the benefit of a level recreation area more than twice the size of the former playground and it will be available for both school and community use. A junior playground of 1.3 acres is being built in one of the projects. Cooperation in Pittsburgh is facilitated by the fact that the chairman of the housing authority is the city councilman in charge of the park and recreation bureaus and that officials and technicians of the local city planning commission are also serving the housing authority.

Cooperation in Preventing Delinquency.—In view of the close relationship between the lack of suitable recreation opportunities and delinquency, it is only natural that police, court, and probation officials should turn to the recreation department for aid in preventing delinquency and in dealing with first offenders. The form of cooperation varies. In some cities the juvenile court or probation department turns the young offender over to the recreation executive or to the director of the playground in the neighborhood in which he lives. The boy or girl is required to report regularly to the recreation worker who encourages the child to participate in the recreation program. In one city juvenile protective committees composed of two or three persons living in the vicinity of each playground assist the playground directors in dealing with children whose names are submitted each month to the recreation department by the juvenile court. Boys and girls on probation are largely in the hands of the recreation worker and the committee members, who report to the court. When unsatisfactory neighborhood conditions are reported in another city, the recreation department, either directly or through some other education-recreation agency, organizes activities for the children or youth of the district.

---

[1] A committee report published by the National Recreation Association, 1939.

Coordinating councils in which public and private groups are represented, and in which the recreation department plays an active part, have made studies of neighborhood conditions and leisure-time activities and have cooperated with police and court officials in bringing troublesome children into contact with facilities and programs provided by the department. The head of a juvenile division of one police department cooperates with the recreation executive by helping boys who have committed misdemeanors and minor offenses adjust themselves to the playground program, and in organizing activities for their own group. Through information submitted by the juvenile court and officials of city welfare agencies, the recreation authorities in another city sought out problem boys who were induced to come to the playgrounds and who were subsequently enrolled in a boys' club playground program sponsored by the junior board of trade.

Workers at Large.—One of the most successful instances of effective service by a local recreation department in the prevention of delinquency is the plan providing for workers at large inaugurated in 1930 by the San Francisco Recreation Department. These workers are assigned to districts of the city and concentrate their efforts in neighborhoods of heaviest delinquency. "Unrestricted by the responsibilities of supervising or directing the activities at a particular recreation center, they move freely through their areas and refer individual boys and groups of boys to the various public and private recreation centers in the vicinity."[1] They keep in close touch with agencies in the district and become familiar with their functions and resources. They likewise get to know the people of the district, particularly the gangs, and discover the subversive influences. Their chief task is to help the young men and boys find the leisure-time activities which they most desire and which would be most helpful to them. Striking results in the reduction of juvenile delinquency and youthful crime and in the rehabilitation of individuals and groups have been reported. A Central Coordinating Council consisting of the Chief of Police, Chief Probation Officer, Superintendent of Schools, and Superintendent of Recreation was set up to guide the plan, and subsequently district councils of like nature have been formed in several neighborhoods.

Service Rendered by Other Departments.—The following references to cooperation extended by other departments to the recreation authorities briefly suggest the nature and scope of such relationships:

Police.—Provides safe coasting places at city streets, sets aside play streets, furnishes police for special events, assists junior safety clubs and playground police

---

[1] *The Director-at Large Plan in Recreation Work*, San Francisco Recreation Commission, 1936.

organizations, furnishes meeting places for boys' recreation activities, sponsors safety contests.

Water.—Furnishes water for pools and buildings and for flooding areas for skating, permits use of its properties for fishing, picnicking, and other activities.

Fire.—Permits use of fire hydrants for street showers and in some instances operates them, floods skating rinks, loans ladders and equipment, permits its buildings to be used for recreation activities, cooperates in fire prevention week.

Lighting.—Furnishes lights and equipment for festivals, pageants and special functions, installs and repairs lighting and other electrical equipment.

Health.—Provides regulations for sanitation at pools and beaches and makes periodic water analyses, holds physical examinations for participants in strenuous activities, conducts health activities on playgrounds, and cooperates in disease prevention.

Public Works.—Furnishes topsoil, sand, stone, or other materials, removes rubbish, transports equipment used at special events, and loans equipment such as steam roller.

Welfare.—Selects children to attend municipal camp, assists with Christmas toy campaigns, calls attention to children with special play needs.

Museum.—Prepares special exhibits for recreation department groups, makes arrangements for visits by playground children to the museum, assists with art, craft, or nature programs, provides meeting places, conducts classes, lectures, and demonstrations.

Reference has been made earlier to relationships with the courts, the city finance authorities, city attorney, planning commission, engineering department, harbor authorities, and other public bodies. Mention should also be made of the cooperation extended by other governmental agencies—county, state, and Federal. Examples are the lease of United States forest lands to several city recreation departments as sites for municipal camps, and the widespread allocation of personnel and funds through emergency agencies. In all these relationships the objective of the recreation department is not the special advantage which it may gain for itself, but the opportunity afforded for a fuller recreation service to the people of the city.

COOPERATION WITH PRIVATE AGENCIES

According to Prof. Martin H. Neumeyer of the University of Southern California, studies of community agencies conducted by coordinating councils "have revealed that overlapping of agencies and the necessity of combining organizations are not so serious a problem as the strengthening of existing agencies, the need of new facilities, the enlargement of the program of activities, and the integration of efforts."[1] The prevalence of this situation in most American cities accounts in part at least for the extensive and expanding cooperation between public and private agencies serving the recreation field. Much of this cooperation exists between the recreation department and a single agency as, for example,

[1] "The Los Angeles County Plan of Co-Ordinating Councils," *Sociology and Social Research*, May–June, 1935, p. 460.

a Y.W.C.A. which permits the recreation department to use its facilities for community dances, as in Lancaster, and which in turn may benefit from the use of the department's facilities, leadership, and training program. More significant, perhaps, is the increased participation by recreation departments in local councils of social agencies, particularly in the work of their leisure-time section.

Cooperation in Reading, Pennsylvania.—Perhaps the best way of indicating briefly the range and character of the relationships between a recreation department and other local organizations is to paraphrase a section of the annual report of the Superintendent of the Recreation Department in Reading, Pennsylvania. In this city, both the public schools and the recreation department are members of the Council of Social Agencies, and the recreation executive participates actively in its work. The list of services and relationships which follows includes a number of governmental, as well as private agencies:

The department has a very interesting relationship with other agencies and organizations in the total planning of the leisure-time program. Our cooperation with them is listed briefly herewith:

1. Council of Social Agencies. The Superintendent of Recreation served on the executive committee as vice-chairman of the Leisure Time Division, helped plan the monthly program of the division and participated in the discussion of problems, planning, and activities. He also assisted the Youth Survey Committee in making a survey of what young people between 16 and 26 years are doing in their leisure time. The Recreation Department was represented on the Committee of the Council's Garden Division.

2. Junior League Recreation Center Committee. Met with Junior Leaguers in the interests of this Center financed by the League. Monthly meetings held.

3. Interracial Recreation Center Committee. Helped determine policies in the operation of this center. Meetings held four times a year.

4. Federal Emergency Education—Recreation—Youth Council. Superintendent served as secretary. Monthly meetings held to discuss program, reports, and policies of WPA and NYA workers loaned to this department and other leisure-time agencies.

5. WPA Projects. Helped in planning band and orchestra programs for the Music Project, sponsored the dramatic and sewing projects, and supplied information on all municipal recreation for the Guide Book.

6. Reading Music Festival. Acted as publicity chairman for this great community music enterprise. Chorus of 1,000 and orchestra of 125.

7. Reading Musical Foundation. Served as a trustee. This Foundation sponsors free public band concerts, the symphony orchestra, and the choral society.

8. Municipal Music Committee. Acted as secretary and helped plan the annual National Music Week Celebration and Christmas music on Penn Square.

9. Playground Federation. Acted as coordinator for 27 neighborhood playground associations. Meetings held four times each year.

10. National Recreation Association, N.Y.C. Worked with them in new studies of recreation activities and facilities, and assisted them in their financial program within Reading and Berks County. Also called upon them for advice and suggestions.

11. National Youth Hostel Association. Served on their National Advisory Council and as president of the Pennsylvania area. Helped stimulate interest in inexpensive overnight places for youth who like to hike or bicycle.

12. Kiwanis Boys' and Girls' Work Committee. Assisted them in the selection of camp personnel and camp programs for the Kiwanis Preventorium.

13. Camp Fire Girls' National Projects. Acted as their local sponsor in the study of "Community Recreation Resources."

14. Boy Scouts. Served on their camp committee.

15. County Recreation Board. Assisted them in training their workers and in planning their summer playground programs.

16. Municipal Camp Committee. Served as a member in making a study of the possibilities of a free municipal camp for children.

17. National Park Service. Gave them suggestions on the development of the New French Creek Area.

18. Reading Council of Christian Education (Interdenominational). Conducted a 12 weeks' training course for workers interested in "Recreational Leadership for Church and Community."

19. Reading Fair Association. Operated a model playground, a playground handicraft exhibit and produced a pageant for them.

20. The recreation superintendent worked with the Garden Division of the Woman's Club and the College Club in arranging for the beautification of playgrounds, the D.A.R. in providing playground citizenship awards, the American Legion and the Reading Times in supplying funds for the operation of boys' baseball teams.

The preceding list, to which should be added the many relationships with other local public departments, indicates the varied ramifications of the service rendered by the recreation department. It incidentally throws light upon the duties of a recreation executive and the way he spends his working hours.

COOPERATION WITH COMMUNITY ORGANIZATIONS

The chapters describing various features of the recreation department's service indicated that in many ways it assists local organizations in carrying on their recreation projects. In return, recreation departments receive valuable aid from many local groups, the nature of which can merely be suggested by citing a few examples. The parent-teacher associations have been loyal allies on frequent occasions by sponsoring referendum campaigns, furnishing volunteer playground leaders, "rescuing" recreation budgets, and cooperating in the promotion of home play. Junior leagues have furnished funds for conducting indoor centers, have organized and financed junior garden clubs and library service at community buildings. Colleges and universities have permitted recreation departments to use their athletic facilities during the summer months, admitted playground boys and girls to football and baseball games, assisted in music and drama programs, cooperated in recreation training institutes, and furnished student leaders to help with the department's program. Automobile clubs, junior chambers of commerce, the American Legion, and other groups have furnished awards for safety patrols, organized boys' baseball leagues, and sponsored community dances and holiday celebrations. Service clubs have been especially helpful in furnishing funds and leadership for specific projects, as in Detroit where the Kiwanis Clubs for several years sponsored day outings for underprivileged boys and girls at Belle Isle, the city's beautiful island "playground."

The American Red Cross gives advice regarding the development and operation of aquatic facilities, assists with learn-to-swim campaigns, and furnishes instructors for first-aid and lifesaving classes. Athletic, music, drama, garden, art, and other clubs furnish volunteer leaders, and assist in planning programs and in organizing city-wide tournaments and special events. Perhaps no group of organizations has been more helpful than the playground mothers' clubs, the playground and community center councils, dads' clubs, and playground federations which have raised money for equipment, furnished transportation, and actively supported the department's program. Industries, churches, newspapers, women's clubs, labor organizations, all help—in fact there is probably no type of organization which in one or more cities is not serving the recreation department.

AN EXAMPLE OF COMMUNITY COOPERATION

The old saying that too many cooks spoil the broth hardly applies in the case of many community undertakings. It is true that responsibility for seeing that they are carried through successfully must be clearly designated, but the very fact that a large number of individuals and organizations have a share in a project goes far in assuring its success. The following account of a community-wide project in which the local recreation department had a leading part illustrates the possibilities of cooperative effort directed toward a worth-while objective.

The manner in which the Recreation Department in Aurora, Illinois, took advantage of a centennial celebration to secure a municipal camp is a story of resourcefulness and remarkable community effort. In a conference with the Centennial Association president, the recreation director learned that one of the features was to be an exhibit of antique vehicles and equipment with a painted canvas background in one of the city parks. Since the Recreation Department had secured a lease on a property which it hoped to acquire for a camp, the idea of having a real pioneer village on this site was suggested to the association. The difficulties in securing the needed labor and materials seemed to doom the idea, but after the possibilities of meeting this problem were presented and carefully investigated, the Centennial Commission approved the project. The recreation director was then appointed chairman of the Pioneer Village Committee. The following statement is taken from his account of the wholehearted cooperation which resulted in the success of the project.[1]

A local company lent a motor grader which for two weeks filled up the swampy area which was to serve as the village square and also a drag line for constructing a drainage ditch. Another firm furnished equipment for laying the water lines and a loader for loading gravel, which was hauled from the city gravel pit by a fleet of trucks and drivers furnished without charge by the local Truckers' Association. The railroad furnished from 1,200 to 1,500 telegraph poles for the cabins and the utility and telephone companies supplied an additional number. The Carpenters' Union constructed the cabin of Sam McCarthy, founder of Aurora, and the Contractors' Association built the town hall. The telephone company erected a flagpole, the Kiwanis Club built a town well, and foot bridges were constructed by the Lions Club. A group of plumbers installed toilet facilities sufficient to accommodate the large numbers using the camp, and an appeal to the officials of the gas and electric company brought five truckloads of linemen to the village after their day's work was over.

In spite of setbacks and unforeseen happenings the village opened on schedule. It was made up of a blacksmith shop, a general store, the cabin of Sam McCarthy, the city's founder, twin dwelling cabins, a single cabin, a trading post, a schoolhouse, a town hall, and a church. When camping time rolls around next season the blacksmith shop will become a camp kitchen; the trading post, the dining hall. The McCarthy cabin will be the camp master's quarters; the twin cabins, schoolhouse, and the single cabin will provide living quarters for overnight campers. The town hall will be converted into an assembly building and will house activities during stormy weather. The church will be kept as a church to remind the campers of the spiritual aspects of camping and nature study.

Cooperation did not end with the construction of the village for during the celebration the Boy Scouts set up a camp, acted as guides and guards, and assisted in cleaning up the grounds. The American Red Cross supplied a tent and gave first aid as necessary, and the local utility

[1] Russell A. Perry, "When the Civic Celebration Was Over," *Recreation*, July, 1938, p. 237.

company lent an ambulance for emergency use and the services of its lifesaving expert. During the eighteen days the village was open, it was estimated that there were more than 100,000 visitors, and special programs were presented each evening by local patriotic, industrial, civic, and racial organizations.

All of those participating in the construction of the village had the satisfaction of knowing that they were taking part in a project which would greatly benefit the children of Aurora under the leadership of the Playground and Recreation Department. Groups sharing in the enterprise included most of the churches of the city, all of the schools, many merchants and manufacturers, civic clubs, a number of fraternal organizations, parent-teacher groups, labor organizations, utility companies, business associations, and the railroad.

IN CONCLUSION

In the minds of many people, the recreation department is primarily a part of the machinery of local government. They think of it chiefly in terms of areas and facilities, supervisors and caretakers, playground schedules and athletic leagues, budgets and reports, or as a means of keeping children and young people out of mischief during their leisure hours. As the preceding chapters have shown, the recreation department is all these things, but it is a great deal more. Most of these are merely means for achieving its larger objectives to develop personality, to build a finer community spirit, and to contribute fully to the enrichment of life for the people of the city. Recreation authorities are increasingly recognizing their larger responsibility and are adjusting their programs to meet more fully the increasing demands for a richer, more satisfying human service. The evidence presented in this chapter indicates that the recreation department is not an isolated unit of the local government but is vitally related to all other community forces, and that its work is closely integrated with that of all other agencies serving the leisure-time interests of the people.

The 1937 report of V. K. Brown, Director of Recreation of the Chicago Park District, gives a striking illustration of the new emphasis upon recreation values, objectives, and achievements. Without any statistics, lists of activities, and other facts usually presented in such annual reports, it records developing attitudes toward life, the practical application of democratic principles, and the effects of competent and sympathetic leadership upon the lives of children, youth, and adults. It considers the contribution which recreation can make to the advance of civilization and to the cultivation of the ideals of democracy. Recreation authorities are challenged to measure up to the possibilities of their task in the following words:

So, since recreation consists of what people do together, since it involves the enthusiasms and purposes which most profoundly affect their social development, it follows that if in affording opportunity to people to engage in their leisure doings together we should emphasize the neighborly spirit, take bitterness out of competition, develop more of sharing and less of contention, we might indeed effectively "promote the general welfare" and contribute in essential ways to the strengthening of our democracy.

BIBLIOGRAPHY

The following bibliography listing material relative to the subjects considered in this volume affords a guide to supplementary reading and a list of valuable reference sources. It does not include publications describing recreation activities, but information concerning such material and bibliographies on various types of recreation activities are available from the National Recreation Association. In addition to the titles listed in the following pages, publications issued by community recreation agencies, such as annual reports, information folders, staff guides, directories, and program materials, furnish data of great value to teachers, students, and recreation workers.

I. RECREATION—ITS NATURE, EXTENT, AND SIGNIFICANCE

Books

ADAM, T. R.: *The Museum and Popular Culture*, American Association for Adult Education, 1938.

ATKINSON, R. K.: *The Boys' Club*, Association Press, 1939.

BELL, HOWARD M.: *Youth Tell Their Story*, American Council on Education, 1938.

CABOT, RICHARD C.: *What Men Live By*, Houghton Mifflin Company, 1914.

Chicago Recreation Survey, Chicago Recreation Commission and Northwestern University, 1937. Vol. I, "Public Recreation"; Vol. II, "Commercial Recreation"; Vol. III, "Private Recreation."

Encyclopaedia of the Social Sciences, The Macmillan Company, 1934. Articles on recreation, leisure, and related subjects.

GLUECK, ELEANOR T.: *The Community Use of Schools*, The Williams & Wilkins Company, 1927.

Handbooks of Adult Education in the United States, American Association for Adult Education, 1934, 1936.

JACKS, L. P.: *Education through Recreation*, Harper & Brothers, 1932.

KEPPEL, F. P., and R. L. DUFFUS: *The Arts in American Life*, McGraw-Hill Book Company, Inc., 1933.

LEE, JOSEPH: *Play in Education*, The Macmillan Company, 1915.

LUNDBERG, GEORGE, *et al.*: *Leisure, a Suburban Study*, Columbia University Press, 1934.

LYND, ROBERT S., and HELEN M. LYND: *Middletown*, Sec. IV, "Using Leisure," Harcourt Brace & Company, Inc., 1929.

MACGOWAN, KENNETH: *Footlights Across America*, Harcourt Brace & Company, Inc., 1929.

MITCHELL, ELMER D., and BERNARD S. MASON: *Theory of Play*, A. S. Barnes & Company, 1934.

MORRISON, R. C., and M. E. HUFF: *Let's Go to the Park*, Wilkinson Printing Company, 1937.

NATIONAL RECREATION ASSOCIATION:[1]

[1] Titles listed under National Recreation Association both here and on succeeding pages are published by the association unless otherwise specified.

Adventures in Recreation, by Weaver W. Pangburn, A. S. Barnes & Company, 1936.
The Child and Play, by James E. Rogers, D. Appleton-Century Company, Inc., 1932.
County Parks, by George D. Butler, 1930.
Music in American Life, by A. D. Zanzig, Oxford University Press, 1932.
The New Leisure Challenges the Schools,[1] by E. T. Lies, 1933
Proceedings of the Twenty-second National Recreation Congress, 1937.
Proceedings of the Twenty-third National Recreation Congress, 1938.
Proceedings of the Twenty-fourth National Recreation Congress, 1939.
NEUMEYER, M. H., and E. S. NEUMEYER: *Leisure and Recreation,* A. S. Barnes & Company, 1936.
OVERMYER, GRACE: *Government and the Arts,* W. W. Norton & Company, Inc., 1939.
PATTEN, MARJORIE: *The Arts Workshop of Rural America,* Columbia University Press, 1937.
PENDRY, ELIZABETH R., and HUGH HARTSHORNE: *Organizations for Youth,* McGraw-Hill Book Company, Inc., 1935.
RAINWATER, CLARENCE E.: *The Play Movement in the United States,*[1] University of Chicago Press, 1922.
Social Work Year Book, Russell Sage Foundation. The issues of this publication contain articles on the current status of recreation, boys' and girls' clubs, camps, youth programs, community centers, settlements, and other related subjects.
STEINER, JESSE F.: *Americans at Play,* McGraw-Hill Book Company, Inc., 1933.
WOODS, ROBERT A., and ALBERT J. KENNEDY: *The Settlement Horizon,* Russell Sage Foundation, 1922.
Youth Serving Organizations, American Youth Commission, 1937.

Magazine Articles

"The Amusement Industry," *Recreation,* February, 1938, p. 639.
BRAUCHER, H. S.: *Recreation.* The editorials beginning with the July, 1931, issue contain some of the best statements available on the subjects covered by this section.
Building America, April, 1936. Recreation issue.
CALKINS, EARNEST E.: "The Lost Art of Play," *The Atlantic Monthly,* April, 1933.
CURTIS, HENRY S.: "A Brief History of the Playground Movement in America," *The Playground,* April, 1915, p. 2, and May, 1915, p. 39.
CURTISS, HAROLD L.: "Opportunities for Recreation in the National Forests," *Recreation,* January, 1938, p. 591.
GLOSS, G. M.: "Ultimate Understanding for Recreational Planning," *The Journal of Health and Physical Education,* December, 1938, p. 602.
"Increasing America's Recreation Facilities," *Recreation,* December, 1936, p. 448.
JACKS, L. P.: "Leisure Time—A Modern Challenge," *Playground and Recreation,* December, 1930, p. 475.
LIES, E. T.: "The New Leisure: Drafting a Program," *The New York Times Magazine,* Dec. 3, 1933, p. 3.
LINDEMAN, EDUARD C.: "Youth and Leisure," *The Annals of the American Academy of Political and Social Science,* November, 1937, p. 59.
MORGAN, JOY ELMER: "The Leisure of Tomorrow," reprinted from *Journal of the National Education Association,* January, 1930.

[1] Out of print.

"National Government Services through Recreation," *Recreation*, January, 1935, p. 465.

PLANT, JAMES S.: "Recreation and the Social Integration of the Individual," *Recreation*, September, 1937, p. 339.

"The Public Library in the Program of Leisure Time," *Recreation*, February, 1935, p. 530.

Recreation,[1] May, 1931. A twenty-fifth anniversary number containing articles on the beginnings and development of the community recreation movement in the United States.

Recreation, December, 1937. A Joseph Lee memorial issue.

Recreation Year Book. This annual publication, issued in the June number of *Recreation* (formerly *The Playground*) contains a statistical report of organized recreation facilities, leadership, and service in American communities.

RICHARDS, ESTHER L.: "Mental Health and Play," *Recreation*, September, 1932, p. 286.

STEINER, JESSE F.: "Challenge of the New Leisure," *The New York Times Magazine*, Sept. 24, 1933, p. 1.

WALDMAN, HENRY S.: "Recreation and Crime," *Recreation*, January, 1939, p. 547.

WALLACE, ROY SMITH: "How Much Recreation Is Essential?" *Recreation*, November, 1932, p. 274.

WORMAN, E. C.: "Trends in Public Recreation," *Recreation*, August, 1938, p. 267.

Miscellaneous

AMERICAN ASSOCIATION OF SCHOOL ADMINISTRATORS: *References on Leisure Education*, National Education Association, 1937.

LEE, JOSEPH: *Play as an Antidote to Civilization*, National Recreation Association, 1911.

"Leisure-time Leadership," Works Progress Administration Recreation Projects, Works Progress Administration, 1938.

MAUGHAN, KENNETH O.: *Recreational Developments in the National Forests*, Bulletin of the New York State College of Forestry, Syracuse, N. Y., 1934.

Municipal and County Parks in the United States, 1935, National Park Service, 1937.

NATIONAL PARK SERVICE: *Recreational Use of Land in the United States*, National Resources Committee, 1938.

NATIONAL RECREATION ASSOCIATION:
Children's Play and Juvenile Delinquency, 1928.
Is Park and Recreation Service a Governmental or Proprietary Function of Municipal Government? 1932.
Recreation, A Major Community Problem, 1936.
Thirty-two Years of Service—The Story of the National Recreation Movement, 1938.
"Park Recreation Areas in the United States," *Bulletin* 462, U. S. Bureau of Labor Statistics, 1928.
"Park Recreation Areas in the United States, 1930," *Bulletin* 565, U. S. Bureau of Labor Statistics, 1932.

Publications and reports of the Federal, state, and municipal recreation agencies, including state reports of the National Park, Parkway, and Recreational Area Study.

Report of the New York Committee on the Use of Leisure Time,[1] National Recovery Administration, 1934.

---

[1] Out of print.

SILVER, ABBA HILLEL: *Recreation and Living in the Modern World*, National Recreation Association, 1930.

STEINER, JESSE F.: *Research Memorandum on Recreation in the Depression*, Social Science Research Council, 1937.

Surveys. For references to recreation surveys, see p. 529.

WEINBERGER, JULIUS: "Economic Aspects of Recreation " reprinted from *Harvard Business Review*, Summer, 1937.

Year Book—Park and Recreation Progress, National Park Service, series beginning with 1937 issue.

II. LEADERSHIP

Books

BUSCH, HENRY M.: *Leadership in Group Work*, Association Press, 1934.

COMMISSION OF INQUIRY ON PUBLIC SERVICE PERSONNEL: *Better Government Personnel*, McGraw-Hill Book Company, Inc., 1935.

MERRIAM, LEWIS: *Public Service and Special Training*, McGraw-Hill Book Company, Inc., 1936.

MITCHELL, ELMER D., and BERNARD S. MASON: *The Theory of Play*, Chap. XX, "The Play Leader," A. S. Barnes & Company, 1934.

NATIONAL RECREATION ASSOCIATION:
The Child and Play, by James Edward Rogers, Chap. VII, "Leadership in Play," D. Appleton-Century Company, Inc., 1932.
Playgrounds, Their Administration and Operation, by George D. Butler, Chaps. V to X, A. S. Barnes & Company, 1936.
Recreation for Girls and Women, by Ethel Bowers, Chap. VIII, "Leadership," A. S. Barnes & Company, 1934.

NEUMEYER, M. H., and E. S. NEUMEYER: *Leisure and Recreation*, Chap. XIX, "Recreation Leadership," A. S. Barnes & Company, 1936.

SMITH, CHARLES F.: *Games and Game Leadership*, Chap. I, "The Leadership of Games and Recreations," and Chap. XIV, "The Leadership of Social Recreation," Dodd, Mead & Company, Inc., 1932.

TEAD, ORDWAY: *The Art of Leadership*, McGraw-Hill Book Company, Inc., 1935.

Magazine Articles

FARRA, KATHRYN: "Being Honest with and about Volunteer Workers," *Better Times*, Jan. 1, 1934.

GRANT, GLEN O.: "Los Angeles Trains for Enlarged Leisure," *Recreation*, October, 1933, p. 316.

HOSMER, GLADYS E.: "Board or Bored," *The Survey*, Apr. 15, 1931, p. 92.

LA PORTE, WILLIAM R.: "Training Recreation Leaders," *Journal of Health and Physical Education*, May, 1934, p. 20.

OVERSTREET, H. A.: "Professional Leadership in the Field of Public Recreation," *Recreation*, December, 1939, p. 483.

PANGBURN, WEAVER W.: "The Institute Comes to Town," *Recreation*, August, 1936, p. 245.

ROBINSON, BRUCE B.: "The Professional in Recreation and His Responsibility for Personality Development," *Recreation*, September, 1938, p. 323.

"Summaries of Group Discussions at the Recreation Congress Section Meetings," *Recreation*, December, 1929, p. 539. Theme: leadership.

"Volunteer Leadership in the Recreation Movement," *Recreation*, January, 1933, p. 480.

Miscellaneous

BROWN, V. K.: "The Capture of Leisure for Use in Volunteer Service to Government and the Community,"[1] *Proceedings of the Twenty-second National Recreation Congress*, National Recreation Association, 1937.

BURTON, HAROLD H.: "The Role of the Layman in the Recreation Movement," *Proceedings of the Twenty-third National Recreation Congress*, National Recreation Association, 1938.

JEFFREY, IDELLE SCOTT, and JULIA F. CAPEN: *Developing Volunteers*, The Womans Press, 1939.

JOHNSON, GEORGE E.: *Why Teach a Child to Play?* National Recreation Association, 1909.

LAMBIE, MORRIS B.: *Training for the Public Service*, Public Administration Service, 1935.

NATIONAL RECREATION ASSOCIATION:

Four-year Undergraduate Course for Training Recreation Leaders, 1934.

Methods of Securing and Maintaining Standards in Community Recreation Work Personnel. In preparation. A committee report.

Outline of Suggested Courses for College Undergraduates Looking to Volunteer Recreation Leadership, 1938.

Standards of Training, Experience, and Compensation in Community Recreation Work, 1938. A committee report.

Suggested Examination Questions—Public Recreation Positions, 1938.

Suggestions for Recreation Institutes, 1934.

Survey of Salaries Paid to Recreation Workers—1938, 1939.

What Recreation Executives Do, 1925.

Recreation Leadership as a Career, The Institute for Research, 1936.

Reports of College Conferences on Training Recreation Leaders, University of Minnesota, 1937, and University of North Carolina, 1939.

The Training of WPA Workers in the Field of Recreation, Works Progress Administration, 1937.

III. AREAS AND FACILITIES

Books

American School and University, A Year Book Devoted to the Design, Construction, Equipment, Utilization, and Maintenance of Educational Buildings and Grounds, American School Publishing Corporation, issued annually since 1928.

HANMER, LEE F.: *Public Recreation*, Committee on Regional Plan of New York and Its Environs, 1928.

HOLY, RUSSELL A.: *The Relationship of City Planning to School Plant Planning*, Teachers College, Columbia University, 1935.

LAMAR, EMIL: *The Athletic Plant: Equipment, Layout, and Care*, Whittlesey House, McGraw-Hill Book Company, Inc., 1938.

LEE, MABEL: *The Conduct of Physical Education*, Sec. V, "Facilities for the Physical Education Program," A. S. Barnes & Company, 1937.

LUEHRING, F. W.: *Swimming Pool Standards* (Indoor), A. S. Barnes & Company, 1939.

NASH, J. B.: *The Administration of Physical Education*, Chap. VIII, "The Physical Education Plant," A. S. Barnes & Company, 1931.

[1] Out of print.

Park and Recreation Structures, National Park Service, 1938.   Vol. I, "Administration and Basic Service Facilities"; Vol. II, "Recreational and Cultural Facilities"; Vol. III, "Overnight and Organized Camp Facilities."

NATIONAL PARK SERVICE: *Recreational Use of Land in the United States*, National Resources Committee, 1938.

NATIONAL RECREATION ASSOCIATION:
  New Play Areas—Their Design and Equipment, by George D. Butler, A. S. Barnes & Company, 1938.
  Parks—a Manual of Municipal and County Parks, by L. H. Weir, Chaps. II to V, A. S. Barnes & Company, 1928.
  Playgrounds, Their Administration and Operation, Chaps. II to IV, by George D. Butler, A. S. Barnes & Company, 1936.

SCOTT, C. A.: *The Essentials of Swimming Pool Sanitation*, Lightner Publishing Company, 1931.

SERBY, MYRON W.: *The Stadium*, The American Institute of Steel Construction, 1930.

Swimming Pool Data and Reference Annual, Hoffman-Harris, Inc.   Issued annually.

TAYLOR, A. D.: *Camp Stoves and Fireplaces*, U. S. Forest Service, 1937.

THOMAS, G. C. J.: *Golf Architecture in America*, Times-Mirror, 1927.

WILLIAMS, JESSE F., and C. L. BROWNELL: *The Administration of Health and Physical Education*, Chaps. XII to XV, W. B. Saunders Company, 1934.

Magazine Articles

ALLEN, F. ELLWOOD: "Planning a Community Recreation Building," *Recreation,* March, 1939, p. 649.

ALLEN, F. ELLWOOD: "Sunbeams for Footlights—The Design and Construction of Playground Theaters," *Recreation*, April, 1939, p. 3, and May, 1939, p. 73.

BALLARD, EDWARD B.: "When Winter Dons Her Mantle White," *Recreation*, December, 1936, p. 431.

"Bases of Design for Community Theaters," *Architectural Record*, October, 1939, p. 78.

BASSETT, E. M.: "Legislation for Parks and Recreation Spaces," *The Playground*, January, 1925, p. 574.

Beach and Pool, published monthly.

BOBST, GLENN G.: "Planning for the Future," *Recreation*, February, 1940, p. 611. Lighting recreation facilities.

BROWN, V. K.: "New Features in a Swimming Pool," *Parks and Recreation*, October, 1931, p. 76.

CLEGG, GILBERT: "Playground Planning and Layout," *Recreation*, June, 1935, p. 151.

EVERLY, ROBERT E., and JOHN MCFADZEAN, "When Park and School Systems Work Together," *The Nation's Schools*, September, 1939, p. 22.

HOYT, RAYMOND E.: "Planning the Recreation Building," *Recreation*, August, 1934, p. 221.

HYATT, CHAUNCEY A.: "Swimming Pool Developments of the Past Decade," *Parks and Recreation*, May, 1932, p. 575.

"Lighting of Outdoor Recreation Facilities," *Recreation*, February, 1938, p. 665.

"Minimum Standards for Recreation Facilities," *Recreation*, July, 1938, p. 241.

MULHOLLAND, J. V., "The Multiple Use of Recreation Facilities," *Recreation*, April, 1929, p. 28.

NICHOLS, C. P. L.: "Planning the Recreational Swimming Pool," *Parks and Recreation*, June, 1939, p. 529, and July, 1939, p. 569.

Recreation, August, 1931.   Recreation in Real Estate Subdivisions.

ROSS, ROBERT J.: "The Design and Construction of Golf Courses," *Parks and Recreation*, August, 1934, p. 422, and September, 1934, p. 17.

TAYLOR, A. D., "Landscape Construction Notes," a series, *Landscape Architecture*, 1922–1923.

The Bulletin, U. S. Golf Association. Published six times a year.

WEIR, L. H.: "Planning the Picnic Grounds," *Recreation*, June, 1933, p. 126.

Miscellaneous

A Swimming Pool for Health and Happiness, Portland Cement Association, 1937.

ADAMS, THOMAS: *Playparks*, Coronation Planting Committee, 1937.

BARROWS, ALICE, and LEE SIMONSON: *The School Auditorium as a Theater*, U. S. Department of Interior, Office of Education, 1939.

"Building Types—A Reference Study on Community Recreation," reprinted from the *Architectural Record*, June, 1937.

BUTLER, GEORGE D.: "Recreational Planning in Relation to School-plant Planning," reprinted from *The American School Board Journal*, December, 1934, and January, 1935.

CHENEY, CHARLES H.: "Recreation and City Planning in the United States,"[1] in *Proceedings of the First International Recreation Congress*, National Recreation Association, 1932.

CLEGG, GILBERT: "Milwaukee Playgrounds, "reprinted from *American Landscape Architect*, 1932.

Community Playgrounds, Extension Service, Massachusetts State College, 1938.

DAY, LOUIS J., and C. W. STEDMAN: *A Treatise on Swimming Pool Design*, Josam Manufacturing Company, 1937.

FELDMAN, J. W.: *The Effects of Playgrounds on Land Value*, National Recreation Association, 1929.

HUUS, R. O., and DOROTHY I. CLINE: *Municipal, School and University Stadia*,[1] Public Administration Service, 1931.

Information on playground apparatus, gymnasium construction, the lighting of recreation areas, swimming pool equipment, and related subjects is available in publications issued by manufacturers of equipment. Lists of such companies may be secured from the National Recreation Association.

Lighting for Night Tennis, Bureau of Municipal Research and Service, University of Oregon, 1939.

Minimum Sanitary Requirements for Swimming Pools and Bathing Places, Illinois Department of Public Health, 1938.

MURPHY, LINTON J.: *Planning the Outdoor Swimming Pool*, Engineering Extension Service, Iowa State College, 1931.

NATIONAL RECREATION ASSOCIATION:

Donated Parks and Play Areas, 1929.

Municipal Golf—Construction and Administration, 1927.

Plans for Playground Shelters (5) *and Recreation Buildings* (2), 1934.

Play Space in New Neighborhoods, 1939. A committee report.

Space Requirements for the Children's Playground, 1934.

Standards in Playground Apparatus, 1929. A committee report.

Surfacing Playground Areas, 1932. A committee report.

Surfacing Playground Areas—A Supplement, 1937.

Types of Municipal Recreation Areas, 1937.

Nature's Plan for Parks and Playgrounds, The Regional Planning Federation of the Philadelphia Tri-state District, 1932.

[1] Out of print.

BIBLIOGRAPHY

RAITT, C. B.: "Municipal Recreation Camps," reprinted from *Parks and Recreation,* March–April, 1924.

Reports of the Standard Court for Tournament Play Committee, U. S. Lawn Tennis Association, 1936.

Spalding's Athletic Library Series, American Sports Publishing Company. Contains official playing rules and directions for laying out fields and facilities for many games and sports. Many of the volumes are reissued annually.

Swimming Pools and Other Public Bathing Places, American Public Health Association, 1935. A committee report.

WALTZ, CLARENCE F.: "Construction and Maintenance of Baseball Fields," *Bulletin* 7, The Athletic Institute, Inc., 1935.

IV. ACTIVITIES AND PROGRAM PLANNING

Books

GREENBIE, MARJORIE B.: *The Arts of Leisure,* McGraw-Hill Book Company, Inc., 1935.

GULICK, LUTHER H.: *A Philosophy of Play,* Charles Scribner's Sons, 1920.

JOHNSON, GEORGE E.: *Education by Plays and Games,* Ginn and Company, 1907.

LEE, JOSEPH: *Play in Education,* The Macmillan Company, 1915.

LEE, MABEL: *The Conduct of Physical Education,* Chaps. II and III, A. S. Barnes & Company, 1937.

LEHMAN, H. C., and P. A. WITTY: *The Psychology of Play Activities,* A. S. Barnes & Company, 1927.

LUNDBERG, GEORGE A., et al.: *Leisure, A Suburban Study,* Columbia University Press, 1934.

MITCHELL, ELMER D., and BERNARD S. MASON: *The Theory of Play,* Chaps. V to VII, XVII, and XIX, A. S. Barnes & Company, 1934.

NATIONAL RECREATION ASSOCIATION:
Partners in Play, by Mary J. Breen, A. S. Barnes & Company, 1936.
Playgrounds—Their Administration and Operation, by George D. Butler, Chaps. XI, XII, and XV, A. S. Barnes & Company, 1936.
Recreation for Girls and Women, by Ethel Bowers, A. S. Barnes & Company, 1934.

OVERSTREET, HARRY A.: *A Guide to Civilized Leisure,* W. W. Norton & Company, Inc., 1934.

RIGGS, AUSTEN FOX: *Play: Recreation in a Balanced Life,* Doubleday, Doran & Company, Inc., 1935.

SLAVSON, S. R.: *Creative Group Education,* Association Press, 1937.

Magazine Articles

BROWN, V. K.: "As to Competition," *Recreation,* June, 1932, p. 130.

BROWN, V. K.: "Chicago Pioneers on New Frontiers," *Recreation,* August, 1935, p. 245.

DIMOCK, HEDLEY: "How Effective Is Our Education for Leisure?" *Recreation,* December, 1936, p. 427.

DODGE, DORA: "Why Not Give the Girl a Chance?" *Recreation,* October, 1934, p. 319.

EGINGTON, DANIEL P.: "Modern Principles of Education for Leisure Time," *Recreation,* September. 1934, p. 274.

ENGLISH, CHARLES E.: "Program Building," *The Playground,* January, 1927, p. 553.

GRANT, GLEN O.: "Much Ado about Nothing," *Recreation,* October, 1937, p. 403. A report of boys' and girls' recreation interests.

Leisure Time Studies. *Recreation*, March, 1934. Summaries of several studies.
SVENDSON, MARGARET T.: "Is Play Vanishing from the Playgrounds?" *Recreation*, June, 1932, p. 123.

Miscellaneous

CALKINS, EARNEST E.: *Care and Feeding of Hobby Horses*, Leisure League of America, 1934.
COOK, WILLIAM R.: *Organizing the Community's Resources for the Use of Leisure Time*, Canadian Welfare Council, 1938.
GARDNER, ELLA: *Development of a Leisure Time Program in Small Cities and Towns*, Children's Bureau, *Publication* 241, 1937.
GLOVER, KATHERINE: "Youth—Leisure for Living," Committee on Youth Problems, Office of Education, *Bulletin* 18-11, 1936.
HILLER, MARGARET: *Programs One Way and Another*, The Womans Press, 1939.
LEE, JOSEPH: *Certain Basic Assumptions Underlying the Work of the National Recreation Association*, National Recreation Association, 1934.
LEE, JOSEPH: *Play and Playgrounds*, National Recreation Association, 1908.
NATIONAL RECREATION ASSOCIATION:
Fundamentals in Community Recreation, 1923.
Leadership, Organization, and Program Making in Boys' Club Groups, 1939.
Leisure Hours of 5,000 People,[1] 1934.
Recreation for Your Community, 1938.
What Can We Do in Our Town? 1932.
Recreation Centers for Young Children, Recreation Department, Board of Education, Newark, N. J., 1938.
Three Thousand Books of Leisure, Leisure, 1939.
VAN HORN, OLIVE O.: *Individual Satisfaction in Adult Education*, The New York Adult Education Council, 1936.
"Youth—How Communities Can Help," Committee on Youth Problems, Office of Education, *Bulletin* 18-1, 1936.

V. THE OPERATION OF AREAS AND FACILITIES

Books

FARLEY, G. A.: *Golf Course Commonsense*, the author, 1931.
GLUECK, ELEANOR T.: *The Community Use of Schools*, The Williams & Wilkins Company, 1927.
Life Saving and Water Safety, The American Red Cross, 1937.
NASH, J. B.: *The Organization and Administration of Playgrounds and Recreation*, Chaps. XX, XXII, XXIII, and XXV, A. S. Barnes & Company, 1927.
NATIONAL RECREATION ASSOCIATION:
The New Leisure Challenges the Schools,[1] by E. T. Lies, Chap. IX, "Recreational Opportunities of Non-school Youth and Adults," 1933.
Parks: A Manual on Municipal and County Parks, by L. H. Weir, Chap. XIII, "The Recreation Service Division," A. S. Barnes & Company, 1928.
Playgrounds—Their Administration and Operation, by George D. Butler, A. S. Barnes & Company, 1936.
NORTON, EDWARD V.: *Play Streets and Their Use for Recreational Programs*, A. S. Barnes & Company, 1937.

[1] Out of print.

Swimming and Water Safety, Boy Scouts of America, 1931.
Swimming Pool Data and Reference Annual, Hoffman-Harris, Inc.   Issued annually.

Magazine Articles

BROWN, V. K.: "Results of Modernizing a Bathing Beach," *Parks and Recreation*, September, 1934, p. 21.

CHRISTIANSEN, MILO F.: "The Club—An Effective Medium in the Community Center," *Recreation*, September, 1935, p. 307.

DEERING, TAM: "Municipal Golf Makes 'Hole in One'," *Recreation*, August, 1938, p. 286.

DRYDEN, MAUDE L.: "New York Tries Out New Methods of Education," *Recreation*, May, 1936, p. 58.

DRYDEN, MAUDE L.: "Winter Day Camps in New York City," *Recreation*, March, 1936, p. 596.

DRYDEN, MAUDE L.: "Neighborhood Day Camping in New York City," *Recreation*, May, 1938, p. 79.

EVANS, BEN: "A Center That Knows No Depression," *Recreation*, October, 1932, p. 319.

FELDMAN, J. W.: "Developing the Community Center Program," *Recreation*, October, 1934, p. 331.

FELDMAN, J. W.: "Developing Community Center Loyalty," *Recreation*, November, 1932, p. 389.

GARVER, PAUL T.: "Recreation on a Municipal Lake," *Recreation*, July, 1937, p. 237.

HEMENWAY, H. S.: "Let's All Go to School," *Recreation*, February, 1937, p. 539.

KRIM, ALAN: "Developing Clubs in Community Centers," *Recreation*, September, 1937, p. 349.

LANTZ, THOMAS W.: "Securing the Use of Schools as Community Centers," *Recreation*, October, 1936, p. 347.

"Life Guard Protection at Bathing Beaches," *Parks and Recreation*, June, 1932, p. 646.

MADSEN, PAUL: "At the Portola Recreation Center," *Recreation*, September, 1937, p. 371.

NICHOLS, C. P. L.: "Planning the Recreational Swimming Pool," *Parks and Recreation*, July, 1939, p. 569.

NORTON, GORDON L.: "Indoor Recreation According to Hoyle," *Recreation*, November, 1938, p. 445.

Parks and Recreation, December, 1931, Winter Sports Number.

WHITE, EVA W.: "Community Centers in School Buildings," *The Playground*, September, 1923, p. 319.

Miscellaneous

BLACKHAM, LOUISE P., and KATHRYN FARRA: *Clubs in Forty-eight Settlements in the City of New York*, Welfare Council of New York City, 1931.

BOWERS, ETHEL: *The Community Center as a Neighborhood Club House*, National Recreation Association, 1936.

BROWN, V. K.: *First Steps in Stadium Operation*, American Institute of Park Executives, 1927.

CURETON, THOMAS K., JR.: *A Water Program for Camps*, The American Red Cross, 1929.

DRYDEN, MAUDE L.: *Day Camping*, National Recreation Association, 1939.

GARDNER, ELLA: *Short-time Camps*, U. S. Department of Agriculture, 1939.

Manual for Caddies, Chicago Park District, 1937.

McCloskey, Mark A.: "Community Centers," *Social Work Year Book,* 1939, Russell Sage Foundation, 1939.

National Recreation Association:
Conduct of Community Centers, 1936.
Conduct of Playgrounds, 1936.
Municipal Golf: Construction and Administration, 1927.
Playground Honor Point Systems, 1938.
Winter Sports, 1934.

Perry, Clarence A., and Marguerita P. Williams: *New York School Centers and Their Community Policy,* Russell Sage Foundation, 1931.

Safety Activities for Supervised Playgrounds, National Safety Council, 1931.

Swimming Pools and Other Public Bathing Places, American Public Health Association, 1935. A committee report.

Trull, Edna: *Municipal Auditoriums,* Public Administration Service, 1931.

VI. Program Features and Services

Books

National Recreation Association:
Music in American Life, by A. D. Zanzig, Chap. XVII, Oxford University Press, 1932.
Partners in Play, by Mary J. Breen, A. S. Barnes & Company, 1936.

Van de Wall, Willem: *The Music of a People,* American Association for Adult Education, 1938.

Magazine Articles

The following articles will be found in the magazine *Recreation,* unless otherwise specified.

Alexander, William P.: "Recreation on the Nature Trail," December, 1932, p. 438.
Altick, Richard D.: "Community Dances in Lancaster," September, 1935, p. 302.
"Arts and Crafts for Playgrounds," May, 1938, p. 63.
Attwell, E. T.: "Recreation for Colored Citizens in the New Democracy," January, 1937, p. 491.
"Bicycling—The Wheels Go Round and Round," July, 1938, p. 234.
Bowers, Ethel: "A Home for Hobbies," July, 1932, p. 175.
Bowers, Ethel: "Centers for Girls," August, 1939, p. 283.
Bunke, Erna D.: "Serving Your Community Institutions," June, 1932, p. 135.
Caulkins, E. Dana: "Recreation in Westchester County," August, 1933, p. 218.
Co-Recreation. Several articles in September and October, 1939.
Foster, Marie V.: "Music as a Playground Activity," May, 1938, p. 100.
Foster, Marie V.: "Musical Arts,'' March, 1935, p. 586.
Gardening,[1] March, 1938.
Glore, Harry F.: "A Recreational Symphony Orchestra," January, 1933, p. 490.
Handlan, John W.: "It's Thar, Effen You Know How to Git It," September, 1937, p. 365. Accomplishments of a music survey.
Hobbs, Mabel F.: "The Place of Drama in Recreation," July, 1935, p. 211.
Hobbs, Mabel F.: "The Children's Playground Theater," *The Playground,* March, 1928, p. 663.
Hurley, John M.: "Hartford Celebrates Christmas—And the Nativity is Presented," February, 1939, p. 616.

[1] Out of print.

KELLY, FRED: "Boystowns for Cleveland Youth," November, 1939, p. 437.
LINDEMAN, EDUARD C.: "Recreation Rehabilitates the Shut-in." October, 1937, p. 417.
"Louisville's Fifth Annual Play Contest," March, 1937, p. 591.
MADDEN, MABEL: "Cincinnati Plans a Merry Christmas," November, 1932, p. 363.
MARSH, CHESTER G.: "Enlarging the Arts and Crafts Program," May, 1938, p. 97.
MEYER, KARL: "Austin's Symphony Orchestra," December, 1939, p. 509.
MULHOLLAND, JAMES V : "Playing in the Parks of New York," April, 1936, p. 3.
"A Museum for Children," September, 1938, p. 341.
"A Nature Program on a Playground," May, 1938, p. 68.
"Nature Recreation," April, 1940.
"A New Recreation Frontier," March, 1937, p. 599. Service to shut-ins.
NEWCOM, JAMES R.: "Santa Claus and his Fairyland on Parade," November, 1938,
    p. 435.
NORTON, GORDON L.: "Card Playing in the Modern Recreation Program," February,
    1939, p. 609.
"People Laughed," April, 1937, p. 32.   An account of service to flood victims.
"Play Past Sixty," September, 1936, p. 301.
"Public Provision for the Play of the Pre-school Child," *Playground and Recreation*,
    September, 1930, p. 331.
"Refurbishing the Playground Program," May, 1938, p. 87.
"San Francisco's Junior Museum," October, 1937, p. 415, and April, 1938, p. 27.
SCOTT, WALTER L.: "A Recreation Department Meets an Emergency," August, 1933,
    p. 215.
SHRIVER, PAUL: "The Flower Market Tot Lot Playground," June, 1933, p. 120.
"The Season in the Playground Theater," September, 1931, p. 337.
"Toy Loan Centers," October, 1938, p. 388.
WELTY, IRENE D.: "The Pennsylvania Folk Festival," September, 1935, p. 311.
"When the Finale Is a Pageant," May, 1938, p. 83.
WILLIAMS, HORTENSE L.: "Recreation for Crippled Children," June, 1932, p. 139.
"Your Museum," February, 1938, p. 667.

Miscellaneous

GRANT, GLEN O.: *City-wide Contest for Better Back Yards*, National Recreation Association, 1933.
Industrial Athletic Association of Metropolitan Oakland, Industrial Athletic Association and Recreation Department, Oakland, Calif., 1939.
NATIONAL RECREATION ASSOCIATION:
    Adventuring in Nature, 1939.
    Community Recreation for Industrial Workers, 1934.
    Drama Tournament Suggestions, 1936.
    Gardening—School, Community, Home, 1940.
Program Suggestions for the Enrichment of Adult Life,[1] prepared by the National Recreation Association for the National Education Association, 1933.

VII. ORGANIZATION AND ADMINISTRATION PROBLEMS

Books

COLCORD, JOANNA C.: *Your Community, Its Provision for Health, Education, Safety, and Welfare*, Russell Sage Foundation, 1939.
DOELL, C. E., and R. J. THOMPSON: *Public Park Policies*, Parks and Recreation, 1930.
GLUECK, ELEANOR T.: *The Community Use of Schools*, The Williams & Wilkins Company, 1927.

[1] Out of print.

BIBLIOGRAPHY 529

HUUS, RANDOLPH O.: *Financing Municipal Recreation*, George Banta Publishing Company, 1935.

KING, CLARENCE: *Social Agency Boards*, Harper & Brothers, 1938.

NASH, J. B.: *The Organization and Administration of Playgrounds and Recreation*, Chaps. X, XII to XIV, and XXXI, A. S. Barnes & Company, 1927.

NATIONAL RECREATION ASSOCIATION:
Charges and Fees, 1932.
County Parks, by George D. Butler, 1930.
Parks—A Manual of Municipal and County Parks, by L. H. Weir, A. S. Barnes & Company, 1928.
Playgrounds—Their Administration and Operation, by George D. Butler, Chaps. XVI to XXIII, A. S. Barnes & Company, 1936.

PRESTON, EVERETT C.: *Principles and Statutory Provisions Relating to the Recreational, Medical and Social Welfare Service of the Public Schools*, Teachers College, Columbia University, 1935.

The Superintendent Surveys Supervision, Eighth Year Book of the Department of Superintendence, National Education Association, 1930.

Surveys. A list of community recreation survey reports is available from the National Recreation Association.

TRUXAL, ANDREW G.: *Outdoor Recreation Legislation and Its Effectiveness*, Columbia University Press, 1929.

Magazine Articles

BRIGHTBILL, C. K.: "Calendar for Public Recreation Administration," *Recreation*, November, 1938, p. 462.

"Board Members," *Bulletin 152*, Russell Sage Foundation Library, December, 1938.

BROWN, V. K.: "How Many Are Served?" *Recreation*, November, 1938, p. 457.

BUTLER, GEORGE D.: "Standards for a Recreation System in a Community of 100,000," *Recreation*, February, 1933, p. 532.

FELDMAN, JACOB W.: "Attendance Taking on the Playground, Can It Be Effectively Standardized?" *Recreation*, July, 1931, p. 227.

"For the Price of a Single Movie," *Recreation*, April, 1937, p. 19. An account of a recreation referendum campaign.

HJELTE, GEORGE: "Statistical Study of Service and Costs of Public Recreation," *Playground and Recreation*, March, 1930, p. 715.

"Human Needs," *Parks and Recreation*, November, 1939, p. 95. A panel discussion broadcast.

JOHANBOEKE, KARL G.: "Waging War on Juvenile Delinquency," *Recreation*, November, 1933, p. 382.

LANTZ, THOMAS W.: "The Board of Recreation Commissioners," *Recreation*, February, 1939, p. 619.

NASH, J. B.: "Improvement of Recreation Facilities," *The Annals of the American Academy of Political and Social Science*, September, 1938, p. 133.

PANGBURN, W. W.: "Newark Plans for Play," *Recreation*, January, 1933, p. 459.

PERRY, RUSSELL A.: "When the Civic Celebration Was Over," *Recreation*, July, 1938, p. 237.

Recreation Year Book, published annually in the June issue of *Recreation*.

ROBINSON, WILLIAM G.: "Correlation of Public and Private Agencies in the Recreation Field," *Recreation*, March, 1935, p. 563.

"They Voted 'Yes' for Recreation," *Recreation*, March, 1933, p. 561.

"Use of Radio in the Local Recreation Program," *Recreation*, February, 1938, p. 657.

VARGA, H. E., and EDWARD A. LEVY: "Public Recreation in Cleveland," *Recreation*, September, 1938, p. 333.

WILLIAMS, ARTHUR: "Twenty-five Years of Recreation Legislation," *Recreation*, May, 1931, p. 80.
WIRTH, THEODORE: "Fees and Charges for Public Park Services," *Recreation*, February, 1939, p. 601.
WORMAN, E. C.: "Trends in Public Recreation," *Recreation*, August, 1938, p. 267.

Miscellaneous

THE ATHLETIC INSTITUTE: Bulletins on financing competitive athletics, athletic forms and records, and related subjects.
A Descriptive Bibliography of Surveys and Special Studies, Community Chests and Councils, Inc., 1936.
The Director-at-large Plan in Recreation Work, San Francisco Recreation Commission, 1936.
Fees and Charges for Public Recreation, National Park Service, 1939.
HJELTE, GEORGE: *Recreation Budget Making and Administration*, National Recreation Association, 1925.
LANTZ, THOMAS W.: *Cooperative Planning for Education-Recreation Services*, National Recreation Association, 1935.
Municipal and County Parks in the United States, 1935, National Park Service, 1937.
NATIONAL RECREATION ASSOCIATION:
  Is Park and Recreation Service a Governmental or Proprietary Function? 1932.
  A New Formula for Determining Summer Playground Attendance, 1938. A committee report.
  Office Organization and Equipment, 1928.
  The Organization of Municipal Recreation Programs, 1938.
  Recent Trends in Local Governmental Control of Year-round Recreation, 1938.
  Recreation Cost Records, 1938. A committee report.
  Recreation Records, Reports, and Information, 1937.
  Schedule for the Appraisal of Community Recreation, revised, 1940.
  Suggestions for a Public Relations Program in a Public Recreation Department, 1937.
  Suggestions for a Recreation Survey, 1938.
  Survey of Salaries Paid to Recreation Workers—1938, 1939.
  Ten Point Publicity Program for Public Recreation, 1934.
  "What Legislative Action is Necessary for Adequate Recreation Service Today?" *Proceedings of Twenty-second National Recreation Congress*, 1937.
  What Recreation Executives Do, 1935.
Park Recreation Areas in the United States, U. S. Bureau of Labor Statistics, *Bulletins* 462, 1928, and 565, 1932.
Public Reporting, Public Administration Service, 1931. A committee report.
RIDLEY, CLARENCE E., and HERBERT A. SIMON: *Measuring Municipal Activities*, International City Managers' Association, 1938.
RIDLEY, CLARENCE E., and HERBERT A. SIMON: *Specifications for the Annual Municipal Report*, International City Managers' Association, 1939.
Social Services and the Schools, The Educational Policies Commission, National Education Association, 1939.
Standard Classification of Municipal Revenues and Expenditures, National Committee on Municipal Accounting, 1939.
STEINER, JESSE F.: *Research Memorandum on Recreation in the Depression*, Social Science Research Council, 1937.
Toward Better Records, Association Press, 1937. A manual.
WHITE, R. CLYDE: *Public Welfare Board and Committee Relationships*, American Public Welfare Association, 1937.

INDEX